DISCARD

AMERICAN AND SOVIET SOCIETY:

A Reader in Comparative Sociology and Perception

AMERICAN AND SOVIET SOCIETY:

A Reader in Comparative Sociology and Perception

Edited by
PAUL HOLLANDER
University of Massachusetts

PRENTICE-HALL, INC.   Englewood Cliffs, New Jersey

AMERICAN AND SOVIET SOCIETY:
A Reader in Comparative Sociology and Perception
Edited by Paul Hollander

© 1969 by *Prentice-Hall, Inc.*
Englewood Cliffs, New Jersey

Translations from *The Current Digest of the
Soviet Press* are published weekly at Columbia
University by the Joint Committee on Slavic
Studies appointed by the American Council
of Learned Societies and the Social Science
Research Council, are copyrighted by the
Joint Committee on Slavic Studies and are
reprinted in this book by permission.

PRENTICE-HALL INTERNATIONAL, INC., *London*
PRENTICE-HALL OF AUSTRALIA, PTY. LTD., *Sydney*
PRENTICE-HALL OF CANADA, LTD., *Toronto*
PRENTICE-HALL OF INDIA PRIVATE LTD., *New Delhi*
PRENTICE-HALL OF JAPAN, INC., *Tokyo*

Current printing (last digit):

10   9   8   7   6   5   4   3   2   1

Library of Congress
Catalog Card Number: 68–28876

PRINTED IN THE UNITED STATES OF AMERICA

AUTHORS

A. ALEXANDROV, M. GARIN, AND N. SHTANKO: Special correspondents for *Izvestia*.

G. F. ALEXANDROV: Soviet philosopher. Professor Alexandrov has written *A History of Western European Philosophy* (English edition 1949) and *Joseph Stalin, A Short Biography* (English edition 1947).

DANIEL BELL: Professor of Sociology at Columbia University. He is the author of *The End of Ideology* (1960) and edited *The Radical Right* (1963).

A. BOGOMOLOV: Professor in the Philosophy Faculty of Moscow University. Author of *History of Bourgeois Philosophy in the Epoch of Imperialism* (1962).

DANIEL BOORSTIN: Professor of American History at the University of Chicago. Professor Boorstin's publications include *The Image* (1962), *America and the Image of Europe* (1960), and *The Americans: The Colonial Experience* (1958). He also edited *An American Primer* (1966).

I. BRAZHNIK: First Deputy Chairman of the Council for Religious Affairs of the USSR Council of Ministers. Editor of *On Religion: An Anthology* (1963).

I. BURKOVA: Special correspondent for *Literaturnaya Rossiya*.

V. CHEPRAKOV: Professor in the Political Economy Department of the Higher Party School of the Central Committee of the CPSU. He is the author of *Basic Features of State Monopoly Capitalism* (1959) and *The Common Market* (1963).

D. CHESNOKOV: Chairman of the Historical Materialism Department of the Philosophy Faculty of Moscow University. He is the author of *Communism and the Individual* (1964).

V. E. CHUGUNOV: A Soviet legal scholar. His publications include *Criminal Court Proceedings in the Chinese People's Republic* (English edition 1961) and *Criminal Process in the Czechoslovakian Republic* (1956).

G. DROZDOV: Russian Republic First Deputy Minister of Social Security.

CORA DUBOIS: Professor of Anthropology at Harvard University. Professor DuBois specializes in problems of cultural change. Her publications include *The People of Alor* (1944) and *Foreign Students and Higher Education in the United States* (1956). She has been engaged since 1961 in a study of values and institutional change in an Indian town.

S. EPSTEIN: Soviet journalist.

Y. FILONOVICH: Soviet political philosopher. He is the author of *Soviet Deputy* (1958) and *Youth on the Komsomol* (1952).

GEORGE FISCHER: Associate Professor of Sociology at Columbia University. Professor Fischer's publications include *Russian Liberalism* (1958), *Soviet Opposition to Stalin* (1952), and *Science and Politics: The New Sociology in the Soviet Union* (1964).

ROBERT E. FITCH: Dean of the Pacific School of Religion. Dr. Fitch is the author of *The Decline and Fall of Sex* (1957) and *Religion, Morality and Law* (1956).

Y. FRANTSEV: A member of the Academy of Science of the USSR and a past editor of *Pravda*. Professor Frantsev has served as president of the Academy of Social Sciences of the Communist Party of the Soviet Union and as the first president of the Soviet Sociological Association. He is presently chief editor of the journal *Problems of Peace and Socialism*. His publications include *The Construction of Communism* (1959) and *Conversations on Religion and Knowledge* (1962).

MAURICE FRIEDBERG: Professor of Slavic Languages and Literature and Director of the Russian and East European Institute at Indiana University. His publications include *Russian Classics in Soviet Jackets* (1962) and *A Bilingual Collection of Russian Short Stories* (1964).

M. GARIN: Special correspondent for *Izvestia*.

KENT GEIGER: Professor of Sociology at Wisconsin University. He is author of *The Family in Soviet Russia* (1968) and co-editor of *Soviet Society* (1961) with Alex Inkeles.

A. GERTSENZON: Doctor of Jurisprudence. Author of *The Understanding of Crime in Soviet Criminal Law* (1955) and *Introduction to Soviet Criminology* (1965).

G. E. GLEZERMAN: Chairman of the Dialectical and Historical Materialism section of the Academy of Social Sciences of the CPSU. Professor Glezerman's writings include *The Laws of Social Development* (1960) and *Questions on the Theory and Practice of Communist Upbringing* (1962).

CHARLES Y. GLOCK: Professor of Sociology at the University of California, Berkeley. He has written *Survey Research in the Social Sciences* (1967) and co-authored *To Comfort and to Challenge* (1967) and *Religion and Society in Tension* (1965).

ERICH GOLDHAGEN: Assistant Professor of Political Science and Director of the Institute of East European Jewish Studies at Brandeis University. Professor Goldhagen often writes on Jewish affairs in East Europe and the Soviet Union.

SCOTT GREER: Professor of Sociology at Northwestern University. Professor Greer's specialty is urban sociology; he is the author of *The Emerging City* (1964).

G. GRUSHIN: A Soviet sociologist affiliated with the Institute of Public Opinion. He is co-author of *Confession of a Generation* (1961) and author of *Free Time* (1967).

MICHAEL HARRINGTON: Mr. Harrington is the author of *The Other America* (1962), *The Accidental Century* (1965); and *Toward A Democratic Left* (1968).

JULES HENRY: Professor of Anthropology at the University of California at Davis. Professor Henry's publications include *Jungle People* (1941) and *Culture Against Man* (1963).

PAUL HOLLANDER: Associate Professor of Sociology at the University of Massachusetts (Amherst) and associate of the Harvard Russian Research Center. He has written several articles on various aspects of Soviet society and is completing a comparative study of American and Soviet society.

ALEX INKELES: Professor of Sociology at Harvard University. He is the author of *Public Opinion in Soviet Russia* (1950), *The Soviet Citizen* (1959) (with Raymond Bauer), *What is Sociology?* (1964), and *Becoming Modern* (with D. H. Smith and H. Schuman, forthcoming).

PETER JUVILER: Associate Professor of Government at Barnard College. Professor Juviler writes frequently about Soviet family policy and problems. He is co-editor of *Soviet Policy-Making* (1967).

ALLEN KASSOF: Associate Professor of Sociology at Princeton University. He is the author of *The Soviet Youth Program* (1965) and editor of *The Prospects for Soviet Society* (1968).

V. KELLE: Head of the Section of Historical Materialism of the Philosophy Institute of the Academy of Sciences of the USSR. Author of *Historical Materialism* (1962).

KENNETH KENISTON: Associate Professor of Psychology, Department of Psychiatry, Yale Medical School. He is the author of *The Uncommitted* (1965).

M. KHALDIYEV: Formerly chief of the Agitation and Propaganda Department of the RSFSR Communist Party. Now a member of the Auditing Commission of the Central Committee of the

CPSU. He is the author of *Questions of Party Life* (1967) and *Leninist Principles in the Work of the Komsomol* (1963).

A. G. KHARCHEV: Professor of Philosophy affiliated with the Institute of Philosophy of the Academy of Sciences of the USSR. Professor Kharchev's specialty is the study of the Soviet family. His publications include *Marriage and Family in the USSR* (1964) and *The Problem of Value in Philosophy* (1966).

GABRIEL KOLKO: Associate Professor of History at the University of Pennsylvania. Professor Kolko has written *Wealth and Power in America* (1962) and *The Triumph of Conservatism* (1963).

I. S. KON: A sociologist affiliated with the Philosophy Faculty of Leningrad University. Author of *Positivism in Sociology* (1964).

F. KONSTANTINOV: Member of the Soviet Academy of Sciences and Director of the Institute of Philosophy of the Academy. Author of *Bases of Marxist Philosophy* (1964).

E. LISAVTSEV, V. MASLIN, AND N. OVCHINNIKOV: Soviet journalists who write on political themes.

F. S. MAKHOV: Soviet legal scholar.

HERBERT MARCUSE: Professor of Philosophy at the University of California at La Jolla. Professor Marcuse is the author of *Eros and Civilization* (1955), *Reason and Revolution* (1941), and *One Dimensional Man* (1964).

DAVID MATZA: Associate Professor of Sociology at the University of California, Berkeley. Professor Matza specializes in the study of deviant behavior. He is the author of *Delinquency and Drift* (1964).

G. MDIVANI: Soviet playwright and film critic. Author of *Plays* (1955) and *A Young Man* (1966).

ALFRED G. MEYER: Professor of Political Science at the University of Michigan. His publications include *Leninism* (1957), *The Soviet Political System* (1965), and *Marxism* (1954).

C. WRIGHT MILLS: The late Dr. Mills was Professor of Sociology at Columbia University. His many publications include *The Power Elite* (1956), *White Collar* (1951), and *Character and Social Structure* (with H. H. Gerth) (1953).

I. MINDLIN: Soviet journalist and political commentator. Author of *Great Program Document of Communism* (1948).

G. M. MINKOVSKY: Candidate of jurisprudence and Director of the All-Union Institute for the Study and Prevention of Crime. Publications include *Courts in the USSR and the Countries of Capital* (1954).

B. MOCHALOV: Secretary of the Party Committee of Moscow University.

BARRINGTON MOORE, JR.: Lecturer on Sociology at Harvard University. His publications include *Soviet Politics: The Dilemma of Power* (1950), *Terror and Progress USSR* (1954), and *The Social Origins of Dictatorship and Democracy* (1966).

WILBERT E. MOORE: Dr. Moore is a sociologist affiliated with the Russell Sage Foundation. His work has focused on problems of industrialization and social change. Dr. Moore is a past president of the American Sociological Association. His publications include *Industrial Relations and the Social Order* (1946), *Social Change* (1963), *The Impact of Industry* (1965), and *Order and Change* (1967).

M. MOTSENOK: Soviet writer and journalist.

DANIEL P. MOYNIHAN: Former assistant secretary of labor in the United States government, now Director of the Harvard-M.I.T. Joint Center for Urban Affairs and affiliated with the Kennedy Institute of Politics at Harvard University. While in the service of the Labor Department, he authored the report entitled "The Negro Family: The Case for National Action."

R. N. NISHANOV: Secretary of the Central Committee of the Uzbek CPSU.

E. NITOBURG: A Soviet journalist and specialist in Latin America. Publications include *Paraguay* (1964), *The Politics of American Imperialism in Cuba* (1965), *Salvador* (1953), and *Venezuela* (1959).

F. OREKHOV: A Soviet journalist.

G. B. OSIPOV: Deputy Director of the Institute of Concrete Sociological Research of the Academy of Sciences of the USSR and President of the Soviet Sociological Association. Professor Osipov has edited *Sociology in the USSR* (1966), *Industry and Labor in the USSR* (in English) (1966), and authored *Contemporary Bourgeois Sociology* (1964).

S. S. OSTROUMOV: A legal scholar at Moscow University. Publications include *Crime and its Causes in Pre-revolutionary Russia* (1960) and *Soviet Legal Statistics* (1952).

TALCOTT PARSONS: Professor of Sociology at Harvard University and past president of the American Sociological Association. His many publications include *The Structure of Social Action* (1937), *The Social System* (1951), *Societies: Evolutionary and Comparative Perspectives* (1966), and *Sociological Theory and Modern Society* (1967).

V. PEREVEDENTSEV: Candidate of Economics affiliated with the Institute of Economics and the Organization of Industrial Production of the Siberian Branch of the Soviet Academy of Sciences. Professor Perevedentsev specializes in problems of demography and labor supply. He is the author of *Population Migration and Labor Problems of Siberia* (1966).

M. PERFIYEV: A philosopher affiliated with the Philosophy Institute of the Academy of Sciences of the USSR. Author of *Criticism of Bourgeois Theories of the Political Organization of Soviet Society* (1964).

G. PETROSYAN: A Soviet sociologist-economist affiliated with the Institute of Economics of Armenian Branch of the Academy of Sciences who specializes in leisure time studies. He wrote *Leisure Time of Workers in the USSR* (1965).

M. PETROSYAN: A Soviet philosopher. Author of *Humanism* (1964).

RICHARD PIPES: Professor of History at Harvard University. He has written *Social Democracy and the St. Petersburg Labor Movement 1885–1897* (1963), *The Formation of the Soviet Union* (1954), and edited *Revolutionary Russia* (1968).

I. POMELOV: A Soviet journalist and political commentator. Author of *The Indestructible Unity of the Party and People* (1955) and *The Revolutionary Course of the CPSU* (1966).

Y. RAIZMAN: Soviet film director. Recipient of the Order of Lenin and six Stalin prizes.

DAVID RIESMAN: Henry Ford II Professor of the Social Sciences at Harvard University. He is a student of American society and character, the author of *The Lonely Crowd* (1950), *Abundance for What?* (1964), and co-author of *Conversations in Japan* (1967).

LEO F. SCHNORE: Associate Professor of Sociology at the University of Wisconsin. Professor Schnore is the author of *The Urban Scene* (1965) and *Urban Research and Policy Planning* (1967).

EDWARD SHILS: Professor of Sociology at the University of Chicago. Professor Shils is the author of *The Torment of Secrecy* (1956), *Political Development in the New States* (1962), and numerous influential articles on sociological topics.

G. SHINAKOVA: Soviet journalist who often writes on sociological themes for *Literaturnaya gazeta*.

A. SHPEYER: A Soviet legal investigator.

V. SHUBKIN: Senior Scientific Associate of the Institute of Economics and the Organization of Industrial Production of the Siberian Branch of the Soviet Academy of Sciences. Professor Shubkin is a specialist in the use of mathematical methods in economics and sociology. He is the author of *Quantitative Methods in Sociology* (1966).

O. I. SKHARATAN: Candidate of Historical Sciences and Senior Scientific Worker, Institute of Ethnography of the Academy of Sciences of the USSR.

PITIRIM SOROKIN: The late Professor Sorokin was professor of sociology at Harvard University and a past president of the American Sociological Association. His many publications include *Sociological Theories of Today* (1966), *Social and Cultural Mobility* (1959), and *Principles of Rural and Urban Sociology* (with C. Zimmerman) (1929).

RODNEY STARK: A sociologist attached to the Survey Research Center of the University of California, Berkeley. Mr. Stark is the co-author of *Religion and Society in Tension* (1965).

ROBERT STRAUS: Professor of Sociology affiliated with the College of Medicine of the University of Kentucky. He is the author of *Drinking in College* (with S. D. Bacon) (1953).

B. SVETLICHNY: A Soviet architect. Author of *Today and Tomorrow in Our Cities* (1961).

GRESHAM SYKES: Professor of Sociology affiliated with the University of Denver School of Law. Professor Sykes' specialty is criminology. His works include *Crime and Society* (1956) and *The Society of Captives* (1958).

N. TROYAN: A Soviet psychiatrist.

A. VASKBERG: Soviet writer and journalist.

A. VALENTINOV: A Soviet engineer.

ERNEST VAN DEN HAAG: Professor of Psychology and Sociology at the New School for Social Research. Publications include *Passion and Social Constraint* (1963).

W. LLOYD WARNER: Professor of Sociology at Michigan State University. Professor Warner specializes in the problems of class structure of American society. He has written *The Status System of a Modern Community* (with Paul S. Lunt) (1942), *The Social Systems of American Ethnic Groups* (with Leo Srole) (1945), *The Social System of the Modern Factory* (with J. O. Low) (1947), and *American Life: Dream and Reality* (1962).

ROBERT WEISS: Lecturer on Sociology in the Department of Psychiatry at Harvard University. Professor Weiss is the author of *Processes of Organization* (1956).

STANTON WHEELER: Sociologist affiliated with the Russell Sage Foundation and Yale University. Dr. Wheeler is the author of *Juvenile Delinquency* (1966).

ROBIN M. WILLIAMS, JR.: Professor of Sociology at Cornell University and past president of the American Sociological Association. His publications include *American Society* (1960) and *Strangers Next Door* (1964).

A. YANOV: Soviet journalist who often writes on sociological themes for *Literaturnaya gazeta*.

D. YEREMIN: Soviet writer, recipient of a Stalin Prize for literature in 1952. Author of *Sun Over the Steppe* (1965) and *Kind People* (1963).

Y. A. ZAMOSHKIN: Doctor of Philosophy and chairman of a section of the Institute of the International Labor Movement. Professor Zamoshkin is also one of the editors of the journal *Voprosy Filosofii*. He is a frequent critic of American sociology. He is the author of *The Crisis of Bourgeois Individualism and Personality* (1967).

A. ZDRAVOMYSLOV: Sociologist affiliated with the Philosophy Faculty of Leningrad University. Professor Zdravomyslov specializes in the sociology of labor. His publications include *Man and His Work* (with V. Yadov) (1967).

L. ZHUKOVITSKY: A Soviet journalist who often writes on sociological themes.

DEDICATION

To the Czechoslovak People,
Longtime Students of Comparative Totalitarianism
and Experts on Soviet Society

ACKNOWLEDGEMENTS

Professors Alex Inkeles and David Riesman of Harvard University read the outline and projected table of contents of the book and made helpful comments both with regard to the objectives of the reader and the selections to be included. Professor Kent Geiger of the University of Wisconsin also read the first outline and gave me much useful advice about topics to be covered. Miss Vida Taranovski of Radcliffe College did many of the original translations from Russian. Mr. Edward Everett of Harvard University performed most of the demanding administrative work involved in obtaining the permission rights for the materials to be reprinted. Mr. Martin Whyte, also of Harvard University, prepared the "Authors" section. Miss Mary Towle and Miss Brenda D. Sens proofread the contents in the short time at their disposal with admirable thoroughness.

The Russian Research Center of Harvard University provided not only facilities for research while the reader was being prepared (as it did during the past five years) but also a stimulating and congenial intellectual environment.

CONTENTS

III. SOCIAL STRATIFICATION 123

IV. THE FAMILY: MARITAL AND SEXUAL RELATIONS 155

V. SOCIAL PROBLEMS 217

Crime and Juvenile Delinquency, 221

Discrimination—Ethnic Minorities, 284

Leisure, 321

Leisure in the U.S.

Leisure in the U.S.S.R.

The Effects of Alcohol, 351

The Effects of Alcohol in the U.S.

The Effects of Alcohol in the U.S.S.R.

Mass Culture, 360

Mass Culture in the U.S.

Mass Culture in the U.S.S.R.

Youth, 373

Youth in the U.S.

Youth in the U.S.S.R.

Old Age, 395

Old Age in the U.S.

Old Age in the U.S.S.R.

Rural Areas, 405

Rural Areas in the U.S.

INTRODUCTION

THE OBJECTIVES OF THE READER

It might surprise some readers that this author felt compelled to explain and justify his enterprise, as if editing an anthology were a somewhat shady undertaking provoking the disdain of one's colleagues and the rumblings of his own conscience. In contemporary American publishing and academic life, anthologies, i.e., collections of articles (or excerpts of books) which had appeared before in print, are widespread and sometimes appear to have become substitutes for books both from the point of view of authors and their readers. For the latter, anthologies save time and intellectual trouble. They represent shortcuts to information, if not to erudition. They help one become acquainted with the ideas, or the gist of ideas of many writers quickly and relatively painlessly. There are, of course, many notable exceptions which cannot be subjected to such criticism. From the authors' point of view the anthology is also a shortcut to getting something between covers. Few would dispute that it is easier and quicker to edit than to write a book. We have today in the social sciences almost as many readers as books. Originally readers were justified by the desire to make inaccessible materials readily available. Yet most readers are hardly scholarly compilations of fugitive or esoteric reading matters. Rather they are reprints (often not the first) of materials published elsewhere not necessarily a long time ago and still in print. Producing them seldom requires much originality, hard work, or imagination. Their requirements lie elsewhere: in the conditions of the

1

market, the demands of introductory courses for easily digestible materials, and the prestige rewards of the profession.

Under these conditions I found myself first reluctant, later embarrassed, in contributing to the flood. It seemed that I was in the classical situation of doing exactly that which I deplored when others did it. Characteristically, the origins of this book could be traced to the publisher, who suggested that I compile a reader on Soviet society, toward which I felt no inclination. It later occurred to me that a comparative reader on American and Soviet society and sociology could be a more valuable and more original undertaking. Still later I added the theme of cross-national perceptions. In the end, rightly or wrongly, I persuaded myself that I was abandoning my objections against readers in order to make an intellectual contribution. I am certain that such feelings are not exactly unique.

In any event it seemed to me that a reader ought to be more than a convenient compilation of information, or a cautious sampling of ideas. My major hope was that the systematic juxtaposition of American and Soviet materials, like any other opportunity for comparison would help to expose the reader (as well as the editor) to something new, something he would not otherwise notice, appreciate, or understand, if he read the same materials in isolation from each other.

As its sheer bulk suggests, this volume tries to accomplish an immoderate number of objectives. At the most elementary level it is a compilation of sociological writings about the two societies organized around their major institutions and problems as observed by their leading sociologists (sometimes social scientists of related disciplines) or—in the Soviet case—sometimes by others without social scientific qualifications who, however, perform analogous roles. At a second level the book is an exercise in comparative sociology. This is accomplished by the juxtaposition of the analysis of identical (or corresponding) institutions in two different societies.

Third, the writings brought together provide a sizeable case study in cross-national perceptions, since about half of them represent the perception of sociologists of the institutions and problems of a society other than their own. I felt that it would be particularly interesting to present the assessments of American sociologists of Soviet institutions, and much less familiar for the American reader, the assessments of Soviet sociologists of numerous aspects of American society.

The goals of the undertaking could also be summarized as follows:

1. To provide an advanced and substantial introduction for the comparative (or non-comparative, for that matter) study of American and Soviet society.
2. To provide an exploration in the sociology of knowledge by examining the characteristics of American and Soviet sociology in relation to their respective social settings and with the help of the self-appraisals of the respective members of the disciplines.
3. To provide a case study in comparative social perception; in this respect

the book offers an opportunity to consider the factors influencing the positions taken across the national and ideological boundaries, and might stimulate the reader to reflect on the various possible sources and patterns of distortion, polemics, structured omission, animosity, and just and unjust criticisms. He might also be prompted to ponder the impact of supposedly shared attachments to canons of scientific procedure and objectivity, the part played by distance, ethnocentrism, ideology, value commitments, political factors, adequate or inadequate information, the choice and availability of data, etc.

4. The volume also might serve some purpose for those interested in broader theoretical issues. It could easily be used as a testing ground of several current, as well as traditional, sociological concerns, concepts, and theories (supplying material for debating their relevance and usefulness), such as social change, modernization, industrialization, political integration, capitalism, communism, pluralism, totalitarianism, structural differentiation, convergence, and others.

5. Last, but not least, the volume provides considerable information about Soviet society and sociology that indeed is not too easily accessible, including several original translations.

THE ORGANIZATION OF THE MATERIAL AND THE PRINCIPLES OF SELECTION

The seven parts of the book reflect a somewhat conventional perception of the major social institutions and problems. They encompass the most frequently discussed aspects or components of any society with the conspicuous exception of the economy, which in conjunction with consumption is discussed to some degree in the part on stratification. In addition several selections do provide, by implication or otherwise, at least glimpses of the economic sphere in the two societies. Still I am aware of the insufficiency of this coverage. The lengthy catalogue of social problems is nonetheless incomplete. In the final analysis, the editor's interest determined what should be included or excluded. Naturally an effort was made to reconcile these interests with the generally agreed upon professional definitions of social problems. One part is included because of an interest in the profession as such, namely Part VI, "Appraisals of Sociology." Little documentation is needed to suggest that the condition and characteristics of sociology in any society are among the revealing indices of the nature of the social order as a whole. This relationship has little to do with the substantive accomplishments of sociology itself.

The other part of the reader not strictly relevant to the systematic, institutional comparison of the two societies—Part VII, "Are the Two Societies Becoming Alike?"—reflects the current interest among social scientists and the public in this question. Here too, however, the selections are drawn from

sociological sources, and the opinions voiced also contribute to the comparative assessment of the two societies.

Throughout the volume an effort was made to limit the selections to the
writings of sociologists—not because their writings are necessarily superior
or more informative or detached than other social scientists' (or even non-
social scientists'), but because it simplified the criteria for selection and
because I was interested not only in the characteristics of the two societies,
but also in the sociologies each has produced. However, not even sociologists
always express themselves on every relevant subject of sociology and on
every aspect of social existence; therefore I found it necessary at times to
resort to non-sociological sources. This was also necessitated by the cross-
national angle of the book: sociologists in every society have more to say
about their own society (and take greater care to avoid ignoring any of
its aspects) than about others. Recourse to non-sociological sources was
especially inescapable in some instances of selecting the Soviet writings.
Because Soviet sociology is a young discipline, it has yet to engage itself in
every important subject of sociological inquiry. In the Soviet context I also
had to contend with the problem of distinguishing a sociologist from a non-
sociologist, since the distinction between sociologist and other social scientists,
and between sociologist and party functionaries or journalists concerned with
sociological matters, is still often blurred. More than in the U.S., authoritative Soviet statements on sociologically important subjects frequently come
from non-sociological sources. I have largely accepted the professional self-
definition of Soviet sociologists, although some of my American colleagues
might object, and perhaps with reason, because at times I have included those
who might uncharitably be called professional party hacks. However, the
fusion between the sociological and political-ideological role still often
encountered in the Soviet Union is in itself an interesting and significant
feature of Soviet sociology, and as such should not be ignored. It must be
noted that Soviet sociologists themselves are aware of the problems of their
professional identity.[1]

In selecting statements on each subject and representing the American
and Soviet perceptions of it, I was partly guided by a desire for what might
be called representative diversity. Whenever possible I tried to capture
differences of opinion on the same issue, not between the American and
Soviet voices (that was almost unavoidable on most topics), but among
American and Soviet sociologists respectively. It was easier to find differences
of opinion among American sociologists—particularly in their assessments of
their own society—than among the Soviet. Greater unanimity is a fact
of life of Soviet sociology, although areas of disagreement do exist (for
example in the discussions of the Soviet family), which whenever encountered
were eagerly included. The relative unfamiliarity of a given subject or the

---

[1] Cf. for example, V. Mikhailov and V. Perevedentsev, "Great expectations," Literaturnaya gazeta, *Current Digest of the Soviet Press,* July 12, 1967, pp. 17–19.

amount of new information available on it often determined a selection's inclusion.

There is a slight quantitative imbalance in the whole volume favoring Soviet writings. Soviet sources are less familiar to the American reader, and thus a slight overexposure to them might be justified. This extra attention to the Soviet side is also reflected in the short introductions which precede each part of the book, and again, a more ample commentary on the Soviet writings seems justified. These short introductions were not intended as complete summaries, and they were not designed to deprive the reader from reaching his own conclusions about any given section of the book.

On the whole, in making the selections I had three major criteria: Relevance to the given topic; representativeness, assured to some degree by quoting distinguished authors; and recency, inasmuch as possible. However, established reputation in itself was not a major criterion, especially in the Soviet case where there are few established reputations in sociology so far.

PROBLEMS OF COMPARATIVE SOCIOLOGY IN
RELATION TO THE U.S. AND U.S.S.R.

An anthology provides its editor with an excellent opportunity to avoid, if he so desires, stating his own views on the topics at hand. He can let the selections (like the proverbial facts of the social sciences) "speak for themselves," as they do within limits, and let them convey his attitudes. I would also like to state more explicitly my view of some of the issues raised by this volume and its contributors. Enough diversity exists among the selections to obscure the leanings of the editor.

There are many possible theoretical approaches to editing an anthology on American and Soviet society, and a corresponding variety of value premises. It is impossible to be completely eclectic or open-minded in selecting the materials no matter how dear are the goals of diversity, representativeness, and objectivity. The easiest might have been to organize the volume around the theme of the growing, or unexpected (yet shrewdly discerned) similarities between American and Soviet society. This would have pleased several groups of readers and students of the subject—the optimists hopeful of a synthesis of the best features of both societies, as well as the gloomy critics who find it difficult to decide which of the two societies is more unappealing. It also would have pleased those who believe on purely theoretical grounds in the growing similarity of all modern societies. A critical demonstration of similarities might also have delighted many who are contemptuous of the false claims of superiority made by the spokesmen of both American and Soviet society. Moreover, by stressing similarities I would have benefited from creating the impression of objectivity and lofty disdain for taking sides, and achieved almost total immunity from either the label of "cold warrior" (often applied to those critical of Soviet society) or that of leftist sympathizer. A strong sense of the differences between any two contemporary societies tends to be accompanied by a preference for one. (It is easier to be impartial about the past.) Consequently, discerning similarities between American and Soviet society has become the best way to avoid the "stigma" attached to having ideological predilections for the American. Although there is no logical or theoretical basis for it, most of those, at least in the United States, who express a keen sense of the differences between American and Soviet society tend to be partial to the American. The number of those who perceive sharp differences and prefer the Soviet is exceedingly small for reasons too numerous to discuss here. Suffice it to say, that those most alienated from and critical of American society no longer place the Soviet Union at the apex of social progress.

At the same time I should point out that a demonstration of similarities between the two societies would not, under any circumstances, please my potential Soviet readers and fellow sociologists. They view such efforts with deep suspicion as part of a more sophisticated campaign to denigrate their society. We will sample their views on this subject in Part VIII.

In any event I did not choose the theme of growing similarities because I disagree with it and because I consider its implications misleading. This does not mean that I deny, or that the volume fails to reflect, the areas where similarities are discernible and possibly increasing. What I reject is the notion that similarities have so increased as to call into question fundamental differences between the two societies. That still leaves us with the perennial question of comparative studies as to what is more significant in a given case, the differences or similarities? To which the time-honored rejoinder is that it depends on the purposes at hand. The issue, of course, is not limited to the relationship between American and Soviet society; it can very well be raised in connection with other contemporary societies which are becoming similar in some ways, remaining dissimilar in others, and evolving new differences in other areas of social life and organization. Underlying the issue of similarities and differences among contemporary societies is the basic, irreducible question of whether a given social scientist is more interested in discovering similarities or differences, and not only in regard to societies. Admittedly the interest in differences can be carried suicidally far, at least from the standpoint of sociological-theoretical fruitfulness. But there are also dangers in the overzealous pursuit of similarities for the sociologist, of which the most obvious is the growth of indifference to empirical facts, to reality as experienced by most men, trained or untrained in the social sciences. Sensitivity to similarities is in close kinship with the generalizing impulse. If this volume errs on the side of highlighting the differences between the two societies (and I am not sure that it does), it is because I feel that in the U.S. awareness of their precise nature is still surprisingly limited. This is primarily due to lingering misconceptions about

Soviet society among the general public and non-specialists in the social sciences, despite a freer flow of information and better relations between the two countries. Perhaps, paradoxically, better relations led to a premature decline of popular (as well as scholarly) interest, as if a less threatening image of the Soviet Union had disqualified her from being a preeminent subject of attention. This being the case, some efforts were made to convey through the selections some of the peculiarities and genuinely contrasting features of Soviet society. It could be argued that to appreciate the similarities between the two societies the differences must first be known, or any alleged awareness of similarities remains a theoretical edifice built on sand. Furthermore, there is no inherent affinity between a clear awareness of the differences between one's own and a strange society and ethnocentrism, contrary to a belief implicitly held by many Americans. Being aware of such differences, as noted earlier, *need not* amount to making value judgments, although it often does.

Thus one of the premises of this reader is a strong sense of the differences between American and Soviet society. That there are important differences would not be denied by most students of the problem. The disagreements arise in evaluating their significance, in specifying their exact nature, and perhaps the most critical, in finding adequate terminology and theoretical propositions with which to characterize and explain them. The last problem is particularly acute today when the rapidity of social change often leaves social scientists grasping for new concepts with which to capture the bewildering transformations of the social landscape. Here again the Soviet Union presents special problems. For several decades there was a degree of consensus among American specialists on Soviet society as to the best ways to characterize it and the most auspicious concepts or models to use. The consensus centered upon the model or concept of "totalitarianism," and it was widely accepted that the "totalitarian syndrome" adequately described and explained the nature of the Soviet social system.[2] The gist of the model was an emphasis on new, intensified, and historically unique forms of centralized political control over society made possible by modern technology and motivated by intense ideological commitments, sometimes referred to as "secular-religious." There is, of course, more to this model, as will be shown in some of the later selections (especially in Part II). After Stalin's death, and in particular, after Khrushchev's rise to power, a slow erosion of faith in the continued applicability of the totalitarian model has set in. The concept was attacked for a variety of reasons. First, it was said that it simply ceased to describe adequately the post-Stalin Soviet Union because of the social changes which have taken place. Also it was felt that the concept itself, with its pejorative connotations (of oppression, terror, regimentation) lent itself to cold war propaganda and impeded better rela-

---

2 Cf. for example, C. Friedrich, *Totalitarianism—A Symposium* (Cambridge: Harvard University Press, 1954).

tions between the U.S. and the Soviet Union. Belatedly, it was also discovered by some that it *never* made much sense, since there is no such thing as a "total" control or domination either of society or of the individual. It is another matter whether or not the concept implied the *realization* of, as opposed to the *aspiration* for, total control. According to may who still consider it useful, the concept draws attention to objectives and measures *aimed at* maximizing controls, rather than asserting that such controls are established facts in totalitarian societies.[3] Be as it may, when the dust of the dispute settles there are few Western and particularly American students of Soviet society who would rely on the totalitarian model *alone* to describe Soviet society, but there are not many either who would banish the concept entirely from their analysis.[4] Actually the difficult is not limited to the Soviet case; it is common to any shorthand description of any huge, complex society. The Soviet Union is, among other things, a totalitarian society. The U.S. is, among other things, a capitalist society. Britain is, among other things, a monarchy. All three are (among other things) highly industrialized, though in this case "highly" can hide a variety of differences, notably the fact that in the U.S. and Britain less than 8 per cent of the labor force is employed in agriculture, whereas in the Soviet Union over 30 per cent is so employed. It seems to me that if we do want to use a shorthand term or descriptive label which conveys *some* of the important differences between American and Soviet society, we might still describe the Soviet as totalitarian. It is not the full truth, but a considerable and characteristic part of it. We might similarly wish to designate American society as "affluent" or "capitalistic" or "pluralistic"—labels which each convey by necessity only a fraction, though perhaps an important one, of the complex and varied American realities. Still, we do need shorthand descriptive terms, if for no other reason, for efficiency in communicating and thinking. Every single concept designed to sum up complex realities does injustice to its empirical referents. All we can do is to try to minimize the injustice. This, of course, is the old issue of ideal types of which Max Weber made us fully conscious. It could still be argued that we are in need of new and improved concepts or descriptive labels for both Soviet and American society. Unfortunately, they have yet to be devised. Of course, one way out of the dilemma is simply to say that both American and Soviet societies are modern, industrial, and complex. But, of course, so are dozens of other societies in Europe and elsewhere. Unless we want to submerge all these in a bland generalization focusing on their similarities, we must use the old labels or invent new ones. The point is that being modern (in itself an elusive concept), industrial, urban, and complex simply does not exhaust all or even the major attributes or dimensions of societies. They can be all these things and still be quite different

[3] For two recent discussions of the concept cf. Hugh Seton-Watson, "Totalitarianism Reconsidered," *Problems of Communism,* July–August 1967, and by this author, "Observations on Totalitarianism, Bureaucracy and the Comparative Study of Communism," *Slavic Review,* June 1967.

[4] Cf. Alex Inkeles, "Models in the Analysis of Soviet Society," *Survey,* July 1966.

from one another, as both social scientific evidence and personal experience tell us. Just as there are no identical social environments for individuals, so there are no identical historical environments for societies. Historical differences of origins and development linger on perplexingly and in defiance of accurate measurement. (Not that there is a shortage of measurable indices of differences between the Soviet Union and the U.S.) More will be said on this subject in the introduction to Part VII.

DIFFERENCES AND SIMILARITIES BETWEEN AMERICAN AND SOVIET SOCIETY

In the following I would like to summarize what appear to be the decisive differences between American and Soviet society.

1. In the political realm, it is the enormous contrast between an imperfectly pluralistic (and democratic) as against an imperfectly totalitarian (and authoritarian) society. In addition there is nothing in the U.S. corresponding to or resembling the role and character of the Party, the Communist Party of the Soviet Union. On the other hand, the Soviet Union does not have a built-in source of conflict comparable to the presence in American society of the Negro minority although, as will be shown later, minority problems and discrimination are not totally absent from Soviet society.

2. In the economic sphere we encounter the much discussed difference between a society with a generally high standard of living (whatever index is used) against one which has only recently and partially left the ranks of underdeveloped nations. Here we should also note that Soviet industrialization until the last decade had borne relatively few fruits in the form of consumer goods and services. The provision of both still remains spotty and insufficient in quantity and quality. Food production has also remained a chronic problem of the Soviet economy. There is, of course, also the structural difference between a private enterprise economy and a state-owned economy. The significance of this difference, however, may be somewhat exaggerated by the defenders and apologists of each type of economy. It is especially difficult for a non-economist to make comparative judgments about their respective efficiency. Each economic system has certain strengths and weaknesses. At any rate, I would like to suggest that if the American economy appears more efficient, and it is in most respects, this does not necessarily result from the magic of free enterprise or private property, but it may very well be correlated with other factors. These factors are the qualities and motivation of the American labor force, advanced techniques of management and organization, certain established social values functional for the achievement of high productivity, and the accumulated historical advantages of the American economy accruing both from resources and the human material.

The difference between a state and a privately owned economy has another important consequence more relevant for the political than for the economic sphere. Providing and controlling employment opportunities is in any society a major lever of social control and sanctions. Where the state is the single employer its power to control, punish, or reward is considerably enhanced.

3. The U.S. is an almost totally urban society, but the Soviet Union is only partly urban. The U.S., with certain important regional exceptions, has come close to attaining what has been a long-standing and much talked about aspiration of the Soviet leadership: closing the gap between town and country. Not that such a synthesis, at least in its American form, is necessarily desirable. There are also qualitative differences between American and Soviet urbanization. Many Soviet cities are still inhabited by first-generation city dwellers, whose peasant backgrounds are much in evidence. Perhaps the attitudes and values of American Negroes rapidly transplanted from the rural South to urban areas in the North may be a parallel situation; but the traditional values of the two groups are very different. It would seem that the "psychic mobility" of the American Negro is somewhat greater than that of the Russian peasant despite handicaps of race.

4. There is no element or faction in the American political system, either in power or within realistic reach of it, which would contemplate or wish for the ideological-indoctrinational remolding of the entire population, or the creation of "The New American Man" corresponding to the New Soviet Man (or the New Communist Man). Nobody in or near a position of power in the U.S. seriously entertains—whether he is a politician, educator, clergy-man, or social scientist—the radical improvement of the human species or significantly changing human nature. There may be a belief in progress and the limited perfectibility of man, corresponding in some measure to the similar Soviet belief; however, no serious or systematic steps comparable to the gigantic Soviet political-educational effort have ever been undertaken. While this difference may seem to be intangible or abstract, it does affect the concrete policies and the institutions of the two societies. It is expressed among other things in the pervasiveness of Soviet political propaganda. It could also be defined as the difference between a system (the Soviet) which retained a substantial part of its original, utopian beliefs and wants to transmit them, and one (the American) which has not.

5. Though related to the presence or absence of political pluralism, the differences in the freedom of expression are important enough to be mentioned separately. These differences are reflected both in institutional arrangements and widely distributed personal-psychological attitudes in the respective populations. These differences are among the sharpest and most easily observable.

6. The formal dominant belief or value systems of the two societies are also noticeably different. A variant of Marxism-Leninism on the one hand, as against a somewhat diluted mixture of the values of Judeo-Christianity, the French Enlightenment, and bourgeois free enterprise. In addition there are further differences resulting from the Anglo-Saxon versus Russian-Slavic

cultural tradition. To be sure all this still allows for some similarities in values. This will be discussed in Part I.

These differences coexist with a number of similarities between the two societies. I will also try to summarize these in the following:

1. Both societies are revolutionary in their origin, although, of course, the actual nature of the revolutions was quite different. The beginnings of both societies can be traced in a sense to the deliberate decision taken by a small number of people who wanted to initiate a radical departure from their hitherto customary existence, and to change the "human condition." This strain was prominent among the first settlers of America (and on a less exalted level among the later ones), and it does present a degree of resemblance to the motives of the early Russian revolutionaries.

2. Both societies are military superpowers, with all that it implies: immense economic burdens, advanced military technology, and farflung international-political commitments and concerns.

3. There are widely shared *popular* values and aspirations in the realms of leisure, comfort, and consumption, and to a lesser extent in those of education and achievement.

4. Both the U.S. and U.S.S.R. are basically secular societies although this is partially concealed in each: in the U.S. by the formal adherence to religious beliefs and the continued existence of religious institutions; in the Soviet Union by the social-ideological role of Marxism-Leninism that does fulfill many functions analogous to religion, particularly for the political elite.

5. Finally, we should note similarities resulting from the sheer size of the two countries, both in area and population. The availability of land area had important social consequences, not only in the patterns of early settlement and expansion (from an early Russian-European versus Eastern-Seaboard core area) but also in the continued presence of geographical (and often attendant social) mobility. One might also speculate about the characterological consequences of opportunities for exploration within the same political-national boundaries. The latter, however, were more pronounced in the U.S. than in pre-revolutionary Russia and the Soviet Union where the settlement of distant parts was less a matter of personal initiative. Size is also relevant in both societies to the growth of huge bureaucratic structures and organizations.

In conclusion I would like to propose that the differences outweigh the similarities: that is, the statistical, institutional, historical, and theoretical differences are supported by the response of the average member of each society, who experiences a profound "cultural shock" when moving from one to another. He feels unmistakably confronted by a different tone and style of life which prolonged exposure deepens rather than erases. In other words the differences have a more tangible and observable impact on daily life than the similarities—another circumstance that makes them more important.

Two societies and two sociologies

The differences between American and Soviet sociology are fairly accurate measures of the differences between the two societies. The discipline of sociology, its products, and practitioners are unlikely to escape the imprint of their larger social environment, partly because society has a stake in the findings of its sociology. The greater the commitment to the perfection of its values and institutions and the stronger the belief in the influence and power of ideas, the more anxiously the guardians of a given social order will keep watch over the social sciences. This fact explains some of the major differences between American and Soviet sociology. Thus, it might be argued that there is more freedom of expression and inquiry in American sociology because ideas are usually treated less seriously due to the Anglo-Saxon intellectual tradition of pragmatism and empiricism. On the other hand, in the Soviet political-ideological tradition, ideas are treated as "weapons," and there is a somewhat exaggerated sensitivity to the interdependence of ideas and institutions, belief and action, theory and practice. There is also, in the Soviet Union, a much more explicit and clearly articulated (indeed ceaselessly reiterated) official belief in the historical superiority of the Soviet social order. This in turn explains why social criticism, or at any rate, serious social criticism is not among the officially designated or tolerated preoccupations of sociology. Yet, it is in itself significant that sociology is permitted to exist.

Soviet sociology, among other things, reflects the transitional state of Soviet society. We must remember that it emerged in the post-Stalin period (in the late 1950's) and its appearance signaled the recognition that not only ideological but also empirical, social-scientific statements about society are legitimate and relevant. As long as a perfect congruence between ideological propositions and social reality was postulated, sociology had no reason to exist. As long as it was asserted that there was a complete harmony between Soviet social institutions and the needs of the Soviet people there was equally little justification for its existence. Whenever it is claimed that social institutions are perfectly integrated with each other and the individuals functioning within their framework well adjusted to them, there are hardly any grounds to initiate sociological inquiry. Thus among the ultimate preconditions for the emergence of Soviet sociology we find the admission, grudging and implicit as it may be, that the perfect fit between society and the individual is yet to be attained.

In the U.S. social criticism has traditionally been a popular pastime not only of social scientists but of many other articulate and literate members of society. Perhaps, one might argue without detracting from its benefits and achievements, the freedom of social criticism in the U.S. has indicated the limited importance attributed to it. It is actions not words that matter in the American ethos, where few would compare ideas to weapons, even if they are critical ones. This circumstance might explain in part, for example, the shock and astonishment the late Senator McCarthy created by stressing the deeply subversive consequences of attachment to certain ideas.

There are a few more obvious yet important differences between American and Soviet sociology, besides those concerning the boundaries of legitimate social criticism.

1. American sociology is older, more developed, and more differentiated both in method and theoretical orientation. It is also more entrenched in academic life.

2. In the Soviet Union the philosophical-ideological orientation and value premises are more readily admitted, indeed often flaunted, by sociologists. In the U.S. scientific detachment is the ideal.

3. Soviet sociology is more problem-oriented, more applied, more directly tied to the needs of society, as defined by the political leadership.

4. There are also immense contrasts in style (which result from the orientation cited in point two). The Soviet style is far more polemical, dogmatic, assertive, and permeated by Marxist-Leninist terminology; the American style is much more tentative (often too much so), abstract, and characterized most frequently by the terminology of structural-functionalism; it is also more burdened by jargon and further removed from the non-sociological discourse. On the other hand, if American sociologists are as self-righteous as their Soviet colleagues often seem to be (especially when they discuss American society and sociology), they do an immensely better job of hiding it and giving the impression of reasonable detachment and objectivity.

In surveying the similarities and differences between the two sociologies we must also consider briefly the issue of "mirror images," especially since much of this book consists of the cross-national perceptions of American and Soviet sociologists. Do their respective perceptions of the other society resemble each other? Do they project to the other society what they are most familiar with in their own? Do their perceptions of each other's institutions and social problems mirror one another? Pleasing as it would be to one's sense of symmetry, the answer must be a qualified, but firm "no." The perceptions in question are fundamentally divergent, ideology being the crucial divider. There is little in the belief system (if it amounts to that) or professional values of most American sociologists, and certainly those included in this volume, that would predispose them to a conception of Soviet society that postulates impending doom, downfall, or disintegration. This has no connection with their liking or not of the U.S.S.R. None of them anticipates radical change, of such or any other nature. At the most, many of them entertain cautious visions of slow change, or gradual evolution to a stage they might consider preferable to the present one. They perceive Soviet institutions as viable, durable, and in most cases, well adapted to Soviet historical conditions. Americans in general, and sociologists in particular, believe that things are getting better, not worse, in the Soviet

Union. Soviet sociologists on the other hand discuss American society on the premise of a historically ordained disintegration and decline. They perceive American society as riddled with contradictions, and insoluble ones for that matter, and American institutions as badly adapted to the needs of American people and out of tune with historical progress. Their image of American society is also basically conspiratorial: behind every facet of American life lurk the malevolent designs of the ruling circles, the power elite, the controllers of the monopolies or the military-industrial complex. In some of this they freely borrow from the American social critics. Their perception of American society is far less benevolent than the image of Soviet society held by most American sociologists.

The Soviet perceptions of American society are also more undifferentiated, more prone to oversimplification and to the heavy-handed juxtapositions of darkness and light. Though there have been improvements, the overwhelming impression still corresponds to the above description. This impression at any rate applies to the public, printed version of these perceptions. The roots of these perceptions are to be found not only in the part Soviet social scientists (especially those writing about bourgeois societies such as the U.S.) must play in the ideological struggle, but also in the rigid adherence to Marxism which predisposes one to a dichotomized world view. Soviet sociologists generally seem to have a greater difficulty in understanding American society and its complexities than vice versa. Another cause for this is the inadequate information and the long period of general isolation from the world outside the Soviet Union, which is only now coming slowly and incompletely to an end.

There are, however, some similarities between the two sets of perceptions: some American views of Soviet society are also somewhat conspiratorial, portraying every aspect of Soviet social life as determined by the pursuit of political power and controls and by the goals set by the political leadership. While it is easier to justify this approach to the Soviet social order, which is far more heavily politicized and tightly integrated, the mere exercise of political power cannot sufficiently explain many features of present-day Soviet society. A further similarity in Soviet and American perceptions of each other is the propensity to separate the "regime," "elite" or "leadership," from the people, the masses, or the "ordinary" Russians and Americans. Again, a sharp dividing line is more plausibly applied to Soviet society rather than to American, since American political leaders, parties, and groupings are visibly more dependent on popular support than their Soviet counterparts. (This difference will be further explored and clarified in Part II.) Such similarities, however, do not add up to a "mirror image."

The purpose of these comparisons has not been to glorify American sociology. If American sociology is richer, freer, and more diverse than Soviet sociology, as I believe it is, it is due to the combination of many fortunate circumstances which made it the most productive discipline compared not only to the Soviet but also to other Western sociologies.

Among these fortunate circumstances are chronological maturity, ample support for research the pluralistic (and perhaps happily indifferent) social-political environment, and particularly the limited government concern with sociological inquiry. Government and political institutions in general ignore the political-ideological significance of sociological research (public opinion polls excepted) often to the dismay of some American sociologists. Of course, government financed and initiated research does exist, and some of it is a counterpart to applied Soviet research designed to further societal efficiency. However, the financial support American sociology receives from public funds has not yet made it dependent on political agencies and interests, although some would probably question this. On the whole most American sociologists, are not ill at ease about the source of their research support (with the possible exception of the Defense Department and CIA), nor do they feel any constraint or obligation toward their benefactors concerning their findings and the theoretical orientation they adopt.

American and Soviet sociology differ from each other because each is stamped by its respective social environment. There is, however, a smaller difference between the two sociologies than between the two societies. (Paradoxically, the two sociologies have most in common in their concern with social problems.) While this might please those who would interpret it as an expression of the unifying force of science, there is little reason to believe that the two sociologies will move significantly closer to each other unless their parent societies do the same.

I

SOCIAL VALUES,

BELIEFS, AND IDEOLOGIES

We have selected three American and one Soviet social scientist for a sketch of American values. We have done so in order to capture the diversity of American viewpoints and approaches. Boorstin's piece is critical-philosophical; Parsons focuses on the major American values in relation to ongoing social change, while Dubois provides a well-rounded summary statement. In view of the considerable unanimity of the Soviet perceptions, one excerpt from Zamoshkin's recent book seemed to provide an adequate sampling of the Soviet perspective. Perhaps we should note that "values," "value systems," "value commitments" are concepts not typical of the Soviet sociological discourse. In general it would be futile to expect to find a terminology identical to that used by the Americans. Yet, while there are terminological differences between the Soviet and American writings presented (and even among the Americans), they all are addressing themselves essentially to the same problems: What do Americans value highly? What do they believe in? What are their major and ultimate aspirations? Where do they seek the meaning and satisfactions in life?

It would be unreasonable to expect close agreement on these matters, and it should surprise few if the Soviet evaluation will substantially differ from the American, although there will also be some areas of agreement.

Perhaps the single major difference between Dubois' and Parsons' views compared with Zamoshkin's is that the former regard American values as viable, well-established, reasonably stable, and functionally relevant to the lives of Americans, while the latter does not. Boorstin comes closest to

Zamoshkin in stressing the undesirable consequences that an attachment to American values create: inflated, unrealistic, and often unrealizable expectations. In effect, Boorstin suggests that Americans get into trouble for taking their values too seriously, in particular for believing unconditionally that theirs is a society of unlimited opportunities. However, unlike Zamoshkin, he does not look upon this as a state of affairs resulting from the deliberate designs of a small group of bad people.

Since we are more familiar with the criticisms Americans make of their own society and its values, we should examine somewhat more closely the picture Professor Zamoshkin presents. It is not a cheerful one. He feels that American beliefs and aspirations are corroded and corrupted by a rampant, vulgar materialism, by the notorious cash nexus. This is the orthodox Marxist diagnosis of the ills of capitalist society, which culminate in alienation. He is most concerned with the aspect of alienation expressed in the worship of material objects and the creation of a false system of values centering on consumption. (This of course is hardly news since Veblen.) Zamoshkin does depart from classical Marxist analysis in acknowledging that there is an abundance of consumer goods in the United States—rather than just grinding poverty—which is available to wide segments of the population even if it must be purchased amidst anxiety and on installments. He emphasizes not so much the debasing effects of poverty and exploitation as the spiritual impoverishment Americans suffer because of their obsession with consumer goods. Another innovation of his critique, from the orthodox Marxist point of view, is his concern with advertising and what he calls bourgeois "official propaganda." (The latter is not clearly defined and appears to belong to the species of Soviet projections, i.e., the transfer of unappealing phenomena present in the Soviet social setting to the American.) It might also be noted that in his emphasis on the importance of advertising and bourgeois ideology, we are encountering a trend in Soviet social thought prominent since Lenin: the importance of ideas as determinants of social institutions and processes.

Needless to say, criticisms of this kind are not peculiar to Soviet observers. Many, if not most, American sociologists are unenthusiastic to say the least about advertising, conspicuous consumption, status anxiety, status symbols, and much else that our Soviet critic includes in "consumer psychology." In point of fact, Zamoshkin relies heavily on American sociologists in making his case. C. Wright Mills, Vance Packard, Harold Rosenberg, and William H. Whyte are among those he quotes. There would be more disagreement among American sociologists on whether or not work lost its value and meaning—among others, Parsons and Dubois would disagree—and on the evaluation of individualism, which for Zamoshkin is a disorganizing, undesirable phenomenon (as well as unrealizable). On the whole we might say that he parts company with most American observers and social critics not at the descriptive but at the analytical or diagnostic level. For most of the Americans, the phenomena criticized are distasteful and distressing but not necessarily inherent and irremovable characteristics of American life. And even if seen as inherent, their sources are found not invariably in the nature of capitalism or the economic system, but elsewhere, as for example in certain historical experiences, in secularization, in social and geographic mobility, and in other factors conducive to uncertainties in the sphere of values. For Zamoshkin the erosion or breakdown of moral standards is an inherent feature of capitalist social-economic relations on the one hand, and on the other the result of deliberate manipulation perpetrated by the exploiting minority, those in control of the big corporations and advertising agencies. In his scheme there is no room for accident or unintended consequences in the social world (at any rate not in a capitalist society), where everything happens with a purpose and everything hangs together with a degree of implausible interdependence. His model of American society is definitely a conspiratorial one. Thus, for instance, it would seem to him that the unwholesome flux of American values came about at least in part because moral uncertainties and decadence best suit the "ruling circles" and because the consumer psychology leads to a docile, apolitical disposition that diverts the population from the big social-political issues of the day. At the same time it is also true that he views this consumer psychology in part as *a response* to being excluded from effective social-political participation and to the frustrations the average American encounters in trying to live up to the American myth and expectation of success. In this respect his analysis is heavily Mertonian.

We must also point out that Zamoshkin is not attempting to provide a detailed or comprehensive description of American values. He is only concerned with those related to the concept of "consumer psychology." He does not specifically discuss some of the values Dubois deals with, although we can safely infer that he does not think Americans are generally egalitarian or optimistic. He would probably strongly deny the existence of an overall value system, arguing that different social classes have different values and that dominant values are merely foisted upon society by the ruling classes and function as opiates. His major premise, shared by all Soviet observers of American society, is that of decline and decadence. Such a perspective derives from the Marxist-Leninist analysis of capitalism seen as a historically doomed social system. While Soviet sociologists have in some ways modified their application of Marxism-Leninism to the world today, the basic thesis postulating the decline of capitalism remains. In fact, the emphasis on *moral* degeneration and decadence has intensified lately, possibly as a result of the continued viability of the political and economic institutions of the societies Soviet spokesmen call capitalist.

It is in itself significant that while American values tended to be discussed, both by the American and Soviet social scientists with primary reference to the individual or the average American, the major referent in discussions of Soviet values is the official ideology, Marxism-Leninism. Relatively little is said about the beliefs and aspirations of the individual Soviet citizen or

the average Soviet man. This is as true of the writings of the American as
of the Soviet authors. It is not entirely speculative to suggest two reasons
for this. One is the relative ignorance, at least from the point of view of
systematic social science evidence, of what the typical values of Soviet
citizens are. The other reason is that in the Soviet case there is a far more
clearly articulated and codified official value system (most recently designated
as "The Moral Code of the Builder of Communism" in the 1961 Party
Program), which is a good deal less vague than the dominant values of
American society which are nowhere codified in a similarly explicit and
authoritative manner. A subject of heated argument is where the official
Soviet values end and the popular or unofficial ones begin, and what the
nature of the conflict and congruence is between the two.

If we compare the discussion of Soviet values with that of the American
ones, the first thing we notice is the magnitude of disagreement between
the Soviet and American appraisals, a disagreement far greater than that
which characterized the two sets of views on American values. The most
obvious reason for this can be found in the difference between the societal
self-appraisal of American and Soviet sociologists. Soviet sociologists are
not social critics—they are social apologists, at least as far as the major or
fundamental social institutions of their society are concerned. Rarely are
American sociologists, on the other hand, totally committed apologists of
their society; and even when they identify with it, they appear to show
some self-restraint, or a sense of detachment, or at least a lack of unconditional blindness toward its defects. This is also a matter of style. American
social scientists, as a rule, do not express themselves in the style of the
editorial or sermon or election campaign, speech, or poster. Perhaps this is
only a matter of professional convention or custom and has nothing to do
with genuine detachment or objectivity. Yet the result is unmistakable:
they convey an impression of greater detachment and objectivity than their
Soviet colleagues. An article by an American sociologist cannot be mistaken
for a campaign speech or Sunday sermon or newspaper editorial. It is much
easier to confuse some of the products of Soviet sociologists with a Pravda
editorial or an Agit-Prop pamphlet. Sometimes the same people write both.
The Soviet discussion of what amounts to the Soviet value system is marked
by a shrill, defensive, polemical, and self-assertive tone. Numerous questionable claims are made for Soviet values. According to them, these values
are totally consistent (no contradictions here as in the case of American
values, pointed out by Boorstin among others), scientific, unique (yet
incorporating everything that is progressive from the past), organically
related to Soviet institutions, and superior to all other values. They "miracul-
ously" transform man. They dissipate selfishness. They are both the
foundation and product of the new society and the New Soviet Man.

American commentators could not agree less. Marcuse, himself a heretic
Marxist (from the Soviet point of view), finds no fundamental difference
between Soviet and traditional Western values, not a "single moral idea or

syndrome of moral ideas that is not common to Western ethics." In his estimation, shared by other Western observers, Soviet official values resemble most closely those of Victorian-bourgeois society modified to take into account certain political objectives. Developing his argument further, we might find agreement between Soviet and American values on such fundamentals as equality of opportunity, veneration of achievement (in the Soviet case qualified by politicized or collectivist criteria), effort, sense of duty, optimism, future orientation, and so on. Marcuse even compares the Soviet valuation of work to the Calvinist work ethic. Beyond this we might suggest that Soviet official values derive from a long tradition of Judeo-Christian-Enlightenment lineage, sharpened by Marx and harnessed to the goals of the Soviet social order as defined by the leaders in power. There is, however, at least one crucial difference: Soviet values represent a more relativized version of this tradition—they admit of few, if any, moral absolutes. What counts is the direction, rather than the substance of any specific act or behavior. Moral-ethical imperatives are situation-specific, at least in the more esoteric of the Soviet ethical discourse.

Goldhagen focuses his attention on the functions Soviet values perform for the ruling elite; he considers them the opiate of the rulers rather than of the masses. This is an interesting contrast to the Soviet perception of American values, which are seen as opiates of the masses while the elites remain cynically and manipulatively aloof. Goldhagen also notes the increasing difficulties Soviet leaders are beginning to face when the major values of Soviet society are supposedly being realized in the course of approaching the stage of communism. The alleged threshold of utopia or fulfillment presents delicate ideological and psychological problems. It can reveal the internal contradictions of the official value system and ideological propositions. According to Goldhagen there is considerable confusion as to the nature of communist society, which in turn reveals the lacking originality and realizability of Soviet values. He perceives a sense of restlessness in the attitude of the Soviet political elite which precludes the attainment of any stable, utopian equilibrium. We might add that if he is right, this attitude has something in common with the restless achievement-orientation of many Americans for whom fulfillment remains elusive and for whom ends become means and means become ends. Perhaps the attainment of communist society on the societal level is not wholly unlike the achievement of success on the personal, each tending to recede into the distance as the pursuer approaches.

VALUES, BELIEFS,

AND IDEOLOGIES IN THE U.S.:

The American View

The Dominant Value Profile
of American Culture

CORA DUBOIS

1. EFFORT-OPTIMISM

Work is a specific value in American society. It is not so much a necessary condition of existence as a positive good. It is a specific instrumental value through which man strives to reach not only the goal of his own perfectibility but also the goal of mastering a mechanistically conceived universe. But in values Vaihinger's "law of the preponderance of the means over the ends" is frequently operative. Thus work becomes a goal in itself and in the process may acquire the quality of activity for its own sake. Thus recreation, although theoretically the antithesis of work, nevertheless in its activism shows many of the aspects of work. "Fun" is something that most Americans work hard for and at, so that they must be warned at forty to give up tennis for golf, or hunting trips for painting. Touring, whether at home or abroad, acquires the

Reprinted by permission of Cora DuBois and the American Anthropological Association from Cora DuBois, "The Dominant Value Profile of American Culture," American Anthropologist, LVII (December 1955), 1232–39.

quality of a marathon. And this in turn is closely associated with another specific value linked with the effort-optimism syndrome, the importance placed on education. However, as we shall see later, the educational effort acquires a particularly American cast when taken in conjunction with the other two focal values, material well-being and conformity. In sum, as many foreigners have observed, American life gives the impression of activism. The directives, as well as the virtues and vices, associated with this optimistic activism are numerous: "If at first you don't succeeded, try, try again"; or, in the more contemporary idiom, "Let's get this show on the road." The optimistic quality that pervades the American mood is clearly conveyed by the "bigger ergo better" mentality; the "never say die"; the "up and at 'em."

Vigor, at least as motility, connotes biologic youth. The cult of youthfulness in this society is again a specific value frequently commented upon by foreign observers. This observation is borne out by the popularity of the heroes manufactured in Hollywood and in the world of sports, by the advertisements of styles and cosmetics. As the average age of the population increases, this value is already showing signs of being given new interpretations in terms of geriatrics, etc. This will be alluded to again in following paragraphs.

2. MATERIAL WELL-BEING

If indeed effort is optimistically viewed in a material universe that man can master, then material well-being is a consistent concomitant value. Not only is it consistent within the value system, but it has been amply demonstrated in our national experience. It has been manifest in the American standard of living. The nation's geographic frontier and its natural resources, combined with an era of invention, have convinced most Americans of the validity of such a proposition. In the American scene progress and prosperity have come to have almost identical meaning. So deeply convinced are most Americans of what is generally called "prosperity" that material well-being is close to being considered a "right" due to those who have conscientiously practiced the specific value of work. The congruence of this view with the new science of geriatrics, social insurance, and the growth of investment trusts is obvious. It represents a consistent adjustment of specific values to a changing situation. However, as the situational context changes it may weaken the present linkage between effort and optimism with the resulting devaluation of both and thereby set up a new strain for consistency that may alter the present configuration of the American value system.

One of the most common stereotypes about the United States is its materialism. Viewed in the context of the value system presented here, materialism is less a value *per se* than an optimistic assertion of two value premises (mastery over material nature and the perfectibility of man) that have operated in a favorable environment. What foreign observers may call materialism, with derogatory or envious innuendos, is to the American a success that carries the moral connotation of "rightness"— of a system that proves itself or, as Americans would say with complete consistency, that "works." Within the frame of American value premises, success phrased as material well-being resolves the material-spiritual opposition and becomes a proof of right-mindedness. "Hard work pays off." The old and widely known proverb that "Virtue is its own reward" has a particularly American slant, meaning not that virtue is in itself a reward but rather that virtue is rewarded.

If hard work is a "good thing" in a material universe and since it has been rewarded by material well-being, consistency requires that manual labor should be accorded dignity or, at least, should not be considered undignified. Furthermore, manual labor is an unambiguous manifestation of that activism alluded to earlier.

The salience of material well-being as a focal value in American life leads into many by-ways, some of which confuse and confound members of societies founded on a different value configuration. In military terms, for example, Americans are so profoundly convinced of the correctness of the material well-being formula that logistics forms our basic strategy. Personal heroism, though it may amply exist, is not assumed to be the fundamental requisite for victory, as it is in France. In American terms, victory is won by the sheet of matériel laid down in front of advancing infantry and by the lines of supply that must be built up to provide such a barrier between hand-to-hand combat.

In the same vein, there is little room in the American middle-class value system for the realities of physical pain, brutality, and death. Since they are nonetheless natural and undeniable, they are given a highly stylized treatment in detective fiction, newspapers, and movies that provide an acceptable discharge of tension created by the discrepancy between values and reality. Many Americans are alienated and morally repelled when they encounter the poverty and misery prevalent in certain lands. They manage to go through life untouched experientially even by those in our own population who have not succeeded—those who exist hopelessly in rural or urban slums or those who are victims of physical or psychic disasters. We have provided for the latter so effectively that they are whisked away into institutions that our national surpluses permit us to provide comparatively lavishly. Death itself has been surrounded with appurtenances of asepsis. Evelyn Waugh's *The Loved One* could never have been written with India as a setting. The compelling quality of this value emerges when we consider world statistics on human welfare facilities. In this respect, the United States is consistently in the lead. Yet, if we compare these statistics with the outbursts of compassion that a newspaper account of a "blue baby" will elicit, we become aware not only of the power of this focal value but also the resultant constellation that might be summarized as compulsive compassionate activism.

3. CONFORMITY

Viewed historically it seems probable that conformity is a more recent focal value in American culture than effort-optimism and material well-being. It may represent one of the valuational changes induced by the strain for consistency assumed earlier in the paper to be one of the forces that alter value systems. Over a century ago De Tocqueville saw with singular clarity the potential threat to national solidarity inherent in the values of individual liberty, on the one hand, and of the sovereignty of enfranchised masses, on the other hand. In the contemporary American value system, conformity represents an attempt to resolve this dilemma. The France of today, with a comparable dilemma, has still to find a resolution.

If the premises of perfectibility and equality are linked with the focal value labeled effort-optimism, then each middle-class American may legitimately aspire to maximal self-realization. But, if man is to master through his efforts a mechanistic universe, he must cooperate with his fellowmen, since no single man can master the universal machine. In other words, people are individuated and prized, but if they are to cooperate with their fellowmen for mastery of the universe or, in more modest terms, of the immediate physical and sociopolitical environment, too great a degree of individualization would be an impediment. Also since the American value premises—in contradistinction to much of the rest of the world—include equality, the realization of the self in such a context would not necessarily imply the development of highly personalized and idiosyncratic but rather of egalitarian traits. Self-cultivation in America has as its goal less the achievement of uniqueness and more the achievement of similarity. This is a proposition many Frenchmen, for example, find difficult to grasp. The Japanese, with their stress upon self-cultivation in order more perfectly to discharge the obligations they owe their family and society, might come closer to understanding this American formulation.

The assimilation of diverse immigrant groups to middle-class American values has been one of the remarkable socio-political achievements of the nation and testifies to the compelling vigor of its value system. As resources and space were more fully manned, the very lack of tolerance for differences that facilitated assimilation was finally to curtail the admission to this country of those who presented such differences.

Earlier in our history self-reliance and initiative were specific values attached to the focal value of liberty. Today these specific values have a new focus. Individual self-reliance and initiative are attached to the promotion of the commonweal and to the progress of society. Conformity has replaced liberty as a focal value to which these specific traits are attached. Cooperation has been added as a specific value that has facilitated the shift-over. The present American value system manifests a highly effective integration of the individual to society.

The ramification of this nexus into the sphere of education has been alluded to already. Education is envisaged as a means by which all men through effort can realize themselves. But since co-operativeness is a specific value also asserted into this equation, education comes to be envisaged as a means to make more men more effective workers and better citizens. The land-grant colleges, the vast network of public schools, and the system of free and compulsory education with its stress on education for citizenship and on technical skills have set the American educational system apart from that of many other countries. In the American context the linkage between conformity, effort-optimism, and material well-being leads inevitably to mass education with the emphasis on the common man rather than the uncommon man, to its technical and practical cast, to what

seems to many observers its low standards. Simultaneously, to many Americans schooling has acquired the weight of a goal rather than a means. A college degree is a "good thing" in itself, whether or not the education entailed is prized. This concatenation does not lead one to expect perfection as a directive for performance in American life.

In a society where cooperation and good citizenship are valued and where the commonweal is served by having each man develop himself through his own efforts, a generous friendliness, openness, and relaxation of interpersonal relations are not only possible but desirable so long as the associated expanding economy furnishes the situational possibilities. Rigid class structures and protective privacies are inconsistent with the values here enumerated. Doors need not be closed to rooms; fences need not be built around properties. The tall hedges of England and the enclosing walls of France are not appropriate to the American scene, where life faces outward rather than inward. If every individual is as "good as" the next and all are good citizens— what is there to hide? The open front yards, the porches, or more recently the picture windows that leave the home open to everyone's view, the figurative and literal klieg lights under which our public figures live are all evidence of the value placed in American life on likeness and the pressure exerted for conformity. This is very different from saying that American middle-class individuals are in fact all alike. It means merely that likeness is valued.

The American hostility to figures in authority has been frequently noted, and in this connection the almost placatory informality and familiarity of American manners that serve to play down status differences have been pointed out. The apparent contradiction between the striving for upward mobility and the distrust of those who achieve preeminent positions can now be seen in more balanced terms. If the argument advanced here is correct, upward mobility is valued as successful activity, but when it reaches a point where it outstrips the premise of equality and the focal value of conformity it borders on *hubris*.

In this connection then the relaxed, friendly manner of American life so frequently commented upon by foreign observers can be gauged in the broader context of an adjustment to incompatible values. The search for popularity, the desire to be liked, the wish to be considered a "good fellow," are searches for reassurance that, in striving to achieve all the ends implied by the focal value of effort-optimism, one has not exceeded the bounds set by the other focal value of conformity. That this process can operate at any level of actual achievement, from the presidency of the United States to chairmanship of an Elks Club committee, need not be stressed. It is the boss, the politician, the teacher, the "big shots" who are disvalued figures to the extent that their superordinate position implies authority. It is the movie star and the baseball hero who are valued figures since their preeminence connotes no authority but at the same time drama-

tizes the meteoric rise to fame and popularity through hard work and youthful striving.

Another aspect of American social life is thrown into relief in the effort to balance effort-optimism, material well-being, and conformity and their linked specific values. In the business and financial world, despite conservative tendencies, there has been a steady trend toward consolidation and standardization. Although the familiar and now perhaps inappropriate hue and cry is still raised about monopoly and big business, the latter, at least, serves the greater material well-being of the American mass consumer, whose values are geared to conformity. "Big business" is consonant with the American value system here portrayed so long as the owners of such enterprises are pictured as the American middle class, so long as savings are invested in the stocks and bonds of these enterprises so that the middle class shares "equally" in its successes, and so long as the authorities in such enterprises are presented as servants of the people. In these terms the American value system is served. The dangers of a too extreme individualistic power-centered authority are thus allayed, and competitive rivalry is brought under control.

Youth in the Context of American Society

TALCOTT PARSONS

...In my own work it has proved useful to formulate the dominant

Reprinted by permission of Daedalus, Journal of the American Academy of Arts and Sciences, Boston, Massachusetts. From Talcott Parsons, "Youth in the Context of American Society," Daedalus (Winter 1962), pp. 100–106.

American value pattern at this very general level as one of *instrumental activism*. Its cultural grounding lies in moral and (eventually) religious orientations, which in turn derive directly from Puritan traditions. The relevance of the pattern extends through all three of the religious, moral, and societal levels, as well as to others that cannot be detailed here. It is most important to keep them distinct, in particular, the difference between the moral and the societal levels.

In its religious aspect, instrumental activism is based on the pattern Max Weber called "inner-worldly asceticism," the conception of man's role as an instrument of the divine will in building a kingdom of God on earth. Through a series of steps, both in internal cultural development and in institutionalization (which cannot be detailed here), this has produced a conception of the human condition in which the individual is committed to maximal effort in the interest of valued *achievement* under a system of normative order. This system is in the first instance moral, but also, at the societal level, it is embodied in legal norms. Achievement is conceived in "rational" terms, which include the maximal objective understanding of the empirical conditions of action, as well as the faithful adherence to normative commitments. It is of great importance that, once institutionalized, the fulfillment of such a value pattern need not be motivated by an explicit recognition of its religious groundings.

One way of describing the pattern in its moral aspects is to say that it is fundamentally individualistic. It tends to maximize the desirability of autonomy and responsibility in the individual. Yet this is an institutionalized individualism, in that it is normatively controlled at the moral level in two ways. First, it is premised on the conception of human existence as serving ends or functions beyond those of physical longevity, or health, or the satisfaction of the psychological needs of the personality apart from these value commitments. In a sense, it is the building of the "good life," not only for the particular individual but also for all mankind—a life that is accounted as desirable, not merely desired. This includes commitment to a good society. Second, to implement these moral premises, it is necessary for the autonomous and responsible achievements of the individual to be regulated by a normative order—at this level, a moral law that defines the relations of various contributions and the patterns of distributive justice.

The society, then, has a dual meaning, from this moral point of view. On the one hand, it is perhaps the primary field in which valued achievement is possible for the individual. In so far as it facilitates such achievements, the society is a good one. On the other hand, the building of the good society (that is, its progressive improvement) is the primary goal of valued action—along with such cultural developments as are intimately involved in social progress, such as science. To the individual, therefore, the most important goal to which he can orient himself is a contribution to the good society.

The value pattern I am outlining is activistic, therefore, in that it is oriented toward control or mastery of the human condition, as judged by moral standards. It is not a doctrine of passive adjustment to conditions, but one of active adaptation. On the other hand, it is instrumental with reference to the source of moral legitimation, in the sense that human achievement is not conceived as an end in itself but as a means to goals beyond the process and its immediate outcome.

This value pattern implies that the society is meant to be a developing, evolving entity. It is meant to develop in the direction of progressive "improvement." But this development is to be through the autonomous initiative and achievements of its units—in the last analysis, individual persons. It is therefore a society which places heavy responsibilities (in the form of expectations) on its individual members. At the same time, it subjects them to two very crucial sets of limitations which have an important bearing on the problem of youth.

One of these concerns the "moralism" of the value system—the fact that individualism is bound within a strongly emphasized framework of normative order. The achievement, the success, of the individual must ideally be in accord with the rules, above all, with those which guarantee opportunity to all, and which keep the system in line with its remoter values. Of course, the more complex the society, the greater the difficulty of defining the requisite norms, a difficulty which is greatly compounded by rapid change. Furthermore, in the interest of effectiveness, achievement must often be in the context of the collective organization, thus further limiting autonomy.

The second and for present purposes an even more crucial limitation is that it is in the nature of such a system that it is not characterized by a single, simple, paramount goal for the society as a system. The values legitimize a *direction* of change, not a terminal state. Furthermore, only in the most general sense is this direction "officially" defined, with respect to such famous formulae as liberty, democracy, general welfare, and distributive justice. The individual is left with a great deal of responsibility, not only for achieving *within* the institutionalized normative order, but for his own interpretation of its meaning and of his obligations in and to it.

Space forbids detailing the ramifications of this value system. Instead, it is necessary to my analysis to outline briefly the main features of the process of social change mentioned above. The suggestion is that the main pattern of values has been and probably will continue to be stable, but that the structure of the society, including its subsystem values at lower levels, has in the nature of the case been involved in a rapid and far-reaching process of change. This centers on the process of differentiation, but very importantly it also involves what we have referred to as inclusion, upgrading, and increasing generalization. I shall confine my discussion here to the structure of the society, though this in turn is intimately connected with problems concerned with the personality of the individual, including his personal values.

Differentiation refers to the process by which simple structures are divided into functionally differing components, these components becoming relatively independent of one another, and then recombined into more complex structures in which the functions of the differentiated units are complementary. A key example in the development of industrial society everywhere is the differentiation, at the collectivity level, of the unit of economic production from the kinship household. Obviously, in peasant economies, production is carried out by and in the household. The development of employing organizations which are structurally distinct from any household is the key new structural element. This clearly means a loss of function to the old undifferentiated unit, but also a gain in autonomy, though this in turn involves a new dependency, because the household can no longer be self-subsistent. The classical formula is that the productive services of certain members (usually the adult males) have been alienated from the organization directly responsible for subsistence and thus lost to the household, which then depends on money income from occupational earnings and in turn on the markets for consumers' goods.

These losses, however, are not without their compensations: the gain in the productivity of the economy and in the standard of living of the household. This familiar paradigm has to be generalized so as to divest it of its exclusively economic features and show it as the primary characterization of a very general process of social change. First, it is essential to point out that it always operates simultaneously in both collectivities and individual roles. Thus, in the example just given, a new type of productive organization which is not a household or (on more complex levels) even a family farm has to be developed. The local community no longer consists only of farm households but also of nonproducing households and productive units—e.g., firms. Then the same individual (the head of the household) has a dual role as head of the family and as employee in a producing unit (the case of the individual entrepreneur is a somewhat special one).

By the extension of inclusiveness, I mean that, once a step of differentiation has been established, there is a tendency to extend the new pattern to increasing proportions of the relevant population of units. In the illustrative case, the overwhelming tendency that has operated for well over a century has been to reduce the proportion of households which are even in part economically self-sufficient, in the sense of a family farm, in favor of those whose members are gainfully employed outside the household. This is a principal aspect of the spread of industrialization and urbanization. The same logic applies to newly established educational standards, e.g., the expectation that a secondary-school education will be normal for the whole age cohort.

Normative upgrading means a type of change in the normative order, to which the operation of units, both individual and collective, is subject. It is a shift from the prescription of rules by a special class or unit in a special situation to more generalized norms having to do with more inclusive classes of units in wider ranges of situations. Thus the law that specifies that a railway engine must be equipped with a steam whistle to give warning at crossings has by court interpretation been generalized to include any effective warning signal (since oil-burning locomotives are not equipped with steam). But in a sense parallel to that in which differentiation leads to alienation from the older unit, normative upgrading means that the unit is left with a problem, since the rules no longer give such concretely unequivocal guidance to what is expected. If the rule is general enough, its application to a particular situation requires interpretation. Such upgrading, we contend, is a necessary concomitant of the process of differentiation.

When we speak of norms, we mean rules applying to particular categories of units in a system, operating in particular types of situations. For example, individual adults may not be employed under conditions which infringe on certain basic freedoms of the individual. The repercussions of a step in differentiation, however, cannot be confined to this level; they must also involve some part of the value system; this is to say, the functions of the differentiated categories of units, which are now different from one another, must not only be regulated but also legitimized. To use our example again, it cannot be true that the whole duty of the fathers of families is to gain subsistence for their households through making the household itself productive, but it becomes legitimate to support the household by earning a money income through work for an outside employer and among other things to be absent from the household many hours a week. At the collectivity level, therefore, a business that is not the direct support of a household (such as farming) must be a legitimate way of life—that is, the unit that employs labor for such purposes, without itself being a household, must be legitimate. This requires defining the values in terms sufficiently general to include both the old and the new way of life.

The values must therefore legitimize a structural complex by which economic production and the consumption needs of households are met simultaneously— that is, both the labor markets and the markets for consumers' goods. For example, this structural complex is of focal importance in the modern (as distinguished from medieval) urban community. The value attitude that regards the rural or the handicraft way of life as morally superior to the modern urban and—if you will—industrial way (a common attitude in the Western world of today) is an example of the failure of the adequate value generalization that is an essential part of institutionalizing the process of structural change.

To sum up, we may state that both the nature of the American value pattern and the nature of the process of change going on in the society make for considerable difficulties in the personal adjustment of individuals. On the one hand, our type of activism, with its individualistic emphases, puts a heavy responsibility for autonomous achievement on the individual. On the other hand, it subjects him to important limitations: he must not only be regulated by norms and the necessity of working cooperatively, in collective contexts; he must also interpret his own responsibilities and the rules to which he is subject. Beyond that, ours is a society which in the nature of its values cannot have a single clear-cut societal goal which can be dramatically symbolized. The individual is relegated to contributions which are relatively specialized, and it is not always easy to see their bearing on the larger whole. Furthermore, the general erosion of traditional culture and symbols, which is inseparable from a scientific age, makes inadequate many of the old formulae once used to give meaning and legitimation to our values and achievements. This is perhaps true in particular of the older religious grounding of our values.

Extravagant Expectations

DANIEL BOORSTIN

...We expect too much of the world. Our expectations are extravagant in the

Reprinted from Daniel Boorstin, "Extravagant Expectations," The Image. New York: Atheneum Publishers, 1963, pp. 3–6.

precise dictionary sense of the word— "going beyond the limits of reason or moderation." They are excessive.

When we pick up our newspaper at breakfast, we expect—we even demand —that it bring us momentous events since the night before. We turn on the car radio as we drive to work and expect "news" to have occurred since the morning newspaper went to press. Returning in the evening, we expect our house not only to shelter us, to keep us warm in winter and cool in summer, but to relax us, to dignify us, to encompass us with soft music and interesting hobbies, to be a playground, a theater, and a bar. We expect our two-week vacation to be romantic, exotic, cheap, and effortless. We expect a far-away atmosphere, if we go to a near-by place; and we expect everything to be relaxing, sanitary, and Americanized if we go to a faraway place. We expect new heroes every season, a literary masterpiece every month, a dramatic spectacular every week, a rare sensation every night. We expect everybody to feel free to disagree, yet we expect everybody to be loyal, not to rock the boat or take the Fifth Amendment. We expect everybody to believe deeply in his religion, yet not to think less of others for not believing. We expect our nation to be strong and great and vast and varied and prepared for every challenge; yet we expect our "national purpose" to be clear and simple, something that gives direction to the lives of nearly two hundred million people and yet can be bought in a paperback at the corner drugstore for a dollar.

We expect anything and everything. We expect the contradictory and the impossible. We expect compact cars which are spacious; luxurious cars which are economical. We expect to be rich and charitable, powerful and merciful, active and reflective, kind and competitive. We expect to be inspired by mediocre appeals for "excellence," to be made literate by illiterate appeals for literacy. We expect to eat and stay thin, to be constantly on the move and ever more neighborly, to go to a "church of our choice" and yet feel its

guiding power over us, to revere God and to be God.

Never have people been more the masters of their environment. Yet never has a people felt more deceived and disappointed. For never has a people expected so much more than the world could offer.

We are ruled by extravagant expectations:

(1) *Of what the world holds.* Of how much news there is, how many heroes there are, how often masterpieces are made, how exotic the nearby can be, how familiar the exotic can become. Of the closeness of places and the farness of places.

(2) *Of our power to shape the world.* Of our ability to create events when there are none, to make heroes when they don't exist, to be somewhere else when we haven't left home. Of our ability to make art forms suit our convenience, to transform a novel into a movie and vice versa, to turn a symphony into mood-conditioning. To fabricate national purposes when we lack them, to pursue these purposes after we have fabricated them. To invent our standards and then to respect them as if they had been revealed or discovered.

By harboring, nourishing, and ever enlarging our extravagant expectations we create the demand for the illusions with which we deceive ourselves. And which we pay others to make to deceive us.

The making of the illusions which flood our experience has become the business of America, some of its most honest and most necessary and most respectable business. I am thinking not only of advertising and public relations and political rhetoric, but of all the activities which purport to inform and comfort and improve and educate and elevate us: the work of our best journalists, our most enterprising book publishers, our most energetic manufacturers and merchandisers, our most successful entertainers, our best guides to world travel, and our most influential leaders in foreign relations. Our every effort to satisfy our extravagant expectations simply makes them more extravagant and makes our illusions more attractive. The story of the making of our illusions—"the news behind the news"—has become the most appealing news of the world.

We tyrannize and frustrate ourselves by expecting more than the world can give us or than we can make of the world. We demand that everyone who talks to us, or writes for us, or takes pictures for us, or makes merchandise for us, should live in our world of extravagant expectations. We expect this even of the peoples of foreign countries. We have become so accustomed to our illusions that we mistake them for reality. We demand them. And we demand that there be always more of them, bigger and better and more vivid. They are the world of our making: the world of the image.

Nowadays everybody tells us that what we need is more belief, a stronger and deeper and more encompassing faith. A faith in America and in what we are doing. That may be true in the long run. What we need first and now is to disillusion ourselves. What ails us most is not what we have done with America, but what we have substituted for America. We suffer primarily not from our vices or our weaknesses, but from our illusions. We are haunted, not by reality, but by those images we have put in place of reality.

To discover our illusions will not solve the problems of our world. But if we do not discover them, we will never discover our real problems. To dispel the ghosts which populate the world of our making will not give us the power to conquer the real enemies of the real world or to remake the real world. But it may help us discover that we cannot make the world in our image. It will liberate us and sharpen our vision. It will clear away the fog so we can face the world we share with all mankind.

VALUES, BELIEFS,

AND IDEOLOGIES IN THE U.S.:

The Soviet View

The Development of "Consumer" Individualism in the United States

Y. A. ZAMOSHKIN

The fact that work has lost social prestige in the U.S.A. is inseparably linked also with the development and diffusion of a special kind of psychology—a bourgeois, consumer psychology, the typical product of the spiritual crisis being experienced by contemporary American capitalism. This psychology among the ruling classes is the natural concomitant of social parasitism—the inescapable feature of monopoly capitalism which is openly reactionary and an obstacle of historical progress.

Simultaneously, the consumers' psychology also becomes diffused among the common people of society. Here it often turns out to be a concomitant and consequence of the crisis in American efficiency...in particular, of the crisis in specific, traditional, and individual stimuli of work. It appears also as a

Original Translation

Reprinted from Yuri A. Zamoshkin, The Crisis of Bourgeois Individualism and Personality. Izdatelstvo "Nauka," Moscow, 1965, Chapter 10, pp. 233–249.

peculiar reaction to social conditions, which make labor more joyless, burdensome, and dehumanized. Not being in a position to display personal initiative in the realm of entrepreneurial activity, or to be creative in the sphere of production, doomed to being the accessory of machines and of depersonalized, auxiliary functions, bound by the routine of bureaucratization, people often search for escape in the sphere of personal consumption, the sphere of daily life, in the family and in entertainment. Personal consumption, daily routines and entertainment, as the case may be, become subordinated to the standards of a narrow Philistine existence.

...At the present time much is written and said in the U.S.A. about the consumer psychology. Writers, artists, journalists, teachers, and sociologists show a most serious concern with this. Among the first to show the rapid and widespread development in the U.S.A. of a purely and narrowly consumer attitude toward life were Wright Mills and D. Riesman.

...Of course, bourgeois sociologists

33

usually idealize the bourgeois personality of the initial period of capitalism. But all of them are correct when they point out that "puritanical virtues" in the U.S. today are increasingly losing their value *from the point of view of bourgeois public opinion,* and are considered by this opinion an anachronism.

The consumer psychology, the subject of this discussion, is, as a rule, *a special variety of individualistic psychology,* of individualistic consciousness, in which the emphasis has shifted from the sphere of productive activities to the sphere of personal consumption.

The characteristics of this variety have two internal sources: on the one hand, the consumer psychology arises as a logical consequence of the natural development of individualism among the big monopolistic bourgeoisie; on the other hand, it is a product of the degeneration and decomposition of individualism in the consciousness of those people who experienced the transition from the small and middle bourgeois status to that of the wage-laborer without any rights, and to the corporation employee.

Those in the first group can display their individualistic passions in the sphere of bourgeois production, in the sphere of business, but they prefer the parasitic life of wealthy, hedonistic idleness. Those in the second group can no longer realize their individualistic ideals and aspirations in the sphere of production or business, although they are still haunted by them. For them the bourgeois style of life becomes the last *practicable empirical support* for individualism. Being objects of exploitation, bureaucratic coercion and manipulation, outside the walls of their homes, these people try to find the opportunity for the display of personal initiative in their private life and the realm of personal consumption. Thus is born the bourgeois psychology of the "little man," of the petty bourgeois individualist. . . .

Objects of personal consumption become the signs of consumer success: a more expensive house, a new car, a new refrigerator, a new TV set or in general money spent on consumer goods or entertainment.

Naturally, the subject of this discussion is such a "small" man, the petty bourgeois who in contemporary America has at his disposal limited, minimal, financial means for the realization of some kind of "consumer" individualism.

At present we can observe in the U.S. the conversion of the consumer psychology into a branch of the *official bourgeois ideology.* The process is designed to make a Philistine out of the "average" American, who thinks only about the means to satisfy his private egotistical aspirations within the confines of the bourgeois life style and who is obedient to the will of the ruling classes in the realm of economy and politics. Spontaneously arising in the conditions of contemporary capitalism, this psychology is seized upon by the organs of mass propaganda controlled by the corporations and the imperialist government and in turn has become transformed into an instrument for the spiritual corruption of the masses. Appearing as the consequence of the crisis and decay of contemporary American capitalism, the consumers' individualistic ideology and psychology are becoming the tools for deepening this crisis.

Mass propaganda more and more proves to be oriented toward the glorification of "small joys of daily life," as though they alone define "genuine success." This propaganda represents the common, average man as the embodiment of the "true" happiness and satisfaction of life, and the bosses in business and politics in whose hands power and capital are concentrated are depicted as "martyrs" and "sufferers." These themes are rehashed in a thousand ways. The characteristic example is the movie "The Man in the Gray Flannel Suit," made in Hollywood in 1959, in which, on the one hand, the ordinary employee is glorified, who prefers the joys of his family circle and leisure to the enjoyment of a "brilliant career" in the world of "big business." Juxtaposed to him is the image of a capitalist tycoon obsessed by business success, possessing both power and a fortune, but a stranger to the "art of consumption" and "the pleasure of leisure and daily life," and therefore "unhappy." Needless to say, such propaganda serves as a special instrument of illusory "consolation" for the ordinary American whom monopolistic capitalism has transformed into its slave without any rights. It also serves as a means of disguising growing social contrasts, and the unheard-of parasitic splendor of the ruling classes.

The fact that propagandizing a consumers' attitude to life is becoming in the U.S. today the predominant trend in the movies, the press, television, and radio, is related not only to political and ideological factors and motives. It is also closely connected with the logic of monopolistic commerce, with the necessity for commercial advertising, with the striving of the corporations to create a commodity market under conditions of savage competition and with the lowering of the purchasing power of the masses of the population.

. . . Bourgeois official propaganda and corporations' advertising usually depict the average contemporary bourgeois man in the U.S. with his consumer psychology as a morally healthy and happy person satisfied with himself and his

life. Actually, the development of narrow consumers' attitudes to life *exerts a demoralizing and destructive influence on man.*

The consumer psychology as a manifestation of a degenerating, petty, barren individualism begets and aggravates all these negative phenomena in the moral and spiritual life of a person. We characterized them in detail when we spoke in general about the demoralizing influence of individualism.

Anomie feeds on consumer psychology as the latter reflects man's total indifference to labor and its social and historical value. Its carriers are also totally indifferent to the public wealth in the genuine sense of that word, and to the historical issues which confront their society. Such a man's philosophy and program for life, according to Mills, is limited to the desire "to receive his share of the wealth surrounding him, exchanging the least effort for the most satisfaction."[1] He does not care about anything else. For this reason the consumer psychology is often the embodiment of moral relativism. A. Kaplan relates such American phenomena as "the deadening of the spirit and the corruption of moral life" to "materialism" (here again this concept appears in a vulgar, typically bourgeois, distorted form), i.e., the deformed pursuit devouring all of man's energy and thoughts, a pursuit only for objects and material wealth for personal consumption.[2]

. . . The level of expectations, standards and demands of consumption are inflated first of all by the efforts of the official propaganda, which unrestrainedly extols and idealizes "the American way of life" and by the commercial

[1] W. Mills, *The Ruling Elite*, p. 431.
[2] E. Morison, ed., *The American Style*, New York: 1958, pp. 27–28.

advertising which strives to provide a market for the products of the corporations. On movie and TV screens, in the pages of newspapers and magazines, the American continually sees a repetitive idealized picture which depicts some family living in a comfortable house, riding in the latest model car, dressed in the latest fashion, eating, drinking cocktails, playing golf and continually buying the most diverse objects. And all this is presented as a model for imitation, as a standard without which supposedly man's self-esteem and satisfaction in life are inconceivable. People are constantly pressured to buy, buy, and buy everything that is produced by corporations which compete with each other and strive for high profits.

...The result is constant intensification of the discrepancy between the standards of consumption, created by the bourgeois fashion, and the real financial opportunities of the majority of the population. Man is forced into expenses larger than his real financial position allows and is obliged to strain himself to the utmost, going into debt. The commercial practice of monopolies helps him in this, creating various forms of consumer credit. As a result the masses of Americans live in debt, they fight for each dollar, but the debts continue to grow. W. H. White in his investigation of the style of life of white collar workers paid special attention to the growth of debts, one of the causes of which is the "excessive stimulation" of consumption. He pointed out the sizeable and growing consumers' debts incurred for the purchase of objects, and debts owned to banks as a typical phenomenon in the life of the average American. According to his evidence, the percent on these debts actually reaches 10 to 12%.[3]

The growth of debts, the constant awareness of the increasing gap between the standards of consumption imposed by the bourgeois mass propaganda-advertising as well as the submission to the public opinion it creates, and the actual opportunities of the majority of the population; all this gives rise to spiritual tension and irritation, bitterness and even despair in many Americans, which leads to the most varied social pathologies. Not without reason, according to the evidence of Packard, advertising agents call themselves sometimes "the merchants of discontent."[4]

...The artificiality and compelling nature of the standards of consumption in the U.S. are also connected with the fact that the articles destined for personal consumption under capitalism are often less important as actual means of consumption than they are for defining the social value and status of an individual. In their present role objects and articles of consumption which are the product of man's labor become a certain force estranged from man, external in relation to his personality, apparently self-sustaining, capable of bestowing on man social prestige, and being a symbol of his success *independently* of his personal qualities and personal activities.

This transformation of articles of consumption into symbols of social significance is reflected and being consolidated in the psychology of "consumer" individualism and in the first place in the psychology of those individualists who are deprived of the real opportunity to achieve success as bourgeois entrepreneurs.

American commercial advertising deliberately utilizes the above transformation. It suggests to man that by buying an expensive object (even if it is

[3] W. H. White, Jr., *The Organization Man.* New York: 1956, p. 350, 359–365.

[4] Vance Packard, *The Status Seekers.* New York: David McKay Co., 1959, p. 308.

more than he can afford) he raises him-self on the social ladder. As Packard accurately observed, advertising per-suades people that "in running deeper into debt, they advance upward."[5]

...the individualistic struggle for the acquisition of objects gives rise, on the one hand, to overt *snobbery,* and con-tempt for those who are not able to acquire these objects which are sanc-tioned by fashion, and on the other hand, creates a persistent petty, soul-corroding and devastating envy of those whose level of consumption is higher. The feverish pursuit of bour-geois fads spiritually cripples people and gives rise to feelings of aggressive-ness, fear, and bitterness.

This grave atmosphere and its influ-ence on daily life, on relations between members of a family, is for example brilliantly described by Steinbeck in his novel *The Winter of our Discontent.* This atmosphere corrupts both children and adults, and leads to the alienation of people close to each other. And not without reason, Bredemeier and Toby consider the concept of "materialism" (interpreted in the sense of a cult of objects) as idential with the concept of "dissociation" ("secularism").[6]

In connection with this the writer is reminded of a conversation he had with one of his American friends, a young professor in one of the colleges located near New York. Answering the ques-tion about the causes for his tragic divorce from his wife (she lives sepa-rately with their two children), the professor opened the *New Yorker,* a magazine popular in the U.S. among white-collar workers and the intelli-gentsia, and pointed to bright pages of numerous advertisements persistently demanding of people and first of all of women to buy, buy, and buy. "You can imagine what a tremendous influence all this exerts on family life, and in particular on the woman raised in a bourgeois family," he said sadly. "What an enormous number of per-sonal tragedies, what a number of neuroses and anguish, all this gives rise to." This atmosphere often pushes man to actual crime, not only in the legal sense but also in that of violations of the elementary norms of humaneness, as happens in the life of the main hero of Steinbeck's novel.

This atmosphere has an especially demoralizing effect on youth, and on adolescents. In order to be "successful consumers" and to get things, the adolescents neglect their work, and their studies. For them it is most im-portant "to obtain money" in order to acquire possessions with a sense of urgency. The absence of this oppor-tunity is one of the causes of the growth of the psychology of "failure," a psy-chology of despair among youth, and one of the causes of the appearance in the U.S. of "an enormous group of people who can define themselves as failures, people who "don't count.""[7] And indeed "to make money" is neces-sary to keep up with the standards of the bourgeois consumer psychology not within the reach of the oppressed ma-jority of American youth. It is not surprising then that those of the young people who become slaves to material things are often ready to commit crime for the sake of these material things.[8]

5 Vance Packard, *The Status Seekers,* pp. 308–311, 313.
6 H. C. Bredemeier, J. Toby, eds. *Social Problems in America,* New York: 1960, pp. 59–60.

7 E. Ginzburg, ed., *Values and Ideals of American Youth,* from *The White House Con-ference on Children and Youth.* New York: 1960, pp. 42, 45–46.
8 *Ibid.,* p. 309.

VALUES, BELIEFS,

AND IDEOLOGIES IN THE U.S.S.R.:

The Soviet View

The Philosopher's Stone

Y. FRANTSEV and Y. FILONOVICH

...Marxism-Leninism has demonstrated that man cannot become truly master of the forces of nature as long as he is fettered by the slavery of wage labor, not until he has built a system on earth where exploitation comes to look as barbarous as cannibalism does for people who have entered civilization. Then people themselves will change. Then a new era will begin in the history of society, in the history of science and technology, in the moral development of man.

This new era did begin, in October, 1917. If we look at the present-day ideological struggle, our opponents of all shades attempt at all costs to belittle the historic significance of the activity of Soviet society. Bourgeois theorists—philosophers, sociologists and economists—and, following their lead, all kinds of apostates from Marxism-Leninism and petty-bourgeois ideologists would like to hide from mankind

Reprinted from Yu. Frantsev and Yu. Filonovich, "The Philosopher's Stone— Talk with Readers," Izvestia *(September 19, 1965). Translated in* Current Digest of the Soviet Press, *XVII, No. 38 (Copyright © October 13, 1965), 28–30.*

the truth about the Soviet people's successes, to distort their achievements and to denigrate and slander the policy of the Communist Party. Therein lies the essence of present-day anticommunism.

However, no tricks will help the anti-communists to conceal the historical fact that Soviet people, led by their Leninist party, are confidently advancing toward the solution of the great tasks of social progress. The Soviet people have demonstrated that the history of the new society, of its first steps and its subsequent development, the history of the formation of new social relations based on public ownership, has begun in our country, while the present-day development of the economic, social and political organization of the Soviet Union toward communism is a most important phase of the modern history of mankind's culture and civilization. That is why the historic deeds of the Soviet people hold the attention of everyone—friends and foes of communism alike. For this is a gigantic experiment, of vital importance for all mankind.

It is now obvious to all that science, if it wholly serves the people, can create much more than gold—it helps to create social wealth and abundance. The progress of science and technology under socialism makes it possible to utilize most productively the wealth and forces of nature in the interests of the working people, to discover new types of energy and to create new materials, to work out new methods of influencing climatic conditions and to conquer space. The application of science becomes a decisive factor in the continuous growth of society's productive forces.

As for the problem of the formation of the new man, our party has, for the first time in history, elaborated and applied a system of scientific views— the teachings of communist upbringing.

Thinkers of the past talked about the rearing of individuals, taken singly. Their prescriptions were as primitive as the recipes of the alchemists, who thought they were finding a "panacea"— a remedy for all ills. Marxist-Leninists have always attached decisive importance to upbringing work among the toiling people in the process of revolutionary struggle. Declaring war on blind spontaneity, aimlessness and unconscious action in the workers' movement, the Party raised high the banner of ideology. Ideological work has always pointed out the path of struggle, and organizational work has always rallied the masses for this struggle. Thus have been forged the remarkable fighters for the people's cause, men of pure heart, daring thought, unbending will.

Goethe once wrote: "Talent is born in calm, character in the world stream." Today we know that even talent fades if it is cut off from the world stream. The mighty current of everyday living sharpens talents, abilities, inclinations and character. Those thinkers who, like Leo Tolstoy, wanted to begin the reconstruction of society with the improvement of the individual followed a wrong path. It was reactionary utopianism to suppose that, far from the revolutionary struggle and above the battle, man can learn and teach others "how to live humanly." V. I. Lenin criticized the utopian socialists because they wanted to nurture the new man in artificial conditions. Vladimir Ilyich angrily ridiculed such views, calling them a game of dolls, a pastime for the Pollyannas of socialism.

"We want," he wrote, "to build socialism out of the people who have been nurtured by capitalism, who have been spoiled and corrupted by it, but who on the other hand have been tempered by it for the struggle. We want to build socialism right away, using the material that the capitalism of yesterday left to the present day, right now, and not people to be nurtured in hothouses, if you wish to amuse yourself with such fables."

To build right now, right away! What revolutionary optimism there is in this Leninist appeal! What faith in the transforming power of free creative labor!

Life has shown how profoundly right he was, the leader of our revolution, the founder of the first working people's state in the world. In the course of radical transformations of the whole social, economic and cultural life of the country, which changed the appearance of the old Russian Empire beyond recognition, thanks to the enormous upbringing work of the Party, a new man grew up on our land: the conscious and active builder of communism, a confirmed collectivist with a communist psychology, which the old world never knew. This man, overcoming incredible difficulties, transformed his ruined country into a mighty socialist power, defended it in fierce battles against all its enemies and set for the world an example of unprecedented persistence in work, of an inexhaustible spirit of innovation in creating new forms of labor and of social discipline, upbringing and mores. This man today boldly and confidently tackles the solution of the grand-scale tasks of the further development of the socialist society, tasks that no one has ever before tried to solve. He creates his life, his history and his future consciously and purposefully, basing himself on the laws of social development as he comprehends them, something no one has ever done before. He grows, together with the new society: In transforming social relations, he thereby transforms himself.

Without this—without a profound remaking of the consciousness of people, of their mores, views and habits—you cannot build communism. There is no more difficult task. The ideologists of the bourgeoisie consider it altogether insoluble, because man, they assert, is wicked by his very nature; he always has been this way—greedy, envious, quarrelsome and selfish—and nothing can change his nature. One of the most prominent apologists of capitalism of the previous century, the English philosopher and sociologist Herbert Spencer, wrote precisely this: "No matter what kind of social organism we may have, the wicked nature of the citizens will always manifest itself through their bad actions. There is no political alchemy that can help to transform leaden instincts into golden mores."

The contemporary standard-bearers of capitalism are equally categorical about the unchanging nature of man. More than that, the experiment of building socialism and the actual successes of science, technology, culture and communist upbringing in the U.S.S.R. and the other countries of socialism infuriate them; now attacking not only the idea but also the unquestionable fact of its realization,

they slander man even more ferociously. The burden of the present-day utterances of even the most "objective" among them is essentially as follows: Yes, socialism managed to develop material production enormously in a short time; yes, it can ensure a high level of welfare of society; yes, the Communists have surpassed us in several sciences, in the training of engineers, in space flights; and they have remade everything in their country—but they will never be able to remake man, to overcome his age-old instincts of the property owner and individualist. That's how it always has been, that's how it always will be!

Life itself refutes the speculations and prognoses of the learned defenders of the old world, and several of them are vaguely aware of this—some with bitterness, others in confusion. . . .

People had been brought up for ages in conditions of a life dominated by class oppression, the power of money and selfishness. For centuries, private ownership mercilessly disunited them, the fight for a "place in the sun" instilled in them a spirit of fierce individualism, taught them hypocrisy and maimed and corrupted them morally. Even after the victory of the socialist system, vestiges of the past remain in people's consciousness and behavior, and they impede and slow down the forward movement of society.

The "leaden instincts," whose power H. Spencer spoke about, not without malicious joy, are hardy and tenacious. But they are being vanquished, and not by political alchemy.

Our revolutionary science—the ideological weapon of the Communist Party and its highly reliable compass—has also been, in combination with revolutionary practice, a powerful means for the formation of the best human qualities. What, by comparison, is the mystical "philosopher's stone" that alchemists of olden times sought, applying their sorcery! What is gold! We have in our hands a truly miraculous method of transformation, our "philosopher's stone"—the philosophy of Marxism-Leninism, with which Soviet society rears a man whose spiritual and moral qualities are worth more than any treasures of the world. . . .

To be sure, the task of the communist upbringing of the masses is still far from solved. In our society, there are still people with parasitic proclivities, loafers and spongers, careerists and sycophants, hooligans and drunkards, breakers of labor and social discipline. But they are all bearers of the last vanishing manifestations of the moral filth of the old, corrupt world. In the struggle against these manifestations, the moral consciousness of the people gathers strength, and new norms of human behavior mature.

The moral code of the builder of communism is taking ever broader and deeper roots in our life. Millions of Soviet toilers already live according to its norms and demands. The influence of its principles on the interrelations and behavior of people is constantly growing. The observance of these principles is becoming an inner need of the advanced Soviet man, enriching and elevating his moral configuration. Of course, this is a complicated process that cannot be oversimplified, because its development is not spontaneous and does not follow a smooth, well-beaten path. But it is impossible not to see the results of this process and its majesty.

In involuntary labor under capitalism man, in the words of Marx, does not assert but negates himself, feels not happy but unhappy, does not freely develop his powers but exhausts himself in physical labor and destroys his spirit. Even many bourgeois sociologists conclude that modern capitalism has destroyed the "spiritual side" of work and deprived it of spiritual content. Therein lies the grave crime of capitalism against mankind.

Can you imagine in these conditions phenomena even remotely resembling the creative activity of the masses, whose wellsprings pulse so strongly everywhere in our country? In the first half of the current year alone, more than 1,400,000 inventions and rationalization proposals submitted by workers, engineers and technicians have been applied in our production. This sentence alone, taken from reports of the Central Statistical Administration, a sentence that has become commonplace for us, if you think about it, refutes all the wicked slander of the enemies of socialism against men of labor. You can't change man, the ideologists of the bourgeoisie repeat over and over again. Meanwhile, the process of moral rejuvenation goes deeper and deeper, unmasking the reactionary fabrications.

Soviet people, through their character, actions, thoughts and aspirations, often drive the representatives of the old world into a corner. Many bourgeois theorists cannot understand how material and moral labor incentives can coexist and be effective in our society. Bourgeois metaphysicians and idealists always believed that the two are mutually exclusive. They do not understand that in abolishing private property, socialism does not in the least abolish material incentives but develops them side by side with moral inducements to work, making the labor that ensures the material requirements of people a social activity of exceptional importance.

Some Western visitors—politicians, businessmen, journalists and writers— cannot see, for instance, why workers who are innovators gladly share their production "secrets" with others and teach (without pay!) their methods to others. They ask our young men and women ad nauseam what high wages lured those who voluntarily have gone off to undeveloped virgin lands and to the remote construction projects of Siberia and the North. The old world has known other movements of people: the "gold rush" to the Klondike, the swarms of migrants leaving exhausted soil, hunger marches. All this was for a crust of bread or for profit, for the mirage of gold. The old world knows of no other motive forces. That is why, in spite of the irrefutable truth of the new life, it stubbornly seeks its "own" explanation for the moral qualities of the people of the socialist system, for their social responsiveness and vital interest in the affairs of their state, for their attitude toward labor, toward the collective and toward each other, for their proud awareness of their dignity, for their feeling that they are the masters of their country.

The ideological servants of imperialism have written mountains of papers attempting to discredit the new communist world and to defend the notorious "spiritual values" of their social system. But it is all in vain. The process of the transformation of the communist principles of work and society into people's personal convictions goes on before the very eyes of mankind. It has been irrefutably demonstrated that people can change, and they are changing, asserting, in the new conditions of their socialist existence, not some "golden mores" but genuinely human relations, the triumph of which will signal the victory of communism.

Questions of Theory: Socialism and Humanism

M. PETROSYAN

...For many decades the enemies of socialism have been trying to prove that Marxism and socialism are inimical to humanism. In searching for substantiation for this false idea they resort to various fictions and speculate on certain unresolved questions in the Soviet socialist state, as well as in the other socialist countries, on existing difficulties and contradictions.

Reprinted from Prof. M. Petrosyan, "Questions of Theory: Socialism and Humanism," Pravda (December 19, 1967). Translated in Current Digest of the Soviet Press, *XVIII, No. 51 (Copyright © January 11, 1967), 22–23.*

The struggle against bourgeois ideology, against its attempts to distort the nature and genuinely humanist goals of socialism, is complicated by the fact that present-day "left-wing" revisionists in the Communist movement, in complete contradiction to the spirit of Marxist-Leninist doctrine, are propagating ideas to the effect that socialism is incompatible with humanism....

1. In the history of the development of social thought, humanism has expressed and continues to express the totality of the social-political, philosophical-ethical, esthetic and other concepts and principles related to the defense of the dignity and worth of

the individual, his liberties and rights and his all-round development, to the defense of humaneness in interpersonal relations, of equality and peace among peoples. In a class society humanist conceptions in the final analysis are determined by the ideology and goals of classes and social forces. The latter also determine the content with which the ideologists of different classes invest the concepts of freedom and the rights of the individual, of his worth and dignity and the very conception of the individual.

Proceeding from everything progressive that has been achieved in the previous development of culture and on the humanist aspirations of the past, Marxism at the same time poses in a new way the problem of humanism and the totality of questions connected with man, his present and his future.

Instead of abstract declarations, illusions and daydreams about the happiness of man, instead of philistine philanthropy and the empty, hypocritical compassion for man in general peculiar to abstract humanism, the essence of the Marxist conception of humanism is a revolutionary, effective struggle for the destruction of the social conditions that doom the majority of mankind to exploitation and spiritual enslavement, a struggle for the victory of socialism.

Marxism links the problem of man with the class struggle of the proletariat, with the liquidation of capitalism and the victory of socialism and communism, with the elimination of national and racial oppression, unjust wars and all other forms of oppression from social relations. This new and genuine love of mankind combines an infinite, selfless love for the working people with an equally vigorous hatred of oppressors and bearers of social evil and injustice....

The present-day reactionary bourge-oisie and its ideology have utterly repudiated the best humanist ideas of the past. A campaign against humanism, as well as against all the democratic gains of the popular masses, against the ideas of social progress; the preaching of misanthropy, violence and racism; apologies for war and piracy; shameless anticommunism—such is the "leitmotiv" of the theoretical research of the defenders of capital. They are called upon to justify the corresponding "practices" of the ringleaders of imperialism: the preparation of a war of annihilation against progressive forces; neocolonialism; and piratical attacks on other countries, an example of which is the American imperialists' war in Vietnam. Antihumanist propensities for the depreciation, depersonalization and oppression of man permeate all spheres of the life of capitalist society.

Only socialism and the progressive democratic forces in the nonsocialist countries are the true successors and continuers of the best humanist traditions of mankind.

2. ...The socialist system has put an end to unemployment, poverty and the inhuman working and living conditions of the popular masses. It has led tens of millions of people out of cellars and hovels. The steady growth of the economy has in the conditions of socialism become the basis for a continuous rise in the working people's well-being. The economic reform now being implemented in the U.S.S.R. is disclosing to a still fuller extent the possibilities of socialist production for a further growth in real wages and an increase in monetary payments and benefits out of public funds. In the current five-year plan these payments and benefits will increase by 40%.

The national-economic plan for the second year of the five-year plan, now being discussed by the U.S.S.R. Supreme Soviet, envisages a further rise in the material and cultural standard of living of the Soviet people. Suffice it to say that real income per capita will increase by 5.5% for the year, approximately 13,000,000 persons will receive new apartments and housing conditions will improve.

The socialist revolution has wrought immeasurable improvements in the lives of the working people. These successes would have even been more impressive had the Soviet state not been forced to wage protracted wars of defense against imperialism and to spend many years in repairing the ruin inflicted on the national economy by those wars.

The half-century of experience of the existence and development of the Land of the Soviets has graphically demonstrated that the goal of socialism is the creation of conditions in which man can make use of the abundance of the good things of life and has everything necessary for physical and spiritual betterment.

Life has cruelly mocked the slanderous fabrications of bourgeois propaganda to the effect that socialism allegedly deprives man of his individual qualities, that it levels men, reducing them to the lowest common denominator. In the processes of building a socialist society, millions of outstanding individuals, brave, daring people filled with creative energy and each in his own way inimitable in the beauty of his personality, have distinguished themselves. These people sprang from the midst of all the toiling classes, of all the socialist nations. . . .

With the victory of socialism society entered a new era of human development. We have in mind, first of all, the formation of a new social type— the socialist individual, characterized by a high level of social consciousness (collectivism, socialist patriotism and internationalism, personal responsibility

to society), which is organically bound up with the distinctiveness and many-sided nature of his individual characteristics. This new, developing individual is distinguished by a harmony of convictions and conduct, a high intellectual level and spiritual wealth—a broad range of interests and the consistently humanist nature of his moral and esthetic principles.

Socialist humanism has nothing in common with liberalism or with a conciliatory attitude toward antisocial acts. Respect for human dignity and for the individual is inseparable from strict exactingness and severe demands with respect to observance of the moral norms of society. . . .

3. As the socialist society develops and grows stronger, the world progressive public becomes more and more convinced of the nobility and beauty of communist ideals, of the fact that the humanist aspirations of mankind are being realized in the Soviet Union and the other socialist countries. . . .

Even such an enemy of Marxism as the French philosopher Merleau-Ponty is obliged to admit that in the Soviet Union, "humanism is a phenomenon of daily life," whereas in present-day bourgeois society "commonly recognized humane principles" have led to "inhumane practice."

Taking into consideration this attitude on the part of various strata of the bourgeois intelligentsia toward socialist humanism, we must subject to fundamental scientific criticism the attempts to identify the Marxist conception of humanism with bourgeois liberalism, to reduce socialist humanism to a mere phase of abstract bourgeois humanism. A number of American and West European philosophers and sociologists, recognizing the growing influence of Marxism, are writing about the necessity of supplementing Marxism with anthropology, the study of man in the abstract and psychoanalysis. This attempt is given candid expression in a number of articles included in the anthology "Socialist Humanism," published in New York in 1965.

Humanism, according to the definition of E. Fromm, editor of this anthology, is "a belief in the unity of the human race and in the ability of man to create himself through his own actions." Although on the face of it this definition is directed against racism, against the idea of the inferiority of individual people and many peoples, it is not difficult to note that the author poses the question of humanism abstractly, in isolation from social-political problems and social attitudes and antagonisms.

Proceeding from this abstract ethical-psychological definition of humanism, the author maintains that theoretically there is no substantial difference between the Marxist and the "Western" bourgeois-liberal conceptions of humanism and that both these "varieties" of humanism are based on "Western traditions."

In denying the Marxist doctrine concerning classes and the class struggle, the ideological opponents of Marxism attempt to emasculate the social essence of socialist humanism. In the same anthology one of the authors asserts that "Marx's humanism is neither a reflection of idealism nor an expression of materialism but is the truth of both, combining them in a new unity." And, relying on these "theoretical" fabrications, he proclaims: "Our generation is better than all preceding generations; it understands that the question is not merely that of the nationalization of private property." Such is the conclusion of self-revealing bourgeois class logic.

The nationalization of private property and the establishment of public socialist ownership of the means of production does not automatically exhaust the resolution of the sum total of questions of socialist humanism. But such a step is the initial, fundamental basis for this solution. Rejection of this step leads to the fallacious idea of the "abstract" moral self-perfection of the individual within the framework of bourgeois society.

It is no accident that in monographs and articles by many contemporary theoreticians of abstract bourgeois humanism one comes across such cardinal problems of humanism in our era as the struggle against the danger of a nuclear-missile war, against the imperialist aggression of the U.S.A. in Vietnam and for the complete liquidation of all vestiges of colonialism.

We undoubtedly have need of a further development of the Marxist-Leninist conception of man. In this connection, we cannot fail to note that the legacy of the classical writers of Marxism-Leninism on questions related to the problem of humanism has still not been studied fully. Criticisms expressed by the founders of scientific communism of the idealist conception of one or another philosophical-ethical question, particularly of the idealist interpretation of the meaning of life, the destiny of man and moral responsibility, often have been regarded as fundamental denials of these conceptions by Marxism. The Marxist conception of the basic nature of man has often been interpreted sketchily, the unity of the social and the individual aspects in analysis of the question of the individual has been ignored, etc. The further development of the Marxist conception of man is possible only on the basis of the present-day level of the development of sociology, anthropology, psychology and other sciences relating to this problem. . . .

VALUES, BELIEFS,
AND IDEOLOGIES IN THE U.S.S.R.:

The American View

The Principles of Communist Morality

HERBERT MARCUSE

According to the Soviet interpretation of its ethical position, we should expect two levels of moral philosophy: one defining the "elementary principles of human morality independent of class content," and another showing the expression of these principles, and their specific realization in "communist morality." However, we are confronted with the problem that there seems to be no systematic exposition of the former which could adequately provide representative material for analysis. The lack of any systematic derivation of the "elementary principles of human morality" is, of course, inherent in the politicalization of ethics: the more the moral values become political values and the more moral behavior becomes right political behavior, the less room there is for *independent* ethical principles, or rather for the derivation of their objective validity. Still, Soviet ethics claims objective validity in so far as the specific goals of Soviet society are to coincide with the universal inter-

From Herbert Marcuse, "The Principles of Communist Morality," Soviet Marxism. *New York: Columbia University Press, 1958, pp. 231–34, 238–42, 243.*

est of mankind, namely, the interest in the realization of freedom for all. But this is also the claim of "bourgeois ethics." *Formally,* the "elementary principles of human morality" assumed by Soviet moral philosophy will thus coincide with those assumed by its antagonist. By the same token, the universally valid principles tend to merge with the specific principles of communist morality. Within the context of Soviet ethics, the former receive their real significance from the latter, which in turn are defined in accord with the development of Soviet society. Therefore, presently, we shall discuss these principles in terms of their social and political function. And from the first step on, we are confronted with the fact that, to a striking degree, the specific principles of communist morality as well as the universal "principles of human morality" resemble those of bourgeois ethics. Just as the Soviet constitution, in the proclamation of the "Fundamental Rights and Duties of Citizens" seems to copy the "bourgeois-democratic" ideology and practice, so do the Soviet statements of ethical principles. It is needless to emphasize the difference between ideology and reality—the fact of imitation or assimilation remains. The world-historical coexistence of the two competing systems, which defines their political dynamic, also defines the social *function* of their ethics.

In going through the enumerations of the highest moral values given in Soviet ethical philosophy, it is difficult to find a single moral idea or syndrome of moral ideas that is not common to Western ethics. Care, responsibility, love, patriotism, diligence, honesty, industriousness, the injunctions against transgressing the happiness of one's fellow men, consideration for the common interest—there is nothing in this catalogue of values that could not be included in the ethics of the Western tradition. The similarity continues to prevail if we look at the specific principles of communist morality.[1] The hierarchy of values stated by Lenin in 1920 is almost literally repeated; the moral norms added to it are hardly more than a reformulation with respect to the situation of a fully and firmly established Soviet state. Soviet patriotism; national pride in the Soviet state; international, national, and individual solidarity; respect for socialist property; love for socialist labor; love, loyalty, and responsibility for the socialist family and for the Party—in order to be able to evaluate the actual function of these commonplace notions, we have to place them in the concrete context in which they are illustrated in Soviet ethics. This context is provided by the discussion of work relations, marriage and family matters, leisure activities, and education, and by their presentation in literature and in the entertainment industry. The moral values converge on the subordination of pleasure to duty—the duty to put everything one has into service for the State, the Party, and society. Translated into private morality, this means strict monogamic relations, directed toward the production and raising of children; discipline and competitive performance in the established division of functions; and leisure activities as relaxation from work and re-creation of energy for work rather than as an end in itself. It is in every respect a *competitive work morality*, proclaimed with a rigidity surpassing that of bourgeois morality—softened or hardened according to the specific interests of the Soviet state (for example, softened as in the treatment of illegitimate children, or if rigidity comes into conflict with the requirements of political loyalty, work efficiency, party discipline, and so forth; hardened as in the punishment for theft or "sabotage" of state property).

One of the most representative exhortations designed to "strengthen communist morale"[2] is entirely centered on work morale. The "highest principles" governing this morale are said to be Soviet patriotism and love for the motherland, which are joined with "proletarian internationalism." They serve as justification for the complete endorsement of work as the very content of the individual's whole life. Not only is work itself honor and glory, and "socialist competition" an unconditional duty, *all* work, under socialism, has a creative character, and any degradation of manual labor impairs communist education. In Soviet society, "love for one's work" is per se one of the highest principles of communist morality, and work per se is declared to be one of the most important factors in the build-

---

1 See also N. I. Boldyrev, *V. I. Lenin i I. V. Stalin o vospitanii kommunisticheskoi morali* (V. I. Lenin and J. V. Stalin on the Training of a Communist Morality) (Moscow, *Pravda*, 1951).

2 "Neustanno vospityvat' sovetskikh liudei v dukhe kommunisticheskoi morali" (Unceasingly Educate Soviet People in the Spirit of Communist Morality), *Kommunist*, 1954, No. 13 (September), pp. 3–12.

ing of moral qualities. In view of the moral value of work in a socialist society, the differences between intellectual and manual labor, between elevated and lowly work, become irrelevant.

...The denial of alienation in Soviet ethics may at first appear as a mere subtlety of abstract theorizing; however, upon closer analysis, it reveals the concrete substance of Soviet ethical philosophy. In canceling the notion of alienation as applicable to Soviet society, Soviet ethics removes the moral ground from under the protest against a repressive social organization of labor and adjusts the moral structure and the character of the individual to this organization. Laboring in the service of the Soviet state is per se ethical—the true vocation of Soviet man. The individual needs and aspirations are disciplined; renumeration and toil is the road to salvation. The theory and practice which were to lead to a new life in freedom are turned into instruments of training men for a more productive, more intense, and more rational mode of labor. What the Calvinist work morale achieved through strengthening irrational anxiety about forever-hidden divine decisions, is here accomplished through more rational means: a more satisfying human existence is to be the reward for the growing productivity of labor. And in both cases, far more telling economic and physical force guarantee their effectiveness. The resemblance is more than incidental: the two ethics meet on the common ground of historical "contemporaneousness"—they reflect the need for the incorporation of large masses of "backward" people into a new social system, the need for the creation of a well-trained, disciplined labor force, capable of vesting the perpetual routine of the working day with ethical sanction, producing ever more rationally ever increasing amounts of

goods, while the rational use of these goods for the individual needs is ever more delayed by the "circumstances." In this sense, Soviet ethics testifies to the *similarity* between Soviet society and capitalist society. The basis for the similarity was established in the Stalinist period.

In the development of Soviet society, the Stalinist period is that of industrialization, or rather "industrial civilization" in the sense outlined by Lenin in his last writings, with the far-reaching principal objective of "catching up" with and surpassing the level of productivity prevailing in the advanced Western countries. Given the starting point for industrialization in the backward state of Bolshevik Russia, this period would correspond to the early stages of capitalist industrialization, after the "primary accumulation" had been completed.

However, the advantageous position of the "latecomer," nationalization of the means of production, central planning, and totalitarian control, makes it possible for the Soviet state to telescope several stages of industrialization, to utilize the most rationalized technology and machinery, advanced science, and the most intensive working methods without being seriously hampered by conflicting private interests. Soviet ethical philosophy formulates the basic values of primary industrialization, but it also expresses, simultaneously, the different (and even conflicting) requirements of the later stages. Soviet ethics must combine the need for "primary" disciplining of the laboring classes with the need for individual initiative and responsibility—the standardized compliance of the human tool with the intelligent imagination of the engineer. It must foster a morale conducive to a long working day as well as to a high productivity of labor, to quantitative as well as qualitative performance. The conditions of backwardness which defined Soviet industrialization have met with those of advanced technology (eighteenth-century with twentieth-century industrialism)—in the political institutions as well as in the ethics of Soviet society. Administrative absolutism faces the effective constitutionalism of the democratic West, a privileged authoritarian bureaucracy must be refined and renewed and kept open to ascent from below. This is required not only by the need to increase the scope and efficiency of the productive apparatus, but also by the obvious competition with the capabilities and realities of the Western world. Increasing cultural and material compensations for the underlying population are indispensable—not only for political reasons, but also on economic grounds; they belong to the "development of the productive forces" which constitutes the backbone of long-range Soviet policy.

Soviet ethics tries to integrate this diversity of economic and political needs and to translate it into a coherent system of moral values. Thus one finds side by side the exhortation to individual initiative and spontaneity and to authoritarian discipline, to Stakhanovist competition and to socialist equality; the glorification of work and the glorification of leisure, of toil and of freedom, of totalitarian and of democratic values. Soviet social philosophy reflects throughout the objective historical contradiction inherent in Soviet society—a contradiction generated by the fact that the principles of socialist economy were made into an instrument of domination, to be applied to a backward country confronted with a far more advanced capitalist world. The need for "catching up" with capitalism called for enforced and accelerated industrialization as the only available road to socialism. While the humanist values attached to the *end* of the road became ritualized into ideology, the values attached to the *means,* i.e., the values of total industrialization, became the really governing values.

...Socialist morality thus succumbs to industrial morality, while the various historical stages of the latter are condensed into one comprehensive unit, combining elements from the ethics of Calvinism and Puritanism, enlightened absolutism and liberalism, nationalism, chauvinism, and internationalism, capitalist and socialist values. This is the strange syndrome presented by Soviet ethics.

Within this syndrome, the repressive elements are predominant. Many of the rules of conduct in school and home, at work and leisure, in private and in public, resemble so much their traditional Western counterparts at earlier stages that they have the sound of secular sermons documenting the "spirit of Protestant-capitalist ethics." They are not too far from Puritan exhortations to good business. The praise of the monogamic family and of the joy and duty of conjugal love recalls classical "petty-bourgeois ideology," while the dissolution of the sphere of privacy reflects twentieth-century reality. The struggle against prostitution, adultery, and divorce evokes the same ethical norms as in the West, while the requirements of the birth rate and the sustained investment of energy in competitive work performances are praised as manifestations of Eros. To be sure, the public exhortations to combine erotic relations with meritorious occupational performance should not be taken too seriously: there is evidence of official and semi-official ridicule and protest, and of widespread private transgression. What is decisive is the general trend, and the extent to which the individual's own evaluation of his personal relationships agrees with the politically desired evaluation.

Relaxation recently has been widespread, but without changing the underlying morality. The trend seems to be toward normalization rather than abolition of repression. In line with tendencies prevalent in late industrial civilization, repression is to be "spontaneously" reproduced by the repressed individuals; this allows a relaxation of external, compulsory repression. . . .

The Glorious Future

ERICH GOLDHAGEN

The idea of progress, the belief in the irresistible advance of human society to ever-greater social and moral perfection, which had been, in the words of the distinguished historian J. B. Bury in his *Idea of Progress,* "the animating and controlling idea of Western civilization," is virtually extinct in the West today. Two world wars, the eruption of inhumanity and barbarism—all the more terrifying for their technological refinement and the ever-present danger of universal nuclear destruction—have banished the optimism characteristic of the nineteenth century. Gloom, pessimism, and uncertainty have enveloped Western civilization. The prophecy of Condorcet that "the perfectability of man is in fact unlimited and can never be reversed" could only evoke a smile in a generation that has witnessed Auschwitz and that is condemned to live in the shadow of the hydrogen bomb.

But the vision of utopia, extinct in the West, continues to shine in the Communist East, deriving its splendor from the artificial illumination of the propaganda engines of *Agitprop.* At the Twelfth International Congress of Philosophers held at Venice in 1958, M. B. Mitin, a leading Soviet philosopher, portrayed the future society to which the Soviet Union is allegedly advancing in terms worthy perhaps not so much of Marx as of his more imaginative predecessors—Condorcet, Saint-Simon, and Fourier. The society to come, he solemnly prophesied, would attain such heights of social perfection that the individuals nurtured by it would develop—"as if by magic"— qualities hitherto possessed only by men of genius. The common man would grow to the stature of a Michelangelo, a Liszt, or a Paganini. Just as Communism would abolish the distinction between rich and poor by providing abundance for all, so would it reduce the differences between the mental capacities and achievements of individuals by liberating the potentialities of man from the oppressive shells of human institutions. To the Western philosophers present, it must have seemed as if the ghost of Condorcet had descended upon Venice in the guise of the Soviet philosopher to preach the doctrine of inevitable progress towards utopia. Some might even have reflected that it was odd, though symbolic, that this Soviet Condorcet combined the lofty vocation of philosophical visionary with the mundane pursuit of police agent and propagandist.[1]

But the theme of utopia is not confined to philosophers alone. In the Soviet Union, economists, writers and a vast army of propagandists have been dwelling on it with increasing frequency, reflecting the guiding and inspiring hand of the Party—the chief dispenser of spiritual nourishment to the Soviet populace.

Addressing a plenary session of the Board of the Writers' Union of the R.S.F.S.R., L. Sobolev, its Chairman and an official guardian of literary orthodoxy, envisaged the future Communist society to be peopled by citizens endowed with intellectual capacities of a degree hitherto confined to a gifted minority. The art of literary creation, instead of remaining the property of a chosen few, will become the natural attribute of everyone. The citizens of Communism, released from the toil to which humanity has been condemned, would take to the pen; and a new golden age of art and literature would dawn upon the human race. Just as "work will become the primary vital need of man, so the mastery of [literary] craftsmanship will cease to be the achievement of single individuals to become the natural practice of every-

[1] Mitin, entrusted by Stalin with the conduct of the campaign against Tito, distinguished himself by such zeal that he earned the Titoist epithet "the best philosopher among the NKVD men and the best NKVD man among philosophers."

one exactly in the same manner in which, under Soviet rule, literacy ceased to be the privilege of the ruling estate and became universal." Soviet society, Sobolev continued, stands in the "forefield" of that golden age, separated from it only by a road of great but surmountable obstacles. In describing the manner in which these obstacles are to be overcome, Sobolev abandoned the mellow and gilded language of the utopian dreamer for the warlike metaphor of the cavalry officer, his former vocation (*Pravda,* May 11, 1960):

We find ourselves in the forefield of Communism. I adduce this military term consciously, because, in the course of the unfolding advance our society is now effecting, we must still overcome some minefields laid thousands of years ago—the so-called survivals of capitalism in the consciousness of people.

Many would be naturally tempted to dismiss such utterances as ritualistic lip service, as mechanical and meaningless recitals of the Marxist creed. But to do so would be to obscure not only the sincere devotion with which many of the Marxist formulas are held, but also the vital role played by utopia in the Communist order.

The secular eschatology of Marxism is one of the ideological and psychological pillars of Soviet society. Just as the power of the Church and indeed the cohesion of the medieval order rested on the belief in the hereafter, so the ideal terrestial future is an essential element of the spiritual foundation of the Communist world. The awe-inspiring firmament of the hereafter was a living psychic reality for medieval man, providing the anchor chain for the power of the Church over his mind. Earthly power was firmly rooted in the heavenly domain, investing the authority of the Church with a claim to obedience equaled by few temporal rulers. All political power seeks to legitimize itself, to rely not on naked force but on the voluntary consent of its subjects. But the Bolshevik claim to obedience could rest on few tangible benefits offered to the people. It has demanded much in toil, suffering, and anxiety, but it has offered little in return, save the assurance that the privation of the present would yield abundant fruit in the undetermined future. Until recently, utopian dreams were the only gratification the regime could supply in plenty.

It would be impossible to determine the efficacy of utopia as an opium for the people. It is doubtful, for instance, that the peasantry was at all susceptible to it, particularly during the collectivization drive. Terror seems to have been a more potent instrument in securing submission to the will of the Party than the blandishments of the glorious future. But if Marx's eschatology has served only imperfectly as an opium for the people, it has been a powerful self-administered opium for the ruling class. It would be difficult to exaggerate the *élan* derived by Bolsheviks from the utopian vision. It has endowed them with an unwavering singleness of purpose, with a missionary zeal that retains, undaunted, the fullness of its fervor even in adversity, and it has imparted to them an immunity to scruples in the pursuit of power.

For the Bolshevik mind, from the very beginning, endowed the future with the dimensions and qualities of a deity —or rather a moloch. Whenever a Bolshevik would be beset by doubts caused by the contradiction between precept and practice, between the humane goal and the inhuman deed, he would summon up the radiant future, thus rationalizing the present, appeasing his conscience, and enabling himself to resume his vocation undisturbed by qualms. Perhaps the power of rationalization conferred by utopia is best revealed in those Communist victims of the Stalinist terror who, languishing innocently in prisons and concentration camps, nevertheless found comfort and justification for their ordeal in the belief that their lot was but part of the heavy toll humanity must pay in order to enter the gates of the future.

...The Bolshevik is one of the purest incarnations of the Faustian Man. He is constantly on the historical road in pursuit of the Goal, overcoming obstacles and warding off enemies. To pause, content with past achievements, would signify that his mission has been completed, his role exhausted, and his claim to total power ended. Totalitarian Communism can dispense neither with enemies nor with utopia.[2]

...One of the contradictions of Communism has always been its demand for absolute obedience and punishment of any sign of resistance to its will on the one hand, and its simultaneous inculcation, through Marxist texts, of the dream of a different social order on the other. A populace exposed to the ubiquitous power of the police and the state, experiencing glaring inequalities in income and status, chained serflike to their jobs, could nevertheless speak aloud about a future state to the fulfillment of which their leaders themselves were pledged, a state in which the police, indeed the very organs of government, would not exist, in which full social equality would reign, and in which every individual would be able to fulfill himself.

Now, with the material conditions for fulfillment of the great promise at last in sight, Soviet citizens, according to *Kommunist,* have begun to raise specific

---

[2] The totalitarian regime must constantly affirm a boundless optimism. For pessimism is the blood-brother of skepticism, and skepticism is the enemy of all absolute creeds. It is, in the words of the *Soviet Encyclopedia,* "one of the forms of the struggle against science and against dialectical materialism."

questions about "the nature of the future organs of government in the villages and cities, about other details of Communist life." An agitator in the Saratov area appealed to Moscow for guidance and knowledge of the future society; for, "deluged" by questions he was unable to answer, he was in danger of "forfeiting his authority as an agitator." One Soviet writer expressed his apprehensions lest an "unreasonable person" might entertain the following notion of Communism: "You rise in the morning and you begin to reflect: Where shall I go to work today—to the factory as the chief engineer, or shall I gather and lead the fishing brigade? Or pehaps fly to Moscow to conduct an urgent session of the Academy of Sciences?" *Kommunist*, quoting this flight of imagination, remarked laconically, "Thus it will not be."

Ideas are a force no dictator can ignore with impunity. The eschatological imagination threatens to become a source of indiscipline, a breeder of "dangerous" expectations incompatible with the total claims of the state. Totalitarian order has to be imposed upon the anarchic vision without, however, robbing it of the enthusiasm and purposefulness that it imparted to its bearers. As early as October 13, 1952, Poskrebyshev, Stalin's secretary and the *éminence grise* of the Soviet system, denounced in *Pravda* "those among us who await the coming of Communism as if it were some heavenly paradise. They sit there and ask themselves: 'When will Communism finally be proclaimed? Will we soon be getting things from society according to our needs?' " Eight years later, the theoretical organ of the Party warned that the treatment of the future society must admit neither "oversimplification" nor "harebrained plans" (*prozhektorstvo*), that "to write now about the future is more complicated than ever before. The days of

utopia, of arbitrary flights of fancy, have passed, giving way to higher responsibility in analyzing reality and in foresight." And Khrushchev, at the Twenty-first Party Congress, sought to dispel with oracular authority the "vulgar" conception of Communism "as a formless, unorganized, and anarchic mass of people. No, it will be a highly organized and arranged cooperation of workers. In order to direct machines, everybody will have to fulfill his functions as a laborer and his *social duties* at a determined time and in an established order." (Italics added.)

It was in the course of purging Marxist eschatology of its heretical elements that the Party gained a clearer conception of the ultimate goal of its endeavor. What had heretofore been a tacit and only half-conscious conception became a more articulate vision.[3] Upon inspection, that vision reveals the hallmarks of a dream typical of Party bureaucrats. If utopia mirrors the imaginary fulfillment of desires thwarted by reality, then the utopia of the Party bureaucrats—the *apparatchiki*—reflects lust for unobstructed power: a perfected totalitarianism. As such, it bears a greater affinity to the ideals of Sparta or the *Republic* of Plato, to Rousseau's ideal state or to Thomas More's *Utopia,* than to the vague vision of Marx, although it is not altogether alien to it. Some strands of the Marxist ideal future are lifted from their original context, severed from the libertarian elements to which they had been organically linked, and woven into a new pattern that Marx would scarcely recognize.

3 Vladimir Dedijer records, in his biography of *Tito* (New York: Simon and Schuster, 1953, p. 296), a statement by Malenkov at the founding conference of the Cominform in 1947, that the Soviet Union was about "to adopt a fifteen-year plan of the transition from socialism to communism...drawing in detail upon the utopian socialists."

...The Communists aspire to "leap" from the "necessity" of compromising with *stykhiinost* into the realm of absolute "freedom" from it, to sway the wayward course of social change into a narrow channel fixed by the Party. But it is doubtful that the complex course of history can be made fully to obey the dictates of a political machine. The mark of unpredictability is written on all historical action. Almost every historical deed breeds unintended consequences. "Man makes his own history, but he does not know the history he is making." Will the Party be exempt from this rule, which has hitherto governed human destiny?

But perhaps, in their heart of hearts, the Communist leaders cherish less the ideal goal than the pursuit of it. Tension and struggle are the pith and marrow of their endeavor. They lend meaning and purpose to their existence. The reward of ultimate conquest would be intolerable ennui. The mantle of philosopher-king ruling a populace trained to unswerving obedience would ill fit an *apparatchik* who has imbibed the ethos of perpetual struggle. . . .

II

THE POLITY

Three American and one Soviet selection will elucidate the nature of the American political system. Once more we chose several American authors to accommodate divergent points of view. There is near unanimity among Soviet authors on this as on many other aspects of American society.

Shils addresses himself to the essentials of political democracy not peculiar to the United States. Bell's article is concerned with the overall character of American society, but it is especially relevant for an understanding of political life in the United States. While Shils and Bell are in basic agreement on the nature of the American polity, Mills registers vigorous dissent. Orekhov, a Soviet political commentator goes further than Mills in denying any semblance of political democracy in the United States; he is, on the other hand, a good deal less informed and more doctrinaire than Mills.

The major issues in establishing the principal characteristics of the American polity are the degree of dependence of political leaders and parties on economic interest groups, the extent and importance of popular participation, and the decline of representative government over time. Whether or not this is a mass society is relevant from the political point of view. People living in a mass society are supposedly "atomized," a condition which is neither conducive to wholesome participation in public affairs, nor does it help to resist undemocratic political tendencies.

In the eyes of Shils and Bell, and probably the majority of American social scientists, this is a pluralistic society with a pluralistic polity. As

Shils explains, this arrangement precludes not only the concentration of power but also the premise that any particular segment of the population is vastly superior to another and has a monopoly of historical insight and prescriptions for perfecting society. Pluralism also refers to the limited or moderated competition among political groups, limited because there is a basic consensus on certain values and because it is carried out within the limiting framework of law. (From the Soviet perspective it is precisely this consensus that makes the competition of established parties unauthentic or phony.) The basic assumption of such a society is that limiting the power of the government is desirable. Such an assumption is totally alien to Soviet political philosophy and practice. Soviet observers of Western political institutions either ignore this checks-and-balances aspect of the polity or ridicule it as an example of bourgeois hypocrisy and formalism. From the Soviet Marxist-Leninist point of view, it is futile to attempt to devise representative political institutions as long as economic power is unequally distributed. Correspondingly it is superfluous to worry about the nature of political institutions and distribution of power once economic inequalities and exploitation have been abolished, since it is the latter which precludes genuine democracy. This, at least, is the orthodox position. As many Western students of Marxism and Soviet society have noted, the very existence and emergence of the Soviet political system exemplifies the fact that political power does not always derive from economic power. Moreover, Soviet political practice in general supports the argument of those who credit political institutions with a high degree of autonomy.

While both Mills and Orekhov are animated by the debunking impulse and both seem inclined to an idealization of the good old days (when American democracy worked better), they are separated by a gulf in their respective levels of understanding the American polity. It is not surprising that Mills, a native observer, does better, while Orekhov has to contend both with distance and the necessity to apply ideological preconceptions. In particular, the complexity of American politics eludes him and he cannot give up the time-honored Soviet notion that American politicians are nothing but the puppets of Wall Street. His discussion of "political education" programs conducted by large corporations sounds more like the corresponding Soviet institution than an American undertaking. Once more we confront the typical Soviet predisposition to view America (and other Western societies) in terms of the Soviet experience. As other Soviet observers, he fatally misjudges and exaggerates the extent of the politicization of American life. Denying the difference between the two major American political parties is also a venerable tradition of the Soviet political analysis of the United States. There is, however, much truth in his article: obviously there is an important relationship between running for office and wealth as well as between socioeconomic class and political participation. The relationship, however, is far more complex and contradictory than one would guess from reading Orekhov and his colleagues.

The presence or absence of political democracy is not among the hotly debated issues in the discussions of the Soviet political system. Western analysts, including those sympathetic to the Soviet Union, agree that democracy in the Western sense and tradition does not exist. Sharper differences of opinion arise in explaining and evaluating this absence. The major concern of most Western observers has been to determine the extent of the absence of political democracy and the nature of the decision-making process and to build an appropriate theoretical model with which to describe and understand the Soviet polity. The latter problem has been aggravated since Stalin's death, when the major model—totalitarianism—has been questioned under the impact of change. Kassof's article reflects the ongoing reevaluation of the applicability of the concept.

From the Soviet perspective the Soviet political system has been the most and the only truly democratic one, in which, under historically determined conditions, the entire people participate effectively in government and are led by the most progressive, enlightened political entity history has ever seen—the Communist Party of the Soviet Union. The Party is, among other things, a quasi-sacred, metaphysical entity, a meeting ground of the various elites of society, a recruitment agency for the highest political decision-makers and the ultimate source of ideological guidance and legitimacy. Two of the Soviet articles discuss the current role and mutual relationship of the Party and State, with an emphasis on the enduring and undiminished leadership functions of the Party during the transition from socialism to communism. We should note here that the "withering away of the State" has been among the most controversial and apparently unrealizable propositions of Marxism. It has created great trouble for Soviet ideologues, especially with the alleged approach of communism bringing abundance and terminating all imperfections of the social world, including the necessity of coercion by the state.

A more realistic appraisal of the role of the Party is provided by Meyer's analysis, which helps us understand this political institution without parallel in the United States. Some realities of the role of the Party in Soviet life are also revealed in the third Soviet article dealing with "Party Work in Institutions of Higher Education." This is essentially a catalogue of the difficulties which beset a particular Party organization (the one at the University of Moscow). It is more than likely that many of the problems discussed here are not peculiar to this one unit of the Party; otherwise the important theoretical journal of the Party would not have devoted a long article to them. (In general it is a safe assumption that whenever a Soviet journal or newspaper castigates particular localized shortcomings they are widespread.) The article is critical of three phenomena: 1) the indifference of academic people to party work; 2) the weakness of the educational-ideological work of the Party at Moscow University; and 3) the ossification of the Party organization in question. ("For example, in the mechanics and mathematics department for the past 15 years the same 25 to 30 scientists have been elected to the department Party bureau over and over.") Without too much reading between the lines, it seems clear that this particular Party organization is anything but a vital, respected, or relevant institution at Moscow University. We cannot, of course, make any estimates as to *how* typical this situation is. It is possible that in the university setting the Party is a more irrelevant institution than elsewhere—partly because of the more critical attitudes of academic intellectuals and partly because, being established professionals (or on their way to becoming such), they need the Party less to improve their status in society. Finally, it is also possible that the article reflects the greater demands made upon the Party by its leadership when it functions in the university setting and especially in Moscow where foreign students also attend. One can infer from the article that contact with foreign students is viewed as a mixed blessing, and preparation for it requires extra ideological measures, so that "prompt replies to burning questions" can be given.

Insofar as the Party is the most important, indeed the only truly functioning political institution in the Soviet Union, it continues to receive a great deal of attention from both Soviet and American social scientists. Perhaps in the future its role might change and its dominance over Soviet life be altered; however, for the present the nature of the Party holds the key for an understanding of the entire Soviet political system. As long as the Party continues to claim and enforce its infallibility there can be little serious argument about the character of the Soviet polity.

Finally, we have also included two articles illustrating the dimensions of and responses to political dissent in the two societies. In both instances of dissent, the Berkeley riots in the United States and the activities of two writers in the U.S.S.R., the writings selected are unsympathetic. (Since smuggling abroad manuscripts critical of Soviet society is considered treasonable in the U.S.S.R., we could not have found any Soviet-published material sympathetic to the writers. We could, of course, easily have found favorable American commentary on the Berkeley dissenters.)

We chose these two cases of dissent because of their prominence in recent years and because of a certain similarity between the two: in both instances those involved strongly rejected their respective social system (less openly and dramatically in the Soviet case); in both instances the carriers of dissent were young, articulate, and associated with academic-intellectual environments; in both instances their rejection and social criticism had a certain romantic coloration. These are, of course, the only similarities. In the United States the dissidents engaged in open and effective political organization, held meetings and talks, disseminated their political literature unhindered, and defied successfully the supporters of the established social-political order, if not nationwide at least in an important local setting. They encountered comparatively mild penalties only after physically obstructing the functioning of the University, but never because of their views, speeches, writings, or organizational activities. The two Soviet writers, by contrast, were found guilty and sentenced to seven and five years of hard labor respectively, for no other reason than sending abroad their manuscripts containing veiled, though genuine criticism of the Soviet system.

The excerpts following illustrate what might be called "establishment reactions" to political dissent. Clearly the Dean of a School of Religion in the U.S. had as little sympathy toward the leftist Berkeley rebels as the editorial writers of the Soviet Party and Government newspapers had toward the two writer-critics. Nonetheless there is a world of difference between the reactions. The American critic analyzes the dissenters without venom and in relation to an overall decline of values and authority in the United States and uses the opportunity to engage in a more general criticism of the conditions facilitating the Berkeley riots. By contrast, Soviet spokesmen view their dissidents as isolated pathological deviants whose views and activities are totally unrelated to the nature of contemporary Soviet reality.

THE POLITY
IN THE U.S.:
The American View

The Rule of Law,
The Separation of Powers,
Pluralistic Politics

EDWARD SHILS

THE RULE OF LAW:
THE SEPARATION OF POWERS

The legal order which guarantees the pluralistic society is the rule of law—

law made within the framework of a constitution, written or unwritten, by elected representatives, executed by a partially autonomous administrative staff and adjudicated by an independent judiciary.

The rule of law limits the powers of the government, both externally and internally. It is the limitation by law of the discretionary power of the executive over the other spheres of government and over the citizen; it is also the external and internal limitation of valid spheres of legislative action by constitution and custom, by tradition and morals. The rule of law is infringed when any one of the constituent authorities abdicates the functions appropriate to its partially autonomous sphere within the total system of authority or seeks so to expand it that it encroaches on the autonomy of another sphere. A bureaucracy which acts without reference to law infringes on the rule of law as much as a legislature which seeks to dominate the decisions of the judiciary. A legislative body which abandons its responsibilities to the populace which has elected it diverges from the rule of law as much as does a legislative which renounces its constitutional powers to the executive.

The rule of law rests at bottom on the belief widely and deeply diffused throughout the society that there is a sacred element in the law as such. The sacredness of the law is not confined to the law; it infuses the institutions through which it is made, applied, and adjudged. Like the pluralistic system as a whole, of which the rule of law is a part, it rests on the belief in the sacredness of a complex constellation of values, no one of which is always greatly superior to any other. Just as in the larger pluralistic system, each major and minor sphere has its own life, its own powers, and its own obligations of mutual adaptation, so in the rule of law each of the four sectors—the electorate, the legislature, the executive, and the judiciary—has its own autonomous realm and its obligations to the other realms which make up the system of the rule of law.

The rule of law is a delicately balanced affair and it must withstand battering from many sides. The populistic mentality, when it has full sway, denies the claims to autonomy of the legisla-tive which it views as its mouthpiece, of the executive which it views as its instrument and of the judiciary which it views as the resistant custodian of a law which sets itself above the will of the people. Politicians are jealous of bureaucrats, whom they regard as rivals; bureaucrats with their greater detailed knowledge and their feeling of intimacy with the situation, sometimes dislike and bridle at the restrictions which the law places in the way of their doing what seems best.

In the United States the rule of law is deeply rooted in the interests of institutions and in a powerful tradition. Alongside of it, however, runs a current of thought and sentiment, a disposition towards ideological enthusiasm and political passions, which proclaim great crises and announce their disbelief in the capacities of ordinary institutions and their leaders to resolve them.

The American people are recurrently pulled in two directions: respect for the conventions of institutions and regard for the rights of others, and the opposite of these. There is a broad antinomian strand in the American people quite apart from the ordinary criminal element which even the best ordered of societies produces. There are times and areas of an exceptional irreverence and disrespect towards the law in the United States; it is widespread, if not often intense, in most sections of the population and it is perhaps more passive than active. The general attitude of the population towards nearly all municipal regulations, the not infrequent attempts to bribe officials, the only recently reduced tendency in certain regions to "take the law into one's own hands," the fact that in the 1930's hundreds of thousands of educated persons could without repugnance and without thought of the implications lend their support to a political organization which was committed in principle, even though at the time not in practice, to the un-constitutional revolutionary overthrow of the existing governmental and legal order, the toleration of small-scale urban civil wars during the 1920's and their intermittent revival since then, the whole fiasco of the observance of the Eighteenth Amendment—all of these instances and many others add up to the conclusion that, as far as one important prerequisite of the rule of law is concerned, American propensities are sometimes not quite all they should be.

Insistence, therefore, on the niceties of the rule of law is not likely to be an unchallenged response of Americans to crises. The disrespect for law is partly a function of the disrespect for the makers of the law, and that in its turn is reflected in the conduct of the makers of the law themselves. The populistic mentality and their own lack of disci-plined self-respect impel them towards actions which conflict with the rule of law. . . .

PLURALISTIC POLITICS

Pluralism is not a single political position. It is the postulate of numerous political positions. Conservatism and liberalism, laissez-faire and socialism, traditionalism and rationalism, hierar-chy and equalitarianism, can all fall within the area of pluralism. Pluralism is conservative by contrast with revolu-tionary extremism, pluralism is liberal by contrast with reactionary extremism. It is only by contrast with the extremes of alienation from social order and orderly change that pluralism appears to be a single position.

Conflict and diversity, change and criticism, are integral to the mutuality of pluralism. So is the order based on affinity. No single party can ever claim that its position and its position alone embodies pluralistic principles. A mod-erate socialist party, a moderate bour-geois party, a moderate party of small businessmen, a moderate party of big businessmen, a moderate Christian party, a moderate free-thinker's party, a regional party, and above the parties which amalgamate many traditions and interests like the American parties can all fall within the circle of pluralism. What places them there is the modera-tion of their demands, their desire for a little more of what they think is good rather than the complete and immedi-ate fulfillment of every dream and im-pulse.

Parties and beliefs which are satis-fied to remain within the circle of plu-ralism define their goals, regardless of their substantive content, as small in-crements. A socialist party, whose socialist aspirations are fulfilled when, as in Great Britain, publicly operated institutions, industries, and services, employ 25% of the gainfully occupied as compared with 15% before the intro-duction of socialism, and a conservative party which accepts the principle of health insurance but thinks that it should be done through private initia-tive and through privately owned insur-ance institutions, which, in other words, is satisfied if the standard of private responsibility is respected, can both equally be pluralistic in the social policy and politics which they espouse.

Pluralistic politics is marked also by the moderation of political involvement. A lukewarm "politicization" is a fea-ture of pluralistic politics. This is par-ticularly so among the lower levels of the membership of the political bodies, but it must obtain, at least relatively, among the elites. Politicians in a plural-istic society must be more than politi-cians, even though politics engages most of their energy and interest. They must also be concerned with objects other than political objects and they must look at them from a nonpolitical point of view. Politicians must enjoy the excitement of the political conflict or they would not care to be politicians; but if most of them care only for that the boundaries of pluralism will be overrun.

Pluralistic politics, regardless of political standpoint or platform, requires from its practitioners a spread of interest beyond the range of politics; it also prohibits emotional intensity, especially emotional excitement continuing over long stretches of time or running on without intermission. Intense passions at election time do not harm pluralism if they fade away quickly thereafter and do not flare up except momentarily between elections.

The apocalyptic mentality sees every issue as a conflict between diametrically opposed alternatives, and it sees the carriers of these alternatives as opposed to each other completely, fundamentally and continuously. The pluralistic mentality, believing the alternatives fall within a narrower range, believes also that the proponents of the alternatives also have more in common with each other than do apocalyptic politicians. The smaller the gap between the alternatives, the closer the positions of their proponents, so that the fundamental political positions are separated from each other, not by deep cleavages or disjunctions, but by gradual variations. Thus, small increments of achievement are acceptable because all pluralist politics rejects the apocalyptic point of view which counts as important only the differences between salvation and damnation. While small increments of achievement are valued, small variations in the properties of associates, colleagues, and rivals, are not endowed with vital significance.

Pluralistic politics requires a sense of affinity among the elites and a common attachment to the institutions and apparatus through which political life is carried on.[1] It requires some slight distance between leaders and led, not great enough to lead to a sense of utter separateness, but large enough to support self-esteem and independence of judgment.

No single party and no single social policy can be put forward as the sole embodiment of a pluralistic point of view. Democrats and Republicans, Conservatives and Labourites, Radicals, Socialists and MRP, Christian Democrats and Socialists, can all be accommodated within the confines of the political system as long as they observe the standards presented above: restriction of the political sphere and interest, gradual increments of change, the shading off and overlapping of differences, and the affinity of elites.

Only extremism is excluded. Yet many of the difficulties of the present situation come from the failure, both among conservatives and liberals, to recognize that the really crucial dividing line in politics is between pluralistic moderation and monomaniac extremism.

It has been too easy for moderates of the different positions to think that their true allies were those who appeared to espouse in a more dramatic and aggressive form their own substantive values, while their greatest enemies were those who were opposed to their substantive programs. Liberals and radicals have thought that revolutionaries and Communists were their allies, but were more impatient and insistent and

[1] The strength of the forces of civility in the battle against the flood of populism was evinced in the refusal by the Select Committee of the Senate to regard Senator McCarthy's re-election in 1952 as a vindication of his actions. It said: "This is a matter for the Senate and the Senate alone. The people of Wisconsin can only pass upon issues before them. They cannot forgive an attack by a Senator upon the integrity of the Senate's processes and its committees. That is the business of the Senate."

less compromising than themselves. They believed that the revolutionaries and Communists were their allies because the extremists, too, seemed to be interested in equalitarian and humanitarian values and in the use of critical reason in social policy. The conservatives have erred in thinking that Fascists, Nazis, nativist-fundamentalists and McCarthyites were their allies because, even though their methods were distasteful, they claimed to be concerned with the protection of tradition and with the maintenance of private property. Large sections of the major parties in most Western countries have committed the mistake of believing that they have had more in common with those who claimed to represent their values by extreme and accentuated methods than they had with those who opposed them within a framework of moderation. . . .

The Theory of Mass Society

DANIEL BELL

...a sombre melancholy weighed on people's souls. . . . It would sometimes seem as if this period had been particularly unhappy, as if it had left behind only the memory of violence, of covetousness and moral hatred. . . . The feeling of general insecurity [was heightened] by the chronic form wars were apt to take, by the constant menace of the dangerous classes, by the mistrust of justice. . . . It was, so to say, bad form to praise the world and life openly. It was fashionable to see only its suffering and misery, to discover everywhere the signs of decadence and the near end—in short to condemn the times or to despise them.

—J. H. Huizinga, *The Waning of the Middle Ages*

The sense of a radical dehumanization of life which has accompanied events of the past few decades has given rise to the theory of "mass society." One can say that, Marxism apart, it is probably the most influential social theory in the Western world today. While no single individual has stamped his name on it—to the extent that Marx

From Daniel Bell, *"The Theory of Mass Society,"* Commentary, *July, 1956, pp. 75–83. Reprinted from* Commentary, *by permission; copyright* © *1956 by the American Jewish Committee.*

is associated with the transformation of personal relations under capitalism into commodity values, or Freud with the role of the irrational and unconscious in behavior—the theory is central to the thinking of the principal aristocratic, Catholic, or Existentialist critics of modern society. These critics—Ortega y Gasset, Paul Tillich, Karl Jaspers, Gabriel Marcel, Emil Lederer, Hannah Arendt, and others—have been concerned less with the general conditions of freedom in society than with the freedom of the *person* and with the possibility, for some few persons, of achieving a sense of individual self in our mechanized society. And this is the source of their appeal.

The conception of the "mass society" can be summarized as follows: The revolutions in transport and communications have brought men into closer contact with each other and bound them in new ways; the division of labor has made them more interdependent; tremors in one part of society affect all others. Despite this greater interdependence, however, individuals have grown more estranged from one another. The old primary group ties of family and local community have been shattered; ancient parochial faiths are questioned; few unifying values have taken their place. Most important, the critical standards of an educated elite no longer shape opinion or taste. As a result, mores and morals are in constant flux, relations between individuals are tangential or compartmentalized, rather than organic. At the same time, greater mobility, spatial and social, intensifies concern over status. Instead of fixed or known status, symbolized by dress or title, each person assumes a multiplicity of roles and constantly has to prove himself in a succession of new situations. Because of all this, the individual loses a coherent sense of self. His anxieties increase. There ensues a search for new faiths. The stage is thus set for the charismatic leader, the secular messiah, who, by bestowing upon each person the semblance of necessary grace and of fullness of personality, supplies a substitute for the older unifying belief that the mass society has destroyed.

In a world of lonely crowds seeking individual distinction, where values are constantly translated into economic calculabilities, where in extreme situations shame and conscience can no longer restrain the most dreadful excesses of terror, the theory of the mass society seems a forceful, realistic description of contemporary society, an accurate reflection of the *quality* and *feeling* of modern life. But when one seeks to apply the theory of mass society, analytically, it becomes very slippery. Ideal types, like the shadows in Plato's cave, generally never give us more than a silhouette. So, too, with the theory of "mass society." Each of the statements making up the theory, as set forth in the second paragraph above, might be true, but they do not follow necessarily from one another. Nor can we say that all the conditions described are present at any one time or place. More than that, there is no organizing principle—other than the general concept of a "breakdown of values"—that puts the individual elements of theory together in a logical, meaningful—let alone historical—manner. And when we examine the way the "theory" is used by those who employ it, we find ourselves even more at a loss. . . .

. . . From the viewpoint of the mass-society hypothesis, the United States ought to be exceptionally vulnerable to the politics of disaffection. In our country, urbanization, industrialization, and democratization have eroded older primary and community ties on a scale unprecedented in social history. Yet, though large-scale unemployment during the depression was more prolonged and more severe here than in any country in Western Europe, the Communist movement never gained a real foothold in the United States, nor has any fascist movement on a European model arisen. How does one explain this?

It is asserted that the United States is an "atomized" society composed of lonely, isolated individuals. One forgets the truism, expressed sometimes as a jeer, that Americans are a nation of joiners. There are in the United States today at least 200,000 voluntary organizations, associations, clubs, societies, lodges, and fraternities, with an aggregate (but obviously overlapping) membership of close to 80 million men and women. In no other country in the world, probably, is there such a high degree of voluntary communal activity, expressed sometimes in absurd rituals, yet often providing real satisfactions for real needs.[1]

"It is natural for the ordinary American," wrote Gunnar Myrdal, "when he sees something that is wrong to feel not only that there should be a law against it, but also that an organization should be formed to combat it."[2] Some of these voluntary organizations are pressure groups—business, farm, labor, veterans, trade associations, the aged, etc.—but thousands more are like the National Association for the Advancement of Colored People, the American Civil Liberties Union, the League of Women Voters, the American Jewish Committee, the Parent-Teachers Associations, local community-improvement groups, and so on, each of which affords hundreds of individuals concrete, emotionally shared activities.

[1] Between 30 and 40 million of the 80 million U.S. joiners work at their voluntary jobs. In 1950, 2 million volunteer workers pounded sidewalks for the Community Chests (the fund-raising and disbursing bodies in each community for local hospitals and social service agencies) and raised $200 million. Other thousands raised over $100 million for the United Jewish Appeal, $67 million for the Red Cross, $30 million for the National Foundation for Infantile Paralysis, $20 million for the National Tuberculosis Association, $13,-600,000 for the American Cancer Society—in all about a billion dollars a year for philanthropy. In 1950 there were 17,000 conventions —national, regional, or state, but not counting district or local—held in the U.S., attended by 10 million persons. In Atlantic City, famed seaside resort, 244,000 individuals went to 272 conventions ranging from the American Academy of Periodomology to the Telephone Pioneers of America. (Figures compiled by *Fortune* magazine research staff.)

[2] Gunnar Myrdal, *An American Dilemma* (New York, 1944).

Equally astonishing are the number of ethnic group organizations in this country carrying on varied cultural, social, and political activities. The number of Irish, Italian, Jewish, Polish, Czech, Finnish, Bulgarian, Bessarabian, and other national groups, their hundreds of fraternal, communal, and political groups, each playing a role in the life of America, is staggering.[3]

Even in urban neighborhoods, where anonymity is presumed to flourish, the extent of local ties is astounding. Within the city limits of Chicago, for example, there are 82 community newspapers with a total weekly circulation of almost one million; within Chicago's larger metropolitan area, there are 181. According to standard sociological theory, these local papers providing news and gossip about neighbors should slowly decline under the pressure of the national media. Yet the reverse is true. In Chicago, the number of such newspapers has increased 165 per cent since

[3] In December, 1954 for example, when the issue of Cyprus was first placed before the United Nations, the Justice for Cyprus Committee, "an organization of American citizens," according to its statement, took a full-page advertisement in the New York *Times* (December 15) to plead the right of that small island to self-determination. Among the groups listed in the Justice for Cyprus Committee were: The Order of Ahepa, the Daughters of Penelope, the Pan-Laconian Federation, the Cretan Federation, the Pan-Messinian Federation, the Pan-Icarian Federation, the Pan-Epirotic Federation of America, the Pan-Elian Federation of America, the Dodecanesian League of America, the Pan-Macedonian Association of America, the Pan-Samian Association, the Federation of Sterea Ellas, the Cyprus Federation of America, the Pan-Arcadian Federation, the GAPA, and the Federation of Hellenic Organizations. We can be sure that if, in a free world, the question of the territorial affiliation of Ruthenia were to come up before the United Nations, dozens of Hungarian, Rumanian, Ukrainian, Slovakian, and Czech "organizations of American citizens" would rush eagerly into print to plead the justice of the claims of their respective homelands to Ruthenia.

1910; in those forty years, circulation has jumped 770 per cent. As sociologist Morris Janowitz, who studied these community newspapers, observed: "If society were as impersonal, as self-centered and barren as described by some who are preoccupied with the one-way trend from *'Gemeinschaft'* to *'Gesellschaft'* seem to believe, the levels of criminality, social disorganization and psychopathology which social science seeks to account for would have to be viewed as very low rather than (as viewed now) alarmingly high."[4]

It may be argued that the existence of such a large network of voluntary associations says little about the cultural level of the country concerned.

[4] Morris Janowitz, *The Community Press in an Urban Setting* (Glencoe, Ill., 1952), pp. 17–18. More recent research, particularly by British sociologists, has questioned the idea that the modern society inevitably tears down primary ties. As Peter Willmott put it succinctly: "Stereotypes die hard, even among sociologists. Ever since Tonnies and Durkheim proclaimed the decline of the family, the notion has persisted that in urban industrial societies it is rootless and atomized, confined to parents and dependent children, isolated from relatives. Only in recent years has this impression been challenged—by field inquiries in London and other English cities, even in such unlikely places (one would have thought) as Detroit and San Francisco. These have suggested that the kindred may be an important source of companionship and support in the heart of the modern city" ("Kinship and Social Legislation," *British Journal of Sociology*, June, 1958, p. 126). The chief British studies are those by Michael Young and Willmott, in Bethnal Green, entitled *Family and Kinship in East London* (London, 1957), and the researches of the Institute of Community Studies, headed by Michael Young, particularly Peter Townsend, *The Family Life of Old People* (London, 1957). Among the American studies cited by Willmott are: *A Social Profile of Detroit: 1955* (Ann Arbor, 1956); Morris Axelrod, "Urban Structure and Social Participation," *American Journal of Sociology*, February, 1956; Wendell Bell and M. D. Boar, "Urban Neighborhoods and Informal Social Relations," *American Journal of Sociology*, January, 1957.

It may well be, as Ortega maintains, that cultural standards throughout the world have declined (in everything?—in architecture, dress, design?), but nonetheless a greater proportion of the population today participates in worthwhile cultural activities. This has been almost an inevitable concomitant of the doubling—*literally*—of the American standard of living over the last fifty years.[5]

The rising levels of education have meant a rising appreciation of culture. In the United States, more dollars are spent on concerts of classical music than on baseball. Sales of books have doubled in a decade.[6] There are over a thousand symphony orchestras, and several hundred museums, institutes and colleges are purchasing art in the United States today. Various other indexes can be cited to show the growth of a new middlebrow society. And in coming years, with steadily increasing productivity and leisure, the United States will become an even more active "consumer" of culture.[7]

It has been argued that the American

[5] For a scholarly summary on American living standards, see William Fielding Ogburn, "Technology and the Standard of Living in the United States," *American Journal of Sociology*, January, 1955, pp. 380–86. Data on cultural participation can be found in F. B. Turek, "The American Explosion," *Scientific Monthly*, September, 1952.

[6] Malcolm Cowley, in his essay on "Cheap Books for the Millions," points out that there were few book clubs in 1931, when a broad survey of the book publishing industry was made, while in 1953 there were seventy-four clubs that recommended books for adults. "The fear had been," he writes, "that the clubs would encourage a general uniformtiy of taste in the American public, and instead they were, to some extent, encouraging a diversity" (*The Literary Situation* [New York, 1955], p. 101).

[7] Some further ambiguity in the use of the mass-society concept derives from the confusions in the use of the anthropological and the humanist meanings of the word "culture." Thus some critics point to the "breakdown"

mass society imposes an excessive conformity upon its members. But it is hard to discern who is conforming to what. The *New Republic* cries that "hucksters are sugarcoating the culture." The *National Review,* organ of the "radical right," raises the banner of iconoclasm against the domination of opinion-making in our society by "the liberals." *Fortune* decries the growth of "organization man." Each of these tendencies exists, yet in historical perspective there is probably less conformity to an overall mode of conduct today than at any time within the last half

century in America. True, there is less bohemianism than in the twenties (though increased sexual tolerance) and less political radicalism than in the thirties (though the New Deal enacted sweeping reforms). But does the arrival at a political dead center mean the establishment, too, of a dead norm? I do not think so. One would be hard put to find today the "conformity" *Main Street* exacted of Carol Kennicott thirty years ago. With rising educational levels, more individuals are able to indulge a wider variety of interests. ("Twenty years ago you couldn't sell Beethoven out of New York," reports a record salesman. "Today we sell Palestrina, Monteverdi, Gabrielli, and Renaissance and Baroque music in large quantities.")

The curious fact, perhaps, is that no one in the United States defends conformity. Everyone is against it, and probably everyone always was. Thirty-five years ago, you could easily rattle any middle-class American by charging him with being a "Babbitt." Today you can do so by accusing him of conformity. The problem is to know who is accusing whom. In December, 1958, the *Reader's Digest* (circulation twelve million) reprinted an article from *Woman's Day* (circulation five million) with the title, "The Danger of Being Too Well-Adjusted." The point of the article is that great men were not adjusted, and the article quotes a psychiatrist who says that "we've made conformity into a religion"; we ought to remember, however, that each child is different "and ought to be."

Such citation is no proof that there is not "conformity" in the middle class; but if there is, there is also a great deal of anxiety and finger-pointing about it. Certainly those who live on the margin of society—the Upper Bohemians, whose manners soon become the style for the culture—seek frantically to find

---

of local folk or regional practices—speech differences, cooking, songs, dances, humor—and their replacement by uniform national patterns as an indication of the leveling of the mass society and of the decline of culture. These changes, which are real, are meaningful, however, only in anthropological usage, as a change from parochial to more universal cultural forms. But such changes are not *necessarily* a judgment about the humanist quality of the culture. (It is curious that in the past the breakdown of rustic forms was seen as a necessary prelude to the growth of a "high culture." Today the breakdown of the rustic forms is seen as part of the destruction of humanist culture.) The distinctions should be made clear. The anthropological concept of culture is relativistic. It implies no judgment of any one culture and cannot be used as a stick to criticize "high culture." The fact that the nature of satisfactions has changed from country dances and folksy humor to Brazilian sambas and Broadway flippancy is analytically a different question than that of the character of the culture. As these criticisms are made, one deals with the presumed disorganization of society, the other with the quality of the culture. Again, it is the purpose of this essay to point out that the invocation of the notion of tradition (*Gemeinschaft,* etc.) to make a judgment about the disorganization of the society is scientifically spurious and conceals a value. The other criticism, which is serious, lies outside the scope of this essay. (For a discussion of the issues of "high" vs. "middle-brow" culture, see Clement Greenberg, "The Plight of Our Culture," *Commentary,* June and July, 1953. See also, Mary McCarthy, "America the Beautiful," *Commentary,* September, 1947.)

different ways of emphasizing their non-conformity. In Hollywood, where Pick-fair society in the twenties counter-feited a European monarchy (and whose homes crossed Louis XIV with Barnum & Bailey), "non-conformity," according to *Life* magazine (in its jumbo Entertainment issue of December 22, 1958—readership twenty-five million), "is now the key to social importance and that Angry Middle-Aged man, Frank Sinatra, is its prophet and reigning social monarch." The Sinatra set, *Life* points out, deliberately mocks the old Hollywood taboos and is imitated by a host of other sets that eagerly want to be non-conformist as well. Significantly—a fact *Life* failed to mention—the reigning social set and its leaders, Sinatra, Dean Martin, Sammy Davis, Jr., are all from minority groups and from the wrong side of the tracks. Sinatra and Martin are Italian, Davis a Negro. In earlier times in American life, a minority group, having bulled its way to the top, would usually ape the style and manners of the established status community. In Hollywood, the old status hierarchies have been fragmented, the new sets celebrate their triumph by jeering at the pompous ways of the old. . . .

. . . The additional sardonic fact is that the man in the gray flannel suit, the presumed target of the Beatniks, is, as Russell Lynes pointed out, especially if he is in advertising, or the entertainment media, an Upper Bohemian himself. The job is accepted as a means of obtaining an income in order to sport and flaunt his presumed, idiosyncratic tastes in dress, food, travel, and the like.[8] The problem for all these

multiple sets is not conformity but added novelty.

To add one more paradox, the early theorists of mass society (e.g., Simmel) condemned it because in the vast metropolitan honeycombs people were isolated, transient, anonymous to each other. Americans, sensitive as they are to the criticism of others, took the charge to heart and, in building the postwar suburbs, sought to create fraternity, communality, togetherness, only to find themselves accused of conformity. In the new, recent trend of people returning to the city, it is clear that, in recoil, people will once again establish barriers and will thus bring on the charge, in the next inspection by European sociology, of anonymity, isolation and soullessness, and *anomie*.

. . . At this point, it becomes quite apparent that such large-scale abstractions as "the mass society," with the implicit diagnosis of social disorganization and decay that derive from them, are rather meaningless without standards of comparison. Social and cultural change is probably greater and more rapid today in the United States than in any other country, but the assumption that social disorder and *anomie* inevitably attend such change is not borne out in this case.

---

[8] "In the richly appointed Lake Shore Drive apartment of Chicago financier Albert Newman, the guests chatted animatedly, gazed at the original Picasso on the wall, and the Monet, the Jackson Pollock. On tables and shelves stood Peruvian fertility symbols, jade bracelets, sculptures that looked like the super- structure of a Japanese battleship. . . . [The guests] had come to meet 32-year old Allen Ginsberg of Paterson, N. J., author of a celebrated, chock-full catalogue called *Howl* ("I saw the best minds of my generation destroyed by madness, starving hysterical naked."). . . . At length poet Ginsberg arrived wearing blue jeans and a checked black-and-red lumberjacking shirt with black patches. . . . With the crashing madness of a Marx Brothers scene run in reverse, the Beatniks [Ginsberg and two friends] read their poetry, made their pitch for money for a new Beatnik magazine, *The Big Table*, and then stalked out. . . . The trio was an instant hit with the literary upper crust. . . . [The next evening] at the Sherman Hotel, the Beatniks read more poetry for a curious crowd of 700 (who paid $1 and up) . . ." (*Time*, February 9, 1959).

The Political Directorate
The Theory of Balance

C. WRIGHT MILLS

The perfect candidate for the Presidency of the United States was born some fifty-four years ago in a modest but ramshackled farm house in the pivotal state of Ohio. Of a sizable family, which arrived from England shortly after the *Mayflower*, he grew up on the farm, performing the traditional chores and thus becoming well acquainted with all farm problems. When he was in high school his father died, the farm was sold, his strong and sensible mother moved the family to a nearby small town, and the struggle began.

The future President worked in his uncle's factory, quickly becoming a practical expert on all labor and management problems, while putting himself through college. He arrived in France during World War I just in time to make clear, for a full six months, that, in another war with more time, he would undoubtedly be a statesman of note. Returning home, he went to the state law school for two years, married his high-school sweetheart, whose grandfathers fought with the Confederate armies, opened his office, and joined the local party club, as well as the Elks, and in due course the Rotary Club, and attended the Episcopalian church. He is having a very

Abridged from The Power Elite *by C. Wright Mills. Copyright © 1956 by Oxford University Press, Inc. Reprinted by permission.*

busy life now, but he can stand such strains, for it is as if his constitution was built for them. During the 'twenties, he represented a group of small factories in their relations with labor, and was so successful that during the 'thirties there was no labor trouble of any consequence. Other companies, noting this as a remarkable fact, also engaged him, and thus, with the publicity, he became mayor of his city in 1935.

As the soldier-statesman and labor-relations expert took hold of the reins, both business and labor acclaimed the skill and vigor of his administration. Although an absolutely regular party man, he remodeled the city government from top to bottom. Came the Second World War, and despite his two young sons, he resigned his mayoralty to become a lieutenant colonel, and a member of a favored general's staff. He quickly became a statesman well versed in Asiatic and European affairs and confidently predicted everything that happened.

A brigadier general, he returned to Ohio after the war and found himself the overwhelming choice for governor. For two terms he has been swept into office, his administration being as efficient as any business, as moral as any church, as warm-hearted as any family. His face is as honest as any business executive's, his manner as sincere as any salesman's; in fact, he is something of both, with a touch of grimness and homely geniality all his own. And all of this comes through, magnetically, straight to you, through the lens of any camera and the microphone as well.[1]

...Many of the images of politicians that prevail today are, in fact, drawn from earlier epochs. Accordingly, 'The American Politician' is seen as a valuable originator but also a cheap tool, a high statesman but also a dirty politician, a public servant but also a sly conniver. Our view is not clear because, as with most of our views of those above us, we tend to understand our own time in accordance with the confused stereotypes of previous periods.

The classic commentaries of American politics—those of Tocqueville, Bryce, and Ostrogorski—rest upon nineteenth-century experience—generally from Andrew Jackson to Theodore Roosevelt. It is, of course, true that many of the trends that determined the political shape of the long middle period are still at work influencing the type of politician that prevails in our own political times—especially on the middle levels of power, in the Congress. But during the twentieth century, and especially after the First World War, other forces have greatly modified the content and the importance in America of political institutions. The political establishment of the United States has become more tightly knit, it has been enlarged in scope, and has come up closer to virtually all of the social institutions which it frames. Increasingly, crises have arisen that have not seemed resolvable on the old local and decentralized basis; increasingly those involved in these crises have looked to the state to resolve them. As these changes in the shape and practice of the

state have increased the power available to those who would gain power and exert it through political institutions, new types of political men have become ascendant.

...Within American political institutions, the center of initiative and decision has shifted from the Congress to the executive; the executive branch of the state has not only expanded mightily but has come to centralize and to use the very party which puts it into power. It has taken over more initiative in legislative matters not only by its veto but by its expert counsel and advice. Accordingly, it is in the executive chambers, and in the agencies and authorities and commissions and departments that stretch out beneath them, that many conflicts of interests and contests of power have come to a head —rather than in the open arena of politics of an older style.

These institutional changes in the shape of the political pyramid have made the new political command posts worthy of being struggled for. They have also made for changes in the career of the type of political man who is ascendant. They have meant that it is now more possible for the political career to lead directly to the top, thus by-passing local political life. In the middle of the nineteenth century—between 1865 and 1881—only 19 per cent of the men at the top of the government began their political career on the national level; but from 1901 to 1953, about one-third of the political elite began there, and, in the Eisenhower administration, some 42 per cent started in politics at the national level —a high for the entire political history of the United States.[2]

---

[1] The lead to this chapter is adapted from Robert Bendiner, 'Portrait of the Perfect Candidate,' *The New York Times Magazine*, 18 May 1952, pp. 9 ff.

[2] Only about 20 per cent of the political elite of 1789–1825 had done so; the historical average as a whole is about 25 per cent. Unless otherwise cited, all statistical data presented in section 1 of this chapter come from an original

From 1789 right up to 1921, generation after generation, the proportion of the political elite which has *ever* held local or state offices decreased from 93 to 69 per cent. In the Eisenhower administration, it fell to 57 per cent. Moreover, only 14 per cent of this current group—and only about one-quarter of earlier twentieth-century politicians —have ever served in any *state legisla-*

ture. In the Founding Fathers' generation of 1789–1801, 81 per cent of the higher politicians had done so.

...Not wishing to be disturbed over moral issues of the political economy, Americans cling to the idea that the government is a sort of automatic machine, regulated by the balancing of competing interests. This image of poli-

---

study of the origins and careers of the occupants of the positions cited below between 1789 and June 1953. For an earlier release of materials from this study, which did not include the Eisenhower administration, see C. Wright and Ruth Mills, 'What Helps Most in Politics,' *Pageant,* November 1952. Cf. also H. Dewey Anderson, 'The Educational and Occupational Attainments of our National Rulers,' *Scientific Monthly,* vol. xxxx, pp. 511 ff; and Richard B. Fisher, *The American Executive* (Hoover Institute and Library on War, Revolution and Peace; Stanford University Press).

If we would understand the higher politician, we must collect information about not one or two, or even fifty, but about the several hundred statesmen who have occupied the highest political offices, and in that simple sense, are the political elite. The statistics presented in this note concern the 513 men who between 1789 and June 1953 occupied the following positions: President, Vice-President, Speaker of the House of Representatives, Cabinet Member, and Supreme Court Justice. To call any selection of men 'the statesmen' or 'the political elite' is to invite disagreement about their selection. In this selection, I have tried to include only the very pinnacles of the American government. The major omission involves the legislators: even to include the committee chairmen of the House and Senate over such a long period was beyond my means of research. Yet such men are the prototypes of 'the politician.' In this section, however, I am not interested in the American politician at large, but in those who have been at the formal head of the government. Whether they are party politicians or not is one thing I am trying to find out. It is quite true that at times leading members of the Senate, and even governors of key states, have exercised *national political* power without ever having served in one of the top governmental positions studied here. But many senators and governors are caught in the net which I have

thrown: of the 513 men, 94 have been governors and 143 have been United States Senators. I do not contend, of course, that those who occupied these positions and who later occupied one of the positions from which I have selected the 513 statesmen were the most powerful and important senators and governors. 'Party politicians' as such are discussed in ELEVEN: The Theory of Balance.

Six out of ten of the 500-odd men who have come to the top of the government during the course of United States history have come from quite prosperous family circumstances, being comfortable boys whose fathers were usually the prosperous and often the wealthy men of local society. Their families— which were among the upper 5 or 6 per cent of the American population—could well afford to give them distinct advantages in the selection and pursuit of their careers: 28 per cent are from the distinctly upper class of landed wealth, big merchants, industrialists, financiers of nation-wide prominence, or professional families of great wealth and national standing; 30 per cent are from the prosperous upper-middle class of businessmen, farmers, and professionals, who, although not of national stature, nevertheless were quite successful and prominent in their respective localities.

Two or three out of ten (24 per cent) have come from that middle class which is neither rich nor poor; their fathers were generally respected businessmen or farmers, or were in the professions of law and medicine—or were dead at the time the future statesmen left school, leaving their otherwise prosperous families in less comfortable, but manageable, circumstances.

The final two out of ten (18 per cent) originate in lower-class families—13 per cent from small-business or small-farming families that did not do so well, but could readily hold their heads above dire poverty; and 5 per cent from the class of wage workers or destitute small businessmen and farmers.

Occupationally, in each and every genera-

tics is simply a carryover from the official image of the economy: in both, an equilibrium is achieved by the pulling and hauling of many interests, each

restrained only by legalistic and amoral interpretations of what the traffic will bear.

The ideal of the automatic balance

tion, the statesmen have come from business and professional families in much greater proportions than the proportions of such families in the population at large. Professional men in the occupied population have never exceeded 7 per cent, and over the years have averaged about 2 per cent; but 44 per cent of this political elite have come from such fathers' homes. Businessmen have never exceeded 10 per cent of the total American labor force, but 25 per cent of the political elite have been sons of businessmen. Farmers have never dropped below 18 per cent and have averaged over 50 per cent of the working force, but only 27 per cent of the political elite come from farmsteads. Moreover, the 'farmers' whose sons have entered the political elite have been much more often prosperous than not.

It has seldom been a disadvantage for a man bent on entering politics to have a father who is the governor of the state or a senator in Washington. Even an uncle or a father-in-law in such positions can be very helpful. At least 25 per cent of these higher politicians have had fathers who were in some kind of political office about the time the sons left school, and when the political connections of all relatives are considered, we find that at least 30 per cent of the statesmen *are known* to have had such political connections at the time they were setting out on their careers. In this there is some decrease: before the end of the Civil War, about four out of ten, after the Civil War, about three out of ten, had political connections among relatives.

There have been, of course, political dynasties in American politics. Yet, it can safely be said that throughout United States history well over half of the higher politicians have come from families *not* previously connected with political affairs. They come more frequently from families highly placed in terms of social and economic position than political influence.

Since so many of the higher politicians come from families with distinct advantages to offer, it is not surprising that no less than 67 per cent of them have graduated from college. Even today—the historical peak of American education—only 6 or 7 per cent of all the people in the United States old enough to have gone, have, in fact, gone to college. But in the first quarter of the nineteenth century, when very few people indeed were college-

educated, 54 per cent of the men then holding high political positions had graduated from college. Generally, each generation of the higher politicians has included larger proportions of college graduates, thus paralleling, on a much higher level, the educational history of Americans at large.

Moreover, the colleges they attended have more often been of the Ivy League than is the case for the ordinary college graduate. Harvard and Princeton lead with about 8 per cent each of all the higher politicians among their alumni; Yale is third with about 6 per cent. Slightly over one-quarter attended Ivy League schools, and well over one-third of those who went to any college went to Ivy League schools. If one includes such famous schools as Dartmouth and Amherst, then one-third of all the higher politicians, and 44 per cent of those who ever spent any time in college, went to top-notch Eastern schools.

Over half of these men grew up on the Atlantic seaboard, and were educated in the East. That the proportion is so large in spite of the Western expansion is largely a reflection of the national hold the densely populated Middle Atlantic states of New York, Pennsylvania, and New Jersey have held in the origins of top politicians. Despite the immigration to the United States of 40 million foreign-born between 1820 and 1953, only 4 per cent of the American statesmen have been foreign-born. Only 2 per cent of them grew up outside the United States—and most of this handful are of The Founding Fathers' generation.

The higher politicians in America have not only been politicians; in fact, only five of these 513 followed no career other than politics before entering their top positions. During the entire history of the United States, about three-fourths of them have been lawyers; almost one-fourth have been businessmen; handful—some 4 per cent—have followed other careers. The industrialization of the American economy is directly reflected in the fact that over three times as many were businessmen immediately after the Civil War as just before it. Since then that fact has remained more or less constant: nearly one-third of the higher politicans since World War I have been businessmen; over 40 per cent of the most recent men, those of the Eisenhower administration, have been.

reached its most compelling elaboration in eighteenth-century economic terms: the market is sovereign and in the magic economy of the small entrepreneur there is no authoritarian center. And in the political sphere as well: the division, the equilibrium, of powers prevails, and hence there is no chance of despotism. 'The nation which will not adopt an equilibrium of power,' John Adams wrote, 'must adopt a despotism. There is no other alternative.'[3] As developed by the men of the eighteenth century, equilibrium, or checks and balances, thus becomes the chief mechanism by which both economic and political freedom were guaranteed and the absence of tyranny insured among the sovereign nations of the world.

Nowadays, the notion of an automatic political economy is best known to us as simply the practical conservatism of the anti-New Dealers of the 'thirties. It has been given new—although quite false—appeal by the frightening spectacle of the totalitarian states of Germany yesterday and Russia today. And although it is quite irrelevant to the political economy of modern America, it is the only rhetoric that prevails widely among the managerial elite of corporation and state.

It is very difficult to give up the old model of power as an automatic balance, with its assumptions of a plurality of independent, relatively equal, and conflicting groups of the balancing society. All these assumptions are explicit to the point of unconscious caricature in recent statements of 'who rules America.' According to Mr. David Riesman, for example, during the past half century there has been a shift from 'the power hierarchy of a ruling class to the power dispersal' of 'veto groups.' Now no one runs anything: all is un-directed drift. 'In a sense,' Mr. Riesman believes, 'this is only another way of saying that America is a middle-class country...in which, perhaps people will soon wake up to the fact that there is no longer a "we" who run things and a "they" who don't or a "we" who don't run things and a "they" who do, but rather that all "we's" are "they's" and all "they's" are "we's."'

'The chiefs have lost the power, but the followers have not gained it,' and in the meantime, Mr. Riesman takes his psychological interpretation of power and of the powerful to quite an extreme, for example: 'if businessmen *feel* weak and dependent, they *are* weak and dependent, no matter what material resources may be ascribed to them.'

'...The future,' accordingly, 'seems to be in the hands of the small business and professional men who control Congress: the local realtors, lawyers, car salesmen, undertakers, and so on; of the military men who control defense and, in part, foreign policy; of the big business managers and their lawyers, finance-committee men, and other counselors who decide on plant investment and influence the rate of technological change; of the labor leaders who control worker productivity and worker votes; of the black belt whites who have the greatest stake in southern politics; of the Poles, Italians, Jews, and Irishmen who have stakes in foreign policy, city jobs, and ethnic religious and cultural organizations; of the editorializers and storytellers who help socialize the young, tease and train the adult, and amuse and annoy the aged; of the farmers—themselves warring congeries of cattlemen, corn men, dairymen, cotton men, and so on—who control key departments and committees and who, as the living representatives of our inner-directed past, control many of our memories; of the Russians and, to a lesser degree, other foreign powers who

---

[3] John Adams, *Discourses on Davila* (Boston: Russell and Cutler, 1805), pp. 92–3.

control much of our agenda of attention; and so on. The reader can complete the list.[4]

Here indeed is something that measures up 'to the modern standards of being fully automatic and completely impersonal.'[5] Yet there is some reality in such romantic pluralism, even in such a *pasticcio* of power as Mr. Riesman invents: it is a recognizable, although a confused, statement of the middle levels of power, especially as revealed in Congressional districts and in the Congress itself. But it confuses, indeed it does not even distinguish between the top, the middle, and the bottom levels of power. In fact, the strategy of all such romantic pluralism, with its image of a semi-organized stalemate, is rather clear:

You elaborate the number of groups involved, in a kind of bewildering, Whitmanesque enthusiasm for variety. Indeed, what group fails to qualify as a 'veto group'? You do not try to clarify the hodge-podge by classifying these groups, occupations, strata, organizations according to their political relevance or even according to whether they are organized politically at all. You do not try to see how they may be connected with one another into a structure of power, for by virtue of his perspective, the romantic conservative focuses upon a scatter of milieux rather than upon their connections within a structure of power. And you do not consider the possibility of any community of interests among the top groups. You do not connect all these milieux and miscellaneous groups with the big decisions: you do not ask and answer with

historical detail: exactly *what*, directly or indirectly, did 'small retailers' or 'brick masons' have to do with the sequence of decision and event that led to World War II? What did 'insurance agents,' or for that matter, the Congress, have to do with the decision to make or not to make, to drop or not to drop, the early model of the new weapon? Moreover, you take seriously the public-relations-minded statements of the leaders of all groups, strata, and blocs, and thus confuse psychological uneasiness with the facts of power and policy. So long as power is not nakedly displayed, it must not be power. And of course you do not consider the difficulties posed for you as an observer by the fact of secrecy, official and otherwise.

...Undue attention to the middle levels of power obscures the structure of power as a whole, especially the top and the bottom. American politics, as discussed and voted and campaigned for, have largely to do with these middle levels, and often only with them. Most 'political' news is news and gossip about middle-level issues and conflicts. And in America, the political theorist too is often merely a more systematic student of elections, of who voted for whom. As a professor or as a free-lance intellectual, the political analyst is generally on the middle levels of power himself. He knows the top only by gossip; the bottom, if at all, only by 'research.' But he is at home with the leaders of the middle level, and, as a talker himself, with their 'bargaining.'

Commentators and analysts, in and out of the universities, thus focus upon the middle levels and their balances because they are closer to them, being mainly middle-class themselves; because these levels provide the noisy content of 'politics' as an explicit and reported-upon fact; because such views are in

[4] David Riesman, in collaboration with Reuel Denney and Nathan Glazer, *The Lonely Crowd* (New Haven: Yale University Press, 1950), pp. 234–9, 260, 281, 250, 254–5.

[5] George Graham, *Morals in American Politics* (New York: Random House, 1952), p. 4.

accord with the folklore of the formal model of how democracy works; and because, accepting that model as good, especially in their current patrioteering, many intellectuals are thus able most readily to satisfy such political urges as they may feel.

. . .'Balance of power' implies equality of power, and equality of power seems wholly fair and even honorable, but in fact what is one man's honorable balance is often another's unfair imbalance. Ascendant groups of course tend readily to proclaim a just balance of power and a true harmony of interest, for they prefer their domination to be uninterrupted and peaceful. So large businessmen condemn small labor leaders as 'disturbers of the peace' and upsetters of the universal interests inherent in business-labor cooperation. So privileged nations condemn weaker ones in the name of internationalism, defending with moral notions what has been won by force against those have-nots whom (sic), making their bid for ascendancy or equality later, can hope to change the *status quo* only by force.[6]

The notion that social change proceeds by a tolerant give-and-take, by compromise and a network of vetoes of one interest balanced by another assumes that all this goes on within a more or less stable framework that does not itself change, that all issues are subject to compromise, and are thus naturally harmonious or can be made such. Those who profit by the general framework of the *status quo* can afford more easily than those who are dissatisfied under it to entertain such views as the mechanics of social change. Moreover, 'in most fields. . .only one interest is organized, none is, or some of the major ones are not.'[7] In these cases, to speak, as Mr. David Truman does, of

'unorganized interests'[8] is merely to use another word for what used to be called 'the public,' a conception we shall presently examine.

The important 'pressure groups,' especially those of rural and urban business, have either been incorporated in the personnel and in the agencies of the government itself, both legislative and executive, or become the instruments of small and powerful cliques, which sometimes include their nominal leaders but often do not. These facts go beyond the centralization of voluntary groups and the usurpation of the power of apathetic members by professional executives. They involve, for example, the use of the NAM by dominant cliques to reveal to small-business members that their interests are identical with those of big business, and then to focus the power of business-as-a-whole into a political pressure. From the standpoint of such higher circles, the 'voluntary association,' the 'pressure group,' becomes an important feature of a public-relations program. The several corporations which are commanded by the individual members of such cliques are themselves instruments of command, public relations, and pressure, but it is often more expedient to use the corporations less openly, as bases of power, and to make of various national associations their joint operating branches. The associations are more operational organizations, whose limits of power are set by those who use them, than final arbiters of action and inaction.[9]

[6] See E. H. Carr, *The Twenty Years' Crisis* (London: Macmillan, 1949), pp. 82–3.

[7] Edelman, op. cit. p. 32.
[8] Cf. David B. Truman, *The Governmental Process* (New York, Knopf, 1951), pp. 506 ff.
[9] See Floyd Hunter, 'Structures of Power and Education,' *Conference Report: Studying the University's Community* (New Orleans, Center for the Study of Liberal Education for Adults, April 1954), for the composition of such cliques in a single city, and preliminary notes on his forthcoming book on the national scene.

Checks and balances may thus be understood as an alternative statement of 'divide and rule,' and as a way of hampering the more direct expression of popular aspiration. For the theory of balance often rests upon the moral idea of a natural harmony of interests, in terms of which greed and ruthlessness are reconciled with justice and progress. Once the basic structure of the American political economy was built, and for so long as it could be tacitly supposed that markets would expand indefinitely, the harmony of interest could and did serve well as the ideology of dominant groups, by making their interests appear identical with the interests of the community as a whole. So long as this doctrine prevails, any lower group that begins to struggle can be made to appear inharmonious, disturbing the common interest. 'The doctrine of the harmony of interests,' E. H. Carr has remarked, 'thus serves as an ingenious moral device invoked, in perfect sincerity, by privileged groups in order to justify and maintain their dominant position.'[10]

Extremism in the Defense of . . .

ROBERT E. FITCH

"Extremism in the defense of liberty is no vice." Now who was it said that? The rightist leader of the Republican party in a recent presidential election? Or, perchance, the leftist leader of a student revolt disturbing the calm of the Berkeley campus of the University of California as 1964 neared its end?

However that may be, the state of California has found itself undergoing, for the second time within a few months, a trial by ordeal of extremism. Some might say that the people of

California are extremism-prone just as other people are accident-prone. During the late presidential campaign the extremism came from the far right. The people of California were implicated in it so far as their vote in the Republican primaries put that extremism in a position to capture the presidential nomination. Perhaps these people redeemed themselves at the time of the national election. At the present moment the extremism comes from left of center. Both extremisms label themselves apostles of liberty, and the champion of each movement is a would-be liberator of his people.

...A good cause is the first ingredi-

10 E. H. Carr, op. cit. p. 80.

ent in a good revolt. In spite of all the complication of issues, there can be no denying that the students on the Berkeley campus have that good cause. Or at least they had it at the beginning. They are asking for the right to participate as responsible citizens in the political process. They want the right to promote on campus, as they pursue further activities off campus, programs in connection with S.N.C.C., or CORE, or the Democratic party, or the Republican party, or the Black Muslims or what-have-you. Their indignation is aggravated by the fact that this right is already fully enjoyed by students in the California state college system, whether at San Francisco State or Sacramento State or elsewhere.

A good leader is a second ingredient in a good revolt. The students have one in the person of Mario Savio. This leader stands 6 feet 1 inch high, weighs 195 pounds, has been a student of physics, is now a major in philosophy, is a veteran of last summer's crusade in Mississippi, has not been attending classes recently, regrets that his grade average, which stood at 3.9 last year, has been somewhat impaired by his recent political interests. Savio is intelligent, personable, courageous, eloquent, possessed of a dynamic purpose. Or has he more than one important purpose? In a recent interview he confessed, "I suppose I'll end up as a professor."

Another ingredient in revolt is the enormous size and range of what President Clark Kerr has called the multiversity. On the Berkeley campus there are over 27,000 students. One per cent of the total will be a crowd; 2 per cent will fill an ordinary auditorium; 4 per cent will make a mob. (I try to remind myself that in the theological school where I teach 4 per cent of the students would just barely constitute a committee!) Under these circumstances it is hard to tell whether one is dealing with the fringe or with the center of the student body. And if one respects the devices of representative government, it is hard to tell whether this 4 per cent is really representative or is just another willful minority determined to impose its way upon an inert and inchoate mass.

Finally, those who have played at this kind of game before here or elsewhere know that there are three kinds of people who enter into the business. First there is the very small minority of the truly dedicated: those who know the principles for which they fight and who are ready, even eager, to receive the full penalty for whatever course they pursue. But lest some innocent folk should have got mixed up in this company, Mario Savio has promised that he will try, with a defense fund he is raising, to save from martyrdom by the courts those who do not really seek such an honor.

The other kinds of people are the sensation seekers and the power lovers. The sensation seekers are in it just for "kicks." They do not know, nor would they care if they did know, the difference between a Governor Wallace of Alabama and a Governor Brown of California. It is part of the tragedy of our times that in this category are to be found so many of our finest young people. They have been cheated—by parents, teachers, preachers—of any set of great ideals to which they might give themselves, and so they give themselves to whatever chance imperative may come along, preferring adventure to inertia, excitement to emptiness.

With a large number of sensation seekers on hand, a mere handful of power lovers can enter into great affairs. The power lovers, like the truly dedicated, also know the ends for which they strive. But their ends are not those of principle; they seek first to ruin, then to rule.

THE TACTICS OF REVOLT

The tactics of revolt call first for a shibboleth and a song and a militant minority. The shibboleth is "free speech"; the movement is known as the Free Speech Movement— F.S.M. Never mind that free speech is not the issue; it still makes a good shibboleth, and as shouted from loudspeakers on touring trucks during the first days of the revolt it stirred the hearts of true liberals all over town.

As for a song, why not appropriate "We Shall Overcome"? To be sure this battle has nothing to do with civil rights, or with the rights of Negroes. But if the song was good for Mississippi and Alabama, why wouldn't it work in California? Elsewhere this song has come from the lips of brave men and women, has been consecrated by stripes and wounds and imprisonment, has even been baptized by the blood of martyrs. But here we shall see to it that there is no immoderate martyrdom.

As for the militant minority, in a huge university student body one can find a minority of that kind for almost anything. What makes it grow into something that begins to look almost like a majority is a series of well executed maneuvers. First there is the deliberate disobedience of university discipline, with students seated at tables on the campus plaza passing out prohibited literature, while a small body of subdeans goes about taking down names. Then there is the sitdown demonstration around a paddy wagon with a former student inside so that the police are unable to move the wagon away. Later there is the sleep-in at Sproul Hall, the administration building, cluttering the aisles until the police come in and haul out the demonstrators to book them for appearance in court. This is followed by what is intended to be a general strike—the cutting of all classes, with picket lines set up in an effort to persuade members of organized labor not to make the daily deliveries that are necessary to the maintenance of the university plant.

ESCALATING FROM A KERNEL

At the start of such an effort the militant minority may be only 1 per cent; soon it is 2, then 3. The students arrested at Sproul Hall numbered 780. But a fair number of teaching assistants get into the act: they are both students and teachers. Joan Baez comes by to lend the inspiration of her presence and her songs. There are some other eager participants: former students, alumni, friends, state assemblymen. When President Clark Kerr calls a meeting of all students in the Greek Theater, it begins to look as though as many as a third are now sympathetic. And when the Academic Senate meets and votes support of the main requests of the students, it looks as though the faculty has joined the movement.

But the shrewdest—or was it purely instinctive?—element in the tactics was the escalating and sublimating of the objective of the revolt. Here are some of the magic words of Mario Savio:

There is a time when the operation of the machine becomes so odious, makes you so sick at heart that you can't take part, you can't even tacitly take part, and you've got to put your bodies upon the gears and upon the wheels, upon the levers, upon all the apparatus, and you've got to make it stop. And you've got to indicate to the people who run it, to the people who own it, that unless you're free, the machine will be prevented from working at all.

In brief, what we are fighting is the

Thing. The true enemy is the System, the Organization, all those faceless Organization Men who want to make us into the same soulless robots they are themselves. Indeed, which one of us, in this remarkably affluent and self-pitying society of ours, has not drawn himself to be the victim of the Thing? Who would not, if he had an opportunity, strike back at the Thing?

OF LIBERTY AND LAW

All this, of course, is in behalf of liberty. Does liberty have anything to do with law? Or, in an academic context, has it anything to do with intellectual honesty? Because the Free Speech Movement was never a movement for freedom of speech. In his famous *Bloudy Tenent,* Roger Williams gave us a sharp distinction between free speech and free action, and that distinction has been confirmed by important rulings of our own Supreme Court. Indeed, a maximum amount of free speech is possible only when this distinction is rigorously observed.

What the students want is a specific freedom for overt action, the right to recruit members and to solicit funds for off-campus organizations engaged in various kinds of political action. If I take a somewhat sardonic view of their insistence upon this right, it is because I have been a dean on two campuses where it was precisely the students who sought to curtail that right; they were being annoyed by nuisances and they were outraged by the interference and competition with their own agreed-on programs of activity. However, with an enormous student body it might be reasonable to allow the exercise of such a right in a carefully defined area.

There was a point at which the administration decided to concede this particular right to the students, but

reserved for itself the right to penalize those who might later be found to have been connected with unlawful activities. The cry then arose that this was double jeopardy. But double jeopardy has reference only to the courts; if, for instance, a clergyman should be convicted of rape or robbery and were later unfrocked by the church, he would not be suffering double jeopardy. The jurisdiction of the civil corporation is distinct from the jurisdiction of the state.

ADMINISTRATION OR COURTS?

At another point in the battle the students insisted that the whole issue was not something to be decided by the university administration but one that should be settled in the courts as a question of constitutional rights. Yet when the police carried the demonstrators out of Sproul Hall, took them briefly to confinement areas, had them booked and released on bail (with funds raised by some members of the faculty) under the requirement that they appear in court to face charges for violating the law, there were cries of protest and dismay. At first one heard scattered charges of police brutality, but these were contradicted by the evidence of cameras and tape recorders. The underlying conviction, however, was that no policeman at any time has the right to touch the privileged person of a student, and that any court which gives a just judgment must give it in his behalf.

For those who care at all about representative government, it must be noted that the F.S.M. was in deliberate disobedience not only of the university administration but also of the duly elected president and senate of the student body. While sympathy came from the student officers at the beginning, there was a clear break before the sleep-in at Sproul Hall, with the student senate declaring that any more overt action could be only for purposes of harassment and of mischief. It is being alleged that the student government does not really represent the students, many of whom do not choose to take part in the political process on their own campus. But surely failure to take part in the orderly processes of government does not entitle one to promote disorderly activities outside of it. And if the duly elected government of the students does not represent them, then by what criterion can it be shown that a self-appointed minority of 2 to 4 per cent represents them?

THE VALUE VACUUM

At the heart of all this confusion lies the value vacuum. This is the great yawning void, engendered by skepticism, relativism, impressionism, existentialism —which have cast out all structures, patterns, imperatives, laws, principles and standards, leaving only Chaos and Dark Night to rule over the ruin. This is the absence of any belief in a universal and objective moral order. This is the total lack of any moral authority anywhere.

The faculty is a chief contributor to this value vacuum. For one thing, since the good scholar wants to be free to do his research and maybe his teaching, he is tempted to withdraw from commitments to action beyond his professional community, above all to abstain from anything having to do with student discipline; he seeks to appear "non-judgmental" in all areas except those which impinge directly upon his personal concerns. The larger and more impersonal the university, the more desperate is this struggle to achieve a private freedom.

Moreover, the prevalent teaching in our culture—not just in universities but even in churches and seminaries—cuts out the ground of any moral authority. We are historical relativists, who deny any order and direction in the course of human events. We are cultural relativists, who make plain that how they do it in Samoa may be just as good as how they do it in South Dakota, who wonder why how they do it in Mississippi may not be just as good as how they do it in Maine. We are ethical relativists, either lifted up to a transcendent reality forever beyond all ethical distinctions, or immersed in diverse contextual and situational traps where ethical discriminations become as meaningless as they are endless. We are epistemological relativists, so overwhelmed with assorted perspectives and frames of reference that we can discern the True no more than we can perceive the Good and the Beautiful.

The comedy begins when a university community which has been busily cutting out the ground of all moral authority suddenly comes up with its own pet absolute of academic freedom. Actually, devotion to the ideal within departmental rituals is exceedingly restricted. I have known a history department that would hire a confessed Marxist but would not touch a confessing Christian, a philosophy department that would take nothing but logical positivists, a psychology department that cared only for experiments in the laboratory and held the clinic in contempt, an economics department loaded with classicists or neoclassicists which refused to look at an institutionalist. If academic freedom can be bent by such ideological constraints, is it altogether intolerable that it might give an inch or two to the political necessities connected with a state university?

In any case, it makes sense that in the development of the debate at the

University of California the faculty should fall in with the students. The academic senate in Berkeley voted overwhelmingly to petition the regents asking that the chief demands of the students be granted. So the isolated individuals who taken together make up the faculty and the student body of a great university fell collectively into one another's arms. But an embrace in a value vacuum, an embrace without moral authority, an embrace held together by the tenuous bond of a capriciously selected freedom which was not in fact the kind of freedom it pretended to be—what kind of embrace is that?

THE POLITY

IN THE U.S.:

The Soviet View

Dollar Democracy

F. OREKHOV

One hundred and nineteen years ago, a group of Americans collected $200 to help a young Illinois self-taught lawyer run for Congress. Those were to be his campaign expenses. The young lawyer, who had also clerked in a store and worked as a lumberjack, won the election and returned $199.25 to his supporters with these words:

"I did not need the money. I made the canvass on my own horse; my entertainment, being at the houses of friends, cost me nothing; and my only outlay was 75 cents for a barrel of cider, which some farmhands insisted I should treat to."

He was Abraham Lincoln, who eight

Reprinted from F. Orekhov, "Dollar Democracy," International Affairs, Moscow (February, 1965), pp. 29–35.

years later took part in the founding of the Republican Party—which then opposed slavery—and in another six years became the President of the United States and the leader of the war against the slaveholding South. In 1864, he was elected for a second term, and received, among others, a message of congratulations from the General Council of the First International written by Karl Marx.

Lincoln, with his campaign expenses amounting to the price of three packets of cigarettes or seven Coca Colas, is a picture of fabulous thrift and honesty verging on the naive, when compared with modern Congressional candidates. *U.S. News & World Report* gives the following insight into 1964 election expenses. A candidate for the Senate spent on the average about half a million dollars. And this was not the highest price paid for a cosy Senate seat. Alan Cranston, who ran for the Senate in California in the 1964 election (and was defeated), admitted that his campaign expenses came to about $1 million.

Robert Kennedy spent $2 million on his campaign for election to the Senate from the State of New York.[1]

ROLE OF DOLLAR

The barrel of cider is the symbolic level from which the price of American democracy began to spiral ranging from the price of mayor and the various other state and local offices to that of President. As campaign expenses soared, the very possibility of financing them became an increasingly weighty political factor. That was only to be expected: the total cost of the 1952 electoral campaign—Federal, state and local—came to roughly $140 million; in 1956, the figure was $155 million; 1960, $175 million, and 1964, $200 million. In the last 12 years, campaign expenses went up by $60 million, or 43 per cent, although the total number of voters went up by only 19 per cent.

This naturally tends to enhance the role of money in the course and outcome of any electoral campaign in the United States, inevitably increasing the influence of the moneybags, who are prepared to "contribute" sizeable amounts to the campaign expenses of this or that party or candidate.

But this does not warrant the simplification that dollars and those who have them decide everything at the elections. There are other diverse factors working for or against a candidate's nomination and success. But the fact remains that it now takes a great deal of money to

finance an electoral campaign, whatever the other circumstances may be. Money may not, or at least may not always, be crucial, but lack of it certainly blocks any candidate's road to important government offices. The power of the moneybags, which have seized the commanding economic and social positions in the United States, inevitably tells at every step in the functioning of the political system of America's "representative democracy."

Those who donate money to the campaign expenses of parties and their candidates naturally acquire political say and other advantages which tend to be proportionate to their contribution. The candidates themselves as a rule feel under an obligation to their sponsors, and become subservient to them, doing their bidding and standing guard over their specific interests. As a result, the aforementioned Cranston says, "the candidate is alienated from himself. . . . He is transformed into a commodity, in the way best calculated to bring him the maximum profit (votes) obtainable under existing market (campaign) conditions."[2]

American experts believe the common voter needs to be prodded into voting for a presidential or congressional candidate for at least six weeks, the means being similar to those used in commercial advertising: television, radio, the press, billboards, whistle-stop tours and meetings. All this costs a great deal of money, but it is the mainspring of paid democracy.

The means of getting through to the voter must be costly if they are to be within the reach of only a few candidates, above all the millionaires, who are able to pay their own campaign expenses, or those for whom they are prepared to pay. In effect, what mortal can afford to run for any office when an

---

1 *U.S. News & World Report,* Jan. 4, 1965, p. 40.

2 *Fortune,* November 1964, p. 124.

hour television broadcast by President Eisenhower, a presidential candidate in 1952, cost his sponsors $275,000; in 1960, the total cost of radio and television appearances by candidates came to $14.2 million, and in 1964, $22.5 million.

In contrast to the growth of prices for any other line of goods, the cost of election campaigns has the specific feature that it has a direct bearing on political power, and not merely in the sense that the "high-cost" democracy keeps the working people away from government.

The high cost of running for office also effectively keeps out a considerable section of the middle and petty bourgeoisie, apart from those who are prepared to serve the interests of monopoly capital. The astronomic election costs ensure, consolidate and cover up the actual monopoly positions of the top section of the ruling class within the system of "representative democracy".

No wonder the power élite is ready to foot the growing election bill, so that despite repeated suggestions over the past decades for a reform of the archaic system of financing electoral campaigns, it remains essentially unchanged. Any electoral campaign in the United States is still financed by private contributions.

This fact has produced some hypocritical complaints in the American press. Here is one: "One of the unsavoury aspects of our political system is that candidates and parties are forced to depend on the large contributions from individuals or special interest groups."[3]

However, this "unsavoury aspect" of the U.S. political system happens to be one of its oldest and most intrinsic. It is not surprising that even the *New York Times* has no plan to eliminate private contributions; it wants them

more broadly based on "democratic" elements, which would provide a more effective cover, consisting of a mass of small contributions, for the crucial role of the monopolies in financing the elections. Attempts to make up the anti-democratic character of the U.S. electoral system are as old as the system of financing presidential and other elections.

WHO PAYS!

Fortune, the mouthpiece of America's Big Business, says contributions of "political money" for electoral campaigns in the United States are made by people who fall under these five heads:

1. The "political angels," or the "fat cats," that is, the millionaires.
2. Organised labour.
3. Government employees.
4. The underworld.
5. Unorganised voluntary contributors.

This list, correct in itself, gives the impression that nearly the whole of American society takes part in contributing to the campaign funds. Actually, nothing is farther from the truth. Ninety per cent of campaign funds of the parties or individual candidates come from about 1 per cent of the people.[4]

This 1 per cent must be really powerful to provide 90 per cent of the $200 million spent in all electoral campaigns in the United States in 1964. This 1 per cent consists chiefly of "fat cats," or "political angels," the epithet of the latter being a means not only of designating the nature and purpose of their contributions but also of differentiating them from the "theatrical angels," the wealthy patrons who back ventures on the stage.

[3] *New York Times,* July 9, 1964.   [4] *Fortune,* November 1964, p. 280.

The banker Jay Cooke, who financed the Republican Party in the second half of the last century, was one of the first major "political angels" in the United States. With the advent of the epoch of imperialism, this part was played by the Rockefellers, the Harrimans, the Morgans, the Mellons, the Du Ponts, the Fords, the Fields and other millionaire families.

Some, like Rockefeller and Mellon, were more or less consistent in financing the Republican Party, others favoured the Democratic Party, or contributed to the campaign funds of both. The Harrimans started out by making political contributions to the presidential campaign fund of the Republican candidate Theodore Roosevelt in 1904, and then switched to the Democratic Party. The Texas oil baron Cullen sent cheques to the campaign funds of both parties in 20 states.

The political contributions of the "fat cats" were as a rule generous. Between 1896 and 1904, John D. Rockefeller, the founder of Standard Oil, made contributions to the Republican Party totalling $550,000. Edward Henry Harriman, railway magnate and father of the present banker and politician William Averell Harriman, spent $250,000 to send Republican Theodore Roosevelt to the White House in 1904. In the 1950s, the family spent at least $30,000 to elect Averell Harriman Governor of New York (this time from the Democratic Party).

Woodrow Wilson's rise to the White House and his stay there largely depended on the political contributions of "angel" Cleveland Dodge, who spent $130,000 for these purposes between 1912 and 1916. In 1936, the political contributions of the Du Pont family came to more than $620,000, and those of the Pew family, to more than $312,000.

Among the "political angels" who contributed to the Republican Party and Eisenhower's campaign chest in 1952 were John D. Rockefeller, Jr., and his sons ($94,000); the Du Pont family ($74,000); the family of Joseph Pew, Jr. (more than $65,000), the family of Richard Mellon, Henry Ford II, and others. That same year, the Democratic Party and Stevenson's "angels" included Joseph Kennedy, father of the late President Kennedy ($20,000), Albert Greenfield ($16,000), and Marshall Field ($10,000).

All the other contributors, including the organised underworld, do not match up to the "fat cats" either in size of donations or the consequent political influence. Together they account for less than 10 per cent of the "political money." But if we are to believe *Fortune,* "a party or candidate can find in this area some very eager contributors who will demand only a reasonable *quid pro quo.*"[5] It is true that contributors of this class have a much greater part to play in local elections— state and city—than in national campaigns.

As far as the average businessman is concerned, the magazine writes, if he "makes any political donation at all it is likely to be less than what he pays for a couple of theatre tickets. . . . The average businessman. . .is more apt to be wondering how he can escape some politically-minded friend who is dunning him for a campaign contribution."

A Republican Party consultant estimated that in 1952, contributions came from only 2.5 million persons, out of the 34 million who voted for the Republicans, and of them 80 per cent gave less than $10 each. A 1954 survey said political donations are made by one in 18 American families, while 31 per cent would be prepared to contribute at least $5 if requested. But one experienced

5 *Fortune,* May 1956, p. 117.

money-raiser says: " 'They'll give, when you back them into a corner.' Whether they would give much more than $5 is a question."[6]

That is the mood of contributors other than the "fat cats," who are the true masters of the United States: they do not need to be prodded into making political contributions. In fact, they egg each other on, and staunchly defend their right to have a "dollar democracy," as the following shows: "A favourite charge of labour leaders, when a company president does make a substantial political contribution, is that he is exploiting an economic advantage over the mass of voters—i.e., his employees. It is a silly charge. *The right to vote and the right of free speech carry with them the right to support one's views with money. . . .* The U.S. has come a long way from the days of property qualifications for voting, but *it has not yet been asserted that property should disqualify a man from full citizenship* [my italics.—F.O.]."[7]

This angry outburst on the pages of a respectable organ of Big Business is not evidence of strength on the part of the bosses of modern America or of their confidence in themselves or capitalist society; they are thrown off balance by the smallest hint at the true nature and deep contradictions of capitalist relations.

But their nervous irritation tends to put a stamp on the true character of their paid democracy. What they are in fact saying is that the wealth of the tycoon automatically enhances his civil rights, and the poverty of the lowly automatically slashes their civil rights; that, they say, is in the nature of things.

Fortune's insistence that the right to vote and the right of free speech includes the right to back up one's views with money is an admission that it is of the essence of American democracy for a citizen's rights and views to be directly dependent on their fortunes. One American businessman has rankly said: "The opportunity to make big contributions is a civil liberty possessed by a relatively small per cent of the population."[8] That is only one remove from admitting that in the United States civil rights and democracy in general are the privilege of "a relatively small per cent of the population."

On the outside "democracy" is observed even in the registration form for political contributions: the law does not require any statement concerning the size of individual donations, so that the "fat cat" will be listed side by side with the one-dollar donor. This kind of "equality" merely serves to screen from public scrutiny the decisive part played by the "fat cats" in selecting candidates for elective office and using them as their agents thereafter.

WHY CONTRIBUTE?

By contrast with *Fortune,* which is read by a small circle of wealthy men, the popular American press prefers not to go into the financial side of U.S. electoral campaigns. When it does come to stating why some people make large contributions to campaign funds and who they are, the press usually refers its readers to the ancient Greeks, who did likewise many centuries ago, at the "cradle of Western democracy." However, a look nearer home—say Chicago —will explain a great deal more than the practices in ancient Athens. In 1955, one Robert Merriam, was defeated in the mayoral race. He later recounted how the owner of a Chicago gambling den offered him $50,000 if,

6 *Ibid.,* p. 114.
7 *Ibid.,* p. 236.

8 *Ibid.,* November 1964, p. 278.

as mayor, he agreed to fight the policy-racket syndicate which was trying to squeeze small "independents" out of business. All the would-be contributor wanted, said Merriam, was a return to free enterprise in the gambling business.[9]

His was, of course, a modest and, you might say, naive and utopian dream, when compared with the aims pursued by the Rockefellers, Du Ponts, Fords and other magnates in making their contributions to campaign funds. Their demands range over a wide field of internal and external policy. But like the small shareholder of any corporation who cannot prevent the men who have the controlling interest from running the enterprise as they like, the small contributor to the campaign fund can never have his way with the "fat cats" in U.S. politics.

In the 19th century, the main source of campaign funds were men eager to secure cushy jobs in the Administration or at least to retain some office. Even today, government officials who contribute are still relatively numerous, because the contributor's job and career may depend on which of the two parties of monopoly capital—the Republicans or the Democrats—gets in. But individual contributions by officials are as a rule not very big and their total is relatively small.

A contribution on a bigger scale than the average official can allow himself to make may bring an ambassadorial or an even higher post. Many American ambassadors have secured their appointments only by their contributions to the victorious party. Averell Harriman and Joseph Davies, both former ambassadors to the U.S.S.R., were once "political angels" of this kind.

The "political angels" themselves usually give hypocritical explanations,

couched in highly patriotic terms, of their reasons for giving their dollars to the parties and candidates. The most popular reasons are "an almost congenital faith in the rightness of their party's principles," zealousness in the furthering of "their political ideas," "a duty of good citizenship," and the desire "to get the best men into office." But some are much more down-to-earth. The President of the Risdon Manufacturing Company, in Naugatuck, Lewis Dibble, thinks that "no one does such a thing except to obtain a favour, and that is stooping pretty low."[10]

The following example shows the tremendous role of money and the political influence of those who give it on the recipients. Last autumn, following Barry Goldwater's nomination by the Republican Party for the presidential race, Republican Senator Hugh Scott of Pennsylvania, who was trying to get into the Senate for another six-year term, announced his opposition to Goldwater. Some Republican "fat cats," including those in Pennsylvania, warned Scott that they would withhold their contributions to his campaign fund unless he supported the Arizona Senator. Sure enough, Scott altered his stand to lukewarm support for Goldwater, although he did avoid committing himself in the industrial areas, where the population was clearly hostile to the leader of the ultras.[11]

"POLITICAL LODE"

It is no problem for the U.S. moneybags to keep such men as Senator Scott in line: their new headache is the political activity of the trade unions, which have been taking an increasingly wider part in electoral campaigns and

9 Fortune, May 1956, pp. 117, 236.

10 Ibid., May 1956, p. 240.
11 Time, Oct. 9, 1964, pp. 22–23.

contributing considerable amounts to the campaign funds of the candidates they favour. The monopolists regard this development with mixed feelings.

On the one hand, they are alarmed. After all, the contributions by trade unionists are very different from those of the small and middle businessmen, the officials, the crooks or shady businessmen. These elements do not make any demands which clash with those of the real masters of the United States and have no real influence on its policies. The trade unions are quite another kettle of fish. Behind them are millions of workers who, whatever their political mood, clearly have no sympathy for the exploiters, and are demanding that their trade unions should campaign with their own platforms which should differ and even clash with those of the monopolists.

The trade unions are also the most organised social force in the country, and their millions of members provide a solid financial basis which tends to gain in strength. Is it surprising, therefore, that the monopolists are alarmed at the activity of this class of voter who is also prepared to back up his platform with sizeable contributions. After all, he could conceivably support another party instead of the traditional two (the trade unions have tended to give support mainly to the Democrats). The business leaders, whom *Fortune* interviewed in 1956, expressed the most concern about "the increasingly formidable financial role of labour."[12] Goldwater has also expressed concern over the highly important part played by the trade unions—because of their activity and organisation—in defeating him at the last elections.[13] Up to 80 per cent of the 17 million trade union-

ists and four-fifths of their families had voted against him.

But monopoly circles have also expressed other views of the political activisation of the trade unions. The "fat cats" admit this to be an inevitable evil and are prepared to meet them half way in order to make sure of neutralising them. Some have even made a point of encouraging trade-union organisers of campaign funds in the hope of using them for their own ends and even of directing and controlling them.

Those who favour the idea, and they are especially active in the Democratic Party, believe trade-union canvassing for campaign funds is a real "political lode," which should be worked in the grand style. "Northern Democrats were rather pleased to have such a rich political lode to tap."[14]

The working of this "lode" has been going on for some time. Since the day in 1936, when John L. Lewis, President of the United Mine Workers' Union, handed a cheque for $469,000 to the campaign fund of President Franklin D. Roosevelt, a great deal has changed in the scale of trade-union contributions and in the attitude of the monopolists to them. Twenty-eight years ago, this trade-union gift gave Big Business a fit. But in 1952, when the trade unions gave more than $1.7 million to Adlai Stevenson's campaign fund (he was the Democratic Party's nominee) there was hardly a ruffle. A sort of inverse proportion was established between trade-union contributions and Big Business high blood pressure: in 1954, the figure was over $2 million, in 1960, $2.5 million, and in electoral campaigns at all levels in 1964, more than $2.5 million (provisional figure).

The A.F.L.-C.I.O.'s Committee on Political Education backed 31 Democrats running for the Senate in 1964,

12 *Fortune,* May 1956, p. 117.

13 *U.S. News & World Report,* Dec. 21, 1964, p. 56.

14 *Fortune,* May 1956, p. 117.

and not a single Republican. Trade-union leaders believe that "they...can count on support from about 40 of the 100 Senators in the present Congress, and around 200 of the 435 House members."[15] They think the Congressmen elected with their support will help to push through bills meeting trade-union demands, but they have been frequently disappointed.

Nevertheless, the scale and results of trade-union participation in last year's electoral campaigns created an impression on the nation, and this was due not only to the more than $2.5 million in contributions. After all, this is only slightly more than 1 per cent of the total of $200 million spent in the electoral campaigns. The fact is that the "fat cats" sat up and were alarmed by the vigorous political and organisational activity of the trade unions, although some of these men were tempted to exploit the untapped political lode.

The trade unions, chiefly the A.F.L.-C.I.O.'s Committee on Political Education, campaigned in last year's elections on a scale unmatched in the past. Thousands of full-time trade-union organisers and volunteers took part in the electoral campaign. They helped to register voters among workers and their families, engaged in door-to-door canvassing, ran an information service for trade unionists, circulated pamphlets and leaflets, and handed out handbills at factory gates. Many of these criticised Senator Goldwater's political programme and his behaviour in the Senate. The A.F.L.-C.I.O. alone circulated nearly 50 million handbills and 10 million leaflets informing voters of the stand taken by members of Congress on the various bills.

In New York, nearly 5,000 trade unionists volunteered to help register voters and act as poll watchers. Nearly 500 volunteers worked on all the working days during the campaign in some of the 27 locals of the Committee on Political Education in Los Angeles, California. In Chicago, at least 3,500 trade unionists were out on polling day.

DABBLING IN POLITICS

Probably one of the most amazing developments was the advertisement recently put up on an office wall—the building belongs to Rockefeller's Chase Manhattan Bank—which said: "Need for you to be active in politics." Just a few years ago, that sort of thing would have been stranger than a pink elephant in a bank. But there it is. Inside the building there is a political seminar which the board has organised for bank employees.

Nor is this a stunt. According to *Time,* more than 450 companies now have hired full-time public-affairs directors "to stir up political interest among their employees." The magazine writes that "for many companies, fund raising is just the beginning. They have set up special public affairs educational programmes, many of them using how-to-do-it political handbooks distributed by the U.S. Chamber of Commerce."[16] More than 500 corporations have programmes to encourage participation in political campaigns. Among them are the giant U.S. Steel, Alcoa, Westinghouse, Ford and Equitable Life. Borg-Warner's programme is entitled "Participate in Politics." There is, of course, no need to explain on whose side. Minnesota Mining and Manufacturing's programme is called "Citizenship Participation Programme"; Boeing offers its employees a course in "prac-

15 *U.S. News & World Report,* Nov. 9, 1964, p. 103.

16 *Time,* Oct. 9, 1964, p. 67.

tical politics." The U.S. press reports that 750,000 people have already "volunteered" to attend these corporation-sponsored seminars of "practical politics."

Why are the monopolists so eager to provide political education for their employees and even workers? That is undoubtedly their effort to counteract the activity of the trade unions. Their purpose is undiluted. *Time* writes: "Businessmen have realised long ago that corporations have a large measure of responsibility for society. Enlightened self-interest [!] also plays a part; though the vast majority of the programmes are scrupulously non-partisan [!], business leaders naturally hope that some of their political and economic views will brush off on participating employees."

An editorial in *New York Times* welcomes "the attempt by business to promote greater political participation,"[17] but neglects to say that this is above all an attempt to secure control of the political activity which has been growing in the teeth of ruling class opposition. This is the true reason why the boards of many corporations, which a few years ago frowned on political activity on the part of their staff in electoral campaigns, now encourage them and frequently help to nominate some of them for office in local bodies.

They have provided the incentives. Ford, Alcoa and Chrysler allow their staff time off for political activity, while the Chase Manhattan Bank is ever prepared to pay for working hours spent by its staff performing the duties of public office. Its branch offices employ about 200 persons who also hold elective posts, ranging from membership on school committee to the office of mayor in small towns.

17 *New York Times*, July 9, 1964.

In 1963, 156 employees of U.S. Steel were actually helped by the corporation to campaign for office and were elected to state and local bodies. In 1964, 18 of the 42 employees of Boeing who ran for local office were elected; of the 31 employees of Ford's who ran, 9 were elected.

All these are incentives invented by the "fat cats" to line up employees (if not the workers) on their side, since there is no keeping them away from politics altogether.

It is a curious development, these efforts on the part of Big Business to stimulate people to greater participation in politics. Corporations once concentrated on forming "company" unions; they are now taking the next step and are trying to set up "company" political organisations, in an effort to broaden the base of their political influence through the inclusion of the employees. That kind of response to last year's active campaigning by the trade unions betrays a fear on the part of the top sections of monopoly capital over the spread of activity and, what is most important, the mood of the organised workers it tends to create.

The ideological influence of the U.S. bourgeoisie on the working people is still rather strong. While trade unionists have been showing more interest in the elections, the mass of American workers still vote for the Democratic Party candidates, one of the two parties of monopoly capital. The political activity of trade-union organisations has increased, but it still operates within the framework of the two-party system, and the paid democracy of the ruling class. Various elements of the political machine of the U.S. monopolies, especially the Democratic Party bosses, use this fact to their advantage. They are still able to do so. But for how long? That is the vexed question confronting the exploiters.

THE POLITY

IN THE U.S.S.R.:

The Soviet View

The Communisty Party
in a Socialist Society

I. POMELOV

1.—The successful development of the world socialist system depends to a decisive extent on correct interpretation and implementation of the guiding role of the Marxist-Leninist parties of socialist states. Problems of party guidance of society have now acquired particular urgency in both the theoretical and practical contexts, primarily in connection with the entry of a substantial group of fraternal countries into a new stage of their development. More and more countries in which the transitional period from capitalism to socialism has been or is being completed and that have begun or are beginning the construction of a developed socialist society are taking their places alongside the Soviet Union, where socialism triumphed a relatively long time ago and communist construction is already under way.

Implementation of the guidance of a socialist society as an integral social-

Reprinted from I. Pomelov, "The Communist Party in a Socialist Society," Pravda *(February 20, 1967) Translated in* Current Digest of the Soviet Press, *XIX, No. 8 (Copyright © March 15, 1967), 8–9.*

economic system embracing the basic spheres of a country's life is a new task on a large historic scale posed by our epoch. Communist Parties, after assuring the victory of socialist revolutions and the construction of socialism in their respective countries, are today called upon to achieve the full exercise of the advantages of socialism, the full flowering of the material and spiritual forces of the new society. . . .

The entire international experience of the revolutionary struggle confirms the growing role of the Communist vanguard in the construction of the new society.

2.—With the completion of the transitional period in socialist countries, the need for conscious guidance of social processes and, consequently, for ensuring the guiding role of the Marxist-Leninist party not only does not diminish but increases. At the same time, substantial changes determined by objective conditions take place in the content and methods of the party's activity.

The victory of socialism opens up the possibility of fully overcoming random social development and of realizing in practice the advantages of planning. These advantages are disclosed through the conscious activity of the masses, which develops on the basis of the party's scientifically grounded policy.

By the end of the transitional period not only does a qualitatively new social system take shape, but also the country's productive, scientific-technical organism reaches large proportions. At the same time, despite the large and comprehensive economic upsurge and the substantial improvement in the people's living conditions, a great number of unsolved economic problems remain in some countries, especially those that were backward before the Revolution.

Although there are no class antagonisms in a socialist society, it is not yet socially homogeneous. The working class continues to be the most progressive force in the new society; ensuring its leading role and implementing its ideology are necessary conditions for further progress on the path to communism.

Socialism is not yet free of survivals of the old order in economics, in the consciousness and behavior of people, in everyday life. It is entirely clear that the overcoming of alien phenomena and trends, the resolution of contradictions and the consistent implementation of socialist principles in all spheres of public life cannot occur by themselves, automatically.

These circumstances attest to a complication in the guidance of social processes, to rising demands and the vital necessity of a scientific approach to this guidance. Only the Communist Party, which is armed with Marxist-Leninist doctrine and treats the problems of social development creatively, can provide this sort of genuinely scientific approach.

This is why any narrowing of the party's role or restriction of its functions, for example, to the sphere of ideology alone would be totally inadmissible and harmful to the cause of socialism. What would it mean in practice for the party to pursue a line of "noninterference" in politics or economics? It would mean allowing the development of the new society to drift and leaving a wide field open to chaos.

Or let us take a specific problem, such as the party's relations with state and public organizations.

"Noninterference" by the party in their work could lead to a lack of coordination in their activities, which would harm the cause of socialism. It would also be harmful if the party assumed inappropriate operational-administrative functions, that is, if it effectively supplanted all other organizations....

Now we know not only from theory but also from the experience of the U.S.S.R. and other fraternal countries that only the Communist Party, comprising the most conscious and active people from the working class, the peasantry and the intelligentsia, only the party, exerting effectual influence on all forms of public activity and on the work of state and mass organizations, is capable of correctly utilizing all forces and opportunities to strengthen and develop a socialist society and to advance it to communism.

The volume of the party's theoretical work increases in the conditions of victorious socialism. The theory of scientific socialism, which serves as a guiding principle in solving the tasks of socialist revolution and socialist construction, was created on the basis of scientific analysis of capitalism, its natural laws and contradictions, as well as the experience of the workers' movement. Lenin worked out questions of this theory in the early years of Soviet rule, in the initial period of socialist reforms. Scientific socialism has been enriched since then by the enormous collective experience of the socialist countries.

Now there is a real, living socialist society. It is hardly necessary to say how important it is for the new society to know itself in order to influence the processes of its own development and how important it is to make theory more profound and concrete on the basis of analysis of accumulated practical experience. Who else but the Communist Party, the proprietor of Marxism-Leninism, can fulfill the task of a really scientific, objective investigation of socialism and the extraction of correct conclusions for practice?

The elaboration of problems of socialist economic management by Communist Parties in a number of fraternal countries convincingly illustrates the immense vital importance that theoretical research has for perfecting the guidance of the new society. The economic reforms carried out in these countries reflect, with certain concrete differences, a common search for ways of perfecting economic relations, of improving the system of managing the national economy and planning and of strengthening economic accountability and material incentive—in short, of making the most effective use of the advantages of a socialist economy.

A highly important trend in the party's guiding work at the new stage consists in expanding democratic principles of administering the affairs of society, in creating the most favorable opportunities for the growth of the working people's political and labor activeness, in strengthening conscious discipline and in raising the level of organization and the sense of responsibility on the part of officials and all citizens for their work. The Communist Party, constructed on the principles of democratic centralism, which combines democracy and discipline, of equal rights and duties of Communists and of collective leadership, can fully realize the opportunities opened up, as a result of the liquidation of the exploiter classes, for carrying out further construction of the new society through increasingly democratic methods and for ensuring the flourishing of socialist democracy.

The Marxist-Leninist party has a great role in working out the problems of a socialist state's foreign policy. It alone, based on the principles of Marxism-Leninism and proletarian internationalism, is capable of ensuring the correct combination of national and international tasks and of pursuing in the present-day complex international situation a foreign-policy course aimed at creating the most favorable conditions for the construction of socialism and communism, at strengthening the world socialist system, at raising its economic and defensive might, at supporting peoples' liberation movements and at the peaceful coexistence of states with different social systems.

Thus, as in the struggle for the victory of working class rule, as in the transitional period from capitalism to socialism, the working people's masses in a socialist society need a political leader and guide, a strong, cohesive Communist Party. Without this, socialism cannot develop successfully.

3.—The basic political, ideological and organizational principles determining the place and role of Communist Parties in creating the new society are firm. But the content of the tasks that arise at the new stage and the new qualitative structure of the socialist make it necessary to change the methods the Marxist-Leninist parties use to influence the society's development. . . .

In the transitional period, when the hostile exploiter classes attempt to prevent the construction of socialism, coercion and means of power are applied against them. But in this period too the Marxist-Leninist party's chief method of guiding the working people's masses is persuasion, upbringing and organization. It is entirely natural that this method acquires supreme importance in a socialist society, which consists only of the friendly classes of workers and peasants and intelligentsia. Coercion still remains even in conditions of victorious socialism. But it is applied only against criminal and antisocial elements and not against any class or social group. No matter what task in the development of socialist society is considered—whether it is the development of productive forces, raising labor productivity or strengthening the positions of communist ideology—attempts to use coercive methods or administration by fiat to solve these problems can only bring harm to the cause.

The party influences the development of socialist society by elaborating a correct, scientifically grounded policy and carrying it out through Communists and party organizations in the activities of all departments and institutions and in all branches of work. This influence is more effective the broader the front of ideological-upbringing work and the better the organization of propagandizing the ideas of Marxism-Leninism, of propagating the party viewpoint on events, facts and phenomena. . . .

Concern with the quality of the membership, for implementing in practice Leninist norms and the principle of collective leadership in the Center and in rural areas, the regular calling of Party Congresses and Central Committee plenary sessions, of conferences and plenary sessions of local party bodies, the creation of more favorable conditions for the criticism of shortcomings and the development of work in the Marxist-Leninist upbringing of Communists and in organizing the masses for fulfillment of the five-year plan—all this, without question, signifies the growth of our party and the heightening of its guiding role.

4.—It was proved long ago that an encroachment on a Communist Party is tantamount to undermining the guiding role of the working class in the revolutionary struggle. Whereas the position of right-wing reformist elements on this is conducive to strengthening the influence of the bourgeoisie and leads to subordination of the working people to the bourgeoisie's ideology, the position of left-wing sectarian elements in undermining the role of the Communist Party is tantamount to subordinating the working class to petty-bourgeois ideology. As the exponents of the fundamental interests of the working class, Marxist-Leninists have always waged and are waging a relentless struggle against both these trends. . . .

The Educative Role
of the Soviet State

D. CHESNOKOV

1. ...The creative development of the theory of the socialist state was an essential condition for the successes of state construction in the U.S.S.R. Having raised Marxist-Leninist doctrine on the dictatorship of the proletariat to a new stage, our Communist Party drew important theoretical and political conclusions on the attributes and functions of the state under socialism and on the preservation, given specific conditions, of the state in a communist society.

At the modern stage the problems of state construction under socialism become immensely important for all the countries of the world socialist system. The correct solution to these problems requires a further creative development of Lenin's theory of the state and a determined struggle against distortions of it and revisionist and sectarian deviations from Marxism-Leninism.

Disparaging the role of the socialist state, the revisionists demand that it be abolished, that it wither away almost the day after the victory of socialism. It is common knowledge that demands of a similar nature were heard in the U.S.S.R. at the beginning of the 1930s. Trends leading essentially to a disparagement of the socialist state's role have

Reprinted from D. Chesnokov, "The Educative Role of the Soviet State," Pravda (February 27, 1967). Translated in Current Digest of the Soviet Press, XIX, No. 9 (Copyright © March 22, 1967), 6–7.

appeared in our country in the recent past in individual statements and articles devoted to the new Party Program. At times they improperly contraposed the socialist state of the entire people to the state of the dictatorship of the proletariat, and statehood to public self-rule.

Actually the Party Program discusses not radical change in the essence of the socialist state but stages in its development. By the same token, statehood and public self-rule are not mutually exclusive. The birth of socialist statehood is also the birth of the people's self-rule. But at a definite stage in the development of society this self-rule must preserve the forms of state and law. In order to express the people's will and activeness most fully, the people's self-rule through the system of statehood is supplemented by a system of independent, nonstate public organizations. The transition to a stateless system of self-rule will be accomplished not through "bypassing" the state or minimizing its role but through the socialist state, by means of the comprehensive development of its democratic essence. Moreover, the working class, the most advanced, organized force of Soviet society, is filling and will continue to fill its leading role until the complete disappearance of classes and class differences.

No less a danger to communism are

the left-opportunist concepts and leftist errors on the question of the state. They boil down to emasculation of the democratic essence of the socialist state, conversion of the state into merely an apparatus for administration by fiat and coercion, and transference of military methods to the work of state organizations.

The Trotskyites preached such views in the most open fashion, and recently the present leaders of China have been preaching them. Moreover, in the C.P.R. the Mao Tse-tung group has elevated this concept to the rank of official policy. Military methods of command and administration by fiat have become the norm of activity there for not only state but also public organizations. In pressing for an improper strengthening of the army's role in the state, the Chinese leaders are calling for its conversion "into a great school where people master politics, military affairs and culture." Such militarization of the state's ideological upbringing activity fundamentally contradicts the very principles of Marxism-Leninism....

2. ...The fundamental changes that have taken place in the economic, social, political and spiritual life of Soviet society and its growing ideological and political unity require improvement in the methods and style of state leadership and a higher level of Party guidance of the Soviets. An important stage on the path of such improvement was the October, 1964, plenary session of the C.P.S.U. Central Committee, which put an end to manifestations of subjectivism and voluntarism in the approach to solving state problems and had a positive effect on all aspects of the activity of the Party, the state and our whole society.

In the conditions of steady growth of the working people's ideological maturity and political consciousness and comprehensive, full-scale develop-ment of socialist democracy, a further change is taking place in the balance between persuasion and coercion in the work of the state: To a great extent the role of persuasion, explanation and education of people through all means and all links of the state apparatus is growing, not to mention the activity of public organizations. . . .

Coercion by the state comes into force only when manifestations of bourgeois ideology, remnants of private-property mentality and morality or prejudices become the basis of anti-social actions and lead individuals into conflict with the norms and laws of socialist society.

All this determines the further development of the socialist state's educative function in the present-day period. Only people who are stuck in the past and lean toward dogmatism in evaluating life phenomena cannot see this. Their inability to perceive correctly what is new is just as harmful as the views of those who have a nihilistic attitude toward the past and in a spirit of petty-bourgeois liberalism and anarchism deny the necessity of great exactingness and a combination of persuasion and coercion, who believe coercion by the state is incompatible with true democracy. . . .

The socialist state plays a great role in strengthening communist discipline and inculcating a highly conscious attitude toward labor for the good of society. This is determined by the fact that under socialism labor has still not become a vital need for many people, that state control over the extent of labor and the extent of consumption is still necessary. The working class, which exhibits models of comradely cooperation, mutual exactingness and consciousness, heads the movement of the entire people for labor discipline and self-discipline, for a communist attitude toward labor. The necessity of further

raising the working people's consciousness as a major condition for the
growth of labor productivity was once
again pointed out by the C.P.S.U.
Central Committee in the resolution on
the work of Tula Province Party
organizations in fostering socialist labor
discipline.[1]

The socialist state by nature and
intent combines material, political and
cultural-ideological factors, and the
fostering of communist labor discipline
is based precisely on a combination of
these factors and stimuli. Thus implementation of the economic reform leads
to a further strengthening of the principle of the workers' collective and
individual stake in the results of labor.
This undoubtedly promotes a strengthening of labor discipline and the growth
of labor productivity. But successful
conduct of the reform requires an increase in the workers' activeness and
independence and a heightening in each
one of the feeling of responsibility to
the people and the state. After all, the
expansion of the rights of enterprises
and the strengthening of economic incentive also can engender tendencies
toward sectionalism, contraposition of
the enterprise's interests to society's
interests and even moneygrubbing attitudes among individuals. The correct
regulation of material incentives combined with moral incentives, continuous
control over the observance of state
discipline and the fulfillment of state
plans, and the comprehensive development of democracy provide the main
antidote to such negative phenomena....

The safeguarding of public order is
an important type of activity by the
Soviet state promoting the education of
the people in the spirit of communist
discipline and organization. Leninism
regards petty-bourgeois dissoluteness

[1] *Current Digest of the Soviet Press,* Vol.
XVIII, No. 51, pp. 8–9.

and disorganization, antisocial actions
and pilferage as manifestations of bourgeois forces, morals and traditions.
Before the building of socialism these
forces and morals were the exploiting
classes' open accomplices in their struggle against the victorious proletariat.
Since the victory of socialism and the
elimination of the exploiting classes, the
bourgeois essence of antisocial actions
and hooliganism—not to mention crime
—has remained. Such phenomena are
overcome on the basis of further con-
solidating the socialist system, raising
the level of the people's material well-
being and culture and improving all
forms of communist education of the
working people. . . .

The people are always intolerant of
antisocial actions, hooliganism, etc. All
the more are they implacable to these
monstrous phenomena under socialism,
when the social base that nurtures such
distortions has been overcome for the
most part and all the conditions exist
for eliminating in a short time or at
least reducing to a minimum not only
crime but also the antisocial actions of
individuals. . . .

3. With the development of the
Soviet state's educative function, its
tasks in all spheres of cultural construction, public education and enlightenment are growing and becoming complex.

In the hands of the state are concentrated such powerful means of educating the working people as the school,
secondary and higher educational institutions and a farflung network of various cultural-enlightenment institutions.
They have done a great deal, but they
have the opportunity to do considerably
more to mold the new man, who is
a harmonious blend of spiritual wealth,
moral purity and physical perfection. . . .

The expansion of the sphere of the
Soviet state's cultural upbringing activity is bound up with the solution to

a number of problems, primarily economic.

In present-day conditions cultural-upbringing work cannot be conducted without the appropriate material base. Thus, for example, improvement of the upbringing of young people and the organization of cultured leisure for the working people require a further expansion of the network of clubs, libraries and reading rooms, sports facilities, radio facilities and television, and the training of specialists for them. Without a further development of all forms of production training and vocational-technical education, it is impossible to raise the average level of skills of those working in production, which the interests of modern technological progress and the economic reform urgently require. This is why only political naivete or ignorance can explain the inattention of individual leaders to cultural-upbringing work and expansion of the material and technical base of culture and the attempts to contrapose economic construction to cultural construction. After all, quite recently voices were heard in some places demanding curtailment of the construction of clubhouses and other cultural-enlightenment institutions under the pretext of "concern" about economic construction.

Such a vulgarized approach to cultural construction contradicts the correct Marxist understanding of and solution to the question of the correlation of material and spiritual culture in the development of society.

The Party and the government are taking serious steps to strengthen the material base of cultural-enlightenment work. The five-year plan provides for an acceleration of the pace of cultural construction.

Fulfillment of the urgent tasks of cultural construction and the Soviet state's successful execution of its cultural educative function as a whole depends to a decisive extent on the activeness of the Soviets. As a decision of the 23rd C.P.S.U. Congress pointed out, it is becoming especially important to enhance their role so that they make full use of their powers in implementing the tasks of economic and cultural construction and checking up on performance.

The Soviets are a universal organization of the people. As the most inclusive of all public organizations, they are simultaneously agencies of state power. The Soviets are a form of the people's self-rule and the political form of the socialist state. The all-encompassing democratism that expresses the essence of the Soviet state in our time broadens the possibilities of the Soviets and enhances their role in the people's self-education. It can be said of the Soviets that they are not only a school of administration, a school of economic management, but also a school for fostering communist discipline and organization, a school of communism. . . .

* * *

The construction of communism is the creation of its material and technical base and at the same time the development of social relations, the growth of socialist relations into communist relations. This presupposes the upbringing of people in accordance with the special features and principles of a communist society, the molding of a new man possessing a high level of consciousness and comprehensive spiritual culture. Only when this process has been completed will the need for regulation by state and law and, consequently, the state itself wither away. But there is only one path to this—the all-round use of the socialist state for construction of the economy and culture, for the comprehensive development and communist upbringing of every toiler in the socialist society.

Party Work in Institutions of Higher Education

B. MOCHALOV

Rapid development of science and technology is a characteristic feature of the present day. The higher schools, which train highly skilled specialists for the national economy and for scientific, cultural and administrative institutions and which also work directly on many vital scientific problems, play an important role in this process. The 23rd C.P.S.U. Congress resolution on the Central Committee's report stresses that the primary task for institutions of higher education at the present stage is "improving the quality of training of specialists."

Party organizations in higher educational institutions are organizers of and active participants in the creative work of their [institutions'] collectives. For example, Moscow university, which is one of the country's largest educational and scientific centers and which has approximately 50,000 undergraduates, graduate students, professors, instructors and scientific workers in its day, evening and correspondence departments, has a Party organization of more than 5,000 members. This Party committee has the rights of a distinct Party committee.

Reprinted from B. Mochalov "Party Work in Institutions of Higher Education," Kommunist (No. 10, July, 1966). Translated in Current Digest of the Soviet Press, XVIII, No. 36 (Copyright © September 28, 1966), 3–5.

The university's Communists direct the collective's efforts toward achieving top results in research and teaching. The quality of training of Moscow State University graduates is renowned throughout the world. The university's school of mathematics and mechanics and a considerable section of its physics and chemistry departments are among those determining worldwide levels of development in their respective fields. Two-thirds of the present members of the U.S.S.R. Academy of Sciences are Moscow State University alumni. About 40% of the university's present graduating class consists of specialists in the new and latest fields that arise as science progresses. Of course, this does not mean that we do not have unsolved problems or that the reserves for improving the work of Moscow State University have already been exhausted.

The new tasks set by the 23rd C.P.S.U. Congress, requiring higher quality in research and teaching, considerably increase the responsibility that Communists in higher educational institutions have for the efficient organization of their collectives' work. It is becoming a pressing need of the day to further develop inner-Party democracy in primary Party organizations as an indispensable condition for implementing the 23rd C.P.S.U. Congress decisions; this will permit giving thorough consideration to various standpoints on the problems under discussion, activizing Communists and strengthening Party discipline.

Organizational Questions.—Above all, this signifies that the role of all Party members in working out Party decisions must increase. This does not mean, of course, constant harmonizing of opinions, but determining with utmost clarity the collective judgment of Party members on a given matter—the collective will of the Party organization—and carrying this out unconditionally.

Where and how can the collective opinion of Party members be determined? First and foremost, at Party meetings, by open, free and broad discussion. Therefore, to develop inner-Party democracy is in effect to increase the prestige and effectiveness of the Party meetings of a university's primary organizations.

Yet we quite often come across instances of Party meetings that do not entirely fulfill their guiding and organizing roles. For example, frequently debates are closed right after the first few speeches, and purely formal decisions are passed. This does not occur because there is nothing to discuss. There are many questions about which the university's Communists are concerned. It is common knowledge, for example, that the majority of professors and teachers were extremely disturbed by the recent deterioration in the quality of training of specialists that has resulted from poor organization, with the consequence that correspondence and evening courses were made "lighter." There are also many highly controversial problems connected with introducing programmed instruction, shortening the term of study and revising the curriculum.

One reason why far from every meeting satisfies the membership is the limited nature of discussion of the research and teaching process, that is, of basic and vital problems of univer-

sity life. This arises from an incorrect interpretation of the Party organization's place and role in an educational institution. If, it is said, the Party organization has no right of control, then it has no possibility of effectively influencing major problems. Therefore, even to raise issues for discussion at Party meetings is pointless. Another common reason is shortcomings in the work of the given Party organization (an insufficiently thought-out agenda, a vague report, poor preliminary briefing of the membership, and so forth).

The Party has reared an army of Communist scientists and scholars who are capable of coping with the most complex problems in developing science and in training cadres. Take the Party organization of Moscow University. Its 5,000 Communists include approximately 1,200 Doctors or Candidates of Sciences. Of the 39 members of the Moscow State University Party Committee, 30 are professors or docents. The situation is similar in the Party organizations within departments. For example, 11 out of the 16 members of the physics department Party committee have Doctors' or Candidates' degrees in physics and mathematics; 13 of the 15 members of the chemistry department Party bureau are professors or docents. The elected Party officials include eminent scientists and scholars: Academician Yu. Rabotnov, Professors A. Shedlovsky, Yu. Saprykin, I. Berezin, L. Voronin, S. Kovalev, A. Kurylev and others.

I think that the existence in higher schools of sufficiently large primary organizations, together with the composition and extensive teaching experience of their membership, makes it possible for these Party organizations to discuss such important problems as the system and quality of instruction, lines of scientific research and the placing of cadres. The political and professional maturity of the leaders in higher educational establishments, departments and institutes on the one hand and of the mass of Party members on the other guarantee that there will be no substitution for the administration or the learned councils, that there will be no infringement on the rights of deans' or rectors' offices.

An approach of this kind is especially important for the basic mass of Communists; it will enhance their roles in the collective and in particular will increase the effectiveness of the Party meeting. At Moscow State University this applies first and foremost to department Party organizations. If a problem of pressing importance to the collective is put on the Party meeting agenda and if all Party members know that a resolution really has vital significance, their sense of responsibility will greatly increase. There will be fewer instances when a Communist looks on passively during discussion and votes for a hastily conceived decision.

There are still some Communist scholars who try to avoid active public work, who concentrate on work in learned councils and in their departments. At report-and-election meetings they frequently object when they are nominated to Party bureaus. The reason is that every scholar has comparatively little free time for assignments not directly connected with his research and teaching. Naturally, he strives to channel his public activity into the field where it will be most effective and closest to his interests. And the primary Party organization, where vital problems or research and teaching are discussed in depth and efficaciously, should become this field of public activity.

At the same time it is our task to try to have all Communist teachers themselves take the initiative, introduce a fresh stream into Party work and seek

and find a creative approach to examining vital problems in the life of the university and its departments. The public activity of a teacher and scholar is the natural practical manifestation of his Marxist-Leninist world outlook.

A scholar who engages in public activity out of the inner conviction that it is necessary and useful, not merely as a formality, can do a great deal to improve the spirit of a higher school's entire public life. However, at present the bulk of Party work falls upon the small number of Communists who are enthusiasts. For example, in the mechanics and mathematics department for the past 15 years the same 25 to 30 scientists have been elected to the department Party bureau over and over. Of course, these comrades deserve the deepest respect. Their civic consciousness is very high. Nevertheless such a situation is intolerable. For when Party work becomes the domain of a narrow group of active members it gradually begins to pall. And the work itself often suffers from this. From being essentially creative, Party work becomes a succession of habitual acts, mainly monotonously repetitive organizational measures.

Another thing is that the scholar who avoids public work often sets an example for the students. It is no secret that many Y.C.L. members do not have permanent assignments. Sometimes the false idea gains ground that scholarship is incompatible with public work. The best way to overcome this error and to achieve a creative advance in all aspects of a collective's life is by drawing the entire teaching and research staff into public, especially Party, work.

Other practical steps should be taken to develop the activity of Party members. First, the rights of department Party organizations in inner-Party life should be broadened; the initiative of the Party organization should be developed, and responsibility for the collective's affairs should be heightened.

In recent years a number of steps have been taken in this direction at Moscow State University. Party committees have been formed in three of the 14 departments (physics, biology and soil science, philosophy and jurisprudence). Two more Party organizations (in the mechanics and mathematics department and in the industrial engineering service) are about to receive the rights of Party committees. In administrative matters, the departments [fakultety] have been given the exclusive right to decide such important matters as admitting and dropping students and granting stipends. The initiative of Y.C.L. members is being developed; they have been given the opportunity to consider important questions of student life firsthand on the education-and-upbringing committees and dormitory floor councils. The departments are becoming full-fledged, strong organizations, capable of dealing effectively with all the problems that arise in their daily activity.

Strengthening the department Party organizations will increase the importance of the Moscow State University Party Committee. For now the university Party Committee will be called on to deal only with the most fundamental questions of general university life, to supervise and guide intelligently the work of the primary Party organizations and to see clearly the prospects for the university's development. With this in view, a 15-year plan for future development has been drafted, and current Party work plans have been drawn up in accordance with it.

Successful work requires the most attentive attitude to elected Party cadres. Under the procedure in effect before the 23rd C.P.S.U. Congress,

secretaries and members of elected Party bodies were usually changed after two years. The Congress repealed this too stringent time limit for elective Party office and at the same time noted the necessity for strictly observing the principles of systematic renewal of the membership of elected Party bodies and of continuity of leadership. This renewal cannot be stereotyped. As is known, the higher schools have a considerable reserve of Communists with experience in leadership. There is no difficulty here in renewing the membership of Party bureaus and committees.

New people bring with them not only new ideas but also their own individual approaches to the solution of problems. However, even new cadres frequently succumb to the influence of traditions and entrenched practices that are often accepted as the norm—but that actually have not proved themselves. Specifically, I wish to make a few remarks about what the Party leader should be like.

The idea of a certain "standard" Party worker is exceedingly tenacious. It is frequently believed that he must be "firm" and "staunch" in everything. I put these words in inverted commas because their true meanings are frequently distorted. "Firm" describes someone who punishes, teaches, rewards. In fact, a Party leader is a human being with all a human being's strengths and weaknesses. Of course, the weaknesses should be at a minimum. But if they do exist, it is pointless to try to conceal them, to pretend that they don't exist. People see everything, and they do not forgive insincerity. They do not consult such a leader, they do not bring him their problems. Yet the important thing is that different circumstances require manifestation of different qualities; sensitivity and adherence to principle are required in all circumstances.

I happened to witness a conversation between a secretary of a primary Party organization and a girl who had come to complain about a young man who had been false to her once. Everything said was correct, but bureaucratic. A week later the boy and girl came to him together and said that they had made up, that they loved one another. But the secretary insisted out of quasi-principle that the Party take up the young Communist's behavior. Such sanctimoniousness will hardly attract people's hearts to this secretary in future.

Sometimes incorrect ideas of what a leader should be like affect·the choice. A given Party member may have all the requisite work qualities but may not be able (or may not wish) to bang his fist on the table, speaking figuratively, and in every case to scold culprits "in bass tones," yet often people will say: "This Communist cannot be secretary," "He isn't firm," "Nobody will listen to him." Firmness and rudeness are two different things.

The point is that the tasks confronting Party organizations in higher educational institutions are constantly growing more complex, thanks to the development of science and improvement in the educational process. There is no one-dimensional answer to many questions. Both the advice of the collective and experimentation are necessary. And any encroachment by "strong personalities" on an organization's life opens the door to willful decisions, distracts people from a purely business-like attitude to problems, makes members cautious and restrains them—simply because they fear being misunderstood—from going to the Party bureau or Party committee with their ideas. Experience shows that Communists correctly understand their errors, and yelling or superfluous moralizing merely irritates them. The Party organi-

zation needs the development of criticism as much as it needs air, but the criticism must be polite, it must not lower a person's dignity and must help him to understand the substance of the criticism.

At the same time—and this must be stressed once again—a leader can never act as a nursemaid or evade making decisions on complex matters. The membership strives to avoid electing such a secretary. The correct policy is obviously to elect a person whose style of work is in keeping with tested Party requirements—reliance on collective action and on the method of persuasion.

Ideological Work.—The decisions of the 23rd C.P.S.U. Congress heighten the significance of ideology, of questions of the Marxist-Leninist education of cadres. In an organization such as ours ideological work comprises at least nine-tenths of all the work. After all, in higher educational institutions we do not train specialists merely by teaching them their future professions; we train them to be people with a Communist world outlook, with the traits of public figures.

There is much that is particular to the ideological upbringing of the younger generation, especially of students. Young people react sharply and do not tolerate ambiguities. Confronted by this or that specific fact, they sometimes exaggerate by generalizing. In their search for "truth" some young people refuse to wait for the logical course of events but strive to intervene in that course actively; they often make mistakes but in the end, under the influence of public organizations and of our entire life, they find the correct path.

Naturally, ideological work with students must be exceptionally flexible and have maximum mobility. It is necessary to be capable of responding to an unexpected turn of events with prompt, knowledgeable and very concrete replies to students' questions.

A great deal depends on the nature and extent of information. In this respect the most complex situation is that of students; and of all the higher schools in the country, that of Moscow's students, especially Moscow University's, is the most complex. At Moscow State University 2,800 envoys from more than 100 countries of the world study together with Soviet students. Among them are students from socialist countries (Czechoslovakia, Poland, Bulgaria, the Chinese People's Republic, the Democratic Republic of Vietnam and others); from large capitalist countries (the U.S.A., Britain, France, the Federal Republic of Germany, Canada and others); and from states that have won political independence comparatively recently (India, the United Arab Republic, Nigeria, Cameroon and others).

A feature of the body of Moscow State University students who have come from developed capitalist states and from young, developing states is that it includes representatives of the big and middle bourgeoisie, the feudal and tribal aristocracy and the merchant class. These people, brought up in the spirit of bourgeois ideology, sit next to Soviet students at lectures and seminars, meet them at the same tables in student dining rooms, share rooms with them at Student House. Here, within the walls of Moscow University, the bourgeois and communist philosophies often wage a sharp struggle for young people's minds. Face to face, argument against argument; the debates are not about the past, interpreted in tranquil circumstances, but about events taking place today. And an immediate reply must be given to the questions that arise.

Mobility of the means of ideological influence is very important in this struggle. The situation and the tasks change, and the most suitable organizational forms of ideological work are used to conform with them.

One of our most widespread forms of presenting political information is the lecture. Qualified groups of lecturers, specialists in international affairs, art history, literature and economics, are capable of giving prompt replies to burning questions. Such groups are the Party committee's most mobile ideological weapon. Talks and question-and-answer evenings provide good supplements to the lectures, for at these the speakers reply to additional questions asked by the more captious students, hear their doubts, and explain things to them.

The work of the special and social-science divisions [kafedry] within the departments has a special role in the ideological upbringing of students, which is planned to last the entire length of their stay at the university.

By order of Academician I. G. Petrovsky, rector of Moscow State University, all upperclassmen are assigned to teachers or professors in the special divisions for productive, all-round preparation for graduation. Personal guidance by the professor not only of his advisee's academic work but also of his civic upbringing plays an extraordinarily important role.

At the same time, the educators are educated too. This is a many-sided and complex process requiring great experience and a profoundly individual approach on the part of the Party organizations. One of the very popular concrete forms of such work is methodological seminars for scientists and scholars on philosophical problems in the natural sciences and the humanities.

The social-science divisions play a most important role in institutions of higher education. We have 16 such divisions. Teachers of the history of the

C.P.S.U., Marxist-Leninist philosophy, political economy and scientific communism in practical ways help undergraduates, graduate students, teachers and researchers to develop a communist outlook. The best members of the social-science divisions enjoy high prestige. Professors and Docents A. Azarova, A. Kozlov, N. Savinchenko, D. Ugrinovich, A. Tsagolov and N. Spiridonova are very popular among the students. The divisions have considerable scholarly achievements to their credit. The Moscow State University Learned Council awarded a Lomonosov Prize in 1965 to Prof. D. Chesnokov for his book "Historical Materialism."

At the same time, further strengthening of the prestige of the social-science teachers remains a prime task of the divisions' ideological work. This is natural. Considering that the social science staff members bear the main burden in the ideological upbringing of the student body, the Party organization should be particularly attentive to them. There are two tasks here: creation of the best possible conditions for research in the social-science divisions and constant improvement of instruction in Marxist-Leninist theory. These tasks are interconnected, and a great deal depends on the teachers themselves. . . .

Socialist Democracy and the Struggle Against Ideological Subversion

On the eve of the forthcoming Congress of our party, every Soviet person, looking back over the path that has been traversed, notes with a sense of satisfaction and pride how much richer the life of our society has become, how creative principles have flourished in it, how socialist democracy has gained strength, what an increase there has been in the people's confidence in their tomorrow and their desire to do all in their power so that this tomorrow may bring the nation new spiritual and material benefits.

Having put a decisive end to violations of Leninist norms in Party and

Reprinted from an Editorial, "Socialist Democracy and the Struggle Against Ideological Subversion," Pravda *(February 22, 1966). Translated in* Current Digest of the Soviet Press, *XVIII, No. 7 (Copyright © March 9, 1966), 9–10.*

state life and to manifestations of subjectivism, the Party opened up truly boundless vistas for the initiative and activity of the popular masses. All this contributes to the successful solution of the tasks of communist construction and the flourishing of the personality of the citizens of the Soviet land.

The restoration of Leninist norms in our life and the development of socialist democracy have had a most beneficial effect on Soviet culture. Writers and artists create ideologically significant works of high artistic value that foster the inculcation of communist traits in people's characters and exert a powerful influence on millions of individuals.

Soviet writers and artists, completely free in their work, in their choice of subject matter and form of composition, tell the truth about our life, about our great ideas and their embodiment, about the feelings and aspirations of the builders of communism. At the same time, they portray the shady sides of our reality in their works, criticizing everything that hinders our progress. This criticism is trenchant and strict. It reveals the high interest of the Soviet artistic intelligentsia, as of all the country's citizens, in the construction of communism, their solicitude for the welfare of their state, their society, their people.

Art and literature live and develop in our country in a fresh, pure atmosphere of universal, nationwide interest in the creative successes of cultural workers and of solicitude for them.

All this evokes the furious malice of the class enemies of the socialist system, who watch from abroad with growing anxiety how communism is being built in our country, how our society is growing stronger and more consolidated, how our great example is influencing all mankind, the whole world.

In these circumstances the ruling circles of the imperialist countries, resorting to the most diverse forms of struggle against socialism, pay special attention to ideological aggression, to ideological subversion against the socialist countries. They seek by every possible means to carry this struggle into the territory of the socialist countries, trying to catch on the rusty hook of the slogan "peaceful coexistence of ideologies" anyone who might bite on the hypocritical and lying phraseology about the "non-partisanship of democracy," about the "absolute freedom" of creative art, about the "apoliticism" of art, etc.

The Soviet artistic intelligentsia—remembering, as the C.P.S.U. Program stresses, that the peaceful coexistence of states with different systems does not mean a slackening of the ideological struggle—displays the necessary vigilance. Participating actively in the construction of the new society, its members stand firmly on the ground of a communist world outlook and wage an implacable offensive against bourgeois ideology.

But then it happened that two men who, camouflaged as honest writers, accepted a social assignment from our enemies and became in fact the executors of their ideological subversion, managed to sneak into the good, healthy, close-knit family of the Soviet artistic intelligentsia. We are referring to Sinyavsky and Daniel, who were caught red-handed and convicted by a Soviet court. As is known, they secretly and in violation of the law supplied their anti-Soviet compositions to foreign propaganda centers hostile to us, which employed them for purposes of subversive activities against the Soviet government, against the Soviet people.

Our readers remember the circumstances of the case. The trial of the criminals was public, open. It was covered by the press. The court hearings were conducted in strict conformity with the law. The criminals' guilt was fully proved. The just sentence handed down on calumniators met with the approval of Soviet people.

Naturally, in the imperialist headquarters of the ideological war they ground their teeth. The bourgeois press tried to use the trial of Sinyavsky and Daniel as a pretext for launching a new anti-Soviet campaign, expatiating on what it claimed was the violation of freedom and democracy in the Soviet Union. Oh, Messrs. liars and hypocrites. The Soviet people well know what "freedoms" of the capitalist world you advocate and would like to impose on the socialist countries: freedom for the ruthless exploitation by capital of hundreds of millions of working people, freedom for an insignificant minority to control the destinies of peoples, freedom to deceive and oppress the working people, freedom to propagandize war, reaction and malicious slander against the socialist countries, against Communists.

Our class enemies have been driven to frenzy and fury by the trial. They could not have reacted otherwise—this is how it has always been when their intrigues against the Soviet Union have failed.

Unfortunately, the campaign in defense of the two literary subversives, orchestrated on an unprecedented scale in the West, has disoriented some honest people. Apparently, lacking the necessary information and accepting the writings of the bourgeois press, which shamelessly ranks Sinyavsky and Daniel with Gogol and Dostoyevsky and claims that the trial concerned problems of literature and freedom of creative art, some progressive people became alarmed. They began to look for some concealed meaning in the trial of the two anti-Sovieteers: Was the development of democracy in the U.S.S.R. in jeopardy? Could it be that the freedom of creative art was being violated in the Soviet land?

Such far-fetched questions could only puzzle anyone acquainted with Soviet life. After all, the very investigation of Sinyavsky's and Daniel's crimes and the attentive, objective conduct of the trial are graphic proof of the democracy of the Soviet system.

Sinyavsky and Daniel were not tried as writers but as people who had committed criminal actions against the Soviet system, against the Soviet people and their revolutionary achievements.

And the secretariat of the board of the U.S.S.R. Writers' Union was perfectly justified in stating in its open letter published in Literaturnaya gazeta on Feb. 19: "The anti-Soviet actions of Sinyavsky and Daniel have been proved both by documents and by the evidence of witnesses. They were tried not for a special artistic style, as some bourgeois

newspapers claim—they were tried for deliberate calumny against the Soviet Union, against our state and social system, against the multinational Soviet people, against the Communist Party and the Soviet government. It is no accident that their compositions were immediately seized upon by the most rabid anti-Soviet troubadours abroad.

"***Drawing on the active support of millions upon millions of citizens, the Soviet state defends itself by means of its laws against all attempts to revile or undermine its principles and legal foundations."

As the open letter stresses, Soviet writers together with their people have rendered, are rendering and will continue to render their state unswerving support. "We have never concealed this and have no intention of concealing it," say the Soviet writers. "It is precisely because of this that the vile deeds of Sinyavsky and Daniel aroused in us indignation and condemnation, and the court's sentence, which is in keeping with the spirit and the letter of our law, has our approval."

One thing cannot be substituted for another by claiming that the defendants were punished for the "critical spirit" of their "works." Calumny was never a form of criticism, and malicious attacks dictated by hostile intentions can in no circumstances be equated with exposure of shortcomings.

As for the contentions of the foreign defenders of the calumniators with regard to democracy, they are directed to the wrong address. True to the behests of V. I. Lenin, the Soviet people are indefatigably and consistently creating the first truly democratic society in the history of mankind.

Let those who now prate about the "imperfection" or the "incompleteness" of socialist democracy recall how Lenin exposed Kautsky's hypocritical chatter in defense of the "beauties" of a certain "pure" democracy and his condemnation of the Soviet system, which, he claimed, excluded democracy altogether!

Lenin wrote: "The bourgeoisie and its supporters accuse us of violating democracy. We assert that the Soviet revolution has provided an unprecedented impetus to the development of democracy in both depth and breadth, democracy, moreover, for the working people and the masses oppressed by capitalism—therefore democracy for the vast majority of the people, therefore socialist (for the working people) democracy, unlike bourgeois (for the exploiters, for the capitalists, for the rich) democracy."

The Party strengthens and develops socialist democracy, drawing broader and broader masses of the people into the administration of the affairs of the state and society; it has done everything to preclude any repetition of those violations of legality that hampered the development of democracy. This is well known. But it is also well known that democracy is not a form of government that presupposes impunity for crimes. Democracy, as Marxism-Leninism teaches, is a form of the state, one of its varieties. It provides for effective measures against those who try to undermine the state system that was established by the will of the people and that provides the people with real, genuine, and not false, freedom.

Stressing that revolutionary power, acting in the interests of the overwhelming majority of the people, must be firm as iron, revolutionary in its boldness and speed, ruthless in suppressing its enemies, Lenin at the same time foresaw that as the basic task of government ceased to be military suppression and became administration, the court would become the typical form of suppressing enemies. And our court tries criminals under the law.

Having built socialism and started to build communism, we have risen to a new and higher stage in the development of democracy, and this has had a beneficial effect on the whole of social development. But even today, inasmuch as class enemies abroad continue their struggle against us, the Soviet people and the state of the entire people established by them must display unfaltering vigilance against the intrigues of these enemies and must cut them short. It would be strange, to say the least, to expect our court to adopt a "liberal approach" to the enemy's ideological spies, caught red-handed.

A. M. Gorky called on us to give a vigorous rebuff to capitalism, which opposes the creative work of the Land of Soviets from without, and at the same time to make no allowances for those people who, acting within the country, "help its [capitalism's] bandit aims to the extent of their vileness."

We are confident that all who hold dear the cause of democracy and socialism will understand us. Solidarity in the struggle against imperialism, persistence in the defense of the Leninist principles of socialist democracy, unity in evaluating the ideals of socialist humanism and the aims of social progress are of the highest significance for the victory of our common great ideas.

The C.P.S.U. and the Soviet state will continue to strengthen the socialist system in every possible way, to promote the flourishing of the people's creative forces, to protect as sacred every Soviet citizen's individual freedom, to educate all Soviet people in the spirit of selfless devotion to the homeland, in the spirit of unshakable loyalty to the ideas of communism.

The Soviet people, rallied closely round the Communist Party and the government, will continue to build communism in our country successfully, to develop and perfect our society, the most democratic history has ever known. They will continue to repulse energetically the ideological subversion of imperialism.

The Soviet people regard this as their duty to the socialist fatherland. They also regard this as their internationalist duty to the working people of the whole world.

Turncoats

D. YEREMIN

The enemies of communism are not squeamish. With what gusto do they dish up any "sensation" gleaned from the garbage heap of anti-Sovietism! That was what happened some time ago. The bourgeois press and radio started coming out with reports of the "groundless arrest" in Moscow of two "men of letters" who had published anti-Soviet lampoons abroad. What a field day the unclean consciences and equally unclean imaginations of Western propagandists had! And here they are, already painting in sweeping strokes a mythical "purge in Soviet literary circles," alleging that these circles "are extremely alarmed at the threat of a new campaign" against "anticommunist-minded writers" and against "liberal intellectual circles" in general.

The question is: What really happened? What has so heartened the black host of anti-Sovieteers? Why have individual foreign intellectuals, who look out of place in this company, fallen into its embrace? Why do certain gentlemen strike the pose of mentors, all but protectors, of our morals, and

Reprinted from D. Yeremin, "Turncoats," Izvestia (January 13, 1966). Translated in Current Digest of the Soviet Press, XVIII, No. 2 (Copyright © February 2, 1966), 11.

pretend they are defending the two renegades "on behalf of" the Soviet intelligentsia? There is only one answer: In the ideological battles between the two worlds, the enemies of the new society are not particularly scrupulous as to means. And when a couple of turncoats turn up in their trenches, they hasten to heroize them, for want of something better. For those impoverished in spirit, such turncoats are a windfall they have longed for. After all, with their aid one can try to confuse public opinion, sow the poisonous seeds of unprincipledness, nihilism and morbid interest in shady "problems of life."

In brief, the enemies of communism found what they were looking for—two renegades, for whom duplicity and shamelessness had become a credo. Hiding behind the pseudonyms of Abram Tertz and Nikolai Arzhak, for several years they had been secretly sending foreign publishing houses dirty libels against their country, against the Party and against the Soviet system, and having them published abroad. One of them, A Sinyavsky, alias A. Tertz, published articles of literary criticism in Soviet magazines, wormed his way into the Writers' Union, and outwardly shared the aspirations of its Statutes— "to serve the people, to show in lofty artistic form the greatness of the ideas of communism" and "through all one's creative work and public activity to take an active part in the building of communism." The second, Yu. Daniel-N. Arzhak, did translations. But this was all just a false front for them. It concealed something else: hatred of our system and foul mockery of what is dearest to our motherland and people.

The first thing you feel in reading their works is revulsion. It is repugnant to cite the vulgarities in which the pages of their books abound. Both delve into sexual and psychopathological "problems" with morbid lust. Both exhibit the utmost moral degradation. Both bespatter paper with everything that is most vile and filthy.

Here are typical specimens of their writing: "Women looking like castrated men," wrote Daniel-Arzhak in one of his "works," "walk the streets and boulevards. Short-legged, like pregnant dachshunds, or long-legged, like ostriches, they conceal swellings and bruises beneath their dresses, lace themselves into corsets and stuff brassieres with padding where their breasts ought to be."

If it is an Academician being described, then he "downs another glass and behold, he's already stuffing the host's silver into his pockets." If it is a girl secretary in a newspaper office, then she is "available to any proofreader." As for adult women, the less said the better. For instance, certain Solomon Moiseyevich's "wife, a lascivious Russian wench, ran away, after first robbing him and then misbehaving with a 16-year-old barber. He knew women and feared them, and with good reason. But what could he understand of the Russian national character, this Solomon Moiseyevich?!'"

One cannot fail to note here the following detail: Russian by birth, Andrei Sinyavsky hides behind the name Abram Tertz. Why? For purposes of provocation! By publishing anti-Soviet stories and novelettes in foreign publications under the pseudonym of Abram Tertz, Sinyavsky was trying to create the impression that anti-Semitism exists in our country, that presumably an author with the name of Abram Tertz must look for publishers in the West if he wishes to write "candidly" about Soviet life. A miserable provocation, which gives away the writer and his bourgeois sponsors.

They find nothing pleasing in our country, nothing in its multinational culture is sacred to them; they are ready to vilify and defame everything that is dear to Soviet man, whether it belongs to the present or the past. Just imagine what they wrote about Anton Pavlovich Chekhov, the outstanding Russian humanist, whose creative work stirs the good in man. Only the utmost shamelessness could move a pen that traces out such lines as: "Oh, to grab this Chekhov by his tubercular little beard and shove his nose into his consumptive phlegm!" And the Russian classics, the pride of world literature—what do they say about them? "The classics—those are what I hate most of all!'"

These scribblers attempt to sling mud at and slander our Soviet Army, whose immortal exploit saved the peoples of Europe from extermination by Hitlerism.

For Soviet people, for the peoples of the earth, for all progressive mankind, no name is more sacred than the name of the leader of our revolution, Vladimir Ilyich Lenin. After all, Lenin is the age of socialist revolutions and national-liberation movements. He is our era, which has changed the world. He is scientific communism, which is being embodied in man's glorious deeds. Even prominent captains of capitalism have bowed their heads before Lenin—on more than one occasion they have had to admit that the 20th century found in him the greatest transformer of life.

To what a bottomless morass of abomination must a so-called man of letters sink to desecrate with his hooligan's pen this name that is sacred to us! It is impossible to repeat the relevant passages here, so malicious is this scribble, so outrageous and filthy! These blasphemous lines alone suffice for the diagnosis that the authors place themselves outside Soviet society. . . .

THE POLITY
IN THE U.S.S.R.:

The American View

The Party in the
Political System; Membership

ALFRED G. MEYER

If we were to single out one central point on which the Constitution of the USSR presents an unrealistic image of the political system, it might be its failure to account for the role of the Communist Party and its relations with the formal or "constitutional" government structure. The Constitution, in all its 146 Articles, mentions the Party but once, almost as an afterthought, in Chapter X, dealing with the rights and duties of citizens. Article 126 in this chapter reads as follows:

In conformity with the interests of the working people, and in order to develop

the organizational initiative and political activity of the masses of the people, the citizens of the USSR are guaranteed the right to unite in public organizations; trade unions, cooperative societies, youth organizations, sport and defense organizations, cultural, technical, and scientific societies; and the most active and politically conscious citizens in the ranks of the working class, working peasants, and working intelligentsia voluntarily unite in the Communist Party of the Soviet Union, which is the vanguard of the working people in their struggle to build a communist society and is the leading core of all organizations of the working people, both societal and governmental.

The Constitution thus recognizes the Party as the "leading core" of the political system and in this fashion summarizes the work of over 9 million people in a vast and all-embracing web of organizations, engaged in as broad a range of activities as any government of a large modern state. Even the formal participation of the Party in the governmental process cannot be summed up in such laconic fashion. From reading the Constitution, one could never guess, for instance, that decrees or regulations issued by the Party have the force of law within the entire society, or that Party agencies play a decisive role in the recruitment of personnel on all levels of the political system, from the highest to the lowest, whether the office be elective or appointive. Nor would one guess that discussion of public issues takes place almost exclusively within the confines of the Party structure, and that the policies and administrative decisions derived from this discussion are formulated by the Party rather than the "constitutional" government. In fact, from reading the Constitution alone one would not guess that the Soviet political system is governed by the Party far more than by the government itself.

The question has at times been asked, not indeed why a Constitution should have been written which so much distorts actual political relationships within the government, but rather why the Party, which governs the USSR, has troubled to create, in addition to its own sprawling political machine, a separate governmental structure no less sprawling and no less complicated. From all this it is obvious that we shall have to go far beyond the Soviet Constitution to examine the place of the Communist Party within the political system and its precise relations to the formal governmental apparatus.

In beginning with this attempt to place the Party within the total political system, we are reversing the order of presentation customarily observed in books on Soviet government. Usually,

authors begin by outlining the history of the Party and then proceed to present its formal structure; only after this do they get around to a discussion of the way in which this structure meshes with the larger social organization and the functions of the Party within the total system. By reversing this order, the present book may seem to violate the logic of historical presentation, but may add clarity to the reader's understanding of the larger whole within which the Party operates.

. . . In discussing the composition of the CPSU it is essential to distinguish between two basic types of members, the rank-and-file and the *aktiv*. Rank-and-file members are those whose activities as Party members are part-time only, because they earn their living by holding jobs in some non-Party agency. They are thus performing their Party work in addition to their more regular duties. The *aktiv*, in contrast, comprises those people whose employer is the Party and who are therefore full-time Party officials—professional communists, as it were. In this brief survey of the Party membership, we shall begin by talking about the Communist Party as a whole, and then go into some detail first with regard to rank-and-file members, then move up to the *aktiv* and through them to the very top of the party elite.

At its twenty-second Congress in 1961, the Communist Party of the Soviet Union announced that it had roughly 8.9 million members and about 840,000 candidate members. In April of 1963, Mr. Khrushchev announced that the total number of members and candidates had come to exceed ten million.[1] To this number it might be useful, at least for certain purposes, to add the 19 million members of the Party's youth affiliate, the All-Union Leninist Com-

---

[1] *Izvestia*, 26 April 1963.

munist Union of Youth (VLKSM or Komsomol).[2]

The Party might be described as a "cadre" party with a generous sprinkling of industrial workers and a very small peasant component. Whereas some of the working-class members might be actual workers at the bench, the relatively few collective farmers within the ranks of the Party are very likely to hold some leadership position, such as team foreman or farm chairman. The term "cadre" in Soviet parlance is synonymous with "elite" as used by Western social scientists. It denotes the leading personnel of any organization or group, the commanders and their essential staffs. The definition of the CPSU as a cadre party therefore means that its leaders have sought to recruit into its ranks the leading citizens of the Soviet Union, those men and women who hold positions of authority, responsibility, and prestige, those who by virtue of their status within the community are opinion-makers or -manipulators. If we knew the social composition of the Party membership more precisely, we would therefore also have a fairly sensitive gauge of the importance Party leaders attach to various positions within society. As it is, the statistical information we do possess is too vague to be of much use, and we therefore complement our insufficient factual knowledge with unreliable impressions. According to these impressions, the peasantry is vastly under-represented in contrast to, for example, the engineering profession which sends a sizable portion of its numbers into the Party. The most general observa-

tion would be that the higher a person's rank within his profession, the more likely will he be a Party member. Given equal rank, a person holding a line job is a more likely recruit than one holding a staff job—that is, an administrator more likely than a professional expert. Thus physicians or professors are far less likely to be Party members than hospital administrators and deans; statisticians, attorneys, or lathe operators less likely than factory managers, judges, or shop foremen. Many responsible positions or ranks within the society can be expected to be held only by Party members. These would probably include generals in the armed forces, police officers of field grade, public prosecutors, federal or republican cabinet ministers, and perhaps many other categories. . . .

. . . The duties of a Party member may be summarized as follows. First, he is to provide to the individual citizens outside the Party all those services and all that guidance which Party organizations render to organizations and agencies throughout the Soviet political system. In order to be equipped for rendering this service, the Party member must unceasingly educate himself in at least two ways. First, he must become familiar with the Party's general ideology, including knowledge not only of its broad goals, but also of its history, institutions, and procedures, down to the very language spoken by initiates. Second, he must keep himself informed as intimately as possible about current public issues, policies, and goal priorities. The Party member must be both indoctrinated and a well-informed ctizen. The member attains this knowledge through a variety of means. He may receive formal schooling in Party schools, ranging from top leadership academies to lectures and discussions organized by primary organizations. More informally, members

[2] For recent statistics regarding the numbers and distribution of Party members as regards locality, nationality, profession, and the like, see "KPSS v tsifrakh, 1956–1961 gg.," *Partiinaia Zhizn*, No. 1 (1962); also "Kommunisticheskaia Partiia Sovetskogo Soiuza." *Politicheskoe Samoobrazovanie*, No. 7 (1963).

gain information through contact with their primary organizations, through the media of communications—even through the rumor mill, that most informal but effective educational institution which seems to play an important role in the Soviet political system. As any reader who attempts to keep himself informed in a complex world knows, the urge toward self-education is a tremendous burden on any individual, and it is an almost Sisyphean labor, because one can never learn enough. But in addition, the CPSU member is expected to be an activist and model citizen. "Activism," in this context, means serving in a great variety of civic duties, such as election campaigns, civil defense work, or promotions of special projects; the activist might be described as a pace-setter in civic volunteer work. And, more broadly, as a model citizen the Party member is expected to lead a life above reproach. Party members are presumed to be more informed, more intelligent, more self-disciplined moral, and law-abiding than the general citizenry. It may be argued that they have more ample opportunity to conceal their lapses from moral standards, less need to violate many laws, and a good deal of protection, through their political contacts, when they get into trouble. But at the same time courts and other authorities deal more severely with offenders who are in the Party than with those who are not for, they argue, Party members must live up to a higher standard of expectations.

From all this it must be plain that Party membership is a formidable responsibility which a Soviet citizen is not likely to undertake light-heartedly or on the spur of the moment. Obviously, it carries with it a great deal of extra work and extra worry. Moreover, it places the individual in a far more exposed position from that of the ordinary citizen. As his status rises to that of an acknowledged civic leader, his responsibilities also increase, and with them the possibilities of being criticized censured, demoted, and punished. The high and mighty fall harder than the meek and low. The party can be a hard taskmaster, and its severest sanction —expulsion—is difficult to bear. No one leaves the Party voluntarily; hence, to be a former Party member probably is worse than never having been a member at all. An expelled member must feel like an outcast. His status in the Soviet system is analogous to that of a defrocked priest among believers. To these disadvantages of membership one other should perhaps be added: the negative deference which broad strata of the population have given in the past, and may still be giving today, to Party members. Certainly, up to the time of World War II considerable portions of the population, especially among the peasantry and national minorities, looked upon the Party with hatred and contempt. Membership therefore had the effect of alienating the individual from the people, of erecting a wall of hostility between members and non-members. This predisposition, however, may be disappearing; our evidence about it is somewhat dated.

...We have only the sketchiest knowledge about the actual process of recruitment from rank-and-file Party membership into the *aktiv*. It seems to involve several steps, or possible lines of advancement, all of them related to either loyalty or competence, the two major criteria for recruitment of Party members ever since 1917. Among the skills and competences that lead to advancement into the *aktiv*, the most important appears to be managerial success. Directors of economic enterprises who consistently succeed in attaining their production goals; collective farm chairmen who have demonstrated their ability to rouse the energies of the peasants and harness them to the purposes of the regime; production engineers who have shown themselves inventive and forceful in raising the efficiency of their plants; trade union officials who by their personality, bargaining skills, or organizational talent manage to contribute to a rise in the productivity of labor—people with these and similar talents the Party seeks for its own leadership. The skills the Party needs, in short, are competence in the manipulation of men, and the ability to make people identify with the Party's goals and successfully to attain them.

By themselves, however, such skills are insufficient prerequisites for co-option into the Party *aktiv*. They must be supplemented by something we have called political loyalty, but which might more aptly be described as political sensitivity. Let us note first of all that this sensitivity is intimately related to the productive and administrative skills the Party seeks. For one thing, political sensitivity is itself one of the indispensable items in the equipment of the capable administrator, manipulator, or producer; conversely, the shrewd organization man who possesses these various talents soon learns that he will succeed only if he shows himself to be in tune with the prevailing political climate. Lasting success in the Soviet political system can come only to those who show both competence and political sensitivity.

To describe this sensitivity we might break it down into a number of components. Perhaps the most basic element is unquestioning acceptance of the political system, a fundamental conformism or conservatism and a concomitant readiness to adjust one's behavior, goals, and personality to prevailing patterns—the frame of mind David Riesman has called "other-directedness."

Beyond this, however, those who wish to advance in the Party must manifest doctrinal soundness by being able to demonstrate substantial knowledge of the Party's history and sacred writings and by mastering the Party jargon. The aspirant to higher office must be able to express all problems, issues, policies, and events in approved terms and must be able to understand the Party's esoteric code of communication. These aptitudes, in turn, will give him another element of political sensitivity, namely the ability to sense the ever-changing hierarchy of values, standards, and priorities of the top leadership. Political sensitivity is both manifested and improved by a man's loyalty to those top commanders who win—and if he does not have such loyalty, he must at least seem to have it.

The personality syndrome of people who present this kind of image to the Party leadership is that complicated and contradictory mixture of traits that has been dubbed "organization man," a personality type with whom, supposedly, the commanding heights of our governmental, educational, and corporate bureaucracies abound. It is a strange mixture of ruthlessness and subservience, deviousness and sheer hard work; it combines timidity with inventiveness, imagination, and the daring to experiment; high regard for regular procedure, conformity, and fear of responsibility. Moreover, while it presupposes intelligence, it discourages narrow expertise: the professional politician must be a generalist, able to ask questions, to pick brains, to make use of his staff, but not unduly burdened by special knowledge, with the versatility of the dilettante where public issues are concerned.

An attempt to refine this vague image would be intriguing, but it is doubtful whether we have impressions sufficient even for making informed guesses. Among the questions it would be useful to investigate would be, for example, the importance of camaraderie and social contacts within the Soviet political elite. How important a method is it for those who wish to gain entrance into the *aktiv?* A much more complicated and controversial problem would be to compare more carefully the successful professional politician in the USSR with the successful executive in the United States. To be sure, we have pointed out broad similarities of personality requirements, but within these requirements there doubtless are subtle or not-so-subtle differences. The prevalence in the USSR of a formal doctrine, an elaborate official ideology that must be mastered, is one obvious difference. Another seems to be the continued preference of the Party *aktiv* for production engineers, as against the growing predominance of marketing and public relations specialists in the American corporate elite, and lawyers in the political one. Furthermore, it would be interesting to substantiate the persistent impression that the Soviet political elite recruits people of more openly ruthless and violent disposition, persons who are less open-minded and more authoritarian than corporate executives in the United States. Even if these impressions could be substantiated, the findings might have no more than ephemeral validity, if it is assumed that, with its growing heterogeneity and maturity, the Soviet political system too will have increasing need for negotiators and bargainers, for urbane and bland manipulators and persuaders rather than local and provincial replicas of the despotic man of steel who imposed his will on a reluctant and recalcitrant peasant population.

The Administered Society: Totalitarianism Without Terror

ALLEN KASSOF

"As an orchestra conductor sees to it that all the instruments sound harmonious and in proportion, so in social and political life does the Party direct the efforts of all people toward the achievement of a single goal.

"Each person must, like a bee in the hive, make his own contribution to increasing the material and spiritual wealth of society. People may be found who say that they do not agree with this, that it is coercion of the individual, a return to the past. To this my answer is: We are living in an organized

Reprinted by permission of the editors from Allen Kassof, "The Administered Society: Totalitarianism Without Terror," World Politics *(July, 1964), pp. 558–562, 567–568, 572–575. Copyright © 1964.*

socialist society where the interests of the individual conform to the interests of society and are not at variance with them."—Nikita Khrushchev, March 8, 1963.[1]

More than a decade after Stalin's death, the time is ripe for a fresh view of Soviet society. Many of the conventional patterns of analysis, developed largely during the period of Stalinist absolutism, seem to be no longer adequate for this purpose. This article proposes that a new concept, the "administered society," may be useful in summarizing and evaluating recent changes in the Soviet system and in identifying current trends.

Like other ideal-typical concepts, that of the administered society by no means pretends to account for all of the concrete detail of a social order. Instead, it draws attention (through emphasis, and hence a certain exaggeration) to very general features which constitute a society's ethos or prevailing themes— in the Soviet case, centering around the drive of the regime to establish a highly organized and totally coordinated society, and the consequences of that drive.

The administered society can be defined as one in which an entrenched and extraordinarily powerful ruling group lays claim to ultimate and exclusive scientific knowledge of social and historical laws and is impelled by a belief not only in the practical desirability, but the moral necessity, of planning, direction, and coordination from above in the name of human welfare and progress.

Convinced that there should be complete order and predictability in human affairs, the elite is concerned not merely with the "commanding heights," but also to an overwhelming degree with the detailed regulation of

the entire range of social life, including those institutions which, in the West, typically have been regarded as lying beyond the legitimate scope of public authority and political intervention. The rulers of the administered society refuse to grant the possibility of unguided coordination and integration; they believe, on the contrary, that not only the masses but responsible subgroups (for example, the professions) are incapable of maintaining a viable social order on their own, without the precise and detailed supervision of an omniscient political directorate. The elite believes, and through a far-reaching program of education and propaganda tries to teach its subjects, that the only possible good society is one that is *administered*.

The administered society is thus a variant of modern totalitarianism, with the important difference that it operates by and large without resort to those elements of gross irrationality (in particular, the large-scale and often self-defeating use of psychological terror and physical coercion as basic means of social control) that we have come to associate with totalitarian systems in recent decades.

The administered society, however, should be distinguished from the conventional welfare state in that it is not involved simply or principally in creating minimal conditions of social welfare within an otherwise pluralistic political framework, but instead treats welfare as an incidental—and instrumental—element in the larger scheme of social planning and reform. While an administered society may display more or fewer welfare features of a material or service nature, they are neither final goals nor the most im-

[1] Reported in *Pravda* and *Izvestia*, March 10, 1963; translation from *Current Digest of the Soviet Press*, xv, No. 11 (April 23, 1963).

portant determinants of overall policy. To put it another way, the elite regards the promotion of total coordination as itself the ultimate form of welfare under modern conditions.

Plainly enough, the administered society is not the authentic good society of faithful Marxists, for it is characterized by the growing size and importance of an elite party and state bureaucracy, in contrast to the withering away of governmental apparatus which Marxism predicts and upon which it insists.

Nor, finally, should the administered society be confused with a rational technocracy, even though here there are some superficial parallels. The leadership of the administered society, to be sure, is forced to rely on scientific and technical cadres as sources of essential information and in the execution of highly complex economic and social planning. But the political elite is not bound solely or principally by considerations of technical rationality; the technicians and experts operate only under license of the political elite and in terms of the latter's self-proclaimed ultimate knowledge about the proper uses of science and technology in the larger socio-historical setting. The experts, in short, are servants rather than masters or even independent practitioners. They lack the power of veto on grounds of technical rationality over political decisions (though in the end the limits of technology itself, if not the will of the technocrats, of course impose certain restraints). And their potential for independent influence in the society is decisively cut short by the elite's consistent practice of defining *all* decision-making as political and therefore beyond the competence of any group other than itself. Similar considerations are applied —if anything, with more vigor—to the producers of the more "esoteric" goods and services—the artists and writers,

professors and critics and journalists. Like technicians in the more literal sense, they are construed by the elite as turning out "commodities" whose creation, distribution, and consumption demand coordination from above in the pursuit of order and planned progress.

Let us see how this preliminary definition of the administered society can be applied to an understanding of Soviet developments, and with what advantages.

By now it must be clear even to the most reluctant analyst that the cumulative change in Soviet society since Stalin's death is too great to dismiss as merely superficial. The transformation of Soviet society during this period, though by no means a wholesale departure from earlier patterns, nevertheless has been extensive. The conventional label for this change has been "liberalization." The reference point is to the state of Soviet totalitarianism under Stalin and to the degree of departure from that condition.

To be sure, the totalitarian model could only approximate the underlying reality. Even at the zenith of Stalinism, we know, there were major and numerous exceptions to the effective realization of absolute despotism. Piecemeal information such as the testimony of refugee informants showed that many individuals were able to preserve for themselves or to create tiny islands of privacy and to maintain attitudes of doubt and skepticism about the system in the face of the relentless propaganda that penetrated every corner of the society. We know, too, that in the midst of what was surely the most thoroughgoing system of political and social controls ever devised, there were widespread and patterned evasions of official demands in places high and low. The factory manager engaged in self-defensive falsification of production statistics; the peasant stealing time from the collectivized sector to work on his private plot; clandestine listeners to forbidden foreign radio broadcasts—these and other types are amply familiar to students of Stalinist Russia. For those who were caught (as well as for many of the totally innocent) the costs were horrendous, often final. But even at its most extreme the system of surveillance and punishments did not stamp out pockets of resentment, awareness, inner resistance.

Nevertheless, if Soviet totalitarianism under Stalin was not exactly an Orwellian 1984 and if, in important respects, it departed from the analysts' model of the totalitarian society, it came very close indeed (perhaps as close as is possible in a modern complex society) to approximating that model. Extraordinary was the near-completeness, if not actual totality, of the invasion of society by Party and State. The efforts to regulate in minute detail cultural activity, patterns of material consumption and taste, attitudes towards love and friendship, professional routine and aspiration, scholarly research, moral virtue, recreation and leisure, informal social relationships, sex and child-bearing and childrearing—these efforts, though far from always successful, had the most profound effects in creating a condition of unfreedom. If one also recalls the elaborate development of control mechanisms designed to promote the institutionalization of anxiety (that state of affairs in which even the most innocent act is likely to be arbitrarily greeted with harsh and capricious punishment), then it is clear that the Soviet system under Stalin, by any practical definition, was totalitarian.

It is also clear that substantial liberalization has taken place since the dictator's death. But this measure, useful in many ways, creates very serious problems in analysis and evaluation. For although liberalization tells something about where the Soviet system has come from, it does not say very much about where it is *going*. To say that the system is being liberalized is like walking away backwards from a receding reference point, a procedure that gives too little information about what lies on the road ahead. After all, if the society has become less totalitarian, then what is it? To conclude, in effect, that it is still more of the same but somehow less so than it used to be may be essentially correct, but it is not a very satisfactory answer. And the understandable fascination with the political drama of on-and-off-again de-Stalinization has led to a partial neglect of its *social* consequences—in some quarters, too, to an imprecise assumption that political liberalization (the moderation of one-man despotism and the probably genuine efforts to avoid extreme abuses of absolute power) also spells some kind of broad social liberalization (even leading, perhaps, to a form of society more familiar—and less antagonistic? —to the Western experience).

Indeed, it may be that the use of liberalization as the key criterion for measuring changes in Soviet society is responsible for some of the confusion and disagreement among analysts of various persuasions. Thus, those of a conservative or pessimistic disposition have been inclined to deny that the changes are so significant (or that some of them have really taken place) because of the implication that liberalization also means *liberation,* a prospect they reject as too unlikely; while their more optimistic colleagues (especially those who see in Khrushchevism the harbinger of a welfare state) have attached far more significance to the same developments.

The core of the difficulty lies in the fact that, under Stalin, there was an amalgamation of totalism with terror and coercion, and that we may have overlearned a lesson about the necessary association between the two on the basis of that highly convincing record. The concept of the administered society is proposed as a way of saying that there can be totalism *without* terror; it recognizes that the changes in the Soviet Union have been real and vast (after all, totalism without terror is something new); but it insists that, far from developing alternatives to totalism, Soviet society is being subjected to new and more subtle forms of it, and that the Stalinist past is being streamlined rather than rejected. . . .

. . .Far from loosening their grip on the new generation in comparison with their practice in Stalin's time, the Komsomol and Pioneers have been involved in intensive efforts to extend their network of influence, both in membership coverage and in the range of youth activities that they originate or supervise. It is true that some steps have been taken to reduce some of the most extreme consequences of excessive bureaucratization and neglect of local interests and, at the most recent Komsomol Congress in 1962, there was some guarded talk about democratizing the internal structure.[2] But a close examination of the recent Komsomol record suggests that the impulse for such changes comes not so much from a serious intention to democratize the youth program as to alter its widespread reputation as boring, repressive, and offensive in order to make it more appealing to youth. At the same time there has been no sign at all of a withdrawal from interference in personal life; if anything, the reforms are meant to make that interference more effective by replacing swivel-chair

organizers with energetic enthusiasts who will not be afraid to grapple directly with problems of youthful nonconformity.

Certainly it is true, as in other areas of Soviet life, that the resort to coercion and threat has become less important than under Stalin. But their replacement with more reasoned tactics of persuasion should not be taken as surrender of the principle of total involvement and control. On the contrary, the youth program is now regarded as more essential than under Stalin, for it has become increasingly important to remind the new generation—which does not share the caution born of experience in the old days—not to confuse the relatively more benign outward character of Khrushchevism with a grant of autonomy. A genuine test of change in the youth sector would be a surrender (more realistically, a partial surrender) of the organizations' claim to a monopoly over formal and informal youth activities. Concretely, such a step might take the form of allowing youngsters (especially in higher educational institutions) not to join if they have no desire to do so. But there has been no change in the Komsomol's policy of covering an ever-larger proportion of those of eligible age, including 100 per cent of the university students and large majorities of key categories of young professionals. And the Pioneer organization, as before, continues to maintain total coverage in its group. Finally, the content of the youth program (as revealed in recent policy literature) centers around renewed efforts to exercise total control over the young on the grounds that the reforms now make the organizations such benign and authoritative agencies of society that no one could possibly object to their paternalistic concern.

. . .The passion for organization, for perfect coordination and integration of

[2] *Komsomol'skaia pravda,* April 18, 1962, 2. A detailed discussion of the youth organizations since Stalin is given in the author's forthcoming study, *The Soviet Youth Program* (Harvard University Press).

social life—a kind of compulsive's dream of beehive order projected upon an entire society—has partly replaced the original impetus of Bolshevik ideology. The denial that there can be any real conflict in the good society, the belief that all legitimate human needs can be satisfied simultaneously, that interest groups are subversive, that only uninformed selfishness or disregard of organizational principles stands between the present and the utopia of the future —these are some of the ingredients of the new ideology. If it lacks some of the romantic appeal of barricade-storming, it is perhaps no less revolutionary in its consequences, for its purveyors insist that they will not rest until all societies have undergone the transformation to superorganization. Its potential impact on an audience, say, of hard-pressed political leaders and court philosophers of developing nations may be considerable, for the idea of total coordination must tempt many of them as the answer to problems and frustrations of economic backwardness and the awkward necessities of coping with competing political ·interests. And for mentalities especially sensitive to the real and apparent disarray of human affairs or philosophically intolerant of ambiguity in social structure, there is, after all, a great utopian charm in such an image: much like the classical Marxist formula of salvation, it seems to promise a final answer to the centuries-old dislocations generated by modernism and science and a return to a latter-day version of a medieval world where everything—and everyone—apparently had a proper place in the universe.

Assuming this assessment of the basic aspirations of the Soviet regime to be correct, there is the quite different question of how far they are likely to be realized in practice. Naturally it would be unrealistic to expect complete and literal fulfillment of the dream, any more than one could have expected perfect totalitarianism to exist under Stalin. The issue, then, is how closely it will or can be approximated. Without going into the kind of detailed discussion that is far beyond the scope of these early notes, the best that can be done is to suggest some of the factors in a balance sheet of probabilities.

In the background is the ancient dilemma of how to combine personal with public interest in such ways as to put an end to politics. If the record of other complex societies (not to mention the history of the Soviet Union itself) is a guide, we may be excused for having serious doubts about such a grandiose conception. To deny that there is social conflict, as the Soviet leadership essentially does, is not to be rid of it. Even the most superficial reading of the Soviet press daily provides an endless catalogue of the stresses and strains arising from the pursuit of private or group interests against the demands for conformity emanating from the center. Some of the examples are petty, more of them are serious, all of them reflect the underlying tensions of an imperfectly coordinated society; they usually fall short of posing immediate threats to the political directorate but often have cumulative consequences of an unplanned and unintended nature. Moreover, broad areas of deviant behavior and subversive attitudes which once were suppressed by the application of prophylactic terror now have to be handled by more patient and indirect means. It is too early to say whether the new machinery of social control will be as adequate to the task as was pure Stalinism.

Then there is the paradoxical discovery, finally dawning on the regime, that the gradual alleviation of extreme material want that has been behind so many traditional problems may produce new and more subtle issues of control over a long-deprived population experiencing relative affluence for the first time. Failures to satisfy these wants are the obvious danger; success breeds more subtle risks, however, for a rising standard of living (as we have seen in the case of other industrial nations) often results in new forms of emotional investment that are to a great extent antithetical to the high level of public commitment obviously essential in realizing the administered society. We already have some evidence of this in the form of a troublesome youth problem in the Soviet Union: one of the greatest headaches of the post-Stalin regime has been how to prevent the drive for individual advancement and the intoxication with consumption from becoming the basis for a privatism that could easily wreck long-term intentions. So far the problem has been most visible among youth, but there is reason to believe that it is widespread.

To these and equally powerful impediments in the road to the administered society—for example, the articulate and sometimes effective objections of at least parts of the scientific, artistic, and intellectual communities to being as totally mobilized as they were under Stalin—must be added the even more vexing "technical" problem of *how* to administer and coordinate an entire enormous society effectively even in the absence of any special opposition. Yet when all this is said, what stands out is the remarkable success of the Soviet regime, during and since Stalin's day, in making a very impressive start.

Most important is the fact that, during almost half a century of Communist rule, the possibilities for alternative institutional forms have been largely wiped out. Even were the will to democratic or pluralistic institutions substantially present—and it is not—it is highly doubtful that the resources currently available by way of formal structures, source philosophies, or practical experience would go very far. The Bolshevization of a society, if it goes on long enough, is an irreversible process, because it is so intense and so total that it indelibly alters not only earlier institutional forms but the entire pattern of a population's expectations of reasonable and workable alternative possibilities for social order. This is not to say that the Soviet leaders have mastered history, for even a process that is irreversible can move forward in unintended and undesired directions. But the prospects of developing viable substitutes for a social system that has so long been based upon extreme and centralized organization are very poor. Ironically, the regime is probably correct—at least in the case of Soviet society—when it insists that any form of pluralism is impossible. The best that can be expected is a more or less benign totalism within the limits of the administered society, with a very slow erosion of the Bolshevik heritage; the worst, a surrender of good intentions to manage the society without terror and a return in some form to the excesses and cruelties of classical Stalinism.

How one evaluates this situation depends on his general political outlook and his preferences about the good society. Surely no one will deny that the Soviet citizen is, in the most elementary sense, better off today than he was under Stalin. And certainly no one will claim that the Soviet citizen prefers to be brutalized as he was then. Still, the thoroughgoing bureaucratization, the superorganization, of social life contains a special nightmare quality of its own even when shorn (as probably it must be if it is to operate efficiently) of raw psychic brutality and terror. And the easing of the terror, while an obviously welcome development, also has the consequence of diminishing the awareness of living in an essentially closed society and of reducing the capacity to act from moral indignation towards a freer life.

Perhaps the concept of the administered society, in this preliminary form, errs on the side of pessimism by making too much of the dream and not enough of the sheer confusion of reality. Daily life in the Soviet Union is far richer, far more problematical to its rulers, far less certain than an abstraction can depict; no doubt the framework of this modest idea will have to be considerably filled in before it can be of much use in practical analysis. But it does call attention to the inadequacy of the liberalization formula in understanding contemporary Soviet developments and the new ideology driving the regime. And if this is the dream of the post-Stalin leadership, then the Soviet system under Khrushchev may be moving not towards its Western counterparts but even farther away from them. If Khrushchev and his heirs succeed, the developments of the last decade in the Soviet Union will have been only a tactical regrouping on the march from a relatively primitive to a far more advanced variety of twentieth-century totalitarianism.

III

SOCIAL

STRATIFICATION

Stratification is probably the single most emotionally involved aspect of both American and Soviet societies. To some degree each of the two societies owes its existence to the goal of a radical alteration in the established systems of stratification; each represents an effort to change what were considered unfair modes. Stratification, of course, refers to equality and inequality; it is a polite designation for the relatively enduring forms of inequalities which set apart groups or classes of people. In the realm of stratification we may observe similarities between the United States and the U.S.S.R. with less strain than elsewhere (except for social problems). One among these is a gradual, at times barely perceptible, abandonment of the original goals of equality which each society set out to accomplish. In the final analysis, the claims put forward by the spokesmen of both societies were reduced to that of "equality of opportunity," a concept more nebulous and difficult to define than "equality" or "classlessness." Furthermore, by this device apologists of both social systems can shift the blame from their social institutions to the individual: after all, as long as opportunities are equal, the people who do not make the best of their opportunities—not society— are at fault. This is an argument used with varying degrees of explicitness, by both conservative American politicians (though rarely by sociologists) and Soviet propagandists when confronted with disadvantaged groups or "underachieving" individuals in their respective societies. The shriller the acclaim of the social order and the more stubborn the insistence on its virtues, the more likely that the individual will be blamed for being poor, ignorant, dissatisfied, or deviant. But the greater the emphasis on the importance of the social environment in shaping individual destinies, the more paradoxical this position becomes, as is the case in the Soviet Union.[1]

One among the many problems in assessing what constitutes equal opportunity lies in establishing a base line, on a generational basis. Do parents or even grandparents need to have it in order for their children to possess it? How many generations does it take to eradicate the remnants of unequal opportunity and privilege? And what exactly constitutes it? Access to education, good health, uncrowded shelter, nourishing food, stimulating social environment, ability to travel, live under good climate, not suffer unduly strict toilet training...? The list of what constitutes opportunity is endless. Most frequently it refers to equal access to education and the learning of useful occupational skills, plus basic health care and the absence of gross material deprivations. But even if all these things were truly equalized (and they are not, either in the U.S. or the U.S.S.R.), this would be still only the beginning.

Warner's classical analysis of the American class system is largely an empirical one based on his own researches, and it combines subjective as well as objective indices of class affiliation. He takes care to differentiate between social and economic class—a position obviously unacceptable for Marxists. He also points out that there are two kinds of stratification in the United States: local-communal on the one hand and national-societal on the other. His analysis reflects the pluralism and regionalism still present in the United States. Kolko argues that class distinctions, i.e., inequalities, in the United States are enormous and show no sign of diminishing. His conception of class is an economic one.

Not unexpectedly, the two Soviet commentators find the American class system rather bleak. In particular, they set out to demolish two concepts which American and other Western sociologists use to reach more favorable conclusions in considering the class structure of their society: social mobility and the middle class. Essentially the Soviet arguments show that capitalism is not improving; that if it changes at all, it is for the worse. While also castigating the work of bourgeois sociologists, they use their findings whenever possible to buttress their position. However, in the final analysis, our Soviet colleagues are out to "unmask" and "expose" falsehoods rampant in bourgeois society and among bourgeois sociologists.

Until relatively recently, few seemed to have any doubt, on either side of the ideological barricades, that the class structure or stratification system of the Soviet Union was profoundly different from the American. For some, this difference was something to rejoice in; for others, an abomination. It is among the ironies of our times that there has been a convergence in the

[1] This leads to theoretical-ideological problems which are best illustrated by the Soviet treatment of crime in a socialist society to be discussed later.

views of the American critics of Soviet society, who were horrified by "forced" equalitarianism (seen as destructive of talent, diversity, and incentives), and the views of Stalin and his successors, who came out strongly against what they called "petty bourgeois egalitarianism" or "wage leveling," deemed incompatible (as Glezerman noted) both with socialism and communism. Needless to say the questioning of the differences between the two class structures was begun by Western rather than Soviet sociologists. According to Inkeles (and others not quoted in this volume), the decisive factor shaping the system of stratification in the world today is the degree of industrialization and urbanization. It is along these lines that he finds similarities between the Soviet and American case, and in particular, in the role of occupation as the major determinant of class and status position. He found occupation correlated with a host of inequalities: income, education, access to information, job satisfaction, and overall satisfaction with life. More recent writings of Soviet sociologists are edging closer to this viewpoint, such as the one included by Shkaratan noting the existence of what he calls secondary or interclass differences within the working class which are correlated with the complexity of the work performed.

As Skharatan states "...differences in qualifications stemming from differences in education are coming to be the main factor of the emergence of differences within the working class." He might have added: not only within the working class but in general, in every stratum of society. This situation, of course, is also true in the United States and other modern urban societies. Naturally there are exceptions and loopholes. Access to education, or to good education, is in itself predetermined by factors other than the availability of public education or the native talent of the young; it also depends on the income, motivation, and values of an individual's family and on the region where one was born. In the Soviet Union, a child born in a family of kolkhoz peasants, for example in Kazahkstan, has a poorer chance to attend Moscow or Leningrad University (or any university) than the child of a high civil servant, engineer, or scientist living in some of the urban areas of European Russia. The chances of such a child may not be quite as bad as those of an illegitimate child of a Negro mother living on welfare in Mississippi, but they are still rather dim. This is so in part because racial discrimination is not nearly so intense a disqualifying factor in the Soviet Union as in the United States. (More will be said on this subject later in the book.)

The factor of political loyalty vs. political unreliability is of considerable importance in the Soviet Union affecting the availability of "equal" opportunity. Being branded, for whatever reason, as politically unreliable can have wide repercussions even if it does not lead to police action. It can mean loss of job, or transfer to an undesirable place of employment (a distant region for example), loss of housing (or loss of good housing), a negative preference in promotion, loss of access to higher education, etc.

Conversely, the demonstration of political reliability and zeal in public-political participation does lead to preferential treatment in spheres not directly connected with political participation itself. The leverage of the state in such matters is enormous, being the single employer and allocator of all material rewards.

It is likely that there is more conspicuous inequality in the United States than in the Soviet Union. One reason is that affluent idleness is not tolerated in the Soviet Union. For example, while some people receive far more lavish salaries and pensions than others, it is not possible to live on the earnings of investment or the interest payments of money loaned, on clipping coupons, etc. Nor is it possible to devote one's life to ever more fastidious and luxurious styles of personal consumption.

It is perhaps this aspect of the Soviet scene, i.e., the relative limitations on luxurious consumption even on part of the elite group as well as the more comprehensive public welfare benefits, that tones down the otherwise real and sharp differences in income, education, and prestige. Insofar as it is possible to assess, social mobility in the two societies is about the same.

STRATIFICATION

IN THE U.S.:

The American View

Social Class and
Color Caste in America

LLOYD WARNER

SOCIAL CLASS IN A DEMOCRACY

It is impossible to study with intelligence and insight the basic problems of contemporary American society and the psychic life of its members without giving full consideration to the several hierarchies which sort people, their behavior, and the objects of our culture into higher and lower social statuses. They permeate every aspect of the social life of this country. In America, as elsewhere in a world of large populations, complex social structures, and advanced civilization, there are two types of orders of ranking. One form includes those systems, such as factories and governmental organizations, which segment the society—hierarchies which place their members in relations of superiority and inferiority within their own limits but not in the whole community. The other form cross-cuts the community, placing all people in superordinate and subordinate ranks.

Modern social systems are developing increasingly the first, segmentary, type of rank order to solve certain social and economic problems and to maintain cohesion and order in a rapidly changing world. Such institutions as cartels, huge factories, great service enterprises, chain stores, producers' and farmers' cooperatives, and vast mail-order houses, such as Sears Roebuck, are examples of elaborate economic hierarchies which regulate part of the lives of some of the individuals in American society but not the entire life of any individual within their ranks. Nor do they directly control any of the lives of those who do not belong to them. In the sense that these hierarchies directly affect only their members and part, but not all, of the behavior of these members, they are hierarchies that segment society.[1]

[1] W. Lloyd Warner and Paul S. Lunt, *The Social Life of a Modern Community* ("The Yankee City Series," Vol. I [New Haven. Yale University Press, 1941]); W. Lloyd Warner, Marchia Meeker, and Kenneth Eells, *Social Class in America: A Manual of Procedure for the Measurement of Social Status* (Chicago: Science Research Associates, 1949).

The values and the spirit of the rules of social class, color caste, and subordinate minority groups encompass the lives of individuals within their confines. Although this is particularly true of caste, it holds sufficiently true for the others to make the statement accurate. They divide the whole population and determine behavior very much as age and sex classes do. There may be indeterminate social areas, in which it is not clear whether the people or the behavior is clearly in one status or another, or something that is a mixture of both. But, when class or caste is present, it divides the society and those to whom the terms apply into distinct levels.

Social class in America is not the same as economic class. Social class refers to levels which are recognizable in the general behavior and social attitudes of the people of the whole community where the levels exist. Although economic factors are of prime importance and are some of the principal determinants of social class, they are insufficient to account for all social-class behavior or for its presence in contemporary America.[2]

The levels of social class are ranked into superior and inferior levels according to the values of the community. The things wanted and actively pursued and the things disliked and, where possible, actively avoided are distributed unevenly among the members of the whole society, the distribution being controlled by the order of rank of the classes present. In such a system, the old precept, "to him that hath shall be given," is often a powerful determinant of how the available rewards are given to those who compete for them.

The rules and norms of marriage in a social-class system have two modes. The values of social class about marriage are such that it is felt to be proper and correct for a man or woman to marry at his or her own level (endogamy); yet it is also believed to be correct and proper for an individual to marry above or below his social position (exogamy). In all truth it must be admitted that a person who "marries up" is said to have made a "good marriage"; and the fortunes of the other spouse in this marital venture are often recognized by such invidious gestures as raised eyebrows and knowing smiles or by the elaborate explanations of friends and family which point out the great moral, aesthetic, or even monetary worth of the marital partner. Unwittingly and unwillingly, they indicate that the marriage is not an exchange of equal status, that it needs the weight of added material or spiritual properties to balance it satisfactorily; thus the ideals of romantic love are not outraged, and the spirit of justice on which all freely chosen permanent contracts must rest is strengthened and maintained.

In a social-class system, the child inherits the status of its parents. It is the family which socially orients him to, and trains him for, the community. It is the family that establishes his social location; within it he has his early experiences and learns to be a human being and a person.

Although social classes are rank orders placing people and their families in higher and lower orders, they do not permanently fix the status of either the individual or his family in America. Despite the fact that a man inherits the class position of his family, his inherited position is not necessarily the one he will always occupy. From the point of view of the total social system of a community, each class is open to properly qualified people below it. Vertical social mobility, the rise and fall of individuals and families, is characteristic of our class system.

[2] Warner and Lunt, *op. cit.*

SOCIAL CLASS IN NEW ENGLAND,

THE MIDDLE WEST, AND THE SOUTH

The class systems of the communities in the several regions of the United States are basically similar. A good test of this statement is that people who move from one region to another recognize their own and other levels in the new community and know how to adjust themselves. But variations are present, for example, in number of class levels, size of the population of each level, and differences in the culture and social composition of the various strata. Furthermore, the amount and kind of social mobility permitted between two or more levels and the strength of the class system itself differ regionally. In general, the older and more stable regions of the East and South have more highly organized class systems than the West.

On the eastern seaboard of New England there are six recognizable class levels. The upper class is divided into a new and old aristocracy. The so-called "old-family" level at the top provides the keystone to the status arch. Immediately beneath it are the people called the "new families," who are new to the status rather than to the community. They are the fortunate mobile people who have climbed to a level where they participate with the top group in their clubs and cliques. These lower-upper-class people recognize that they are below those born to high position with lineages of several generations. The old families hold their position by virtue of inheritance, validated by the possession of a recognized social lineage; the new families, by competition with others and by translating their material successes into acceptance by their social betters. On the average, the new families, socially inferior to the old ones, have more money, better houses, more expensive automobiles, and other material goods that are superior in dollars and cents to those of their social superiors. But if the success of the new families is due to wealth, their money is felt to be too new; if due to occupational triumph, their achievement is too recent; if the source of their new social power is educational attainment, what they have learned, while highly valued, is too newly learned and insufficient. The inherited culture of an upper class, firmly supplemented by higher education in the proper preparatory schools and superior universities and colleges, is more highly regarded.

The hard core of the upper-middle class, the level below the top two, consists of the solid citizens who are the active civic leaders of the community. They are thought of as the "joiners," for they belong to the associations which are better known to the public and are given more respectful attention by the public press. The upper-middle class feels itself to be, and in fact is, above the Level of the Common Man just beneath it. Its members are acutely aware of being socially inferior to the upper classes. To the upper-middle families that are not anxious to move up socially, this problem is not particularly distressing; but, to those that are socially mobile, the presence of an upper class sufficiently open to make it possible for some of their level to climb into it is a source of continuing frustration or anxious anticipation. Combined, the two upper levels and the upper-middle, comprising about 15–25 per cent of the people of most communities in America, are what might be called the "Level above the Common Man." The upper two classes alone rarely comprise more than 5 per cent of the total population of a city.

The lower-middle class, the top of the Common Man Level, is composed economically of small businessmen, a few highly skilled workmen, and a large number of clerks and other workers in similar categories. Members of this class tend to be extremely proper and conservative. They are joiners, belonging to patriotic organizations, fraternal orders, secret societies and auxiliaries, or other associations based on family membership. They live in the regions of the little houses, with the well-kept but cramped gardens and lawns, on the side streets rather than the better residential ones. The upper-middle class tends to live on the broad residential streets, in the better houses with the larger gardens. Upper-middle-class dwelling areas in the smaller communities are sometimes indistinguishable from those of the class above them.

The men and women of the lower-middle class tend to approach the ideal typical of the Protestant ethic, being careful with their money, saving, far-sighted, forever anxious about what their neighbors think, and continually concerned about respectability.

The people in the upper-lower class are the semiskilled workers, the small tradesmen, and often the less-skilled employees of service enterprises. They, too, are highly respectable, limited in their outlook on the world around them, and are thought of as "honest workmen."

The people of the lowest level, the lower-lower class, by social reputation are not respectable or are the pitied unfortunates. Sometimes they are the new "greenhorns," the recently arrived "ethnic" peoples. These new people throughout American history, with their diverse cultural, linguistic, and religious backgrounds, have migrated here and settled. Starting at the bottom, they begin their slow ascent in our status system. They differ culturally rather than racially from the dominant group in America. Lower-lower-class people live on the riverbanks, in the foggy bottoms, in the regions back of the

tanneries or near the stockyards, and generally in those places that are not desired by anyone else. Their reputation is such that they are believed to lack the cardinal virtues in which Americans pride themselves. Although in standards of sexual behavior many differ from the classes above, others are different only because they are less ambitious and have little desire to fulfil the middle-class goal of "getting ahead." Their reputation for immorality often is no more than the projected fantasy of those above them; as such they become a collective symbol of the community's unconscious!

...The class differences among the communities of the several regions are significant and need comment. The newer regions of America, because of rapid social change and their comparative recency, tend not to develop a superior old-family class. This is true of many of the communities throughout the prairie states of the Middle West. An old-family group may be present in the community and feel some claim to superior recognition, but ordinarily communities in new regions look upon them as no more than the equals of the new-family group. It will take several more generations to validate their claims to a rank above the more recently arrived.

The lower-lower group is smaller in the middle-western towns and Far West because there are fewer recently arrived ethnic peoples and the towns are too new to produce a so-called "worthless" class; furthermore, they are market centers for large agricultural areas, making it less likely that economic forces will help to produce an industrial proletariat.

The lowest white group in parts of the South is smaller and the higher classes larger than elsewhere in America because there is a large rural Negro peasant group on which much of the market economy of the town is founded.

Actually, each class merges into the class above and the one below it. A class system where there is movement up and down by individuals and families in an open social system where there is territorial as well as social movement necessarily makes no sharp distinctions between one class and contiguous ones. The reader should not suppose that all individuals are alike in a particular class, any more than he should assume that all men in our society who occupy the status *father* are alike either as men or as fathers. They do share common characteristics, but clearly diversity and heterogeneity must exist in a society when social change is rapid and individualism is stressed. But, in our recognition of the differences among men, we should not overlook the many similarities which permit the scientist to establish modal types. Despite the variations, the core of the status structure of America, as it has been studied in various communities throughout the United States, remains remarkably the same. Although there are regional and cultural differences, the basic arrangement of the social classes and the kinds of people in them show far greater similarities than differences.

The Quality of Economic Life:
Myth and Reality

GABRIEL KOLKO

Insofar as economic power in the United States derives from savings and income, it is dominated by a small class, comprising not more than one-tenth of the population, whose interests and style of life mark them off from the rest of American society. And within this class, a very small elite controls the corporate structure, the major sector of our economy, and through it makes basic price and investment decisions that directly affect the entire nation.

"The historic ethos of American life" may be "its bourgeois hungers, its class-

Reprinted by permission from Gabriel Kolko, Wealth and Power in America. *New York: Frederick A. Praeger, Inc., 1962, pp. 127–132.*

lessness, the spirit of equality," as Louis Hartz suggests in *The Liberal Tradition in America* (1955), but these are surely not the dominant realities in its social and economic structure. American society is based on a class structure, and it pervades most of the crucial facets of life.

More than any other factor, the American class structure is determined by the great inequality in the distribution of income, an inequality that has not lessened although the economy's unemployment total has dropped from 12 million to a much smaller but still substantial figure. A sharp inequality of income has remained despite a generation of encroachments by laws, wars, and crises at home and abroad. If the form this inequality takes has been modified by expense accounts, undistributed profits, undeclared income, and similar complex measures, the nature of the phenomenon has not been altered.

The economically determined class lines in American society have been reinforced by the failure of the lowest-paid groups (largely blue-collar workers) to increase their relative income share since 1938—contrary to the common academic notion that they have. Their occasional ascents to a higher-income bracket usually result from the entry of wife or child into the labor market. And, perhaps most significant of all, the movement of the children of blue-collar workers into white-collar occupations is not necessarily a step upward, since white-collar workers are losing ground in their income standing.

Inequality of income is reflected in inequality of consumption, an inequality so great that contemporary social theories on the "democratization" or "massification" of symbols of economic status hold little relevance to the America of this decade. On the one hand, nearly one-half of the population is financially able to meet only its immediate physical needs, and the larger part of this group, nearly one-third of the nation, are in want of even basic necessities. On the other hand, a small section of the population, at most the top tenth, lives in the prosperous and frequently sumptuous manner that most social commentators ascribe to the large majority of Americans. And within this small section, there exists an economic elite variously described as the "sports-car," "country-club," or "Ivy League" set, depending on its particular tastes. Here are found the major owners of stock and the corporate managers, sharing the same social life and the same set of values.

Sharp inequalities in consumption are the pervasive fact of the American class structure. Privacy and comfort in housing are privileges of the well-to-do, and an increasing number of $250,000-and-up homes are being built throughout the United States—at a time when the few old mansions of the Astors and Morgans are being sold, purportedly because of loss of wealth, but actually because of changes in taste. The type of car one drives is a fairly accurate index of social class; the expensive sports car is purchased when an ordinary car will no longer impart sufficient prestige. Steaks are standard fare in the upper-income ranks; hamburger—which now accounts for one-quarter of beef consumption as opposed to one-tenth before World War II—is the staple of the luckier among the lower-income groups. Life is longer for the wealthy, whose money spares them from some diseases and in general gives them superior medical care. Last of all, higher education at the best institutions perpetuates the advantages of wealth in succeeding generations, while among the poor, vast reservoirs of talent and creativity go unexploited.

The basic economic fact of life for a majority of the population is insecurity. This is the logical outgrowth of their lack of ready savings; a very large majority of the low- and middle-income population have no more than a few months' income saved for financial emergencies.

Yet such emergencies are frequent among low-income families—in part because they are low-income families. The resultant increased rate of illness not only drains their meager finances, even with hospitalization insurance, but often has the disastrous effect of cutting off the earnings of the bread-winner.

Another common emergency for the low-income family is recurring unemployment, a by-product of the business cycle. If the family is covered by unemployment insurance—and over one-third of workers are not—the loss of income during this period is compensated for only very inadequately. If unemployment is very brief, the average family weathers it, although not without suffering reductions in consumption and other difficulties. If unemployment lasts more than several months, it eliminates the average family's savings, and causes a sharp reduction in consumption and perhaps some credit defaults. If unemployment compensation ends, relief is often the only recourse. For millions of Americans, this sequence of events is more than academic; they have experienced the necessity of having to live on $20 or $30 a week.

The insecurity caused by the ever-present possibility of unemployment, illness, or some other cause of financial emergency is made more ominous by the suddenness with which these crises occur. Perhaps more important is the expectation, growing out of personal experience and the observation of family and friends, that there is never enough money with which to meet predictable, certain responsibilities. Children add to the financial burdens of the average worker during the period when his income is greatest. By the time his financial responsibility for his children is ended, his peak earning period is past, and for himself and his wife, there is only the prospect of a continuation of the inadequate living standards of their late youth and early middle age. During the plateau between the children's attaining financial independence and the start of retirement, the average worker may save, but after retirement, he ends his life in want. If, before old age, he lived slightly below the maintenance level, he now drops below the emergency level.

For nearly half the population, these are the harsh facts of economic life—and for most, these facts limit their freedom to conceive or attain noneconomic goals.

It is true, as John Kenneth Galbraith suggests, that poverty is an "afterthought" in the contemporary American economy, but it is not true that the nation is so well off that we should "escape from the obsolete and contrived preoccupation associated with the assumption of poverty." Poverty is an afterthought not because it *has* disappeared, but because social scientists *believe* it has.

In the coming decades, certain conditions giving rise to poverty will grow in importance, and if they meet the same response in future years as they have since World War II, the percentages of the population living at submaintenance and subemergency standards will climb, despite the increase in real income for some occupations. One such factor is the simultaneous numerical growth and relative economic decline of the white-collar class. This trend is a crucial aspect of a group that many social scientists thought would join that "classless" and nebulous category, the middle class. Another element is the mounting number of families headed by women, a low-income group—in part because of wage prejudice. But, above all, there is the persistent growth in the population aged sixty-five and over, most of whom live on penurious Social Security payments or other meager funds.

It is conceivable that the termination of the business cycle, plus a substantial rise in real income, could end poverty in the United States caused by unemployment and low wages. But realization of these two goals is quite unlikely. Too many factors are operating to assure a continuing sequence of recessions, or even worse.

One difficulty in the way of full employment is the rising productivity per-man-hour, and it is certain to become more formidable as automation spreads. The solution obviously is to expand consumption greatly, but only a decisive shift in the distribution of income and purchasing power can accomplish this. A self-defeating factor in wage boosts is the almost invariable business practice of passing along the cost of pay increases to the public. Raising legal minimum wages and extending the coverage to more people will not increase real purchasing power unless accompanied by direct control of prices.

Thus, eliminating poverty caused by unemployment and low wages requires the sweeping sort of political decisions concerning the economy which no administration has proposed or practiced, except during World War II. For this reason, it is probable that the very substantial importance of poverty caused by unemployment and low wages will not diminish in the near future. This static position, plus the rising new trends toward poverty discussed above, and the instability inherent in an extensive credit system—all these factors indicate that poverty will continue to be a basic aspect of the American social and class structure so long as no fundamental changes are made in the distribution of wealth and the autonomous control of the corporate machinery.

Poverty and low incomes in the United States are not, as in underdeveloped nations, an inevitable consequence of deficient industry. In 1958, only three-quarters of the nation's industrial capacity was utilized, and 5 million workers were unemployed. This was true in large part because the poorer half of the nation was not seriously in the market for new automobiles, refrigerators, houses, and goods of every other type. The problem was not in technology, but in economic organization, and at the bottom of this economic inadequacy was the sharply unequal distribution of income and wealth.

Let us ignore for the moment the tremendous industrial development that would be stimulated by the growth of the consumer-goods market among the poorer half of the population. Let us consider only that if the existing industrial machinery were fully exploited, its production would be sufficient to raise markedly the standard of living of those now living below the maintenance level. . . .

STRATIFICATION

IN THE U.S.:

The Soviet View

The Class Character of
the Theory of Social Mobility

G. B. OSIPOV

Bourgeois sociologists are attempting to mask the obviously antidemocratic character of the theories of the "elites" and the unrestrained exploitation of the wage laborers in the capitalist society with the fashionable theory of "social mobility." According to this theory, which is one of the variants of the reformist conception of "class cooperation" between the bourgeois and the proletarian, the individual seems to have the opportunity to cross from one "stratum" to another, and does not have to remain in his "stratum" for life. This movement "upwards" and "downwards" is called "social mobility" by bourgeois sociologists.

...Of course, horizontal mobility is a frequent phenomenon but so far as vertical mobility is concerned, offering the workers an opportunity to move up within the social structure to become "businessmen" and millionaires, is an

Original Translation

Reprinted from G. B. Osipov, Contemporary Bourgeois Sociology, *Izd. Nauka, Moscow, 1964, pp. 247–248, 250–251, 253–254.*

unrealizable utopia conjured up in order to conceal the exacerbation of class contradictions of capitalism. Even bourgeois sociologists themselves are forced to admit this. Thus F. Merrill writes that lately certain factors have appeared which prevent the realization of upward mobility. Amidst the factors reducing social mobility, he considers "the concentration of corporate control." He notes that the possession of shares in the corporations is unequal and in reality belongs to the minority. L. Warner and J. Abegglen explain that the groups in control of the corporations form "the new and powerful elite."

F. Merrill declares that social mobility is being lowered also because the craft hierarchy is collapsing. He notes that "in many branches of mass production the rudimentary skill necessary to operate a machine can be learned in two or three weeks. The skill of a mechanic and a skilled craftsman in many cases is replaced by the skill of a machine. Under such conditions the worker becomes a supplemental part of the machine. He is an easily replaceable part in the process which, although

135

it also requires the masses of anonymous individuals, needs less and less individual skill."

As a result, the road of advancement from apprentice to foreman, manager, and owner is being closed to the worker. The American sociologist R. Bendix writes that "the contemporary worker as he becomes older often does not increase his skill, but loses his viability and productivity. Many skilled workers of course remain, but the most of them are firmly consolidated on the level of a semi-skilled worker."

...American sociologists would like to shift the blame for the reduction of social mobility to the machine. But, in reality the machine is not guilty of this, but the capitalist use of it, and the capitalist conditions of labor are responsible.

...Bourgeois sociologists maintain that work, education, and political activity are channels of "vertical mobility." But how real are these "equal opportunities" for the proletariat? The progress of technology under capitalism increases the intensification of labor, the expenditure of the worker's physical and mental energy per unit of time. As a result, the worker is worn out faster. The feverish tempo of labor is so exhausting that it precludes the spiritual development of the working man. Reaching the age of 40 and 50 such a worker becomes unwanted for the capitalist.

...Automated production under capitalism divides the working class into two unequal parts—the skilled part (technicians and machine operators) and the enormous army of semi-skilled workers. An insignificant amount of time is spent on the instruction of each operation under the conveyor system. Chained to a single operation, the worker remains the accessory of the machine.

The working class which assures the progress of technology and culture, receives only pitiful crumbs of the fruits of this progress. Thus, in the U.S. about 6 million people are illiterate. A substantial number of the children of the poor have no opportunity to study. Only children of well-to-do parents can complete their secondary education. Housing shortage, slums (according to the acknowledgement of the official press, more than 15 million of the population of the U.S. live under exceptionally difficult conditions), malnutrition, social diseases (distrophy, tuberculosis, etc.), and social pathologies (alcoholism, prostitution) are the constant companions of the working class in the capitalist society.

THE MYTH OF THE SOCIAL "TRANSFORMATION" OF THE CLASS STRUCTURE OF CAPITALISM

The myth of the "transformation" of the class structure of capitalism is being destroyed by the blows of the capitalist reality itself. The sole masters of property usually are large stockholders, and workers, if they acquire two or three shares, have no voice in the business of the joint-stock society.

"The fear of revolution, the successes of the socialist countries, the pressure of the labor movement force the bourgeoisie"—as stated in the Program of the CPSU—"to partial concessions in relation to wages, the conditions of labor, and social security. But the rising prices and inflation wipe out these concessions. The wages lag behind the material and cultural needs of the worker and his family, which grow with the development of society. Even the relatively high standard of living in a small group of developed capitalist countries is based on the plunder of the peoples of Asia, Africa, and South America, on an unequal exchange, on discrimination against female labor, on the fierce oppression of Negroes and immigrant laborers, and also on the stepped-up exploitation of the workers of those countries. The bourgeois myth about "total employment" has turned out to be a cruel mockery—the working class constantly suffers from mass unemployment, from uncertainty about tomorrow. Despite the partial successes of the working class's economic struggle, as a whole its position in the capitalist world is deteriorating."

The myth about "people's capitalism" is sung not only by the loyal and overt ideologists of the bourgeoisie, but also by various kinds of reformists, right socialists, who still attempt to put on the mask of "leftist" terminology.

...In order to mask the anti-popular, exploitative essence of contemporary capitalism, the reactionary, bourgeois sociologists and social philosophers created quite a number of legends about the so-called "people's capitalism." In numerous works these bourgeois sociologists and social philosophers said that "a people's capitalism" allegedly exists now in the United States of America and certain other capitalist countries.

The theory of the "transformation" of the class structure of capitalism into some new class structure while preserving the relationships of domination and oppression is utopian and, consequently, unscientific. This theory is the recurrent social myth of contemporary bourgeois sociology.

Bourgeois Theories
of the "Middle Class"

G. F. ALEXANDROV

Bourgeois sociology which advances apologetic theories justifying and defending capitalism, uses widely the concept of the "middle class." Alongside the genuine middle strata, the concept includes a significant part of the proletariat and the majority of capitalists. The English sociologist G. Marshall declares that "almost the entire

Western society is turning into an enormous middle class."[1]

Bourgeois investigators differ in their definitions of the "middle class." Some emphasize the subjective evaluation of classes, others attempt to find objective criteria. The former reach their conclusions mainly on the basis of interviews. But can one demand from the respondent a correct determination of his class affiliation, if even specialists are not always in a position to ascertain in which social category one should place one or another group of the population?

Original Translation

Reprinted from G. F. Alexandrov, et al., eds., The Urban Middle Strata of Contemporary Capitalist Society, Izd. Nauk, USSR, Moscow, 1963, pp. 55–56, 62–63.

[1] Transactions of the Third World Congress of Society, vol. 3, p. 15.

The answers to the questionnaires depend on the class consciousness of the respondent and on the way the question was raised. The use, for example, of terms like "middle," "lower," and "upper" classes will lead to a different distribution of responses than the use of the concepts "bourgeoisie," "petty bourgeoisie," and "the working class."

Among the objective criteria for the determination of the "middle class," the bourgeois theoreticians single out mainly the source and level of income and the nature of work. However, in using these criteria, it would be necessary to acknowledge the existence of countless classes. If one takes as a basis of class division the source of income, then the petty bourgeoisie alone will be divided into a whole number of classes. The petty bourgeois, according to the sources of income, break down into owners of land, and of industrial, commercial, and other enterprises. One would need a minute breakdown of individuals according to their level of income, and a differentiation among people according to the nature of their labor (mental and · physical). In so doing, a classification on the basis of certain characteristics would contradict class membership arrived at on the basis of others. For example, according to the level of income, it would be necessary to include many petty bourgeois in the same class with poorly paid workers and office workers when, according to the nature of their labor, they should be placed into different classes. In short, such criteria as the source and level of income and the nature of work cannot by themselves serve as a scientific basis for class differentiation. If the application of these criteria proves anything, it is only the complete unsoundness of the bourgeois category of the "middle class."

The merging of various social classes and intermediate groups of the popula-tion into the so-called middle class is necessary for the bourgeois ideologists to demonstrate that supposedly in contemporary capitalist society a gradual dissolution of all classes into one "middle class" is taking place. A necessary consequence of this, according to the bourgeois ideologists, is the disappearance of class conflict and class struggle under capitalism.

. . . The theory of the "middle class" has been especially widely disseminated in the United States of America. Bourgeois historians and sociologists falsify the history of the U.S. They allege that America developed differently from Europe after the revolution—class divisions did not exist in it, the whole population supposedly presenting a more or less homogeneous "middle class." They declare that the majority of Americans possessed land or other property and differed little from each other in their standard of living. Subsequently a differentiation of American society followed, but in the twentieth century the pendulum swung back and once again the U.S. is turning into a "middle class" country.

. . . Historical experience shows that the position of the middle strata has considerably changed in the epoch of general crisis in capitalism and especially in its present, third stage. The vast majority of the urban middle strata has lost the privileged position which it had in the last century. The process of the proletarization of the middle strata has progressed so far in breadth and in depth, that their basic mass has found itself brought down to a proletarian or semi-proletarian level. These strata are neither less deprived nor less exploited and oppressed by the monopolies than the working class. The pursuit of superprofits by the monopolies represents the main obstacle to combining technical progress with social progress for all strata of the population.

Consequently, monopolistic capital is the enemy, not only of the working class, but of all toilers. This is why previously the middle strata by virtue of their economic position were the bulwark of the ruling class rather than the ally of the proletariat, so today resulting from the changes which have occurred in the economic position of the middle strata, there are more favorable preconditions for them to be attracted to the side of the proletariat. In the contemporary epoch increasingly favorable conditions have been created for the unification of the middle strata around the proletariat on the basis of the struggle for peace, for the expansion and renewal of democracy, and for the improvement of living conditions. But, it would be incorrect to suggest that all of the middle strata face the same problems. That is why the study of each strata separately can promote a better understanding of the objective prerequisites and possibilities for winning over the middle strata to the side of the proletariat in the struggle of the toilers against the all-powerful monopoly capital.

STRATIFICATION
IN THE SOVIET UNION:

The Soviet View

From Class Differentiation
to Social Homogeniety

G. E. GLEZERMAN

The changes in the composition of the urban and rural population are being studied by sociologists in close connection with the more general problem of eliminating the dividing lines between classes, social groups which

Original Translation

Reprinted from Voprosy Filosofii, *No. 2. 1963, pp. 39–49. The Academy of Sciences of the U.S.S.R.—The Institute of Philosophy.*

compose Soviet society. If in the past, historical development necessarily proceeded from the social homogeneity of the very early stage of social development, to increasingly greater class differentiation, in our times the historical progress itself raises the issue of overcoming class differentiation and of the transition to a classless society which will be socially homogeneous.

In the years following the socialist revolution in the U.S.S.R., a basic change of the class structure of society took place. A new socialist society arose, which no longer is divided into antagonistic and exploiting classes, a society composed of friendly classes and social groups—the working class, the collective farm peasantry and the intelligentsia. In the same manner, the major and fundamental historical task of the destruction of classes was solved in society in so far as there are no longer such social groups which could exploit others.

However, the building of socialism does not immediately eliminate all class differences. Socialism, as the first phase of communism, inherits from the old society, social distinctions between the town and the country, between mental and manual labor, which no longer express class antagonism, but which have not yet disappeared. There also remain classes of workers and peasants connected with the two forms of socialist property—state and cooperative—kolhoz property.

Naturally, these are classes not in the old, property-based sense of the word. The concept of "class" historically developed in sociology as the reflection of social relationships which polarized society into the haves and have-nots, exploiters and exploited. These relationships no longer exist under socialism; the classes of socialist society are increasingly drawing closer to each other. These classes are still different in their relationship to the means of production, in their role in the social organization of labor, in the forms of the division of social income; however, these differences are no longer basic, they are gradually disappearing, and there is a movement toward a society in which classes will be altogether absent. Thus, the classes of a socialist society are disappearing ones, which are ceasing to be classes. Therefore, most important is not what distinguishes them from each other, but

the common features which join them together. Thus, for example, classes in the U.S.S.R. not only differ in their relations to the means of production, they are also united by their relations to the publicly-owned means of production. The common ownership of the means of common labor, the single goal —the building of communism—these are the things which unite all social groups in the U.S.S.R.

. . . The period of the construction of communism introduces a new stage in the development of class, national and other social relationships. This period is characterized by the disappearance of the major, decisive differences between the classes and by the accelerated obliteration of the remaining class differences. In the sphere of nationality relations, this period is characterized by the further rapprochement of nationalities and the achievement of their complete unity. All this reflects the further consolidation of the social homogeniety of society and its internal cohesiveness.

. . . The obliteration of boundaries between the working class and the peasantry is inseparably linked to the liquidation of essential differences between the city and the countryside. Of course, it would be incorrect to equate these problems. The rural population today is composed not only of the collective farm peasantry—the state farm workers make up a substantial part of it, and so do the local industry, and the rural intelligentsia.

. . . The introduction of the new technology is accompanied by a rapid change in the composition of agricultural workers, by their approaching the professional composition, qualifications, and cultural-technical level of industrial workers. Agricultural work is gradually becoming a species of industrial work, and consequently, the labor of a peasant is becoming similar to that of the worker. If in 1928 the mechanical power available to the peasants composed only 2% of that available to the workers, today it has reached 57%. Formerly, the Russian peasant performed all the work on the farm, and there was almost no specialization of labor, the only representative of industrial (rather handicraft) labor in the countryside being the blacksmith. Today on any collective farm in the U.S.S.R. there are tens of people with different skills: milkmaids, poultry-hands, pig tenders, crop experts, etc. What has been especially important, in the years of building up collective farms there appeared a great number of industrial occupations: tractor and combine operators, mechanics, drivers, electricians, construction workers, etc. The number of tractor and combine operators and drivers has almost doubled in the last twenty years.

...Sociological investigation, conducted in the village Constantinovsko, in the Stavrapolsky region, showed that in the collective farm there are workers in almost 60 categories of specialization. Besides that, among the 202 machine operators questioned, 117 men have 2 or 3 specializations, and 35 have 4 or 5.

In contrast to the working class which grows absolutely and relatively, the number of peasants in the U.S.S.R. is decreasing. The general trend and the dynamics of change in the class structure of the population in the U.S.S.R. under socialism, is shown by the following chart (in % of total population).

...However, the final disappearance of the differences between the working class and the peasantry will not result from a progressive decrease in the numbers of peasantry and their transformation into workers. The decisive step in overcoming these differences consists of the further improvement of collective farms and their convergence with public enterprises. Today collective farms have already significantly approached public enterprises in the degree of concentration and collectivization of production. In the course of the next decade (1961–70) all collective and state farms will become profitable and highly productive enterprises, and in the following decade (1971–80) the transition from the two forms of socialist economy to a unified public economy will gradually take place.

...The growth of the intelligentsia in Soviet society continued during the years of the building of communism. However, this does not mean that a new privileged stratum or class appeared in Soviet society or that a new elite has been formed, as many bourgeois sociologists contend.

...With the passage of time, the intelligentsia will cease to be a special social stratum of mental workers, distinguished from the rest of the people. Gradually, the differences between it and the manual laborers will disappear as a result of the general rise in the culture of the people.

...The growth of the intelligentsia under socialism is the result of rapid

	1937	1939	1959	1961
Industrial and White Collar Workers	45.7	50.2	68.3	71.8
Collective Farm Workers and Handicraftsmen in Cooperatives	48.8	47.2	31.4	28.0
Private Peasants and Handicraftsmen not in Cooperatives	5.5	2.6	0.3	0.2

(Chart from *"The National Economy in the U.S.S.R. in 1961*, Gosstatizdat, Moscow, 1962, pg. 27.)

technological progress, of the growing application of science to production, which increasingly turns into a direct productive force, a result of the planned organization of all public life on the basis of science and finally, a result of the concern of the socialist society with a fuller satisfaction of the people's cultural needs.

To illustrate the last point we might note that the number of workers in public health, education, sciences, culture, etc. will grow between 1960 and 1980 significantly faster than the number of workers in the national economy as a whole.

At the same time, the intelligentsia and the mass of workers and peasants will be drawn together through the nature of their work and their cultural-technical standards.

...The change in the character of labor and the cultural-technical growth of workers brings them closer to engineer-technicians. Characteristically, a new category "worker-researcher" was created in socialist enterprises. Such combination of concepts can be surprising for a man from the capitalist world. There it is customary to view the worker as a person hired to fulfill some operation, and the researcher as an educated man who studies the process. But socialist production united these opposites. Worker-researchers, appearing first at the Omsk time factory, and at other enterprises, have not only executive but also creative functions. Together with the engineers, they work out new technological processes and apply them themselves. Now there are many such people not only in Omsk, but also in Sverdlosk, Zaporozh, Moscow, Kharkov, and other cities. The wide development of a movement to innovate and rationalize in production is also significant, and millions of people are participating.

...The development of a system of public education plays the most im-portant role in assuring such cultural-technical growth. Soviet society was faced with a very serious problem: how to transform the system of education, which for centuries and thousands of years promoted the separation of mental from physical workers, into an instrument uniting all social groups. This problem was solved in our society, first of all, by the introduction of a universal education for the young. Virtually everybody goes through secondary school: at present the universal compulsory 8-year education.

...The system of national education in the U.S.S.R. not only does not create any social partitions, but on the contrary, promotes the merging of social groups, and the levelling of differences between them. While in 1939 only 8.2% of the workers and 1.5% of the collective farm workers had a secondary and higher education, in 1961 40% of workers and more than 23% of collective farm workers possessed such education.

...Naturally there still remain significant differences between the conditions of life and culture of city and countryside. But it is important to stress that class affiliation in the U.S.S.R. no longer plays a decisive role in determining the possibility for a man to get an education, to choose work according to his inclinations and abilities, and to participate in the political life of the country. The disappearance of class segregation is shown by the fact that in the U.S.S.R. there are more and more families which contain people of different professions, and different social groups (for example, families where parents are workers or peasants, and the children belong to the intelligentsia: engineers, teachers, agronomists, doctors, etc.)

...The differences in income between peasants and workers, low-payed and highly payed workers, and between the populations of various regions, are being decreased. The essential role in this process besides raising the lower levels of income to higher ones, is played by the development of public means for satisfying personal needs. Free education, medical care, free or inexpensive child care or support, iron out the differences in material prosperity between childless families and those with few and many children.

...In the process of progress to communism, full social equality, communist equality, will take shape. Such equality, of course, has nothing in common with the petty bourgeois wage-levelling, as alien to communism as to socialism. We are talking about the creation of equal conditions and opportunity for all members of society, for a free development of their abilities and the satisfaction of their needs (which remain different even under communism), and not about the distribution of material and cultural wealth to equal parts, as demanded by wage-levelling.

The program of the CPSU defines precisely "communist equality," which assumes (a) equal position of people in society, (b) identical relation to the means of production, (c) equal conditions of work and distribution, and (d) active participation of all in the management of public affairs.

...Thus, the movement of society to social homogeniety entails: (a) the obliteration of class boundaries, the drawing together followed by the merging of all social groups in society into a united collective of toilers of the communist society; (b) the strengthening of social homogeniety of nationalities, their subsequent drawing together and total unity; and (c) the overcoming of old forms of the division of labor, and the bringing together of different forms of labor.

Naturally, social homogeniety does not preclude differentiation in the oc-cupations and public functions of individuals. Specialization and the division of labor will also not disappear in the future. But differences in the nature of occupations will no longer be connected with differences in the social position of individuals, and to the degree of satisfaction of their needs, and, therefore, they will not be differences of a social character.

The achievement of social homogeniety and total social equality does not signify the elimination of individual differences between people and the equalization of their abilities, although bourgeois sociologists still attribute such nonsense to communists. Social equality presupposes the elimination of all social obstacles from the free development of individuality; it does not however, eliminate the differences between people's abilities.

With the destruction of class differences, individual differences between people, their individual traits and peculiarities, will become more diverse. While in a class society, the individual appears, first of all a representative of his class, in communist society, the individual, freed of the depersonalizing influence of the exploitative social order becomes a *person* in the authentic sense of the word. Man, forever delivered from insecurity and anxiety, will develop fully his personality.

...The possibilities of the development of individual inclinations and tastes, do not contradict collectivization in production, in public and daily life. As a measure of the progress to communism, society will increasingly take responsibility for the gratification of each man's needs but this will not at all lead to regimentation of man's whole life, nor to the levelling of needs. In the communist society, men's needs will be satisfied from public funds, and at the same time objects of personal consumption will be possessed by each member of society. Satisfying personal needs in this manner will allow for the most expedient combination of the collectivity and the individuality.

Total social homogeniety, the greatest diversity of people's abilities and needs, and the full flowering of individuality —such is the communist society toward which the workers of the Soviet Union are moving.

The Social Structure of the Soviet Working Class

O. I. SKHARATAN

Until recently we had no special publications whatever on questions of developments and changes in intraclass structure. Only during the first 15 years of Soviet society was the term "intraclass structure" employed in relation to the structure of our society. Not once has an investigation of the social structure of the Soviet working class been carried out since the First Five-Year Plan. The attempts of a number of researchers (including the author of these lines) to analyze the composition of the working class, attempts made at the end of the fifties and in the first half of the sixties, proved to be little effective because of the absence of a theoretical concept of the structural dependencies within the working class of socialist society and the lack of empirical data compiled under a scientifically valid

Reprinted from O. I. Skharatan "The Social Structure of the Soviet Working Class," Voprosi Filosofii (January, 1967). Translated in Current Digest of the Soviet Press, XIX, No. 12 (Copyright © April 12, 1967), 3–5, 7–8.

program. At best, the authors of these works were able to characterize a few features of the present-day industrial cadres, with more or less accuracy, only from scattered data. Soviet statistics provide a sufficiently clear idea of the technical and production characteristics of our industrial cadres, and their demographic features also, but the statistics of the Central Statistical Administration and of local statistical agencies do not—more exactly, almost do not— show social composition.

Yet study of the intraclass structure is of more than informational interest. Plans for social development cannot be drawn up without taking account of actual class differentiation. The simplest observations of life show substantial differences among various groups of the working class in social activeness, cultural level, etc. Such a problem as the structure of capital investments in the technical modernization of an enterprise —seemingly, strictly a technico-economic problem—is closely connected with tasks of social development, including the task of reducing the gap in qualifications and cultural level between various groups of workers. Questions of the assigning, training, and upbringing of workers at the enterprises likewise cannot be resolved without reckoning with the effect of these measures on the change in the social structure of the working class. The same is true of the policy of distribution of public consumption funds, and of many other aspects of society's daily functioning. Finally, to achieve complete social equality and the organic merging of all social groups presupposes change in the social structure of each social group, including the working class.

Let us consider, first of all, the basic theoretical postulates of study of the social structure of the working class and then examine some of the results of a concrete sociological study of this social structure at Leningrad machine-building enterprises.

...An important task in drawing up a program of concrete sociological research is to determine the boundaries of the object of study. In a developed socialist society, where the boundary lines between social groups are being eroded in the process of social integration, mixed social types arise and it appears difficult to establish the class to which quite large social groups belong. This applies particularly to the technical intelligentsia, an ever growing proportion of the population. All categories of industrial production personnel were included, therefore, among the persons studied in our research.

Both those who do physical work and those engaged in mental work in the branches of material production and distribution, and are employed in industrial enterprises and institutions which are publicly owned, belong to the working class of modern Soviet society, bearing in mind the socio-economic and socio-political characteristics of this

class. This is explained by the common features in the production process (the "aggregate worker") which all these groups of working people exhibit in the socio-economic sense (relationship to the means of production) and in the socio-political sense (leading role in society and in social processes). This fact enables us to view them as the common object of sociological research. It should be noted, too, that in the concrete historical conditions of modern socialist society one can to some extent regard the division into those engaged in mental work and those doing physical work as an aspect of intraclass differences.

...The experience of the construction of socialism in the U.S.S.R. has shown that the basic social differences within the working class after the socialist revolution in countries with a predominantly petty-bourgeois population are founded on qualitative-quantitative differences with regard to property. These stem from the mobility of class boundaries, on the one hand, and the enlargement of the working class through the addition of persons from other classes (mainly the petty bourgeoisie), on the other. Two basic strata are formed in this process: that of the cadre workers, who have no source of income other than wages received from the enterprises or payments from the public consumption funds, and the stratum of those who are becoming workers but are economically connected with petty commodity (usually peasant) pursuits and hence derive incomes from their own private pursuits. This period of development in the working class is, of course, attended by other differences, and other structure organizations exist. The leading and determinant grouping, however, is the aforementioned.

After petty commodity production is eliminated in the country in the course of the socialist transformation of cities and countryside, the basis for the perpetuation of differences relating to the means of production disappears.

The new phase of interclass relations intrinsic to the socialist society leads to rearrangement of the structure of the working class. In a society with uniform social relations, the relationship to the means of production ceases to be a factor of social differentiation within the class. As in the society as a whole, the foreground is taken by differences connected with roles in the social organization of labor, which are determined in turn by the socio-economic heterogeneity of labor.

This group of differences within the working class is genetically connected with the forms of capitalist cooperation in the production process. In the period of the transition from capitalism to socialism these differences were not of decisive, independent importance in differentiation within the working class. With the elimination of the class hierarchy, the remaining socio-economic division of labor acquires direct and immediate (not intermediary, as before) influence on the mechanism of intraclass structure.

The basic social differences within the Soviet working class today therefore are essentially differences in complexity of work, appearing at the surface as differences of working qualifications. How are these differences measured? Commodity-monetary relations are inherent in the production relations of socialism, and hence the law of value also. The value method of expressing social labor is necessary in a developed socialist society also, even if (let us assume) the society functions exclusively on the basis of public ownership. This is connected with the level of development of the economic relations themselves. Abstract labor, which measures differences based on complexity of work, becomes a necessary category here.

The fact that members of one and the same class belong to groups of workers with different skills, holding unequal positions in the system of social production, is decisive today in determining the social importance of the individual. These differences lead to the fact that various groups of the working people have unequal possibilities to develop and improve socialist production. Still unequal, at the same time, is the socio-economic possibility of members of society to engage in work of equal social importance.

In socialist society the social role of a group of persons is determined by the contribution to the development of social production and culture. The historically conditioned inequality of the contribution acts as a most important, determinant element in the structure characteristic of classes under socialism. This is due to the immaturity of socialism as the first phase of communism, since inequality of contribution is not yet determined in decisive measure by the degree of individual talent but depends chiefly on the nature of the work and its social division by virtue of the insufficient development of society's material-technical base. Although all the citizens in a socialist society are equal masters of the public wealth, their factual social inequality in social production is preserved, within certain limits, owing to the aforementioned reasons.

Intraclass division into groups according to their socially heterogeneous labor determines the social cast of the individual and influences the possibility of advancement of those who come from these groups. This circumstance is very important for the development of a scientifically grounded policy aimed at creating a society of complete social equality.

The division of labor into its socially heterogeneous kinds is manifested in the division into organization work and performed work, the division of performed work into mental and predominantly physical work (with the division of the latter into skilled, semi-skilled and unskilled work).

The intraclass structure, thus, is derivative from the type of class structure of society, from the socio-economic system of the society. The process of construction of a society without classes is accompanied by profound structural changes of class groupings, increasingly losing their specifically class features and acquiring qualities comprising the basis for the formation, in future, of a classless society of communist workers.

Such are the methodological foundations for research on the working class. Now let us turn to the experience of concrete research in this sphere, the research mentioned at the beginning of this article.

The Methods and Some Results of the Research.—We conducted the research at enterprises of the machine-building industry in Leningrad. Widely represented in the study were various groups of workers, office employees, engineers and technicians. The proportions of the various social groups to be found in our economic district do not properly reflect the proportions throughout the country in this branch of industry. But the data characterizing the social groups themselves, the scale of variations of features from group to group, to judge from the published results of research conducted in other districts of the country, could, with some corrections, apply to the country's entire working class.

The sample chosen for study was a 1% selection from each locale. Since the hypothesis of groupings in the working class was predicated on the idea of differences in complexity of labor as the dominant factor of social differences, it was possible to base the selection of the

sample on state statistical data on the distribution of personnel by occupations, by grades of skill and by pay. Insofar as the information and the possibilities of sample selection permitted, preference was given to selection on the basis of graduated degrees of complexity of work and the particular features of the production activity of blocs of occupational groups. The workers were grouped in blocs in accordance with the data of the occupational census conducted in 1962 by the economist G. F. Komarov jointly with V. P. Polozov and the author of these lines. Data for calculating the sample aggregate of those groups of industrial-production personnel not recorded in the censuses of state statistical agencies were derived through calculation of indirect data.

...The data obtained fully confirm the aforementioned hypothesis of criteria of differentiation, it seems to me. If we examine the figures characterizing the groups of personnel in the industry, the decline in indices from the first to the eighth group will be quite evident. Moreover, individual deviations in specific characteristics mutually cancel out when we consider the combined indices.

The data furnished by the tables confirm the conclusion that differences in qualifications stemming from differences in education are coming to be the main factor of the emergence of differences within the working class. The average educational level of workers engaged in unskilled physical labor is 6.5 grades; workers doing skilled physical labor have had 8.2 to 8.3 grades of schooling; the highly skilled workers have had 8.8 grades, and so on. This division likewise depends upon the length of occupational training.

It should be stressed that the chief way of moving from one social group into another is to exchange a less skilled occupation for a more highly qualified one, and not by raising one's skill (grade) within the confines of the same occupation; though, as the table shows, the average skill-grades for the groups differing in nature of work also reflect socio-economic differences to some degree (the average grade for lathe operators is 3.2, compared with 4.8 for machine setters and mechanics). But in the main a rise in grade testifies to the acquisition of work skills as age and length of service increase. According to K. Varshavsky's data, at the presently prevailing rate of advancement the worker reaches the highest grade in his occupation in ten years, i.e., at the average age of 27, since the average age for starting work is 17 (*cf.* K. Vershavsky, "Some Forms of Manifestation of the Law Governing Changes in Work at the Present Stage," in *Filosofskiye nauki* [Philosophical Sciences], No. 2, 1965). The qualitative leap in qualifications, leading to a change in social position in society, is connected with a change of occupation, which in turn depends in decisive measure on the level of educational preparation.

Whether the person belongs to one or another social group of the working class decides the degree of activeness and the nature of his participation in production and community life (in rationalization, self-administration, and so on). The highest showings in rationalization work are, characteristically, made by two social groups: the directors of production collectives and personnel combining mental and physical work in their jobs. In the first group, 27.1% regularly participate in rationalization activities; 54.4% are Party members, and 84.2% engage in community activities. These figures confirm the fact that the mechanism of socialist democracy ensures the advancement of the best representatives of the working people, possessing great life experience, civic experience, and production and

technical experience (their average age is 41.8 years, their average previous service in industry 17 years), to positions in organization and management.

As for the second of the aforementioned groups, the data show that the combination of mental and physical labor leads to greatest satisfaction for the individual in production and social activity (15.6% of this group are regularly involved in improving production, 23.4% are Party members, and 79.2% participate in community activities). This same group has the highest percentage of persons fully satisfied with their occupation (80.0% compared with 25.4% among the unskilled workers, 60.9% among lathe operators, and 63.3% among highly skilled personnel engaged in mental work).

An extremely important aspect of the social structure of socialist society is the absence of stable, hereditary social strata. According to the data of the research, 54.2% of the directors of enterprises came from families of manual laborers or collective farmers; about half of them began their careers as workers.

The educational level of even unskilled workers is sufficiently high for advancement to more complicated forms of labor activity (6.5 years of schooling). Characteristically, according to data from research on the causes of labor turnover in Leningrad (1963), 62.8% of auxiliary workers changed their occupation when taking new jobs. Resignations connected with change in social category constitute up to 30% of the turnover at some enterprises. In socialist society this is furthered by the system of vocational and general education available to all. If those who come from low-income families frequently interrupt their study in the system of classroom education, they display the greatest desire for advancement, for study while working. Thus, according to the data from the questioning of the Leningrad machine builders, most of those studying in higher educational institutions without interrupting their work turned out to be persons belonging to families with a monthly income of 30 rubles per family member (7.2%).

It is important to note that the viability of this approach to social grouping of the working people is confirmed by practical workers who are seeking ways of solving problems of regulating the selection of personnel, the admission of applicants to higher educational institutions, etc.

We shall have to deal for many a year to come with the differences among workers according to complexity of work. As we come closer to communism the structure of jobs (reflecting the directly technical division of labor) will conform more and more to the distribution of people according to their abilities (intellectual capacity). For the present, however, it is necessary to regulate the social processes in the direction of equalizing the conditions for advancement. This transition from socially fixed heterogeneous labor to rational distribution of manpower according to personal inclinations and abilities is an important aspect of social progress in the transition to communism. Social heterogeneity and the hierarchy of occupations disappears from the sphere of production relations. Division of labor remains as an aspect of the structure of the productive forces. In the sphere of social relations full social equality manifests itself in the rational distribution of manpower and genuinely free change of occupations. The universal law of division of labor, which in class society manifests itself in the social hierarchy of occupations and fixed position in socially single-type groups by occupation and qualifications, will manifest itself in communist society in social homogeneity of occupations and free exchange of occupation.

STRATIFICATION
IN THE SOVIET UNION:
The American View

Social Stratification
in the Modernization of Russia

ALEX INKELES

Near the core of every revolution lies a problem in social stratification. Indeed, we may define a revolution as a sudden intensification of an established trend, or a sudden break in the continuity of development, in a society's stratification system. Admittedly this definition is not adequate to account for the multiform processes which revolutions generally encompass. I do not argue revolutions are always, or even regularly, "caused" by strains in the stratification systems of society, although quite a good case could be made for that position.[1] But it may certainly be argued that changes in the stratification system are a universal accom-paniment of political and economic revolutions, and that the unfolding of such revolution is always in significant degree reflected in the shifting patterns of stratification. This is no less true of slower processes of social change than those following from political revolutions. It applies equally to more general or diffuse processes of change, such as those summed up in the idea of "the industrial revolution," and to more specific and geographically limited processes such as the modernization of Russia.

Stratification results from the fact that societies distribute or allocate "scarce goods" more or less unequally. By scarce goods we mean all objects or states which are recognized as of value in any society but are in limited supply. The tangible free goods most commonly cited are air and less often water, as against land or money, which are generally scarce. Among the intangibles, all sorts of honors, prestige, and respect are to some degree scarce, as against a state of grace or faith which probably qualifies as free goods. Max Weber distinguished three main realms or

Reprinted by permission of the publishers from Alex Inkeles, "Social Stratification in the Modernization of Russia," The Transformation of Russian Society, Ed. Cyril Black. Cambridge, Mass.: Harvard University Press, 1960, pp. 338–339, 341–342, 348–349. Copyright © 1960 by the President and Fellows of Harvard College.

[1] On the French Revolution, for example, see Elinor G. Barber, The Bourgeoisie of 18th Century France (Princeton, 1955).

"orders" in social life, each with its distinctive allocated object and each yielding its own pattern of differentiation. The political order refers to the pattern for allocating power, the economic order to the allocation of goods and services, and the status order to the allocation of honor, prestige, or "standing" in the community. To these we should, perhaps, add several others, assigning a more independent role to realms which Weber subsumed under the term status, including a whole complex of factors he summed up as "style of life." In modern times we need to give more independent standing to what might be called the realm of "experience"—wherein are allocated access to aesthetic experience and opportunities for the development and expression of individual talents and needs. Another is the realm of knowledge, wherein are allocated the skills, information, and wisdom which are the collective heritage of the society.

Each of these realms or social orders is characterized by a pattern or organization, a set of rules, which determines the allocation of the realm's distinctive scarce good. These rules determine who gets what, when, and how. To the extent that a good is differentially distributed and the differentiation is relatively enduring, we have the fundamental condition underlying the phenomenon of social stratification. All those who have more or less equal chances for a share of the particular good are designated a stratum. Such strata may be sharply separated from each other and even prescribed by law. Such were the Tsarist estates, including the hereditary and personal nobility, honored citizens, large and small merchants, and peasants. Each held precisely defined rights and privileges, such as the right to own serfs or the exemption from corporal punishment. Strata are, however, equally likely to be separated only by imprecise and perhaps even arbitrary dividing lines. This is eminently true in the case of income, where the categories used are generally quite conventional, and modest shifts in the "cut-off" points are of little significance.

...I offer two propositions on the effects of the process of modernization on stratification systems. The first holds that the modernization of a traditional social system leads to a decrease in the degree of differentiation in each of the stratification subsystems or orders. That is, a process of relative homogenization takes place, reducing the gap or range separating the top and the bottom of the scale in income, status, power, experience (self-expression), and knowledge (skill). More important, in each hierarchy modernization brings about a marked increase in the proportion of the total population that falls in the same or adjacent strata near the middle of the distribution.[2] The prototypical elongated income pyramid, for example, becomes truncated; both the broad base and the sharp tip are eliminated, and in its place there is a trapezoid or perhaps even a diamond shape. The distance from the top to the bottom of the scale is reduced, and more people will be found sharing relatively the same position within a narrow range of the total scale. Movement from one to another position on the scale, furthermore, will not be sharply proscribed. Fluidity will characterize the system as a whole, especially with regard to individuals occupying adjacent or close positions in any given status hierarchy.

[2] It is important to stress the location of the "bulge" because in a traditional peasant-based society there is extraordinary homogeneity, or concentration of the majority of the population in a single stratum. Thus in Russia some 80 per cent were peasants experiencing fairly homogeneous conditions. But this bulge was at the bottom of the distribution and in terms of "range" very far removed indeed from the top of the hierarchy.

The second proposition holds that under conditions of modernization there is a tendency to equilibration within the stratification system as a whole, a tendency that is, for standing on any one of the stratification scales to be the same or similar to the individual's or group's relative standing on the other scales. The traditional society abhors discrepancies in standing, but generates them in abundance because of the rigidity of the several stratification orders. By contrast, the modern society is relatively indifferent to such discrepancies, but its greater flexibility in fact tends to minimize their number.

These rather sweeping assertions cannot be fully or even adequately documented in a chapter as limited as this in size and topic. Some few illustrations may, however, serve to suggest the direction in which a fuller account would go. This brief excursion should also help to highlight some of the reservations and restrictions which must be applied to the propositions sketched above.

. . . Knowing only a man's occupation in the modern society, we can predict with reasonable success a host of other characteristics, including the man's standing in the community, his income, education, aesthetic preferences, and housing.

I cannot here cite relevant evidence in any detail. But our report of the findings of the Harvard Project on the Soviet Social System[3] presents detailed evidence of the extent to which a man's position in the occupational structure in Soviet society falls into line with other important characteristics of his situation. The stratification profile presented by each major social group reveals marked consistency in the relative standing of

[3] Alex Inkeles and Raymond A. Bauer, *The Soviet Citizen: Daily Life in a Totalitarian Society* (Cambridge, Mass., 1959).

the group in each of the several subsystems, spheres, or social orders which together make up the larger stratification system. High, middle, or low standing on one dimension is associated with high, middle, or low standing on the other scales measuring the share of scarce goods received by those in various groups. A few illustrative figures involving two groups near the poles of the hierarchy should suffice.

In income those in the professional-administrative category fell overwhelmingly in the highest bracket, 63 per cent earning 6,600 rubles per year or over (in 1940). Only 3 per cent fell in the lowest category earning 3,000 or less. But 60 per cent of the unskilled workers fell in that category, 87 per cent in the two lowest categories combined (earning 4,199 rubles or less). Those who had the well-paid jobs stood at the top of the educational hierarchy as well. In the more recent generation of Soviet citizens we found that at least 75 per cent of the college graduates entered the ranks of the professional and top administrative groups; of the remainder all but 4 per cent were at least semi-professional. At the other end of the scale, those with four years of schooling or less were ordinary workers or peasants by occupation in 85 per cent of the cases, and only 3 per cent were at the white-collar level. The educational measure is particularly useful in highlighting the tendency of modern society to bring the different stratification measures into line. Among those who share humble origin, born into worker or peasant families, it is almost invariably true that those who secure more education also rise in the occupational scale. Thus, of those from such backgrounds who secured schooling for only four years or less, 88 per cent remained peasants or workers. But of those who managed to get beyond secondary school, 79 per cent secured white-collar or professional-administrative jobs.

Another realm of stratification in which the tendency toward equivalence of position in different hierarchies may be noted is that of access to information. On every measure of involvement in the communications network, of the fullness of a man's contact with sources of ideas and information, the professional-administrative group was at the top of the hierarchy, the ordinary worker at the other pole. Of those in the intelligentsia 82 per cent were frequent readers of newspapers and magazines, and 62 per cent frequent radio listeners. The workers fell near the bottom of the scale, with only about 20 per cent being frequently exposed to such channels of official communication.

Finally, we may note that even in the realm of "psychic income," where we measure the gratification and satisfactions of daily living, the same pattern prevails. The professional-administrative group is consistently at the top of the hierarchy with regard to prestige and personal satisfaction; the working class consistently falls near the lower end. When our sample judged the regard or esteem in which selected occupations were held by the population, the highest scores were earned by the professional-administrative occupations. And when we asked the incumbents of various positions how they liked the jobs they held, the professional-administrative group was at the top, with 77 per cent satisfied, whereas the unskilled workers fell near the bottom of the distribution with only 23 per cent reporting satisfaction.

These are but a few of many illustrations which could be introduced to show that there is a striking consistency in the relative standing of each major occupational group on the several different hierarchies of stratification in the USSR. The Soviet Union is of course not unique in this respect. A similar situation prevails in the United States and in other large-scale industrial societies: a general tendency to minimize the discrepancies in the standing of any group as one goes from one to another realm of the stratification system. To put it in more positive terms, modern society tends to encourage comparability, congruence, or equivalence in the position of any group in each and all of the relevant distinctive hierarchies making up the stratification system as a whole.

IV

THE FAMILY: MARITAL
AND SEXUAL RELATIONS

Insofar as family relationships are less influenced by political criteria, one would expect to find more dispassionate sociological discussion of this subject than in the more sensitive areas of ideology, polity, or stratification; however, this is only partly true. Soviet sociologists, committed to a generally critical appraisal of capitalist society and of the United States in particular, cannot exempt the family from the overall indictment of the entire institutional structure. If, in their view, the fundamentals of social arrangements are distorted, it should follow that the family too must be a warped institution under capitalism. Certainly the growing instability of the American family over the last half-century lends plausibility to this argument. Whether or not this instability is inherent in the capitalist socio-economic system or in other factors is, of course, a matter of debate.

The major criticism the two Soviet authors make of the American family is that it is not a good enough provider of emotional gratifications and genuine warmth, being contaminated by the disease of monetary interest, and calculation, and unable to escape the "contradictions" of the larger society. Kharchev inclines to think that this is less so in proletarian families, which, according to him, prefer divorce to adultery and are on the whole more concerned with the "moral quality" of the matrimonial union. Though we are not trying to refute every single misconception Soviet sociologists entertain about American society, it should be noted that this assertion is among the most unsupportable by any empirical evidence. Instead it reflects the ideological convictions of Soviet sociologists about the mythical virtues of the proletariat. Zamoshkin, more familiar with American society (resulting in part from several visits) is more sensitive to the role the family plays in the life of Americans. It is interesting that his description of the American family as the "oasis where one can reestablish a sense of self-esteem...etc.," is highly similar to American descriptions of the Soviet family especially under Stalin when it was seen as the only refuge or island of safety amidst the hardships and endemic insecurity of life outside.

Robin Williams' discussion of the American family is somewhat more abstract and theoretical. He is particularly interested in the effects of changing size and kinship structure. While sensitive to the problems confronting the American family, and particularly those deriving from the expectations of emotional intensity and intimacy, he does not regard the American family as hopelessly crippled by the structure and nature of society. Rather, he seems to feel that its problems result only in part from the typically American social-historical experience, while many others are related to the generally changing functions of the family in modern, urban, secular societies. Significantly enough, these implications of his analysis are strikingly borne out by some of the empirical findings of Soviet sociologists about the Soviet family.

The Soviet writings on the Soviet family are characterized by a contrast more and more frequently encountered in Soviet sociological works dealing with Soviet society. It is the contrast between empirical findings and theoretical conclusions. (This, incidently, is among the criticisms made of Kharchev's work by another Soviet sociologist, Mindlin, quoted below.) Thus, the Soviet family is said to be a fine, flourishing, affection-bound institution free of all the conflicts and contradictions which pollute family life in Western societies. By definition, all conditions have been provided for the most wholesome family relations. At the same time, on the empirical level, there are findings such as the rising divorce rate (a sure sign of crisis in the United States, though not in the Soviet Union), huge increase in the number of unwed mothers, widespread common law marriages, and a persisting housing shortage which deprives young couples of privacy and is often among the causes of divorce or separation. The double standard of Soviet sociologists is also fascinatingly revealed in comparing Kharchev's criticism of an American sociologist for accepting people's self-evaluation of their motives for marriage with his own study of Soviet marriages. The same Kharchev reports with pride that 76.2 per cent of the *Soviet* couples interviewed in his study "regard the prime condition for a lasting and happy marriage to be love...." Yet he observed in his book (in the context of assessing the *American* motives for marriage) that "...science cannot take everything at its face value which people say about themselves...." It is most likely that both in American and Soviet societies people, and young people in particular, believe that they *should* get married for reasons of love, rather than for money, good housing, social status, and other unromantic and calculated motives. It is interesting in this connection to draw attention to another statement made by Kharchev in another article.

In conditions of socialism, where love and the striving for conjugal happiness have become the dominant goal of the marriage contract, the demands made of marriage have risen sharply. And the possibility of contradictions between what an individual expects of marriage and the reality of family life itself has grown accordingly. The new criterion for evaluating a marriage has changed the attitude toward divorce as well: it is juridically and morally recognized in the name of this very right of the individual to 'optimum satisfaction' in marriage.

This point is, of course, precisely the one made by Robin Williams and other American sociologists discussing romantic love, divorce, and high expectations, though not "in conditions of socialism" but in contemporary American society. If both Kharchev and the American sociologists are right in their respective assessments, it would appear that there is a remarkable similarity between the sources of family instability in the two societies.

There are, of course, also obstacles to stable family life which are peculiar to each society. For example, housing difficulties are a paramount factor in the life of Soviet newlyweds, sometimes compelling temporary separation or more typically the sharing of the apartment with in-laws or strangers, and sometimes, as Kharchev mentions, sending children to relatives with more ample housing. These are not the characteristic problems of American families. Nor should anyone in the United States find it necessary to plead, as Kharchev does, for the necessity of families spending their vacations together. In the U.S.S.R. this problem arises from the provision of vacation facilities through the place of employment which often makes no allowances for family ties. On the other hand, Soviet family life is not so threatened, as the American, by the obsession with sex, youth, glamour, and sexual competitiveness. It would also seem that, despite the greater opportunities for Soviet women in various areas of employment and public life, they have so far escaped the role conflicts the equalization of women created in the United States. To some extent this is perhaps due to persisting traditional values in Soviet society which compel women— more so than in the United States—to combine full domestic and full outside occupational roles despite the hardships of such a combination. One would not be likely to find a highly educated and qualified woman in the Soviet Union languishing in a well-equipped suburban home, bemoaning her fate as mere housewife and mother who makes little use of her training. Most Soviet women work, especially the more highly qualified ones, because they will earn as much as a similarly qualified male; few Soviet families can live comfortably on one income; and the prevailing atmosphere and officially fostered "public opinion" is unfavorable to idleness. It would be our guess that only a tiny proportion of Soviet women married to prominent professionals, administrators, or party functionaries do not work, but if not, they are satisfied and have no role conflicts, just as the wives of the newly rich in this country have no role conflicts.

In comparing the equality of American and Soviet women, an interesting paradox emerges. It appears that although in the occupational realm Soviet women have achieved greater equality and have little discrimination to contend with, they are less equal in the home than American women.[1] This indicates an interesting difference in the evolution of the relationship and role of the sexes in the two societies. Soviet women, as a result of the deliberate policies of the regime, attained virtually full equality in the fields subject to institutional control but have been less successful in emancipating themselves in the more intimate, personal spheres of life outside the reach of such controls. This state of affairs reflects the limitations and the quality of social change and social engineering in the Soviet Union which, proceeding from top to bottom, has left relatively untouched certain areas of life, thus allowing certain traditional relationships and attitudes to persist. It is easier to regulate employment and educational opportunities than the attitudes of man to woman or the role relations within the family. In the United States the trend has been the opposite. Institutional control and intervention from above has been more limited, but a more gradual evolution within the family and in the relations of the sexes has taken place over a longer period of time, and has resulted in women's greater equality in their personal relationships with men, in the home, and in the family decision-making process than in the public and occupational realms.

In both the United States and the Soviet Union the relationship between the sexes, in and outside the family, is affected by certain residual puritanical values. These are, however, quite different both in their origins and manifestations. American puritanism is religiously derived, and, as an odd anachronism, coexists with the overpowering preoccupation with sexuality. Using Soviet terminology, sexual puritanism in the United States is a "survival" which is most poorly integrated with the other aspects and values of American life. The major proposition of this puritanism is the counsel of premarital chastity to women, an injunction surrounded by the veritable flood of encouragement to engage in sexual behavior, and to be sexually alluring practically from infancy until ripe old age. Adultery is also disapproved of though widely practiced. The principal concrete manifestation of American sexual puritanism is a legal system that makes divorce difficult and costly and ties it to the pretense of false motives (i.e., there is virtually no state in the United States where people can get divorced purely on grounds of personal incompatibility), and various legal restrictions on the effective dissemination of birth control methods and in particular on access to abortion. There are also other minor manifestations such as dormitory regulations for young women designed, apparently, to prevent them from having sexual relationships after certain hours or in their own rooms.

[1] *Cf.* also the article below "Argument with a He-man."

The Soviet version of sexual puritanism (or prudishness) has two components. One is the surviving traditional values of a peasant society and the other the Neo-Victorian antihedonistic moral code imposed by Stalinist totalitarianism. With the demise of Stalin and the continuing urbanization of Soviet society both ingredients have been weakening, but as some of the articles following indicate, they have yet to disappear completely. Sex and sexual education is still considered a "difficult subject" both by teachers, sociologists, and journalists, and it would seem that there are astonishing pockets of ignorance on the subject in Soviet society. One might also discern further similarities between the crude sexual attitudes of some Soviet and American adolescents and their apparently shared difficulty of integrating the sexual with the emotional experience.

The two American selections on the Soviet family are both concerned, among other things, with the changes in the regime's policy toward the family, which for some time has puzzled many Western observers. In particular the major puzzle was provided by the spectacle of the transformation of revolutionary libertarian policy (apparently aimed at the destruction of the family) into a most conventional, indeed Victorian, set of family policies and official moral standards. We would like to add one to the many interpretations of this shift. Soviet family policies became more rigid, conventional, and restrictive as the regime became fully totalitarian under Stalin in the early 1930's. What we suggest is that freedom and fluidity in family life, in personal, sexual, and emotional relations is incompatible with overall regimentation and repression; that in a totalitarian society the leaders try to liquidate pockets of freedom and libertarianism not only in political but also in personal life. A strict sexual morality, conventional family life, and puritanism in interpersonal relations is more compatible with totalitarianism than freedom and fluidity in these areas. Possibly there are simpler explanations; namely, that the regime could not afford to carry out the radical reorganization of society, which abolishing the family would have entailed, as it lacked the resources to create new institutions for the upbringing and complete socialization of children. Thus the task was left, at least partially, in the hands of the family, which survived with many of its socializing functions neutralized by other agencies.

Since the death of Stalin the general loosening of regimentation and controls came to be reflected in family life and policies. Abortion, divorce, romantic love are once more permissible and not frowned upon, or less so. The emphasis on the total subordination of personal to collective interests has become more muted. Along with other changes which have occurred in the last decade, the Soviet family has begun to reflect the problems of family life which arise in contemporary, urban, secular societies. Instability, the intensification of hedonism, conflict of the generations, and parental permissiveness are among these symptoms the Soviet family appears to share with the American on an increasing scale.

THE AMERICAN

FAMILY:

The American View

Kinship and the Family

ROBIN M. WILLIAMS, JR.

In the American kinship system, (1) the incest taboo everywhere forbids a person to marry father, mother, and children, grandparents, uncle, aunt, niece, nephew.[1] In twenty-nine states intermarriage of first cousins is forbidden; intermarriage of blood relatives is seldom otherwise limited. (2) Marriage is monogamous and there is no prescriptive pattern for kinship marriages. (3) No discrimination is made between paternal and maternal relatives for marriage purposes. (4) Although the "family name" descends through the male line, there is little other emphasis upon the male line of descent. The descent system tends to be bilineal or, more strictly, multilineal.

These characteristics indicate a highly dispersed system of intermarriage and kinship.[2] From any given individual X

the ancestral lines can theoretically fan out indefinitely into the past, so that any of many lines of heredity may be emphasized for some purposes. Similarly the lines of descent dispense among a large number of kin-name groupings.

Thus, (5) there is an emphasis on the immediate conjugal family.[3] In a highly developed consanguine kinship-system, by contrast, the tightest unit is the descent-group of siblings,[4] a group

From Robin M. Williams, Jr., American Society. New York: Alfred A. Knopf, 1965. Composite of excerpts reprinted by permission of the publisher. Copyright 1951 by Alfred A. Knopf, Inc.

[1] See Vernier and Weller, American Family Laws: Introductory Survey and Marriage, Vol. I, pp. 173 ff.

[2] The best structural description is Talcott Parsons, "The Kinship System of the Contemporary United States," American Anthropologist, Vol. XLV, No. 1 (January–March 1943), pp. 22–38.

[3] Margaret Park Redfield, "The American Family: Consensus and Freedom," American Journal of Sociology, Vol. LII, No. 3 (November 1946), p. 175. "The American family—parents and children—appears on the surface as a simple conjugal type with no important or formal connections with remoter kin, no rituals of ancestor worship (except, perhaps, in the case of the D.A.R.'s), and no intricate economic ties. It is a small, compact group of two generations, bound together by ties of affection and functioning to care for the young until they reach years of maturity and can repeat for themselves the process of family rearing."

[4] Cf. Ralph Linton, "The Natural History of the Family," in Ruth Anshen (ed.), The Family, p. 25.

of brothers and sisters whose spouses enter as strangers and remain always somewhat so. In America, the solidarity of spouses is stressed, to the exclusion of in-laws.

The emphasis in modern, urban, middle-class America upon the marriage pair is bound to result, insofar as it is actually carried out, in a greatly simplified kinship structure of nuclear families.[5] This has profound sociopsychological implications, to be examined later.

(6) The immediate family of father, mother, and children tends to be the effective residence, consumption, and social unit. No extended kin-groupings are of more than negligible importance in these respects, except among a few relatively small, deviant population-elements. The doubling-up of families in the same household ordinarily occurs only under economic depression, housing shortage, or extraordinary family circumstances. Even grandparents in the home, once more or less taken for granted, has become unusual.

The relatively independent conjugal unit is regarded as desirable, right, and proper by social consensus. It is felt that each "family" (typically this is simply *assumed* to mean "immediate family") *should* be an autonomous group. It is considered unfortunate if for any reason other relatives have to reside in the household. Except in extraordinary crises parents are specifically expected not to "interfere" with the families of their children.

(7) In urban communities, which are increasingly representative of the country as a whole, the family group is typically a consuming rather than a producing unit. Kinship-units as work groups and productive organizations have largely disappeared except in farming and certain types of small retail businesses. The family producing-unit characterizes societies with relatively little industry and economic specialization. The family farms and the small shops and stores of earlier America combined functions that have been separated in an age of giant corporations, mass industry, and highly specialized occupations. The cooperation of all family members in a common economic enterprise makes for a kinship-grouping quite different from that of the modern urban family. Contrary to some impressions, however, the unity of the old-style rural family did not rest exclusively on *shared* activities (for example, men's and women's work were sharply segregated) but rather on the fact that the activities of each member were family-centered and did not involve potentially disruptive extra-familial associations.[6]

(8) Because the nuclear family is the unit and the kinship system is multilineal, American society little emphasizes family tradition and family continuity.[7] Of course the "old society" families of Charleston, South Carolina, and the Beacon Hill families of Boston, for example, put considerable stress upon lineage and collateral kinship. Significantly, however, such groups are

---

[5] Cf. Margaret Mead's statement: "A primary stress upon the husband-wife relationship results in a bilateral kinship system and a very simple kinship-structure which lacks the continuity of descent-groups...the family founded upon the husband-wife relationship is too unstable and discontinuous a form of organization to provide the type of firm structure which is given by social groups based on blood relationship." *Encyclopaedia of the Social Sciences*, Vol. VI, p. 67.

[6] Cf. William J. Goode, *After Divorce* (Glencoe, Ill. 1956), p. 93.

[7] The following statement is a reasonably accurate description of the modal pattern: "The family is thought of not as an organic structure to be handed on from generation to generation but rather as the individual creation of each generation and enduring rather less than a lifetime." Redfield, "The American Family: Consensus and Freedom," p. 176.

commonly regarded as so exceptional as to be ready subjects for comment. Among many wealthy, "upper-upper" groups there has developed a marked concern with family continuity and tradition, but they are neither types nor "models" for the society as a whole. Significantly also, families wishing to emphasize continuity and tradition often have a difficult time doing so. A thriving business is done in ferreting out genealogies, tracing descent from notable persons, discovering (or inventing) coats of arms, and so on. This desire for family history is specific evidence of the lack of continuity. One does not need a specialized search for traditions, genealogies, and symbols where these things are a solid part of actual family life.

(9) There is comparatively free choice of mates. In fact, American mate-selection is to a considerable extent an application of "free competition" in the institution of marriage. The whole detailed system of "dating" is a unique American arrangement.[8] Within certain legal barriers,[9] the choice of spouses is purely personal; the kin of the prospective mates have no right to interfere. Parents are usually asked to sanction the marriage choice but this convention is residual. The free choice of mates is made possible by the autonomy of the marriage unit. The married pair do not have to fit into an established kinship unit with consequent important and complex repercussions upon many other individuals. This

[8] See the discussion by Willard Waller, "The Rating and Dating Complex," *American Sociological Review,* Vol. II, No. 5 (October 1937), pp. 727–37.

[9] The most important legal barriers concern "race," degree of consanguinity, age, and physical or mental health. Thirty-one states require a physical examination; twenty-five have a waiting period.

autonomy in turn rests upon geographic and occupational mobility.

. . .Since husband and wife constitute the most basic solidary group in the kinship order, they must, partly because of peculiar features of the social stratification system, be treated by the wider community as a unit and thus as social equals in important respects. Were this not the institutional pattern, ordinary social intercourse between the individual family and outside groups would certainly put such serious strain upon the marriage bond as to threaten it. It is not a trivial matter of "mere convention" or "manners" that in the typical middle-class, urban community, if either spouse is invited to a mixed "social" gathering, the other spouse must be likewise invited. For any aggregate of persons becomes a real social group only by being identified as a unit, by sharing a common set of experiences, and hence by sharing a common universe of meanings and symbols. This kind of solidarity is, of course, quite compatible with marked differentiation of sex-roles and with inequalitarian husband-wife relationships; but once we are given a kinship-system of dispersed, multilineal nature built around the marriage bond, the pressures to treat the nuclear family as the primary unit are bound to work toward equalities between husband and wife. And still other social conditions, external to the husband-wife relation itself, affect the roles of husband and wife. Sharp segregation of role-activities within the family probably will be found to be at maximum when there is a combination of low physical mobility, low social mobility, extended kinship connections in the area of residence, high birth rates, and certain types of occupational demands upon the husband. When the married partners engage in many social relationships with a tight-knit social circle of friends and relatives, the roles of husband and wife probably will tend to be clearly segregated.[10]

The so-called emancipation of women has been greatly exaggerated and misinterpreted in much contemporary discussion. Yet there is no doubt that women in the United States have a relatively great amount of freedom. The disappearance of formalized chaperonage is in itself an important indication of emancipation. Our statutory laws have greatly modified the older common-law conceptions in the direction of equalizing the formal rights of husband and wife. Married women may make contracts, own property, make wills, and sue or be sued in their own right. Some court decisions now even affirm that the husband and wife may sue each other. The legal status of such husband-wife suits is still confused and ambiguous, but they mark a radical move not only toward equality of rights in law but also toward an individualization ("atomization") of the legal structure of the family.

Besides legal rights, American wives hold a remarkable set of customary or conventional intrafamilial rights that, although perhaps less rigid and explicit, are hardly less common or less important. Not even in theory is the wife expected to render unquestioning obedience to her husband, much less in actual practice. The marriage relationship most commonly held up as a model is one in which joint decisions are reached. It remains true that general concensus still holds that in the last resort the husband should be "head of the house,"

but it is felt that only in rare circumstances will "partiarchal" rather than "democratic" processes be desirable.

...Probably the most obvious change in the general social position of women has been a blurring of the feminine sex-role in the masculine direction. Some specific evidences may be briefly enumerated:

1. *Legal rights:* women vote, hold public office, practice professions, hold and dispose of property, etc.

2. *Occupational role:* women participate in paid work outside the home on a large scale; they have entered traditionally male occupations.

3. *Educational participation:* there are coeducational school systems, colleges, and universities; graduate studies are open to women.

4. *Recreational patterns:* women participate in active sports, patronize drinking places, etc.

5. *Courtship behavior:* women have a kind and degree of freedom and initiative in courtship not before sanctioned.

6. *"Symbolic" evidences:* women emulate men's clothes in their slacks, tailored suits, etc.

Nevertheless, women's roles remain clearly distinguished in a number of ways.[11] Housekeeping and the care of children is still the primary role of adult women. In 1955, only 29 per cent of all married women were reported to be working. The percentage of married women in the labor force is highest among younger women, urban women, those with no children under ten years of age, and those whose husbands' incomes are in the lowest brackets. In the higher income levels, the working wife seldom has a job equal to that of her husband in status or pay. Despite long agitation for the principle of equal pay for equal work, it is difficult to

---

10 Bott has suggested this hypothesis: "The degree of segregation in the role-relationship of husband and wife varies directly with the connectedness of the family's social network" (op. cit., p. 60).

11 Cf. Parsons, "The Kinship System of the Contemporary United States," pp. 33–36.

find evidence of husbands and wives competing on an equal basis and in large numbers in precisely the same occupations;[12] where women work in wage-earning occupations, it is usually out of the presumed necessity of supplementing the husbands' incomes, and the "career jobs" (white-collar, professional, and business) of married women will typically not be in *direct* competition with men in their husband's occupation.

Much of recent discussion of women's roles appears to be dealing with the problems of the last generation, not this one. The "problem" of the working wife, for instance, is no longer a major issue in most families. It is now widely taken for granted that married women will work for pay outside the home if "necessary," e.g., to supplement the family income, to use special training in the period before children arrive, to fill the days usefully after the children no longer require continual care. The question has shifted from whether wives or mothers should be in the labor market at all to˜when, how, and under what specific circumstances such employment is justified or desirable. Although only a minority of women work, the crucial point is that the opportunity exists, and hence the possibility of choice.

. . .Marriage and family still come first for most American women, even though most of them at some time do work for pay outside the home. Although the "career woman" is an important social type, the percentage of women who follow continuous careers is very small. Few women hold administrative or executive positions, e.g., in the field of education only about 8 per cent of high-school principals are women. Few women attain high political office. And established conceptions of the feminine role exert widespread and powerful influences in many subtle ways. If a woman becomes a doctor, she is likely to specialize in dealing with women and children. If she becomes an electrical engineer, she may be advised (as in an actual case known to the author) to specialize in the design of household appliances. Even the political issues concerning which women have been most active have been closely associated with the traditional "feminine" functions of nurturance and protection—schools, juvenile delinquency, mental health, protective legislation, child labor, and the like.

In short, even in our "emancipated" society there remain persistent and important pressures tending to preserve the roles of women as mothers and homemakers. These pressures are neither wholly arbitrary nor a simple matter of social inertia and the survival of traditional prejudice. If women were to compete for jobs on an equal basis with men, drastic changes would be necessary in the family system, or in the occupational structure, or in both. So long as women bear children, who must be cared for and trained during the extended period of dependency, there must be *some* social arrangement to ensure that the necessary functions are performed. We can imagine a situation in which men, children, and retired elders might take over the major part of child-rearing; or, we can conceive of homemaking and child-rearing functions being performed by professional workers operating through new forms of social organization. *Complete* free-

---

[12] The practice of equal pay for women and men in the same jobs has undoubtedly gained ground in recent years, partly under the influence of the industrial labor unions. However, as late as 1933, the comprehensive survey of the President's Research Committee on Social Trends complained that "it is almost impossible to secure wage data for both men and women doing precisely the same tasks, even within the limits of a single occupation." *Recent Social Trends*, Vol. I (New York, 1933), p. 736.

dom of occupational competition for women would certainly involve one or both of these paths—or the disappearance of stable family units as we know them. At present, the family system is made partly compatible with the employment of many married women by: (1) low birth rates and small families; (2) extrafamily service agencies providing certain household aids and child care; (3) the tendency not to employ women in jobs that compete with those of men in the same socioeconomic class. The last factor, whatever psychological problems it creates for women, tends to reduce the possibilities of a husband-wife competition for status that can be quite disruptive of marriage solidarity.

. . . The great emphasis in American culture upon idealizing romantic love depends closely upon certain features of the basic family system. With the diminution of the extended family and the correlated loss of many previous functions of the nuclear unit, the family's chief function has come to be that of providing affection and security. When choice of mates is relatively free, personal attraction bulks larger in marriage than it could under any system of arranged marriages; it is a commonplace hypothesis in the sociological literature that our emphasis upon romantic love is in part an equivalent for the group support and regulation of marriage in the less diffuse and mobile systems of many other societies. At the usual age of first marriage, the young person is still acquiring emotional independence from the parental family, under the multiple stresses just discussed. The "need" for dependence is strong, and the institutional demand for independence is strong. Under these circumstances, it is necessary to break through complex and deep-seated resistances to marriage and its responsibility and emotional independence without the

help of a clearly defined system of mate choice based upon status and wider kinship regulation. An almost compulsive emphasis upon romantic love emerges in part from this situation.

Furthermore, young people who have been brought up in the relatively isolated and autonomous small-family unit probably bring to a marriage a tendency to depend emotionally upon one or a very few persons, and, in the extreme cases, after marriage are almost completely thrown back upon one another for full emotional response and basic psychological securities. In a mobile, competitive world, so largely dominated by relatively impersonal and segmented social relationships, the courtship process and the marriage relation can thus come to carry a kind of intensity and importance not typical of societies lacking these characteristics. The ideals of premarital chastity and lifelong fidelity in marriage, insofar as they are socially effective, increase this intensity.

It is clear, of course, that romantic love is not confined to America, nor to modern times. It is potentially universal, and actually very widespread in time and space.[13] Nowhere is it completely released from social control. As a matter of fact, the greater the emphasis upon freedom of personal choice of mate, the more likely it is that there will be ways of restricting the "field of eligibles"[14] within which young people may choose. Residential separation, restricted social circles, and a thousand

13 ". . . love relationships are a basis of the final choice of mate among a large minority of the societies of the earth." W. J. Goode, "The Sociology of the Family: Horizons in Family Theory," in Robert K. Merton, Leonard Broom, Leonard S. Cottrell, Jr. (eds.), *Sociology Today* (New York, 1959), p. 194.

14 Numerous studies have shown these facts: ". . . spouses tend to be alike in those status characteristics that are structurally central for their society, such as race, religion, rank, eduaction, and income." W. J. Goode, *After Divorce* (Glencoe, Ill., 1956), p. 98.

social pressures, both the obvious and the subtle, combine to insure that final choices will not be socially capricious.

All the indirect influences or "secondary institutions" that operate to encourage romatic love are at work in a family system that has already freed the spontaneous affective inclinations of the young couple from elaborate restrictions. In proportion as marriages are not arranged, they are left to the choice of the potential partners, and, as institutionalized status (such as social class or caste) is less important, the choice rests more on individual qualities and achievements. Because American society has come to permit considerable personal choice, the pattern of romantic love is encouraged both by the family structure and by a series of indirect consequences of that structure. Of course, the extreme stereotype of romantic love is partly a "cultural fiction." Marriage partners available to any given individual are severely limited in practice by race, religion, social class, propinquity, and so on. Nevertheless, our culture continues to idealize romantic love.

FAMILY STABILITY AND INSTABILITY

Despite many cultural prescriptions supporting the permanence of the marriage tie and the solidity of the nuclear family, American society is characterized by what are commonly regarded as high rates of divorce and other forms of family dissolution. The atomization of the family into separate legal personalities is far advanced; the family is extremely open to external agencies and influences, from nursery schools to radio and from the social worker to the truant officer, the military draft, and even the political party. Kinship obligations sometimes are not strongly upheld, and many of these have been taken over by the state. The effective family unit is, therefore, a small permeable group. It is emotionally intense, but often is not strongly supported by the surrounding society.[15]

There are probably some ten million Americans who hae been divorced, and it is estimated that between one fifth and one sixth of American adults who live out an average lifespan will experience divorce.[16] In addition, the number of marriages broken by separation and desertion probably equals the number dissolved by divorce. The divorce rate per 100 marriages, which was 16 in 1930 and 21 in 1940, climbed to the all-time high of 40 in the postwar year of 1946. By 1951, however, the rate had dropped back to 21.5.[17] The ratio of divorces in a given year to the average number of marriages in each year of the preceding decade is a good index of marriage instability, since most divorces occur within ten years after marriage. This ratio has risen from 6 per cent in 1890, to about 40 per cent in 1947.[18] From 1867 to 1932, divorce occurred in increasingly earlier years of marriage: during 1867–86, a marriage was most likely to break up in its seventh year, but by 1922–32, in its third or fourth year, and today probably in the third year. Although divorce rates are higher

[15] Some modern students of the family have been sufficiently impressed with the signs of family instability to argue that our society faces a major "family crisis." The most prominent exponent of this is Carle C. Zimmerman, *Family and Civilization* (New York, 1947); and *The Family of Tomorrow* (New York, 1949).

[16] William J. Goode, *After Divorce* (Glencoe, Ill., 1956), p. 11.

[17] Kingsley Davis in Fishbein and Kennedy, op. cit., p. 108.

[18] See the estimates cited in the article by Kingsley Davis, "Children of Divorced Parents: A Sociological and Statistical Analysis," *Law and Contemporary Problems* (1944), reprinted in Davis, Bredemeier, and Levy, *Modern American Society*, pp. 680–81.

in urban than in rural areas, divorce has come to the open country; for example there was about one divorce for every four marriages even in the most rural counties of Ohio in the period 1937–47.[19]

Most divorces dissolve *marriages* rather than *families*; apparently about two-thirds of all divorces are childless. In desertions and informal separations, on the other hand, it appears that there is a smaller proportion of childless couples than in the total population.[20] Through a lack of data concerning desertion and nonsupport, however, we must rely chiefly upon divorce as an index of family instability. Judged by divorce alone, the United States certainly has a high rate of family dissolution. Differences among national divorce laws and customs make strict comparison very dubious, but without doubt, family break-up is very frequent in our society, by any standard of comparison.

How is this family instability to be explained? Full causal analysis is impossible here, since a full "historical" treatment would deal with all of American civilization. However, the preceding discussion has provided important clues.

Popular explanations of "the divorce problem" commonly stress the alleged personal incompatibility of the spouses. Yet plainly personal incompatibility explains very little, for why does the incompatibility ever arise, why does it lead to divorce, and why do families often endure even in the face of severe interpersonal tensions? There are structural factors far more basic than the "reasons" commonly advanced for

family breakdown. Marriages dissolve because: (1) divorce or separation is *permitted*; (2) there are few strong internal bonds holding the marriage together; and (3) the marriage-pair or family unit is not well supported by the surrounding social structure. Modern America combines all these features. It permits divorce far more readily than formerly. At the same time the American family has lost many of its former functions—the multiple activities that once centered in and around the home. The family as an almost purely consuming and affectional unit contrasts sharply with the old-style "trustee family"—practically a self-contained social system combining economic production, education, "government," religious functions, and "social security"; including several generations; and comprehending nearly all phases of the individual's life. The sharing of common tasks in a collective enterprise in such families was one manifestation of the close economic and social interdependence of family members.

Modern family instability if often blamed directly upon the loss of multiple functions. It is better to say that the remaining family "bonds" bear too heavy a load and break under it. As the family has become less important, it has also become more important; the scope of family activities has narrowed, the emotional significance of the surviving relationship has, in one sense, increased. High expectations are imposed upon a relatively vulnerable structure. For instance, the ideal of perfect husband-wife compatibility in romantic love conflicts with the fact that many families have few common activities and institutional supports.

From considerations of this kind it is easily possible to build up the impression of extreme fragility in American families. This impression would not be entirely accurate. The high divorce rates

[19] A. R. Mangus, "Marriage and Divorce in Ohio," *Rural Sociology,* Vol. XIV, No. 2 (June 1949), p. 132.

[20] Davis, Bredemeier, and Levi, *Modern American Society,* p. 682; Ernest R. Mowrer, *Family Disorganization* (Chicago, 1939), pp. 99–100.

of the years immediately following the turmoil of the Second World War have declined. Even at the peak of the divorce rate in the United States, higher rates had been found in many nonliterate societies as well as in major political societies (e.g., Japan, Russia, Palestine, Egypt, at various periods).[21] Furthermore, most divorced persons rather promptly remarry—in fact, about 94 per cent of women divorcing at age thirty will eventually remarry. And it appears that the remarriage rate of divorced mothers is not much lower than that of female divorcees generally.[22] To an appreciable extent, we have developed a largely unrecognized subsystem of tandem monogamy—or "sequential polygamy"[23]—in our complex efforts to deal with the new as well as the permanent aspects of the relations of men and women and children in families.

And we must remember, as suggested in passing at several points in earlier discussion, that the image of the relatively autonomous and isolated nuclear family does not accurately describe all of American society. Both in rural and in urban areas, extended kinship relations retain an importance not obvious to superficial inspection. Despite high geographic mobility, most families of procreation retain meaningful relations with their families of orientation. Even in the seemingly impersonal and turbulent metropolitan areas, patterns of visiting and of mutual aid in crises govern relations with kinsmen who are socially accessible.

The American family is not a dying institution. It already has been strengthened by new forces. Although in addition to stresses within the kinship structure, it is subject to multiple strains from other institutions (e.g., occupational structure which interferes in many ways with stable family life), higher birth rates and renewed emphases on family values attest to the continued tenacity of this basic social unit.

[21] Goode, *op. cit.*, pp. 10–11; George P. Murdock, "Family Stability in Non-European Cultures, *Annals,* Vol. 272 (1950), pp. 195–201.

[22] Goode, *op. cit.*, p. 207. A basic point in this connection is made by Goode (p. 216): "Although the rate of divorce is high the existing kinship institutions indirectly move both child and mother back into relatively well-defined statuses, thus fixing responsibility for maintenance, status placement, and socialization of the child."

[23] Jessie Bernard, *Remarriage: A Study of Marriage* (New York, 1956), p. 46: "...probably more persons practice plural marriage in our society today than in societies that are avowedly polygamous." About one out of every eight married persons has been married more than once.

THE AMERICAN
FAMILY:

The Soviet View

The Development of Marriage
and Family under Capitalism

A. G. KHARCHEV

The most optimistic concerning the nature of marriage in contemporary bourgeois society are those sociologists who, like J. Fichter (U.S.A.) believe that the marriage contract and family relations are based only on feelings. He writes that "among Americans such a great significance is attached to romantic love as the essential basis for family life, that we are shocked when one speaks of marriage for comfort, of a marriage broker, or of marriage for financial or social position. . . . In contrast to a financial contract or political obligation, the marriage contract in its context takes into account the change of feelings and desires."[1]

Apparently, Fichter bases his conclusions mainly on self-evaluation, i.e., on what the married people themselves think about their relations. But, to

Original Translation

Reprinted from A. Kharchev, Marriage and the Family in the U.S.S.R., *Izd. Mysl., Moscow, 1964, pp. 85–86, 87–88, 91–92, 95, 98, 103–104.*

[1] J. Fichter, *Sociology* (Chicago, 1957), p. 259.

whom is it not clear that as long as even bourgeois public opinion is squeamish about marriages of convenience (and in this Fichter is indisputably right), no one who enters into such marriages, with the exception of hardened cynics, will parade his true aims and motives, but would rather profess to have nobler bases for marriage. Moreover, the meaner the motives, the greater the efforts to hide or camouflage them. Therefore, science cannot take everything at its face value which people say about themselves and make it the basis for theoretical propositions.

. . . Consequently, Fichter's statement about romantic love as "the essential basis of family life" in contemporary America can be applied only to a part of the families, mainly to working families. So far as he attempts to generalize his proposition to all property-owning families, he comes into conflict both with facts and with the evidence of a number of people sufficiently well informed about life in contemporary bourgeois society.

If one assumes that all Americans

really reject "marriages for financial position" and "marriage brokers," then how can one explain the success of such an establishment as, for example, the "Helen Brooks" marriage bureau, selecting men and women for a 100 dollar fee? If the bureau manages to find the appropriate mate for the client, it extracts from him a few hundred dollars more, depending on how much the spouse is worth. It is difficult to believe that the objects of "romantic love" find each other this way. All the more so as in the card index of the bureau the clientele is classified not by aesthetic and moral attributes but mainly according to status and income. If one takes into account that the "Helen Brooks" bureau "contracts" on the average of 3.5 marriages a week, and that in New York there are several tens of these bureaus registered (in Manhattan there are eight) then it emerges that marriages contracted with the aid of brokers are far from being a rare phenomenon in the largest city of the U.S.A.

...Noting all these contradictions in the marital and family relations of contemporary capitalist society, we don't mean to suggest that marriages based on love are completely absent from the bourgeois social environment, or that belonging to the propertied class always and everywhere entails the primacy of calculation over feeling. Moreover, it cannot be disputed that the process of female emancipation, affecting in one way or another also the women who belong to the propertied class, has strengthened the striving for romantic love not only among workers, but also among the bourgeois youth. But if in the case of the working youth this striving can be realized in marriage, under corresponding material conditions with respect to the bourgeois youth the realization of the same aspiration signifies as a rule the repudiation of one of the best opportunities for a sizeable enlargement of capital, a break with tradition, the danger of being deprived of parents' blessing, and consequently of the parents' inheritance, and finally it signifies the threat of "sanctions" from those elements of "society" which consider "unequal" marriages a betrayal.

...It is true that all this can be avoided if romantic love develops between people who "suit" each other economically too, but as is generally known, such cases are very rare and cannot be considered typical of marital relations in contemporary bourgeois society.

As a result, even if the striving for romantic love exists among contemporary bourgeois youth, it does not destroy the conflict between "the principle of ownership" and the "principle of the family," but reinforces and exacerbates it.

...In the book *Sisters of the Night* by J. Stearn it is shown that today in the United States of America side by side with professional prostitution, the prostitution of students and working women is widespread. In describing one of the "establishments" whose owner is called Willy, the author notes that the women involved are virtually in the bondage of the owner. He takes all the money which they "earn" and uses his fists if he meets with even the smallest objection. It is practically impossible to tear oneself away from this establishment, and hence many of its inhabitants end their lives in suicide.[2]

...Thus, prostitution as a phenomenon accompanying the proprietary marriage and organically connected with it, continues to exist in contemporary bourgeois society and enjoys if not the direct, at least the indirect support of the ruling class. Only its forms have

[2] J. Stearn, *Sisters of the Night* (New York. 1956), pp. 62–64.

changed in response to new conditions: formerly there existed clearly marked, mostly legal centers of trade of human commodities, now this trade is better "dispersed" and camouflaged, and consequently, more ubiquitous and effective. Formerly the circle of women involved in prostitution was comparatively sharply divided from the rest of society; at present this boundary has become highly relative and fluid since, as has already been stated, many of the "B-girls," "call girls," etc., work or study; added to this are the irregular, part-time prostitutes. The "upsurge" in the numbers of the latter is usually connected either with the deterioration of the material condition of certain groups in the population, or with temporary rise in the demand for prostitutes. In all these changes one can hardly detect any element of progress.

... Discussing the increasing spread of adultery in contemporary bourgeois society, some Western writers, and especially sociologists, tend to find the main cause of this trend in the economic and spiritual emancipation of women rather than in the intensification of the internal contradictions of proprietary monogamy. But even if one agrees with the view that this emancipation has to some extent affected matrimonial fidelity, this only confirms the existence and intensification of the contradictions mentioned. It means that until the emancipation matrimonial fidelity was not an organic part of marriage, but was maintained only by fear and by the dependent position of women. One must not forget that adultery is significantly older than emancipation, and most importantly, that those classes in bourgeois society in which the emancipation of women has been carried out most completely and consistently, primarily of the proletariat, suffer the least from adultery. This integrity of the proletarian marriage derives first of all, from the nature of its motives (mutual feeling and not economic advantage), and secondly, from the absence of economic interest in the continuation of the marriage in the event of discord between husband and wife. Therefore, while a propertied husband and wife prefer adultery to divorce, a proletarian couple prefer divorce to adultery, since their most precious possession is the moral quality of marriage.

Thus the family in contemporary bourgeois society is changing in two directions. The first has been promoted by the development of private property relations and the social practice of the parasitic strata of the bourgeoisie. It is connected with the growth and the strengthening of the utilitarian-economic, businesslike element in marital and family relations, it entails the sharpening of the contradictions created by them. The second change has resulted from the economic and spiritual progress of society under capitalism and by the social practice of the workers. It is connected with the emancipation of women, the predominance of equal relations between the sexes, the conversion of marriage to a voluntary union of man and woman based on personal choice.

The Crisis of Bourgeois
Individualism and Personality

Y. A. ZAMOSHKIN

It is not by accident that today in American sociological literature family problems are given enormous significance. In order to understand more profoundly the meaning of this constant emphasis of the role of the family in the life of the contemporary American, one can turn, for example, to an article very typical of this preoccupation, written by Professor L. J. McKinley, appearing in the book, *Values and Ideals of American Youth*. McKinley, recognizing the growth of social diseases of the personality on a mass scale among adolescents in the U.S., relates these diseases to the dehumanized, estranged, functional-bureaucratic relationships between people. At the same time he thinks that essentially the family is the only source of genuine, human relations in the contemporary world not poisoned by conventionality, competition, and selfish commercialism. He maintains that "Only the family can give a young man a sense of his personality, and create a unity of common aspirations and individual goals."[1]

The family, in the eyes of many

Original Translation

Reprinted from Yu. A. Zamoshkin, "The Crisis of Bourgeois Individualism and Personality," Izd. Nauka, Moscow, 1966, pp. 252–253.

[1] E. Ginsberg, ed., *Values and Ideals of American Youth* (New York, 1961), p. 312.

people in the U.S., appears to be that oasis where one can reestablish a sense of self-esteem and achieve harmonious and humane relations combining the shared efforts and interests of the whole family with the development of the individuality of each member. Is this really the case? The facts of life show that the family in contemporary American society is very often not in a condition to fulfill this task. The family is an internally subordinate part, a cell of the overall social organization (especially at the present time when it often no longer has independent productive or socio-political functions). Therefore the family inevitably carries upon itself the imprint of social relationships and social contradictions characteristic of society in general, in our case that of the contemporary capitalist society in the U.S.

Coming into the family, man brings with him the whole complex of ideas, moods, feelings, internal spiritual contradictions and torments deposited in his consciousness while in the sphere of productive or business activity, as a result of his contacts with the economic, political, ideological attitudes of American state-monopoly capitalism. And it is natural that the American family often becomes a particular accumulator of social contradictions which are characteristic today of the U.S. A typical example is the family of J. Houly, the main hero of Steinbeck's novel, *The Winter of Our Discontent*. This family, which from the beginning seems to the reader, and even to the hero himself, a kind of oasis where one can hide from the brutal world of competition, buying and selling, and from the inhuman attitudes of the surrounding reality, subsequently itself turns out to be only a particular segment of that same reality.

THE SOVIET
FAMILY:

The Soviet View

On Some Results of the Study
of the Motives for Marriage

A. G. KHARCHEV[1]

The family is one of the most complex of social institutions. The fact that there are so many sides, so many aspects, to family relationships makes it possible for a large number of social factors to influence them. These range from the ratio between men and women in a country's population to the nature of the morality dominant in the given society. Most important among these factors is the economic system, which influences the status and development of the family as an institution both directly and through other aspects of social life: the position of women in society, the standard of living, government policy and law, social ideology and psychology, etc. Therefore, the triumph of socialism in the USSR led to a corresponding change in the field of marriage and family relationships and to the appearance of a new, socialist type of family. Socialization of property in the means of production resulted in a fundamental change in the nature of the very need for marriage: from an economic necessity it was transformed into a moral one.

As Friedrich Engels once observed, under the conditions of dominance of private property, the monogamous family "is based on the dominance of the husband, with the clearly-defined purpose of producing children whose descent from the father is not subject

Reprinted by permission of International Arts and Sciences Press from A. G. Kharchev, Nauchnye doklady vysshei shkoly. *Translated in* Soviet Review, *V, No. 2 (Copyright © Summer 1964) 252–253.*

[1] Paper presented at 8th International Seminar on the Family, Oslo.

to doubt, and this unchallangeability of descent is essential because the children will, in the course of time, as direct descendants, come to possess the property of the father" (Marx and Engels, *Selected Works* [Izbr. proizv.], Vol. II, Gospolitizdat, 1955, p. 208). The same thing, essentially, although in less clearcut form, is granted in a number of contemporary sociological publications in the West: "The family," we read, for example, in one of them, "not only distributes the wealth, but accumulates property of various types in the form of capital. For individual and social progress it is quite important that this accumulation proceed in a specific and orderly fashion from generation to generation" (*Sociological Theory*, New York, 1956, p. 274).

The freeing of family and marriage relationships from subordination to concerns of accumulation and transmission of private property by inheritance had inevitably to exert an influence upon the nature of those relationships and, above all, upon the motives for marriage. By motives we understand everything that impels people to marry, including both the major and "secondary" goals of marriage. For all their diversity, it is possible to reduce them to two forms:

1. Motives deriving from the essence of marriage, from the human desire for motherhood and fatherhood and intellectual, moral and esthetic strivings, of which the highest is love.

2. Motives alien to the essence of marriage, depriving it of significance in and for itself, and transforming the selection of the future mate into merely a means of achieving goals external to the marriage relationship itself (increase in wealth, the receipt of economic, political or administrative benefits and advantages, etc.).

Both groups of motives have been operative in all socio-economic systems starting with that of slavery. But a private-property economy provides a stimulus for the motives that deprive marriage of its real essence and therefore, as Marx once put it, "at a higher stage of development *the principle of private property contradicts the principle of the family*" (Marx and Engels, *Works*, [Soch.], Vol. I, p. 334). On the other hand, a socialist economy and the entire system of social relationships existing under socialism create the atmosphere "most favorable" to marriage for love and sharply reduce the opportunity for "marriage of convenience."

Suffice it to say that in the majority of bourgeois countries, despite all the efforts of the progressive strata of society, economic, political, legal and, in particular, moral-psychological discrimination against women persists, while in all socialist countries women are equal with men in the opportunity to get jobs, in payment for their work, in civil rights and in the eyes of society. At the end of 1960, women in the USSR numbered 53% of all employed persons with higher education and 63% of all with higher and secondary education in professional skills (*The National Economy of the USSR in 1960. Statistical Yearbook* [Narodnoe khoziaistvo SSSR v 1960 godu. Statisticheskii ezhegodnik], Moscow, Gosstatizdat, 1961, pp. 661, 662). Thus, the socialist system eliminates the economic and social bases for the dominance of man in the family and thereby sharply accelerates the operation of the tendency, arising even under capitalism, to convert marriage into an equal and voluntary alliance of man and woman.[2]

[2] Professor Nelson Foote comments on the family in the United States today: "The stablest families, as demographers have repeatedly demonstrated, are found among people in the 'professional class' or 'professional group' .... Members of this group usually favor

But on the other hand, we know that the changes toward socialism in the USSR took place under conditions of serious economic and social difficulties associated, in the first place, with civil war and devastation, then with World War II and the fascist occupation of a considerable portion of the country, and finally under conditions in which the threat of a new world war had not yet been eliminated.

As a result, despite the immense improvement in the material well-being of the people and in housing construction,[3] the standard of living in the USSR does not yet in all respects measure up to the opportunities inherent in socialism. Moreover, the death of millions of men at the front led to a great disproportion between the male and female populations in the USSR after World War II. According to the 1959 census, there were 20,700,000 more women than men in the country. And while today this applies primarily to people in the middle and older age groups (over 32), ten to fifteen years ago it was typical of a younger segment

liberal divorce laws, larger employment of women (married women included) and greater equality between man and wife in the family circle. Marriages between persons in this group usually involve young people of approximately the same age. They marry across ethnic, class, and religious lines more freely than do others." (*Problemy sotsial'nykh izmenenii XX veka. Obzor dokladov Tret'ego Mezhdunarodnogo sotsiologicheskogo kongressa. Amsterdam, avgust, 1956 god,* Moscow, Izd-vo Sov. Nauka, 1957, p. 52.)

3 The real incomes of workers (including elimination of unemployment and reduction in the working-day) multiplied by a factor of 5.8 from 1913 to 1962, and the real incomes of the peasants (including those used to increase the indivisible capital and reserves of the collective farms) by a factor of about seven. The housing available in towns and urban settlement rose from 180,000 square meters in 1913 to 1,014,000 square meters in 1961. (*SSSR v tsifrakh v 1961 godu. Kratkii statisticheskii sbornik,* Moscow. Gosstatizdat, 1962, pp. 348, 350, 381.)

of the population. Naturally, all this influenced the thoughts, psychology and behavior of human beings, and complicated the struggle against the old property-holding, petty-bourgeois, anarchistic and other traditions in relationships between the sexes. Therefore one cannot regard the present status of marriage and the family in the USSR merely as a consequence of the socialist transformation of the economy and the social structure. In the sphere of personal and everyday life there is, along with the predominant progressive and socialist tendencies, still a good deal that is negative. However, this is not a product of socialism, but, as a general rule, of those extremely difficult historical conditions under which socialism was fated to develop. This must be borne in mind both in considering marriage and family relationships in the USSR and in comparing them with the institution of marriage and the family in bourgeois lands.

* * *

In the USSR, special studies of motives and practices in marriage have been a rarity. The question was usually regarded as one of the problems to be dealt with in overall study of the family and family life (see S. Ia. Vol'fson, *The Family and Marriage in Their Historical Development* [Sem'ia i brak v ikh istoricheskom razvitii], Moscow, Sotsekgiz, 1937; N.A. Kisliakov, *Family and Marriage Among the Tadzhiks* [Sem'ia i brak u tadzhikov], Moscow and Leningrad, USSR Academy of Sciences, 1959; S.M. Abramzon, K.I. Antipina, G.P. Vasil'eva, E.I. Makhova, and D. Sulaimanov, *The Way of Life of the Collective-Farm Peasantry of the Kirgiz Villages of Darkhan and Chichkan* [Byt kolkhoznikov kirgizskikh selenii Darhan i Chichkan], Moscow, USSR Academy of Sciences, 1958; *Viriatino Village in the Past and Today*

[Selo Viriatino v proshlom i nastoiash-chem], Moscow, USSR Academy of Sciences, 1958; *The Family and Family Life of the Collective Farmers of the Baltic Region* [Sem'ia i semeinyi byt kolkhoznikov Pribaltiki], Moscow, USSR Academy of Sciences, 1962, and other works).

Inasmuch as data directly descriptive of the goals and intentions of persons entering into marriage are confined to their own opinions and value judgments, we have, in addition to studying these opinions, made an attempt to obtain some indirect evidence of an objective nature. The role of parents in marriage, the relation between the ages of bride-groom and bride, the duration of ac-quaintance before marriage, the rise in marriages across ethnic lines, etc., fall into this category.

With the object of shedding light on these matters, we conducted, toward the end of 1962, a questionnaire survey of the persons getting married at the Leningrad City Registration Bureau (ZAGS), and also analyzed the data of these bureaus for the Uzbek SSR, the city of Kiev, the town of Tiumen', and Mga Raion of Leningrad Oblast.

It appears to us that the following circumstances testify to the representa-tive nature of the data obtained in the Leningrad City Registration Bureau:

1) a majority (about 85%) of all marriages in which the ages of both parties do not exceed 30, and about half of all marriages in the city are registered there;

2) persons marrying for the second or subsequent times are not registered at that office. Thus, the very regulation governing this institution assures that the marriages studied are the most typical;

3) the structure of the population of Leningrad is a sort of "optimal model" of the structure of the country's urban population in its entirety (a high percentage of skilled industrial workers and of scientific and technical profes-sionals, a large stratum of persons employed in culture and education and of students and a minimal proportion of persons not directly engaged in work for socialist society);

4) the study extended over a com-paratively long period of time (two months). A total of 500 couples were questioned, and 300 more question-naires were filled out as a check against the results obtained.

The persons queried consisted of 21% workers, 10% engineering and technical personnel, and 28% students, plus white-collar workers, physicians, and people in science, culture and education, the arts and military service.

The question pertaining directly to people's ideas as to the motives for marriage was formulated as follows: "What, in your opinion, is the prime condition for a lasting and happy mar-riage?" This formulation made it possi-ble to transfer the "stress" from the factors that led to the choice of the particular individual (which might have been regarded as "interference in per-sonal affairs") to the general moral bases of these factors. This, in our view, diminished somewhat the prob-ability of untruthful answers.

Of all the couples who filled out the questionnaire, 76.2% regard the prime condition for a lasting and happy mar-riage to be love or love plus community of views, mutual confidence, sincerity, friendship, etc.; 13.2% regarded equity of rights and respect as primary; 4% named love and housing conditions; 1.6%—love and material well-being; 0.6% named the presence of children and 0.2% said "a realistic view of life." The remaining 4.2% gave no reply. Even if we assume that many of those who failed to reply held views similar to those who gave preference to material factors, the total number of such persons would still constitute only some 5% of those getting married. This ratio indicates that the moral approach to marriage has come to predominate in Soviet society.

However, the preference given to the moral approach should not be interpreted as indicating any inclination toward asceticism. Sample oral interviews showed that the people getting married understood the full importance of economic security in married life, but when the moral and material conditions for marriage were in conflict or not in harmony, the moral were given preference. This is particularly indicated by the answer to the following query in the questionnaire: "Where do you intend to live after you get married?" The present housing shortage often faces young people in love with the dilemma of postponing marriage and waiting till they get housing, or of marrying despite unfavorable material circumstances. Which choice is favored? 9.4% replied: "We hope to obtain a new place to live"; 7.6% intended to live in the groom's present quarters (without parents); 7.6% in the bride's, also without parents; 19.6% with the groom's parents; 16% with the bride's parents; 2% "part of the time with the groom's and part of the time with the wife's parents"; 15.6% intended to rent a room; 9.8% expected to remain in dormitories for the time being; one pair (0.2%) was leaving for Siberia after the marriage; the others answered "we don't know" (1.4%) or gave no answer. The decision to marry of that portion of the youth who do not enjoy normal living conditions is associated with its confidence that, in view of the fact that the USSR has the world's highest rates of public and cooperative housing construction they will be able to obtain an apartment in the relatively near future.

Summation of the findings on the role of parents in marriage yielded the following results. Of 500 couples, 79.6% had asked their parents' agreement before deciding to marry and 77.8% obtained it, 1% "got it, but not at once," and in four cases (0.8%) the groom's parents objected. 13% did not ask the parents' agreement but informed them. In 3.4% of the cases "our parents don't yet know we're married"; two couples (0.4%) have no parents; and the remaining 18 couples (3.6%) did not respond to this question. Thus, the overwhelming majority of the marriages (78.8%) were concluded with the knowledge and agreement of the parents. As was demonstrated by sampling conversations with newlyweds after they had filled out the questionnaires, in all these cases the choice of partner was made by the person getting married; the parents merely gave their approval to the choice. Thus, parents have not been ousted from a part in the marriage of their children but their role has changed significantly as compared to the past.

The results of ethnographic study of marriage and family relationships in the USSR testify to the clear dominance of moral over material motives, both in choice of a partner and in the decision to marry.

Before the Revolution, marriage among the ruling classes, as well as among the peasantry and the urban petty bourgeoisie, jointly constituting the overwhelming majority of the population of the Russia of that day, was normally accompanied by the payment of a dowry or bride-price or other economic transactions. Today, all ethnographic expeditions observe that the institutions of dowry and bride-price are no longer mass phenomena. In cases in which marriage is still accompanied by monetary arrangements, this is usually condemned by public opinion. Such arrangements are sometimes even concluded by parents against the will of the young couple. Moreover, the dying out of these institutions is characteristic not only for the central regions of the USSR but also for formerly backward ethnic borderlands, and even of areas that have become part of the Soviet Union comparatively recently. It is interesting to note that the new marriage customs at times even find expression in language: in Fergana Region of Uzbekistan the popular name for the ZAGS (Bureau for Registration of Documents of Civil Status) is *"kholadim,"* which means, "I wish, I want" (see O.A. Sukhareva and M.A. Bikzhanova, *Past and Present of the Village of Aikyran* [Proshloe i nastoiashchee seleniia Aikyran], Tashkent, 1955, p. 195).

With respect to the role of parents in marriage, ethnographic studies modify somewhat the conclusions we have made on the basis of the Leningrad data, inasmuch as these studies deal with rural areas and districts with strong vestiges of patriarchal traditions. Thus the expedition headed by S.M. Abramzon found that in the Kirgiz village "by no means all marriages concluded by mutual agreement between the partners receive the approval of the parents on both sides, although in the majority of cases the parents did not stand in the way of the wishes of the young people. About half the marriages were concluded without obtaining the agreement of the parents of one of the parties, most frequently against the wishes of the girl's parents" (Abramzon *et al.*, *op. cit.*, p. 241). However, these cases of parental interference in choice of marriage partner are local in nature relative to the total number of marriages in the country, and are transient in terms of the direction of development of family and marriage relationships in the USSR.

To our question as to the circumstances of acquaintance that led to the marriage, we obtained the following replies: 9% of couples knew each other from childhood (lived in the same building or immediate neighborhood); 21% met at work; 17.5% at school; 27.2% at places of recreation (community center, dance, skating-rink, theater); 5.7% at house parties; 5% at summer vacation spots; 5.2% through mutual friends; 3.3% through relatives; 0.7% lived in the same dormitory; 1.6% met on the street and the other 3.8% in other places (streetcars, trains, hospitals, libraries, and at a mathematical elimination competition). Thus, about one-half the marriages are the result of acquaintances not associated either with place of residence, work or study. This relative independence of choice of marriage partner from occupational or residential localization is also to be seen in the countryside. But here it is limited by the very conditions of rural life, which continues to be a "compact" phenomenon confined within each village. V. Iu. Krupianskaia reports, for example, that "as a result of the fact that population mobility is greater than before the Revolution, boys and girls working outside their home village very frequently get married where they are working. But we heard repeatedly that the youth continue to prefer to marry fellow-villagers" (*Selo Viriatino...*, pp. 225–226). There are both positive and negative aspects to this tendency to expand the socio-geographic domain from which one's future life-partner is selected. To the degree to which it increases the possibility that the individual chosen will correspond more fully to the moral and esthetic ideals of the individual entering marriage, it certainly will improve the prospects of the marriage. But at the same time there is an increasing possibility of chance evaluation and decision in choosing a mate, inasmuch as the knowledge of a person one obtains through contact on the job or in daily life cannot always be replaced by some other form of verification. A person's internal nature often does not correspond to his outward appearance or even to his behavior in some comparatively brief period of time.

Soviet scholars have as yet made no attempts to study "stages of courtship." But it would seem that we have not lost much by this, for the conclusions Western sociology is coming to in this regard do not as yet go beyond trivial assertions to the effect that people first meet, become acquainted, date, and then these dates either break off or end in marriage. This sequence apparently is not affected by the societal differences in the modern world and therefore exists in all countries where patriarchal power of parents over children and men over women does not exist.

Of considerably greater sociological interest is the question of the length of acquaintance preceding marriage. Summation of the responses to this question enables the following conclusions to be drawn (data in %) in Table 1.

Although these figures hardly parallel the nature of the marriage and family relationships that ensues, they are, however, the only objective source for our judgments in this field.

Judging by these data, most marriages (58.5%) are the result of comparatively long-term acquaintance (over two years) and this means, one must assume, of tested feelings and a serious,

morally-motivated decision. This also applies, although certainly to a lesser degree, to marriages preceded by acquaintance of one to two years' duration (23%). Only in cases totalling less than one-fifth of all marriages (18.5%) may doubt arise that the individuals who have entered them have had the chance really to get to know each other and make sure of their feelings.

*   *   *

A study of the ages of persons entering upon marriage may be useful in determining the motives and essence of marriage in two respects: 1. The average at marriage gives us an idea of the degree to which natural need in this respect is in accord with social conditions or is distorted by the latter. 2. The relation between age of the two parties provides some indication of the degree to which the marriage is free of utilitarian calculations and factors, for, as H. Bowman correctly observes, among the factors explaining "why young people marry older ones," "a powerful social status, and prestige is far from the least important" (H. Bowman, *Marriage for Moderns,* New York, 1942, p. 166).

Different and often even contradictory trends are characteristic of different parts of the USSR, as far as average age at marriage is concerned. Thus, according to L.N. Terent'eva, "comparison of data on the age of persons marrying during the years of bourgeois dictatorship in Latvia and prior to that, as far back as before 1917, with those for two years after 1940 shows that there was a rise in age of marriage

TABLE 1

A few days	Under 3 mos.	3 to 6 mos.	6 mos. 1 year	1 to 2 years	2 to 3 years	3 to 5 years	5 to 8 years	Since childhood	Total
0.7	2.9	9.3	5.6	23.0	25.6	14.8	9.1	9.0	100

during the first years after establishment of the Soviets. In later years, this age declined considerably, to 24–25 for men and 21–23 for women" (*Sem'ia i semeinyi byt...*, p. 81).

Another picture may be seen in Uzbekistan. Here are data obtained from ZAGS documents for that republic over a twenty-year period (in %) (see Table 2).

to buy land and tools. All this increased the number of late marriages and led to a rise in average age at marriage. Consequently, the reversal of the process indicates that these factors had ceased to be operative and that marriage has come to be governed not by factors external to it, but by the desires and personal choice of the individuals entering into marriage themselves.

TABLE 2

	Men	Women	Men	Women	Men	Women
18 and under	2.2	35.0	4.0	16.8	2.4	12.8
19–22	19.0	27.7	16.4	37.7	19.4	36.3
23–26	31.1	17.1	19.0	19.0	28.2	15.3
27 and over	47.7	20.2	60.6	26.5	50.0	35.6
	100	100	100	100	100	100

Consequently, while this twenty-year period showed comparative stability of mean age at marriage for men (the only major fluctuation was in the immediate postwar year of 1946), this age rose steadily for girls. The number of marriages of girls 18 and under dropped by nearly two-thirds. At the same time there was a considerable rise in the percentage of marriages in which the bride was between 19 and 22, or over 26. True, this increase occurred to some degree as a result of the influx of Russians and Ukrainians after the war and was less typical of the indigenous people, but this only modifies our conclusion somewhat, without changing its essence.

Thus, we face two trends in change in the average age at marriage: a reduction in Latvia and a rise (among women) in Uzbekistan. What is the explanation in each case? In the presocialist Latvian countryside, marriage was governed first by the age at which a son came to own a farm or a portion of one, and secondly upon the accumulation of the dowry. Farm laborers usually postponed marriage, hoping first to accumulate some sum of money

In Uzbekistan, on the other hand, before the changes to socialism, forced giving of under-age girls in marriage was widely practiced. As the table indicates, this tradition remained in substantial force in 1937. It goes without saying that as equality of rights for women took stronger root, along with their increasing economic independence and cultural advancement, this tradition could be expected to disappear gradually. One of the indicators of this is the regular reduction in the number of early marriages of girls and the gradual equalization of the marriage age of men and women.

Thus, these tendencies, despite the significant differences between them, actually constitute an expression of the same process: the liberation of marriage and the humanization of its motives.

In order to determine the approximate relationship between the ages of groom and bride in marriage in the USSR today, a selective study of marriage records was made at the registries in Kiev, Tiumen's and Mga Raion of Leningrad Oblast. In our opinion, the choice of these places meets the requirement that the sample be representative both geographically and in terms of the society. Kiev is one of the largest industrial and cultural centers in the country, and has the style of life characteristic of large cities. Tiumen's is a comparatively small regional center. Finally, Mga Raion was chosen as an ordinary (and in that respect typical) rural district.

All told, 600 cards were studied, 200 from each of these places. No special selection of the cards was made: all the marriages concluded during a given time interval were considered. (The length of the interval depended upon the number of marriages recorded by the given ZAGS per day.) It seems to us that such an approach assured the discovery of general trends considerably better than a special system of selection could have done, in that it preserved the relationship which had objectively taken shape among the various categories and types of marriages during a given period.

The study yielded the following results in Tables 3, 4 and 5.

It should be said in explanation of these tables that in cases in which the groom was younger than the bride, this difference usually did not exceed three or four years, and was usually one or two years.

The data on the relationship of ages at marriage permit us to identify certain trends in this field of marriage and family relationships, independent of or little dependent upon local conditions.

We note, in the first place, that in the overwhelming majority of marriages the difference in age between partners does not exceed six years (81% in Kiev, 84.5% in Tiumen', and 89% in Mga Raion).

Marriages in which the partners are of the same age or in which the age difference is minimal (not over three years) number over two-thirds of the total, and marriages in the top range of difference (twenty years and more) are virtually nonexistent because there are only isolated instances of these. Even marriages in which the husband is ten or more years older than the wife are comparatively rare, ranging from only 4.5% (Mga District) to 9% (in Kiev).

Of no less interest is the fact that marriages in which the groom is younger than the bride are comparatively numerous. On the basis of a study of the statistics of natural population movement in 1924–1925, V. G. Peschanskii, a Soviet demographer of that day, concluded that there was a tendency for "men 25 years of age and older to take wives younger than themselves." But grooms of 18 or 19 married older women in one case out of three (*Natural Movement of Population of USSR. 1923–1925* [Estestvennoe divizhenie

TABLE 3

MARRIAGE AGE RATIOS IN KIEV (1959, in %)

			RATIO OF AGES OF GROOMS TO BRIDES					
			Groom older					
Age of bride	*Groom younger*	*Same ages*	*1–3 years*	*4–6 years*	*7–9 years*	*10–12 years*	*13 years and more*	*Total*
Under 20	1.0	1.0	1.0	2.5	—	—	—	5.5
20–24	8.0	9.5	22.5	8.5	5.5	2.0	—	56.0
25–28	3.0	0.5	4.0	1.5	0.5	0.5	0.5	10.5
29–32	2.0	1.0	2.0	1.5	0.5	—	—	7.0
33 and older	3.5	0.5	5.0	2.5	3.5	2.0	4.0	21.0
Total	17.5	12.5	34.5	16.5	10.0	4.5	4.5	100.0

TABLE 4
MARRIAGE AGE RATIOS IN TIUMEN' (1959, in %)

RATIO OF AGES OF GROOMS TO BRIDES

| Age of bride | Groom younger | Same ages | Groom older | | | | | Total |
			1–3 years	4–6 years	7–9 years	10–12 years	13 years and more	
Under 20	—	0.5	7.0	5.0	2.0	1.5	—	16.0
20–23	6.5	6.0	19.0	9.5	4.0	—	—	45.0
24–29	10.0	1.5	4.5	1.5	2.0	0.5	—	20.0
30 and older	6.0	2.5	3.0	2.0	1.5	3.0	1.0	19.0
Total	22.5	10.5	33.5	18.0	9.5	5.0	1.0	100.0

TABLE 5
MARRIAGE AGE RATIOS IN MGA DISTRICT (1959, in %)

RATIO OF AGES OF GROOMS TO BRIDES

| Age of bride | Groom younger | Same ages | Groom older | | | | | Total |
			1–3 years	4–6 years	7–9 years	10–12 years	13 years and more	
Under 20	0.5	1.5	7.0	5.0	2.0	—	—	16.0
20–24	9.5	7.0	18.0	7.5	2.0	0.5	0.5	45.0
25–28	7.0	2.0	3.5	1.0	0.5	—	—	14.0
29–32	6.5	0.5	0.5	0.5	0.5	—	—	8.5
33 and older	6.0	0.5	3.0	2.0	1.5	1.5	2.0	16.5
Total	29.5	11.5	32.0	16.0	6.5	2.0	2.5	100.0

naseleniia Soiuza SSSR. 1923–1925], Moscow, TsSU SSSR, 1928, pp. XXVII-XXVIII). Whereas the first of these two observations may be ascribed to the fact that physiological evaluation of the woman was the prime consideration, the latter was also often based on the economic advantages then to be gained by marrying spinsters and widows (a larger dowry, a peasant farm holding ready at hand, etc.), which were particularly important for grooms who had not yet established themselves, economically speaking.

Today, as we see, the situation has changed substantially. Marriages in which the woman is considerably older that the man and in which, as A.A. Luts has correctly noted, "economic considerations were self-evident" (Sem'ia i semeinyi byt..., p. 101) have virtually disappeared. Marriages in which the bride is one to three years older than the groom are much less apt to be associated with material considerations. Moreover, the fact that they are fairly common may be regarded as evidence of the change in the attitude toward women, and in the criteria of female beauty and of choice of a bride in the direction of increasing importance of intellectual, moral and esthetic factors in these criteria as against physiological ones.

Along with these common trends which, precisely because of their universality, are obviously due primarily to the economic and social system obtaining in the USSR, there are certain differences among the places studied. These differences have to do primarily with the ages at which women marry. Whereas in Kiev the number of women marrying early (20 or younger) is only

5.5% of the total, in Tiumen' and Mga Raion it is 16%. At the same time, the number of women marrying at 33 and older is 21% in Kiev, and only 16.5% in Mga District.

The former circumstance is obviously due to the fact that in small towns and in the villages there is a comparatively smaller percentage of students, a group that usually postpones marriage until the completion of education or, at least, until the senior years. At the same time, the countryside offers greater opportunities for newlyweds to find the things they need to set up housekeeping, housing above all.

With respect to the second circumstance, it may be explained both by

torical period. Taking this into consideration, let us make an attempt to compare the data on the relationship of ages at marriage in 1920, when the socialist revolution in our country had just taken place; in 1940, when socialism had triumphed not only politically but economically, and in 1960, representing the present period in the development of Soviet society. These data are the result of selective study of marriage records in the Leningrad ZAGS archives. All told, 3,000 records were studied, 1,500 of them for the city of Leningrad (Kirov and Kuibyshev Raions) and 1,500 for Leningrad Oblast (Mga Raion). The results of the study are as follows in %:

TABLE 6

RELATIONSHIP OF GROOM'S AND BRIDE'S AGE AT MARRIAGE

Year and place of marriage		Groom younger	Same age	Groom older					Total
				1–3 years	4–6 years	7–9 years	10–12 years	13 years and more	
1920	City	12.5	6.5	25.5	24.0	16.0	8.0	7.5	100
	Country	13.0	4.5	23.5	22.5	17.0	6.0	13.5	100
1940	City	28.0	4.5	20.5	30.5	8.0	4.0	4.5	100
	Country	16.5	10.0	26.0	24.5	10.5	4.0	8.5	100
1960	City	33.5	6.5	28.0	18.5	8.5	3.0	2.0	100
	Country	30.5	10.5	32.0	16.0	6.0	2.5	2.5	100

the fact that in the countryside there is a considerably smaller number of second marriages than in the large cities and by the fact that the disproportion between the male and female populations which came into being in the USSR after the war has made itself felt to a much greater degree in the countryside than in the city.

The correlation between the ratio of ages at marriage and the motives for marriage, as well as the dependence of both these factors upon the economic and societal relationships dominant in society, are seen with particular clarity when data are analyzed not for one year but for a number of years separated by a comparatively lengthy his-

These data indicate primarily that there has been a steady reduction, in the USSR, in the percentage of marriages with a large difference in age between the parties. The percentage in which the husband is older by 13 years and more dropped with particular sharpness. Marriage in which the husband was seven and more years older than the bride, which were 31.5% of all marriages in the city in 1920, and 36.5% in the countryside, were 16.5% and 23%, respectively, in 1940, and in 1960, only 13.5% and 11%. Simultaneously, we observe a regular increase in the number of marriages between equals, the age difference between the parties being minimal (not over three years). Further, it must be borne in mind that in 1920, in marriages in which the bride was older than the groom, the difference in age was considerably greater than in 1940 and 1960. Therefore the data on marriages in 1920 showed that most of them were unequal, while in 1940 and 1960 the overwhelming majority could be regarded as equal marriages.

Thus, the present ratio of age at marriage in the USSR is certainly not accidental but a logical result of the progress and consolidation of socialist principles in the life of Soviet society. It testifies to the rising influence of these principles both upon the motives in choice of a mate and on the marriage itself.

Naturally, the sociological data we have presented are not a sufficient basis for broad general conclusions encompassing the country as a whole. However, they do to some degree describe the trends presently operating in the USSR in the field of marriage and family relationships and, in particular, of motives for marriage.

To begin with, we observe that people see the chief value of marriage not in its material but in its moral consequences, and the fact that it serves as the social sanction for love. Marriage based upon the love and mutual respect of the partners is regarded for all practical purposes as the only morally acceptable form of marriage.

Entry into marriage is the result of the personal choice and personal decision of the future partners. This decision is based primarily upon individual feelings and experience, although in the majority of cases it is made with the knowledge and approval of the parents. Upon entering into marriage, people seek to assure themselves of the necessary minimum of material conditions for their lives together and it would appear that occasionally the choice of

the future mate itself serves as a means of attaining this goal. However, even in these cases utilitarian calculation is not the sole stimulus to the conclusion of a marriage alliance but is primarily an "auxiliary" motive. This is indicated indirectly by such an objective fact as the tendency toward "equalization" of the ages of groom and bride at marriage. When material and moral aspirations conflict it is usually the latter that win out.

In the USSR, the moral prestige of the institution of marriage is particularly high. However, the number of divorces is still comparatively large. According to data of 1960, there were 12.1 marriages per 1,000 in the population, as against 8.5 in the USA, 7.5 in England (excluding Scotland and Northern Ireland), 7.0 in France, and 9.4 in West Germany. At the same time the number of divorces, also per 1,000 population, were 1.3 in the USSR, 2.2 in the USA, 0.5 in England, 0.6 in France, and 0.8 in West Germany (*Narodnoe khoziaistvo...1960, op. cit.*, p. 204).

When we compare these data, it must be borne in mind that in the Catholic countries of Europe and in part in the USA, the percentage of divorces is reduced artificially by church prohibition. In the USSR, however, the percentage of divorces increased primarily as a consequence of postwar difficulties, primarily material in nature, as well as due to the fact that not all marriages were sufficiently firmly based in the psychological and moral sense.

This permits us to conclude that as these temporary factors are overcome, the actual motives for marriage in the USSR will increasingly approximate the moral ideal for relationships between the sexes, and the institution of marriage itself will become stronger and more stable.

Leningrad Chair of Philosophy, USSR Academy of Sciences

The Old in the New

I. MINDLIN

Need it be said how great is the general interest in questions of the family and marriage? Nonetheless, our social sciences, particularly philosophy, have not overly favored this side of life with their attention; moreover, a number of problems connected with family and marital relations were not open to scientific consideration during the period of the personality cult. It was held that the decrees extant in this sphere disposed of all problems. But questions of the family and marriage did not attract the fixed attention of sociologists even after the interdictions disappeared.

In view of this state of affairs, it is difficult to overestimate the importance of A. G. Kharchev's substantial book,[1] which is essentially the first attempt at a thorough sociological study of these questions.

In the first three chapters, "Marriage and the Family as Objects of Sociological Research," "The Social Nature of Marriage and the Family," and "Trends in the Development of Marriage and the Family Under Capitalism," the author gives a critical analysis of fundamental principles and tendencies of foreign (mainly American) sociology. He shows convincingly that modern bourgeois sociology, in spite of all its scientific pretensions, has not gone very far from the Domostroi [a 16th-century treatise on social, religious and family conduct.—Trans.] in its views on the family and marriage. Apart from the fact that bourgeois sociology suffers from conscious idealism and petty "idea-less empiricism," if one may so express it, this sociology is incapable of providing even an approximately true picture of family and marital relations. This is, above all, because the theory of woman's inferiority hovers like original sin over the reasoning of Western sociologists.

The Great October Revolution was not only a social revolution, it was a revolution in way of life, including family and marital relations. Wrote V. I. Lenin: "We have not left stone upon stone, in the true meaning of these words, of those base laws on the unequal rights of woman, on the constraints on divorce, on the infamous formalities which surround it, on the non-recognition of illegitimate children, searching for their fathers, etc.; laws, the vestiges of which are numerous in all civilized countries, to the shame of the bourgeoisie and capitalism." This represented a world-historic advance and placed Soviet civilization on an enormous height from the very first days of its existence.

Reprinted from I. Mindlin, "The Old in the New" (a review of Kharchev's work on family), Novy Mir. (December, 1964). Translated in Current Digest of the Soviet Press, XVII, No. 8 (Copyright © March 17, 1965), 277.

[1] A. G. Kharchev, "Marriage and the Family in the U.S.S.R. An Experiment in Sociological Research." Mysl [Thought] Publishing House, Moscow, 1964. 325 pp.

Churchmen, lawyers and bourgeois sociologists saw in all this the "destruction of the stability of the family hearth," and in general the abolition of the institution of marriage in the U.S.S.R. A. G. Kharchev, in attempting to repulse these attacks, might have relied with success on Lenin's well-known statement cited above. Unfortunately, in reproducing the quotation, his book omitted the words "constraints on divorce, the infamous formalities which surround it, the non-recognition of illegitimate children, searching for their fathers, etc." And actually, as we see further on, A. G. Kharchev defends many of the positions of the 1944 Decree, which contradict the Leninist spirit of legislation on the family and marriage.

This Decree, as is known, introduced birth certificates with a line crossed through the space for the name of the father [if the child was born out of wedlock] and thereby established the concept of the "illegitimate child" (together with this concept, the insulting sobriquet of "single mother" or "unwed mother" entered our life); it introduced multi-stage divorce procedure, etc. A. G. Kharchev justifies these principles by the fact that they are to prevent a frivolous attitude on the part of the woman toward "sexual life." But why only on the woman's part? After all, Engels said that the family should develop in the direction of making monogamy actual for men also. In agreeing to grant a deceived woman the right to recover alimony, A. G. Kharchev is preoccupied with working out legal criteria to distinguish such women "from the sexually dissolute and those who seek to prey upon wealthly alimony-payers" (?). While admitting that the "divorce procedure" sometimes creates situations reminiscent of the "filth of the divorce trial," which V. I. Lenin resolutely opposed, the author is extremely frugal with concrete recommendations. It is difficult to perceive any consistency in this, especially if one recalls the data cited by the author on Leningrad, where 28% of the divorces have as their cause marital infidelity, 21% loss of love or incompatibility of character, and 17% the inability to have children or sexual separation. Thus, 66% of the divorces are motivated by the most intimate, deeply personal relations between people.

A. G. Kharchev not only does not accept the legislation of the '20s and '30s, does not merely defend a number of the principles of the 1944 Decree, which broke with the Leninist spirit of this legislation, but as a sociologist does not take into consideration the objective information that he himself has presented in the book rather fully. Can one really draw the conclusion that there has been an increase in the "moral authority of the very act of registering marriage" from the fact that in 1925 ten marriages were contracted per 1,000 persons in the population and that now the rate is 12 per 1,000? After all, the author admits that despite the duty to register, unregistered marriages "still are quite widespread."

In 1945 there were 282,000 "unwed mothers," while in 1960 there were nearly 2,700,000, and of these approximately 400,000 had two or more children. A large number of unregistered marriages are reflected in these figures; it may also be supposed that quite a few of the so-called "unwed mothers" are de facto married to the fathers of their children, who have not legalized divorce with their former families because of the obstacles in the way of divorce. That such a supposition is well founded may be judged from the data which the author collected in Leningrad. It turns out that "nearly 20% are cases in which both are divorced persons or one of them is already in another (de facto) marriage and has children by it."

On the basis of the objective sociologic data cited in the book, the conclusion suggests itself that the elimination of the very concept of "unwed mother" and "illegitimate child," besides being a colossal moral gain, would greatly simplify family ties. However, instead of drawing this conclusion, A. G. Kharchev urges the introduction of betrothal, formal engagement, as a panacea. It goes without saying that one can, along with the author, regret that the words "fiancé" and "fiancée" are used less and less frequently in their actual meaning and have acquired an ironic connotation. But one need hardly create an artificial "third stage" in courtship by means of an official betrothal preceding marriage.

Let us note, incidentally, that the assertions about the careless attitude of our young people to marriage is not confirmed by the objective data quoted in the book. Thus, from the Leningrad Palace of Marriages' questionnaires it follows that only 13% of the marriages take place after a short acquaintance (of under six months); the remainder take place after a longer acquaintance: from one to two years (23%), from two to three years (26%), from three to five years (15%), from five to eight years (9%), and finally, after acquaintance since childhood (9%). What might be called unofficial betrothal is thus encountered: a considerable period of time between the decision to marry and the registration of the marriage.

It is not a search for palliatives, with which the book's author is occupied, that is needed to further strengthen the moral foundations of family and marital relations, but making our legislation conform with the moral code of a builder of communism, and, consequently, returning to the Leninist posi-

tions on this question. Instead of this, A. G. Kharchev recommends moving further in the "channel of basic ideas and goals" proclaimed in the July, 1944, Decree. The book asserts that the virtue of the Decree is that it increased the social authority of the mother and stimulated a growth in the birth-rate. Is this so? Let us turn to the statistics. They testify that in 1961 the birth-rate had decreased by 25% in comparison with 1940. According to the data of the 1959 census, a quarter of all families did not have children, and of the remaining number half of the families were raising only one child.

But what conclusion does the author draw from this data, which requires great attention and reflection? He is worried most of all that having few children may conflict with the collectivist goals of our upbringing! For this reason A. G. Kharchev notes with satisfaction that between 3% and 4% of all families have more than three children, but he does not help us properly to consider another fact, that one of the reasons for the absence of children or the small number of children in many families is that the woman is too busy. The working day of a married woman, who works at a job and runs a household, is so long that in effect it is almost impossible for her to establish a family with two or three children if her parents or her husband's parents do not share the mother's responsibilities.

In conclusion, let us mention the problem of the future family, raised by A. G. Kharchev in the last chapter. He rightly criticizes the assertions of those who consider that under communism the family will not be preserved as a social institution. Among these he names I. Yefremov, author of "The Mists of Andromeda." A. G. Kharchev says that the family will be preserved under communism, that love for children, the feeling of fatherhood and motherhood and reciprocal feelings not only will not die, but will develop still more. This is true. But it is hardly possible to agree with one of the author's assertions. A. G. Kharchev considers that even under communism, when there will be only the "moral sanction in marriage," there will nevertheless remain a "necessity for special moral arbitration, and at times even for compulsion on the part of society with regard to certain of its members." Thus he assumes not only that the law should "develop" in the "channel of basic ideas and goals" of the Decree, but he also attempts to force future morality into its bed of Procrustes. Isn't it clear that this position of the author diminishes the theoretical and practical value of the experiment he has conducted in sociological research?

A Valuable Study

I. S. KON

The timeliness of sociological investigation of marriage and the family requires no proof; it is self-evident. In recent decades Soviet literature has not produced a single major complex study of this subject. The last serious Soviet sociological work, S. Ya. Wolfson's "Family and Marriage in Their Historical Development," appeared in 1937. Since then marriage and the family have been written about primarily in exclusively juridical or ethical contexts, which is, of course, completely inadequate. A. G. Kharchev's book[1]

Reprinted from I. S. Kon, "A Valuable Study" (another review of Kharchev), Nauchny doklady vysshei shkoly (1965). Translated in Current Digest of the Soviet Press, XVII, No. 19 (Copyright © June 2, 1965), 13–14.

1 A. G. Kharchev, "Marriage and Family in the U.S.S.R.: An Experiment in Sociological Research," Mysl [Thought] Publishing House, Moscow, 1964, 324 pp. [For another review of this book, see Current Digest of the Soviet Press, Vol. XVII, No. 8, pp. 9–10.]

therefore represents the first contemporary attempt at a sociological study of this extensive problem (more accurately, not problem but rather sphere of social life), and this in itself makes the work interesting to the widest circle of readers.

The first chapter of the book is devoted to marriage and the family as a sociological question. The second treats the social essence of marriage and the family; the third, the trends in development of marriage and the family under capitalism; the fourth, the influence of the socialist revolution on marriage and family relations; the fifth, marriage in the U.S.S.R.; the sixth, the size and structure of the Soviet family; the seventh, its basic social functions. The eighth and final chapter is devoted to the prospects for the development of the Soviet family in the conditions of the full-scale building of communism. And all this is not speculative ratiocination but rather theoretical generalization from a huge mass of the most diverse factual data. Needless to say, all problems are not elucidated in the book with equal depth, but they are all raised in earnest, on the basis of a rich fund of source material.

A. G. Kharchev has studied and made very skillful use of the extensive bourgeois literature on the sociology of marriage and the family. While criticizing the theoretical concepts and methods of bourgeois sociologists in a convincing and well-reasoned manner, the author at the same time makes able use of the factual material they have gathered, as well as those of their observations and comments on particular questions that he regards as correct. This comes out with the greatest sharpness in the second and third chapters, although the polemic with the bourgeois authors continues throughout the book. While the entire book rests firmly on Party positions, it is at the same time free of the vulgar-nihilistic attitude to non-Marxist sociology that still occasionally rears its head in certain works, to the obvious detriment of Soviet scholarship.

The factual data relating to the Soviet family are rich and varied. A. G. Kharchev has made use of the works of sociologists (Wolfson), ethnographers (Kislyakov, Abramzon, Antipina, Bikzhanova, et al.), economists (Prudensky), jurists (Sverdlov) and psychologists (Yakobson). The generalization of such diverse data is in itself interesting. But A. G. Kharchev relies just as much on his own sociological research as on the literature. This includes his data on the correlation and dynamics of marrying ages, motives for marrying, reasons for divorce, on nationally mixed marriages, on the structure of the Soviet family, etc.

The monograph under review contains many—in places even too many —facts and figures regarding various aspects of Soviet family life. But this does not reduce it to a mere compilation of facts. They are all subordinated to the theoretical task the author has set himself of ascertaining the fundamental nature and laws of development of the socialist family.

Many theoretical and practically important questions are set forth for the first time in Soviet literature by A. G. Kharchev. An example is his concrete analysis of the structure of roles in the Soviet family, showing the change in the position of the woman not only in work and public activity but also within the family. His study of the functions of the Soviet family, especially its role in raising children, is interesting. As we know, the gradual disappearance of the production function and reduction of the consumer function of the family have been interpreted by certain foreign authors as symptoms of its gradual "withering away." Echoes of these views have also penetrated into Soviet literature, particularly in connection with the development of the system of communal child care (round-the-clock nurseries, boarding schools, etc.). A. G. Kharchev demonstrates the groundlessness of these views, showing on the one hand the need for the family in rearing children, especially young ones, and on the other hand the great moral and psychological importance of this for parents themselves. Of great interest are the data A. G. Kharchev has gathered on nationally mixed marriages in the U.S.S.R., which shed light on one aspect of the national question.

In dealing with diverse problems in the life of Soviet society, the author speaks of the difficulties and contradictions of our everyday life connected, for example, with the housing problem and analyzes them from a correct Party standpoint. Not contenting himself with a description and explanation of social processes, A. G. Kharchev also offers certain practical proposals aimed at improving our legislation on marriage and the family, sex education for young people, etc. In this respect the book under review is of interest not only to sociologists but also to practical workers.

A generally positive evaluation of A. G. Kharchev's work does not imply, of course, that it has no shortcomings. The very scope of its subject matter makes for a certain inadequacy in the treatment of individual questions. This holds true for both general theoretical and concrete sociological problems.

A. G. Kharchev does not trace the historical evolution of the forms of marriage and the family, and rightly so, as this would be a subject for an independent study, or even many studies. Nonetheless, this does not release the author from the obligation to be accurate in his passing observations relating to this question. The author maintains that in contemporary foreign ethnography "theories denying the matriarchy have collapsed" (p. 9). This is not so. The existence of the matriarchy (not to be confused with the maternal family!) is now regarded as more controversial than ever before. On page 27 the author speaks of the "punalua family" [a primitive form of family organization in Hawaii.—Trans.] as of something beyond question. But we know that this matter has been under debate in Soviet ethnography since as far back as 1952. Reservations on these matters must be noted.

In Chapter 3, "Trends in the Development of Marriage and the Family Under Capitalism," A. G. Kharchev cites much interesting data. But his characterization of the "disorganization of the family" (p. 104) is incomplete, and in addition he confuses two different, though mutually related, processes: the disintegration of the family and its disorganization. The disintegration of the family, as evidenced in the reduc-

tion of its size and change in its structure, is a normal process of any modern industrial society. As to its disorganization, expressed in the growing number of divorces, etc., this is a much more complex process, and A. G. Kharchev rightly points out that certain trends observable under capitalism are either absent in the U.S.S.R. or far less pronounced. At the same time, his analysis of the so-called "sexual revolution" in the West would have been far more profound had he linked it to the trend toward destruction of the personality characteristic of modern capitalism.

What is most complicated with regard to A. G. Kharchev's own concrete sociological investigations is the problem of representativeness of data. Sometimes he gives percentages without indicating the number of cases studied. Some of his conclusions are based on selections of data and on statistical calculations that are more hypothetical than fully demonstrated. Subsequent investigations must introduce the necessary corrections.

A weak spot in the book (and this is typical of Soviet literature on marriage and the family in general) is the sexual-psychology aspect. The question of marriage and the family cannot be seriously discussed without bringing in the problem of sex. Man's sex life is no less a product of history than is its legal and moral regulation. Nevertheless, this aspect of the problem of marriage is as a rule treated with embarrassment. A. G. Kharchev speaks about it very obscurely. More over, his individual excursions into sexology do not transcend the limits of "worldly wisdom" and reveal no familiarity with specialized literature. This applies not only to the problem of sexual adjustment in marriages but also to premarital sexual relations.

He reports that in our country as well as abroad "a large number of young people entering marriage have had previous sexual experience" (pps. 203–204). But he views this problem exclusively through the prism of the moral upbringing of youth. Yet the problem is much more complicated. We know that in all developed countries the physical maturity of adolescents now comes much earlier than in the past, sometimes two or three years earlier. But social maturity (precisely social, and not merely the "moral maturity" of which A. G. Kharchev writes), presupposing a definite education, etc., comes much later. Hence arises a complex social problem that moral upbringing alone, for all its importance, cannot resolve. What is required is joint efforts by sociologists, teachers and physicians. And this above all requires overcoming the hyprocritical fear of sex questions that has long exerted a negative influence on the study of the sex-psychology aspect of marital relations.

On the whole, A. G. Kharchev's book is a serious and interesting work, which will undoubtedly assist in further intensive study of the sociological problems of marriage and the family.

Once More on the Family

A. G. KHARCHEV

Editors' Note: Pravda No. 206 printed A. Kharchev's article "The Family Is a Cell of Society." Both the subject of the article itself and its treatment of the problem excited the lively interest of the readers, as attested by the countless letters received by the editors. For all their differences, the letters are permeated with a firm certitude of the large and yet growing significance of the family, the necessity of its further strengthening. At the same time, readers endeavor to discern what the reasons are for particular difficulties and contradictions in the development of marital-family relations in the U.S.S.R. and what ways there are for removing these reasons.

At the editors' request, the writer of the article answers the most typical questions raised in the letters.

1. ...If we speak of the exploiter classes, marriage for them, as we know, is based predominantly on capital, on private gain and on private (but by no means personal) property, and has

Reprinted from A. Kharchev, "Once More on the Family," Pravda (*November 23, 1966*). *Translated in* Current Digest of the Soviet Press, *XVIII, No. 47 (Copyright* © *December 14, 1966), 22–23.*

the purpose of accumulating this property and passing it on through inheritance. Such a marriage is not so much a union of people as a union of estates, of capital.

Under socialism, the decisive motives for entering into marriage have a predominantly moral nature (love, attraction, mutual respect). In other words, it is not the material factors but the personality, the moral and physical qualities of a man and woman, that advance to the foreground.

Needless to say, all this by no means cancels the reality of the organic tie of the present-day socialist family with personal property, the necessity of some minimum material security for the normal existence and functioning of the family collective. And I can only agree with those readers who oppose the insouciance of some young people who go into marriage before they are capable of earning their own livelihood (to say nothing of supporting a family), attempting to build their family felicity "on papa's dole." Such marriages are seldom solid and happy.

But material security per se is only one of the conditions for normal family life.

Our society supports and bolsters the family as the form of social communion that most fully meets people's need for personal happiness, motherhood or fatherhood, and is one of the most important factors in the raising of children.

In conditions of capitalism, where marriage and family life are subordinate to economic and property interests, people regard a conflict between their personal feelings, drives or inclinations and their marital-family status as somehow fitting and proper. And if attempts are made to resolve this conflict, this is done, as a rule, outside the confines of the marriage. It is for this reason that K. Marx and F. Engels considered adultery and prostitution "the natural supplement" to the proprietary marriage.

But in conditions of socialism, where love and the striving for conjugal happiness have become the dominant goal of the marriage contract, the demands made of marriage have risen sharply. And the possibility of contradictions between what an individual expects of marriage and the reality of family life itself has grown accordingly. The new criterion for evaluating a marriage has changed the attitude toward divorce as well: It is juridically and morally recognized in the name of this very right of the individual to "optimum satisfaction" in marriage.

All these changes in the approach to marriage and in marital-family relations themselves are objectively necessary and progressive. But they presuppose a high level of moral maturity in people.

2. Can it be said, however, that all Soviet citizens possess highly developed senses of conscience, duty, honor, personal dignity, that they have the correct notion of happiness and the meaning of life? Unfortunately, no. Moral awareness still frequently lags behind our economic development. This circumstance is pointed out in a number of letters received by the editors. At the same time, P. I. Kulakov (Tula Province) writes, "the method by which survivals of the past penetrate the consciousness of man remain a mystery for many people."

The fact is that not one method exists, but a multitude. Many deviations from the norm of communist morality can scarcely be called survivals, for their source lies not so much in the feudal-capitalist past as in negative phenomena arising in the socialist society. Among these have been such phenomena as the material and psychological consequences of the war, economic difficulties, the low moral level of some parents or of whole families and, finally, shortcomings and errors in the system of moral upbringing itself. . . .

A number of important aspects of the shaping of morality (the culture of emotions, the esthetics of behavior, etc.) for a prolonged period remained outside the field of vision of our upbringing institutions. The demand that young people be better prepared for marriage is enunciated with special persistence in readers' letters. "It is necessary to write about the sex question, and necessary too that the Y.C.L. and the schools take this up," we read in a letter from N. T. Papin (city of Gryaz, Lipetsk Province).

Some readers, when opposing hypocritical reticence about "ticklish" problems that arise for young people, unwittingly go to extremes. For example, one reader protests against the showing of films in which the collisions of familial relations are depicted. But not all films are alike. It is necessary to draw a strict distinction between the truly vulgar films (which do, alas, make their way onto our screens) and real art. . . .

Needless to say, it would be simplification in the extreme to assume that all the influence of art boils down to imitation alone. The higher a man's esthetic cultivation, the less of a role will imitation play in his perception of works of art, which means the more significant will be the place occupied in this perception by the experiencing and contemplation of the reality reflected in art, the comparison of it with the life experience of the viewer (reader, listener) himself, his analysis and reassessment of his own acts in the light of the esthetic ideal incorporated in the work of art.

Consideration of the question helps us discern yet another reason for the lag of moral consciousness behind the economic and social development of Soviet society. It consists in the inadequate efficacy of the use of art as a "teacher of life" because of the esthetic "subliteracy" of a segment of the population, including young people.

The lag of moral consciousness in turn creates strife between the new objective situation in the field of marital-family relations arising as a result of the socialist revolution and the reflection of the given situation in the minds of certain people. This makes itself felt both in the practice of raising a family and in family relations themselves. A substantial number of marriages are fraught with mutual dissatisfaction and conflicts.

Let us cite a few characteristic figures. An analysis of 1,000 divorce cases in Leningrad showed the following. Out of these thousand unsuccessful marriages, 3.1% lasted only six months, 7.3% one year, 10.7% two years or less, and 20.5% four years or less. In 8.3% of the cases, conflicts began between the spouses suing for divorce right away; in 10.8%, after one or two months; in 17.5%, after three to six months; in 15%, after seven to 12 months; in 12.5%, in the second year; and in 35.9%, after two years of conjugal life.

These figures lead to one more thought: Even serious love (to say nothing of the varying degrees of "simple infatuation") in and of itself still does not ensure a painless transition from "the single state" to conjugality and family life. Many problems arise here—from adjustment to each other's personalities and habits to mastery of the new roles of mistress and master of the house, of mother and father. And this requires not only mutual love but also cognizance of the responsibility of the young people starting a family for its future; it requires from each of them a sense of duty, patience, often even a capacity for self-sacrifice and a number of other qualities whose lack threatens the young family with disintegration. Newlyweds—and readers write about this as well—are especially in need of moral support from their elders, from parents and society, which they do not always receive.

Before the Revolution marital ties were reinforced by the wife's dependency on the husband, a de facto pro-scription of divorce, religious fear, and so forth. Socialism eliminated these "watchdogs," for they contradict the very substance of communist ideology and are demeaning to human dignity. The center of gravity in the regulation of marital-family relations shifted from outside compulsion to the moral and psychological "forces of cohesion"; feel-ings of love, kinship, duty, family solidarity and responsibility. However, these forces—again, because of the insufficient moral maturity of some mar-riage partners—sometimes are too weak to counteract the difficulties and tribu-lations the family encounters and must overcome, growing stronger and happier in the process. . . .

The individual's personality, a per-son's attitude toward the opposite sex, toward his elders and toward society, his moral traits, largely repeat, as a rule, the respective elements in the make-up of the family in which the person grew up and was taught. But inasmuch as not all Soviet families at this time, as a number of letters point out, are yet coping with this educative function of theirs, while some of them are doing outright harm to the development of children, the fate of upbringing often depends almost entirely on public child-care institutions.

Questions of control over the behavior of minors in their leisure hours and of their acclimation to labor are now arising with particular keenness. In this connection, one of the proposals voiced in the letters deserves attention, in our view. "The unruly ones are the prov-ince of the militia, the schools, and the Party, Y.C.L. and trade union organi-zations, but children who so far do not fall into this category are left on their own," S. V. German from Ivanovo writes. "But can't we organize labor camps for them, where they might work

not for the purpose of earning money but for an athletic uniform, say? How proud the adolescent would be—he earned it himself!—and for some fami-lies it would be a real help: They live at the adults' expense, after all, and opportunities within the family are limited. Why not let them work, we have our work to do! Of course, this might cost us some effort, but they do want to work. They are romanticists, after all, and simply loitering in the courtyard is a bore to them." The writer of this letter is a mother herself, and she knows well whereof she writes. The Y.C.L. and the Academy of Peda-gogy must search persistently for new forms of upbringing, must not be afraid to experiment, to rely more boldly on the initiative of the young people them-selves, to trust them more. Excessive tutelage always blunts one's faith in one's own powers, one's sense of responsibility, which is the psycholog-ical foundation of morality.

3. However, it would be one-sided at best to assert that the solidity and well-being of the family collective depends solely on the moral complexion of those who start the family. Without excep-tion, all the readers who sent letters to the editors about the article "The Family Is a Cell of Society" agree that many conflicts, disorders and misunder-standings in family life occur because of poor organization of everyday life, and that the people responsible for living arrangements and services to the population still fall far short of squar-ing accounts with the Soviet family.

For example, a letter from N. Sit-nikov, Rostov-on-Don, reports the following case. A young husband and wife, both specialists with a higher edu-cation, were sent to work in a district of Bashkiria. After living four years there in substandard quarters, they finally sent their child to the wife's parents and set out themselves for Kaliningrad Province in hopes of better things. And again, "several years have passed now, and their life is still unsettled. The child is growing estranged from the parents and the parents from the child, and mutual recriminations are beginning—" And who knows what the finale to the worsening discord in this once happy family will be?

Housing difficulties in large cities can be understood and explained. But the creation of at least rudimentary living conditions in "the sticks," especially for young specialists, depends in large part not on objective but on subjective reasons—on whether or not certain managers have struck upon this simple truth: Home life is important not only for its own sake but also for its very great influence on people's production activity, not to mention its influence on their world outlook and disposition.

The readers' letters cite many examples attesting to the great harm inflicted on the solidity, unity, and social participation of the family by a lack of everyday and children's institutions, family rest homes and lodgings. T. F. Onipchenko and A. P. Malyshev, two Muscovites, offer a number of practical proposals on this score: 1) that women with children must have priority over women without children in the selection of vacation time and must receive at least a few additional days off; 2) couples should have their vacations predominantly together; and 3) in the summer period, or perhaps even generally, the procedure for distributing passes to rest homes should be changed in such a way that predominantly families, rather than "loners," will be able to rest there, and to this end passes should be given to a whole family at once, if possible.

A. D. Matveyeva from the city of Donetsk, Rostov Province, in turn, believes that in cities a temporary shortage of children's institutions can be compensated to some degree by activating the housing offices' work with children. "It is necessary to enlist specialists on pension to take charge of hobby groups," she writes, "and the apartment house administrations must set aside space for this and must seek out ways and means for rewarding people who work with children."

Readers point out the inadequacy of measures for the development of everyday services to the population. As a rule, the work here so far has boiled down merely to expansion of the existing network of service establishments, which is quite necessary, of course. However, we cannot forget the other side—the categorical need to perfect the very operating principles of these establishments. There is no point in even talking about a breakthrough in the organization of everyday services until every employee therein has an economic stake in giving the largest possible number of clients the best possible service. Aside from state everyday services, there obviously should be a more intensive development in rural localities of the network of cooperative dining rooms, barber shops, tailor shops and shoe-repair shops.

Only competition for customers can engender truly exemplary socialist service. And after all, very, very much depends on this—from the country's overall prestige to people's day-to-day mood, their interrelations at work and in the family.

The readers' responses to the article "The Family Is a Cell of Society" once more confirm that marriage, the family, and child-rearing are not simply "personal life" but a large and important sphere of social existence, where personal interests are interwoven with public and state interests. By eliminating the antagonism between the individual and society, socialism creates the most propitious conditions for the further progress of these important social institutions. But in order to turn this possibility into reality, it is still necessary to exert great efforts. One of the letters puts it well: "Logical does not mean automatic; progress takes work."

Delicate Topic

M. MOTSENOK

It is quite logical that our press, particularly the young people's newspapers, should turn to topics of morals and ethics. The man of the communist tomorrow is being formed physically and ideologically in our times. This is why articles, sketches, feuilletons, correspondence and letters about behavior on the job and in everyday life, about the family, happiness and love, are appearing more and more often in the newspapers. A newspaper article on a topic concerning morality, if the article is correct by communist ethical and esthetic criteria, leaves a deep impression on the reader. In such instances one can see that the newspaper is passed from hand to hand, the article is discussed and commented on, and the readers write to the editor expressing their views on the questions raised.

In the case of some articles published by newspapers, however, the writers and editors are intruding into fields of human relations about which one does not speak aloud. There has even appeared a newspaper department headed "About Delicate Topics." Perhaps the journalists raising these "delicate topics" are filled with noble impulses. But they sometimes forget that on any question and in any genre the ability to write a lively piece is secondary to deep understanding of the essence of the topic, knowledge of the subject, and absolute observance of a sense of proportion and tact. All the more is this necessary in writing on "delicate" topics.

"There are matters about which it is not good or necessary to speak," wrote Alexei Tolstoy. "These are things that are personal, subtle and delicate." Enthusiasm for "delicate" topics leads to sensationalism, melodrama and an unhealthy interest. This is what happened with the Perm journalists working for the newspaper Molodaya gvardia [Young Guard].

An article "Love at 14" occupied a good deal of space in one of its issues. This was a journalist's reflections from the courtroom. In the dock sat one girl of 14 and another of 17. Of course they had earned condemnation for parasitism, thieving, drunkenness and dissolute behavior. But it was not this that preoccupied the writer of the news

Reprinted from M. Motsenok, "Delicate Topic," Sovetskaya pechat (April, 1964). Translated in Current Digest of the Soviet Press, XVI, No. 21 (Copyright © June 17, 1964), 19–20.

story. His attention was concentrated on "premature sex life."

The journalists set forth *for discussion* by their 45,000 readers: "How could it have happened that these girls, who are still incapable of becoming either wives or mothers and who have not yet experienced love, began to lead a sex life?" The answer followed: "Naturally, only boys and girls who have not been taught any esthetic sense indulge in such love"(!). The writer and editor turned indignantly to young readers: "Is it really so hard to try to refrain from sex at least until adulthood?"(!) Hotheads proposed: "Decisive measures are necessary, perhaps even a law that would increase the responsibility of parents. Then there would be fewer criminals, and the matter of sex problems would improve"(!).

The article under the sensational headline "Love at 14" was preceded by the newspaper's "position-paper" article, "Tomorrow Will Be Too Late." From it the reader learned that apparently there are boys and girls who hold "free-love parties" and "saturnalias." The editors sought readers' comments. And the newspaper began to break out in the words "sex life," "sex problem" and "sexual relations." The whole province took up the pen! A full page was filled with readers' letters. Learned and unlearned responded to the editors' call.

"There is a great deal of literature on questions of sex education and sex life," one of the readers announced. Hurry, boys and girls, read it! Another reader submitted the "valuable" proposal that the Perm Publishing House immediately issue in a large edition a book that would "tell in simple and easily understandable form everything that young people need to know initially about sex," etc., etc.

The comrades at Golos shakhtera [Miner's Voice], published at the Kizel Coal Trust, also do not ignore "delicate" topics. They described with relish how a miner's wife surprised her husband with a lover, locked the door on them, went off to call the people's volunteer detachment and then the militia itself, rushed in with the militia and pulled her frightened husband out of his hiding place.

Vulgarity and the savoring of "piquant" matters is profoundly alien to our press.

As C[lara] Zetkin related in her memoirs about Lenin, he said that preoccupation at meetings and by the press with questions of sex relations is harmful and dangerous and could easily encourage excessive stimulation and excitation of sex life in some individuals. Young people especially need lively joy and cheerfulness. Healthy sports—gymnastics, swimming, outings, physical exercise of all kinds—a diversity of intellectual interests, study, analysis, research, and all this, as far as possible, in combination! All this gives young people more than interminable speeches and discussions on sex.

If the journalists wished to talk about maintaining young people's health and strength, they would have many opportunities and many excellent examples. But both Molodaya gvardia and Golos shakhtera write very little about examples of real, sound families, about the jobs of motherhood and fatherhood, and about duty and friendship.

This same Molodaya gvardia printed a serial report, "A Person Is Known by the Company He Keeps," in three issues. The central figure in the account, a woman, was in jail; the investigation had been completed and she was awaiting trial. A special correspondent received permission to interview her in jail. He did not come to the meeting empty-handed; he brought her a "parcel"—cigarettes! One can judge the "depth" of this interview from these lines:

"Behind bars, the most hardened cutthroats become timid vegetarians, frightened chicks, very understanding persons."

As the upshot of his conversation with the imprisoned thief, the journalist concluded:

"She felt herself all alone in the world. She had not known real friendship.*** She had not known real love, but had been a beautiful mannequin in a gang of drunken fellows.***"

The most exacting lawyer would envy such a "defense."

What are the roots [of the girl's life of crime]? The journalist writes: "It begins with the fact that we turn away from persons less educated than we, persons who are not smart, who are simply fools."

As far as fools go, that's great!

What good did this jail interview do? It provided a sensation for the newspaper. The writer went about with a swelled head, declaring that it was a real scoop.

Some journalists on the newspaper Solikamsky rabochy [Solikamsk Worker] also are infected with the baleful disease of sensationalism and melodrama. Solikamsk is a city of large-scale chemistry and a world center for potassium salt. Potassium combines operate and are being built here, new chemical products are being created. There are many daring dreamers here, and such deeds that there is no need to invent them or indulge in fantasy. There is adventuresome challenge all around! Yet the newspaper printed a letter entitled "Do We Find a Challenge Here?" The journalists prefaced the letter with an introduction calling on the young people of Solikamsk to engage in a discussion of "Do We Find a Challenge Here?"

What was in the letter?

"We have no end of difficulties. The occupation of builder would seem to be to our taste, but here we work without desire, life is boring and stale*** Many people take part in amateur arts circles*** and attend schools for working youth. But all this goes on somehow prosaically, without spark, in routine fashion*** They tell us: 'What was it like for Pavel Korchagin and the Young Guards? Learn from them how to live!' These are examples from bygone years. What about modern times?*** Where are they, the romantic heroes? In books and films. But in life? Where does a real challenge lie buried, behind what locks is it hidden? Where? Where?"

A "peg" for discussion, even if it be a rusty peg! Literally the next day—that is, in the next issue—the newspaper printed the first response from a reader. An investigator of the city prosecutor's office spoke out. Effectively, too! He poured oil on the fire. The title was, "Challenge, but Not the Right Kind." The investigator described cases of hooliganism, drunkenness and thievery, which still occur among young builders, and called all this "criminal romance." He concluded: "The situation among young people is alarming, very alarming." The headline "Do We Find a Challenge Here?" is becoming a regular rubric in the newspaper. The secretary of the city Young Communist League committee entered the discussion: "You write, Tamara, that there is much dullness and boredom in life, and you cite convincing examples and cases." But there had been no such cases or examples in the letter.

The "discussion" brought no good. Often the journalists' efforts are not directed at bringing good. How much better it would have been if the Solikamsk newspapermen had shown the real challenge and drama of our days vividly, interestingly and thoughtfully. The challenge and the drama are bursting to get into the newspaper. The once-forgotten Solikamsk region, so forgotten that even the assignment of the position of provincial governor was regarded as a punishment—this region has become a republic of large-scale chemistry. How this region has changed! How many great deeds are performed there daily, how many wonderful people are there! Create, dare, try, journalist! And if you do tackle a delicate theme, do it skillfully, with sense and not sensationalism, without vulgarity or melodrama.

A Difficult Subject

A. VASKBERG

At long last, people have begun to talk openly about a subject long considered unworthy of public attention, if not forbidden. Zdorovye [Health], Semya i shkola [Family and School] and other magazines have carried a number of articles about sex education, though considering it, to be sure, only from the medical and pedagogical standpoint. In the July 2 Literaturnaya gazeta, the investigator A. Shpeyer "opened" the doors of a courtroom where a rape case was being tried and gave some of his thoughts on the reasons for sex crimes.[1]

This big and pressing problem is at last in the center of public attention. So there is now hope that it will be solved—after all, there is no problem that collective thought and collective effort cannot solve.

Reprinted from A. Vaskberg, "A Difficult Subject," Literaturnaya Rossia (October 7, 1966). Translated in Current Digest of the Soviet Press, XVIII, No. 40 (Copyright © October 26, 1966), 20–21.

[1] Current Digest of the Soviet Press, Vol. XVIII, No. 28, pp. 10–11.

Before a teacher first enters a classroom, he has had many years of study, for an untrained teacher cannot teach anything. Education of the educator—that is where practical pedagogics begins. Therefore, to speak of sex education for young people means to speak first of sex education for adults.

The very combination of words will probably seem strange at first. But let us descend from the summits of theory to the valleys of life and look into the courtroom, as did A. Shpeyer. Not during a rape trial, but during an ordinary divorce case.

The plaintiff puts his case listlessly: His wife reproached him for not spending enough time with the family. Her reproaches irritated him, especially because he had his own complaints about her "with regard to domestic matters." The wife, hereinafter called the respondent, raises no objections: It is all true, and she nods her head sadly. He is sad too, as he squeezes out the meaningless words, obviously aware that he must say something.

The judge reads the decision aloud:

"The divorce is granted." Thousands of human lives have passed before her eyes in her many years of work. Perhaps that is why she realizes full well that it was not domestic details that caused this family's break-up. She has a definite and uneasy feeling that a deep dissatisfaction with intimate aspects of life exists here, unproclaimed, unexpressed and unanalyzed, a source of embarrassment and grievance, but existing nonetheless and constantly exerting its influence.

Gentility and tact kept these people from opening the door of their apartment wide before the public. So they hastily concocted a "respectable" motive for their divorce. While their real pain and trouble that kept them from being happy remained locked up inside.

In the fraternal socialist republics (Czechoslovakia and Yugoslavia), a doctor who is a specialist in sexual neuropathology and hygiene talks with the prospective bride and groom separately. The informal heart-to-heart talk and tactful advice help the couple to avoid many of the dangers that fill the first days of marriage and can leave an imprint on their future relationship. These dangers arise from ignorance, fear, irresponsibility, a too simple or too complicated "view of things."

No one has ever calculated, nor is anyone likely to, how many marriages have been saved by this prosaic preventive medicine. Were such a calculation to be made, I am certain the figure would be impressive.

A very important (if not the most important) task of sex education is to expose the hypocritical prudishness that exists even today in so-called "questions of sex." Silence about what plays an important part in everyone's life will not fail to have its consequences. For some reason it is deemed improper to speak to a doctor "about this." As a

matter of fact, there are no such doctors: Nobody trains them, and there would be nowhere for them to practice.

Let us be frank: The level of many people's knowledge of sexual physiology is extremely primitive, and—worse still —those same people consider this level entirely sufficient to qualify them not only to express an opinion but also to pass judgment.

I recall one divorce case that was greatly complicated by the obtuseness of certain precocious "moralists." It so happened that a man of hot blood had been married by a kind registry office to a frigid, supercilious woman, loftily indifferent to everything earthly. She viewed her husband's restlessness as nothing more than depravity and capriciousness. This opinion was fortified when she discovered her husband was unfaithful. The result of this quite ordinary domestic drama was a complaint to the trade union committee.

The complaint having been lodged, it had to be investigated. The hapless husband was called in and scolded.

The husband was naive enough to explain man-to-man why he was not getting along with his wife. He was held up to ridicule. They declared him a lecher. He was branded as a bearer of "private-property survivals."

Incidentally, it should be noted that epithets like "dissolute" and "lecher" are sometimes employed with excessive zeal, whether they apply or not. With the help of these words it is easy to fight off many unsolved problems, but they cannot solve these problems.

Several years ago I attended the trial of a 16-year-old schoolboy charged with rape. All the juridical signs of rape were present, so there were no grounds to consider the trial unlawful.

The important thing is this. The schoolteachers said the boy was quiet, withdrawn and even shy, that he kept away from the other boys and girls and from adults. "Whoever would have thought it!" was all they had to say about what had happened.

Yet it is precisely they—teachers and parents, responsible for rearing not only future citizens but also future men, future husbands and fathers—who should have stopped to reflect.

They had not noticed the signs of rapidly developing sexual emotions in the boy. His inability to control his desires played a malicious trick on him: He ended up letting go with his fists.

The court was lenient toward him. The sentence was comparatively mild. The work colony took his age into consideration and released him long before the end of his term. And what happened? In less than three months he was back in the dock. For rape.

This time, as you can guess, there were no allowances made.

All right, a crime must be paid for with the full severity of the law. That is clear. But after the sentence was handed down—a harsh sentence—I talked with the "recidivist rapist," who had just turned 18. He was sincerely surprised when I conversed about womanliness and love. He simply did not understand what it was all about.

What had they been teaching him? How had they been "educating" and "re-educating" him? After all, it is clear that more than mere "labor activity" was needed to re-educate this boy, that his psyche should have been subjected to intelligent (and skillful!) influence, that the rudiments of the esthetics of feeling should have been imbued in him. After all, to any man the least bit cultivated all the ups and downs of love, its joys and disappointments, are as important as the "conquest." And the boor, the esthetically blind and deaf man, has no interest in all this. He wants the "result."

However, refinement of feelings does not drop from the sky. It has to be instilled. And probably no field of education is more subtle and complex than this.

"Everyone says you must teach this, but no one tells you how," a schoolteacher once complained to me. She may be right: This should indeed be taught, at least to teachers—both present and future. Otherwise we end up with the kind of thing that happened about two years ago in a large and deservedly famous city: Having heard so much talk about the need for sex education, the teachers called the older schoolchildren together in the city's largest clubhouse and gave them the kind of public lecture suitable, if at all, only for a specialized seminar in a medical college. A highly important matter of genuine state significance was steeped in egregious vulgarity.

Leo Tolstoi, the author, incidentally, of not only "Anna Karenina" and "Resurrection" but also "The Kreutzer Sonata," wrote the not very well-known (but nevertheless remarkable) article "On Relations Between the Sexes," an emotionally charged response to the book "Diana, a Psychophysiological Experiment in Sexual Relations." L. Tolstoi noted that the author "talks about things deemed improper (calling things, as is proper, by their right name)" and that this book "can have ***a beneficial effect on***young people suffering from excesses and misconceptions." The great writer felt it necessary that the book be spread "among adult men," "particularly among boys who are being destroyed by ignorance alone," and that this would be, in Tolstoi's words, "a genuine beneficence."

But where do we have any books aimed at adolescents and called upon to satisfy their intelligent interest in questions of sex, their justified curiosity, so horrifying to some hypocritical educators? Isn't it clear that the lack of such literature is an antihuman phenomenon and testifies to an indifference to the great force and tremendous significance of natural human feelings in everyone's life?

In such matters a vacuum never remains a vacuum, and the place of the nonexistent book and the tongue-tied educator is taken by overly "authoritative" coevals or by foul-mouthed older persons.

If books were available boys and girls could learn a good deal from an intelligent narrator, free from pharisaical affectations and vulgar relish!

The very existence of a book would be edifying, for the "nimbus" of taboo around intimate questions of sex would disappear. If what girls whisper about in corners were written down in a book available in every library and bookshop, then there would be no room for ambiguities and innuendos.

What I mean, of course, is not simple instruction or "bald utilitarianism" but skilled shaping of the mind and heart, and books in which socio-ethical and medical-physiological questions are closely interwoven.

But we do not have such books now and do not expect to have any in the foreseeable future. Yet Russia long had the good tradition of not removing these human problems from the sphere of public discussion. Almost 200 years ago the university printshop of the eminent Russian educator N. I. Novikov published one of our country's first books on the question of sex—"Instruction to Fathers and Mothers on the Physical and Moral Education of Children." The unknown author wrote in a style that may seem exceedingly florid to us now but that his contemporaries must have found vividly graphic.

Who nowadays will converse with young people, with adolescents, and with their mothers and fathers in modern language but with that same vividness, with that same emotionality? There should be honesty in such a conversation and depth, and—most important—good sense!

It is difficult to disagree with V. Kaverin, who wrote several years ago that "the broad panorama of our society with which literature deals should include questions of love and family, the personal relationships with which society cannot help occupying itself and on which social development and progress depend.*** For when love goes unmentioned even in literature, society stops thinking about it too, and then what appears is something that might cautiously be termed love without love, that is, relations that are, of course, necessary to continue the human race but that do not make life more beautiful; rather, they cheapen and debase it."

The trouble is that physical (and physiological) development outstrips spiritual development. The process of developing personality, a process that engages family, school and society, lags behind the maturation of men and women, whom Nature shapes without the slightest effort. The gap between these two processes is growing wider. What is contributing to this is something to which the philosopher I. Kon paid special attention in his interesting article in Molodoi Kommunist:

"As medical statistical research shows, in the majority of developed countries adolescents arrive at sexual maturity earlier, sometimes two or three years earlier, than they did a century ago. This is due to improved nutrition and medical services and to certain psychological factors."

It is the aim of sex education to

narrow this gap to a minimum; the ideal would be to instill stable moral principles in adolescents even before nature completes its "shaping."

This is why any attempt to delay everything connected with sex education "until later" rebounds with a vengeance. After all, we try to instill industriousness in a person long before he goes to work, and patriotism and civic consciousness long before he becomes an active member of society.

Let us not be afraid to say that society is responsible for how every citizen's personal life turns out. For a person is not only a citizen. He is a human being.

And nothing human is alien to him. It is not for nothing that this was a favorite saying of Marx, who understood that everything human in a human being is not only natural but also beautiful.

Yes, beautiful—but only, of course, if it is truly human. In other words, if it is ennobled by culture. (Remember Chekhov. Well-bred people, he wrote in a well-known letter to his brother Nikolai, "try as much as possible to tame and ennoble the sexual instinct.") This is why sex education is first and foremost cultural education. It is no accident, after all, that truly well-bred families deal with the sex problem without hyprocrisy and vulgarity and find the correct and necessary words for talks with their children on this critical subject.

I cannot recall a single case in which a truly cultivated and emotionally rich person has been a rapist or corrupter of minors. The "heroes" of such trials are always persons with few interests, wretched taste, and limited ideas of beauty.

Incidentally, a few words about these trials. I agree with A. Shpeyer that they provide considerable food for thought, even when the accused is not really a rapist in the juridical sense (and this happens often) but "merely" an ill-bred, dissolute, cynical person, sometimes no worse than the girl, who for some reason plays the role of the "victim" in such a trial.

There's nothing easier than to "brand" and "condemn" and then decide that you have thereby made your contribution to the fight for morality. In fact, however, the whole thing is much more complicated.

Sex education is a tremendously important problem that cannot be solved in an offhand manner. Dissoluteness in some young people has been caused by the war, which took away their fathers, embittered their mothers and stole their childhood, and by the housing shortage, which has compelled some of them, from childhood on, to spend their free time in the streets. And by the influence of translated foreign literature and foreign films, some of which are beautiful and touching but in which the immature boy or girl, alas, notices only the outward form of the events.

The above list makes no claim to completeness. But even as it is, it indicates how complex the problem is. What will be the result if only the courts deal with it? And if, in addition, only the male portion of those who violate our morals have to pay?

It will become very simple to solve the problem. Only in that case it will never be solved. What is required is the efforts of writers, sociologists, teachers, doctors and jurists, and of public opinion, the role of which we still underestimate.

Izvestia in the Family Circle:
Argument With a He-man

A. VALENTINOV

Twelve billion working days—that is what the annual labor women spend on housework is estimated at. This gloomy figure has been the subject of commentary by our press. "Workers, teachers or scientists—at home these women are still all housewives," it was explained in one article. "On their shoulders lie the cares of comfort, clothing and cooking." Hence the conclusion that therefore they read very little, rarely go to the theater and in general lag behind life. The suggestion was made urgently to develop the cooking industry and the network of everyday services. The C.P.S.U. Program was quoted to the effect that "the vestiges of the unequal position of women in domestic life must be completely eliminated."

Nothing can be said against such ideas. Everyone would be satisfied if, starting tomorrow, housework and everyday services were to be mechanized to the utmost. But unfortunately that will not happen either tomorrow or the day after. The experience of the big cities, not to mention the more remote rural areas, suggests that it is a very troublesome job to arrange communal services well. It is obviously not a task for one year. And in 1966 and 1967 we shall prefer to dine at home

Reprinted from A. Valentinov, Izvestia (March 6, 1966). Translated in Current Digest of the Soviet Press, *XVIII, No. 10 (Copyright* © *March 30, 1966), 25–26.*

and not in a dining room; the washing, housecleaning and mending of clothing will eat up the same millions and billions of hours. . . .

Let us take a look at this expression: "He helps her around the house with the work." These words are uttered with approval, but to me they are absurd. As a matter of fact, in a majority of families the husband and wife both work, which means that both have equal opportunities for housework, but he, you see, only helps her, that is, he might not do it, whereas she has to do it. But why? . . .

A great many things that had seemed for centuries to be "settled" have been done away with before the very eyes of our generation in Russia. But here is a little something that has been preserved. A soldier takes care of himself almost completely, and a sailor trusts no one else to iron his trousers before he goes ashore. But at home he can sit tranquilly in front of the television set or click dominoes while his wife irons those same trousers. And some "good housewife" makes excuses for this lazybones: "Tell my husband to wash clothes and fix dinner? I can just imagine him fixing it. Better let him take care of his man's affairs." I would like to hear just what particular affairs these are: Perhaps it means moving a cupboard from one corner to another or, say, replacing a fuse that has blown? You will agree that all of these chores are, so to speak, of a sporadic nature.

This was not really arranged by us but came from the remote times when the following dogma was born: "The world is the home of the man; the home is the world of the woman." One would think that there is no point in proving that the world has long since become the possession of both halves of the human species, but, look here, the home—

"This is demagogy," the "he-men" object. "Equality of the sexes in our conditions does not at all mean a strict division into two halves of all everyday concerns. The very nature of woman imposes on her duties which the most ideal man is unable to perform." But no one is thinking of breaking down an open door. There is no need to prove that only a woman can breastfeed a baby. But while she is doing so, even a man who is not ideal is capable of scrubbing the floor and peeling potatoes. There are not really so many chores with which only a woman can cope; there are not really so many of these "sacred duties"—they exist more in words than in fact. Everything is far more prosaic and dull. It is simply that while she irons his shirt and darns socks (woman's duties) he reads the evening newspaper or plays "rooster," waiting patiently while she cooks the dinner (also her sacred duty!). And after dinner he does not start washing the dishes (it's not a man's duty) but starts discussing a most important problem: Will his favorite team, the Tinsmiths, transfer to group E? There it is in reality: "Better let him take care of his man's affairs!"...

I do not know if any statistical calculation has been made of the amount of strife that arises in families in which, in the bitter observations of women, they must work a second shift at home after their day's work. Whether or not divorces follow in the wake of this kind of strife is not so important. But it is terribly important that it leaves people, especially children, who have been affected.

And it is not only the family that loses by this, but all of society. It loses by virtue of the fact that the cultural outlook of the "good housewives" might be broadened, that they might be more beneficial to production and might rear their children better; it loses by virtue of the fact that they are for ever not getting enough sleep and are worn to a frazzle over the endless household bustle; it loses morally because the wonderful formula of "friend, comrade and brother" does not take root within those walls where some people tranquilly loll about on sofas while at the same time others right beside them wear themselves out. And, therefore, the solution of this problem is a political task, just as the eradication of drunkenness is.

This problem must be solved, as people said in olden times, by the whole community. In any case, it is clear that no one needs this deception—the assertion that women have every opportunity to compete with men while failing to relieve women of at least half of the household duties.

And it is necessary to begin with the "he-men." It is imperative that they be asked: "Would you really like to see your little Lyalka or Katyusha, whose braids you love to stroke and whom you love to carry piggyback, turn into a worn-out woman after some 15 or 20 years? Hurrying home after work with heavy shopping bags and at home not knowing what to start first? Would you like to see, after she has graduated from a school or even an institute, the great joy of her life become a good piece of meat she has bought or a well-ironed shirt?"

Unfortunately, it is not to individual persons that such questions ought to be put. But it is difficult to speak in a low voice to a large audience. That is why this hackneyed theme had to be taken up. That is why I have dared to write to the newspaper.

THE SOVIET
FAMILY:

The American View

Soviet Families

PETER JUVILER

Informed Western opinion about Soviet family policy runs the gamut from the view that "Soviet parents are bringing up their children pretty much as the regime wants them to,"[1] to the forecast that the Communists consider the family an intolerable obstacle to the formation of the new, collectivist Soviet man, and are out to destroy it. Nothing before the fall of Khrushchev seemed to indicate to the pessimists any deviation of the Soviet march via a post-Stalinist "revolution from above" towards a collectivised affluence that destroys the family as a unit of parents and children, and nothing after the fall of Khrushchev discouraged the conclu-

sion that "the socialisation of the family and the public rearing of children are feasible and in earnest."[2]

At first glance, the evidence supports the view that the family is "withering away." The regime is in fact far from satisfied with family upbringing of the younger generation, and prophets of the Soviet family's demise have no difficulty in establishing a communist motive for its elimination. They can point, moreover, to the anti-familial strain in the communist heritage, from Plato's Republic to the social revolution under Lenin which disintegrated, disorganised, and attacked the traditional religious basis of family ties. Stalin's conservative "revolution from above," with its call for "strong families" and glorification of motherhood, could be looked upon as no more than a necessary interlude before the on-

Reprinted by permission of the publisher from Peter Juviler, "Soviet Families," Survey (Copyright © July, 1966), pp. 51– 53, 56–61.

[1] Alex Inkeles and Raymonds Bauer, *The Soviet Citizen: Daily Life in a Totalitarian Society* (Cambridge, 1961), p. 230.

[2] Albert L. Weeks, "The Boarding School," *Survey*, No. 56, p. 84.

slaught was renewed, and a third revolution from above inaugurated as part of the party's programme for the "full-scale building of a communist society," as confirmed by the congresses in 1959 and 1961. They usually cite an article "Workers' Life and Communism," written by the venerable economist, Academician S. G. Strumilin, and published in 1960 during the discussion of the 1961 programme of the Communist Party.[3]

Children, said Strumilin, should be raised apart from the parents, from birth, in special wings of the "working and residential communes" where all Soviet people would be living in a few decades. Society, he wrote, could raise children much better than their parents could. Parental doting in the relatively isolated family environment made children selfish and individualistic, two traits unworthy of the men and women of the future communist society. Parents might visit their children periodically to bring them needed "vitamins of love." Their family life would be reduced, therefore, to the companionship of a loving couple (as in Engels' image of the future monogamous family). They would have no household chores and no problems of child-rearing to worry about.

This article, however, has been overrated as a sign of Soviet intentions, as even a cursory glance at the reaction to it will show. Strumilin's proposals for socialised child-rearing outside the family were attacked as "a caricature of communism" while heated and sentimental articles extolled the joys of filial and parental love. Khrushchev openly repudiated Strumilin's scheme at the 22nd congress: "Those who maintain that the family will become less important in the transition to communism and that with time it will disappear are entirely wrong." Paraphrasing his

remarks, the 1961 programme, a conservative document, in its only sentence bearing directly on family relations, asserts that they "will be freed once and for all from material considerations and will be based solely on mutual love and friendship." A. G. Kharchev, head of the Philosophy Department of the Leningrad branch of the U.S.S.R. Academy of Sciences, has devoted part of the first post-Stalin Soviet sociological treatise on the family to rejecting Strumilin's communes. Under communism, he tells his readers, "the sole family function which will wither away, not develop...is housekeeping." After Khrushchev's fall, Kharchev published a chapter entitled "Means of Further Strengthening the Family of the U.S.S.R.," in which he tied the need for family stability to the "important role of the family in Soviet society, especially in rearing the younger generation."[4]

Moving from theory towards current Soviet practice, one can note that architects who, Strumilin said, were drawing up plans for the communes, must have filed them away. From talks at the Moscow Experimental Architectural Institute (MITEP) in 1964, I gathered that prevailing opinion there had never favoured the communes. An exhibit of new housing projects at the House of Architects in 1964 showed models of the most advanced, "microdistrict," pilot housing project, now being built in southwest Moscow, one of the projects which are to set the pattern for years to come. It does not include plans for boarding students in its school complex, which is designed to accommodate all the children living in the project. Families will occupy separate apartments with bedroom space for the children. In planning apartment sizes, MITEP's architects have been

[3] S. Strumilin, 'Rabochii byt i kommunizm,' *Novy mir*, No. 7, 1960, pp. 203–220.

[4] A. G. Kharchev, *Brak i semya v SSSR: opyt sotsiologischeskogo issledovaniya* (Moscow, 1964), pp. 231, 318.

guided not by social blueprints for socialising upbringing, but by the results of demographic surveys of the size of families which are on the waiting lists for apartments in Moscow. In short, improved housing should bring families more, not less, physical privacy, unless the party makes a sudden turn in policy at present nowhere in evidence.

The truth appears to lie somewhere in between the finding that all is well with the Soviet family and that it is slated for deliberate extinction. Trends in boarding schools, family law, and family life seem to indicate that the regime is dissatisfied but that it seeks to eliminate eventually only most of the economic functions of the family and to leave with the families a small but vital share in child-rearing.

...The Bolsheviks attempted to undermine the patriarchs and "emancipate" women by enforcing paternal obligations whether incurred in or out of wedlock, allowing non-medical abortions, recognising unregistered marriages, permitting automatic divorce. Stalin advanced one step towards depriving the family of its economic functions and bonds by collectivising the private peasants and nationalising most small-scale private enterprise. Otherwise he retreated for the sake of the birthrate and family stability by forbidding therapeutic abortions (1936) and, in the edict of 8 July 1944, dissolving all paternal obligations incurred out of registered wedlock, recognising only registered marriages, establishing state aid for unwed mothers instead of paternal support, making divorce complicated and expensive.

A regime which was out to break up the family would logically return to or even surpass the radicalism of the 1920s. This did not happen after Stalin. His heirs have inched back only part way towards "Leninist principles of freedom of marriage and divorce, equality of all children whether born in or out of wedlock." Would-be reformers—lawyers, judges, scientists and intellectuals, the publications *Semia i shkola* and *Literaturnaya gazeta*—demanded this for many years in heated debate, but the long-awaited new family law which would eliminate illegitimacy and substantially liberalise divorce procedures did not appear in 1964 as many, women especially, had hoped. The Party decision not to repeal the 1944 edict affected some eight million extra-marital offspring of all ages, the five million mothers who had given birth to them out of wedlock, and some 300,000 couples divorcing annually.[5]

Only piecemeal reforms have filtered through the sieve of bureaucratic and professional caution. Divorce practice was liberalised in 1955. This meant fewer refusals thereafter, but a continuation of the obstacles inherent in the complicated and lengthy procedure and the high fees. Still, many couples simply

[5] Arkadii Vaksberg, 'Vosvrashchayas k staroi teme,' *Literaturnaya gazeta*, 30 July 1964. Only 1.97 million unwed mothers are listed in *Narodnoe khozyaistvo SSSR v 1963 godu*, p. 512, as receiving state grants for their children. Yet 'over five million' unwed mothers is most probably on the low side. To the above-mentioned 1.97 million must be added the millions of mothers no longer listed because their illegitimate children are over twelve and no longer qualify for grants (the number of unwed mothers receiving grants reached a peak in 1957), or the mothers disqualified because (1) they live with the fathers of their children out of registered wedlock, (2) they have not reported their children, (3) the natural fathers have adopted the children to give them their names and material rights of children born in wedlock, (4) they are receiving support by court order from men who had once undertaken permanent support of their children and then reneged, (5) they have opted to place their children in state homes. A leading Soviet expert on the family told me in 1964 that there were about five million unwed mothers; their number has of course risen since then, even though the number of illegitimate children under 12 or 18 has fallen.

established *de facto* marriages rather than go through official divorce complications. Hence divorce obstacles served to harm the interests of women and weaken rather than strengthen family ties, since many new families had no legal protection.[6] Finally, at the end of 1965, a compromise divorce law provision appeared rather than the comprehensive new All-Union Basic Family Law which the reformists had been awaiting. Under the decree of 10 December 1965 divorces are a little simpler and less expensive. It retained the petition and 10 ruble filing fee; abolished publication of newspaper notice (often published after a long wait and usually costing 40 rubles); retained the first reconciliation hearing in the People's Court (usually ineffective), and moved the second, final hearing from the city or provincial court to the same People's Court; retained divorce registration fees of 50-100 rubles.[7]

Taken together, the other concessions of the regime to the family since Stalin do not amount to a campaign against it. Under Malenkov judges were allowed to use a loophole in the law to enforce support suits against fathers of extra-marital children not because they were the fathers but on the ground that they had at one time undertaken to support them.[8] Khrushchev's regime repealed a 1936 ban on nontherapeutic abortions "in order to let a mother

decide for herself whether or not to have her child, and in order to prevent the harm to women caused by abortions outside hospitals."[9] Abortions are free for working women, Soviet health officials told me. Housewives and students pay city clinics only 5 rubles and rural clinics 2½ rubles for each abortion. Moscow University's clinic offers this service to the women students. I attended a lecture on the use of contraceptives and the harm of abortions given at Moscow University in 1964 to a mixed audience as part of the campaign to encourage the use of contraceptives in a country so unfamiliar with them still that some college students expressed the belief that if men used them they would become impotent. The woman university physician wanted to clear the men out of the lecture hall. "Men have no place here", she said. But the visiting specialist demurred. "No, you stay. I am glad to see you men here. . . . You have plenty to do with your wives' abortions." Other concessions by the regime included the repeal of a 1934 decree establishing the blood guilt of the relatives of a defecting serviceman, freeing persons with only one or two children (i.e., most Soviet parents) as of 1 January 1958 from paying a "birth stimulation" tax imposed in 1944; raising paid maternity leave from 77 to 112 days for urban working women (1956); extending maternity leave and pension benefits to peasant women (1964); and removing most priorities in college admissions which persons with two years' work experience had enjoyed since 1958, thus redressing the balance more in favour of the graduates straight out of secondary schools (1965).

In the context of these limited concessions, the inroads on family functions

6 *Sorok let sovetskogo prava 1917–1957*, vol. II (Leningrad, 1957), p. 281. One or both parties to 20 per cent of a sample of divorce cases in Leningrad had extramarital children in new families at the time of divorce, largely because of delays in obtaining divorces. A. G. Kharchev, 'Brak i semia v SSSR: Opyt sotsiologicheskogo issledovania' (doctoral dissertation, Leningrad Department of Philosophy of the USSR Academy of Sciences, 1963), pp. 288–289.

7 *Vedomosti verkhovnogo soveta SSSR*, No. 49, 1965, item 275.

8 Peter Juviler, 'Marriage and Divorce,' *Survey*, No. 48.

9 *Sbornik zakonov SSSR i ukazov prezidiuma Verkhovnogo Soveta SSSR 1938–1958* (Moscow, 1959), p. 550.

made by Khrushchev—the surviving
boarding schools, the stepped up grass
roots social controls, confiscatory legislation to discourage speculation—hardly
add up to a social revolution.

"Today there is no more conservative
society than Soviet society," wrote
Mihajolo Mihajlov in *Moscow Summer
1964*. "The slightest change, even a new
kind of tie, song, or trouser leg width,
provokes great resistance." Conservatism
has been the word in family policy too,
even though present divorce grounds
and abortion laws would be considered
radical in many parts of the world.

Before Stalin, Bolshevik radicals like
Alexandra Kollontai urged young people on to "free love." In some localities
enthusiasts "nationalised" women. Lenin
disapproved of such extremism. Today,
in Soviet Russia as in the West, the
sexual revolution comes from below,
not above. Official conservatism came
in with Stalin and his 1929 model
charter for a youth commune which
banned a "licentious sex life." "The
sexual question," read the charter, "can
be correctly decided in one way only;
steadfast and lasting marriage founded
on love."[10]

There is a direct link between the
moral tone and traditionalist morality
manifested in this youth commune
statute and Kharchev's authoritative
book, *Marriage and Family in the
USSR*. Kharchev's views on sex would
gladden the hearts of many parents,
college administrators, and clerics. No
pre-marital sexual relations or trial marriages for him, though he favours
betrothals, an institution swept away
along with church controls in 1917. Yet
it is quite clear from Kharchev's book
that the Western sex revolution, or
what he calls "the Western pattern of
sexual 'freedom' or more precisely,
sexual anarchy," prevails as well under

[10] Klaus Mehnert, *Youth in Soviet Russia*
(London, 1933), pp. 214–215.

the "socialist way of life." Leningrad,
with the lowest reported birthrate,
seems to have the highest legal abortion rate, three abortions for every live
birth. Twenty per cent of the many
abortions are had by women under 24;
the majority of these are unmarried.
This gives direct testimony of the
"spread of pre-marital promiscuity
among women." Among the causes of
the high urban incidence of pre-marital
relations, Kharchev lists cramped housing, alcoholism due to boredom, and
"the ideology and psychology of the
bourgeois world." He mentions too the
"growing independence of students and
working youth, especially in the cities,
from the control of family and neigh-
bours."

Soviet family and sexual relations are
coming to resemble their Western counterparts in other ways too. As in the
West, a slowly increasing part of socialisation takes place outside the family—
in schools, youth activities, peer groups.
Over the long haul, families have lost
some of their economic-productive functions too, though in the USSR mostly
through direct state intervention rather
than spontaneous economic growth.

Although wide family ties are cherished, the residual family unit has been
shrinking in the Soviet Union as in the
West from the extended family of at
least three generations to the so-called
nuclear family of two generations.

Resignedly accepting the new times,
a Russian grandmother faces the problem of being also a mother-in-law and
concedes that "It is better to live on
one's own if possible. Suppose that I'm
staying with my son. He comes home
from work late and his wife is already
asleep. I wait up for him, making tea,
sit down with him. He tells me everything about his work and his household
affairs. He shared all his confidences
with me when he was a boy. In the
morning his wife asks: 'What has made

you so talkative? You never tell me anything, but you are always gabbing with your mother'." Such a *babushka* remains the proverbially indispensable babysitter and stander-in-line and a stubborn link with the church. But her changing life personifies the impact of industrialisation on a majority of Soviet families, whatever their ethnic backgrounds: the decline in economic interdependency, the consequent shift towards stronger emotional ties and greater mobility. This has brought about a steady disintegration of the matriarchal family. Only one family in four packs more than two generations under one roof.[11]

As in other modernising countries, Soviet family relations are becoming less authoritarian, but also, with the loosening of economic and religious ties, more widely subject to break-up and divorce. Official statistics show a divorce rate in the USSR of 1.3 per thousand population per year compared with 2.2 in the United States. But in Moscow the divorce rate is 3.6, the highest reported in the USSR. Families are smaller, especially in European Russia outside the Caucasus.[12] 'The conflict of

generations' and youthful rebelliousness are leading themes in literature and press discussions, as they are in the West. Doting white-collar parents show concern that their children get into college and marry well. The regime has tried to introduce romance into marriage with its new secular wedding ceremonials. Political crises could bring periods of setback, but the basic trends in family life over the long run are towards companionate marriage, greater physical privacy, and continuing high or even higher national divorce rates. If anything withers away in the USSR within this century, it will not be the conjugal, two-generation family. It will be certain special reflections of the austere, directed, terrorised, war-torn family in a period of total social mobilisation from which the Soviet Union seems to be just emerging.

I have in mind such symptoms as the prudery in matters of sex education and manuals of marital relations; the sparse rituals of courtship; the casual, honeymoonless adjustment to marriage; the contrast between the warm affection of grownups for children when time permits and the way-station aspect of the home when it does not; the massive, sometimes brutal impact of state restrictions on religion; the modesty of family possessions; the austerity of budgeting in all except well-to-do families; the specially heavy load carried by working women; the housing still so cramped that, for example, more than half the marrying couples polled at Leningrad's Wedding Palace expected to have to begin their married life with parents or in dormitories; and the still vital role of family entrepreneurship in feeding Soviet people.

[11] Kharchev, *op. cit.*, pp. 231–233.
[12] Divorce rates are lower and the birthrate higher, in the country than in the city, and above all in areas inhabited predominantly by non-Russian indigenous nationalities south and east of Moscow (*e.g.* in the Caucasus and Central Asia). Moscow and Leningrad have the highest divorce rate (annual registered divorces per thousand population) of 3.6 with a 10.8 marriage rate in Moscow, and 3.4 with a 11.1 marriage rate in Leningrad. They have the lowest recorded birth rates (annual births per thousand population) of 12 in Leningrad and 13 in Moscow. Divorce rates in Central Asia and the Transcaucasus are only 0.4 and 0.5 respectively, birth rates 35.9 and 32, with a national high of 40.6 in Azerbaidjan. The national divorce rate is 1.3, birth rate 21.2, and marriage rate 9.1. For the more urbanised USA the divorce rate is 2.2, birth rate 21.6, and marriage rate 8.8. All figures are for 1963. For most complete Soviet figures to date, see

Vestnik statistiki, No. 1, 1965, pp. 86–96. The divorce rate rose in 1964 to 1.5. *Narodnoe Khoziastvo SSSR v 1964 g.* (Moscow, 1965), p. 120.

Perhaps social revolution was brewing for Soviet families in the heyday of Khrushchev's power. Even if this were so, it had run aground by the mid-sixties on practical difficulties, bureaucratic opposition, and professional objection.

Stalin's "revolution from above" won the devoted support of his "promoted ones." They benefited by it. Now the Soviet power elite, they have in effect vetoed even the pale reflection of the old social upheaval that brought them to the top.

For years the Soviet regime will continue to face the same problem with the family that it did before Khrushchev's fall. It seeks to strengthen the Soviet family for the sake of the children's healthy emotional development and the avoidance of social disorganisation. Yet particularisms of outlook and interest in the "strong" family stand in the way of the ideal of collectivism and unity around the common task of building communism. Despite all this, the family remains both socially irreplaceable and morally desirable in the official Soviet view. Coexistence of family and state is likely to be permanent if not always peaceful.

The Soviet Family

KENT GEIGER

The onset of the modern age has moved the Soviet family along in a direction now quite familiar. It has become smaller in size, its membership composition has altered and many of the functions it formerly performed have been relinquished or weakened. The large Russian family, extended in a lineal and often also collateral direction, seems about to disappear entirely; the Soviet birthrate has fallen drastically over the past decades; and larger economic and social organizations have taken over activities that used to be done by the family as a unit. The pattern of changes to be observed in

Reprinted by permission of the publisher from Kent Geiger, "The Soviet Family," Comparative Family Structures, Meyer F. Nimkoff, ed. Boston: Houghton-Mifflin Co., 1965, pp. 301–304, 326–328.

the family systems of the Soviet ethnic minority groups is similar, even though the socio-cultural starting points were sometimes quite different from those of the dominant Slavic majority.

Whether "justifiable" in order to build communism, or "outrageous," whether seen as "temporary" (and all such views are found among the Soviet people), Soviet citizens usually agree that life has been economically hard. Hardship also has long been a major orienting factor in family life, and while the "lack of money" is one way to define it, we can also deal with hardship in terms of lack of space and lack of time. Because of crowded housing conditions, the Soviet home, especially among middle and working classes, has seldom furnished the space to become the source of new strength, the place for relaxation and easy freedom, that "haven from the pressures of society," which the modern family home has afforded in other lands. Along the time dimension, too, it has become a byword that the Soviet people are "busy." To the hours of the regular workweek must be added those spent in over-time, extra-jobbing, obligatory meetings, travel back and forth from place of work, and the daily chores of living. The last-named has frequently assumed awesome proportions. Daily shopping, queuing for a turn in a communally shared kitchen, bringing up water from the basement, courtyard or (in the smaller towns) from a central well or water tower, searching for and hauling firewood or coal, working in the family garden—all these have been typical daily chores for Soviet families.

Taken together, small space and little free time exacerbate each other's effects. From the point of view of family activities the scarce hours of freedom from duties, external and domestic, are apt to be spoiled. And conversely, the little space that is available is very likely to be entirely consumed by sustenance activities and other tasks made necessary by crowded daily time schedules.

How have these twin and mutually reinforcing factors affected the atmosphere of Soviet family life? There is of course no single answer. In the first place it has been made less attractive, both to those living in a family and to those contemplating it. But the paradoxes of family life are many, and frequently the time and space shortages are converted from "obstacles" into the main goals of family life. There are traces of a class-specific attitude. The rank-and-file of the peasantry are too concerned about food and clothing to be overly preoccupied with the housing situation and the harassment of a busy schedule. They are also better supplied

with space which, although primitive, is at least little different from the usage of tradition. Among the upper classes, who are best provided for on the material side, the main aim has come to be focused on the time dimension. Finding hours to be together for recreation has become a main family goal for many a hard-working factory manager, party and government official or other member of the elite. For this reason also there is some evidence that elite families are little interested in owning their own homes, which help soak up what little free time they have with extra travel hours and chores.

The squeeze of poor housing is psychologically most painful among the Soviet middle classes, probably because families on this level are badly housed and yet far enough up in the class system to see the possibility of something better. To them "busyness" has an immediate and highly-prized goal: better housing, so they tend to be less likely to feel their family life impoverished by shortage of time. Their motto is often like that of the young Soviet engineer who observed: "In the Soviet Union you have to work and you have to study, and there is no time for anything else."[1]

If more time together is of central importance in the upper class, and better housing in the middle class, in the lower and working classes of the Soviet cities the picture is less monothematic. Family life among the workers seems to split into three sub-patterns along these dimensions. Among the bottom category life is typically little more than an extension of the routine and tradition of the village. Often living on the outskirts of cities, the husband is a factory worker and the wife may still be a collective farmer; in any case, she is

[1] Life History Interview No. 190, p. 22, Protocols of the Harvard Project on the Soviet Social System.

still close to the chickens, cow and vegetable plot. On this level, just as in the collective farm family, life is busy but horizon, aspiration and dissatisfaction are all limited. The top-level working-class family is similar in organization and spirit, and merges readily with the middle class; better housing is crucial. In between is the group from which comes the Soviet version of the proletarian family of nineteenth-century capitalism. Like the English workers described by Engels, they live in the most primitive urban housing, have little expectation of doing better in the foreseeable future (because of the lack of skills, advancing age, poor political or work records and so on) and tend "to have only two pleasures."[2]

A recent observer generalized that "Soviet man spends very little time at home or with his family."[3] Aside from work, he spends his time, paradoxically, in two rather extremely distinct ways. First, he occupies himself with party and trade-union meetings, production conferences, comrades' courts and so on. Here again he is in a context which is highly organized, but officially sponsored, and he participates in these activities as an individual.

At the other extreme, the Soviet man tries to avoid social contexts in which there are too many people and too much organization. This can be done in the anonymity of nature, the movie theater, the city park, the crowds and in the streets of the large city. The city streets as the place, and strolling as the activity, play a very special role for members of Soviet families, especially in the lives of the young people.

...By and large the Soviet leaders have made their peace with the family. There is very little, if any, talk these days about the "withering away of the family," a topic which was quite prominent for almost the first 20 years of Soviet history. On the other hand, regime-family relations are far from sublime, and on one question in particular the current state of affairs reminds one of the "peaceful coexistence" which Khrushchev declared the proper policy in regard to capitalist societies. This has to do with the matter of where the line should be drawn between public life and private life, or, to put it more bluntly, limits of personal freedom.

There is no doubt that the Soviet people as individuals, from top hierarchy to lowly peasant, prefer maximum privacy and anonymity in their family lives. For many years it was almost a rule of survival for the average citizen to exert extra effort to obtain this. As one man put it: "I worked for my wife and she worked for me and I told nobody what went on at home.[4] Even the most loyal and indoctrinated of Soviet citizens, leading Party and Government officials, have always drawn a sharp line between their public and personal lives.[5]

Yet for some 30 years, with little sign of diminishing intensity, there has been a struggle over where the line should be drawn between the legitimate interests of the individual and his family and the legitimate interests of the regime. In the record of public discourse the controversy appears repeatedly. The "no-man's land" is the area in which people behave in ways the

[2] Friedrich Engels, *The Condition of the Working Classes in England in 1844.* London: F. K. Wischnewetsky, 1892, p. 128.

[3] Joseph Novak, *The Future is Ours, Comrade: Conversations with the Russians.* Garden City, N.Y.: Doubleday & Co., 1959, p. 35.

[4] Life History Interview No. 167, p. 16, Protocols of the Harvard Project on the Soviet System.

[5] The fact that this is slightly less true of Khrushchev may be explained in terms of his particular personality traits, rather than as a change in policy.

regime does not approve, but for which legal prosecution is not appropriate. Here is a typical example:

In Moscow this spring there was an announcement about an important event: 200 tenth-grade children from the Proletarski District, having graduated from school, made up their minds to set off for the new projects in Altai. There was a lot of fuss made about this. It was written about, and talked about on the radio. In the middle of July, in Biisk, I met these children in the new hostels of a huge project. There were not 200 of them, but only 40.
"Why are there only 40?"
"The rest were not allowed to come," sighed a sturdy girl with large eyes.
"Who did not allow them?"
"Their papas and mamas."
Ah, those tender-hearted mamas and papas. Their parents played on their filial feelings, moved them to pity, frightened them, and cooled their ardent young hearts with the talk of the philistine.[6]

The official position on this issue has not changed since the mid-thirties. It is well-stated in the same source:

We have liquidated the social and economic bases of amoral behavior. But this does not mean that we do not find alien influences in our environment. The norms of the old way of life are displayed most frequently of all in the family. That is explained by the fact that family daily life relations do not yet stand in the field of vision of the party organizations. With this there can be no reconciliation.[7]

Two relevant facts are clear. Among the people the opinion is widely shared and not infrequently openly expressed that there is a realm of life—religious belief, family life, informal relations in general—which ought to remain private.

[6] From *Leningradskaia Pravda*, August 31, 1958, cited in Allen Kassof, "The Soviet Youth Program: Socialization in a Totalitarian Society." Unpublished doctoral thesis, Harvard University, 1960, p. 328.
[7] *Ibid*.

Secondly, official agencies, local Party organizations and various work, neighborhood and apartment house "collectives" are very reluctant to take action which intrudes upon this belief.

Notwithstanding, the line remains adamant in principle. Two official doctrines are involved to support it. The first denies in axiomatic fashion that there is any conflict of interest between Soviet society and the Soviet family. The second holds, after Lenin, that "at the basis of communist morality lies the struggle to strengthen and perfect communism." From this it follows that any "survival" impedes the struggle to build communism, and that therefore any item of behavior or belief in family life which detracts from the public interest is immoral and subject to interference.

How is one to evaluate the behavior of the Soviet rulers? For what reason does the Soviet regime still today insist that there is a "single, correct viewpoint from which actions, conduct, every step in public and private life, must be evaluated?" The answer, of course, is in the nature of Soviet totalitarianism itself. Experience to date, in the U.S.S.R. as elsewhere, while it does not prove, certainly suggests strongly that there is something "pluralistic" about society, and that the family is an institution which cannot be shaped, controlled or subjugated beyond a minimum degree by political doctrine or power. But to this likelihood, as to a number of others, the totalitarian mind is closed.

Perhaps the most significant conclusion to which the study of Soviet family life leads is that, in spite of temporary and partial reverses, the family, along with religion and the church, science and education, is a slow-working but effective enemy of totalitarianism. In the long view of history this special mission—to afford privacy and some protection against the pressure of totalitarian encroachment upon the individual—may prove to be the Soviet family's most important function.

V

SOCIAL PROBLEMS

If the presence of social problems is a sign of some sort of a "developmental maturity" or even modernity, then clearly not only American but also Soviet society is mature and modern. It is indeed in this sphere that the propositions of convergence theory are most tempting.

By linking social problems to modernity we did not mean to imply that all was well in past societies, or in those of the contemporary world which cannot be called modern.[1] Modernity and social problems are linked in two ways. Social problems tend to follow rapid social change and in particular the decline of well-established, traditional, informal social controls and beliefs. Since Durkheim, much sociological attention has been focused on this issue and there is little new we could add to it here. The second type of relationship between modernity and social problems is more perceptual. What we are suggesting here is that numerous phenomena regarded as social problems also existed in the past, but were simply not considered "problems," either because they were viewed as ineradicable (or natural or inevitable) or because there was little aggregate awareness of them. For social problems to emerge they must be identified as such and accompanied by a belief in the corrigibility and perfectibility of both human nature and social institutions. Without these factors, a problem consciousness simply cannot arise. It is a hallmark of modernity to conceptualize unpleasant,

---

1 By modern societies, we mean those which are highly technological, urbanized, and secular, where most products are mass produced and the use of machines is widespread not only in manufacturing but also in agriculture.

undesirable, or disturbing features of society as "problematic," that is to say, subject to correction, alleviation, or change rather than immutable features of the social world and human nature. Consequently social problems are also closely related to expectations.

It follows that the definition of what constitutes a social problem is a subjective, elusive, and even arbitrary matter closely tied not only to expectations but to values and philosophies. One should therefore expect to find profoundly different social problems in the U.S. and U.S.S.R.; however, this is only true in part. There are a surprisingly large number of social situations and behaviors which are defined in both societies as problematic, as undesirable. Their common denominator is disruptiveness and the undermining of social cooperation, morale, and efficiency. For example, crime, juvenile delinquency, alcoholism, the misuse of leisure, the hardships of old age, job placement (or lack of it) for the young, rural depopulation, urban overcrowding—these are some of the phenomena which are considered social problems in both the U.S. and the Soviet Union, as well as in other societies. At the same time we must note that even some of these are defined divergently, reflecting the different prevailing value premises in the two societies. For instance the definitions of crimes or of their gravity varies considerably, just as the conceptions of what amounts to the misuse of leisure. Of course, each of our two societies has problems peculiar to it: for example, housing shortage in the Soviet Union and drug addiction in the U.S., stealing state property in the Soviet Union and organized crime and gambling in the U.S. Even the same social institution and its influence may be viewed differently, as the case of religion illustrates. If there is a social problem linked with religion in the U.S., it is the decline of religious norms and beliefs or the difficulty of the churches in adapting themselves to contemporary conditions and needs. By contrast, in the Soviet Union religion is perceived as a social problem because it has not yet disappeared completely and still has some influence over the behavior and attitudes of some people.

In selecting the social problems to be included in this volume we used two criteria. One was the indigenous criteria used in each society respectively; the second, the consensus of Western sociologists about what constitutes a social problem. The two criteria do not necessarily coincide. In addition the presence of some problems might simply be denied in one society. For example, according to Soviet sources, there are no minority problems in the U.S.S.R. and discrimination is nonexistent. Consequently there are no printed Soviet sources available on Soviet anti-Semitism for example, and we had to rely on American discussions of it.

There is considerable variation in the amount of material available about each social problem included. In particular there is not enough discussion across the national boundaries of the social problems of the other society. Perhaps it would be too much to expect to find American sociologists concerned with problems of old age in the Soviet Union, or urban overcrowding, and other issues. Correspondingly Soviet sociologists, though more interested in writing about the seamy side of American life, have yet to devote sufficient attention to every American social problem. Consequently in this section we had to depart from the general structure of the book and limit the discussion of social problems to the juxtaposition of self-appraisals and dispense with the views "from the other side," except for three topics for which we found sufficient materials to select from: crime and delinquency, leisure, and ethnic discrimination.

Although our list of social problems is lengthy, we do not consider it exhaustive. No doubt many other issues in each society are defined as problematic by some or most people; on the other hand, some readers might not regard some of the items included as serious problems. We might also note that, on the whole, the American public, social scientists, and government officials are more willing to acknowledge the existence of social problems. On the other hand until the last decade there has been a great reluctance, indeed refusal, in the Soviet Union to admit the existence of any social problems, since such admissions would contradict the image of the ever-increasing perfection and historically superior nature of the social order that was allegedly established. Over the last decade, an interesting change of attitude has taken place in the U.S.S.R. following the relative political relaxation. It has become ideologically permissible to discuss and even study social problems in a compartmentalized manner—in isolation from what are considered the fundamentals of the social system. We do not know, because of the lack of comprehensive statistics spanning several decades, to what extent the new public and social scientific concern with these matters reflects an intensification of the problems. Probably some of them are related to growing urbanization, improved living standards, and decline of police terror, as well as to demographic changes. Still it is more likely that without the degree of political and ideological liberalization that has occurred, they could not be ventilated in public. Thus we might also conclude that the admission of the existence of social problems in the U.S.S.R. is a sign of the increased security of the regime which is no longer pathologically determined to repress and conceal its deficiencies and blemishes and no longer fearful that facing some of them might undermine the whole edifice. Finally it is also probable that the newly developed public and social scientific attention to these issues is part of the quest for greater societal efficiency and for better information about malfunctioning in the system. Still the fundamental official Soviet attitude remains a denial that the problems represent a serious defect or failure of the system, or that they are in any way similar to their counterparts in American and other Western societies. In the latter these problems are said to be inherent and ineradicable features of the institutional framework, born out of the manifold contradictions and injustices of capitalism. In the Soviet Union, a socialist society (in transition to communism), they are on the contrary alien to the nature of the social order and are either survivals of the past or imports from abroad, but in any event, somehow incidental and unrelated to the basic fabric of society.

Occasionally, as will be seen in some of the selections, a Soviet social scientist shows dissatisfaction with this viewpoint and questions the usefulness of the concept of survivals (of which more will be said later.).

The American approach to social problems is very different. Rather than trying to conceal them, many Americans have an almost masochistic preoccupation with them, and their revelation and ventilation supplies much of the contents of the mass media and social scientific literature. There are good explanations for this attitude in the U.S. First, there has been a long standing tendency toward societal self-analysis, perhaps having to do with the relative newness of the society as a whole, certain aspects of which are still not quite taken for granted. Americans may believe in the superiority of the American way of life, but they are also fascinated with all that is nasty and wrong with their society. The description of social problems, or some of them, makes good reading, listening, or watching, and the mass media is fully aware of this. In particular social problems connected with violence, be it ordinary crime or race riots, receive enormous coverage in response to public interest. Certainly as far as publicity is concerned, the U.S. is an open society and a most unsecretive one. Americans also feel a general compulsion to be informed, at least of the current and sensational events, situations and problems in their society. Perhaps publicity also functions as an alternative to action, as if it were believed that ample public discussion of a problem will somehow lead to its disappearance. For all these and possibly other reasons, there is not and has not been a dearth of information about most American social problems, although some receive much more attention than others. As long as the sensationalistic (or the scholarly) urge to expose, reveal, debunk, or demythologize exists, there are few defects of American life which can for long escape being dissected in public.

There are also powerful traditions in American sociology which contribute to the wide awareness of social problems. In its beginning, sociology in the U.S. was primarily a problem-oriented discipline, aspiring to contribute to the alleviation of social ills. While this tradition declined following the 1930's, it has never completely disappeared and considerable segments of the discipline have continued to work in the early tradition. It is not without significance either that the "social problem" courses are the ones most frequently offered by departments of sociology and attract the largest number of students and that such texts have also been the most numerous with enormously high circulation. It is of course another question whether or not all this attention has helped to solve these problems or merely offered a way to soothe our social conscience.

Crime and Juvenile
Delinquency

American and Soviet social scientists agree that crime in the United States is widespread, serious, and much of it violent. There is also considerable similarity in their relating it to many social institutions, practices, and values which are not criminal in themselves. We might note in passing, that these similarities are not acknowledged by Soviet sociologists. They claim that their American colleagues try to deny the magnitude or seriousness of crime in the United States and to divert attention from its social roots. The article by the American authors indicates (as do many other American writings not included) that these assertions have no substance.

An interesting and neglected aspect of American delinquency is expressed in the excerpt by a Soviet author, who finds a clearcut relationship between cold war propaganda and juvenile crime. However, it is yet to be demonstrated how much awareness there is among juvenile delinquents of the cold war or the possibilities of nuclear destruction, and if it exists, how it influences the propensity to delinquent behavior. Contrary to the Soviet suggestion, there is more typically an inverse relationship between crime and war psychosis (or political unrest), since war psychosis helps to syphon off some of the impulses which promote many forms of delinquency.

The Soviet excerpt also provides a familiar example of projection in the allegation that juvenile crime in the United States is blamed on communist influences. While we are not given a precise source of the alleged remark by F.B.I. Director Hoover, even assuming that he made it, it can hardly be considered a typical or widespread explanation. At the same time, as some of the Soviet articles included will also show, it is widely held in the Soviet Union not only by propagandists but also by social scientists that capitalist propaganda and corruption is responsible for much of the crime in the U.S.S.R.

In recent years the concern with crime in Soviet society has increased enormously, as is indicated by the richness of material we had to select from. Curiously enough, once the ideological platitudes are left behind and Soviet investigators reveal their concrete findings, numerous similarities emerge between crime in the two societies—in particular, its concentration among the lower socio-economic strata of the cities. Not without reason, some of the Soviet authors are becoming uneasy about the usefulness of the theory of survivals, which with every passing day becomes more and more inapplicable and useless in explaining the criminality of Soviet citizens reared under the new social system. Significantly, Soviet sociologists betray a curious insensitivity to the interdependence of social processes and institutions when attempting to understand crime in their own society, while they display a keen and even exaggerated sensitivity to this inter-dependence in the United States. Their major effort appears to be to isolate crime or criminal behavior from other areas and institutions of life, and especially from the fundamentals of the Soviet social system. For example, isolated teachers or schools might be blamed for juvenile delinquency, but the educational system as a whole is not questioned; the mechanisms of job placement in a given locality might be deplored for not providing promptly satisfactory employment opportunities for the young, but the system of employment as a whole is not criticized. Nor is there any serious effort comparable to that of Matza and Sykes to find a relationship between the attitudes and values of delinquents and those in society at large, or to trace the broader social origins of acquisitiveness, violence, escapism, and anti-social behavior. Still more interesting is the fact that a society seemingly less concerned with sex, less inundated with pornography, and spared of sexual titillation also produces its share of youthful rapists and sex criminals as the Soviet article indicates. The Soviet article on the criminal personality argues, not unlike an American arch-conservative, that the criminals themselves are to blame if they did not attain "the proper education and level of culture," if they did not avail themselves of all the opportunities their society provided. Apparently the author has abandoned even a pretense of pointing to a social causation for crime, citing detail after detail (e.g., 95 per cent of the sample never participated in any civic activity) to show that the criminals are unworthy people who ". . .possessed in the overwhelming majority of cases every opportunity to choose an honest path."

It is perhaps not surprising that if virtue is said to reside in the institutions of society then it must be the individual who is at fault for his misbehavior. In no society is it possible to account for crime in a sociological manner without venturing into the field of social criticism. This is precisely the problem Soviet social scientists face in trying to discard the theory of survivals and in explaining crime without casting doubt on the soundness of major social institutions. While American sociologists may not be more successful in creating theories of crime which have powers of prediction, they do not have to (and they do not) avert their eyes from any facet of their society in pursuing the factors associated with it.

One thing seems clear, which should be no cause for embarrassment to Soviet social scientists: the rise in many types of crime in the Soviet Union, as in the United States, is connected with rising expectations and a growing intolerance of material frustrations. Soviet data show, as well as American, that there is more crime among disadvantaged and deprived groups, whatever the exact source of deprivation. Perhaps crime especially among juveniles is among the unacclaimed signs of the Soviet Union's becoming a truly modern, urban, secular society.

CRIME AND DELINQUENCY
IN THE U.S. :
The American View

Juvenile Delinquency
and Subterranean Values

DAVID MATZA and GRESHAM SYKES

Current explanations of juvenile delinquency can be divided roughly into two major types. On the one hand, juvenile delinquency is seen as a product of personality disturbances or emotional conflicts within the individual; on the other hand, delinquency is viewed as result of relatively normal personalities exposed to a "disturbed" social environment—particularly in the form of a deviant sub-culture in which the individual learns to be delinquent as others learn to conform to the law. The theoretical conflict between these two positions has been intensified, unfortunately, by the fact that professional pride sometimes leads psychologists and sociologists to define the issue as a conflict between disciplines and to rally be-

Reprinted by permission of the American Sociological Association and Gresham Sykes, from D. Matza and G. Sykes, American Sociological Review, XXVI, No. 5 (October, 1961), 712–719. Copyright 1961 from ASR by Matza and Sykes.

hind their respective academic banners.

Despite many disagreements between these two points of view, one assumption is apt to elicit common support. The delinquent, it is asserted, is deviant; not only does his behavior run counter to the law but his underlying norms, attitudes, and values also stand opposed to those of the dominant social order. And the dominant social order, more often than not, turns out to be the world of the middle class.

We have suggested in a previous article that this image of delinquents and the larger society as antagonists can be misleading.[1] Many delinquents, we argued, are essentially in agreement with the larger society, at least with regard to the evaluation of delinquent behavior as "wrong." Rather than standing in opposition to conventional ideas of good conduct, the delinquent is likely to adhere to the dominant norms in belief but render them ineffective in practice by holding various attitudes and perceptions which serve to neutralize the norms as checks on behavior. "Techniques of neutralization," such as the denial of responsibility or the definition of injury as rightful revenge, free the individual from a large measure of social control.

This approach to delinquency centers its attention on how an impetus to engage in delinquent behavior is translated into action. But it leaves unanswered a serious question: What makes delinquency attractive in the first place? Even if it is granted that techniques of neutralization or some similar evasions of social controls pave the way for overt delinquency, there remains the problem of the values or ends underlying delinquency and the relationship of these values to those of the larger

society. Briefly stated, this paper argues that (a) the values behind much juvenile delinquency are far less deviant than they are commonly portrayed; and (b) the faulty picture is due to a gross oversimplification of the middle-class value system.

THE VALUES OF DELINQUENCY

There are many perceptive accounts describing the behavior of juvenile delinquents and their underlying values, using methods ranging from participant observation to projective tests.[2] Although there are some important differences of opinion in the interpretation

---

[1] Gresham M. Sykes and David Matza, "Techniques of Neutralization," *American Sociological Review*, 22 (December, 1957), pp. 664–670.

[2] Frederic M. Thrasher, *The Gang*, Chicago: University of Chicago Press, 1936; Clifford R. Shaw and Maurice E. Moore, *The Natural History of a Delinquent Career*, Chicago: University of Chicago Press, 1931; Albert K. Cohen, *Delinquent Boys: The Culture of the Gang*, Glencoe, Ill.: The Free Press, 1955; Albert K. Cohen and James F. Short, "Research in Delinquent Subcultures," *Journal of Social Issues*, 14 (1958), pp. 20–37; Walter B. Miller, "Lower Class Culture as a Generating Milieu of Gang Delinquents," *Journal of Social Issues*, 14 (1958), pp. 5–19; Harold Finestone, "Cats, Kicks, and Color," *Social Problems*, 5 (July, 1957), pp. 3–13; Solomin Kobrin, "The Conflict of Values in Delinquent Areas," *American Sociological Review*, 16 (October, 1951), pp. 653–661; Richard Cloward and Lloyd Ohlin, "New Perspectives on Juvenile Delinquency," (unpublished manuscript); Dale Kramer and Madeline Karr, *Teen-Age Gangs*, New York: Henry Holt, 1953; Stacey V. Jones, "The Cougars—Life with a Delinquent Gang," *Harper Magazine*, (November, 1954); Harrison E. Salisbury, *The Shook-Up Generation*, New York: Harper and Brothers, 1958; William C. Kvaraceus and Walter B. Miller, ed., *Delinquent Behavior: Culture and the Individual*, National Education Association of the United States, 1959; Herbert A. Bloch and Arthur Niederhoffer, *The Gang*, New York: Philosophical Library, 1958; Beatrice Griffith, *American Me*, Boston: Houghton-Mifflin, 1948; Sheldon Glueck and Eleanor Glueck, *Unraveling Juvenile Delinquency*, New York: Commonwealth Fund, 1950.

of this material, there exists a striking consensus on actual substance. Many divisions and subdivisions are possible, of course, in classifying these behavior patterns and the values on which they are based, but three major themes emerge with marked regularity.

First, many observers have noted that delinquents are deeply immersed in a restless search for excitement, "thrills," or "kicks." The approved style of life, for many delinquents, is an adventurous one. Activities pervaded by displays of daring and charged with danger are highly valued in comparison with more mundane and routine patterns of behavior. This search for excitement is not easily satisfied in legitimate outlets such as organized recreation, as Tappan has indicated. The fact that an activity involves breaking the law is precisely the fact that often infuses it with an air of excitement.[3] In fact, excitement or "kicks" may come to be defined with clear awareness as "any act tabooed by 'squares' that heightens and intensifies the present moment of experience and differentiates it as much as possible from the humdrum routines of daily life."[4] But in any event, the delinquent way of life is frequently a way of life shot through with adventurous exploits that are valued for the stimulation they provide.

It should be noted that in courting physical danger, experimenting with the forbidden, provoking the authorities, and so on, the delinquent is not simply enduring hazards; he is also creating hazards in a deliberate attempt to manufacture excitement. As Miller has noted, for example, in his study of Roxbury, for many delinquents "the rhythm of life fluctuates between periods of relatively routine and repetitive activities and sought situations of greater emotional stimulation."[5] The excitement, then, that flows from gang rumbles, games of "chicken" played with cars, or the use of drugs is not merely an incidental by-product but may instead serve as a major motivating force.

Second, juvenile delinquents commonly exhibit a disdain for "getting on" in the realm of work. Occupation goals involving a steady job or careful advancement are apt to be lacking, and in their place we find a sort of aimless drifting or grandiose dreams of quick success. Now it takes a very deep faith in the maxims of Benjamin Franklin—or a certain naiveté, perhaps —to believe that hard work at the lower ranges of the occupational hierarchy is a sure path to worldly achievement. The delinquent is typically described as choosing another course, rationally or irrationally. Chicanery or manipulation, which may take the form of borrowing from social workers or more elaborate modes of "hustling"; an emphasis on "pull," frequently with reference to obtaining a soft job which is assumed to be available only to those with influential connections: all are seen as methods of exploiting the social environment without drudgery, and are accorded a high value. Simple expropriation should be included, of course, in the form of theft, robbery, and the rest; but it is only one of a variety of ways of "scoring" and does not necessarily carry great prestige in the eyes of the delinquent. In fact, there is some evidence that, among certain delinquents, theft and robbery may actually be looked down upon as pointing to a lack of wit or skill. A life of ease based on pimping or the numbers game may be held out as a far more admirable goal.[6] In any event, the delinquent is frequ-

[3] Paul Tappan, *Juvenile Delinquency*, New York: McGraw-Hill, 1949, pp. 148–154.

[4] Finestone, *op. cit.*

[5] Miller, *op. cit.*

[6] Finestone, *op. cit.*

ently convinced that only suckers work and he avoids, if he can, the regimen of the factory, store, and office.

Some writers have coupled the delinquent's disdain of work with a disdain of money. Much delinquent activity, it is said, is non-utilitarian in character and the delinquent disavows the material aspirations of the larger society, thus protecting himself against inevitable frustration. Now it is true that the delinquent's attacks agains property are often a form of play, as Cohen has pointed out, rather than a means to a material end.[7] It is also true that the delinquent often shows little liking for the slow accumulation of financial resources. Yet rather than saying that the delinquent disdains money, it would seem more accurate to say that the delinquent is deeply and constantly concerned with the problem of money in his own way. The delinquent wants money, probably no less than the law-abiding, but not for the purposes of a careful series of expenditures or some long-range objective. Rather, money is frequently desired as something to be squandered in gestures of largesse, in patterns of conspicuous consumption. The sudden acquisition of large sums of money is his goal—the "big score"—and he will employ legal means if possible and illegal means if necessary. Since legal means are likely to be thought of as ineffective, it is far from accidental that "smartness" is such an important feature of the delinquent's view of life: "Smartness involves the capacity to outsmart, outfox, outwit, dupe. . ."[8]

A third theme running through accounts of juvenile delinquency centers on aggression. This theme is most likely to be selected as pointing to the delinquent's alienation from the larger society. Verbal and physical assaults are a commonplace, and frequent reference is made to the delinquent's basic hostility, his hatred, and his urge to injure and destroy.

The delinquent's readiness for aggression is particularly emphasized in the analysis of juvenile gangs found in the slum areas of large cities. In such gangs we find the struggles for "turf," the beatings, and the violent feuds which form such distinctive elements in the portrayal of delinquency. As Cloward and Ohlin have pointed out, we can be led into error by viewing these gang delinquents as typical of all delinquents.[9] And Bloch and Niederhoffer have indicated that many current notions of the delinquent gangs are quite worn out and require reappraisal.[10] Yet the gang delinquent's use of violence for the maintenance of "rep," the proof of "heart," and so on, seems to express in extreme form the idea that aggression is a demonstration of toughness and thus of masculinity. This idea runs through much delinquent activity. The concept of *machismo*, of the path to manhood through the ability to take it and hand it out, is foreign to the average delinquent only in name.

In short, juvenile delinquency appears to be permeated by a cluster of values that can be characterized as the search for kicks, the disdain of work and a desire for the big score, and the acceptance of aggressive toughness as proof of masculinity. Whether these values are seen as pathological expressions of a distorted personality or as the traits of a delinquent sub-culture, they are taken as indicative of the delinquent's deviation from the dominant society. The delinquent, it is said, stands apart from the dominant society not only in terms of his illegal behavior but in terms of his basic values as well.

---

[7] Cohen, *op. cit.*
[8] Miller, *op. cit.*

[9] Cloward and Ohlin, *op. cit.*
[10] Bloch and Niederhoffer, *op. cit.*

DELINQUENCY AND LEISURE

The deviant nature of the deliquent's values might pass unquestioned at first glance. Yet when we examine these values a bit more closely, we must be struck by their similarity to the components of the code of the "gentleman of leisure" depicted by Thorstein Veblen. The emphasis on daring and adventure; the rejection of the prosaic discipline of work; the taste for luxury and conspicuous consumption; and the respect paid to manhood demonstrated through force—all find a prototype in that sardonic picture of a leisured elite. What is *not* familiar is the mode of expression of these values, namely, delinquency. The quality of the values is obscured by their context. When "daring" turns out to be acts of daring by adolescents directed against adult figures of accepted authority, for example, we are apt to see only the flaunting of authority and not the courage that may be involved. We suspect that if juvenile delinquency were highly valued by the dominant society—as is the case, let us say, in the deviance of prisoners of war or resistance fighters rebelling against the rules of their oppressors—the interpretation of the nature of delinquency and the delinquent might be far different.[11]

In any event, the values of a leisure class seem to lie behind much delinquent activity, however brutalized or perverted their expression may be accounted by the dominant social order.

[11] Merton's comments on in-group virtues and out-group vices are particularly germane. The moral alchemy cited by Merton might be paraphrased to read:

> I am daring
> You are reckless
> He is delinquent

Cf. Robert K. Merton, *Social Theory and Social Structure,* Glencoe, Ill.: The Free Press, 1957, pp. 426–430.

Interestingly enough, Veblen himself saw a similarity between the pecuniary man, the embodiment of the leisure class, and the delinquent. "The ideal pecuniary man is like the ideal delinquent," said Veblen, "in his unscrupulous conversion of goods and services to his own ends, and in a callous disregard for the feelings and wishes of others and of the remoter effects of his actions."[12] For Veblen this comparison was probably no more than an aside, a part of polemical attack on the irresponsibility and pretentions of an industrial society's rulers. And it is far from clear what Veblen meant by delinquency. Nonetheless, his barbed comparison points to an important idea. We have too easily assumed that the delinquent is deviant in his values, opposed to the larger society. This is due, in part, to the fact that we have taken an overly simple view of the value system of the supposedly law-abiding. In our haste to create a standard from which deviance can be measured, we have reduced the value system of the whole society to that of the middle class. We have ignored both the fact that society is not composed exclusively of the middle class and that the middle class itself is far from homogeneous.[13]

[12] T. Veblen, *The Theory of the Leisure Class,* The Modern Library, 1934, pp. 237–238.

[13] Much of the current sociological analysis of the value systems of the different social classes would seem to be based on a model which is closely akin to an outmoded portrayal of race. Just as racial groups were once viewed as a clustering of physical traits with no overlapping of traits from one group to the next (e.g., Caucasians are straight-haired, light-skinned, etc., whereas Negroes are kinky-haired, dark-skinned, etc.), so now are the value systems of social classes apt to be seen as a distinct grouping of specific values which are unique to the social class in which they are found. The model of the value systems of the different social classes we are using in this paper is more closely allied to the treatment of race presently used in anthropology, i.e., a

In reality, of course, the value system of any society is exceedingly complex and we cannot solve our problems in the analysis of deviance by taking as a baseline a simplicity which does not exist in fact. Not only do different social classes differ in their values, but there are also significant variations within a class based on ethnic origins, upward and downward mobility, region, age, etc. Perhaps even more important, however, is the existence of subterranean values—values, that is to say, which are in conflict or in competition with other deeply held values but which are still recognized and accepted by many.[14] It is crucial to note that these contradictions in values are not necessarily the opposing viewpoints of two different groups. They may also exist within a single individual and give rise to profound feelings of ambivalence in many areas of life. In this sense, subterranean values are akin to private as opposed to public morality. They are values that the individual holds to and believes in but that are also recognized as being not quite *comme il faut*. The easier task of analysis is to call such values deviant and to charge the individual with hypocrisy when he acts on them. Social reality, however, is somewhat more intricate than that and we cannot take the black and white world of McGuffey's Readers as an accurate model of the values by which men live.

Now the value of adventure certainly does not provide the major organizing principle of the dominant social order in modern, industrial society. This is especially true in the work-a-day world where so much activity is founded on bureaucratization and all that it implies

with regard to routinization, standardization, and so on. But this is not to say that the element of adventure is completely rejected by the society at large or never appears in the motivational structure of the law-abiding. Instead, it would appear that adventure, i.e., displays of daring and the search for excitement, are acceptable and desirable but only when confined to certain circumstances such as sports, recreation, and holidays. The last has been frequently noted in the observation that conventions are often viewed as social events in which conventional canons of conduct are interpreted rather loosely. In fact, most societies seem to provide room for Saturnalias in one form or another, a sort of periodic anomie in which thrill-seeking is allowed to emerge.

In other words, the middle-class citizen may seem like a far cry from the delinquent on the prowl for "thrills," but they both recognize and share the idea that "thrills" are worth pursuing and often with the same connotation of throwing over the traces, of opposing "fun" to the routine. As members of the middle class—and other classes— seek their "kicks" in gambling, nightclubbing, the big night on the town, etc., we can neither ignore their use of leisure nor claim that it is based on a markedly deviant value. Leisure class values have come increasingly to color the activities of many individuals in the dominant society, although they may limit their expression more sharply than does the delinquent. The search for adventure, excitement, and thrills, then, is a subterranean value that now often exists side by side with the values of security, routinization, and the rest. It is not a deviant value, in any full sense, but it must be held in abeyance until the proper moment and circumstances for its expression arrive. It is obvious that something more than the delin-

---

distribution of frequencies. Most values, we argue, appear in most social classes; the social classes differ, however, in the frequency with which the values appear.

[14] Robert S. Lynd, *Knowledge for What,* Princeton: Princeton University Press, 1948.

quent's sense of appropriateness is involved, but it is also clear that in many cases the delinquent suffers from bad timing.

Similarly, to characterize the dominant society as being fully and unquestioningly attached to the virtue of hard work and careful saving is to distort reality. Notions of "pull" and the soft job are far from uncommon and the individual who entertains such notions cannot be thrust beyond the pale merely because some sociologists have found it convenient to erect a simplified conception of *the* work values of society. As Chinoy and Bell, and a host of other writers have pointed out, the conditions of work in modern society have broken down earlier conceptions of work as a calling and there are strong pressures to define the job as a place where one earns money as quickly and painlessly as possible.[15] If the delinquent carries this idea further than many of society's members might be willing to do, he has not necessarily moved into a new realm of values. In the same vein it can be argued that the delinquent's attachment to conspicuous consumption hardly makes him a stranger to the dominant society. Just as Riesman's "inside dopester," Whyte's "organization man," and Mills' "fixer" have a more authentic ring than an obsolete Weberian image in many instances, the picture of the delinquent as a spender seems more valid than a picture of him as an adolescent who has renounced material aspirations. The delinquent, we suggest, is much more in step with his times. Perhaps it is too extreme to say with Lowenthal[16] that "the idols of work have been replaced by the idols of leisure," but it appears unquestionable that we are witnessing a compromise between the Protestant Ethic and a Leisure Ethic. The delinquent conforms to society, rather than deviates from it, when he incorporates "big money" into his value sytem.[17]

Finally, we would do well to question prevalent views about society's attitudes toward violence and aggression. It could be argued, for one thing, that the dominant society exhibits a widespread taste for violence, since fantasies of violence in books, magazines, movies, and television are everywhere at hand. The delinquent simply translates into behavior those values that the majority are usually too timid to express. Furthermore, disclaimers of violence are suspect not simply because fantasies of violence are widely consumed, but also because of the actual use of aggression and violence in war, race riots, industrial conflicts, and the treatment of delinquents themselves by police. There are numerous examples of the acceptance of aggression and violence on the part of the dominant social order.

Perhaps it is more important, however, to recognize that the crucial idea of aggression as a proof of toughness and masculinity is widely accepted at many points in the social system. The ability to take it and hand it out, to defend one's rights and one's reputation with force, to prove one's manhood by hardness and physical courage—all are widespread in American culture. They cannot be dismissed by noting the equally valid observation that many people will declare that "nice children do not fight." The use of aggression to demonstrate masculinity is, of course,

[15] Daniel Bell, *Work and Its Discontents,* Boston: Beacon Press, 1956. Ely Chinoy, *Automobile Workers and the American Dream,* Garden City, N. Y.: Doubleday and Company, 1955.

[16] Leo Lowenthal, "Historical Perspectives of Popular Culture," in Bernard Rosenberg and David M. White, ed., *Mass Culture: The* *Popular Arts in America,* Glencoe, Ill.: The Free Press, 1957.

[17] Arthur K. Davis, "Veblen on the Decline of the Protestant Ethic," *Social Forces,* 22 (March, 1944), pp. 282–286.

restricted by numerous prohibitions against instigating violence, "dirty" fighting, bullying, blustering, and so on. Yet even if the show of violence is carefully hedged in by both children and adults throughout our society, there is a persistent support for aggression which manifests itself in the derogatory connotations of labels such as "sissy" or "fag."[18]

In short, we are arguing that the delinquent may not stand as an alien in the body of society but may represent instead a disturbing reflection or a caricature. His vocabulary is different, to be sure, but kicks, big-time spending, and rep have immediate counterparts in the value system of the law-abiding. The delinquent has picked up and emphasized one part of the dominant value system, namely, the subterranean values that coexist with other, publicly proclaimed values possessing a more respectable air. These subterranean values, similar in many ways to the values Veblen ascribed to a leisure class, bind the delinquent to the society whose laws he violates. And we suspect that this sharing of· values, this bond with the larger social order, facilitates the frequently observed "reformation" of delinquents with the coming of adult status.[19] To the objection that much juvenile behavior other than simply delinquent behavior would then be analyzed as an extension of the adult world rather than as a product of a distinct adolescent sub-culture we can only answer that this is precisely our thesis.

[18] Albert Bandura and Richard Haig Walters, *Adolescent Aggression,* New York: Ronald Press, 1959, ch. 3.

[19] See, for example, William McCord, Joan McCord and Irving K. Zola, *Origins of Crime,* New York: Columbia University Press, 1959, p. 21.

DELINQUENCY AND SOCIAL CLASS

The persistence of the assumption that the juvenile delinquent must deviate from the law-abiding in his values as well as in his behavior can be traced in part, we suspect, to the large number of studies that have indicated that delinquents are disproportionately represented in the lower classes. In earlier years it was not too difficult to believe that the lower classes were set off from their social superiors in most attributes, including "immorality," and that this taint produced delinquent behavior. Writers of more recent vintage have avoided this reassuring error, but, still holding to the belief that delinquency is predominantly a lower-class phenomenon, have continued to look for features peculiar to certain segments of the lower class that would create values at variance with those of the rest of society and which would foster delinquency.

Some criminologists, however, have long expressed doubts about the validity of the statistics on delinquency and have suggested that if all the facts were at hand the delinquency rate of the lower classes and the classes above them would be found to be far less divergent than they now appear.[20] Preferential treatment by the police and the courts and better and more varied means for handling the offender may have led us to underestimate seriously the extent to which juvenile delinquency crops up in what are euphemistically termed "relatively privileged homes."

Given the present state of data in this field, it is probably impossible to come to any firm conclusion on this issue. One thing, however, seems fairly

[20] Milton L. Barron, *The Juvenile in Delinquent Society,* New York: Alfred A. Knopf, 1954.

clear: juvenile delinquency does occur frequently in the middle and upper classes and recent studies show more delinquency in these groups than have studies in the past. We might interpret this as showing that our research methods have improved or that "white-collar" delinquency is increasing—or possibly both. But in any event, the existence of juvenile delinquency in the middle and upper classes poses a serious problem for theories which depend on status deprivation, social disorganization, and similar explanatory variables. One solution has been to change horses in the middle of the stratification system, as it were, shifting from social environment to personality disturbances as the causative factor as one moves up the social ladder. Future research may prove that this shift is necessary. Since juvenile delinquency does not appear to be a unitary phenomenon we might expect that no one theoretical approach will be adequate. To speak of juvenile delinquency in general, as we have done in this paper, should not obscure the fact that there are different types of delinquency and the differences among them cannot be ignored. Yet it seems worthwhile to pursue the idea that some forms of juvenile delinquency—and possibly the most frequent—have a common sociological basis regardless of the class level at which they appear.

One such basis is offered, we believe, by our argument that the values lying behind much delinquent behavior are the values of a leisure class. All adolescents at all class levels are to some extent members of a leisure class, for they move in a limbo between earlier parental domination and future integration with the social structure through the bonds of work and marriage.[21]

[21] Reuel Denney, *The Astonished Muse*, Chicago: University of Chicago Press, 1957.

Theirs is an anticipatory leisure, it is true, a period of freedom from the demands for self-support which allows room for the schooling enabling them to enter the world of work. They thus enjoy a temporary leisure by sufferance rather than by virtue of a permanent aristocratic right. Yet the leisure status of adolescents, modified though it may be by the discipline of school and the lack of wealth, places them in relationship to the social structure in a manner similar to that of an elite which consumes without producing. In this situation, disdain of work, an emphasis on personal qualities rather than technical skills, and a stress on the manner and extent of consumption all can flourish. Insofar, then, as these values do lie behind delinquency, we could expect delinquent behavior to be prevalent among all adolescents rather than confined to the lower class.

CONCLUSION

This theory concerning the role of leisure in juvenile delinquency leaves unsolved, of course, a number of problems. First, there is the question why some adolescents convert subterranean values into seriously deviant behavior while other do not. Even if it is granted that many adolescents are far more deviant in their behavior than official records would indicate, it is clear that there are degrees of delinquency and types of delinquency. This variation cannot be explained simply on the basis of exposure to leisure. It is possible that leisure values are typically converted

See also Barbara Wooton, *Social Science and Social Pathology*, New York: Macmillan, 1959; Arthur L. Porterfield, *Youth in Trouble*, Austin, Tex.: Leo Potishman Foundation, 1946.

into delinquent behavior when such values are coupled with frustrations and resentments. (This is more than a matter of being deprived in socio-economic terms.) If this is so, if the delinquent is a sort of soured sportsman, neither leisure nor deprivation will be sufficient by itself as an explanatory variable. This would appear to be in accordance with the present empirical observations in the field. Second, we need to know a good deal more about the distribution of leisure among adolescents and its impact on their value systems. We have assumed that adolescents are in general leisured, i.e., free from the demands for self-support, but school drop-outs, the conversion of school into a tightly disciplined and time-consuming preparation for a career, the facilities for leisure as opposed to mere idleness, will all probably have their effect. We suspect that two variables are of vital impor-

tance in this area: (a) the extent of identification with adult symbols of work, such as the father; and (b) the extent to which the school is seen as providing roles to enhance the ego, both now and in the future, rather than as an oppressive and dreary marking of time.

We conclude that the explanation of juvenile delinquency may be clarified by exploring the delinquent's similarity to the society that produced him rather than his dissimilarity. If his values are the subterranean values of a society that is placing increasing emphasis on leisure, we may throw new light on Taft's comment that the basic values in our culture are accepted by both the delinquent and the larger society of which he is a part.[22]

[22] Donald R. Taft, *Criminology,* New York: Macmillan, 1950.

Crime in the American
Social Structure

STANTON WHEELER

Given the limitations of official criminal statistics, it is perhaps unwise to attempt to set forth the seemingly most important facts about crime in the United States. It is conceivable that with adequate and valid measures many of these "facts" would change drastically. Nevertheless, there seems to be

Reprinted by permission of the publisher from S. Wheeler, "Crime in the American Social Structure," Social Problems, Howard Becker, ed. New York: John Wiley & Sons, 1966, pp. 210–225.

enough evidence, gathered from a variety of sources, by diverse methods, to support at least the following brief description of crime in the United States.

1. Crime rates are high, and may be getting higher. To say that a rate of crime is high is to suggest a criterion that distinguishes a high rate from a low one. Here we mean simply that crime rates in the United States are apparently among the highest in industrialized societies. Because of the lack of strict comparability of crime statistics

from one political system to another, this judgment rests largely on informal observation of persons familiar with crime problems in a range of countries. Particularly with regard to violent crimes, there is relatively little doubt among such persons that the problem of crime in the United States is greater than in most other countries.

The number of persons officially charged with being delinquent or criminal in any one year is, however, small. In most analyses it ranges from one to 4 or 5 per cent of the population. If we ask, however, how many persons will either have been arrested or have appeared in court during their lifetime for a delinquent or criminal charge, the rate is of course substantially higher.

Evidence for the rise in the crime rate in recent years comes largely from the official statistics compiled by the FBI. Taking only those offenses they believe most reliably reported, as discussed earlier, the crime rate for 1963 is up some 30 per cent over the rate for 1958.[1] The actual number of crimes increased about 40 per cent, whereas the population of the United States increased only 8 per cent over that time period, leaving an overall increase in the crime rate of approximately 30 per cent. Most of this increase was due to an increase in property crime; the rate of increase for murder, forcible rape, robbery, and aggravated assault was only 12 per cent.

2. The vast majority of offenses are property crimes. This judgment is especially subject to the limitations of official statistics, because offenses against the person, notably those involving mutual consent, such as many types of sex offenses, are unlikely to be reported to the police. In any event, the work of the police, the courts, and the

prisons is primarily with property offenders, rather than offenders against the person. Of the total of 2,259,081 offenses treated as most serious in the "Uniform Crime Reports," 77 per cent involved the property crimes of burglary, larceny of 50 dollars or over, or auto theft, and of the remaining 23 per cent, about one-third involved crimes of violence against the person, apparently committed for *reasons* of gaining property, that is, robberies.[2]

3. Despite a preponderance of property crimes among the more serious offenses, the amount of personal violence is high—probably higher than in most Western nations, a view which necessarily rests on subjective comparison as well as evidence. Specifically, our homicide rates are much higher than those of European countries, as are our rates of assault.

4. A characteristic feature of American criminality is the presence of organized crime—the development of large-scale organizations for criminal activities. Traditionally, what has been organized is the control and distribution of illicit goods and services—alcohol during prohibition, narcotics, prostitution, and gambling. In addition, there are the organized efforts to control various legitimate business activities, such as labor unions, vending machine operations, and the like. Although the total number of major crimes charged to "organized crime" is probably small, its cost and its pattern within our central urban areas provide a distinctive element of American society.[3]

5. The United States has much youth-gang crime. Here again, it is the patterning, rather than the total numbers, of such crime that is important. Gang violence in our major urban cen-

[1] Here and in following sections, official FBI data are taken from "Uniform Crime Reports," 1963.

[2] *Ibid.*
[3] Gus W. Tyler, *Organized Crime in America* (Ann Arbor: University of Michigan Press, 1962).

ters has been a prevalent part of the American urban scene. It is found especially in our largest cities such as New York and Chicago, but it is far from unknown in other areas as well. In recent years similar patterns appear to be developing in Western Europe, as represented, for example, by the Mods and Rockers in England, the *raggeri* in Sweden, and similar youth groups elsewhere.

These features—the high proportion of property crime, and the amount of violence, organized crime, and youthful gang activity—are salient characteristics of crime in the United States. A parallel series of characteristics emerges when we examine those charged with commission of crimes.

1. Crime rates are many times higher for males than females. The 1963 FBI data suggest an overall arrest ratio of eight males for each female. The ratio of male to female crime is greater for property offenses than for personal offenses, and the ratio tends to decline under conditions when crime rates are at their highest. That is, the ratio of male to female crime tends to decline in our urban centers among young people, and among other segments of the population that tend to have higher crime rates.

2. Official crime rates tend to be highest among those in the lowest socioeconomic groups. Whenever studies have been conducted that relate crime to one's location in the socioeconomic order, those at the bottom tend to have the highest rates. The extent to which this is true varies under different conditions, but the general point has been made in many studies. It is the case, however, that the impact of socioeconomic status shows its effect most strongly the further one goes into the criminal adjudication process. Nye and Short, using the self-reported delinquency method described earlier, found

no evidence of higher delinquency rates among their lower-class adolescents.[4] Their finding has recently been confirmed for a large urban area by Akers.[5] At the most serious level tapped by this self-reporting measure, however, Akers' lowest socioeconomic group did report higher rates of offense. Thus the apparent relation of socioeconomic status to crime probably indicates both some true difference in the amount of serious crime committed by lower- and middle-class persons, and an impact of police and judicial procedures that is likely to lead to higher rates of arrest, court action, and conviction among those socially and financially less capable of fighting for their release.

Not all the seemingly discriminatory action is chargeable to negative bias or the lack of funds, however. Many court officials feel that, especially among delinquents, removal from poor environments into institutions may be more beneficial than leaving them in unfavorable environmental settings. Such action is taken in the name of humanity and therapy, but its consequence is the application of what society regards as a more severe reaction. Again, an important feature of the relationship between crime and socioeconomic status is that "white-collar crime," for reasons indicated earlier, is not likely to be included in these statistics.

3. Crime rates tend to be highest during middle and late adolescence, declining rapidly with the onset of adulthood. Here again, it is difficult to obtain adequate measurement, because adolescents are frequently handled by special

[4] F. Ivan Nye, James F. Short, Jr., and V. J. Olsen, "Socio-Economic Status and Delinquent Behavior," in F. Ivan Nye, *Family Relationships and Delinquent Behavior* (New York: John Wiley & Sons, 1958).

[5] Ronald L. Akers, "Socio-Economic Status: A Retest," *The Journal of Research in Crime and Delinquency,* 1, 1 (January 1964), pp. 38–46.

administrative procedures. They are less likely to be fingerprinted, and less likely to have official records with the FBI. But such evidence as is available suggests strongly that crime is primarily a young man's activity.[6]

4. Crime rates tend to be highest in the central areas of our major cities, with the rates being much lower in small towns and rural areas. This differential is especially true for property crimes, much less so for offenses against the person, where the differential between rural and urban rates is far less extreme.[7]

5. Crime rates tend to be higher than average among certain minority groups, and lower than average among others. Most forms of crime tend to have relatively high rates among Negroes, Puerto Ricans, and Mexican-Americans living in our large urban areas; the rates tend to be lower than average for populations of Japanese and Chinese ancestry. A large portion of the differential rates for the minority group members appears to be related to the frequent concomitants of minority group status, especially those already enumerated, living in the central sectors of cities and low socioeconomic status. Additional features that may partly account for the differentials between the Oriental and Negro rates relate to typical family structures, which are usually solid and strong among Orientals and more frequently weak or broken in the Negro population. In those few attempts that have been made to compare rates among different racial groups, holding constant such features as socio-economic status, there still appears to be some differential in the rates by race, although it is difficult to find comparable units because of the association between race and poor socioeconomic conditions.[8]

This brief list of characteristic features in American crime invites the question: Why? What is there about the character of American society that gives it these specific properties? A convincing and thorough answer to this question is impossible at this time, since so little is objectively known about how we compare with other countries, and since in any case it is so difficult to attribute *causal* significance to one or another of the ways in which we differ. It can be shown, for example, that the homicide rate in Norway is much lower than in the United States. But in attempting to tell why Americans kill each other at a higher rate than Norwegians do, we might list a combination of *any* of the vast number of other ways Norway differs from the United States: growth rate, size, nature of the political system, rate of industrialization, racial composition, rate of urbanization, average level of income, range in level of income, differences in patterns of child-rearing. Or among characteristics that are conceptually closer to crime, there is the difference in police systems, in public attitudes toward law and its enforcement, differences in the severity of punishment for offenders, in the rate of their detection, and so on.

Occasionally there are techniques for statistically controlling some of these forms of variation, thus removing their influence, so that we can see whether

[6] See the data described in Walter B. Miller, "The Impact of a 'Total-Community' Delinquency Control Project," *Social Problems*, 10, 2 (Fall 1962), p. 168.

[7] For a review of area differences, see Terence Morris, "A Critique of Area Studies," reprinted in Marvin E. Wolfgang, Leonard Savitz, and Norman Johnston, eds., *The Sociology of Crime and Delinquency* (New York: John Wiley & Sons, 1962), pp. 191–198.

[8] Guy B. Johnson, "The Negro and Crime," *Annals of the American Academy of Political and Social Science*, 271 (September 1941), pp. 93–104; Earl R. Moses, "Differentials in Crime Rates between Negroes and Whites Based on Comparisons of Four Socio-Economically Equated Areas," *American Sociological Review*, 12 (August 1947), pp. 411–420.

the effect still remains. In this instance, for example, we might be able to compare homicide rates among rural and urban people in both Norway and the United States, to see whether the overall difference is caused by the varying rates of urbanization. Typically, however, such comparisons are difficult because the necessary data are lacking. It is thus nearly impossible at present to explain the characteristic features of American crime in an intellectually compelling and satisfying way. But we are not prevented from using the knowledge that can be gathered in an attempt to piece together a plausible account of the characteristic differences. It should serve to forewarn us, however, of the possibility of error and of the great need for more systematic comparative studies that make possible a clearer assessment of the conditions related to crime in different societies, and an explanation of changes in volume of crime over time and place.

In presenting and assessing these accounts, we should remember that some are addressed to the *general character* of crime in America—its various types and amounts. Others are addressed more to an explanation of the *distribution* of crime among various segments of the population. (These differences correspond roughly to the different sets of facts just noted.) The theories also differ in generality; some point to features common to modern industrial societies and are useful in explaining why crime patterns may be different in such societies from the patterns found in the pre-industrial or developing nations; others point more directly to factors that distinguish the United States from other industrial nations.

Finally, the arguments reviewed here are designed to explain differences in the rate or quality of crime, not to describe in detail the process by which a given person becomes criminal. Even

for social categories in which rates are highest, some individuals do not commit offenses. It requires a more detailed review of their personal background experience to explain why, within the same broad category, some persons do and others do not become criminal. We turn to some of these problems in a later section.

The disruption of social relationships. Some efforts to account for variations in crime rates focus on disrupted social bonds and the consequent weakening of motives for conformity to conventional standards.[9] The central notion is that personal stability and willingness to abide by conventional norms depend on the stability of social patterns and relationships. Individuals bound up closely with persons from groups that they know and admire would be unlikely to violate the norms of such groups. And for most groups, most of the time, the norms include conformity to the law. Proponents of this view hold that any condition that leads to a weakening of social bonds, or to the development of conflict and dissension in place of cultural uniformity and homogeneity, may so weaken motives for conformity that individuals are willing to commit criminal acts.

Such conditions are typically found in modern industrial societies. First, rates of social change are rapid, so that new generations face new conditions. This means a possible break-up in the continuity of training and socialization, and therefore a potential weakening of ties across age-graded positions in the life cycle.

[9] This is the general position of those who stress social disorganization as a cause of crime. For a relevant review, see Albert K. Cohen, *Delinquent Boys: The Culture of the Gang* (Glencoe, Ill.: The Free Press, 1954), Chapter 1. See also Ralph H. Turner, "Value Conflict in Social Disorganization," *Sociology and Social Research* (May–June 1954), pp. 301–308.

Second, not only is there rapid change in general social conditions, but there is also likely to be rapid change in the position of given individuals in the social order. High rates of social mobility, either upward or downward, produce disrupted social relationships and a weakening of solidarity.[10]

Third, increasing social differentiation and heterogeneity may lead to the disruption of social relationships among groups occupying differing statuses and engaged in different functions, even *within* such groups. When the bonds are broken between them, the possibility of variant group values and interests emerges, along with conflict among the various segments. Such relationships may allow the development of deviant subcultures giving expression to values opposed to those of the conventional society. Clear examples in our own society include those sorts of urban subcultures devoted to organized crime, gang delinquency, and the like. Adolescence appears crucial here, since so much of the adolescent's time is spent with his peers rather than with those directly engaged in traditional adult roles. Under these conditions it is not surprising to find an upward surge of deviant movements, either political, delinquent, or bohemian, among adolescents and young adults.[11]

It is important to note three things about this reasoning. First, it is not necessary to argue that only those persons who personally face these conditions are likely to feel the weakening of the social and normative order. Rather, when these conditions are found in society, many will be exposed to their indirect consequences. For example, even though a youth may grow up with a stable family life and retain most of his childhood friends, he is still likely to be exposed to rapid changes in communication and transportation systems, the occupational and educational structure, and other major institutional settings.

Second, as Cohen and others have clearly noted, this line of reasoning does not expalin why motives for the commission of crimes are present in the first place.[12] Only if there is a relatively steady (although perhaps random) push or motivation toward the commission of criminal acts will these conditions of disrupted social relationships result in crimes.

Third, these conditions are general, whereas crime is specific. The same conditions are alleged to be related to the production of mental disorder, suicide, the formation of deviant political groups, revolutions, and almost all other forms of behavior defined as socially deviant. It would not be surprising to find that many of these forms of deviation have elements in common and therefore are responsive to common conditions. The question remains: Why do these conditions sometimes lead to the commission of crimes, sometimes to radically different forms of deviance? Part of the answer may be suggested below.

The nature of role and status definitions. Other ideas focus on the major status and role structures of society. The definitions of appropriate behavior for males versus females, adolescents versus adults, lower-class youths versus middle-class youths, may predispose, if not require, characteristic forms of criminal behavior. One of the leading reasons for the predominance of male

[10] The original argument is found in Emile Durkheim, *Suicide: A Study in Sociology*, trans. by John A. Spaulding and George Simpson (Glencoe, Ill.: The Free Press, 1951).

[11] See David Matza, "Position and Behavior Patterns in Youth," in Robert E. L. Faris, ed., *Handbook of Modern Sociology* (Chicago: Rand McNally, 1964), pp. 191–217.

[12] Cohen, *op. cit.*

over female crime is that males are expected to provide material goods and services. They are also expected to play more aggressive and instrumental roles, whereas females are expected to be more passive and expressive. The combination of these role definitions provides a basis for expecting high rates of male crime compared to female crime, especially since the bulk of all crimes is property offense. We might also expect that where *different* definition of male and female roles emerge, there should be changes in the rates of crime between the sexes. Thus it has been argued that as women's roles become more masculine, as in some labor forces, the female crime rates also rise.[13]

When we look more closely at the manner in which crimes are committed, this difference between male and female role definitions appears clearly. In an interesting analysis of male and female crime, Grosser showed that delinquent girls' pattern of participation in delinquent activities was radically different from that of delinquent boys.[14] Not only are the girls much less likely to become involved in delinquent activity at all, but when they do become involved, it is typically with sexual promiscuity, or with helping males engaging in offenses. It is uncommon for girls to be involved in the more serious patterns of delinquency except through their participation in heterosexual affairs.

Another set of role and status definitions that may influence rates of crime are those associated with different positions in the social stratification system. Since today many of those Americans who compose the lower levels in the stratification system are members of ethnic and cultural minorities, these patterns of role definitions are in some respects tied in with ethnic status. Some investigators, such as the anthropologist Walter Miller, feel that there is a core set of values and problems in lower-class culture that distinguishes it from other levels in the system and increases the probability that anyone raised in that culture will engage in violations of the law.[15] On the basis of long-term experience in the study of lower-class street corner groups, Miller has arrived at a set of what he calls "focal concerns" of lower-class culture that differentiate it clearly from other positions in the social order. These include:

1. "Trouble"—various forms of unwelcome or complicating involvement with society's agents, such as police, welfare investigators, and others.

2. "Toughness"—skill in physical combat plus a surrounding set of values that emphasizes the ability to "take it," lack of sentimentality and a contempt for anything smacking of femininity.

3. "Smartness"—being able to outwit, dupe, and in general outsmart others.

4. "Excitement"—a value placed upon thrills, taking chances, and flirting with danger.

5. "Fate"—a value that assumes most of the important events in life are beyond one's control and governed by chance, destiny, or circumstance.

6. "Autonomy"—on the level of expressed values, though not necessarily in actual behavior, an emphasis on the importance of not submitting to others' demands, a resentment of external controls or restrictions—especially coercive authority.

Miller's point is that an orientation toward this set of concerns will neces-

13 Edwin Sutherland and Donald R. Cressey, *Principles of Criminology* (Philadelphia: Lippincott, fifth editon, 1955), pp. 111–114.

14 George Grosser, "Juvenile Delinquency and Contemporary American Sex Roles," unpublished Ph.D. dissertation, Harvard University, 1952.

15 Walter B. Miller, "Lower Class Culture as a Generating Milieu of Gang Delinquency," *Journal of Social Issues*, 14, 3 (1958), pp. 5–19.

sarily involve some in unlawful activity such as fighting and disturbing the peace, and that it creates situations in which unlawful activity it likely to emerge. The craving for excitement leads to auto theft, or the stress on toughness leads to the return of verbal insult with physical attack. It is not that lower-class cultural values *demand* violation of the law, but rather that they help create circumstances where violation is more likely.

Culturally defined expressions of appropriate behavior also relate to crime through what some have called the "sub-culture of violence."[16] It appears that Negro communities and Southern white communities are more likely to condone the use of aggression as a response to problems. Rates of homicide are generally higher in the South than in the North, even when racial differences in homicide rates are removed. Many homicides result from intially innocuous arguments among intoxicated persons. No clearcut set of social controls keeps a verbal dispute from becoming physical, a physical dispute from becoming a fight with deadly weapons, and so on. Indeed, according to a study of some 500 homicides in Philadelphia over a five-year period, 26 per cent were "victim precipitated"—the person who was killed *began* the dispute that led to his death.[17]

Role and status definitions, like our previous category of disrupted social relationships, do not operate uniformly on all members of a given status category. Some persons more deeply internalize the norms of their settings, and others are in positions where these normative pulls or pushes are felt less

strongly. These processes do give a basis, however, for expecting higher rates of delinquent and criminal behavior among some segments of the population than among others.

The struggle for success and response to failure. One of the most influence sets of ideas about crime causation has been developed by a long list of scholars, stemming primarily from the French sociologist, Emile Durkheim, with a major restatement by Merton and additional contributions by Cohen, Cloward and Ohlin, and others.[18] These ideas about crime are typically embedded in a broader series of issues about the genesis of other forms of deviant behavior; we shall restrict our account to the portion bearing most closely on crime and delinquency, and for the most part to Merton's statement of the problem.[19]

The central notion involves a distinction between cultural goals and the institutionalized and legitimate means by which they may be achieved. The goal is what is worth striving for— the item or condition of value toward which we direct our activity. The legitimate means are the various procedures by which we can seek to achieve the goal without violating social or legal norms.

Merton's argument derives from this distinction in two ways. First, societies differ in the relative emphasis they give to the goals themselves, or to the institutionalized means for achieving them. Some, which we might think of as "rule-oriented," heavily stress proper and correct procedures—the norms telling how one is allowed to compete for the goals. Others place the emphasis on the goals rather than the legitimacy of the means for their achievement.

16 Thomas Pettigrew and Rosemary Spier, "The Ecology of Negro Homicide," *American Journal of Sociology*, 67 (May 1962), pp. 724–730.

17 Wolfgang, Savitz, and Johnston, eds., *op. cit.*, p. 329.

18 Durkheim, *op. cit.*

19 Robert K. Merton, "Social Structure and Anomie," *American Sociological Review*, 3 (October 1938), pp. 677–682.

Second, people *within* a society differ in their proximity to the legitimate means for achieving the goals. Some are in positions that provide easy access to the goals through legal means for achieving them; others are in positions where access to such means is difficult. The central concept here is one of *differential* opportunity or access.

By combining these ideas, we can arrive at predictions about the relative rates of crime within and between societies. In comparing different societies, for example, the prediction must be that societies placing emphasis on personal goal attainment, without similar emphasis on the legitimate means for achieving the goals, will tend to have generally high rates of crime and other forms of "innovating" behavior designed to achieve the goals by whatever means. Merton has argued that the United States is such a society—that we have extolled the value of success without a balance of attention being given to the legitimate means for achieving it. If opportunities were easily accessible to all, there would be no problem, since it would be possible to achieve the goals by legitimate means. But no society has so eliminated the struggle, and it is questionable whether the goal would be worth striving for if everyone could easily attain it. It is, of course, difficult to test these notions because we have no measure of the extent to which a society emphasizes, in its cultural values, goals versus means. No thorough attempt has been made to rate societies on these dimensions. Nevertheless, this idea is one of the important bases for expecting differential rates of crime among societies.

This line of reasoning is applied more frequently to individuals within the same society. Here the argument is straightforward: crime rates will differ according to the extent of "disjuncture" between the goals persons internalize and their socially structured opportunities for achieving them. In American society, where the goal of material success seems dominant, and where the legitimate means to such success typically call for high levels of education and professional training, we would expect high crime rates among those least able to obtain good vocational or professional training.

It is important to note that our prediction does not imply that, anywhere and everywhere, persons of lower socioeconomic standing will have higher rates of crime. This will only be true, so the argument goes, when a cultural goal is set for them and is therefore in most instances internalized by them as an important aim in life, at the same time that their position makes it difficult to compete for this goal. If the society stresses some other goal, say spirituality, and if lower-status persons are in no worse position to compete for this goal than others in society, we would not expect a differential rate of deviant behavior on these grounds. Or, to take a more familiar case, if the goals held out to members of society differ depending on their location in the system, as in some caste systems, we would not necessarily expect the same result. For it is where they stand *in relation to the goals which they seek* that we use to predict their rate of deviant behavior, not where they stand in any absolute sense.

As a plausible account, this reasoning goes far in helping us interpret some of the findings already discussed. Certainly it is true that persons in the lower part of the social order are disadvantaged in their capacity to compete for monetary success. And since that success, on the basis of other values in American society, is expected to be won primarily by males rather than females, we could expect a greater drive toward crime among males. If ethnic and racial minorities have been exposed to the same values or goals, we would expect their crime rates to be higher. Indeed, we might expect relatively well-organized paths of criminal behavior to emerge as routes to financial success for those less likely to attain it through legitimate patterns. Such paths are suggested by the disproportionate ties of political corruption and organized crime to lower-status ethnic groups in our society.

This theme has been criticized, modified, and extended since its original publication in the 1930s. Some have questioned whether the cultural goal of success is indeed held out to all or even a large percentage of persons across the social strata; they have pointed to the evidence that persons in lower social strata do not expect their children to proceed far up the educational ladder, are less likely to expect to hold professional jobs, and so forth.[20] The question is what number of persons hold such achievement goals *compared to the number of available positions;* the balance between the two is difficult to judge.

A closely related issue is the extent to which upward mobility is closed to those near the bottom. Current programs that provide support for poor but talented students, that provide retraining for school drop-outs, that provide special nursery school training as a preparation for entering elementary school, are all designed to achieve greater equality of opportunity. To the extent that such programs are successful, *and* to the extent that this theory is correct, crime rates should fall as more persons are given access to opportunities for developing their skills and talents. In any

event, the question here is primarily one of magnitude, since there is little question that some persons, because of their ethnic, cultural, or personal family backgrounds, are in poorer positions to struggle for success than others. And it is largely in such groups that relatively high official crime rates are found.

Another important modification of the theory has been offered by Cloward.[21] Cloward raised the question: What are the opportunities for success in the criminal world? If we can ask how opportunities for achieving success by legitimate means are distributed throughout the social structure, does it not make sense to ask the same question about illegitimate means? Crime is not a simple reflex action emitted without any prior training or preparation. Most crimes are not of that form, and many persons are not in positions where they can learn to use the necessary means effectively. How many students who read this chapter can hotwire a car, find a fence for stolen property, have the audacity to be a successful con man, have the manual dexterity and training to be a successful pickpocket or safecracker, have the social ties to gain entry to organized gambling syndicates? The question is not silly and the point is clear. Many students would find it difficult to acquire such skills, even if they were motivated to learn. To draw any clear predictions about the probable rates of crime in differing social statuses, we need to know what access the various statuses provide their occupants for both legitimate and illegitimate opportunities.

These (and other) qualifying ideas suggest that the theory of illegitimate or deviant means has been rich in its capacity to create new thoughts, leading to refinements and modifications in the

[20] Herbert Hyman, "The Value Systems of Different Classes: A Social Psychological Contribution to the Analysis of Stratification," in Reinhard Bendix and Seymour Martin Lipset, eds., *Class, Status and Power* (Glencoe, Ill.: The Free Press, 1953).

[21] Richard A. Cloward, "Illegitimate Means, Anomie, and Deviant Behavior," *American Sociological Review,* 24 (April 1959), pp. 164–176.

theory. Unfortunately, evidence providing efficient tests of these ideas is more difficult to come by. Hopefully, evidence will emerge from current efforts to provide equal opportunities and the associated effort to evaluate such programs.

A historical tradition of lawlessness. A final set of ideas about crime in America uses an historical mode to explain the seemingly high rate of crime and violence. It does seem that a combination of historical factors has given rise to conditions with less effective restraints on crime than those in other countries. Our Puritan heritage meant that many human vices were strongly condemned. Emphasis on legal control has meant that laws have been passed to prevent them. Thus gambling, bookmaking, the use of alcohol, premarital and extramarital sexual relations, and other forms of behavior are criminal in many, if not all, jurisdictions of the United States. One pressure toward higher crime rates has come from the simple fact of passing numerous laws in an attempt at legal control of personal conduct.

At the same time, the settling of a vast country required strength, aggressiveness, and manliness. The most successful man was likely to be the most aggressive and powerful, rather than he who lived closest to the letter of the law. Moreover, many of those who settled the country did so partly to escape past histories of failure or deviance. Some of the early settlers of our country arrived here after being banished from England for criminal offenses. In short, the condition seemingly necessary for successful expansion and settlement of the country, coupled with the personal backgrounds of many of the early settlers, was hardly supportive of a passive, mild, and peaceful way of life.[22]

Our methods for responding to criminal behavior were equally aggressive and violent. In the absence of settled legal and protective institutions, local groups often took the law into their own hands, and lynch law emerged as a form of violence supported by many elements in the social order, including lawbreakers and law enforcers. Such activities are by no means limited only to our historical past, as is obvious from recent events in connection with the civil rights movement.

With the settling of the West many of the central problems of crime reappeared in our growing cities. Here the combined forces of ethnic immigration and corruption in politics led to high rates of organized crime in urban politics. And again, lest we imagine that such problems died in the 1920s and 1930s with the Capone era, evidence suggests that there were large numbers of gangland killings in such cities as Boston in the 1960s. The pattern of violence has been traced clearly for one county in southern Illinois—admittedly not a typical instance. From the late nineteenth century to the early part of the twentieth, Williamson County had a pattern of violence that included a massacre of strikebreakers in connection with union strife and several murders precipitated by family feuds, the Ku Klux Klan, and gangster rivalry.[23]

It is thus possible to argue that America is a society with violent traditions. The forms of violence have varied with the changing conditions of social life, especially the settling of previously unsettled land and the growth of major cities. Currently, a great deal of attention is given to violent youth crime. It is receiving the attention previously devoted to the gunmen of the West and the corruption in the syndicates of our

[22] Mabel A. Elliott, "Crime and the Frontier Mores," *American Sociological Review,* 9 (April 1944), pp. 185–192.

[23] Paul M. Angle, *Bloody Williamson* (New York: Alfred A. Knopf, 1952).

urban areas. This recent attention is in no sense the first time public concern has been expressed about youth crime. For example, here is an account of youth gangs in late nineteenth-century New York City:

The gang fights of those days were fearsome. On the Fourth of July in 1857, the Dead Rabbits from the Five Points district [now being torn down for an urban renewal project] clashed with the Bowery Boys in Bayard Street. Sticks, stones and knives were freely used. Men, women and children were wounded. A small body of policemen, sent to quell the disturbance, was repulsed after several of these were wounded. Finally the Seventh Regiment was summoned from Boston, and the city militia called out. By the time the riot was put down, late in the evening, six had been killed and over a hundred wounded.[24]

The amount of violence may also vary by region of the country. There is good evidence, as noted earlier, that the violent tradition is more widespread in our Southern regions than in other areas. Not only are the actual rates of violent behavior such as homicide higher in such areas, but values supporting the use of weapons and guns appear to be stronger. A recent public opinion poll showed that 53 percent of Southerners believed it should be legal to have loaded weapons in homes, compared with smaller percentages in other regions.[25] There is even one study suggesting that those who migrate from the South to the North or West show the effect of their Southern heritage in that they have higher rates of homicide in the Northern communities than do those who have always lived in the North.[26] These observations have the character of variations on a theme and should not obscure the fact that violent traditions are part of our total cultural heritage.

This set of ideas differs from the previous ones primarily in that it is less general as an explanation of high crime rates. It pertains to historical conditions unique to the United States and is thus of little help in explaining variations in rates of crime in other countries. But it is clear that many of its elements have much in common with the three sets of ideas presented above. Sharpening, modifying, extending, and clarifying the relevance of these plausible accounts is one of the major tasks confronting social scientists interested in crime.

[24] Wayne Phillips, "The Relative Rumble," *Columbia University Forum,* 5, 4 (Fall 1962), p. 40.

[25] Thomas F. Pettigrew, *A Profile of the American Negro* (Princeton, N. J.: Van Nostrand, 1964), p. 148.
[26] Pettigrew and Spier, *op. cit.*

CRIME

IN THE U.S.:

The Soviet View

Juvenile Delinquency in the
United States and England

F. S. MAKHOV

INTRODUCTION

There exist in the contemporary English language two words which fill with dread the hearts of many thousands of fathers and mothers in the United States and in England. These two words compel the members of parliamentary commissions to spend long hours in fruitless sessions, and the police forces to enlarge their staffs. The words "juvenile delinquency" filled the pages of American and English newspapers and magazines in recent years. "National calamity," "terrible danger," "the highest wave," "the black cloud," are only some of the screaming headlines one often finds on the pages of the bourgeois press when the subject is the delinquency of children.

There are many unsolved problems in the capitalist society. Economic crises, chronic unemployment, and a general cultural decline have for some time

Original Translation

Reprinted from F. S. Makhov, Yurid'cheskaya Literatura, *Moscow, 1964, pp. 3–5, 95–98.*

been integral traits of that "flourishing paradise" proclaimed constantly by the ideologists of capitalism. The examples of the United States of America and England tell the story of the growth of children's and youth's delinquency, and provide an analysis of young peoples' offenses disclosing the social, economic, and political roots of the given phenomenon.

In the last ten to fifteen years juvenile delinquency in the U.S. and in England has reached such catastrophic proportions that this problem is often considered "the number one social problem." Thus, the authors, Raab and Selznick, of the book, *Major Social Problems,* published in the U.S.A. in 1959, begin their work precisely with the problem of juvenile delinquency pushing into the background such issues as unemployment, racial discrimination, the crisis of the educational and social security systems, etc. The same opinion is held by the American sociologist Kirson Weinberg, expressed in the book, *Social Problems of Our Time* (published in New York in 1960), and by many other authors (B. Fine, M.

Newmeyer—U.S.A., D. Watson—England, and others).

Juvenile delinquency in the U.S.A. and England is one of the most acute social problems. However, bourgeois sociology, taking advantage of the sensational character of this phenomenon, attempts to lead the wide popular masses away from the solution of other still more important issues like, for example, unemployment, and racial discrimination. That is why a lot of sociologists in the U.S.A. and in England, at the order of their masters, attempt to view children's delinquency as the most acute domestic problem, not saying a word about the fact that juvenile delinquency itself is a product of exploitation, of a deep social inequality and the sharpening of class conflict.

At the same time, frequent attempts are made in the West to present the delinquency of children and adolescents as a phenomenon rooted in purely subjective motives of biological and psychological character.

One cannot agree with such an appraisal. That is why this booklet attempts not only to show the essence and growth of juvenile delinquency, but also to recount the causes of this growth, paying the most attention not to subjective but to objective causes.

In the U.S.A. and in England, juvenile delinquency is often compared to an infection. The best preventive means against infectious diseases are, as is generally known, vaccinations. To find a "vaccine" against juvenile delinquency in the conditions of bourgeois society is impossible without smashing its base completely. Juvenile delinquency in capitalist countries is not a "disease" which can be healed with the aid of some or other means. It is a constant companion of bourgeois civilization, and its dark spectre beclouds the lives of an ever-growing number of children and adolescents.

Marxism-Leninism considers delinquency in capitalist countries not a passing phenomenon, but a constantly operative factor, a social defect inescapably inherent in bourgeois society, a phenomenon deeply rooted in the capitalist system itself. That is why it is impossible to solve this problem only through the improvement of housing conditions or with the aid of a legal-correctional system .. . .

"THE POLITICS OF THE COLD WAR, THE SPREAD OF THE ATOMIC PSYCHOSIS AND ITS INFLUENCE ON THE PSYCHE OF THE ADOLESCENTS"

. . ."Cold war" politics and the atomic hysteria in the U.S.A. and England is the second factor whose influence on juvenile delinquency is passed over in silence by bourgeois sociology.

The years of preparation for war and the war years have always resulted in a sharp increase of child and adolescent delinquency. In the work, *Social Problems of Our Time*, Kirson Weinberg indicates that according to the data of 76 courts in the U.S.A., they handled 52 thousand cases in 1938, 85 thousand cases in 1945, and 20 thousand in 1947.

With the beginning of war in Korea the curve of child delinquency again rose. Thus, in 1950 the number of offenses was 5% higher than in 1949, and in 1951 it was 9% higher than in 1950.[1]

In the course of the whole period of the "cold" war, delinquency among minors in the U.S.A. continued to grow steadily. . . .

. . .However, the ruling circles in England and the U.S.A. attempt to blame the growth of child and adolescent delinquency in their countries on

[1] S. Kirson Weinberg, *Social Problems in Our Time* (New York 1960), p. 130.

"the activity of Communists." In July 1960 at the convention of the Republican Party of the U.S.A., the director of the FBI of the U.S.A., Hoover, noted in his speech that for the last 14 years the number of capital crimes increased three times faster than the growth of the population. He stated: "At present America finds itself at the climax of a terrible moral crisis." How did Hoover explain the increase in the number of murders, rapes, and slaughter committed by youth? It turns out that the growth of crime among minors in the U.S.A. is nothing other than "a consequence of the spreading of the communist contamination."[2]

...But no matter how much the American and English statesmen try to shift the blame from a sick head to a healthy one, no matter how much the bourgeois researchers attempt to ignore the true causes of this phenomenon, it is clear to every clear-thinking person that it is not "the communist menace" but the preparation for a new world war which cripples the soul of tens and hundreds of thousands of children, destroys everything that is reasonable, lucid, and lively in a child's imagination, and makes the rising generation into murderers and vandals. What can a child understand of the notorious theory of "brinkmanship," a theory which is the basis of the security of the Western countries? What can a youth think if he daily hears that the Soviet Union is preparing to attack the United States of America and therefore it is necessary to build bomb shelters?! Is it an accident that 47% of all hospital beds in the U.S.A. and 45% in England are occupied by patients with mental disorders?

...The atomic psychosis, like an enormous, terrible octopus with its cold tentacles seizes more and more children and adolescents. An American art teacher, Nancy Lawson, announces that "more than half of her students are afraid of radioactive contamination. The children cannot draw a clean, sky.... They always draw on it the mushroom cloud of an atomic explosion...."[3]

---

2 *Leningrad Pravda* (July 27, 1960).   3 *Newsweek* (Nov. 20, 1961), p. 15.

CRIME

IN THE U.S.S.R.:

The Soviet View

Theoretical Conference: Antisocial Phenomena, Their Causes and the Means of Combating Them

...Material for a theoretical conference devoted to problems of combating antisocial phenomena is published in this issue. The material has been prepared by Prof. I. I. Karpets, Doctor of Jurisprudence, and Prof. V. N. Kudryavtsev, Doctor of Jurisprudence. Of the total aggregate of problems in it, the following have been singled out:

1. The social nature of antisocial phenomena. 2. The causes of the persistence of antisocial phenomena in a socialist society. 3. The means and methods of combating antisocial phenomena.

It will not be possible at the conference to dwell in a uniformly detailed way on all aspects of these complex problems; therefore, it is primarily the questions that are most compelling for the particular categories of its participants that should be highlighted in the preparation of reports and speeches. The use of local material on the state

Reprinted from Kommunist *(August, 1966). Translated in* Current Digest of the Soviet Press, *XVIII, No. 36 (Copyright © September 28, 1966), 9–11.*

of the struggle against antisocial phenomena is extremely useful. Personnel of the militia agencies, the courts, and the prosecutor's office can be enlisted for reports on this. It would be useful if during the theoretical conference its participants were to offer practical suggestions aimed at intensifying the struggle against antisocial phenomena, such as might be generalized and put into practice in the localities.

* * *

Our country is successfully advancing along the path of social-economic, political and cultural progress. In the course of building the new society the awareness, and political involvement of Soviet man are growing. The norms of the advanced morality of the builder of a communist society have become for the absolute majority of Soviet people an organic part of their convictions and the basis for conduct at work and in private life. At the same time there are in our country persons who violate the rules of the socialist community and who commit crimes.

Antisocial phenomena and crime are alien to the very nature of the Soviet system. They will be eradicated as progress toward communism is made. But this does not mean that crime will disappear by itself, automatically. A persistent day-to-day struggle must be waged against it, and it is essential to create an atmosphere of implacability toward the bearers of morals that are alien to us, toward hooligans and persons who flout socialist legality. Herein lies the very great importance of the documents recently adopted by the C.P.S.U. Central Committee, the U.S.S.R. Council of Ministers, and the Presidium of the U.S.S.R. Supreme Soviet. . . .

I. THE NATURE OF ANTISOCIAL PHENOMENA

1. Antisocial phenomena are human acts that are detrimental to the interests of Soviet people and socialist society, that retard its development.

Among antisocial phenomena are first of all violations of the rules of conduct for citizens in the society. Inasmuch as these rules of conduct have been established by acts of law or are the norms of morality, people's antisocial acts are themselves either violations of laws established by the state or immoral acts. In the first instance, antisocial acts entail liability under the law; in the second, they become the object of public censure. It should be stressed that there are no clearcut, impassable boundaries between law and morality. Law and morality in the socialist society are closely interrelated. Violations of Soviet laws, which protect the interests of the people, are immoral actions, and they are condemned from the standpoints of both law and morality.

Antisocial behavior is not a manifestation of the biological traits of human nature but is of a socially and historically conditioned nature. His-

torically, crime arose with the stratification of society into classes. . . . It is precisely because this chief cause of excesses has been liquidated in socialist society that a solution to the task of reducing and eventually eradicating crime in our country is becoming a real possibility.

Lacking the desire or having no opportunity for discovering the social roots of crime in the capitalist society, many bourgeois scholars relate crime to heredity, personality, national and racial characteristics, the type of nervous system, etc.

Of course, special traits of a person's psychological make-up, aspects of his character and personality, are of no small importance in his behavior, but social factors are the determinants. A human being is not born a criminal, but he can become one. Moreover, character and personality themselves are not innate qualities; they are also molded under the influence of the external environment.

It is true that many bourgeois scholars now also recognize the relationship between crime and social phenomena. But at the same time they conceal the fact that all the social causes of crime in capitalist society (unemployment, exploitation of the masses, etc.) arise from the nature of the capitalist system, the class-antagonistic character of bourgeois society, which is inherent in capitalism.

What is typical of the capitalist world, where the principle of "dog-eat-dog" is in force, cannot be carried over to socialist society, which consists of friendly classes and is based on the principles of mutual aid, cooperation and mutual respect among people. . . .

2. Under socialism crime is not engendered by the social system itself. It "invades" socialism from exploitative socio-economic formations and in this sense can be regarded as a survival of

the past in the minds and behavior of people.

The still-persisting views, customs and habits inherent in the ideology and mentality of an exploitative society lie at the root of the majority of antisocial phenomena. Hooligans, parasites, swindlers, thieves, bribetakers, speculators and other violators of Soviet laws are vessels of a mentality and morality alien to us. . . .

An antisocial phenomenon such as drunkenness is a legacy of the past. It goes against the rules of the socialist community, leads to large material losses, impairs people's health and destroys families. Simultaneously, drunkenness is the source of many serious crimes.

It is often asked: What survivals of the past could there be in someone born after 1917? After all, he has never lived under capitalism! But the fact is that the thesis of crime as a survival of the past does not pretend to explain the "mechanics" of the origin of antisocial views in one individual or another. In contending that egotism, venality, drunkenness and disrespect for women are "survivals of the past," we are merely emphasizing that all these phenomena are peculiar to the preceding social-economic formations but do not arise from the nature of socialism and have no place in our society.

Survivals of the past remain in the consciousness, behavior and lives of people long after the fundamental social-economic causes that engendered them have disappeared. Ugly practices and traditions that have developed for centuries are often deeply rooted in the way of life. For example, let us take such a "custom" as "washing down" one's pay, which does no small amount of harm. It can be encountered even among young people, who adopt it from their elders as a kind of "tradition.". . .

The thesis of the disappearance of

crime in a communist society occasionally gives rise to the question: "Can it really be guaranteed that individuals will not commit antisocial acts under communism?" Needless to say, no such guarantee can be given. V. I. Lenin wrote: "We are not utopians and do not in the least deny the possibility and inevitability of excesses by individuals" in the future society. At the same time, the fundamental difference between crime as a social phenomenon and the existence of individual antisocial acts should be explained.

3. The thesis of the social nature of antisocial phenomena does not absolve a person from personal responsibility for his acts. On the contrary, it requires of people a conscious discipline and strict observance of the laws and rules of the socialist community.

Recognition of the possibility of a choice for man in his behavior lies at the basis of the concept of legal liability. The lawbreaker is punished precisely because he resorts to an antisocial act of his own volition. The fact that the consequences of that act at times go beyond what the lawbreaker himself intended does not remove the question of his responsibility. . . .

It should be emphasized that a person who is aware of his responsibility to society not only will not commit one or another antisocial act himself but also will not ignore the unrestrained hooligan, the rowdy, the drunkard or the pilferer of socialist property. Participation in the struggle against antisocial phenomena is the civic duty of every honest toiler, every conscious member of the socialist society.

II. THE CAUSES OF ANTISOCIAl PHENOMENA

1. How can backward views and habits that are wholly extrinsic to socialist society be preserved in its

midst and poison the minds of individual persons? In other words, why do individuals commit crimes and what are the specific causes of antisocial phenomena?

The "mechanics" of the existence and occurrence of antisocial views and acts vary.

First of all, let us note that imperialist propaganda of the "attractions" of the so-called "free world" and the spread of bourgeois views of individualism sometimes exert an influence on a certain segment of the population. But bourgeois propaganda proves absolutely ineffective where it is offset by well thought-out measures that expose its deceitful character. Sociological research done in the Baltic area has shown that Western propaganda is powerless to influence the younger generation if the interests of young people are fully satisfied and their energy and craving for activity are countenanced and encouraged in every way. . . .

Socialism creates all the conditions for the rearing of the new man. But these conditions are not developed in the proper way in every family or in every labor collective. There are still fairly frequent cases of the evil influence of the "street," the disintegration of family ties and abnormal interpersonal relations at work or in private life. . . .

The family teaches what is good, but it can also lay a bad foundation. Criminological studies of juvenile lawbreakers show that more than 50% of them grew up in so-called unhappy families. In a number of these families (about 30%) the father drank, the parents brawled and quarreled in the presence of the children and violated the elementary rules of conduct. Frequently the juvenile had grown up fatherless or motherless.

The negative consequences of the war also undoubtedly had an effect on the upbringing of juveniles. For example, an investigation of minors convicted in the 1950s for hooliganism disclosed that 68% of them had lost one or both of their parents. And at present the largest age group of criminals comprises people whose childhood or adolescence coincided with the war years or the difficult years of the postwar reconstruction period.

In many cases excessive outside demands on the time of both parents impeded the correct upbringing of juveniles who embarked on a path of lawbreaking. According to selective studies, 80% of the cases of crimes by minors are related to a lack of supervision. At the theoretical conference it would be useful to discuss practical ways of eliminating lack of supervision over children.

Shortcomings and difficulties in upbringing work within the family can be largely offset by the positive influence of the school, the work collective, Young Pioneer and Y.C.L. organizations, etc. But when these shortcomings are not offset by anything and, what is more, are aggravated by the poor work of the school and other institutions, the very complex of circumstances that are unfavorable to the rearing of juveniles and that mold their views and habits in sharp contradiction to the prerequisites of communist morality can form.

Prompt job placement for those who, for one reason or another, have dropped out of school constitutes, along with intensified guidance for young people working in production or pupils in vocational-technical schools, an essential link in upbringing work with minors. Sociological research shows that lawbreaking is done primarily by juveniles who are not in school or working.

Formalism and stereotype in the rearing of the younger generation, inadequate consideration of the level of preparation and the national and age composition of the working people and a lack of concreteness in upbringing work lead to a situation where ideological work with young people frequently proceeds without effect. It sometimes fails to reach precisely the categories of juveniles who are not divested of antisocial views and habits and are therefore all the more in need of an educative influence.

Lapses in ideological work constitute one of the major reasons for the incorrect, sometimes abnormal, development of the personalities of juveniles and adults. Probably everyone acknowledges this idea, but unfortunately by no means every Party, Y.C.L. and trade union worker or enterprise executive draws the correct conclusions from the fact. . . .

The greatest difficulties are encountered in the organization of upbringing work with people who have already begun to commit antisocial acts. But even here the collective is capable of a great deal. A bold, individual approach to the person who has stumbled, based on detection of the causes of his antisocial behavior, makes it possible to choose precisely the form of influence that will be the most practical in the specific case. For one person a comradely chat may be enough, while strict day-to-day supervision must be established over another. The collective is an important force if it acts in a friendly, purposeful way, never failing to act upon any case of violation of the norms of the socialist community and, at the same time, not antagonizing the person but showing attention to and concern for his needs.

2. Shortcomings in upbringing work alone cannot fully explain the existence of antisocial phenomena. Laxity in upbringing work and its inadequate efficacy in turn require explanations.

Practice shows that violations of the norms of the socialist community are engendered, as a rule, by an intricate complex, an aggregate of causes and conditions.

Diverse shortcomings in the activity of state agencies and public organizations are part of the conditions that promote the preservation, and sometimes even an intensification, of antisocial phenomena. Laxity, a negligent attitude of officials toward their duties, an inability to organize the work properly—all of this hinders the struggle against crime. More than 40% of the thefts of state and public property are committed in conditions where control is lacking and the proper accounting for material values is absent. In 20% of these cases, the thefts were facilitated by inadequate safekeeping of the property. There are frequent cases of lax inspection, poor organization of intra-agency checkups and inventory of property, etc.

Among the circumstances that encourage hooliganism and other violations of public order, one can point to the poor organization of the militia's patrol service and of the work of the people's volunteers in safeguarding public order. . . .

Factors of a material nature have a definite place among the circumstances that promote the continuation of antisocial phenomena, although the role of these factors under socialism is by no means the same as in a capitalist society. The majority of crimes there, in the final analysis, are engendered by the social relations inherent in capitalism and by economic factors connected with unemployment and the poverty of the working masses. One thing is characteristic of the law violations committed in socialist society: The overwhelming majority of them are not caused by material difficulties. For example, a Latvian Republic investigation of juveniles who had commited thefts disclosed that only 3.7% of them related these crimes to one material circumstance or another (for example, family difficulties because the father spent his pay on drink). The remaining lawbreakers committed thefts for hooligan motives, out of malice or a false "sense of adventure," in "following the example" of an older friend, etc.

There are still low-paid categories of working people in our country, the population is not adequately supplied with all goods; despite the large amount of housing construction there are difficulties with housing, and so forth. The difficulties that actually exist and the still unresolved social problems create conditions for the preservation of a private-property mentality among a certain segment of people. A shortage of certain goods creates a favorable medium for speculation, abuses of office and bribetaking. Cultural deprivation and a low educational level are closely linked to drunkenness, crime, and other antisocial acts. An unfavorable atmosphere for molding the personalities of children and juveniles often develops in the crowded communal apartments.

At present there are still no possibilities of freeing women from many arduous household and everyday chores. At the same time, prejudices and harmful mundane traditions connected with an incorrect attitude toward women continue to survive among a segment of the male population. Hence arise conflicts in family life.

The Soviet state and society are doing everything necessary to meet the fast-growing material and spiritual needs of the Soviet people as fully and comprehensively as possible. As the material and technical base of communism is created, increasingly broader opportunities for solving other social problems are also created. It is not by chance that the Party Program links the eradication of crime to such highly important factors in the progressive development of society as an increase in the material security, cultural level and consciousness of the working people.

III. THE MEANS OF COMBATING ANTISOCIAL PHENOMENA

1. From what has been said, it is apparent that the measures needed to eradicate antisocial phenomena cannot be reduced to some short-lived campaign. They must be a complex of socio-economic, ideological and legal means.

The forms for combating antisocial phenomena are divided into two main groups: a) steps to prevent antisocial phenomena; b) measures of state coercion and public influence with respect to persons who have committed antisocial acts. . . .

The July 26, 1966, decree of the Presidium of the U.S.S.R. Supreme Soviet "On Increased Liability for Hooliganism"[1] placed in the hands of the public strong new levers for bringing influence to bear on people who commit antisocial acts and crimes. In particular, it granted the right to deprive people who have committed hooligan actions of bonuses and reduced-rate passes to rest homes and sanatoriums and to cancel their priority in obtaining housing. These measures will be a sufficiently serious warning for persons who are not malicious lawbreakers. Also of no small importance is the provision of the decree (Art. 18) that increases safeguards for citizens who combat hooliganism.

The decree dispels the illusion of those "petty" hooligans who hitherto sometimes counted on an "easy rest" during a period of serving out an administrative arrest. Physical labor without pay, charging for the cost of food and

[1] *Current Digest of the Soviet Press,* Vol. XVIII, No. 30, pp. 5–6.

upkeep, withholding wages on the job —these are measures that should compel them to think over their behavior. . . .

A number of proposals for combating drunkenness and alcoholism have appeared in our press. Frequently the authors of these proposals have focused their attention on only a single measure (such as punishment for drunkards). But the struggle against drunkenness, and other antisocial phenomena as well, can be successful only if a complex of statewide and local measures is put into effect. That is precisely why comprehensive, painstaking work by administrative, economic and public organizations to eradicate drunkenness is envisaged in the decisions of the C.P.S.U. Central Committee, the Presidium of the U.S.S.R. Supreme Soviet and the U.S.S.R. Council of Ministers on measures for intensifying the struggle against violators of public order and for increasing liability for antisocial acts while in a state of intoxication.

To illustrate, we cite a complex of measures for combating drunkenness and alcoholism, arising from a review and generalization of the working people's proposals:

a) economic measures. Practice a gradual "supplanting" of vodka and other strong alcoholic beverages. Expand the production of natural fruit juices, wines and nonalcoholic beverages, and extensively advertise these beverages. Expand the network of public-catering enterprises and provide for the opening of additional restaurants, cafes, dining rooms, snack bars, etc., in order to meet the population's needs for such enterprises fully;

b) cultural and educative measures. Widely publicize the struggle against drunkenness and alcoholism and intensify antialcohol propaganda and health education work on questions of combating drunkenness. Expand the network of clubs and other cultural-enlightenment institutions and also athletic facilities. Organize young people's leisure time at their places of residence. Start the regular issuance of newsreels and feature films that show extensively the enormous damage that drunkenness inflicts on health, the rearing of children, the family and all Soviet society;

c) administrative measures. Forbid the sale of alcoholic beverages to persons who are in a state of intoxication and to minors. Limit the times and places at which alcoholic beverages may be sold. Extend the powers of the militia agencies to suppress drunkenness in public places. Make it a criminal offense to entice minors into drunkenness.

Make full use of the coercive measures stipulated by legislation in force, as well as measures of public influence, in the day-to-day struggle against alcoholism. Conduct compulsory treatment for alcoholics in closed labor-therapy prophylactic institutions.

It is quite clear that the above list of working people's proposals aimed at intensifying the struggle against drunkenness does not encompass all the possible ways and forms of combating this antisocial phenomenon. However, it shows that the approach to combating any antisocial phenomenon should be well-founded and versatile, taking into account economic, cultural, educational and administrative aspects and not relying on partial measures.

During the theoretical conference it is advisable to discuss the range of measures that should be implemented in combating drunkenness under local conditions.

The experience of work by Party organizations in a number of cities shows that where the struggle against antisocial phenomena is approached in an integrated way and on the basis of well thought-out plans, the effort yields perceptible results.

The organization of the struggle against juvenile crime in Leningrad can be cited as an example. Preventive upbringing work with minors in the city is of a precisely thought-out nature. Its basis is a plan of practical measures, worked out by the Party organization, for intensifying the struggle against crime and violations of public order. In line with this plan, 400 children's playrooms have been opened under the housing offices, the number of Red Corners has increased from 250 to 622, and eight courtyard stadiums and 2,000 playgrounds have been newly built and equipped. More than 34,000 children were engaged in 110 different hobby clubs and athletic squads in 1964. In 1965 this figure greatly increased. One or two amateur performing clubs with memberships of 200 to 300 teenagers, including so-called difficult ones, have been set up in almost every microborough. As a result of this purposeful work, the crime rate among juveniles, in spite of the increase in the child population in the city, declined 44% during 1961–1965. . . .

Widespread enlistment of the public in the struggle against crime, especially in recent years, was perceived by some people in the localities as a course toward slackening the activity of state agencies in the punishment of lawbreakers. This is not so, of course. The participation of the public does not exclude and does not replace the work of the militia, the prosecutor's office and the courts but supplements it. The widespread use of measures of public influence on lawbreakers must not lead to unpunished violations. Persons who break the law must be called to account. At the same time, it must be stressed that the struggle against crime and other antisocial phenomena is a struggle for legality and law and order in the country. Overcoming crime is possible only within the framework of established legal norms and on their strict basis. To leave lawbreakers unpunished means to weaken the preventive force of the law. Just as dangerous are the exceeding of legal measures of punishment and, worse still, injustices committed with respect to the innocent. Strict observance of the law is an extremely important obligation and duty of personnel of the militia, the prosecutor's office and the courts. . . .

Some Causes of Juvenile Delinquency in the U.S.S.R. and Measures to Prevent It

G. M. MINKOVSKY

The concept of the nature and causes of juvenile delinquency in socialist society is a constituent part of the general concept of the nature and causes of crime in the U.S.S.R.[1] Juvenile delinquency is social in nature and is shaped by an entire series of phenomena and processes of a material, ideological and organizational character in the life of society.

The causes of juvenile delinquency and the conditions fostering these causes

Reprinted from G. M. Minkovsky, "Some Causes of Juvenile Delinquency in the U.S.S.R. and Measures to Prevent It," Sovetskoye gosudartsvo i pravo (May, 1966). Translated in Current Digest of the Soviet Press, XVIII, No. 30 (Copyright © August 17, 1966), 9–11.

[1] Cf. A. A. Gertsenson, "Introduction to Soviet Criminology," Juridical Literature Publishing House, Moscow, 1965; N. F. Kuznetsova and S. S. Ostroumov, "On the Causes and Conditions of Crime," in Vestnik MGU [Annals of Moscow State University], No. 4, 1965; V. N. Kudryavtsev, "The Category of Causality in Soviet Criminology," in Sovetskoye gosudarstvo i pravo, No. 11, 1965; I. I. Karpets, "On the Nature and Causes of Crime in the U.S.S.R.," in Sovetskoye gosudarstvo i pravo, No. 4, 1966; A. M. Yakovlev, "The Struggle Against Recidivist Crime," Nauka [Science] Publishing House, Moscow, 1964; "The Work of Investigation Agencies, the Prosecutor's Office and the Courts in the Prevention of Crime," State Juridical Publishing House, Moscow, 1962, et al.

do not remain unchanged in the process of the development of socialist society. Their range and sphere of operation shrink and their character changes. To study them, therefore, a concrete historical approach is essential.

During the first years after the war, for instance, juvenile delinquency was connected largely with the direct effects of the war (loss of parents, enforced interruption of schooling, the worsened material situation, etc.) Between 65% and 70% of the juvenile delinquents had lost one or both parents (owing mainly to wartime circumstances). Up to 70% of the thefts perpetrated by adolescents were due to unsatisfactory material conditions, etc. By the mid-fifties the state's purposeful steps for the care of orphans, as well as the successes achieved in the restoration and development of the national economy and in raising the living standard of the population, had in the main liquidated the influence exerted on juvenile delinquency by these consequences of the war.

At present the proportion of juvenile delinquents who are orphans is, according to sample data, down to almost half what it had been in the first years after the war, and in only 3% to 4% of the thefts could the direct influence of material conditions be traced (and these, as a rule, stemmed from such circumstances as drunkenness of the parents, desertion of the family, etc.). A great part of the crimes committed by young people are now connected with negative influences within the family and in the everyday environment. Timely identification and elimination of the source of such influence is, needless to say, a more complicated task than arranging care of orphans, whose very return to normal conditions of upbringing was in itself of decisive significance.

In considering the present state of juvenile delinquency we must bear another important circumstance in mind. The 1960s were marked by an increase in the 14-to-18-year-old group in the population. From 1961 to 1965 alone this age group increased in many localities by an average of 40%. At the same time, the number of young people living in cities also increased (in 1940 urban dwellers constituted one-third of the total population, in 1964 more than one-half). If we remember that about 75% of all juvenile crimes are committed in the cities, then in the light of these social-demographic processes there should have been at least a proportionate increase in the scope of measures for providing schooling, job placement and recreational facilities for young people, and other, special, preventive measures. Miscalculations in some cities and provinces in this respect created a disproportion between the rate of increase in the number of accommodations for pupils in the schools (including schools and classes with an extended school day) and in children's cultural and upbringing institutions, as well as the number of vacancies in the teachers' schools, etc., and the real need for such accommodations, with the result that the implementation of preventive measures was seriously hampered.

In this connection the drafting of scientifically validated norms "tying"

the number of children's cultural and upbringing institutions of various kinds and the number of accommodations within them to the size of the age-group in question—norms per 10,000 or per 100,000 juveniles—is a quite urgent task of the Soviet science of city planning and of pedagogical science.

Studies conducted in Moscow, Leningrad and some Union republics (the Belorussian, Lithuanian and others) show that constant attention to the problems of the upbringing of young people, to providing the personnel and the material base for the measures being carried out, with regard for the dynamics of the social and demographic processes, make for a decline in juvenile delinquency. In Leningrad, for example, the number of juveniles who committed crimes fell 37% in five years (from 1960 to 1964). This decrease was the logical result of the preventive work undertaken under the guidance of the city's Party organizations by Soviet and economic agencies, by the courts, the Prosecutor's Office and the militia, together with the general public.[2]

For a complete solution of the juvenile delinquency problem the local measures must, needless to say, be combined with an extensive system of nationwide measures, and general preventive measures should be combined with the special measures taken through the court agencies, the Prosecutor's Office and the militia.

The aforementioned data permit us to draw the indisputable conclusion that in socialist society the rate of decline in juvenile delinquency is not automatically retarded by growth in the juvenile popu-

[2] The U.S.S.R. Prosecutor's Office, the Russian Republic Prosecutor's Office and the All-Union Institute for the Study and Prevention of Crime have prepared a special methodological circular about Leningrad's experience, based on data derived from a study of it.

lation and urban population. The conclusions of foreign criminologists that growth of juvenile delinquency is inevitable in developed countries are based on the analysis of urbanization's effects under capitalist conditions and are absolutely unacceptable for explaining and forecasting the dynamics of crime in socialist society.

The social causality of juvenile delinquency in the U.S.S.R. does not signify that juvenile delinquency is predetermined by the nature of the socialist system. The phenomena and processes underlying juvenile delinquency are the result of the effect of survivals of the past in economics, ideology, culture and everyday life. They are related to the level of development of society's material resources. The question of the material factors is usually treated in criminological literature from the standpoint of their direct influence upon shaping motivation and intent. But there is another aspect of the problem, far more important in the present conditions of our society: how the volume of resources allocated to improve the conditions of upbringing of the growing generation is affected by the level of development of society's material resources and by the urgency of the national-economic tasks being carried out at the given moment.

The process of creating the conditions for eliminating juvenile delinquency (and crime in general) cannot help but be of a prolonged nature. The phenomena from which crime stems in the first phase of communist society—phenomena which are survivals and remnants—are alien to our system, but their existence is an objective fact. The study of these phenomena provides the basis for nationwide and special measures for the prevention and gradual eradication of crime. At the same time, the nature and structure of juvenile delinquency depend not only on the general phenomena and processes that determine the existence of crime in society, but upon particular features of the social conditions of the life and upbringing of the young generation and the extent to which the growth peculiarities of young people are taken into account.

Figuratively speaking, juvenile delinquency now serves as a specific index of shortcomings in upbringings by the family, school and public organizations.[3] We shall try to take a closer look at the importance of negative influences exerted by unfavorable conditions of upbringing by the family and immediate environment, as well as by shortcomings in upbringing work in school and on the job.

Unfavorable Conditions of Juvenile Upbringing in the Family and Immediate Daily Surroundings as Source of Formation of Anti-Social Views and Habits.—Of the utmost importance for further successes in the struggle against juvenile delinquency are the general social and special measures to improve family upbringing and create healthy surroundings for children and teenagers by increasing state and public aid to the family for the prevention of child neglect, for the pedagogic enlightenment of parents and for intensified struggle against negative influences upon minors in the family and in everyday life. According to sample data obtained by the institute, 80% of the cases of juvenile delinquency are related to neglect. Particularly characteristic is the fact that about half the crimes committed by young people occur after 10 p.m., when the adults should have seen to it that the youngsters were at home. At the same time, far from all cases of neglect are due to the parents' disregard of their responsibilities.

[3] N. R. Mironov, "Strengthening Law and Order—A Program Task of the Party," State Juridical Publishing House, Moscow, 1964, pp. 183–184.

According to the data we derived from a study of several schools, children by single mothers constitute about 10% of all school-age children. (This percentage has been dropping gradually year by year.) When planning preventative measures one cannot ignore the contingent of children reared in unfavorable conditions owing to the divorce of their parents. The number of divorces per 10,000 of the population increased in the first half of the fifties, but has now leveled off; and about half of the divorced have children.[4]

It is characteristic that the proportion of lawbreakers among youngsters reared in incomplete families is, according to data from various investigations, 50% to 200% greater than in the control groups. This is understandable, since a single parent in most cases has been unable to watch over the youngster properly.

The same situation may arise sometimes in a formally complete family owing to illness, a prolonged business trip or special working conditions of one of the parents. In a study of a sample group of Leningrad juvenile delinquents it was found that this situation obtained in 14% of the cases. From this it is clear how important it is to extend the system of patrons, to establish child-counseling instructors' jobs in the apart-

ment house committees, and to develop the network of extended-day schools and boarding schools, etc., if the struggle against juvenile delinquency is to be successful.

Estimates show that a high rate of development of the system of extended-day schools and boarding schools (the number of accommodations in the extended-day schools is to increase 20% in 1966) must be maintained over the next five years to fill the urgent need for such schools.

Determined objection must be registered to the proposal, set forth in the press, to reorganize the boarding schools as extended-day schools. The latter, for all their importance and promise, cannot replace the boarding schools where most youngsters without normal family conditions are now to be found. Data from sample investigations show, among other things, that more than 40% of the boarding school pupils are children of incomplete families, and 46% are from large families. In these circumstances, any attempt to "economize" at the expense of the boarding schools will lead to the opposite results.

To ensure the intensive development of the measures of state and public aid to the family in raising its children, it is imperative to enlist more widely the resources of the local authorities, industrial enterprises, public organizations and the public itself. The organizational form applicable here could be, in our view, a revived and modified version of the All-Union V. I. Lenin Fund which existed until 1938.

State and public aid to the family in the upbringing of its children should not be limited to incomplete and disrupted families. One should not forget that the basic family of socialist society is the family with working parents. As we know, drawing women into work lessens the possibility of watching over the behavior of children (what with

---

[4] It should be noted that the total number of divorces per 10,000 of the population has not essentially exceeded the level for the twenties (in 1924, 11; 1960, 13; 1963, 13). See G. I. Kursky, "Selected Articles and Speeches," Juridical Publishing House, Moscow, 1948, p. 177; "Women and Children in the U.S.S.R.," State Statistical Publishing House, Moscow, 1961, p. 87; "The National Economy of the U.S.S.R. in 1963," State Statistical Publishing House, Moscow, 1965, p. 106. The fact that the number of divorces per 10,000 at the end of the fifties was between double and triple the 1950 level is evidently connected with the change in legal practice facilitating divorce for families factually separated.

the still considerable burden of house-keeping).[5] In addition to the aforementioned measures, it may be particularly important to reduce and change the working hours of women with children, and also to give them the right to work half time (with proportionate pay).

It should be emphasized that the elimination of child neglect alone will not solve all the problems of the struggle against juvenile delinquency within the sphere of the family and everyday life. No less urgent is the task of combating incorrect upbringing and bad examples on the part of parents and others surrounding the child.

One of the causes of a youngster's irresponsibility and egotistical attitude to those around him is "the accustoming of children to unjustified gratification of their desires."[6] This problem has become especially timely in connection with the rapid growth in the material level of the population, creating objective conditions for some parents to satisfy their children's immoderate demands, which in turn stimulates similar demands on the part of their classmates at school and their comrades at work and at home.

Equally dangerous is a family's combination of "lip service to Soviet ideology" with Philistine talk and dishonest doings,[7] undermining the youngster's respect for his elders, inhibiting his public activeness and infecting him with rebelliousness and cynicism. It is

the family atmosphere, the place occupied in it by the youngster, the adults' example and the attitude the family has formed to society that largely determine the direction which the moral development of the youngster's personality will take. Hence the prime preventive importance of developing the system of educating parents, as well as intensifying public control over the upbringing of children.

At the same time, the necessary measures must be urgently taken to normalize living conditions for the upbringing of children wherever the latter are persistently subjected to negative influences by their parents and their immediate daily surroundings.

Studies of the conditions of family upbringing of juvenile delinquents have shown that there was habitual heavy drinking by the parents in 25% to 30% of the cases, constant family quarreling and fighting in 50%, immoral behavior in 7% to 10% of cases, etc. Equally significant is the fact that only 8% to 10% of the employed youngsters who committed crimes while intoxicated had learned to drink after they had begun to work; the remainder had learned to drink long before, under the influence of their parents or their everyday environment.

The Children's Rooms of the militia and now required to keep a register, with the aid of the community organizations, of "difficult" families, regardless of whether youngsters in these families have broken the law or not. Work of this sort, if conducted on a full scale, permits us to take timely preventive measures, including lodging the youngster in a children's home; suing for deprivation of the parents' rights, with simultaneous eviction of [one or both of] the parents for inability to live as a family; hailing the parents before the commissions for the affairs of minors or before comrades'

[5] According to G. V. Osipov and S. F. Frolov, women spend up to 40 hours a week on housekeeping, i.e., five to six hours a day ("Sociology in the U.S.S.R.," Vol. II, Moscow, 1965, p. 236). A. G. Kharchev cites the data of a number of investigations fixing that expenditure of time at four to five hours a day (A. G. Kharchev, "Marriage and the Family in the U.S.S.R.," State Political Publishing House, Moscow, 1964, p. 258).

[6] A. S. Makarenko, "Collected Works," Vol. IV, Pedagogical Textbook Publishing House, Moscow, 1961, p. 37.

[7] Ibid.

courts; instituting criminal proceedings against them under Art. 210 of the Russian Republic Criminal Code, etc.

In Leningrad, where a steady decline in juvenile delinquency has been evident in recent years, there has been a considerable (sixfold) increase in the number of persons tried under Art. 210 of the Russian Republic Criminal Code. In the struggle against juvenile delinquency the great preventive value of this trend in investigatory and court practice cannot be doubted.

Some investigators try to ascribe concrete crimes a priori and directly to the material circumstances and housing conditions of the family in which the youngster was reared. In our opinion, these investigators are wrong. Unfavorable circumstances of this kind can, of course, make proper upbringing difficult, but the chief factor is the essence, the nature, of the influence exerted by the parents.[8]

An urgent task of Soviet criminology is, therefore, depth study of unfavorable conditions of upbringing of minors at home and in their everyday surroundings and the drafting of measures to eliminate negative influences stemming from these conditions.

Shortcomings in the Organization of Educational and Upbringing Work in the General Schools, Trade Schools and On-Job Training, and Their Effects

Upon the Behavior of Minors.—Most of the juvenile delinquents lag behind their coevals by two to three years in educational level.[9] Only 10% to 15% of them are at an educational level corresponding to their age. The contingent of minors who break the law consists, in other words, mainly of pupils who have been left behind to repeat a grade or are school drop-outs.

When a youngster drops out of general school before completing it, he is prematurely "released" from the bonds of school discipline and from the pedagogical demands which stimulate development of the habits of proper social behavior, and his positive social ties are disrupted. The same process occurs when a youngster is left behind to repeat a grade, for this considerably weakens his ties with his schoolmates, leaves him dissatisfied with his situation, and weakens his interest in study. Lagging behind in level of general education makes for impoverishment of the personality and for a low cultural level, which in turn facilitates the assimilation of antisocial views and habits, breeds instability in the face of alien influences, and, in a dangerous situation, hinders self-control and the correct self-evaluation of motives and actions.

The solution of this problem is quite difficult, requiring a series of statewide measures, including the organization of thorough study of the personality and the conditions of family upbringing of each pupil and an individual pedagogical approach to each. This in turn calls for improved training of teachers (including those specializing in work with "difficult" youngsters); the introduction of a record of student behavior

---

[8] In this connection we should note that the housing conditions of families of juvenile delinquents do not differ substantially from the housing conditions of those in control groups. At the same time, attention is drawn to the low educational and cultural level of many persons in whose families juvenile delinquents have been reared (40% to 50% of the parents of such children had only elementary education); according to the data of N. G. Yakovlev (from an investigation in Omsk), 80% of the parents employed in industry had low skills or were entirely unskilled. The need for differentiated educational propaganda and special attention to precisely such families is, therefore, self-evident.

[9] Cf. "The Public in the Struggle Against Juvenile Delinquency," Riga, 1964. This index, as shown by the researches of N. I. Gukovskaya, V. I. Ivanov, E. F. Kuranova and A. F. Troshin, did not change in 1965.

and evaluation, to be transferred with the pupil if he is transferred to another school; instituting the position of classroom teacher carrying only a small teaching load (at least in the crucial fifth to eighth grades); reducing the size of classes; elimination of the system of several shifts in schools; differentation of types of schools, including the establishment of separate schools and classes for over-age and "difficult" children (like those established in Leningrad); and an intensified struggle against "covert" expulsion from school in the guise of transfer of pupils to schools that do not offer a general education or to evening schools.[10]

The time has come, in our opinion, for a substantial reorganization of instruction and upbringing in the schools along the lines of thorough intensification of civic and legal upbringing, of molding a sense of collectivism and of responsibility for one's actions and of moral tempering of the personality. Without solution of these key problems it is impossible to complete the establishment of conditions for the eradication of juvenile delinquency.

Shortcomings in job placement of minors and in their upbringing on the job also exert a negative influence on the behavior of teenagers, helping to give them antisocial views and habits. About 50%–60% of the juvenile delinquents investigated are youngsters holding jobs; about 20%–30% of them attend school, and about 10%–20% neither study nor work. Comparing this with the structure of control groups leads to the conclusion that the greatest number of criminal manifestations occur among the contingent of those who are neither studying nor working: The pro-

portion of non-studying and non-working youngsters among the criminals is 15% to 20% greater than the proportion of such youngsters in the control groups. The incidence of crime among working youth is about 150% greater per 10,000 than among the pupils of trade schools and 13 times as much as among school children. The crime rate among trade school pupils is in turn five times as high as among the school children. The relatively higher intensity of crime among working youth and trade school pupils is due largely to the weakening of guidance and supervision over their development, over the way they spend their time, their contacts, interests, etc., on the part of their families and also on the part of management and the collectives at their place of work (or training) as compared with the supervision in general schools. Parents regard the youngster holding a job or attending a trade school as an adult: the family's contact with the collective in which he is being brought up is reduced; his routine and the daily course of his activities change and this likewise cuts down the supervision of him by his family. It is not by chance, incidentally, that about 30% of the crimes committed by trade school pupils are committed during the period of their on-job training.

The youngsters' work load on the job and the absence of outside prompting to improve his education—prompting he was used to while at school—cause many in this contingent to discontinue their studies. It is characteristic that about 40% of all under-age workers attend evening schools or take correspondence courses, but the percentage who do this among working youngsters who have committed crimes is only one-third of this.

At the same time, working youth who belong to this category find that they have a reserve of free time in the

10 According to data from Tallinn, the number of minors who "transferred" to the schools for working youth in 1963–1964 before completing eight grades was 50% greater than the number who got jobs.

evening. Owing to the narrowness of their interests, they spend this time loafing on the streets or join in chance drinking parties. An investigation conducted in Leningrad showed that among a group of working youngsters who committed crimes in 1964 and 1965 only 6% had attended technical study circles and only 5% had taken part in amateur arts. A similar study conducted in Omsk showed that only 14% of the group of

youngsters in question had engaged in sports, only 2% in amateur arts, and so on.

Thus, the problem of struggle against crime among working youth is in great measure a problem of encouraging them to study, of organization of their leisure, of widening their horizons, elevating their cultural level and drawing them into the life of the collective.

A Difficult Subject

A. SHPEYER

Criminal cases dealing with sex crimes are heard in closed session.

One might thus get the impression that most cases of this type have extremely "private" significance and must be mentioned in public as little as possible. Indeed, rapists are scoundrels and degenerates. Let the investigatory and court agencies deal with them.

During the examination of each specific case the need for "closed doors" really is imperative. It is necessary to respect the human modesty of the victims, their self-respect and sense of personal dignity. Vulgar, gutter curiosity about all kinds of "tidbits" must be frustrated, not fed.

I am deeply convinced, however, that a definite connection exists between rape, a purely criminal act, and the problem of sex education for the young —if not a direct connection, not a

Reprinted from A. Shpeyer, "A Difficult Subject (on sex crimes)," Literaturnaya gazeta (July, 1966). Translated in Current Digest of the Soviet Press, XVIII, No. 28 (Copyright © August 3, 1966), 9–11.

merely schematic one either. The social nature of the problem is indisputable, and to keep discussion of it behind closed doors is inadmissible. This can only do harm: We all know where a hush-up of vitally important questions can lead.

I wish to note at the outset that the "heroes" of my notes will not be hardened criminals who are moved to crime by all the baseness of lives pitted against society. I should like to describe a few cases involving ordinary adolescents, so to speak. Their parents, relatives and friends seemed to have been satisfied with them, and there is nothing in their life stories to foreshadow their crimes.

Ask any investigator which cases he regards as the most difficult, and he will unhesitatingly name rape among the first three or four categories. Ask any judge in which cases he has to struggle hardest to find the truth, and the answer will be the same.

They are dangerous, these crimes. And the soil from which they spring is even more dangerous. To find the roots and rip them up—that is our aim. There are many paths to it. I shall tell about a few.

The statistics show that the majority of these crimes are committed by youths and adolescents, and that their victims are usually girls 20 years old or younger.

Some time ago I finished an investigation of several rape cases, and here is what struck me most: All of those involved without exception, both the young men and the girls, had an utterly obtuse idea of honor, manly dignity, maidenly modesty and the equality of the sexes; they all had a utilitarian view of intimate relations. Everything was mixed up, everything was encrusted with licentiousness and cynicism, bravado and indifference, mindless imitation and ordinary boorishness.

It is said that "life will teach them." Many people think so, especially parents. I have fought against their complacent "life will teach them"! I have tried to explain things, have tried to understand such parents.

I did battle with the mother of a red-haired lad whose case I investigated. This weary, aging woman gave me a hard time all the way: She is a teacher, so she herself teaches something to children. She kept instructing me too, patiently and monotonously, as if displeased with my failure to comprehend. She tried to convince me that the youngsters would get over their wild oats, that almost all of them pass through this stage. They would come to their senses by themselves when they grew up. She listened to my objections and reproaches politely, with half-closed eyes, but heard nothing, for she did not want to.

Finally came her meeting with her son, and bitter atonement. I hadn't noticed his eyes that day. As always he was twisting, fidgeting, turning his head, and vigorously rubbing his mop of red hair. Toward the end he said,

in what seemed to be a cheerful, cavalier manner: "Mama, don't expect your son to be good. I'm a criminal now." He was led away before she had time to object. But her eyes showed plainly that she wanted to argue with him, with me, with all the world.

Another women blinded with material love implored me not to believe the victim, or the witnesses, or her son (who had confessed to his crime), or anyone else, because her son, her baby, could not have done such a thing! What do you think was her chief argument? Here it is: He did not yet know anything at all about intimate relations. He still had a child's idea of the problems of sex, because his parents had always shielded him from the "shameful" subject.

But he had learned about it nevertheless. Not from his father or his mother, not the way be should have learned it—gradually, with the help of tactful, knowing preceptors—but from his pals, his older friends in the courtyard, as they boasted, half drunk, about their amorous exploits. He had learned it in a distorted, vulgar way, from gutter language and dirty jokes.

His pal and fellow-defendant had traveled a somewhat different path, a "literary" one, so to speak. A pudgy little fellow with protruding, transparent ears, the little fingers of his puffy hands delicately extended, this "book lover," if such he can be called, breathlessly recalled how his parents had hidden a "wonderful volume" of Apulius from him in the kitchen cupboard, and how he had found it anyway.

The book had been secreted from the boy because he would seek what was "forbidden" in it, but he had found what he was looking for.

Apulius was hidden away, and hiding places were found, too, for reproductions of classical paintings, which might, God forbid, depict a nude. As if these masterpieces could only corrupt the youth, and could never kindle in him a love of beauty. They were protecting him, it seems—but at the same time they would tell double-entendre jokes, adding their own drunken commentary.

I recall another criminal case, which involved several victims. All the crimes had been committed by the same man. He was 23 years old. I shall never forget my final talk with this young fellow.

His father had died at the front, and a new "papa" soon turned up at home. After a while this "papa" was exchanged for a still newer one. Mama had made the boy call them all "Papa," and she beat her only son mercilessly when he objected—for after all, he remembered who his father was and had not yet learned to dissemble. But he was forced to call them "Papa" and taught to play the hypocrite. The "papa" kept changing as he grew. More than once he would wake up at night and notice, first with surprise and loathing and later with indifference, that he had never before seen the man lying beside his mother. His mother! This is how he received his "schooling," how he mastered what he should have learned ten years later, how the mystery for him was turned into swinishness. A normal child was mutilated, becoming first a spoiled adolescent and then a cynical youth. He shrugged off the word "love" and had not the faintest notion of respect for a woman.

He complained about nothing, blamed no one but himself and simply related the facts.

Now about some of the victims. The word "victims" somehow does not square with the lives they led, with their behavior. If only you could hear with what relish they described their evening parties, which were more like orgies. Yes, it all ended in full-fledged rape, so to speak. Yes, the culprits should be mercilessly punished and isolated from society. One is troubled by the persistent thought, however, that it may be worthwhile to protect society with equal zeal from some of these so-called "victims," these girls who can drink almost as much as the fellows, who turn a dance into an obscene spectacle. I would not hesitate to say that their way of life and conduct sometimes smack of provocation, whereby they become their own victims.

The chief gathering place of these young men and women, who later turned into defendants and victims, was a club in a densely populated borough of Moscow and the dance hall next door. Two centers of culture, so to speak.

Sex crimes: The very term indicates that all such crimes are connected with various aspects of intimacy, one way or another. If this is so, it means we must study the sphere of emotion and the sphere of sex, both together. So don't blame me or accuse me of blasphemy when in the investigation of these crimes I touch on such sacred things as the pure and lofty relations between people who love each other. I want to know what these 16- to 20-year-old products of the eight-year and ten-year schools, some of them even having two or three years of higher education, had heard about the great and immortal examples of love, whose force and persuasiveness have not diminished through the centuries, through the changing epochs.

Needless to say, being well-read cannot be equated with having cultivated feelings, but there is undoubtedly a connection between the two. Experience has taught me this.

And another thing: How often we adults, even if we don't want to, inculcate in young souls a sense of our superiority over those who lived, loved and suffered yesterday and over the way they did so. Think back upon this: Haven't you been left with an ironic attitude toward all chivalry since childhood?

One of my acquaintances recently was visited by a young man, a perfectly up-to-date student and athlete, who sank to his knees and asked for his daughter's hand. No one found this funny; it was moving, noble and fitting to the situation.

As I was finishing my investigation of an unfortunate case one evening, the door suddenly opened and two people came in; the accused and his victim. In every previous meeting with this large-eyed, exceptionally neat girl I had visualized clearly her begging this lout with the heavy red hands to leave her alone, and then weeping. Later, he himself had told how he had been ready to call it off, but "things somehow happened that way." Now they were harmoniously chattering away, saying they were in love and wanted to marry. Then came a few businesslike inquiries as to how this would affect the further course of the case. It was all so squalid, so commonplace and humdrum.

Perhaps it was from this kind of casualness, this humdrum feeling, that one thread led to the tragedy. And another thread led from excessive and perverted familiarity. And still another from philistinism and narrow-mindedness, from indifference. And still others—

*   *   *

I'm not going to generalize. Generalization requires perspective, and I am in the thick of events. This is the easiest way to fall into subjectivism. I have merely recounted a few case histories. After all, when you recount something, you yourself get a new look at it.

Study of the Criminal Personality from the Materials of Criminological Research

S. S. OSTROUMOV and V. E. CHUGUNOV

We are all aware of the vast practical and scientific significance of the problem of studying and preventing crime and of researching its causes and the conditions giving rise to it. That is why one of the principal provisions of Soviet criminal procedure is the demand that the reasons and conditions making

Reprinted by permission of International Arts and Sciences Press from S. S. Ostroumov and V. E. Chugunov, Sovetskoye gosudarstvo i pravo *(April 1966). Translated in* Soviet Review *(Copyright © Summer 1966), pp. 13–21.*

possible the commission of the crime be determined in each criminal case, and that measures be taken to eliminate them. But if the most characteristic, the most typical features in the development of criminality are to be discovered, and if its essential causes and conditions are to be determined (and this is a most important task of criminology), we cannot rely upon the study of individual cases and persons. Because these typical, essential characteristics in the realm of criminality manifest themselves in the form of statistical regularities, criminology must therefore make use of the statistical method on the very largest scale, i.e., it must base its conclusions upon mass-scale observations. "We must remember the rule," wrote Lenin, "that in social science... we deal with *mass-scale* phenomena and not individual cases."[1] Therefore, criminology, like the other social sciences, is required "to make broader and fuller use of the richest statistical material. For statistics, like concrete investigations, are the air without which science suffocates and is distorted into dead scholasticism."[2]

In this article, the question of study of the criminal personality and its role in the total system of causes of crime will be examined on the basis of the findings of concrete studies conducted by the law schools of Moscow and Voronezh universities.

Antisocial views, traditions, and habits are causes of crime. The vitality of such vestiges of the past is explained by the fact that consciousness lags behind social existence, by the presence of a capitalist world that is hostile to us, and by the continuing shortcomings in material and cultural services to citizens and in their upbringing. Vestiges of the past are rooted in the mode of life and the minds of millions of persons long after the disappearance of the economic conditions that gave rise to them. These vestiges are responsible for the fact that the commission of crimes is an objective possibility.

One of the most important tasks of criminological research lies in discovering the concrete conditions under which this possibility is transformed into a reality, inasmuch as many people who are infected by vestiges of the past are not at all condemned to commit crimes. It is only particular conditions

that, like catalysts, activate and vitalize such vestiges. For embezzlement [khishchenie] to occur, conditions such as the following must exist: poor accounting of valuables in an enterprise where the given individual is employed, poor supervision ov.. their utilization, an atmosphere of in.., --ality, misuse of alcohol, etc. Cons quently, particular conditions are, as it were, a connecting link betwen a given cause (let us assume, cupidity and selfishness as specific types of vestiges of the past) and a given consequence (embezzlement).

Criminal statistics provide a quantitative characterization of the causes and conditions facilitating the commission of particular categories of crimes. For example, the motives for so heinous a crime as intentional homicide were: a desire for gain—8.8%, revenge—19.1%, jealousy—11.3%, the attitudes of a rowdy—29.4%, fights arising in the course of an argument—20.7%. These repulsive vestiges of the past came to the fore under the influence of particular catalyzing agents, such as alcohol for example. We need only state that 67.8% of all intentional homicides were committed in a state of intoxication.[3] According to the courts of Moscow and Moscow Region, 73.1% of those convicted under Article 102 of the RSFSR Criminal Code and 81.6% of those convicted under Article 108, Part 2, of the RSFSR Criminal Code committed their crimes while intoxicated.[4]

These statistical data offer a clear picture of the quantitative aspect of the causes and conditions making for crime, but they provide no answer to an important question. Why is it that these causes and conditions result in

[1] V. I. Lenin, *Soch.*, Vol. 21, p. 218.
[2] *Kommunist*, 1963, No. 16, p. 33.
[3] *Voprosy kriminalistiki*, 1964, No. 11, p. 71.
[4] *Voprosy preduprezhdeniia prestupnosti*, 1965, No. 1, p. 40.

socially dangerous acts on the part of only a negligible number of people with firmly established individualist views and habits, while the majority observe the norms of socialist law and morality? To find an answer to this question it is necessary to study the data on the personalities of lawbreakers.

A study of criminality that is detached from detailed research into the personality of the criminal leads, as past experience has shown, to sterile, scholastic constructs in the spirit of the classical school of criminal law. One cannot but observe that our criminologists do not yet ascribe the necessary significance to the need for careful study of the subjective, psychological characteristics of the criminal, his temperament and character. Study of these aspects of the criminal personality is still often regarded as almost slipping back to the standpoint of Lombroso. We hold that these features of the personality are also in need of serious attention. Study of the personality of the criminal must be all-embracing. A man's psychological characteristics, his temperament and character, and traits such as thoughtlessness, withdrawal, reticence, cruelty, faintheartedness, etc., play an important role in people's general conduct, and particularly in criminal behavior. Identical objective conditions have different effects upon different individuals upon being refracted through their psychological make-up.

Of course, one should not exaggerate the role of the individual's personal characteristics in the commission of crime and thus seek help in biology, which has no place in Soviet criminology. But neither can one disregard the psychological traits of the individual. And it is exceedingly important to emphasize that individual personality traits are the product of the conditions under which the person has lived, been raised, and has functioned. Consequently, for all the importance of the individual's subjective characteristics, his actions and deeds depend upon concrete external conditions and circumstances. These subjective conditions can only promote or inhibit the commission of crimes; they certainly do not render it inevitable that a particular individual will be a criminal, as the bourgeois bio-criminologists would have us believe. Thus, by changing objective conditions in a given direction, one may have a restraining influence upon unstable individuals.

In studying the personality of the criminal it is first necessary to elucidate the conditions that, as it is phrased in criminology, have had a negative influence upon his moral development. Only after this may one take concrete measures to eliminate the conditions discovered or to reduce the influence they exert, i.e., to engage in crime prevention. In order to study more concretely and purposefully the conditions exercising a negative influence upon individuals infected with vestiges of the past, it is necessary to direct attention to such criteria as the sex and age of criminals.

STUDY OF DATA ON THE SEX AND AGE OF CRIMINALS

Data of a sampling survey conducted in the Central Black Earth Economic District show that 88% of crimes in 1963 were committed by men and 12% by women. Among the women, 80% of the crimes consisted of speculation, 11% of embezzlement, 4% of homicide, 2% of stealing [*grabezh*], and 1.2% of hooliganism. As we know, the 1959 census showed men to comprise 45%, and women 55%, of the total population. The considerable predominance of males in the total number of convicted persons obtains not only among adults, but also among minors. Thus, data from a complete survey of the Lenin District of Moscow show that girls have numbered between 7% and 3.5% of the total number of convicted minors during the past four years. In the Latvian SSR, girls numbered 5% of the minors brought to trial in 1959 and 1960.[5]

boys and girls. The result is that the committees do not develop special forms of prevention of lawbreaking among juveniles."[6]

According to the data of a complete survey in the Central Black Earth Economic District, the ages of the convicts break down as follows (with the figures for embezzlement and hooliganism[7] singled out; see the table below).

Indices (%)	Under 18	18–25	26–30	31–40	41–50	51–60	Over 60	Total
All crimes	7.0	31.0	20.6	30.0	7.0	2.6	1.8	100
Of which: Embezzlement of socialist property	8.0	24.2	21.9	26.4	10.0	4.9	4.6	100
Hooliganism	6.0	28.1	23.3	30.0	10.0	2.6	—	100

Without in any way taking an anthropological position on the matter, we cannot ignore the physical, psychological, and physiological differences between the sexes. The distinctive features of crime among men and women, to which very little attention has thus far been paid, must certainly be considered in carrying out prophylactic measures in general, and in preventing crime among minors in particular.

Commenting upon the fact that the overwhelming majority of juvenile lawbreakers are boys, E. V. Boldyrev has written: "This points to the need for a differentiated system of preventive measures, proceeding from the utterly obvious need for considerably broader preventive work among boys and for the development of special, sex-differentiated forms of character training for minors. The committees on the affairs of minors underestimate this fact and, thus far, in organizing general preventive measures, do not provide for satisfaction of the interests and needs of

It is clear from these data that more than a third of all crimes (38%) are committed by youth under 25, including 32.2% of the embezzlement of socialist property and 34.1% of the hooliganism. With respect to a number of other dangerous crimes, this group of young people is predominant or at least exceeds its average for all criminal violations.

STUDY OF DATA ON THE MATERIAL STATUS OF CRIMINALS

Examination of the synthesized indices of a number of criminological investigations brings us to the conclu-

5 Preduprezhdenie pravonarushenii nesovershennoletnikh, Riga, 1963, p. 37.

6 See E. V. Boldyrev, Mery preduprezhdeniia pravonarushenii nesovershennoletnikh v SSSR, "Nauka" Press, Moscow, 1964, pp. 134–135.

7 We have chosen to use the age data on criminals guilty of embezzlement and hooliganism because these two types of crime are dominant among the socially dangerous acts committed—the former comprising 33.8% and the latter, 41.4%. Consequently, these two offenses account for over three-fourths (75.2%) of all crimes.

sion that in the period of transition from socialism to communism, as distinct from the preceding period, economic factors have generally ceased to be the dominant and immediate cause of crime. Such social phenomena as unemployment and childhood without adult supervision, which gave rise to crime in the first years of Soviet government and under the conditions of the New Economic Policy, have long receded into the past.[8] The fact that it is still impossible, under the conditions of socialism, to completely satisfy the steadily increasing material needs of all Soviet citizens has, in the main, an indirect rather than a direct, immediate influence upon criminals. Such persons—bearers of vestiges of the past—commit crimes in the overwhelming majority of cases not because of material

in the Central Black Earth Economic District. The data on the incomes of persons who have committed crimes involving property show that these crimes are committed, for the most part, by persons who are materially well-off. Thus, 58.8% of those studied had an income of 40 rubles per month per member of the family, and one-third had 60 rubles per month or more. Studies of repeaters show these percentages to be, respectively, 63% and 37.7%, while among youth, i.e., persons under 30 who have committed crimes involving property, the figures are 72.9% and 43.7%.

This conclusion is confirmed by data from a complete survey of juvenile law-breakers in Moscow's Lenin District in 1964. The earnings of their families are shown in the table below.

Monthly earnings of family of criminal	100 rubles or less	100 to 150	150 to 200	200 to 250	Over 250	Total
In %	14.6	31.4	34.9	12.4	6.7	100.0

difficulties, but due to private-property, egoistic attitudes, an unwillingness to consider the public interest, a desire to live at the expense of others and to satisfy by any and all means their "enlarged" individual requirements.

This conclusion is confirmed by the data of the sampling survey conducted

If we consider the family to average 3.5 persons[9] we see that a clear majority of juveniles who engaged in crime did not do so at all because of material need.

INVESTIGATION OF DATA ON HOUSING CONDITIONS OF CRIMINALS

Is it perhaps that unsatisfactory housing, particularly the inconvenience of shared apartments, created an unbearable situation, with all the negative consequences deriving from this? Not so long ago this played some role in the moral shaping of the personality,

[8] During the New Economic Policy, when there were more than a million unemployed and declassed elements in the country, criminals (thieves in particular) came primarily from that milieu. This is confirmed by the following data, which characterize the direct relationship between thievery and the socio-economic position of the criminal. Dentention of male thieves in Moscow in 1923 breaks down as follows: per 1,000 persons in the population, 0.7 were workers, 0.4 were employees, 5.4 were unemployed, and 93.5 were declassed elements (*Prestupnyi mir Moskvy*, Moscow, 1924, p. 156).

[9] *Naselenie mira,* "Mysl'" Press, 1965, p. 136.

Indices (%)	Had own home	Had own apart- ment	Had a room	Lived in dormi- tory	Lived in private apart- ment	No dwell- ing	Total
All criminals surveyed	49.3	20.5	9.3	7.2	11.7	2.0	100.0
Of which:							
Repeaters	50.0	17.3	10.3	5.0	13.1	4.3	100.0
Plunderers of public property [raskhititeli]	58.0	21.0	7.0	4.0	10.0	0	100.0

particularly that of juveniles. But the vast scale of housing during the past decade has solved this problem to a considerable degree. Poor housing conditions, with the resultant possibility of hostile relationships among neighbors and the negative influence of such relationships upon minors, etc., are today not of major significance among the causes of crime. We cite highly revealing data on the housing circumstances of criminals at the time of their crimes, drawn from a selective survey in the Central Black Earth Economic District (see the above table).

Thus, except for 4.3% of repeaters from outside the area, the remaining categories of lawbreakers lived under satisfactory conditions prior to the commission of their crimes. These data are indicative not only for the Central Black Earth Economic District. Thus, according to a survey of Moscow's Lenin District, 65.2% of the juvenile lawbreakers lived, prior to conviction, in families with over five square meters

of housing space per person, 34.9% having their own apartments.

Thus, material circumstances and living conditions have ceased to play a basic role in shaping antisocial views and habits. The center of gravity in this matter has shifted, in our opinion, to the sphere of ideological relationships, to the region of level of culture and consciousness of persons who are bearers of various vestiges of the past.

STUDY OF DATA ON CRIMINALS' LEVEL OF EDUCATION AND CULTURE

The data of these surveys provide clear evidence of a direct relationship between criminality and low general education and culture. We present a table compiled on the basis of processing the results of a sampling survey in the Central Black Earth Economic District, and characterizing the level of education of lawbreakers:

Indices (%)	Illit- erate	Pri- mary	Incom- plete second- ary	Sec- ond- ary	Incom- plete higher	Higher	Not deter- mined	Total
All criminals surveyed	2.6	45.6	37.7	8.2	0.5	0.4	5.0	100.0
Of which:								
Plunderers of public property	3.2	43.4	38.0	7.9	0.5	0.4	6.6	100.0
Hooligans	1.8	52.4	35.4	7.5	0.2	0.5	2.2	100.0
Murderers	4.4	40.0	47.4	8.2	—	—	—	100.0
All repeaters surveyed	3.3	48.7	39.0	7.0	—	0.5	1.5	100.0
Of which, 4 or more convictions	5.0	52.5	32.5	10.0	—	—	—	100.0

As we see, 85.9% of all the criminals surveyed had less than eight years of schooling, and 2.6% were illiterate. The level of education was still lower among murderers and hooligans, and particularly among habitual criminals. It is interesting that while the 1959 census showed 1.5% of the USSR population as illiterate (chiefly elderly individuals and persons suffering from chronic diseases or physical inadequacies[10]), the percentage of illiterates among criminals, particularly murderers and dangerous habitual criminals of youthful age, exceeds the percentage in the population at large by 100 to 200%.

Thus, it was not living conditions and material circumstances that prevented lawbreakers from attaining the proper education and level of culture. On the contrary, they had all the possibilities for this, but did not wish to make use of them because their impoverished interests were oriented in a certain direction: to drink, lead dissipated lives, enrich themselves at the expense of the labor of others, and live as parasites. This is the source of their complete disdain for civic activity, and the absence of interest in creative literature, magazines and newspapers, the theater and films on the part of many of them. Of the lawbreakers surveyed, 95% had never participated in civic activity of any kind, 55% had not read creative literature, 41% had not read papers or magazines, 79.5% had not gone to the theater, 15.6% had not even attended movies, 24.5% had not been radio listeners, and only 1.2% had engaged in sports and 4.9% in mechanical hobbies.

As already noted, 88.6% of all crimes were committed by persons under forty years of age. Consequently, these were people with every opportunity to improve their general level of education.

However, only 4.4% were attending an educational institution of any kind, whereas over 50% of the general population was engaged in learning in one form or another. The lack of desire to learn explains the fact that 40% of those held to criminal responsibility had no trade of any kind, whereas only 1.9% of the industrial workers of the USSR lacked vocational skills.[11] We add that 11.6% of those held to criminal responsibility did not wish to work and maliciously evaded socially useful labor.

Our attention is attracted by the fact that nearly nine-tenths of the convicted juveniles between 16 and 18 years of age should have had 8 to 10 years of schooling. But the survey of Moscow's Lenin District showed that 66.2% of them had 7 years of schooling, while only 28.2% had 8 or 9 years. Consequently, the majority of the juvenile lawbreakers did not, for various reasons, have the schooling corresponding to their ages. This is also confirmed by a number of studies made by the USSR Institute on the Causes and Prevention of Crime. Thus, of the juvenile criminals of 1963 whose cases were studied, 85.4% did not have the education corresponding to their age. A similar picture was observed in Latvia, where only 10% of the juveniles whose cases were studied had received educations corresponding to their age levels.[12]

STUDY OF DATA CHARACTERIZING
FAMILY, SCHOOL, AND WORK SITUATION

Favorable family conditions, as well as the beneficial effects of work and of character building in the group, play an enormous role in the moral shaping of

10 *Ibid.*, p. 141.

11 *Ekonomicheskaia zhizn'*, Oct. 23, 1961.
12 *Voprosy preduprezhdeniia prestupnosti*, 1965, No. 1, p. 13.

the personality. The investigations conducted showed that 7.2% of the lawbreakers lived at the time of the crime in families in which father, mother, or brother had been convicted of a crime; in 21.4% of the cases, relationships within the family were bad. All this had a significant influence in developing traits of character such as quickness of temper (13.5%), habitual lying (20.1%), and obstinacy (10.4%).

According to the data of Moscow's Lenin District, only 53.9% of the convicted minors were living with both parents, 30.7% lived with their mothers, 1.1% with their fathers, 8.8% with a stepmother or stepfather, and 5.5% were orphans.

Data on the undiminishing number of suits for divorce and for child maintenance in Moscow's Lenin District testify to the disintegration and unhappy conditions in certain families, and, consequently, the creation of conditions negatively influencing the moral shaping of juveniles. (From 1961 to 1964, inclusive, there was nearly a 5% increase in divorce cases, and maintenance suits increased by almost 15%.) In many cases the lack of normal family conditions led to lack of adult supervision, failure in school and, sometimes, expulsion, to the desire to avoid work and to spend time in the street. Only 8% of all the individuals convicted in Moscow's Lenin District were neither working nor in school, but in the Krasnaia Presnia District of Moscow this figure attained 22%, and in Latvia —28.4%.[13] All this led many juveniles first to mischief, then to minor infractions of the law, and finally to crime. Data for Moscow's Lenin District show that 19% of the convictions were of individuals who had previous police records, and 30.4% had committed petty hooliganism.

Inasmuch as two-thirds of the lawbreakers had jobs, it is clear that their recreation at work and residence had been inadequately organized, and this often led to the formation of groups first of mischief-makers, then of criminals, and to the appearance of the evil figure of the adult inciter. Our data show that, from 1962 to 1964, between 75.8 and 80% of crimes were committed in groups, and 17 to 39% of these had the participation of adults. It is characteristic that the total period of employment of lawbreakers prior to their being held to criminal responsibility, and especially at their last jobs, was short. It was less than one year among 40% of all criminals and 52% of repeaters. It is clear that the influence of work upon the personality, and the educative role of the collective, were very limited here. This would explain the negative references that places of employment provided for 40% of the lawbreakers.

The pernicious influence of alcohol upon crime is well known. And we find that 56.9% of the persons convicted committed their crimes while intoxicated. But it is characteristic that the overwhelming majority of the minors who committed crimes when sober did so either to steal alcoholic drinks or money to buy them. All this confirms once again that it is not material conditions that are responsible for crime, but inadequacies of upbringing in the family, at school and at work, which cause juveniles to depart from the normal course of life and to be unsupervised, with all the consequences resulting from this. The interests of juvenile lawbreakers differed sharply from those of pupils who made good and excellent grades, as may be seen from the above table.

This table is instructive. It indicates

---

13 E. V. Boldyrev, *op. cit.*, p. 137; *Preduprezhdenie pravonarushenii nesovershennoletnikh*, p. 52.

		INTERESTS		
Indices	Sports	Amateur artistic groups	Civic activity	Pursuits in various clubs
Lawbreakers	20%	8.6%	2.3%	—
Pupils making good or excellent grades	60%	65%	67%	33%

quite convincingly that many violations of law are committed by juveniles because they have no activities that interest and attract them, and because of the inertness or inability of certain teachers in organizing the leisure time of children in general and of "difficult" children in particular. That remarkable teacher, S. T. Shatskii, wrote with justice: "A busy atmosphere, and interesting work particularly, creates a good working atmosphere, in which every outburst of a disorderly nature is unpleasant to the children themselves."[14] On the other hand, unoccupied leisure time and detachment from the collective often have the result that a juvenile begins, for lack of things to do, to engage in mischief and rowdyism, to associate with bad company and sometimes to fall into crime.

Habitual criminals have a corrupting influence upon unstable youth, and particularly upon minors. This is facilitated by the manner in which sentences are served, among other things. According to the sampling survey in the Central Black Earth Economic District, only 58.3% of recidivists served their full terms, while 30% were given conditional early releases. This sort of "humanism" had the consequence that 3.9% of those granted conditional early releases committed another crime within one month of release, 7.8% within 3 months, 17.1% within 6 months, 18.3% within a year, and 23.8% within three years. Thus, half of the recidivists had

14 S. D. Cherepanov, S. T. Shatskii i ego pedagogicheskie vyskazyvaniia, Moscow, 1927, p. 116.

committed another crime within a year after being freed. We note that of the recidivists granted conditional early releases, 64.3% had had one previous conviction, 20% — two, 10% — three, 5%—four, and 0.7%—five or more. Need we say that this faulty practice of giving conditional early releases to habitual criminals, which still exists, unfortunately, creates the impression not only upon them, but also upon an unstable segment of the population infected with vestiges of the past, that crimes will go unpunished?

*   *   *

As the results of our studies have shown, a number of objective conditions influence the manifestation of anti-social views and habits by certain persons and lead them to commit crimes. A careful study of the conditions that have a negative influence upon the moral development of the personality is decisive in eliminating and, therefore, preventing crime. People sometimes draw the conclusion that everything depends upon these objective conditions and that the individual bears the least responsibility. The individual is allegedly under the "fatal" influence of the objective conditions, and he is virtually compelled to commit crime. Fatalism of this sort does not withstand criticism and must be entirely discarded by Soviet criminology. Even the far from complete factual data adduced in this article offer convincing proof that it is not conditions of material life that drive the "safe-guarders of the traditions of capitalism" to the path of crime. Everything turns on the level of consciousness and culture of these individuals, on their unwillingness to study, work, and take recreation as do Soviet people, and on their desire to live as parasites and to satisfy their egoistic needs by whatever means come to hand.

The question arises as to whether we can really reduce everything to objective conditions, without making rigorous demands upon the criminal himself who, as we see it, possessed, in the overwhelming majority of cases, every opportunity to choose an honest path. Much is now being said and written about this. We totally reject the unscientific view that criminal behavior is allegedly compelled by external circumstances and is entirely dependent upon the peculiarities of the "personality stereotype" of the individual. One of the authors of the present article has already expressed himself on this subject.[15]

The problem of free will in criminal law is beyond the scope of the present article, and therefore we do not deal with it here. We note only that inasmuch as man possesses the ability to select his course of behavior, it is up to him, in our opinion, to direct his mind and will toward a given goal. We hold that in the overwhelming majority of cases, a citizen of our country has every opportunity to choose freely, within various conditions, among courses of conduct, and that this is the basic prerequisite for correct solution of the problem of responsibility for crime. Lacking the opportunity to go into this question in detail, we confine ourselves to noting that, in studying crime, it is necessary to direct the most serious attention both to the objective external conditions promoting the commission of crimes and to the personality of the criminal himself. An all-round study of these objective and subjective conditions, on the basis of concrete sociological research, will make possible a more successful solution of the task of eliminating crime and removing all the factors that give rise to it.

15 *Sotsialisticheskaia zakonnost'*, 1963, No. 10, pp. 91–92.

CRIME

IN THE U.S.S.R.:

The American View

Reflections on
Soviet Juvenile Delinquency

PAUL HOLLANDER

...can we really speak of the causes of crime in capitalist society without showing the organic link between capitalism and crime? Obviously not... the whole capitalist mode of life makes for increasing juvenile deliquency.

Soviet Review, January 1961.

...we know that the fundamental social cause of excesses, which consist in the violation of the rules of social intercourse, is the exploitation of the masses, their want and their poverty.

Lenin in *State and Revolution.*

It would be a big mistake to think that the very fact of living in the land of the Soviets, in the conditions of socialist reality, presupposes a Communist world outlook in a young person.

Pavlov, Secretary of the Young Communist League, *Komsomolskaya Pravda,* Dec. 29, 1965.

In the 1960's, juvenile delinquency has achieved the status of a Soviet social problem. For those who think that Soviet society, if undemocratic, is at least free of the characteristic evils of capitalist societies—such as crime and delinquency—this is an obvious disappointment. Others, skeptical of Soviet

An original contribution based in part on a paper entitled "The Problem of Delinquency in the United States and the USSR" delivered by the author at the annual meeting of the American Sociological Association in 1966.

achievements gain considerable satisfaction from the failure to eradicate crime not only among the adults but even among the purer, younger generations. For those impartial spirits who gleefully contemplate the universal corruption of all modern societies, the emergence of Soviet juvenile delinquency must be a perversely satisfying phenomenon confirming their judgment of the inherent evils of every industrial, mass society.

It is interesting to note that proponents of the "convergence hypothesis" while suggesting a growing institutional

275

resemblance between American and Soviet society, particularly in the realms of economics, science, education, and bureaucratization, failed to predict or emphasize the convergence of social problems."[1] Today it is becoming increasingly clear that while the above-mentioned institutional convergence is questionable, the Soviet Union is "catching up" with the United States in the production of social problems, paramount among them juvenile delinquency.

The social scientific study and public discussion of juvenile delinquency is a comparatively recent phenomenon in the U.S.S.R., and it has so far provided little insight into the quantitative dimensions of the problem. Much of what we know about Soviet juvenile delinquency comes from the Soviet press, from its numerous, if impressionistic accounts of juvenile misbehavior, the descriptions of court cases, and the ideological discussions of the problems and its remedies. This publicity itself is a fairly recent development. The

gradually diminishing reluctance of the Soviet authorities to openly discuss and study delinquency is a residue of the Stalinist reticence about the ventilation of social problems. To reveal social problems, and particularly problems involving youth, is far more traumatic in Soviet than in American society. In the Soviet Union, the utopian conceptions of the social order and its unlimited perfectibility have never been officially abandoned. Throughout Soviet history, from Lenin to Khrushchev, spokesmen for the regime never tired of conjuring up visions of the perfect society and claiming to sense its perceptible approach. The outlines of communist society continue to be painted in vivid, if somewhat vague, colors. Deliberate and large-scale social engineering remains the principal method of tackling social transformations and handling the malfunctioning of institutions. Under such conditions, the persistence, or re-emergence, of social problems represents both a serious ideological issue and a practical challenge, particularly when the problems in question have their embarrassing counterparts in capitalist societies. Anti-social behavior on the part of the young must appear doubly threatening since it casts doubt on the efficiency of the socialization processes the regime has developed over decades. Therein lies the difficulty of the theory of survivals,[2] which postulates that deviant behavior has its source in the attitudinal legacy of the past which survives even after the old social order has been destroyed. While this may have

[1] For discussions and various viewpoints and Soviet-American convergence, see I. Deutscher; *The Great Contest*, London: 1960; Z. Brzezinski and S. Huntington: *Political Power: USA/USSR*, New York: 1964; P. Sorokin, *The Mutual Convergence of the US and USSR in Basic Trends of our Times*, New Haven: 1964; A. Inkeles, "Russia and the United States," in P. J. Allen, ed., *P. Sorokin in Review*, Durham: 1963; W. W. Rostow, *The Stages of Economic Growth*, London: 1960; P. Wiles: "Will Capitalism and Communism Spontaneously Converge?" *Encounter*, June 1963; A. S. Feldman and W. Moore, "Industrialization and Industrialism, Convergence and Differentiation," *Transaction of the Fifth World Congress of Sociology*, 1962; A. Meyer, "USSR Incorporated" and Z. Brzezinski, "Reply," in D. Treadgold, ed., *The Development of the USSR*, Seattle, 1964. For a representative Soviet view *cf.*, Yu. Zamoshkin, "Teoria 'edinovo industrialnovo obshchestva' na sluzhbe antikommuniza" (The Theory of a Single Industrial Society in the Service of Anticommunism) in *Marksistkaya i burzhuaznia sotsiologia sevodna*, Moscow, 1964.

[2] M. Shargarodski, The Causes and Prevention of Crime, *Soviet Sociology*, Summer, 1964, No. 1. and A. A. Gercenzon, *Vvedenie v sovetskuiu kriminologiu (Introduction to Soviet Criminology)*, Izd. Iuridicheskaia Literatura, Moscow, 1965, pp. 122–123; also *Stroitelstvo communizma i duchovnii mir tseloveka* (The Building of Communism and the Spiritual World of Man), Izd. Nauka, Moscow 1966, pp. 332–358.

some plausibility for the older generations, its applicability to the younger ones is unconvincing, even when it is alleged that the old can transmit the survivals to the young.

The desire to escape from boredom is among the alleged and probably genuine sources of Soviet juvenile delinquency. Many factors enter into Soviet boredom. First, there is the proverbial drabness of the Soviet environment that has impressed generations of outside visitors, and of which Soviet youngsters complain more and more vociferously.[3] Drabness is not merely a reflection of the low standard of living; it is also a product of the lack of official imagination and the inertia of an overorganized society. An institution that does more than its share in injecting boredom into the life of the young is the Young Communist League, or the Komsomol. The Komsomol meeting is an apt symbol of the intense boredom this venerable organization is capable of generating in the minds of Soviet youth:

We have such meetings, but to tell the truth, were it not for the Young Communist League discipline, no one would attend. After all, we know by heart everything that will happen at them.... More YCL meetings should be held under the crimson sails of romanticism![4]

The "crimson sails of romanticism" persistently elude the activities of the Komsomol as many similar complaints in the Soviet press testify. The entertainments organized by it tend to ossify into bureaucratic, overly supervised routines.[5] What is even worse, most of its activities do not even pretend to be entertaining. However, the Komsomol is not the only boredom-creating agent in

[3] A letter from a young reader in *Izvestia* declared: "There is no real solicitude for our free time.... Why couldn't we be taught how to dance in school?...The main enemy is boredom." *Izvestia,* November 3, 1965, transl. *Current Digest of the Soviet Press* (abbreviated as *CDSP*), November 24, 1965, p. 27; another article criticized Soviet films, saying that "...our films do not satisfy young people's desire for romanticism and heroism." "Give Young People the Romance of an Exploit," *Izvestia,* August 11, 1965, transl. *CDSP,* September 1, 1965, p. 30; another article complained of adult interference with the "spontaneous" leisure time activities of youth. "Boredom with Stuffing," *Pravda,* January 22, 1966; transl. *CDSP,* February 9, 1966, p. 29; More significantly, a survey conducted among secondary students on their leisure time activities linked the misuse of leisure to delinquency. The response to the problem is in many ways similar to that in the U.S.: "So the attitude that free time is a source of criminal inclinations and actions is becoming traditional. Accordingly only emergency measures are taken...Athletic fields and recreation rooms ...are being quickly and haphazardly created. They are necessary but can they alone prevent youngsters from delinquent behavior and help build up an immunity to bad influences?... Why is there so little immunity?" "Senior Pupils after Class," *Komsomolskaya Pravda,* June 16, 1965, transl. *CDSP,* August 25, 1965, p. 15.

[4] "Thirteen Days Around the Clock at Meetings," *Molodoi Kommunist,* No. 2, February 1965, transl. *CDSP,* May 5, 1965, p. 7. The shortcomings of the organized upbringing of youth are also discussed in "Rear Young People in the Spirit of Revolutionary Ideals," *Pravda,* November 28, 1965, transl. *CDSP,* December 22, 1965, pp. 5–6. The article, written by the head of the Soviet Communist Party's Department of Propaganda, noted that "Certain young men and women sometimes fall under an alien influence and slide into a position of skepticism and nihilism."

[5] The case of the so-called youth cafes illustrates this problem. Intended to be informal, friendly and inexpensive gathering places for young people they came under rigid bureaucratic controls. "...a guard meets you at the entrance. He makes sure you aren't trying to smuggle in some vodka. Next you... look at a menu...it lists dishes that haven't been available for a long time. The waitress ignores you...All evening...nothing happens. "Over a Cup of Coffee," *Literaturnaya Gazeta,* September 1, 1964, transl. *CDSP,* November 4, 1964, p. 19. Further difficulties about the youth cafes were detailed in "How the Discussion of Youth Cafes Ended," *Sovetskaya Rossia,* September 22, 1966, trans. *CDSP,* November 16, 1966, p. 26.

Soviet society. The residues of neo-Victorian puritanism—developed under Stalin—still make their contribution. Finally, we must also point out that Soviet boredom is also related to the degree of control to which Soviet citizens are subject. We should not conceive of this control as ceaseless police surveillance. Rather, we might visualize it as a lifelong membership in one huge bureaucratic organization that concerns itself with most details of life.[6] We might even argue that this is a benevolent, paternalistic control. Whether it is or not, an obvious consequence of extensive controls is the routinization and predictability of life. This predictability leaves little room for chance, luck, imagination, or excitement. As such, it is among the most important components of Soviet boredom. At the same time, it also explains the pathetically intense curiosity young Soviet people show toward the world outside (especially the West), and all objects—primarily consumer goods and accessories of entertainment—that originate in it.

We might still ask why has boredom *recently* become more prominently associated with juvenile delinquency in the Soviet Union? Not too originally, we must suggest that increased expectations have played their usual part. The decline of political repression and the rising standards of living since the death of Stalin set off the phenomenon more familiar from the underdeveloped countries: the asymetrical growth of aspirations and their fulfillment. "A revolution" of rising expectations would certainly overstate the Soviet case. Yet, particularly among the young, expectations rapidly outgrew what the regime

could provide in consumer goods, opportunities for leisure, travel, and higher education. That much of Soviet juvenile delinquency looks like a response to such frustrations is one of the major similarities between the sources of juvenile delinquency in the U.S.S.R. and the United States. The United States is probably worse off because American society has been systematically indoctrinating too many generations with unrealistic expectations, a process which, incidentally, continues to form the backbone of the American entertainment and advertising industries. (Nor has American society been noticeably successful in controlling the frustrations thus generated.)

Drunkenness, a social problem in its own right, is also closely associated with Soviet juvenile delinquency:

Last year more than 2000 intoxicated young men were arrested in one Leningrad borough alone. Out of every ten violators of public order, nine are drunk. A group of juvenile delinquents serving sentences in corrective labor colonies for minors were questioned. The overwhelming majority of them said that the chief cause of their violations of the law had been 'drinking out of boredom.'[7]

We might not rule out the possibility that Soviet juvenile delinquents are showing considerable sophistication in

---

[6] See for further discussion Alfred G. Meyer, *The Soviet Political System,* New York: Random House, 1965, p. 467; Barrington Moore, Jr., *Soviet Politics—the Dilemma of Power,* New York: Harper Torchbooks, 1965, Ch. 12.

[7] "We Continue the Discussion of Free Time: Amuse Me," *Nedelya,* No. 44, 1965, transl. *CDSP,* December 8, 1965, p. 14. Another article stated: "...today such crimes as hooliganism...rape, theft...and other crimes are committed in a state of intoxication." Jurist's Notes, *Izvestia,* January 4, 1967, transl. *CDSP,* January 25, 1967, p. 27. According to yet another source, "...67.8% of all intentional homicides were committed in a state of intoxication." S. S. Ostroumov and V. E. Chugunov, "Study of the Criminal Personality," *Sovetskoe Gosudarstvo i Pravo,* 1965, No. 9., transl. in *Soviet Review,* Summer 1966, pp. 13–21. What we are not told, however, is just how many homicides are committed per year.

the manner Americans do when they have to account for their misbehavior. In America, a respectable explanation on their part usually includes allusions to the sociological causation of which they are well aware—in the Soviet Union a similarly acceptable and respectable explanation appears to be found in boredom, rather than social institutions.[8] The following statement by the Russian Republic Minister for Safeguarding Public Order reflects both this dilemma and the puzzled vexation of the officials with hooliganism, a predominant form of juvenile delinquency:

What is the matter? Why is it that in our wonderful time, when the material well-being and culture of the people is rising steadily this evil is so tenacious? Why is it that the hooligan continues to commit outrages...? The trouble is that the laws are not always and everywhere applied to the full measure. Here and there the public danger of hooliganism is underestimated, tolerance is shown toward foul-mouths and rowdies...conciliatory, indulgent attitude toward a great evil can be observed....[9]

Nevertheless, despite official indignation there are good reasons to believe that Soviet juvenile misbehavior has not yet produced much *serious* crime, and that on the whole, Soviet juvenile deliquency is less vicious, less organized, and less

8 "When a young person lands in the prisoner's dock everyone begins to look for the reasons that led him to crime and some people try to prove that poor organization of leisure is responsible for everything. 'They weren't properly amused,' 'They weren't drawn into activities,' 'There were too few youth cafes and dance halls'—you often hear a lawyer in court utter words to this effect. And his client, a trim, strapping fellow, nods his approval and begins to believe that he became a thug only because of the shortage of youth cafes." "We Continue the Discussion of Free Time: Amuse Me," *Nedelya*, No. 44, 1965, transl. *CDSP*, December 8, 1965, p. 15.
9 "There will be No Indulgence for Hooligans," *Izvestia*, April 21, 1966, transl. *CDSP*, May 11, 1966, p. 45.

differentiated and has fewer sub-cultural supports than in the United States.

An important determinant of the behavior of the Soviet juvenile offender is that delinquent behavior can form a smaller part of his total activities than in the case of his American counterpart. As a rule, the Soviet delinquent can only devote a relatively small amount of time to lawbreaking; he cannot be a school drop-out for long—not, at any rate, in major urban areas—and he cannot shirk socially useful labor for long without attracting the attention of the authorities. This probably has significant implications for delinquent "specialization," for the development of delinquent skills, delinquent associations, and the hardening of deviant attitudes. He may share with his more advanced American colleagues the whole gamut of anti-social attitudes: the disrespect for authority, contempt for routines, rejection of effort, dreams of conspicuous consumption, wine, women, and violence—but the active and sustained pursuit of these goals is less easily accessible to him. The scope of Soviet delinquency is also narrowed down by limited physical mobility. Soviet delinquents cannot run around in cars, not even in dilapidated ones. Nor can they procure armaments for gang warfare (or other purposes) at the friendly neighborhood gun store. It is among the few blessings of life in a totalitarian society that liberal access to firearms is denied. To be sure, knives are wielded among Soviet delinquents as they are in American slums and at times with the same deadly results. Some Soviet juvenile delinquents are also capable of passionless violence more typically found among their American counterparts.[10]

10 "The tragic events of that evening... seem quite mundane: 'After work I went to see my friend. He got hold of another friend. We did some drinking...We went to the movies. From the movies we went through

It would be both theoretically pleasing and in keeping with current fashions to propose that—as most other things—Soviet juvenile delinquency can be explained somehow by industrialization. This simple proposition, though not without a grain of truth, has to be abandoned. At any rate, if juvenile delinquency is related to the *disruptions* (rather than the expectations) associated with industrialization, then the Soviet Union should have had more of it in the 1930's—when it passed through its forced, rapid, most disruptive stages. Yet it appears (though we cannot be quite certain in the absence of statistical data) that there is more of it today when the tempo of industrialization has slowed down and its wounds are largely healed. In suggesting an explanation, we must stress (what is becoming more and more apparent in other contexts), that industrialization is not a monolithic process with identical repercussions everywhere, regardless of the political, historical, and cultural conditions under which it takes place. There is no reason, for example, to expect that the social consequences of industrialization in nineteenth-century England would be similar to those in twentieth-century Soviet Union or that the latter resemble what is happening in the underdeveloped societies of the "third world." Planned and government-controlled industrialization accompanied by intense political repression and regimentation—as was the case in the U.S.S.R. in the 1930's—does not lead to the type of disruptions we know

well are taking place in Africa or Asia. Industrialization accompanied by totalitarian controls and values is not necessarily a disorganizing or liberating force which destroys the established fabric of society and creates an anomic vacuum. Industrialization in a totalitarian institutional framework can be a repressive, cohesive process that often creates more stringent social controls than the traditional ones it has replaced. Soviet industrialization might have destroyed many informal mechanisms of social control, yet produced enough new formal ones to keep social disorganization at bay. The net result has been an increase rather than a decrease of the sum total of controls over the individual. However since the death of Stalin, formal controls have weakened and economic expectations have grown. Political continuity was disrupted, creating a measure of instability and confusion that had implications for the disorientation of youth. Greater contacts with the West, and the U.S. in particular, also played their part in whetting appetites. It might even be true, as Soviet propagandists often claim, that American models of easy and criminal life, filtering through the fragments of Western mass media, also had some effect on the attitudes of Soviet youngsters, who might be as corruptible as the authorities fear them to be.[11]

We must finally consider the major Soviet theories of juvenile delinquency

---

the courtyard. Some guys were standing around there. One of them pushed B. A fight started. I stabbed somebody with my knife and ran away.' Amazing sang-froid, a stunning cynicism! 'I stabbed somebody'! Murder not for robbery or revenge but simply as a matter of course."—Arpund 'Finch' *Izvestia,* July 31, 1963, transl. *CDSP,* August 28, 1963.

[11] "Having learned from bitter experience, the officials of the agencies for safeguarding public order, when they hear of the approaching showing of a film with a provocative title [this refers to foreign crime thrillers the influence of which the article deplores—P.H.], takes steps in advance to reinforce precinct duty rosters." V. Tikunov, Russian Republic Minister for Safeguarding Public Order, "No Visa for the 'Black Mask' ", *Izvestia,* May 28, 1965, transl. *CDSP,* June 16, 1965, p. 14.

in the Soviet Union (Soviet theories of delinquency elsewhere are quite different). Their most characteristic feature is an effort to explain delinquency by locating its origins *outside* Soviet society, being constrained by the determination to avoid seriously implicating the major instituions of their society. This is the reason why Soviet analyses of juvenile delinquency (and crime in general) continue to rely on—though perhaps with less and less conviction—the concepts of "contamination" and "survivals." Both are designed to deflect blame from Soviet society by finding the sources of anti-social behavior "outside" in either the spatial or temporal sense.[12]

Contamination refers to the corrupting Western, bourgeois influences:

How can backward views and habits that are wholly extrinsic to socialist society be preserved in its midst and poison the minds of individual persons?...First of all let us note that imperialist propaganda of the 'attractions' of the so-called 'free world' and the spread of bourgeois views of indi-

vidualism exert an influence on a certain segment of the population.

As regards survivals,

Under socialism crime is not engendered by the social system itself. It 'invades' socialism from exploitative socio-economic formations and in this sense can be regarded as a survival of the past in the minds and behavior of people...In contending that egotism, venality, drunkenness and disrespect for women are 'survivals of the past' we are merely emphasizing that all these phenomena are peculiar to the preceding social-economic formations but do not arise from the nature of socialism and can have no place in our society. Survivals of the past remain in the consciousness... of people long after the fundamental social-economic causes that engendered them have disappeared.[13]

It is significant that alongside these ideologically inspired propositions the concrete findings about juvenile delinquency undermine the obligatory references to survivals and contamination. Moreover the emerging factors associated with Soviet juvenile delinquency are virtually indistinguishable from those found in the despised bourgeois societies. Only the ideologically attuned imagination could discover why factors such as the following differ from those found in capitalist societies:

Criminological studies of juvenile lawbreakers show that more than 50% of them grew up in so-called unhappy families...an investigation of minors convicted in the 1950's for hooliganism disclosed that 68% of them had lost one or both of their parents.... In many cases excessive outside demands on the time of both parents impeded the correct upbringing of juveniles who embarked on a path of lawbreaking.

---

[12] Another time-honored way of averting the criticism of the social order is to blame the individual. In the U.S. only diehard conservatives resort to this explanation, the same people who believe that poverty is the fault of the poor. Thus a recent Soviet article pointed out that "...it was not living conditions and material circumstances that prevented lawbreakers from attaining proper education and level of culture [the latter being seen as the immediate causes of their anti-social behavior—P.H.]. On the contrary, they had all the possibilities for this but did not wish to make use of them because...[they] were oriented...to drink, lead dissipated lives ...and live as parasites...the criminal... possessed in the overwhelming majority of cases every opportunity to choose an honest path." S. S. Ostroumov and V. E. Chugunov, "Study of the Criminal Personality from the Materials of Criminological Research," *Sovetskoe Gosudarstvo i Pravo*, 1965, No. 9, transl. *Soviet Review*, Summer 1966, pp. 17, 20.

[13] Theoretical conference: Anti-social phenomena, their causes and the means of combatting them, *Kommunist*, August 1966, transl. *CDSP*, September 28, 1966, p. 10.

According to selective studies, 80% of the cases of crimes by minors are related to a lack of supervision...[14]

Besides the problems of the home environment, the article also pointed out that "...lawbreaking is done primarily by juveniles who are not in school or working." Implicitly introducing the concept of relative deprivation, the same author also noted that: "One thing is characteristic of the law violations committed in socialist society: the overwhelming majority of them are not caused by material difficulties." There is also an echo of Cohen's observations about the "negativistic, malicious" attitudes of American delinquents: "The remaining lawbreakers committed their thefts for hooligan motives, out of malice or a false 'sense of adventure,' in 'following the example' of an older friend, etc."

While poverty as a source of crime was rejected, the same author observes that:

A shortage of certain goods creates a favorable medium for speculation, abuses of office and bribetaking. Cultural deprivation and a low educational level are closely linked to drunkenness, crime and other anti-social acts. An unfavorable atmosphere for molding the personalities of children and juveniles often develops in the crowded communal apartments.[15]

Another examination of Soviet juvenile delinquency follows the same pattern. After paying ritualistic homage to the notion of survivals, the article enumerates a series of factors which have their exact counterparts in American, and other Western, societies. For example, it noted that half of the crimes committed by young people occurred after 10 p.m., that the proportion of children from broken homes and those of heavy drinking parents was exceed-

ingly high among delinquents, that the educational level of delinquents lagged 2–3 years behind non-delinquents, that school drop-outs and unemployed ranked high and even that parents' trying to "satisfy their children's immoderate demands" played a part in the process. More interesting still, because of the claims of equal opportunity, was the concentration of juvenile delinquency among trade school and working class youth, who apparently face the same difficulties as their American counterparts.[16]

Despite such striking similarities at the empirical level, Soviet sociologists continue to view juvenile delinquency as intrinsically alien to their society. This often results in the paradoxical attitude of criticizing local conditions and authorities in isolation from society at large. Today more and more frequently, Soviet parents, teachers, Komsomol, or Party officials are taken to task for their unconcern or negligence toward young people. What these strictures most typically overlook is that Soviet society, not unlike some others, creates expectations faster than opportunities for their satisfaction and that expectations are more equitably distributed than the possibilities for their fulfillment.

In this sketchy survey we did not pause to assess the influences two other important institutions exert on the behavior of the young and on the development of his expectations: the family and the local community. There are indications that in recent years the cohesiveness of both has decreased. In particular the break-up of rural communities, and even rural families, has proceeded apace with so many of the younger generations leaving for the city.

[14] *Ibid.*
[15] *Ibid.*

[16] "Some Causes of Juvenile Delinquency in the U.S.S.R. and Measures to Prevent It," *Sovetskoye Gosudarstvo i Pravo*, May 1966, transl. *CDSP*, August 17, 1966, pp. 9–12.

It would be interesting to know what is the proportional contribution this group is making to delinquency. There also is sufficient evidence to show that divorce rates have increased, reflecting the growing instability of the Soviet family.

We might thus conclude that hardly any of the ascertainable factors associated with juvenile delinquency are peculiar products of the Soviet social environment. The claims of distinctivness lie elsewhere.

Discrimination—

Ethnic Minorities

Ethnic minorities and discrimination against them is a social problem of far greater gravity in the U.S. than in the Soviet Union. In part this is a result of historical facts. Although serfdom in Russia also had some debilitating effects on the peasantry, they have been less grievous and enduring than the effects of slavery on the American Negro. Also, selfdom was not based on ethnic differences and Russian peasants had the same skin color as the rest of the population, an inestimable advantage in softening the impact of cumulative social deprivation. The combination of the instituion of slavery, its consequences, and the easily discernible physical characteristics of the American Negro have created a far more serious problem in the U.S. Especially in its early phases, the Soviet system made determined efforts to provide effective legal-political safeguards to protect that rights of ethnic minorities. Under Stalin, however, there was a good deal of reshuffling and forcible resettlement of certain minorities whose political reliability was called into question. Still a pattern of friction and discrimination comparable to the treatment of Negroes in the U.S. did not develop in the Soviet Union.

There is virtually no dispute among American and Soviet commentators about the magnitude and gravity of the problems created by racial discrimination and disadvantage in the U.S. The disputes arise at the level of interpretation. From the Soviet perspective, racial discrimination, as every other social problem of American society, arises out of the nature of capitalism. There is some truth in this, although it is not the full truth. Discrimination against Negroes has had its economic benefits in the form of lower costs of labor, real estate speculation, and the overall economic exploitation of much of the Negro population. Discrimination also helped to maintain a degree of social stability by creating a sense of status superiority among the lower socio-economic strata of the white population. It is also easier to maintain belief in the overall soundness of a social system as long as most of its unappealing features are distributed predominantly among one segment of the population—as are poverty, unemployment, low level of education, crime, family instability, bad housing conditions, etc. This belief is further encouraged if the group in question is easily distinguished by external, physical characteristics, and when there is an apparent possibility to account for the plight of the group in terms of inherent, biological defects. The latter, the essence of racism, enables the rest of society to ignore the deficiencies of social institutions and facilitates shifting the responsibility to the victimized group itself. The racist argument is further fortified by the both deliberate and unintentional creation of social conditions, under which the alleged inherent defects are given institutional, environmental support. Thus, for example, the premise that Negroes are intellectually inferior resulted in their being deprived of access to good education, which in turn did create in later generations genuine handicaps, if not inherent, irremovable flaws of personality.

At present the major problems of American Negroes are not those of formal rights and legal disadvantage but informal discrimination, the cumulative results of hundreds of years of total disenfranchisement and the combination of low socio-economic status with easily distinguishable physical characteristics. There is little doubt about it: the situation of Negroes represents the most serious social problem in the U.S., and it would even if there had been no urban riots. The situation of other minorities is not much better. Puerto Ricans, American Indians, Mexican-Americans all share many of the disadvantages Negroes face. On the other hand, anti-Semitism is not a serious social problem insofar as it has not created significant disadvantages for Jews.

Perhaps it should also be added that the forms and intensity of the problem vary among the different regions of the country (rural-urban, Southern-Northern, etc.) and with the historical traditions of each region; it is also influenced by the proportion of Negroes in the population of a given locality. Variations of attitude occur in different strata of the population. In this context it might also be noted that discrimination does not invariably bring economic advantages—sometimes the opposite is true—and in many instances efforts toward integration originate with business leaders. We might also point out that, contrary to Marxist propositions, there is little, if any solidarity between the poor Negro and the poor white in the U.S. and that the white working classes are more prone to racial prejudice than are the middle or upper ones. Of course this propensity is related not to the type of occupation or income, but to levels of education and security.

The minority group which has been the most traditional target of discrimination in the Soviet Union is the Jews. While the magnitude and character of the problem has little in common with that of Negroes in the U.S., the roots of discrimination are also deep and historically determined. Soviet anti-Semitism, like race prejudice in the U.S., is primarily a popular sentiment rather than an institutionally fostered phenomenon. Yet there is also subtle governmental support of this sentiment, expressed primarily in unusually vigorous efforts to compel the cultural integration of Jews and in the equally determined efforts to liquidate Judaism as a religion. Both of these policies are, according to most Western students of the subject, more intense than the corresponding measures against other cultural-ethnic minorities and religions. In addition, informal discrimination is also said to be practiced in certain occupations and educational institutions, as well as in political leadership positions, where the number of Jews is apparently kept to a minimum. These policies are likely to have three sources. One is the lingering cultural tradition of anti-Semitism to which the leadership is not immune. In particular, there is much evidence to show that both Stalin and Khrushchev were outspokenly anti-Semitic. Secondly Jews are regarded with suspicion on political-ideological grounds, a sentiment that grows out of traditional anti-Semitism. They are considered overly individualistic, having more ethnic loyalty than loyalty to the political community or nation, Western-oriented, and worst of all, sympathetic to Israel, a pro-Western state in an area where the Soviet Union has been strenuously trying to establish its influence. Thirdly, anti-Semitic policies, even if veiled, are likely to earn some popular support for the regime in a population traditionally suspicious of, if not openly hostile, to Jews.

A more serious mistreatment of non-Jewish minority groups took place during and after World War II in the Soviet Union.

The Soviet views quoted on these minority problems are not from sociological sources. The existence, past or present, of discrimination against ethnic groups is denied by Soviet authorities and consequently it does not belong to the subjects on which sociologists express themselves or conduct research.

Characteristically, considerable time elapsed before the ouside world began to know about the mistreatment of certain ethnic minorities in the Soviet Union. Apart from the case of Jews, where official and popular discrimination often converged, discrimination against other minority groups was strictly and primarily an official matter which found spectacular expression in their deportation during and after World War II. Ethnic groups officially viewed as security risks were deported under conditions a good deal more inhuman than the correspondingly inhuman internment of Japanese-Americans by American authorities during World War II. The Soviet moves caused considerable loss of life, and in many instances "rehabilitation" was incomplete and did not result in the restoration of the territorial autonomy which the groups enjoyed prior to their deportation. A third difference between such Soviet and American "wartime emergency measures" is that in the Soviet

Union an open and critical analysis or reevaluation of these policies has not yet occurred, whereas in the United States there has been much retroactive public discussion and soul-searching concerning the treatment of the Japanese-Americans. The major Soviet admission of the true nature of the deportations came in Khrushchev's speech at the 20th Party Congress, which has never been made public in the Soviet Union. The published decrees and speeches about rehabilitation (such as those which follow) are full of characteristic official euphemisms reserved for those occasions when some unpalatable truth or major injustices perpetrated by the regime are reluctantly and partially revealed. Thus the official Soviet statements speak of "rehabilitation," "settlement," "resettlement," "reorganization," or "restoration of national autonomy," glossing over the events which preceded rehabilitation. A partial exception to this is found in the more recent decree on the Crimean Tartars, but even there we are only told about "groundless" or "sweeping" accusations which had been made against them, and hardly a word as to what actually happened to them. The decree has noted, however, that they were now living in Uzbekistan and elsewhere rather than in their native regions.

This attitude toward the past is not limited to the mistreatment of minority groups. It is a part of a broader pattern and an outlook that almost instinctively recoils from a thorough and open examination of the misdeeds and mistakes of the past, and has been revealed with particular sharpness in the carefully controlled, qualified, and halting process of de-Stalinization. The concrete manifestations of this attitude have ranged from a total Orwellian silence (consignment to the "memory hole"), to curt, impatient and irritable or euphemistic admissions of "errors," and the refusal to expend much time and energy on the reexamination or reevaluation of past polices, even those which had been quietly abandoned. Stalin is, of course, a partial exception, and at any rate, Khrushchev tried to place the responsibility for the mistreatment of these ethnic groups upon him alone (along with many other posthumous accusations against the once infallible leader). As long as the Party persists in claiming infallibility, even the retroactive admission of serious errors and injustices is avoided, since it is bound to raise more questions than can be answered without some embarrassment. Above all, the full revelation of the injustices of the past could interfere with maintaining a sense of historical continuity and could cast doubts on the legitimacy of the prevailing system and its leadership.

The article by Pipes dealing with various Soviet minorities analyzes the paradoxical developments which have taken place with regard to Russification and presents an overview of the official policies toward the non-Russian nationalities in general. Of particular interest is the resistance shown toward Russification and the tenaciousness of ethnic identification.

In conclusion it might be worth noting that there has been much evidence in recent years that Soviet people are also susceptible to color prejudice. This has come to light following numerous complaints and incidents involving

African students studying in the U.S.S.R. The popular animosity toward them has also been reported by many Western visitors and exchange students, in addition to the writings of Africans themselves. Apparently their hostile stereotypes have much in common with those applied to colored people in the U.S. and elsewhere.

MINORITIES
IN THE U.S.:

The American View

Employment, Income and
the Ordeal of the Negro Family

DANIEL P. MOYNIHAN

The civil rights revolution of our time is entering a new phase, and a new crisis. In the first phase, the demands of the Negro American were directed primarily to those rights associated with the idea of Liberty: the right to vote, the right to free speech, the right to free assembly. In the second phase, the movement must turn to the issue of Equality. This dualism, which has always been present in the civil rights movement, simply reflects the dualism of American democracy. From the outset American society has been committed to the twin ideals of Liberty and Equal-

Reprinted by permission of Daedalus, Journal of the American Academy of Arts and Sciences, Boston, Massachusetts. From Daniel P. Moynihan, "Employment, Income and the Ordeal of the Negro Family," Daedalus (Winter 1965), pp. 745–748, 751, 755, 758, 759, 760–762, 764.

ity. These are not the same things. Nor do they appeal to different persons with the same force. The Declaration of Independence began with a proposition about Equality, but the word does not appear in the Constitution until almost a century later. One reason, surely, is that at the time the Constitution was adopted almost one American in five was a slave.

...As long as Negro demands concentrated on issues of liberty they enjoyed the unquestioned support of the centers of power in American society. Even those who resisted did so in practice, rather than on principle: no one can successfully challenge the principle of liberty in the United States at this time. However, as demands turn toward those associated with equality, this support can only dissipate. Several problems are involved. The first is that of incomprehension. Great portions of the

American middle class simply do not understand the nature of the demand for equality. Typically, they assume such demands are met when equal opportunity is provided. Thus Negro Americans have found their staunchest white allies among newer middle-class groups who for varying periods were excluded from the competitions of American life by quotas and other techniques, but who once admitted were quickly successful. But equality, as a fundamental democratic disposition, goes beyond equal opportunity to the issue of equal results. Here middle-class support begins to dissipate, principles are not clear, concensus does not exist.

Given the ethnic group structure of American life, equality for Negro Americans means that they will have open to them the full range of American economic, social, and political life, and that within the pattern of endeavor that they choose, having assessed the comparative advantages of time, place, and cultural endowment, they will have a fully comparable share of the successes, no less than of the small winners and of the outright failures. The test of American society will be whether it can work out arrangements so that this happens more or less naturally for Negro Americans, as it has more or less naturally happened for other groups. The rules are unwritten, but well enough understood. A certain amount of Freemasonry is not only permitted, but necessary. Some concessions are in order from other groups. It is fatal to make an across-the-board assault: highly developed activities are highly resistant to intrusion; the less developed an activity is, the more opportunity it provides for newcomers. More than a generation must pass before the outcome will be clear. It will be uneven, but nonetheless acceptable.

From the very outset, the principal measure of progress toward equality will be that of employment. It is the primary source of individual or group identity. In America what you do is what you are: to do nothing is to be nothing; to do little is to be little. The equations are implacable and blunt, and ruthlessly public.

For the Negro American it is already, and will continue to be, the master problem. It is the measure of white *bona fides*. It is the measure of Negro competence, and also of the competence of American society. Most importantly, the linkage between problems of employment and the range of social pathology that afflicts the Negro community is unmistakable. Employment not only controls the present for the Negro American; but, in a most profound way, it is creating the future as well.

The current situation and recent trends pose a problem of interpretation which may not have been much noticed. It is that in terms of employment and income and occupational status it is quite possible the Negro community is moving in two directions, or rather that two Negro communities are moving in opposite ones. Obviously such a development would be concealed—cancelled out—in aggregate statistics that list all "nonwhites" together. Anyone with eyes to see can observe the emergence of a Negro middle class that is on the whole doing very well. This group has, if anything, rather a preferred position in the job market. A nation catching up with centuries of discrimination has rather sharply raised the demand for a group in short supply. One would be hard put to describe a person with better job opportunities than a newly minted Negro Ph.D. In a wide and expanding range of employment, there would seem to be no question that opportunities for some are rather more equal than for others, and that for the first time in our history the Negro American is the beneficiary of such arrangements. These facts are reflected in the steadily rising level of Negro aspirations and in efforts by the Negro to acquire the education and training that are the *cartes d'identité* of the Great American Middle Class.

At the same time there would also seem to be no question that opportunities for a large mass of Negro workers in the lower ranges of training and education have not been improving, that in many ways the circumstances of these workers relative to the white work force have grown worse. It would appear that this in turn has led to, or been accompanied by, a serious weakening of the Negro social structure, specifically of the Negro family. It could be that this situation has gone on so long that the Negro potential is already impaired; in any event it would hardly seem possible to doubt that if it persists much longer the capacity of the Negro community to make the most of its opportunities will be grievously diminished. Measures that would have worked twenty years ago may not work today, and surely will not work twenty years hence. A crisis of commitment is at hand.

The moral grandeur of the Negro revolution makes it more than normally difficult to speak of these matters; yet it demands that we do so. The plain physical courage which the Negro leaders and their followers have shown in recent years ought at least to summon in the rest of us the moral courage to inquire just how bad things may have become while we were occupied elsewhere. It is probable that such inquiry will be resented by some and misused by others. So be it. The important fact is that it is not likely to cause any great harm if things turn out not to be so bad as they appeared. On the other hand, if present indications are correct, the only hope we have is to state them and face up to them.

UNEMPLOYMENT

The primary measure of the problem of Negro employment is the rate of unemployment. It is here that the deterioration of the Negro position is most conspicuous. What has happened is that over the past thirty-five years the rate of Negro unemployment, from being rather less than that of whites, has steadily moved to the point where it is now regularly more than twice as great, while, of course, the overall unemployment rate in the United States has remained higher than that of any other industrial democracy in the world. (As I write, unemployment in Japan is less than one per cent.)

The decennial census shows the steady rise in the ratio.

Unemployment Rates	1930	1940	1950
White	6.6%	14.1%	4.5%
Nonwhite	6.1%	16.9%	7.9%
Ratio, nonwhite to white	.92	1.20	1.76

...In contrast to the experience of unemployment, the occupational patterns of Negro workers have clearly improved over the past three and one-half

	1930	1940	1950	1960
Per cent of Nonwhite Civilian Labor Force which is in the South	71.9	72.8	63.0	53.3
Per cent of Experienced Labor Force which is in Agriculture				
White	19.2	16.1	11.4*	6.2
Nonwhite	36.5	30.7	19.5*	9.1

* Based on those employed rather than total labor force.

decades. Slowly they are coming into line with the white work force; but they have a long way to go. The most dramatic and important movement has been out of agriculture. Over one-third of the Negroes were in agriculture in 1930; less than one-tenth in 1960. This movement has been accompanied by migration northward: approximately 70 per cent of the Negro workers were in the South in 1930 and about 50 per cent in 1960.

...The patterns of Negro employment are directly related to those of income. Negro income has risen substantially in recent years, as has employment. But the gap between Negro and white income is not closing; it is widening. And the problems that follow are made more savage by a soaring population.

The principal problem, and the proper focus of public concern, is that of the Negro male worker. His plight does not seem to improve. Income rises. Year-round, full-time workers gained almost $1,000 in the short period from 1957 to 1963. But positions relative to white workers did not improve significantly, nor did the chances of being a year-round, full-time worker.

...The cumulative result of unemployment and low income, and probably also of excessive dependence upon the income of women, has produced an unmistakable crisis in the Negro family, and raises the serious question of whether or not this crisis is beginning to create conditions which tend to reinforce the cycle that produced it in the first instance. The crisis would probably exist in any event, but it becomes acute in the context of the extraordinary rise in Negro population in recent years.

...A Negro child born to a large family is more likely to be reared in a broken family. Such are the strains of rearing large families with marginal incomes and unemployed fathers. In the urban U.S. in 1960 there were 154,000 one-child nonwhite families headed by married men age twenty to twenty-four with wives present. There were 19,000 such families headed by women separated from their husbands, one-eighth as many as whole families. There were a similar number of such husband-wife families with four or more children, 152,000, but there were 39,000 headed by married women separated from their husbands—one-fourth the number with both husband and wife. Poor families break under the responsibilities imposed by a large number of children. Children from these families become the nation's draft rejectees, because— among other reasons—they have spent a basic learning period in an institution too large for its resources and often with one of the instructors missing.

Poverty is both the cause and the result. In 1963 the median income of nonwhite families was $3,465, about half the $6,548 median of whites. The magnitude of the income gap is illustrated by the fact that incomes were lower in nonwhite families with employed heads than in white families with unemployed heads. What the long trend of the gap will be is not, of course, clear, but from 1960 to 1963 the nonwhite median family income as a per cent of white declined from 55 to 53.

In March 1964 nearly 20 million persons fourteen years and over were living in families with annual incomes under $3,000. Nonwhite persons accounted for a quarter of those living in such families. But nearly half of all nonwhite youths under fourteen are living in families with incomes under $3,000. Nonwhites make up 40 per cent of the children living in such families. Using a flexible scale that relates required family income to family size, the Department of Health, Education and Welfare has estimated that 60 per cent of the Negro children in America today are growing up in poverty-stricken families. In these circumstances the stability of the Negro family, still grievously impaired by the heritage of slavery and segregation, would seem to have been weakened still further.

...The first effect is simply that of broken homes. Nearly a quarter of Negro women living in cities who have ever married are divorced, separated, or living apart from their husbands. These rates have been steadily rising and are approaching one-third in, for example, New York City. Almost one-quarter of nonwhite families are headed by a woman, a rate that also continues to rise. At any given moment some 36 per cent of Negro children are living in homes where one or both parents are missing. It is probable that not much more than one-third of Negro youth reach eighteen having lived all their lives with both their parents. The second effect of the deterioration of the position of the Negro male worker has been a sharp increase in welfare dependency among Negro families. It would appear that a majority of Negro youth sooner or later are supported by the Aid to Families of Dependent Children program. In 1961 not quite half of all children receiving AFDC aid were Negro (1,112,106) and half of these were in cities of 250,000 population, where they made up three-quarters of the AFDC recipients. Nonwhites account for almost two-thirds of the increase in AFDC families between 1948 and 1961. The third effect that must be associated with the deteriorating position of the Negro male is the phenomenon Kenneth Clark has described as the tangle of pathology—the complex of interrelated disabilities and disadvan-

tages that feed on each other and seem to make matters steadily worse for the individuals and communities caught up in it.

The cycle begins and ends with the children. A disastrous number begin their lives with no fathers present. Many, in some communities nearly half or more, are illegitimate. In 1963, 24 per cent of all nonwhite births in the nation were illegitimate. Too few live their early years in the presence of a respected and responsible male figure. The mothers, as often as not magnificent women, go to work too soon, if indeed they ever stop. This situation is getting worse, not better. In March 1959, 29.3 per cent of nonwhite women with children under six years of age were in the work force. By March 1964 this proportion had increased to 36.1 per cent! At that moment 56.7 per cent of nonwhite women with children six to seventeen years of age were in the work force—a higher percentage than that of nonwhite women with *no* children under eighteen years of age, which was 50.5 per cent. Although these movements were matched among white women, they clearly have gotten out of proportion among Negroes.

...Obviously, the most pressing question for American social policy is whether the essential first step for resolving the problem of the Negro American is to provide such a measure of full employment of Negro workers that the impact of unemployment on family structure is removed. The assumption would be that only then will the wide and increasing range and level of social services available to the Negro American have their full effect, and only then will there be a Negro population that not only has equal opportunities in the American economy, but is equal to those opportunities.

MINORITIES

IN THE U.S.:

The Soviet View

Black Ghettos

E. NITOBURG

Harlem, Watts—the names are associated with outbursts of Negro unrest and resentment, with the shocking violence with which the American racialists quelled them. The past tense is not altogether appropriate. "The black ghetto," warns the New York *Newsweek*, "remains a timebomb ticking at the heart of every major city." Even more ominous is the warning given by Dr. Kenneth B. Clark, Negro professor, that the Negro ghettos "now represent a nuclear stockpile which can annihilate the very foundations of America." How did these "nuclear stockpiles" come into being and what is the present situation in America's Negro ghettos?

*   *   *

After the Civil War and the abolition of slavery in the United States (1861–65) 91 per cent of the American Negroes were living in the South, almost all of them in the rural South. Fifty years later, on the eve of the First World War, 27 per cent of them were already living in cities, but the rest were still

From E. Nitoburg, New Times, *Moscow (July 12, 1967), pp. 19–21.*

working the land their slave forefathers had worked before them. World War I and industry's urgent need for millions of cheap working hands spurred mass Negro migration to the cities of the North. By 1940 nearly half the Negro population (47.9 per cent) was already living in cities (urbanites then constituted 57 per cent of the total U.S. population).

The city-ward trend observed in the first third of the 20th century gained impetus during the Second World War and the postwar period. From 9 million persons engaged in agriculture in 1940 the figure has now dropped to 4.5 million. The number of farms dropped by nearly half between 1940 and 1965, and more than half in the South, for the prolonged agrarian crisis is bringing the rural Negro population to ruin. The number of Negro farm owners has dropped in this period to one-fourth. The cotton fields, once worked by thousands of farm hands, are now harvested by machines.

The mass exodus of the Negroes to the cities has wrought a radical change in the social and occupational composition of the Negro population. Less than 8 per cent of the able-bodied Negro population is now employed in agriculture. The bourgeoisie and the comparatively prosperous high-salaried Negroes constitute no more than 3 per cent. Ninety-five per cent are wage earners (the figure for whites is 80 per cent).

About nine-tenths of the Negro labor force belongs to the working class in the widest sense of the term. Two-thirds are industrial, transport or building workers. The rest are engaged in the service sphere, agriculture, trade, etc. Generally Negroes are employed in the hardest and lowest-paid jobs.

In the past 25 years the flight of the Negroes from the South has assumed unparalleled proportions. Today a good half of the U.S. Negro population is already living in the North and West. Their number in New York has long since topped the one-million mark, in Chicago it is nearly one million, in Philadelphia, Washington, Detroit and Los Angeles it is about half a million each. Negroes constitute one-sixth the population of New York, one-fifth the population of San Francisco and Los Angeles, more than one-quarter that of Chicago, Philadelphia, Detroit and Cleveland, one-third that of Baltimore and two-thirds that of Washington. Unlike the prewar migration, large numbers of Negroes have now moved to towns in the South as well, owing to the rapid development there of military and related industries in the period 1940–60.

This mass migration of Negroes to the towns has resulted in a higher level of urbanization among them than among whites. The towns now account for 70 per cent of the total U.S. population and about 75 per cent of the Negro population.

*   *   *

The rise of the "black ghettos" was connected with the urbanization of the Negro population. There were freed Negroes living in the towns even before the Civil War, but after the abolition of slavery the number of urban Negroes rose perceptibly. In the old Southern towns the dwellings of the Negroes were scattered, for most of them went into service and found quarters near the homes of the white families they worked for. Under the long-established Southern tradition of race etiquette the Negroes "knew their place."

In the Northern towns settlement followed racial lines for many generations. Whites lived in one section, Negroes in another and generally worse section. This division was as a rule laid down by municipal regulations, which in many cases rested on state laws. Most of these segregation laws were adopted towards the end of the 19th and at the beginning of the 20th centuries.

When in 1915–17 the U.S. Supreme Court ruled the local laws of this type unconstitutional, they were replaced by so-called "restrictive covenants" between landlords and real estate brokers under which all parties to them undertook not to sell or rent houses in white residential areas to Negroes or persons of mixed blood. Every person who bought real estate became a party to such a covenant. Though the segregation laws were annulled, the "restrictive covenants" were recognized as legal until the end of the 1940's.

Little by little, through the operation of the segregation laws and the "restrictive covenants," thousands and millions of Negroes were herded into separate residential areas which soon became overcrowded and unsanitary areas of poverty, unemployment and race unrest. By the time of the Second World War every major city had its Negro ghetto. In New York it was Harlem, in Chicago—the West Side, in Detroit—Brewster, in Cleveland—Hough.

In 1948, the Supreme Court, responding to pressure from the Negro movement and democratic forces, ruled that courts could no longer enforce the "restrictive covenants." The decision did not, however, shake the system set up by them, which still maintains the "color bar" in American cities. In Chicago alone, in the space of two years, racialists blew up 167 houses bought or built by Negroes outside their ghetto area. The unwritten laws of racialism are stronger than Supreme Court decisions.

Segregation has strong backing from the National Real Estate Association, the Property and Home Owners Protection Association, business and other firms owning property in the Negro ghettos. The reason why is easy to understand: in Harlem alone white businessmen rake in 346 million dollars in profit from the 3,898 shops they own in the area.

Big Business is the true owner of the "black ghettos." Harlem, for instance, is in effect the property of big insurance companies, like Metropolitan Life, and of banks conducting real estate operations, which refuse to finance the purchase, repairs or construction of houses whose owners disregard the "restrictive covenants."

Race discrimination in hiring practices and in payment puts at least 13,000–14,000 million dollars in superprofits into the safes of the American monopolies annually. Discrimination in housing likewise yields immense superprofits. Nor is this the only role the black ghetto plays. The difference in pay for whites and blacks is used to split the American working class, and the existence of the ghettos widens the gulf.

The same banks and corporations determine the policies of the Federal government, its housing policy included. The U.S. Commission on Civil Rights stressed in its reports for 1961 and 1963 that responsibility for the continual violation of the Supreme Court decision of 1948 on the "restrictive covenants" lies not only with "the real estate brokers, builders, and mortgage finance institutions," but with the Federal authorities which "are still promoters of residential segregation." Numerous facts are cited in the reports showing that the federal and local authorities encourage residential segregation instead of stopping it, help to preserve the Negro ghettos rather than abolish them.

*   *   *

In view of the anarchy of production prevailing under capitalism, the growth of the urban population and of big industrial centers has led to the formation in the U.S. of close clusters of cities or "urbanized areas." Each consists of a big "central city" surrounded by dozens of smaller economically related satellite towns. Their number came in 1960 to 212. And in them resides nearly two-thirds of the country's population.

An important feature of the "urbanized areas" is their centrifugal tendency: industry and population are flowing away from the "central cities" and tending to become concentrated in the suburbs and satellite towns. The population increase in the suburban zones in the fifties and sixties has been nearly fourfold that of the "central cities." Among the reasons for the shift away from the latter (besides the growing number of industrial enterprises in the suburbs) is the big difference in the price of land, high taxes, contamination of the air of big towns with industrial waste products and exhaust gases, noise, overcrowding, transport difficulties. Possession of motorcars has accelerated the shift to the suburbs.

All this is so, but the major factor is the policy of residential segregation. It is no accident that the Negroes have very little part in the mass exodus to the suburbs. In the first 60 years of the present century the percentage of Negroes in the central districts of the present 212 "urbanized areas" rose from 6.5 to 17, whereas in the suburbs it dropped from 9 to 4.6. That most Negroes cannot afford to buy a plot of land or a car is not the only reason for this. White homeowners do not want to have Negro neighbors and to prevent it take even physical action. As the Civil Rights Commission noted in one of its reports, housing "seems to be the one commodity in the American market that is not freely available on equal terms to everyone who can afford to pay."

The white exodus from the central districts is accompanied by a Negro influx from the Southern states. This is clearly shown by the figures on the 12 major "urbanized areas" to which Negroes migrate from the South: New York, Los Angeles, Chicago, Philadelphia, Detroit, Baltimore, Cleveland, St. Louis, Washington, Boston, San Francisco, Pittsburgh. In these twelve is concentrated one-third of the entire Negro population. American sociologists H. Sharp and L. F. Schnore have estimated that in ten years (1950 to 1960) the central districts of these areas lost over 2 million white residents to the suburbs and acquired 1,800,000 new Negro residents.

Sometimes Negroes are able to move into the homes abandoned by the white who can afford to fly from the city slums to the suburbs, but this does not lead to "integration." The changing racial composition of the "central cities" does not lead to the disappearance of their ghetto. Of 100 big U.S. cities, says American sociologist R. L. Morrill, not one but had a Negro ghetto in 1965.

Far from disappearing, the black ghettos are expanding. Since discrimination and low incomes deprive the Negroes of the choice, they are obliged to settle in Negro neighborhoods. In Watts, Los Angeles' Negro ghetto of sad memory, Negroes constituted 77 per cent of the residents in 1960 and 98 per cent in 1965. The centers of Chicago, in the North, and of Oakland, in the West, have already become predominantly Negro. The ghettos are spreading out. The Civil Rights Commission reports that "there is an ever-increasing concentration of non-whites in racial ghettos, largely in the decaying centers of our cities—while a 'white noose' of new suburban housing grows up around them."

Contrary to American propaganda claims on the "progress" of desegregation, the inkspots of the ghettos on the maps of American cities are steadily spreading. In the past decades, according to K. E. Taeuber, B. Weissbourd, I. F. Kain and other American researchers, residential segregation has increased substantially. Which prompted the *New York World Telegram and Sun* to write recently that if desegregation continues at the same rate as in the past ten years it will take America roughly another thousand years to achieve a desegregated society.

*   *   *

The Negro ghetto is often described as a prison without walls. Its residents are indeed surrounded by an invisible wall of alienation. Though they have not been able to escape from its confines yet, the struggle for abolition of the shameful system of race discrimination and segregation does not subside for a single day.

Revolts in the "black ghettos"—those spontaneous explosions of accumulated resentment—show that the Negro movement has shifted its center of gravity from the Southern states to the big Northern cities. Many leaders of the movement are well aware of this. Early last year Martin Luther King's Southern Christian Leadership Conference moved its headquarters to Chicago, and after careful preparation jointly with other Negro organizations and with trade unions, proclaimed "war on the slums." This campaign, whose activities include the boycotting of schools and firms practicing segregation, meetings, demonstrations and protest marches designed to compel local authorities to abolish the slums, swept many cities in the summer and autumn of last year. Since Chicago remained its center, it came to be called the Chicago movement.

To quiet Negro discontent at least a little the government introduced a new civil rights bill in Congress last spring, this time including clauses on abolition of the race barrier in housing. But it has not yet been passed. The Senate has in effect put this bill in cold storage.

Racism, events show, has strong roots. The soil it grows in is primarily economic. Capitalist America may make some concessions to the Negroes where elementary democratic rights are concerned, but will never voluntarily give up one of its chief sources of profit—race discrimination in the economic sphere.

The experience they acquired in the last ten years and the growing maturity of their movement has led the Negroes to rely less on the "kindness of the overlords" and more on their own strength and determination. This is admitted by American and foreign observers alike.

"... Johnson's new bill," writes the *Paris-Match* weekly, "has met with indifference, irony or hostility among the Negro community." The American Negroes, comments *Le Monde,* "are no longer content to beg for a hypothetical 'second-class integration.' They bluntly demand equality, and not only juridical but economic and political."

It is not new laws, which more often than not remain mere scraps of paper, that the Negro movement now demands ever more loudly and determinedly, but the enforcement of already existing laws.

The Negro Ghetto in Revolt

A U.S. Senator has described the present Negro unrest as America's "gravest domestic crisis" since the Civil War a hundred years ago. Indeed, what is happening in many U.S. cities these days has no parallel in the past. At times it is as if a new Civil War had broken out between the rulers supported by all that is reactionary in American society and the most oppressed and downtrodden section of the nation.

An editorial, New Times, *Moscow, No. 32 (August, 9, 1967), pp. 1–2.*

The unrest has gripped more than 50 cities, many of which look as if they had been attacked by a hostile army. Scores of Negroes killed, thousands wounded, thousands more arrested—tanks patrolling the streets—machine-gun posts at street intersections—block after block of smouldering ruins. The order established in the police-and-troop-invaded Negro ghettos is reminiscent of an occupation regime.

Elsewhere in this issue we print an Open Letter to President Johnson and an Appeal to the American People,

Black and White, published in June by
the Communist Party, U.S.A., which
throw light on the causes of the present
upheaval. The Open Letter shows that
the conflict rending capitalist America,
though racial in form, has deep socio-
political roots. The courageous struggle
for civil rights waged by the Negro
people cannot be separated from their
legitimate demand that the slums and
chronic unemployment be abolished,
that segregation be abolished in schools,
that the entire system of oppression of
the Negroes, which has been a hallmark
of America for more than 300 years, be
extirpated. Desperation accumulated
through the decades and multiplied by
bitter disappointment with the policies
of the Johnson Administration, once so
lavish with its promises to the Negroes,
is what makes the present racial conflict in the U.S.A. so sharp and irreconcilable.

Needless to say the crisis is aggravated by the war in Vietnam. It is not
only a matter of the thinking Negroes'
indignation at the use of their people
as cannon fodder in this war waged by
U.S. imperialism to enslave another people. The Negroes can see that the
Vietnam war, which swallows up anything from $20,000–30,000 million an-
nually, is crushing all their hopes of
winning any improvement, either political or material, in their condition. As
Martin Luther King said last spring,
the Vietnam war "has diverted attention from the civil rights movement. We
must face the fact that the war has
strengthened the forces of reaction in
our country and excited hatred and
violence among our people. The 'great
society' has been shot down on the bat-
tlefield of Vietnam."

The growing protest movement
against the Vietnam war among the
millions of Negroes is unquestionably
one of the main reasons why U.S. im-

perialism is dealing with the black
ghetto rebels so ruthlessly.

The Communist Party's Open Letter
points to another fact that should alert
world opinion when it declares that
"conspiracy is afoot in our land to provoke and slaughter militant Negroes."
The facts offer incontrovertible evidence
of the existence of such a conspiracy
among the U.S. reactionaries who
quake in the face of the determination
displayed by the Negroes but who know
no other way of resolving racial and
national problems than through fascist-
type terror and violence. It is not by
chance that all reactionaries from yesterday's "liberals" to the Birchites and
the Ku Klux Klan have joined forces in
hurling invective at the Negroes and
urging the authorities to discard the
"kid gloves" and strike a blow at the
Negro movement from which it would
not be able to recover for a long time
to come.

The White House has heeded this
advice. The President set up a special
committee of inquiry. To divert attention from the real conspiracy of the
reaction, rumors were passed around
about a Negro "conspiracy" to overthrow the existing system. The FBI set
to work looking for "proof." A drastic
law against "outside agitators" was
hastily put through Congress to prevent
civil rights workers from crossing state
lines. It is by no means excluded that
the next step will be to shift the blame
from the appalling conditions of millions of U.S. Negroes to some malicious
"agitators" out to disturb the peace in
Negro neighborhoods. But few, one
should think, are gullible enough in our
time to be taken in by this hoax.

It is in place to recall that the agitator version was publicly refuted last
year by the present Assistant Secretary
of State Nicholas Katzenbach, then
Attorney-General. Last August, address-

ing a Senate subcommittee investigating the causes of race clashes, he said that the true agitators were "named disease and despair, joblessness and hopelessness, rat-infested housing and long impacted cynicism." He firmly discounted the assertions that riots were fomented by "Communists or black nationalists or terrorists"; they were the product of "generations of indifference by all the American people to the rot and rust and mold which we have allowed to eat into the core of our cities."

Apart from the clumsy attempt to shift the responsibility from the ruling classes on to all the American people, Katzenbach's admission does credit to his insight.

The rampant racism in the United States has evoked indignation throughout the world. With few (but indicative) exceptions, the press and the public condemn the policy of provocation pursued by the U.S. authorities. Particularly sharp is the criticism coming from Africa, Asia, Latin America and other areas swept by the national-liberation movement. Nor could it be otherwise considering the supercilious arrogance with which the United States presumes to teach other peoples "democracy" and "respect for the individual." The fact is, however, that whereas the majority of the African peoples have won political freedom and national independence, the U.S. Negroes, as Martin Luther King put it, are still compelled to fight for the right to be considered human beings, for the right to sit down next to a white man and drink a cup of coffee.

Together with the dirty war in Vietnam, Washington's other war at home is bound to undermine the prestige of the U.S.A. still more in the world arena. Many American political leaders are aware of this. Senator Morton, for instance, is worried that what is happening in U.S. cities might spell national bankruptcy for the United States and loss of leadership in the Western world. But even if it realizes the threat implicit in the Negro unrest, the imperialist bourgeoisie in power is incapable of finding a solution to the country's most pressing social problem and knows of no other recourse than brute force.

The bloody clashes in America's cities once again show how varied and far-reaching for the United States are the consequences of the war it is waging in distant Vietnam. Americans with common sense see that an end to this war could help to alleviate tensions at home as well. What the Negroes want is not more promises but tangible steps to improve their condition.

MINORITIES

IN THE U.S.S.R.:

The American View

The State of Soviet Jewry

MAURICE FRIEDBERG

According to a theory currently fashionable among Western Sovietologists, the abyss that separates the Soviet Union from the United States is gradually narrowing. It has even been suggested that we should speak of a gap rather than of an abyss, and that, if all goes well, the two societies will ultimately converge to the point where they will differ in little but ritualistic nomenclature: the one continuing to call itself "socialist," the other "capitalist."

Whatever the merits of this theory, it does not seem to hold for the Jews in the two countries. As time progresses, the Soviet Jewish community drifts further and further apart from the rest of world Jewry—so much so that at present it is the Western Jews, among all faiths, who can speak with most justification of their separated brethren and pray that this separation be only temporary.

Merely forty years ago, the Jewish community in the U.S.S.R. was only

From Maurice Friedberg, "The State of Soviet Jewry," Commentary *(January, 1965), pp. 38–43. Reprinted from* Commentary, *by permission; copyright* © *1965 by the American Jewish Committee.*

superficially different from Jewish communities everywhere—whether in Poland, Hungary, Rumania; whether in the United States, Argentina, or Palestine. The *shtetl* culture, as American anthropologists have just recently discovered, transcended national frontiers. Until World War II most Soviet Jews still lived within the confines of the Czarist Pale of Settlement in the Western provinces of European Russia. Ignoring the official atheist propaganda, they continued to attend shabby synagogues led by aging rabbis or pious Jews past retirement age and equipped with brittle, yellow prayerbooks printed under the Czars. In spite of the much advertised campaigns for agricultural resettlement, including the abortive Birobidzhan experiment (which apparently tried to channel Zionist sentiments into an acceptable Soviet alternative), most of the Jews of Russia remained in their traditional occupations, except that the petty storekeepers of Czarist times entered the lower echelons of the state bureaucracy. To be sure, the Hebrew language was under a cloud, but so were the other languages of liturgy—Latin, Arabic, and even Old Church Slavonic. It is also true that

Hebrew culture in general, which had experienced a rebirth in Russia shortly before the Revolution, was withering away. (The Habimah Theater, whose "godfather" was Stanislavsky, was only barely rescued by the intercession of Gorki and allowed to emigrate to Palestine.) But *Yiddish* culture did not suffer a similar fate: most of Russia's Jews continued to speak the language; there was a wide network of Yiddish schools; there were several Yiddish newspapers, magazines, and scholarly journals; and there were a number of Yiddish theaters, including Mikhoel's famous Moscow ensemble.

By the eve of World War II, some of these cultural and religious institutions had disappeared. In part this was due to the natural processes of acculturation, and in part to the effort to hasten the assimilation of Jews into "supranational" Soviet life. No Jewish institutions using the Russian language were permitted to take the place of the declining Yiddish institutions. Like other ethnic groups, the Jews were recognized only as a linguistic community; their religion was regarded as merely another variety of the "opiate of the masses" whose continued existence might temporarily have to be tolerated, but was in no way to be encouraged.

During World War II, Russian Jews were swept back into the mainstream of Jewish history by the German invasion. Having contributed their share of blood both to the Nazi holocaust and the Russian war effort, the remnant of Russian Jewry suffered yet another blow in the postwar period. Under Stalin's directives all Jewish institutions, including the wartime Jewish Anti-Fascist Committee, were shut down and most of their leaders, including the faithful Stalinists among them, were killed. The victims of the infamous "anti-cosmopolitan" witch-hunts of the late 1940's were for the most part "assimilated"

Jews who were prominent in Russian cultural life; in their hour of disgrace their Slavic pseudonyms were stripped from them and their shameful Semitic names revealed—a procedure, incidentally, followed by Soviet courts to this day. The Jewish community of the Soviet Union was terrified at the prospect of a show trial of a group of prominent doctors who were to be unmasked as agents of an American-Zionist conspiracy to murder Soviet leaders: the plot was allegedly masterminded by the Joint Distribution Committee, which was still very active in relief work in Eastern Europe, though not in the U.S.S.R. Only Stalin's death in 1953 saved these men—and perhaps the entire Soviet Jewish community—from execution or banishment to concentration camps. If the last seems extreme, it should be remembered that deportations of entire national groups were not unknown in Soviet Russia—it had already happened to the Kalmyks, the Chechens, the Ingushi, and the Volga Germans. Subsequently Stalin's successors freely admitted and duly denounced such acts as "violations of Socialist legality" of which they, high-ranking leaders under Stalin, had allegedly been completely unaware.

The events following Stalin's death revived hope among Russia's Jews and led to a bettering of their general situation. Together with the rest of the population, Soviet Jews today enjoy a considerably higher standard of living than they had a decade ago; moreover, police terror has been significantly relaxed and there is somewhat more personal freedom. The specifically *Jewish* hopes of the Soviet Jews, however, have not come true and they continue to be marked men in the society. Since the Soviet state and the average Soviet citizen regard the Jews as a "nationality" rather than as another religious group, it is useless for the individual Jew to abandon his faith or even to convert. He will still be marked as a Jew by his name or physical appearance, or, if these allow him to "pass," by his internal passport, which every Soviet citizen must produce—when applying for a job, or admission to a school, or a marriage license, or an apartment—and which states that he is a Jew "by nationality." Only children of mixed marriages have the option of choosing the "nationality" of either parent for their passport. There has been some talk of replacing this document with a labor card which would contain no information about the bearer's "nationality," but at present every Soviet citizen still consists, as did his forefathers in Imperial Russia, of "body, soul, and passport."

Numerous studies, moreover, point to a strong pattern of public anti-Jewish discrimination in the USSR. While a number of Jews can be found in various government bodies, including the Supreme Soviet—and even here they are seriously under-represented—it should be remembered that these are purely honorific assemblies. A recent article in *Political Affairs*, the intellectual journal of the American Communist party, pointed out that a large percentage of Soviet Jews are party members; it failed to mention that nominal membership in the party is virtually automatic in a variety of purely technical jobs, and that under Khrushchev no Jews at all were left in the party's *apparat*, which is the real seat of power. Similarly, only two or three Jews remain in the upper echelons of the armed forces —all of them survivors of prewar years—and there are almost none in the diplomatic service, where Jews were once numerous. Jews are still very prominent in the artistic and technical intelligentsia, but most of them established their reputations many years ago. And if, as Soviet apologists like to point

out, there are many Jews among the country's lawyers and doctors, it is also true that in the USSR these are poorly paid professions which entail little prestige and are dominated by women.

A recent study by Nicholas DeWitt, a leading authority on the Soviet labor force, indicates that there is marked discrimination against Jews in the admission policies of institutions of higher learning. DeWitt's findings are corroborated by the testimony of Western scholars and students who have returned from lengthy stays in the Soviet Union under the terms of cultural exchange agreements. Thus with both roads to advancement—the party and the university—closed to them, the younger generation of Soviet Jews now constitutes the one major exception to the pattern of upward social mobility in the Soviet Union. Indeed, the recent trials in which one-hundred and forty persons, most of them Jews, were sentenced to death for embezzlement, speculation in foreign currency, or black market activities point (among other things) to this loss of status. Many of the condemned were convicted of petty offenses, for which they would hardly have risked the death penalty had they not been spurred on by economic necessity or the lack of better opportunities. It is also worth noting that not a single one of their non-Jewish accomplices within the power structure—party bureaucrats, police officials, etc.—was punished with similar severity.

The Jews in the Soviet Union are the victims not only of "official" discrimination; periodically, there are outbreaks of "popular" anti-Semitism as well. Among the more recent were cases of blood-libel in Georgia and Uzbekistan, attacks on synagogues, and the distribution of anti-Semitic leaflets. As a rule these outbreaks are not reported in the Soviet press, which, however, never fails to inform its readers of anti-Semitic incidents in the West such as the practice of defacing synagogues with swastikas that broke out several years ago, or the activities of the American Nazi Party, which are presented as evidence of the resurgence of fascism. One of the principal grievances of the Soviet Jews during the Khrushchev era was that the government, while officially professing its abhorrence of "popular" anti-Semitism, did nothing to combat it—unlike Lenin's government in the 1920's—although the need for such a campaign was greater than ever. Instead there was the campaign against economic offenses, which tended to revive and reinforce the traditional negative image of the Jew. Moreover, while Jewish first names and patronymics are stressed in stories about embezzlers, thieves, and black marketeers, there appears to be a conspiracy of silence about positive Jewish contributions to Russian life. In the recent florid obituaries of the writer Emmanuil Kazakevich, not a word was said about his long career as a Yiddish writer. In the trial this year of the young Jewish poet Iosif Brodsky, who was convicted of the crime of "parasitism" and sentenced to a term of forced labor in the North, the judge repeatedly ridiculed the defendant and two Jewish witnesses, whose Russified patronymics were "corrected" to the Jewish ones appearing on their passports. Khrushchev himself occasionally set the example in Jew-baiting. In a speech last year to Soviet intellectuals, for instance, he digressed from the main subject of his talk to remind his audience that before 1917 various Jewish organizations had collaborated with the Czarist secret police. On the other hand, when Khrushchev said, in reply to a foreigner's query, that Russia's Jews had played a leading role in

Soviet space research, his remarks were deleted from the text of the speech that appeared in the Soviet press.

In his highly informative article in *Foreign Affairs*[1] Moshe Decter adds to the gloomy picture of life in the Soviet Union. The Jews, who have been living in Russia for centuries, are still treated as aliens ("we had to make room for *our* intelligentsia," Khrushchev once declared in an effort to explain why Jews have been removed from important positions). Though considered a foreign and therefore suspect element in Soviet society, they are not permitted to leave the country, a choice many of them would make if they could. As a people they are identified with Judaism, a hostile ideology, and both in turn are identified with the State of Israel, an "imperialist puppet." No other ethnic group in the Soviet Union bears such a stigma: the Lithuanians, for example, are not identified with Roman Catholicism and, by extension, with the "reactionary" policies of the Vatican, nor are the Turkic Moslems held accountable for the policies of Saudi Arabia.

Despite the fact that Jews are officially recognized as a religious group, they are not permitted to set up any central coordinating body similar to those of the various Christian denominations, the Moslems, and the Buddhists; nor do the Jews have any religious publications like the Russian Orthodox *Zhurnal Moskovskoi Patriarkhii* or the Baptist *Bratskii vestnik* ("Fraternal Herald"). Of all the religious groups, only the Jews are prevented from establishing contact with their co-religionists in other countries (the Russian Orthodox Church is now a member of the World Council of Churches, and Soviet seminarians at-

[1] "Status of Jews in the Soviet Union," Jan. '63.

tend Protestant and Moslem institutions of learning abroad); nor are they allowed to organize pilgrimages to holy places abroad (Soviet Moslems, even if only a few, travel annually to Mecca), or to manufacture or import religious objects (Christian churches are permitted to manufacture candles and print Bibles and hymnals, and the Moslems were recently allowed to reprint the Koran in Arabic). When attempts were made to bake and distribute *matzot* privately, a few old men were sent to prison as speculators. While charges of corruption are frequently leveled against the clergy of other faiths, only Jewish synagogues have been branded as centers of anti-state economic activity, like black marketeering, and even of subversive political activity, like meeting Israeli diplomats and supplying them with "slanderous information" about the Soviet Union (presumably a reference to complaints about material hardships and anti-Semitism). To prevent such contacts, a partition has been erected in Moscow's central synagogue, and foreigners are normally allowed only within the enclosed area. Finally, there is no public Jewish religious instruction at all, though we may assume that some parents attempt to teach their own children at home. The training of religious functionaries is limited to a single yeshiva, housed in the Moscow synagogue, which leads a precarious existence; only five students are presently in attendance, and several out-of-town students have been refused Moscow residence permits.

The Yiddish writers shot under Stalin were posthumously "rehabilitated," though not as a group and without any publicity. Jewish cultural life has not been restored, as have the cultural institutions of the Caucasian nationalities, the Kalmyks, and the Volga Germans, which were suppressed

when these ethnic groups were accused of collaborating with the Nazis. A decade after Stalin's death, there is still no permanent Yiddish theater but only occasional Yiddish variety shows by surviving artists of the disbanded theaters. Though generally not very distinguished, these shows are attended by thousands of Jews, including young people whose knowledge of Yiddish is very slight. Yiddish publishing is limited to the bi-monthly journal *Sovietish heimland* and to the small tri-weekly local newspaper *Birobidzhaner shtern* which is published in the Far East and which, incidentally, accepts no outside subscriptions. The total output of Yiddish books for the entire post-Stalin period amounts to fewer than ten titles, mostly classics.

The familiar Soviet excuses for this state of affairs are unconvincing. It is, for instance, untrue that not enough Jews know Yiddish to warrant a state-supported cultural program for them. Ethnic groups far smaller than Russia's Yiddish-speaking community are provided with hundreds of book titles annually and have their own theaters and periodicals. According to the official Soviet census of 1959, there are almost two-and-a-half million Jews in the Soviet Union and of these some 20 per cent—approximately half a million people—claim Yiddish as their mother tongue. It is also evident that the census figures definitely understate the size of both categories. Considering the intensity of semi-official and popular anti-Semitism, there can be no doubt that some Jews attempted to register as non-Jews, particularly in view of the fact that for the first time in the history of the Soviet census no passports were required as evidence and all answers were accepted on faith. As for the Yiddish-speaking group, a Soviet Jewish author writing in a Warsaw Yiddish journal pointed out that many respondents must have given Russian instead of Yiddish as their mother tongue because they "misunderstood" the question of the census-takers. Besides, the number of speakers of any language always far exceeds the number of those who consider it their mother tongue.

Nor is there any foundation to the Soviet claim that the support of Yiddish cultural institutions would be impractical because of the geographic dispersion of the Jews. Minorities such as the Poles and the Germans are also scattered throughout the Soviet Union, yet they have at their disposal various cultural facilities through which they can perpetuate their language.

The absence of any Jewish schools— even in the "Jewish Autonomous Province" of Birobidzhan with its 14,000 Jews—is, of course, the most blatant manifestation of the effort to destroy the cultural life of Soviet Jewry. While still publishing *Sovietish heimland* for the older generation of Jews, the Soviet authorities are seeing to it that Soviet Jewish children will no longer be able to read that periodical. A year ago a Hebrew-Russian dictionary was published but, as far as can be ascertained, Hebrew is taught only in *Christian* theological academies. Several university libraries have impressive collections of Judaica, but not one Soviet university offers a course in Yiddish or Hebrew or in Jewish history, except as part of abstruse programs in philology or archaeology which are open only to advanced students. A number of Russian translations from the Yiddish (Sholem Aleichem, Peretz, Mendele, and several volumes by the authors who were executed under Stalin) have appeared, to be sure, as well as an anthology of Israeli poetry, mostly by Communist authors, including Israeli Arabs. But the only "scholarly" books dealing with Jewish subjects have been a slim biography of Sholem Aleichem

and some crudely propagandistic tracts, officially described as "scientifically atheist," of which the now notorious *Judaism Without Embellishment,* with its Nazi-like anti-Semitic cartoons, is a horrible example.

While Stalin was alive the Communist world was more or less politically homogeneous, at least in its official dogma and goals. However, the Stalinist policies toward the Jewish minorities did not prevail in the newly established Communist regimes of Eastern Europe primarily because their leaders had more pressing problems to tackle. Today there are huge differences between the treatment of Jews in the Soviet Union and in the satellite countries. In the countries of Eastern Europe, tolerance of Jewish communal life appears reasonably secure and permanent— provided, of course, that it does not conflict with the larger aims and policies of the states involved. The degree of tolerance in a given country appears to relate directly to the strength of "liberalizing" influences in its general political climate. Thus, the two most "liberal" countries, Hungary and Poland —which may soon be joined by Rumania—also boast the most active Jewish communities. Hungary has a Central Board of Jewish Communities which is rigidly restricted in its activities but subsidized by the government, as well as a Jewish Theological Seminary, a kosher canteen, and several religious secondary schools. Poland, with a Jewish population of only thirty thousand, maintains a network of state-supported Yiddish day schools, a Yiddish newspaper, a scholarly historical journal, an active Yiddish publishing house, and, most significantly, a state-supported Yiddish theater. The existence of these institutions in satellite countries, along with a reasonably permissive attitude toward emigration, make the Soviet policy of continued suppression of Jewish communal life all the more flagrant, and those Communists—both inside the Soviet Union and in the Western European parties—who appeal for the restoration of Soviet Yiddish culture see it as another step in the struggle against the remnants of Stalinism in the Soviet Union.

Somewhat paradoxically, Stalinists outside the Soviet Union have also seized on the issue of Russian anti-Semitism. Thus, *Hammer and Steel,* the publication of the pro-Chinese "Stalinist" faction of the U.S. Communists, has pointed to the mistreatment of the Jewish minority as a shameful example of Khrushchev's violation of Leninist nationality policies. Or again, only four days before Khrushchev's ouster from power, the New York *Morning Freiheit* printed an article by Samuel Rozin of the Soviet Novosti Press Agency, violently denying a report in a Peking newspaper to the effect that the USSR was setting up "concentration camps for Jews." Indeed, it would be surprising if the pro-Chinese Communist movements—and the Chinese Communist Party itself—were not to exploit the issue of Soviet anti-Semitism again, since one of Peking's favorite themes is the Soviet Union's "great power chauvinism" and its mistreatment of racial and national minorities. It is likely, for example, that the issue will be used by Chinese propaganda in Black Africa, where the fierce Sino-Soviet competition for influence is rapidly gaining in momentum, and where accusations of racial discrimination are not to be dismissed lightly.

In the Soviet Union itself, opposition to the government's semi-official anti-Semitism is widespread among the liberal segments of the artistic intelligentsia, which, while numerically weak, are outspoken and influential. The poet Yevgenii Yevtushenko, author of "Babii

Yar," is the best-known representative of this group. Among the others, the most vocal are the two grand old men of Soviet letters, Konstantin Paustovsky and Kornei Chukovsky; this group also includes persons of Jewish origin, such as Ilya Ehrenburg and the film director Mikhail Romm. Their protests often assume the apparently innocuous form of memoirs, whose loving and nostalgic pictures of Russia's Jewish communities and Yiddish cultural life during the early post-revolutionary years are left to make their own implicit point of contrast with present conditions. Or again, these reminiscences may include descriptions of pogroms in Czarist Russia: the identification of the anti-Semites with the hated police providing another tacit but telling comment.

In their condemnation of anti-Semitism these Soviet writers, young and old, are following the tradition of the humanistic intelligentsia of pre-revolutionary Russia—men like Korolenko, Leskov, Chekhov, Kuprin, and Gorki. It is noteworthy that those writings of this older generation which condemn Czarist anti-Semitism are suppressed in the Soviet Union, even though Korolenko, Leskov, and the others are claimed as "progressive" forerunners of contemporary Soviet thought, and even though their other works are widely disseminated. Be that as it may, the Soviet intellectuals of the 1960's continue to refer to the neo-Stalinist anti-Semites by such traditional names as *pogromshchiki* and *cehrnosotentsy* ("Black Hundreds").

If the intelligentsia tends to oppose the Soviet government's anti-Semitic policies, these policies are quite popular with other elements of the population. This split in public opinion helps to explain the frequent inconsistencies in the Soviet treatment of the Jews. At times of ideological flux and internal instability—and the Sino-Soviet conflict and the spectacular palace revolution in the Kremlin have made the present moment such a time—the various factions struggling for power are more likely to value the support of the intelligentsia, the "engineers of human souls" as Stalin allegedly once called them.

Nor should we minimize the importance of Western intercessions on behalf of the Soviet Jews. Among those who, at one time or another, have expressed their concern over the problem are Bertrand Russell, François Mauriac, Albert Schweitzer, Linus Pauling, the Dowager Queen Elizabeth of Belgium, Martin Luther King, and Bishop James Pike of California. Under Stalin, any foreign intervention was likely to have been totally useless, and possibly harmful, but under Khrushchev the pressure of foreign public opinion proved effective on more than one occasion; it was, for example, successful in shielding Pasternak from police reprisals. There are also indications that persistent Western protests against the treatment of Russia's Jews, if presented in firm but temperate language and coupled with concrete and reasonable demands, do occasionally produce tangible results. The publication of the bi-monthly *Sovietish heimland* (scheduled to become a monthly in 1965) was decided upon "in order to please our friends abroad," as the Soviet Minister of Culture candidly declared. The periodical has obvious shortcomings—an official organ of the Union of Soviet Writers, it parrots official party pronouncements and is marked for its particular zeal in defending the "Jewish policy" of the Soviet Union—but it is, after all, written in Yiddish and it does contain some material of Jewish interest. Second, there is strong reason to believe that the planned "show trials" of Jewish embezzlers and black marketeers—which

would inevitably have unleashed a new anti-Semitic campaign—were called off because of fear of adverse Western reaction. Third, though anti-Judaic and anti-Zionist pamphlets continue to appear, their tone has become considerably milder after the worldwide protests evoked by the appearance of *Judaism Without Embellishment*. The book was subsequently condemned by the Ideological Commission of the Party's Central Committee as "crude and offensive" and allegedly withdrawn from circulation. Fourth, some time ago the Soviet press denounced Israeli diplomats in Moscow for distributing Jewish calendars, which are indispensable to observant Jews, but when the incident was reported in the West, together with the information that no Jewish religious calendars were published in the USSR, such calendars were printed in the fall of 1964 and placed on sale in the Moscow synagogue. Finally, Lord Russell's letters to Khrushchev put the Soviet authorities on the defensive and resulted in public disclosure of some facts and figures about "positive" Jewish participation in Soviet life and Jewish contributions to the Soviet war effort. For example, it was revealed that during the war over one hundred Jews had been awarded the title of Hero of the Soviet Union, the equivalent of the Congressional Medal of Honor. Such facts and figures had been suppressed for two decades and might be of some value in combating anti-Semitism in the Soviet Union. Once made public, they can, of course, be quoted again.

Speculation about the personal attitude toward the Jews held by Brezhnev, Kosygin, Podgorny, Mikoyan, Suslov— or anyone else who may ultimately inherit Khrushchev's mantle—is premature if not altogether irrelevant. But there is every reason to believe that Churchill's advice, in 1953, to negotiate with Soviet leaders while a struggle for succession is in progress, is valid. Though no formal "negotiations" concerning the status of Russia's Jews are possible, Khrushchev's successors, preoccupied with far weightier matters, may prove responsive to foreign intercessions on behalf of the Jews, particularly since all the "errors" and "distortions" in the matter can now be blamed on Khrushchev.

Foreign intercessions are valuable not only because they may effect changes in Soviet policy. They are reported in the Soviet press, and while they are dismissed as either "naïve" and "misinformed" or as "provocationist" and "hostile," depending on their origin, Soviet Jews learn of them and thus no longer feel completely abandoned and friendless. Some criticism of the Soviet treatment of the Jews also appears in Western Communist newspapers, and these are available in the USSR (curiously, Yiddish Communist newspapers are not). In addition, there are occasional broadcasts of news items and cultural and religious programs of Jewish interest, such as those transmitted by the BBC, the Voice of America, Radio Liberty, and Kol Israel. All these may not result in an actual improvement of the position of the Soviet Jews, but their importance in helping to maintain the morale of Soviet Jewry should not be underestimated.

The plight of the Soviet Jews is a very serious one. They are isolated from the major Jewish centers abroad, including those within the Communist camp, and the various communities within the Soviet borders are even cut off from one another. They are deprived of educational facilities and are threatened with the deprivation of their ninety or so remaining synagogues, the only Jewish institutions still theoretical-

ly tolerated. In this isolation, their notion of the outside Jewish world becomes a prey to fantastic rumors which travel from one synagogue to another. Soviet Jews have a very foggy notion of Israel or of the Jews in America. In the era of Telstars and space exploration they still depend on occasional travelers from distant lands for news about their co-religionists.

Nevertheless, it is unlikely that the Soviet Jewish community will simply disappear. Recent visitors to the USSR all report that the thirst for information about Jews abroad, and particularly about Israel, is intense. On major religious holidays the few remaining synagogues are packed, and on Simchat Torah, one can see thousands of young people singing and dancing near synagogues (some 20,000 in Moscow in 1964)—a risky thing to do in the Soviet Union, where it is much safer to be secretly religious than openly observant. In general, there is a strong nostalgia for a necessarily ambiguous "Jewishness."

The Soviet Jewish community is a victim of discrimination and persecution. It may become impoverished economically and spiritually; it may grow ignorant of its cultural and religious heritage. Yet it cannot really "assimilate," because complete assimilation is possible only under conditions of tolerance. This situation, in which the Jews are neither allowed to be Jews nor to assimilate, produces pain and despair, but it also brings about, as a natural reaction, a feeling of revulsion toward the hostile Gentile world and a reversion to values once abandoned. It kindles a renewed interest in the Jewish heritage, and very often a feeling of strong ethnic identity. It is suggestive that not so many decades ago, similar conditions obtaining in Europe produced a generation of Jewish theologians and Zionist leaders.

The Forces of Nationalism

RICHARD PIPES

There was a time—and not so long ago—when merely to assert the existence in Russia of a "national problem" evoked skepticism. This was a reaction common to both émigrés of pre-World War II vintage and Americans knowledgeable in Russian affairs. The majority of Russian émigrés consisted either of nobles, officials, and officers, who denied the existence of this problem on principle, from a misguided sense of patriotism, or of urban intellectuals, who simply had no experience of it: they knew of an agrarian problem, of a labor problem, of a constitutional problem, even of a Jewish problem, but not of, say, a Ukrainian or a Moslem national problem. The latter they were inclined to regard as phantoms raised by German and Austrian propagandists during the First World War in an effort to weaken and dismember the Russian Empire.

The American attitude was, and continues to be, inspired by other considerations. First, there is the unsophisticated approach which takes at face value Soviet assertions that the abolition of private property in means of production and the constitutional guarantee of equality have in fact done away with

Reprinted by permission of the publisher from Richard Pipes, "The Forces of Nationalism," Problems of Communism, XIII, No. 1 (Jan.–Feb. 1964), 1–6. Copyright © 1964 Problems of Communism.

national discrimination and animosities. Behind this kind of reasoning lie many uncritical and largely false assumptions about the nature of nationalism. Is nationalism really a "function" of economics? Do constitutional guarantees of equality assure actual equality—in Russia any more than in the United States? And would equality, even if realized, neutralize nationalism? Such questions are rarely asked by those who believe in what may be called a manipulative solution of the national question.

The more sophisticated and at the same time more prevalent attitude rests on a more or less conscious equation of the American and Russian experiences with national minorities. It assumes that in Russia, as in the United States, gradual assimilation of the minorities is both progressive and inevitable: progressive because it tends toward the establishment of true equality, inevitable because it is backed by superior culture and economic power. How persuasive such considerations can be is best illustrated by the example of an eminent American jurist who was shocked to find upon visiting Soviet Central Asia that native children were attending separate schools instead of Russian ones! Still fresh in memory are comparisons equating the Ukraine with Pennsylvania, and Georgians with the Welsh or Scots.

It is safe to say that such attitudes no longer prevail today, or at least are encountered less frequently than a decade ago. The national problem in the Soviet Union is widely recognized as a true and valid problem: it exists. But if one probes behind this admission, one still finds a very pronounced reluctance to concede that the problem is really something important and enduring. Men of good will are against nationalism, because nationalism has been responsible for so much bloodshed, hatred, and various other forms of irrational behavior. And because men of good will, like men of bad will, so often allow wishes (or fears) to interfere with their judgment of facts, they sometimes think that to recognize the reality of something one does not approve is tantamount to approving it; hence they are inclined to deny reality to that which they disapprove. Thus, though they may concede that the national problem exists, they like to think it will disappear.

NATIONALISM AND MODERNIZATION

It is quite striking that in this respect the attitudes of very many Russians and Americans fully coincide. When the issue is raised, one can hear quite similar responses from intellectuals in Moscow or Leningrad and New York or Washington. Why should this be so? It may well be that behind it lies a very fundamental factor linking American and Russian cultures: an impatience with, and underestimation of, historical roots. For all their differences—and they are very profound—the American and Russian cultures are young cultures, having been essentially molded in the past 250 years, that is, in an era when the prevailing intellectual tendencies have been anti-traditionalist and scientific. They are forward-looking, more concerned with the life to be built than with the life that has been inherited. Both are

imbued by a strong millenial spirit. Having given up many of their own traditions for the sake of modernization, Americans and Russians are not inclined to show undue respect for the traditionalism of other nations, especially when this traditionalism runs contrary to the requirements of modern life. So they tend to deprecate nationalism and advocate assimilation—and, sometimes, to assume that the desirable is also the inevitable.[1]

Now, if we try to take a more dispassionate look at the problems of nationalism and nationality in the modern world, we must acknowledge that they show no sign whatever of becoming less urgent, let alone of disappearing. This is in some respects puzzling, because nationalism runs contrary to the needs of economic development which exert such a powerful influence on contemporary life. Certainly, the maximal use of economic resources requires a degree of rationalization that cannot brook interference from traditionalism. National barriers must be broken, and the ground must be cleared of the old vegetation—sometimes luxuriant, sometimes merely disorderly and lifeless—which centuries of spontaneous cultural growth have produced. The discipline of the clock, the techniques of a money economy, and all the other complex features of modern industrial life are not compatible with national traditions that are

[1] It is curious that in spite of all the propaganda value which the Soviet Union has derived from discrimination against Negroes in the United States, one often encounters scorn for the whole "Negro question" among Soviet citizens. Many Russians have neither much sympathy for the economic plight of the American Negro, which is less acute than their own, nor for the Negro's national aspirations. In this respect, Russian tolerance of American intolerance matches the indifference of some Americans toward the Russians' maltreatment of their national minorities.

usually rooted in agricultural or commercial mores. An ideal economic arrangement would be one in which all states would merge into one world union, and all mankind dissolve into one nation.

If, in fact, such an amalgamation is not taking place, it is because the process of modernization also has a reverse side which preserves and even intensifies national allegiances and distinctions. This is the social aspect of modernization, which finds expression in the levelling of class differences and the involvement of the entire population in the national life. The rational organization of life requires that the whole citizenry be treated as one vast reservoir of manpower; consequently, it calls for democratization (in the social, if not necessarily the political, sense). Now, by pulling into national life the mass of previously isolated and passive population groups, the process of modernization inadvertently promotes nationalism and national differences, because national identity is most deeply rooted among these very groups. To cite but one example, in the days of mercenary armies, nationalism was no factor in the maintenance of military morale, but it has become one with the introduction of the modern non-professional mass army. Mass education and mass literacy also promote national distinctions by institutionalizing local languages, histories, literatures, etc. So does the intelligentsia, whose emergence everywhere accompanies the breakdown of the old class-stratified social structure.

This push and pull exerted on nationalism by the process of modernization has been the essence of the "national problem" of our time. On the one hand, modernization demands cultural levelling; on the other, it releases social forces that are least prone to such levelling. Since the latter tendency is often stronger than the former, because it represents real pressures as against ideal considerations, nationalism has made remarkable headway and is likely to continue to do so.

AMERICAN VS. SOVIET EXPERIENCE

The relentless assimilation of the ethnic groups residing in the United States is certainly a unique instance which neither vitiates these general considerations nor has any bearing on the situation in the Soviet Union. (I leave aside the question of whether the American population is really as much assimilated and culturally integrated as it is often assumed to be.) Some nine-tenths of American citizens are descendants of immigrants who voluntarily severed their native roots and migrated to the United States to start a completely new life. Moreover, because many of them belonged to underprivileged groups of the population in their countries of origin, their ties to their national cultures were quite tenuous in any event. What occurred in American history was a mass-scale renunciation of one nationality in favor of a new one.

Nothing of the sort happened in Russia. The national minorities of that country consist largely of historic peoples who came or were brought under Russian sovereignty between the sixteenth and nineteenth centuries. While some of these nationalities passed under Russian rule more or less voluntarily, they did so in order to secure Russian protection against hostile neighbors, and not with any idea of surrendering their right to self-rule. Today, each has an intelligentsia and an officialdom of its own; they receive much of their education in native languages; they reside on their historic territories, surrounded by places and monuments with strong national associations. The differences between Soviet and American national minority groups could be further elaborated upon, but this is scarcely necessary. It seems obvious that the two situations are fundamentally different: in one case, we are dealing with a new nation created, as it were, through a voluntary multinational effort; in the other, with an ordinary empire of many nations dominated by one. It is meaningful to speak of an American nation, because the inhabitants of the United States refer to themselves as "Americans." Has anyone ever heard an inhabitant of the Soviet Union refer to his nationality as "Soviet"?

One of the reasons why the national problem in the Soviet Union is difficult to grasp is the confusion that surrounds the number of nationalities involved. The figures of 175, 188, or over 200 "nationalities" which are sometimes cited are quite misleading, because they confuse the term "nationality" as understood by the ethnographer and anthropologist with the term as it is used by the historian or political scientist. To the former, any group displaying certain common ethnic characteristics may well be a nationality—the six hundred Tofalars as much as the six million Uzbeks. To the historian and political scientist, on the other hand, a "nationality" all of whose members reside in one medium-sized Caucasian *aul* or Siberian settlement is of no interest whatever. Actually, there are in the Soviet Union only a dozen or so national groups of significance to the student of the national question. The fate of the national minorities and of the "national problem" depends in large measure on them, or, more specifically, on their ability or inability to resist Russification and to evolve viable national cultures.

THE ASSIMILATION PROCESS

This Russification has been carried out by a great variety of methods, some crude, some subtle. The most effective have been connected with the semi-official policy of elevating the Great Russians to the position of the leading ethnic group in the Soviet Union. This policy, formulated by Stalin, has not been repudiated by his successors. In a country where personal relations play so important a function, serving as something of a substitute for the weakly-developed legal system, such an attitude on the part of the rulers has a direct bearing on the life of all the citizens. It means, above all, that the road to prestige, power, and material benefits entails adaptation to Russian culture: in the party, in the army, in the higher educational establishment.

The message of Russian primacy is conveyed to the minorities in a variety of ways, among which one may mention the linguistic (imposition of the Cyrillic alphabet on the Muslim minority), the historiographic (emphasis on the progressive role of conquest by Tsarist Russia), and the religious (more acute persecution of religious bodies other than the Orthodox church). That the ultimate intent of all these measures is the Russification of all the various ethnic groups is made quite clear by the statement in the new party program that "full-scale communist construction constitutes a new stage in the development of national relations in which the nations will draw still closer together until complete unity is achieved." It is fair to assume that the language and culture of the eventual "completely unified" nation will not be Komi-Zyrian, Chukchi, or even Uzbek.

There are many ways in which the reaction of the national minorities can be studied, some quantitative, others not. Useful indices can be obtained from population censuses, which furnish data on such vital matters as population movement, fertility, intermarriage, and linguistic habits. Information of a different kind, less measurable but equally important, can be derived from literary sources, from ethnographic data, and from political intelligence. Only when both these types of data—the quantitative and non-quantitative—are juxtaposed and placed against the historic background of the national groups concerned is it possible to draw meaningful and more or less scientific conclusions about the situation of Soviet minorities.[2]

The publication by the Soviet Central Statistical Administration of the abstract of the 1959 population census, imperfect as this volume is, permits for the first time in a quarter century a study of the vital statistics bearing on the Soviet national minorities. The data it supplies, when compared with those given in the 1926 census, give a better picture than we have ever had of the various nationalities' actual tendencies of development.[3] And none of this information is more significant than the figures which tell, black on white, what

has happened to the linguistic habits of the minorities. In considering these figures, one must bear in mind that the inter-census period (1926–1959) coincided with the most intense Russification effort in modern Russian history. What we now have is, as it were, the fruits of that gigantic and ruthless effort. What do we find?

LINGUISTIC TRENDS

In 1926 Russians constituted 54 percent of the total population of the U.S.S.R. by nationality, but 58.5 percent by language. In other words, in 1926, 4.5 percent of the total population may be said to have been linguistically Russified. In 1959, the corresponding figures are 54.5 and 59.3 percent, giving 4.8 percent as the proportion of those linguistically Russified. The net gain of 0.3 percent represents approximately 600,000 citizens. But even this minute gain disappears if we recall that in the intervening period the Nazis had slaughtered some two million Yiddish-speaking Jews on Soviet soil, reducing the number of Jewish Soviet citizens who consider Yiddish their native language from 1.8 million (1926) to less than one-half million (1959). Thus, the proportion of linguistically Russified non-Russians has actually decreased somewhat. In absolute terms, of course, the number of citizens who speak their national languages has grown far more than the number of those who have become linguistically assimilated. While the number of Soviet citizens who have abandoned their native language in favor of Russian has grown from 6.5 million (1926) to 10 million (1959), the number of those who adhere to their native language has increased in the same period from 60 to 85 million.

---

[2] The author tried to apply both these methods to Central Asia and Transcaucasia in the following articles: "Muslims of Soviet Central Asia: Trends and Prospects," *Middle East Journal*, Nos. 2 and 3, 1955, and "Demographic and Ethnographic Changes in Transcaucasia, 1897–1956," *Ibid.*, Winter, 1959.

[3] Tsentralnoe statisticheskoe upravlenie pri Sovete Ministrov SSSR, *Itogi vsesoiuznoi perepisi naseleniia 1959 goda: SSSR (Svodnyi tom)*, Moscow 1962, pp. 184–243. The data from the 1926 census are drawn largely from F. Lorimer, *The Population of the Soviet Union: History and Prospects*, Geneva, 1946, supplemented by R. Pipes, *Formation of the Soviet Union*, Cambridge: Harvard University Press, 1954, pp. 289–90.

Such, in its broadest aspect, is the impact of thirty years of Russification carried out with all the instruments at the disposal of the totalitarian state. But if we delve deeper into the statistical material and break down the figures for overall linguistic assimilation into figures for each of the various national groups, and, within these, for different age groups, we discover even more surprising facts.

Linguistic assimilation has always been and continues to be most rapid among ethnic groups that enjoy a high level of culture, but whose historic roots, and often ethnic centers, are located outside the Soviet Union. In this category belong, first of all, the groups of Europeans, such as Poles, Germans, or Greeks, between one-quarter and one-half of whom have become linguistically de-nationalized.[4] It also includes the groups representing ancient Oriental cultures, such as Koreans, Chinese, or Persians. In all these groups linguistic Russification is proceeding apace. The reason for it is not far to seek. Members of these nationalities in the Soviet Union regard themselves as isolated fragments of their nations and consequently see no reason to aspire to national self-preservation. *Mutatis mutandis,* the same may be said of the Jews, four-fifths of whom acknowledge Russian as their native tongue—at any rate to the census taker.

---

[4] It must not be assumed, however, that all linguistic de-nationalization benefits Russification. Among Soviet Poles, for example, more than half (756,000) had given up Polish, but of these, two-thirds had opted for Ukranian and Belorussian, only one-third for Russian. (Undoubtedly, many of these Poles preferred to deny their mother tongue for political reasons.) In the case of the Bashkirs, of the 377,000 who had given up Bashkir, 350,000 had adopted Tatar. Among the 94,000 linguistically de-nationalized Uzbeks, twice as many declared Tajik their native tongue as Russian.

More than one-quarter of all the Russified non-Russians belong to this category.

The nationalities with a medium "Russification index" may also be divided into two groups. One consists of the two largest minorities, the Ukrainians and Belorussians, both closely related to Great Russians in terms of origin and culture. If we compare the linguistic data for these two nationalities in the 1926 and 1959 census reports, we find that the proportion of those who consider Ukrainian and Belorussian their native tongues has actually *increased*. In 1926, 87.1 percent of the Ukrainians spoke their native language; in 1959, 87.7 percent. In the case of Belorussians, the increase has been even more significant: from 71.9 to 84.2 percent. Figures by age groups indicate, moreover, that Ukrainians and Belorussians under 20 years of age (*i.e.,* those educated between approximately the end of the war and the year of Stalin's death) are more loyal to their native languages than those of middle age (who had been educated in the 1920's and 1930's)—an indication that there has been no progressive de-nationalization of youth.

The other group in this category consists of nationalities inhabiting the Volga-Ural region, including both Turkic Moslems (Tatars and Bashkirs) and Finnic Christians (Mordvins, Chuvash, etc.). These nationalities have for several centuries been under Russian rule. In fact, they were the first minorities to be conquered by Russians in the sixteenth and seventeenth centuries. They now find themselves in the midst of Russian population centers, cut off from the main body of their Turkic and Finnic relatives, and consequently have a difficult time preserving their identity. Among them the proportion of those who are shifting to Russian is growing, though not dramatically (*e.g.*, Tatar-speaking Tatars have declined from 98.9 to 92.0 percent, Chuvash-speaking Chuvash from 97.7 to 90.0 percent, with the Mordvins showing the greatest decline, from 94 to 78 percent).

If we next turn to the minorities with distinct cultures, living in borderland areas, and with historic roots on their present territories, we find that Russification either has made little or no progress, or has lost ground. The Turkic inhabitants, who constitute the single most numerous minority bloc after the Ukrainians, show an astounding loyalty to their native languages. Except for the Volga Tatars, whom we have discussed above, they show between 97 and 99 percent adherence to their own languages. In some cases (*e.g.*, the Azeri Turks and Turkmens) the percentage of native-speaking citizens is up a bit compared to 1926, in others (*e.g.*, the Kazakhs and Kirghiz) it is a bit down, but in general no linguistic assimilation has taken place. Of the 20 million Moslems (Volga Tatars excepted) in the Soviet Union, only 200,000, or one percent, have become linguistically Russified. The same situation prevails in the Caucasus. The percentage of Georgians who consider Georgian their native tongue has increased from 96.5 (1926) to 98.6 (1959). This also holds true of the Azeri Turks (from 93.8 percent in 1926 to 97.6 percent in 1959). The Armenians, on the other hand, seem to be slowly Russifying, though it is more than probable that the decrease in percentage of those who consider Armenian their native tongue (from 92.4 in 1926 to 89.9 in 1959) has occurred among Armenians residing outside the Armenian republic. Among the Baltic peoples, the proportion of those who adhere to their native languages varies between 95 and 97 percent.

IMPLICATIONS FOR THE FUTURE

The principal conclusion which emerges from these statistics may be formulated as follows: both on territories predominantly occupied by Russians (RSFSR) and on those predominantly occupied by major minority groups, the lines separating the Russians from the nationalities in matters of language are becoming sharper and more distinct. The Russians as well as the national minorities are gaining linguistic hegemony in the areas where they enjoy numerical and administrative preponderance. What is occurring may be described as a process of the emergence of modern nations within the Soviet Union. The smaller nationalities are slowly giving ground by dissolving either among the Russians or among the ethnic groups whose language and culture are most closely related to their own. The major nationalities, on the other hand, among whom one must include the Ukrainians, Georgians, and Turkic peoples of Central Asia, are gaining in cohesion.

Language, of course, is only one of several criteria of national viability, and it would not be sound to base one's whole evaluation on the pattern of linguistic development. But it is a most important criterion. The transition from one language to another is, perhaps, the single most dramatic manifestation of a shift in national allegiance. The fact that it is not occurring among the major peripheral nationalities gives some ground for arguing that the burden of proof in discussing the fate of Soviet nationalities lies on those who foresee their imminent dissolution in a single Soviet nationality.

The practical conclusions which this evidence suggests have bearing not merely on the Soviet Union but on all those areas where a nascent sense of national identity emerges simultaneously with a drive for modernization. It is difficult to conceive how the contrary pulls implicit in modernization, to which reference has been made above, can be reconciled in any other way than through the establishment of independent national states. The national state alone provides within its confines outlets both for economic and other forms of rationalization, on which material well-being and power depend, and for the national sentiments and loyalties which rationalization brings to the surface. Such has been the experience of Western Europe and of all the great multinational states and empires. In Russia, the breakdown of empire almost occurred in the course of the Revolution and Civil War. It was averted partly by force of arms and partly by the creation of a novel political system which combined outward decentralization with unprecedented inner centralization. But from the long-term historical point of view, there is no reason to assume that this solution was anything but a temporary one.

MINORITIES

IN THE U.S.S.R.:

The Soviet View

The Soviet Deportation
of Nationalities

Comrades, let us reach for some other facts. The Soviet Union is justly considered as a model of a multinational state because we have in practice assured the equality and friendship of all nations which live in our great fatherland.

All the more monstrous are the acts

Reprinted from Robert Conquest, The Soviet Deportation of Nationalities. London: Macmillan & Co. (1960) pp. 133, 134, 135, 136. By permission of St. Martin's Press, Inc., The Macmillan Company of Canada Ltd., and Macmillan & Co. Ltd.

whose initiator was Stalin and which are crude violations of the basic Leninist principles of the nationality policy of the Soviet State. We refer to the mass deportations from their native places of whole nations, together with all Communists and Komsomols without any exception; this deportation action was not dictated by any military considerations.

Thus, already at the end of 1943, when there occurred a permanent breakthrough at the fronts of the great patriotic war in favor of the Soviet Union, a decision was taken and executed concerning the deportation of all the Karachai from the lands on which they lived. In the same period, at the end of December 1943, the same lot befell the whole population of the Autonomous Kalmyk Republic. In March 1944, all the Chechen and Ingush people were deported and the Chechen-Ingush Autonomous Republic was liquidated.

In April 1944, all Balkars were deported to faraway places from the territory of the Kabardine-Balkar Autonomous Republic and the Republic itself was renamed Autonomous Kabardine Republic. The Ukrainians avoided meeting this fate only because there were too many of them and there was no place to which to deport them. Otherwise, he would have deported them also. (Laughter and animation in the hall.)

Not only no Marxist-Leninist but also no man of common sense can grasp how it is possible to make whole nations responsible for inimical activity, including women, children, old people, Communists and Komsomols, to use mass repression against them, and to expose them to misery and suffering for the hostile acts of individual persons or groups of persons.[1]

By a decree of January 9th, 1957, the Presidium of the Supreme Soviet of the U.S.S.R. recommended the Presidium of the Supreme Soviet of the R.S.F.S.R. to examine the question and take decisions:

On the reorganization of the Kabardine A.S.S.R. into the Kabardine-Balkar A.S.S.R.,

On the restoration of the Chechen-Ingush A.S.S.R. in the structure of the R.S.F.S.R.,

[1 Excerpt from Khrushchev's speech at the 20th Party Congress.]

On the formation of the Kalmyk autonomous province in the structure of the R.S.F.S.R.,

On the reorganization of the Cherkess autonomous province into the Karachai-Cherkess autonomous province.

In accordance with these decisions the Presidium of the Supreme Soviet of the R.S.F.S.R. passed Decrees on the reorganization of the Kabardine A.S.S.R. into the Kabardine-Balkar A.S.S.R., on the restoration of the Chechen-Ingush A.S.S.R., on the formation of a Kalmyk autonomous province and on the reorganization of the Cherkess autonomous province into the Karachai-Cherkess autonomous province. At the same time the Presidium of the Supreme Soviet of the R.S.F.S.R., for the direction and organization of all work connected with the restoration of autonomies, pending elections of the leading Soviet organs, confirmed organizational committees of representatives of the corresponding nationalities for the Chechen-Ingush A.S.S.R. and the Kalmyk autonomous province.

Direction of work for the implementation of all measures connected with the reorganization of the Kabardine A.S.S.R. into the Kabardine-Balkar A.S.S.R. and the Cherkess autonomous province into the Karachai-Cherkess autonomous province has been entrusted accordingly to the Council of Ministers of the Kabardine A.S.S.R. and the Executive Committee of the Cherkess autonomous province, together with representatives of the Balkar and Karachai peoples.

Comrades, deputies! The practical implementation of measures for the restoration of the national autonomy of these peoples requires a certain amount of time and the carrying out of much organizational work in the preparation of the necessary production, housing and other cultural and everyday conditions in places of former residence.

Great expenditure of material and monetary funds is also required.

Therefore the resettlement of citizens of the stated nationalities who have expressed the desire to return to regions of former residence must be conducted in an organized manner, in small groups, at definite periods and in order of precedence. These periods and order of precedence, and also all practical questions of labor and everyday arrangements will be determined and solved by organs of State power of the autonomous republics and autonomous provinces being formed.

Such an order will make it possible not to permit certain complications and to avoid difficulties for the population of these nationalities in the matter of labor and living arrangements. It should also be borne in mind that unorganized resettlement can do serious harm to the economy of those collective farms, State farms and enterprises in which workers of these nationalities are employed at the present time. It is therefore necessary to guard against all attempts at unorganized resettlement.

Proceeding from these considerations and bearing in mind the need to prepare in advance conditions of a productive and everyday order it is proposed to conduct the resettlement of citizens of Balkar, Kalmyk and Karachai nationality in the territory of the restored autonomies and organize work for them during 1957 and 1958.

As concerns Chechen and Ingush peoples, as being the most numerous, it is proposed to carry out measures connected with the restoration of their national autonomy over a longer period, between 1957 and 1960.

There is no doubt that republics, territories and provinces on whose territory the Balkars, Chechens, Ingushes, Kalmyks and Karachais are living at the present time will render the necessary assistance in the organized conduct of the resettlement of those desiring to return to their former place of residence, and at the same time will create for those people who continue to live in these republics, territories and provinces, every condition for their active participation in economic and cultural construction together with other peoples of these territories and provinces.

In connection with the restoration of the Chechen-Ingush A.S.S.R. (Autonomous Soviet Socialist Republic) by a Decree of January 11th, 1957, the Presidium of the Supreme Soviet of the U.S.S.R. has ratified a resolution of the Presidium of the Supreme Soviet of the Georgian S.S.R. and the Presidium of the Supreme Soviet of the R.S.F.S.R. on the handing over of part of the territory of the Dushet and Kazbek regions from the Georgian S.S.R. to the R.S.F.S.R. (Russian Soviet Federated Socialist Republic) and on the restoration in such manner of the borders between these union republics which existed up to March 7th, 1944.

In ratifying Decrees on the restoration of the national autonomy of the peoples mentioned, it will be necessary to introduce appropriate changes into Article 22 of the Constitution of the U.S.S.R. (*Pravda*, February 12th 1957.) [2]

...Law on confirming the decree of the Presidium of the Supreme Soviet of the U.S.S.R. on the restoration of the national autonomy of the Balkar, Chechen, Ingush, Kalmyk and Karachai peoples.

The Supreme Soviet of the Union of Soviet Socialist Republics decides:

Article 1. To confirm the decrees of the Presidium of the Supreme Soviet of the U.S.S.R. of January 9th, 1957:

[2 Speech and decree at a meeting of the Supreme Soviet on the Rehabilitation of Nationalities.]

On the transformation of the Kabardine A.S.S.R. into the Kabardine-Balkar A.S.S.R.

On the restoration of the Chechen-Ingush A.S.S.R. in the framework of the R.S.F.S.R.

On the formation of a Kalmyk Autonomous Province in the framework of the R.S.F.S.R.

On the transformation of the Cherkess Autonomous Province into the Karachai-Cherkess autonomous province.

Article 2. To confirm the decree of the

Presidium of the Supreme Soviet of the U.S.S.R. of January 11th, 1957: On the transfer of parts of the territories of the Dushet and Kazbek regions from the Georgian S.S.R. to the framework of the R.S.F.S.R.

President of the Presidium of the U.S.S.R., K. Voroshilov

Secretary of Presidium of the Supreme Soviet of the U.S.S.R., A. Gorkin

Moscow, Kremlin, February 11th, 1957.

On Citizens of Tatar Nationality
Who Resided in the Crimea

After the liberation of the Crimea from fascist occupation in 1944, instances of active collaboration with the German invaders by certain parts of the Tatar population living in the Crimea were groundlessly attributed to the whole Tatar population of the Crimea. These sweeping accusations against all the citizens of Tatar nationality who resided in the Crimea must be withdrawn, all the more so since a new generation has entered the working and political life of society.

The Presidium of the U.S.S.R. Supreme Soviet resolves:

1. To revoke the corresponding decisions of state bodies insofar as they

Decree of Presidium of U.S.S.R. Supreme Soviet. Reprinted from Kazakhstanskaya pravda, *Sept. 9, 1967, p. 3;* Kommunist Tadzhikistana, *p. 3;* Sovetskaya Kirgizia, *p. 1;* Pravda Vostoka, *p. 1. Complete text translated in* Current Digest of the Soviet Press *(September 27, 1967), p. 3.*

contain sweeping accusations against citizens of Tatar nationality who resided in the Crimea.

2. To note that the Tatars who previously resided in the Crimea have settled on the territory of the Uzbek and other Union republics, that they have all the rights of Soviet citizens, take part in public and political life, are elected Deputies to the Supreme Soviets and local Soviets of Workers' Deputies, hold responsible positions in Soviet, economic and Party bodies, that radio broadcasts are conducted for them, a newspaper is published in their mother tongue and other cultural enterprises are conducted.

For the further development of areas with Tatar population, Union-republic Councils of Ministers are instructed to continue to give assistance to citizens of Tatar nationality in economic and cultural construction, taking account to their national interests and characteristics.

N. PODGORNY,
Chairman, Presidium of
U.S.S.R. Supreme Soviet.
M. GEORGADZE,
Secretary, Presidium of
U.S.S.R. Supreme Soviet.
The Kremlin, Moscow, Sept. 5, 1967.
Resolution of Presidium of U.S.S.R.
Supreme Soviet: ON PROCEDURE
FOR APPLYING ART. 2 OF APRIL
28, 1956, DECREE OF PRESIDIUM
OF U.S.S.R. SUPREME SOVIET.

The Presidium of the U.S.S.R.
Supreme Soviet resolves:

To explain that citizens of Tatar nationality who previously resided in the Crimea and the members of their families have the right, like all citizens of the U.S.S.R., to live anywhere on the territory of the Soviet Union in accordance with the effective legislation on job placement and passport procedure.

N. PODGORNY,
Chairman, Presidium of
U.S.S.R. Supreme Soviet.
M. GEORGADZE,
Secretary, Presidium of
U.S.S.R. Supreme Soviet.
The Kremlin, Moscow, Sept. 5, 1967.

Leisure

As has been pointed out many times, there is something paradoxical about the association of leisure with social problems. Leisure problems resemble those of a person who earns more than he can spend. As long as his expenditures are self-evidently compelling he has no problems. As long as a person has only enough time after work for sleep and physical maintenance functions, he does not worry about his leisure. Nor do sociologists worry about it. Leisure problems arise when it becomes less obvious how to use the time remaining after obvious necessities are taken care of. Additional complications enter into the situation in modern, secular societies where fewer and fewer things appear preordained and self-evident. First there is the notion that time is valuable and has to be treated as a precious commodity, to be exploited and made good use of. The more purposeful man gets, the more self-conscious he is about his leisure and the more anxious to avoid wasting it. A residual puritanism, the anxiety over the association of leisure and idleness, plays its part in both countries. In the U.S., it is less explicit; in the U.S.S.R. it is more carefully cultivated. In the official value system of the Soviet man, the misuse of leisure is in close kinship with the abhorrence of spontaneity. Just as social goals are set, planned, calculated, and controlled, so should be the personal ones. Time is to be spent usefully, not just enjoyably, although there is no prescribed clash between the two. Self-improvement and collective benefits should jointly flow from the prudent use of free time. In the United States, at least on the surface, attitudes are more relaxed, yet there is a similar haunting fear about the waste of leisure time. Two imperatives characterize the dominant American conceptions of well-spent leisure. It should be active and it should entail the possession of that elusive entity Americans call "fun." As long as fun is had, it does not matter what people do—hence the relative lenience of the American leisure "code"—provided, of course, fun is associated with some energetic activity, preferably in a group context. While the notion of "having fun" is hardly a precise one, certain activities are more readily associated with it than others. Going on a lonely walk or sitting quietly with a book is not a popular idea of fun. Fun teads to imply a lot of boisterous activity, the presence of other people, noise, sound, physical movement, laughter, and perhaps an element of jocular competition.

Another factor intruding upon leisure in modern societies is the presence of the mass media, a ready-made, prepackaged source or accessory of leisure that troubles many social critics. The socially problematic nature of the mass media will be more fully discussed in another section. At this point we only wish to note that there is an influential school of thought that regards heavy reliance on the mass media as unwholesome, stifling individuality, spontaneity, creativity, and good taste. This, at any rate, is the case in Western societies where spontaneity is a valued if rarely attained state. In the Soviet Union reliance on the mass media for recreational needs is not viewed unfavorably. On the contrary, since the mass media is part of the governmental apparatus it is given the role of educating the masses in a useful and purposeful manner, and it offers a good deal more (or less) than pure entertainment. It has plenty of messages, often too many for its audience. It may bore but hardly corrupt the innocent.

A comparison of Riesman and Zamoshkin on American leisure reveals points of agreement. Riesman argues that the importance of leisure grows in proportion not only with its quantitative increase but also with the decline in gratification offered by work. Thus unskilled and semi-skilled workers are most affected, and at the same time, least equipped to extract meaning and pleasure from their growing free time. Soviet sociologists automatically assume that work cannot be gratifying in a capitalist society under conditions of exploitation and alienation. Further, Zamoshkin believes that leisure serves an escape function in an intolerable social environment (i.e., the American) that offers no spiritual satisfaction, sustaining human relationships, or pride in work. Leisure time activities in his eyes are among the opiates capitalism offers to the masses who eagerly seize upon them. The problem is aggravated by the obsession with success, unattainable for the majority. The average American without prestige or status in the occupational or public realm tries to find compensation in leisure time activities which become a form of withdrawal from society. Even sexual conquest and accomplishments become substitutes for financial or occupational success. American leisure thus becomes yet another indicator of "the general crisis of capitalism" and the crisis of individualism. While this argument has considerable plausibility, it remains to be shown that these conditions are characteristic of capitalism or the United States, rather than of modern, secular, urban, mass societies, which create moral uncertainties, routinized jobs, increased social isolation, and surplus free time. Far more doubtful is Zamoshkin's proposition that the American mass media and leisure industry represent a sinister conspiracy to divert the attention of the masses from political issues and activities. It cannot be denied that, by and large, the American mass media is apolitical, sensational, unrealistic, and escapist. What is debatable is the degree to which this represents deliberate planning by the "ruling circles," and to what extent the character of the mass media is determined by political design. The Soviet opinion is especially dubious, since much evidence (including the Soviet case) shows that the demand for escapist entertainment is widespread in most contemporary societies and is hardly something forced upon the protesting masses. Zamoshkin is of course quite correct in suggesting that the mass media and entertainment are thoroughly commercialized in the United States. Most American sociologists would suggest that it is this circumstance rather than the conspiratorial, political-ideological motives of the ruling classes which accounts for much of their poor quality and tastelessness. Regarding the American mass media as an apologist of the capitalist social order and an instrument of embellishing its harsh realities, Zamoshkin once more unwittingly indulges in projecting a feature of the Soviet social environment. In the Soviet Union the mass media and the arts are given, openly and explicitly, exactly this task; namely, the inculcation and strengthening of the belief of the citizen that he lives in the best of all possible social worlds.

There is considerable evidence, as the following Soviet articles reflect, that the socially problematic aspects of leisure in the Soviet Union are not vastly different from those in the United States. Apparently many Soviet citizens are also beginning to confront the stage of bewilderment, which results from having more free time than they are accustomed to, although it is likely that this aspect of the problem is significantly smaller than in the United States and applies mainly to the younger age groups who have fewer obligations and responsibilities. There is also considerable evidence to show that Soviet leisure also has many escapist affinities as far as average attitudes are concerned. The proximity between leisure time activities, heavy drinking, and delinquent behavior is a recurring theme of the Soviet discussions. Nor do the Soviet masses consistently long for serious entertainment or show invulnerability to the temptations of shallow Western-type entertainments.

If cheap sensationalism, vulgarity, sexual stimulation, and violence characterize much of the American mass media and entertainment industries, dullness and boredom cast their shadows over much of the Soviet offerings, which attempt to combine entertainment and edification, recreation and moral uplift. Still, probably the major problem in the Soviet Union is the lack of facilities—not enough movie theaters, dance halls, restaurants, coffee houses, sports fields, etc.—and particularly their uneven distribution over the country. On the other hand, what is available is inexpensive.

Quite possibly leisure in the U.S.S.R. is regarded as a social problem mostly because of its affinity with other more serious problems (such as mentioned above) and also because its improper utilization might invite a hedonistic, anti-social, or overly individualistic outlook incompatible with the attributes of the New Soviet Man. Thus it is quite likely that leisure might have been prematurely elevated to the rank of a social problem because of the ideological sensitivity of the Soviet leadership, which is unwilling to give up its hard-won gains in disciplining and reeducating the masses who are beginning to be tempted by greater affluence and comfort.

LEISURE
IN THE U.S.:
The American View

Some Issues in
the Future of Leisure

DAVID REISMAN and ROBERT WEISS

We want in this article to explore some of the problems in the use of the leisure which technological and organizational development have brought within our reach. Primarily, we shall be concerned with the consequences for the industrial worker of the new phase of the Indus-

Reprinted from David Riesman and Robert Weiss, "Some Issues in the Future of Leisure," Social Problems, IX, No. 1 (Summer, 1961), pp. 78–86, by permission of Social Problems *and The Society for the Study of Social Problems.*

trial Revolution in which the level of productivity is almost independent of the input of human energy, and leisure consequently is available to just those men who might once have found themselves condemned to endless days in the plant. Secondarily, we shall be concerned with the members of professional and managerial strata for whom work appears to be losing its centrality though their hours of work and its psychic arduousness decline little, if at all.

WORK AND LEISURE FOR THE INDUSTRIAL WORKERS

It is a political and economic problem to ensure that leisure be the consequence of technological developments, and not simply unemployment. This first, and basic, problem is far from solved. Wage protection alone is not the answer, although Galbraith has cogently argued[1] for maintaining the purchasing power of the unemployed at almost the level they realized while employed. Such a measure fails to give to men the structuring of the day, the feeling of personal adequacy, and the relatedness to society that only work provides for most adult male Americans. It is true that if industrial workers are asked in a survey why a job is important, they tend to respond with matter-of-fact phrases like "You have to work to eat," or "That's the way the society works." Yet these conventional remarks cover the fact that for most of them holding down a job is necessary to a sense of responsible, and respectable, adulthood.[2] Not only do they feel that it is a man's role, in an outworn phrase, "To bring home the bacon," but a sizeable minority of them explain the value of marriage on the basis that it provides a man with a family for whom he may work.[3] (A paradoxical reversal of the image of the man trapped into marriage and a life of servitude.) To be sure, there are exceptions in those groups and communities which have adapted to widespread, endemic unemployment. Young single men awaiting military service or some other voice that will give their life direction may, in place of a steady job, seek to prove their manliness by what is ironically called juvenile delinquency. So too those discriminated against in the job market, such as Negroes and Puerto Ricans in Harlem, may find other patterns of masculinity.

In a society where most men work, the job furnishes a metronome-like capacity to keep in order one's routine of waking and sleeping, time on and time off, life on and life off the job. As surveys show, however, only a minority of industrial workers have any interest in the jobs themselves; it would be amazing to find a job so satisfying that a man would be anxious to continue with it after the day is over. Occasionally a skilled machinist will take a dour pride in his ability to turn out a blue-printed piece, or in his ingenuity in outwitting the time-study man, but these accomplishments seldom suffice to sustain his interest during a long day spent setting and nursing a turret lathe. Moreover, as Robert Dubin has argued, not even the community that springs up on the shop floor is of great moment to the production workers,[4] although his membership in it and liking for it may be essential in permitting him to get through the day.[5] His relations with his fellows are neither deep nor is there any expectation that they will be permanent. Indeed, no matter how friendly the work group to which he belongs, the industrial worker is likely to assume that his next job will furnish him

[1] John Kenneth Galbraith, *The Affluent Society*, Boston: Houghton-Mifflin, 1958.

[2] Material on the functions of work is based on a study by R. S. Weiss and R. L. Kahn, supported by a grant from the Institute of Labor and Industrial Relations, The University of Michigan—Wayne State University. See also R. S. Weiss and R. L. Kahn, "Definitions of Work and Occupation," *Social Problems,* 8 (Fall, 1960), pp. 142–151.

[3] Based on unpublished results of a survey conducted by the Survey Research Center, University of Michigan, 1953.

[4] Robert Dubin, "Industrial Workers' Worlds: A Study of the Central Life Interests of Industrial Workers," *Social Problems* (January, 1956), pp. 131–142.

[5] Donald Roy, "Banana Time," *Human Organization,* Vol. 18, No. 4 (Winter, 1959–60), pp. 158–168.

with an equally good group of men to work with. Save in the form of car pools, work contacts are almost never carried off the job. (Not that this is necessarily regrettable: contacts off the job may be regarded as all the more refreshing because they differ or appear to differ from those on the job.)

Given the lack of intrinsic interest in work, it is not surprising that during the last century the lower ranks of industrial and office workers have taken part of the gains of productivity in the form of time off rather than in the form of increased pay. Up to a certain point, this drive to reduce hours is a drive also to increase one's chances to be human: it is when waking time outside of work comes to equal or exceed waking time at work that the marginal utility of further free time or unpaid time may come into question. Even so, the drive to reduce hours continues. Partly, it is maintained by the sheer momentum of the revolution by which the working class has become the new leisure class. Partly, it reflects the boredom of the school child, who wishes at least in fantasy that every day were a holiday. Partly, it reflects the growing cynicism concerning work about which Paul Goodman writes in *Growing Up Absurd*.[6] Indeed, in the light of the purposes a job serves, reduction in the hours spent at work does not require any redefinition of the importance of work: so long as one has a job, requiring some substantial fraction of time, work has met its most important requirement for the industrial worker. Yet when free time is empty and resembles a temporary layoff more than it does an anticipated weekend, men begin to be restless; many complain that the day is filled by small tasks requested by their wives. It seems to us that the reduction of the workweek may, for many men, be coming increasingly close to the point where it is not so much a matter of giving a disliked employer less for more, than it is a matter of getting more "free" time than one knows what to do with

One development, of course, anticipated by Veblen, has postponed this day of reckoning; namely, that the free time has been time to expose oneself to all the stimuli for acquiring new consumer tastes, which in turn require new sources of income. What has happened, where the six-hour day has been introduced, is that many men have taken on second jobs.[7] The unions are sharply opposed to the practice, on ideological grounds, since it defeats the aim of a reduced workweek for members, and on practical grounds, since it means there are then fewer jobs to go around. Yet the practice is insidious, and in union circles, it is whispered that even union officials have taken on a second job as a real estate agent or bartender or cab driver. The most obvious explanation, and the one offered by union officials, is that the men are money-hungry. But this is an insufficient explanation. These same men would object violently to working on holidays such as the Fourth of July, let alone Christmas, irrespective of double or triple time wages. Few of them, we would guess, would be willing to work seven days without a break, and most would object to having different days off instead of Saturday and Sunday. Rather, what has happened is that they have free time that is not clearly earmarked for leisure. It is as though their jobs suddenly turned from full-time to three-quarter time, and they must decide whether to loaf in that extra quarter time available or to go out and

---

6 Paul Goodman, *Growing Up Absurd*, New York: Random House, 1960.

7 Harvy Swados, "Less Work—Less Leisure," in *Mass Leisure*, Eric Larrabee and Rolf Meyersohn (eds.), Glencoe, Illinois: Free Press, 1958, pp. 353–363.

earn some money. Given the indebtedness for housing and consumer goods that is endemic in America, many members of this group could hardly help feeling that they had no right to work only part-time so long as they are up against it financially. And, in addition, there is a built-in cumulativeness about many consumer goods: a house can always be added to or improved; a car is a standing invitation to travel and to evenings out on the town; a television set, an invitational mirror of the good life.

It is hard to see any way out of this spiral in the distribution of leisure to industrial workers. Given incomes inadequate to aspirations, and aggressive selling through the mass media and elsewhere, with resulting indebtedness, is it likely that the individual who is in debt will accept a thirty-hour or a twenty-hour week, without looking for another job? What indeed are the alternatives for him? He has now more time than necessary to recuperate from work's pressures or compensate for its demands: increase in the amount of leisure means that not only will there be more time for compensatory activities —to the extent that this is a primary function of leisure—but that there will be less need for such activities. Thus, recuperation from work's pressures as a rationale for the use of leisure time may no longer loom so large. Even if recuperation remains important, a man may decide that another job of a very different sort is just as "recreational" as one more evening spent bowling or looking at television or driving about.

An ironic commentary on the pressure toward a reduction in the workweek is provided by a study in which industrial workers were asked what they would do if they had an extra hour a day; most of them responded: "Sleep."[8]

8 Reported by Rolf Meyersohn.

While for a few this may bespeak an over-full life, and for others a general irritation with a nettling or silly question, the answer seems to us to symbolize the lack of interests and resources that could give point to the leisure time that is now available. A study of the impact of the four-day week in a situation where it was too unpredictably scheduled to permit other employment on the additional day off, indicates that this additional day was less of a boon for the workers than they had originally anticipated.[9] The extra day off was not a day off for the children, so there was an empty house during school hours; nor was it a day off for the wife, so there was house-cleaning and vacuuming, with the man in the way. In this plant, a small aircraft manufacturing company in southern California, the four-day week was scheduled for one week out of four. Though originally anticipated with high hopes, it was soon disliked: television, loafing, ballgames, all these were felt to be weekend activities, and fell flat during the workweek. One wonders whether, even in California, this reflects residual Puritanism, analogous to the feeling that it is wicked to go to the movies in the morning. It certainly does reflect the social or festive nature of much valued leisure, as well as the difficulty in developing a program for the use of a sizeable increase in leisure time when other members of the family and the community are not equally free.

When we talk of programming, in fact, we come to a characteristic which seems most common within working class groups: the lack of the middle-class pattern of postponed gratification and planning ahead, if not actual con-

9 Rolf Meyersohn, "Some Consequences of Changing Work and Leisure Routines," paper presented to the Fourth Congress of Sociology, Section on Leisure, Milan-Strezza, Italy, September, 1959.

tempt for it. Only a few of these men use increased leisure to prepare themselves for higher vocational tasks. Only a few turn out for union meetings, and fewer still evidence any interest in improving the lot of the occupational group to which they belong or in taking a hand in the decisions that may affect them in the future. So, too, Great Books courses or union education programs seem to attract few workers. The necessary ideology which seems to be lacking in the United States is said to be found in some Communist countries, notably Yugoslavia which recruits a proportion of the workers for educational and agitational tasks. The level of secondary education is also lacking that one finds in a country like Denmark or Japan that leads many workers to become active, lifelong readers—although in the United States, before the Civil War, energetic workmen did flock to the Mechanics Institutes in that first burst of enthusiasm for science and literacy that our present educational system both harnesses and attenuates.

In this situation, most industrial workers appear to fall back on their families as the enclave within which leisure is to be spent. The long drive on Sunday, with its combination of aimlessness and togetherness, is traditional in this group. Leisure time away from the family, "with the boys," is defined as time for blowing off steam, and is limited to what is thought to be physiologically and psychologically necessary. Of course, this is not the whole story. Many workers cultivate fairly expensive and time-consuming hobbies, such as hunting. Some attend art classes for adults, and a handful may join the predominately middle-class groups devoted to amateur music. A very few take part in voluntary associational activities; by and large these are staffed by the upper social strata.

It is discomforting to reflect on the complexity and scope of the programs that would be required to overcome this legacy of passivity and aimlessness. What sort of adult education program could meet these workers halfway in helping them plan their leisure in terms of lifelong opportunities? What sort of change of perspective on the world and the self is required before muted and barely realized dissatisfactions can become a lever for individual development?

At the level of the society the problems are no less grave. Where the recreationist works for the public rather than the private sector, he has as little leverage at his disposal as the city planner has. One of us recently had the chance to observe the enormous resistance that developed in a small Vermont community to the idea of a recreation leader that the town should build a swimming pool as a war memorial rather than some monument: the project was fought by the town's elders as frivolous and a waste of money, in spite of the fact that the nearby rivers had become too polluted for swimming. Only an enormous civic effort finally carried the project through, and now "everyone" can see what a boon it is to children and their parents, to farmers and workers after a hot day, and to otherwise idle teenagers who can display themselves on the high dives, or if they swim well enough, make a little money and gain some sense of responsibility from helping act as lifeguards around the pool. One consequence of the political weakness of public recreation is a tendency to over-ideologize particular leisure-time activities, exaggerating their importance and their potential contribution to individual character and the fabric of society. The President's campaign for physical fitness as a way of beating the Russians is an illustration.

College sports have clearly suffered in this way; the proposition that team sports contribute to character building has resulted primarily in increased shock when it is reported that football players may more nearly work for a school than attend it, or that some basketball players are on a gambler's payroll. Yet it is hard to see how social forms adequate to the new leisure can be developed without an ideology that will mobilize people and strengthen the power of the few groups who are now concerned with the preservation of wilderness areas, the setting aside of land in our sprawling metropolitan belts for the play of adults and children, and the general release of resources other than commercial ones for experimentation and research in the field of leisure. In comparison with the organizational forms developed for the integration of work effort, there barely exist social forms for the utilization of leisure. Yet such comments evoke the whole paradox of freedom and planning. Leisure is supposed to be informal, spontaneous, and unplanned,[10] and is often defined as unobligated time, not only free of the job but free of social or civic obligations, moonlighting, or more or less requisite do-it-yourself activities. One result of this outlook, however, is to discourage whatever planning is possible (except, perhaps, in terms of the family, not always the optimal unit for leisure when one thinks of the development of its individual members). When we confront such problems, we are inclined to think that significant changes in the organization of leisure are not likely to come in the absence of changes in the whole society: in its work, its political forms, and its cultural style.

[10] See, in this connection, David Riesman, Robert J. Potter, and Jeanne Watson, "Sociability, Permissiveness, and Equality," in *Psychiatry: Journal for the Study of Interpersonal Processes*, Vol. 23, No. 4 (November, 1960), pp. 323–340, and by the same authors, "The Vanishing Host," in *Human Organization*, Vol. 19, No. 1 (Spring, 1960), pp. 17–27.

LEISURE

IN THE U.S.:

The Soviet View

The Psychology of "Escapism"
and "Fun Morality"

Y. A. ZAMOSHKIN

The Philistine psychology and narrow consumers' attitude to life are often expressed in the "small" man's striving to escape into the sphere of entertainment during his leisure time, from the weight of exploitation, from the joyless wage labor, the routine and drabness of daily life, from the oppression of the state-monopolistic bureaucratic organizations, from constant anxiety, which is engendered by the threat of unemployment, crises, war, political and social catastrophes. These "escapist" tendencies are characteristic of a man who himself experiences the destructive social consequences of the general crisis of capitalism, who is frightened by the symptoms of this crisis, but who doesn't yet comprehend the real way out of this crisis, who is unaware of the perspectives linked to the anti-monopolistic struggle and the communist movement. At the same time, this is a psychology

Original Translation

From Yu. A. Zamoshkin, The Crisis of Bourgeois Individualism and Sociology. *Moscow: Izd. Nauka, 1966, Chapter 11, pp. 250–270.*

of a man who no longer believes in the possibility of the realization of individualistic ideals of success in business or work, and who attempts to hide from his consciousness of "failure" which persistently pursues him in working, official, and business relations.

...Extensive, empirical sociological investigations by such well-known American specialists as E. Katz and P. Lazarsfeld have shown that for many people in the U.S., leisure and especially entertainment, which they can depend on during leisure time, are distinctive means of psychological escape from feelings of depression and loneliness generated by the dehumanized bureaucratic reality, that reality which deprives the individual of "an adequate participation in public life."[1]

What do those "joys of leisure" mean in practice, in which the "little" man whom we described attempts to find the means of psychological escape from social reality? In reading American literature, and acquainting oneself with the materials of empirical investigation,

[1] J. T. Klapper, *The Effects of Mass Communication* (New York: 1960), p. 312.

with the data of numerous polls, you unwillingly arrive at the conclusion that very often hopes and expectations connected with leisure appear to be linked to the idea of family life, the hopes for a happy life, and happiness through close contact with one's intimates.

...The most important and most popular leisure activities in the U.S. are commercial entertainments, created and fabricated by the movie industry, television, radio companies, newspapers, magazines, and publishing houses of pulp literature, by the companies which organize sports events, syndicates which maintain chains of night clubs and burlesque shows, by enterprises which produce records, etc. *It is precisely these entertainments which also often serve as the basic means for the satisfaction and realization of "escapist" tendencies and aspirations* which appear in the consciousness of the "little" man, the average American citizen. Such amusements are simultaneously nourishing and developing these tendencies and aspirations and in every possible way profiting by them.

The movies, television, radio, the press, etc., all that in the U.S. it is customary to call "the means of mass communications," play an enormous and perhaps an ever-increasing role in the spiritual life of the contemporary American. It is sufficient to indicate that 98% of American homes have radios, and 86% have television sets (it is computed that each typical TV viewer spends 3 to 5 hours out of 24 in front of the TV), that 45 million Americans frequent movie theaters weekly, that 1750 daily newspapers with a circulation of 58 million copies (plus 555 Sunday papers with a circulation of 19 million copies) are published, and 8000 magazines with a circulation of 400 million copies yearly; publishers release well-known comics in the quantity of 700 million copies yearly, and about

60% of the whole population reads basically poor literature (serious literature is read by only 10–15%).[2] Many more such facts could be cited.

Powerful means of mass entertainment exert an enormous pressure on the ordinary American, lying in wait for him at every step, enticing him with the help of the most sophisticated advertising techniques, striving to make him submit to their influence, and striving to compel him to surrender to them the lion's share of his leisure time.

...Naturally the functions of the cinema, television, radio, the press, etc. cannot be reduced merely to the provision of commercial entertainments. Their first function was and remains *political and ideological propaganda,* the cultivation of the apology of American capitalism, its institutions, ideas, principles, and "way of life." Besides that, one of their basic functions is commercial advertising.

...The basic type and orientation of entertainment is of the *escapist* variety, i.e., whose goal is to provide man with the means "to escape reality." According to J. T. Klapper, one of the main authorities in this field, "both critics-publicists, and individual investigators have for a long time been expressing concern over the significant increase of escapist themes in the products of mass media."[3] "Escapist" products act as a kind of social narcotic which gives man an artificial and temporary oblivion from the real state of affairs. Amusement of this kind is attained first of all through *spiritual narcotization* of people, the stupefaction of their consciousness, and the intoxica-

2 E. Emery, P. H. Ault, W. K. Agee, *Introduction to Mass Communications* (New York: 1960), pp. 129–130. W. Schramm, ed., *Mass Communications* (Urbana: 1960), p. 495. B. Rosenberg and D. M. White, eds., *Mass Culture* (Glencoe: 1957), p. 123.
3 J. T. Klapper, *op. cit.,* pp. 166, 179–180.

tion of their senses and emotions. P. Lazarsfeld and R. Merton wrote that "the mass media can be included among the most effective narcotics."[4]

How do movies, television, radio, the press, etc. attempt to achieve a narcotic effect? How do these modern narcotics act upon the personality of the Americans?

First of all, the commercial mass entertainments strive for the narcotic effect by leading man away from disturbing social contradictions, characteristic of his social environment, to *an artificially created world, a world of illusions, myths, and dreams.*

...An American who in real life cannot hope to achieve what is generally considered success from a traditionally individualistic point of view, and whose only prospect is of being a wage earner without any rights, at the state-monopolistic organization, this is the man movies, television, radio, etc. attempt to "entertain" with an illusory sense of "participation" in the success of other people. Such a man is continuously shown the most intimate details of the personal life and life style of prosperous people, those who have capital, prestige, and power. This device has been called "false identification" in American literature. Its purpose is the temporary, artificial and illusory diversion of those who are failures from the point of view of individualistic bourgeois standards of success in real life. False identification also serves the purpose of banishing a sense of failure by means of the colorful depiction of other people's successes.

...Thus it is evident that there is a very close connection between two basic functions of the mass propaganda in the U.S.: the function of creating narcotic, "escapist" entertainment and the function of providing an ideological apology of the bourgeois reality. The powerful instruments of mass propaganda which present themselves as means of mass entertainment, in creating deceptive illusions, disorient people, distracting them from the acute conflicts and contradictions in the U.S.

..."Escapist" mass entertainments further enormously the emergence of that moral-psychological condition which we conditionally designated as "anomie" in this book. This is a condition of moral laxity, nihilism and cynicism. A man who is acutely aware of the contrast between his real social existence and its idealized forms, ideological stereotypes, and its moral symbols created by mass propaganda and mass entertainment often stops believing in anything. Surrounded on all sides by artificial, false, embellished pictures of social existence and relations in the U.S., he becomes infected by a mood of scepticism. This process takes place in the consciousness of many Americans, especially among the young people.

...At the present time much is said in American sociological and socio-psychological literature about the emergence and spread in the U.S. and among young people in particular of a special kind of morality which most investigators call "fun morality." This is a morality of night clubs, parties, and drunken orgies, a morality resting upon the cult of the automobile and fast driving, on the cult of "hot" jazz, whiskey, and sexual relations of the most coarse and unregulated kind. This is the morality of the so-called hipsters, young people with a shuffling walk, depraved eyes, and impudently scornful facial expression, who devote all their time to the pursuit of entertainment.[5]

This species of "morality" emerged as a type of protest (engendered by the conditions of the moral crisis in contem-

---

[4] W. Schramm, ed., *op. cit.*, p. 502.

[5] M. Wolfstein, N. Leites, *Movies: A Psychological Study* (Glencoe: 1950).

porary America) against the bigotry and hypocrisy of the "formal" code of "puritanical" morality, and against the conventionality of bourgeois norms. However, this protest is essentially *bourgeois-anarchistic,* it is the rebellion of the petty bourgeois, the Philistine, who is in a state of "anomie," having become a cynic and a pleasure seeker. This morality is the extreme, the most naked form of that consumers' individualism which we discussed earlier.

Appearing as a distinctive protest against the "formal" code of bourgeois "puritanical" morality, the "fun morality" *with the active help* of the mass media subsequently develops its own "formal" code, its regulations and demands, which young people must follow under the threat of losing their contemporaries' respect, and under the threat of ostracism. In this way, the demands and rules of the "fun morality" acquire a compulsory character. In spite of inward, personal inclinations, people often find themselves drawn into a circle of some or other entertainment, submitting to the fashion and tradition accepted in one or another group, and company of friends. In case of insubordination, loneliness awaits, and the threat of loneliness is the real tragedy of man in the U.S.

...The corruption of man's consciousness, senses and emotions in the U.S. becomes clearly apparent in matters which concern sexual life. At present the American society displays a great preoccupation with sex displayed in the unrestrained advertising of sensuality in movies, television, and in literature, a sensuality of the most coarse kind, which amounts to open pornography and pathology.

The study of erotic materials, programs, films and publications presented to the American reader and viewer reveals certain characteristic tendencies which are not uninteresting from the point of view of our analysis. The fact is that an artificial excitation of the senses and emotions in the realm of sexual relations very often is intended to serve as a kind of safety valve to compensate for the *inadequate individualism* of the average contemporary American. To this average man, who in daily life is a mere object of depersonalized suppression, manipulation and levelling on the part of the bureaucratic state-monopolistic organizations and institutions, who is pursued by the consciousness of "failure" in the competitive struggle for bourgeois "business success,"—to this average man it is constantly suggested that in the sphere of sexual relations he can find the means for "psychological compensation." It is suggested to him that victories in the competitive struggle for maximum "sexual attractiveness and irresistibility" supposedly can serve as a substitute for the victories in the realm of business competition, that acquiring "prestige" through "sexual success" is in the final analysis more important for the restoration of a lost sense of self-esteem than the acquisition of real capital, real power in the world of business.

LEISURE

IN THE U.S.S.R.:

The Soviet View

A Sociologist's Notes:
A Free Evening

A. G. KHARCHEV and M. PERFILYEV

Editors' Note.—Sociologists, Young Communist League workers, doctors, and educators are devoting much attention to the problem of young people's leisure time.

When boys and girls have only a minimum of responsibility at home and are not enrolled in night school or in correspondence courses at an institute, they sometimes find themselves with nothing to do once the working day is over. It is too early to go to bed. A whole evening lies ahead. How can they fill it?

Not everyone knows how to organize his free time, to make full and interesting use of it. This is borne out by sociological studies. One such study is described below.

*   *   *

Leningrad sociologists recently decided to find out how young people spend

Reprinted from A. G. Kharchev and M. Perfilyev, "A Sociologist's Notes: A Free Evening," Nedelya. Translated in Current Digest of the Soviet Press, XVII, No. 46 (Copyright © December 8, 1965), 14–15.

their leisure time and how this affects their work and moral outlook. Investigation confirmed that there is a direct relationship between an individual's work and his behavior in society. Some 4,000 young workers from several industrial enterprises and research institutes responded to a questionnaire.

It turned out that approximately 40% of the young people polled found themselves with four to five hours a day free from study, household chores, etc.; approximately 30% had from two to three hours' free time; while the rest, for the most part representatives of the "weaker sex," had less. Ninety per cent said they had at least four hours of leisure on Sundays. However, more than half of the young people, chiefly those with a lower level of education, replied that they gave no thought at all to the best and most useful way of spending their free time.

The questionnaire showed that the majority of those polled preferred to spend their free time at home or visiting relatives and friends. Other forms of leisure-time activity were reported in the following order: hiking, going to the movies, engaging in sports, visiting cafes and restaurants, and playing cards and dominoes. The lower the general educational and cultural level of those questioned, the more rarely does one come across such words as theater, concert hall, exhibit, museum, youth cafe. These forms of leisure are characteristic chiefly of those who to some extent plan their free time.

Pastimes that are not connected with spiritual interests and that are accompanied by drinking lead to no good. Last year more than 2,000 intoxicated young men were arrested in one Leningrad borough alone. Out of every ten violators of public order, nine are drunk. A group of juvenile delinquents serving sentences in corrective labor colonies for minors were questioned. The overwhelming majority of them said that the chief cause of their violations of the law had been "drinking out of boredom."

In the Hungarian People's Republic we once had occasion to talk with a comrade who was studying the problem of young people's leisure. He told us that in Budapest one can pass an evening in a restaurant or cafe for the price of a cup of coffee and a piece of pastry, or at most a glass of dry wine. "How do these enterprises pay their way?" we asked in surprise. "In the first place," he replied, " 'pumping' money out of the customers is not the only way to meet costs; you can make more room in the restaurants and cafes and lower overhead costs. In the second place, the moral costs, not the economic ones, must be given priority here. After all, it is clear that young people will not permit themselves to behave in public places as they might in private apartments and dachas."

Study of the causes of divorce in Leningrad has shown that approximately half of the divorces result from the husband's drinking. And think of the harm alcohol does to the national economy! It is the cause of thousands of lost man-days, diminished output and increased spoilage in plants and factories. The industrial enterprises we investigated reported hundreds of cases of absenteeism and tardiness due to drinking every year. On Mondays and the days after holidays labor productivity usually falls off markedly and cases of defective work and accidents become more frequent. Here are your "profits" from the sale of alcoholic beverages!

These difficulties arise in large part because we have too few recreational facilities that are genuinely cultural and are capable of attracting young people. A few years ago youth cafes were opened throughout the country. But why should they be restricted to young people? What is wrong with young people spending an evening there with their older comrades, rather than in a "special capacity"? Is the continuity of generations necessary only in labor and public activities? It is useful and interesting for people of different ages, occupations and tastes to associate. However, this is not the main point. What is far more important is that there are very few of the youth cafes. It is a problem to get into one of them. Each evening during the "rush hours" lines form at their doors. And even when you do get a seat at a table you don't feel comfortable and relaxed—the line out on the street doesn't get any shorter, and people keep peering impatiently through the windows wondering when a place will be free. So these enterprises began to die even before they were born.

It is apparent that these cafes are becoming less, rather than more, popular. Only 5% of those questioned spend their free time in them. Some did not even know they existed. The "Poets' Cafe" in Leningrad has so far been given no real support by the writers' organization. Naturally, then, it cannot play the role intended for it. And although everyone realizes that decisions alone are not enough, that a taste for everything new must be cultivated, the new is still taking root very slowly.

Unfortunately, in their economic and organizational structure the youth cafes are indistinguishable from public catering enterprises and continue to be conventional "trade points." The cafes' workers are concerned about receipts, which here too are the decisive index. And the only way to increase these receipts appreciably is to sell alcoholic beverages. In public catering, alcoholic beverages still account for about one-third of the plan.

The Leningrad Television Studio received a letter from A. Chigrinets, a resident of the city. "At the corner of Malaya Pushkarskaya and Sablinskaya Streets," she wrote, "there are a buffet, a beer-and-soft-drinks stand, and a dining room. Liquor and vodka are consumed here virtually all day long. Walk two blocks down Bolshoi Prospect and again you see signs: 'Wine and Champagne,' 'Beer and Soft Drinks,' 'Cognac.' And it's the same all along the avenue. There are always drunks gathered around these establishments. Among them are many young people."

The letter hardly needs any commentary. Yet the trade and public catering officials are making no real efforts to change the situation.

Young people love sports. At first glance everything is just fine in this area. According to the figures of one Leningrad borough sports council, the borough has approximately 50,000 sports participants. Actually, this figure is about five times too large. Yet more than 80% of the residents of this borough who were questioned said they would very much like to engage in sports! They would like to, but they can't—because the sports facilities will not accommodate all of them; because the physical culture workers are interested only in training masters of sports and setting records; because to get into a section it isn't enough merely to like sports, it's absolutely essential to have talent in one particular sport or another.

The stadiums and athletic fields of our cities are clearly inadequate. Yet facilities could be created with the help of Y.C.L. members. An example is the stadium recently erected in the small Donetsk Province city of Dzerzhinsk. But such cases are rare.

Where do the sports organizations get the astronomical figures that appear in their records? It seems that they list everyone who has ever been issued a sports society membership card and who pays membership dues, even though it is common knowledge that by no means everyone who receives such a card takes part regularly in athletics. The records also include people who even once during the year participated in intrashop competitions, as well as young men subject to military service who have had to pass the tests for their Ready for Labor and Defense badge. Most paradoxical of all is the fact that an individual who signs up for, say, three types of sports gets counted three times rather than once in the records.

The correct organization of leisure for city youth is unthinkable without clubs and Palaces of Culture. But these establishments, too, are ruled by a financial plan. Some clubs and Palaces of Culture have to all intents and purposes been converted into movie houses. Only auxiliary premises remain for mass work, and this work itself is so regimented that young people have long since lost the habit of just dropping in casually. According to data from the poll, fewer than 25% of the young workers and only 2% of the intelligentsia visited the clubs last year, and they came mainly for films and dances.

The conclusion is not very comforting: The majority of boys and girls spend a large part of their free time in the courtyards and streets.

Strange as it may seem, the Y.C.L. and trade union committees and public education departments devote little attention to the leisure of young people. The result is that "a child with seven nurses has no one to look after it." In the past five years the Y.C.L. committees in the boroughs we surveyed have devoted not a single plenary session or a single committee meeting to a discussion of the leisure of young Leningraders. Each year enterprises and institutions receive scores of notices from the militia concerning violations of law and order by young people. But it often happens that not only is there no discussion of these cases in the collectives, nothing whatsoever is done about them.

It is difficult to say at present just what should be done to make the clubs, sports organizations and cafes attractive to boys and girls, to make them enjoyable and interesting all the time. But one thing is clear: A serious search must be made for a solution, and everything should be tried. People whose responsibility it is to organize the leisure of young people must answer for this, just as engineers answer for the construction and operation of enterprises and agronomists for the fate of the harvest. We must always remember that the morale and work of young people depend on how they spend their free time.

On the Rational Use of the Off-Work Time of the Working People

G. PETROSYAN

The creation of the material and technical base for communism during the course of the next 20 years is the main economic task of the Soviet people. The solution of this task presupposes not only a sharp upsurge in the country's productive forces but also the further improvement of social relations. Ideological work is one of the most impor-

Reprinted from G. Petrosyan, Voprosy ekonomiki. Translated in Current Digest of the Soviet Press, XV, No. 33 (Copyright © September 11, 1963), 3–4.

tant sectors of the struggle for building communism. Therefore the Party devotes great attention to the communist upbringing of the working people, to the comprehensive spiritual and physical development of the member of society. "As the time spent on material production is reduced," the Party Program says, "ever greater opportunities are afforded to develop abilities, gifts and talents in the fields of production, science, technology, literature and the arts. People's leisure will be increasingly devoted to public activities, cultural intercourse, mental and physical development and artistic endeavor. Physical culture and sports will become a firm part of the everyday life of the people."

In the light of the Party Program's instruction, the problem of the rational use of the off-work time of the working people is acquiring exceptionally great economic and socio-political importance. The amount of off-work time and the way it is used reflect in a certain sense the level of development of society's productive forces, as well as the opportunities for people's spiritual and physical development.

The classical writers of Marxism-Leninism attach great importance to the problem of free time. Under communism, Marx wrote, "the real wealth is the developed productive force of all individuals. The measure of wealth will then be no longer working time but free time."

The Communist Party, guided by the great teaching of the founders of scientific communism, is putting into practice their instructions on the necessity for shortening the working day and increasing off-work time. The seven-year plan for developing the national economy envisages the creation of conditions for a transition to a workweek of 30 to 35 hours with two days off. This means that our country will have the shortest working day in the world. As a result of the transition to a six- and seven-hour working day, the working time of the working person has already been reduced by more than 50 full working days a year. There will inevitably be a further increase in the working people's off-work time in the future in consequence of additional reductions in working time. Therefore the rational use of the ever-growing amount of free time has already become an important task of communist construction. If it is to be solved correctly, it is first necessary to clarify whether all off-work time or only a part of it should be considered free time.

It is characteristic of the research of bourgeois economists that they use off-work time and free time synonymously. Some of them, for instance S. Braun, not only identify off-work time with free time but even artificially exaggerate the actual amount of such time by including in it losses of working time occasioned by the very existence of capitalism, specifically unemployment, occupational traumatism, etc. True, Braun makes a reservation by calling such free time "undesirable," but this does not change the essence of the matter. Such a position on the part of bourgeois economists is understandable. They pursue the aim of concealing the true dimensions of the working people's free time.

Unfortunately, our literature, too, often fails to distinguish between off-work time and free time.

In our view, off-work time and free time differ both in amount and in content. Off-work time is a broader concept than free time. Off-work time is the total time providing for simple and expanded reproduction of the working forces.* Free time is that part of the total off-work time providing for expanded reproduction of the working forces. The off-work time of working people can be divided into two parts. The first part consists of the time spent in sleeping, eating, housework, personal toilet, [samoobsluzhivaniye—literally, "self-service"], etc.—that is, time spent in the direct satisfaction of an individual's natural requirements. The second part consists of the time spent in rest, in studying and improving one's skills, in fulfilling public duties and satisfying

* ["Reproduction"—*vosproizvodstvo*—is to be understood as "refreshment" or "restoration." The meaning of "simple" and "expanded" in this Marxist formulation is explained in the next few sentences.—Trans.]

cultural needs. It is this part of off-work time that constitutes the free time of working people, in that its use is not connected with the mandatory satisfaction of natural and physiological requirements. The individual uses it for his own spiritual and physical development, for spending with the family or friends [literally "society."—Trans.], for leisure and relaxation, on the basis of the free choice of one means or another of employing it. Thus free time represents only a part of off-work time.

Free time is necessary for the harmonious development of the individual. This, needless to say, is in no way to demean the importance of labor for the all-round development of the individual. Labor, having created the individual, always remains primary and definitive in his development; the meaning and the beauty of life lie in labor. Labor and rest are merely the mutually alternating and interrelated means of the individual's vital activity. Therefore along with the labor carried out during working time, a large role in ensuring the all-round development of the members of a socialist society is played by free time and its rational use. Since the measure of society's wealth, as we move forward to communism, more and more becomes the amount of free time rather than the amount of working time, the constant increase of free time is just as important a task of communist construction as the steady reduction of working time. The importance of reducing working time lies precisely in the fact that this permits an increase in free time.

Free time can be increased not only by further reducing working time but also by increasing the share of off-work time represented by free time. A reduction in working time does not necessarily always lead to an equal gain in free time. If the rational use of off-work time is prevented by housing or service difficulties, shortcomings in the organization of public catering and trade, a shortage of children's preschool institutions, etc., this substantially curtails the effectiveness of reducing the working day. Therefore questions of making rational use of off-work time and of exposing shortcomings affecting such use are of enormous practical importance for increasing free time. The Communist Party and the Soviet government are creating all the conditions necessary to enable the working people to make the fullest use of their free time and to employ it to the greatest benefit. This is necessary for the formation of the new man—the member of the future communist society.

The first serious studies of the time budgets of working people in our country were carried out in the 1920s and 1930s. There followed a long period during which attention to the problem of off-work time slackened. Not until the end of 1958 did a number of scientific organizations undertake comprehensive investigations of the problem, in view of its enormous political and practical importance. In 1958–1960 an experimental time-budget study covering 20,000 man-days was carried out in Siberia, while in all during this period the time budgets of approximately 28,000 man-days were studied by various scientific and public organizations. However, this work was of an experimental nature and therefore the data obtained could not serve as the basis for more extensive and cardinal generalizations.

Analysis of these data indicates that the absolute magnitude of off-work time is relatively constant. The structure of off-work time, however, is extremely variable. It is influenced by a number of factors: the age and family situation of the worker, the composition of his family and the age of the children, the presence of "helping" members of the family (those who do not work in state enterprises or institutions and can give the working members of the family assistance in housework, bringing up the children, etc.), the amount of income and housing space per person, study and general-education level, type of occupation, existence of communal services, etc.

The structure of off-work time differs for different days of the week (weekdays, Saturdays, Sundays) and also is affected by the season of the year and by the branch of the economy in which the working people are employed. It is influenced, too, by other objective factors (family cooperation, whether the family has household appliances and machines, the distance between home and work, the working people's job experience and skills, the existence and distribution within the city of a network of service, children's, trade, cultural-enlightenment and medical institutions, public catering enterprises, urban transport, etc.).

The way our country's working people budget their time bears striking testimony to the enormous advantages of socialism over capitalism. Even before the transition to the shorter working day, an average of 66% to 68% of the working people's total time—i.e., more than two-thirds—was off-work time. Even on weekdays, the working people of our country already have approximately three hours of free time at their disposal, and in the long-established industrial and cultural centers they have even more. In describing the specific nature of the free time of the working people in a socialist society, it must be emphasized that their free time does not follow exhausting work for an exploiter but free and creative work for themselves.

The amount and content of free time are determined by the level of development of productive forces and the char-

acter of production relations in each social formation. Under capitalism, the existence of private ownership of the means of production and the private nature of the appropriation of the results of labor result in enormous amounts of free time for the parasitic classes, which they spend fruitlessly and negligible amounts of free time for the working people, for the intelligent use of which capitalism does not create the necessary conditions. In a society in which the exploitation of man by man reigns, free time, as Marx noted, takes the form of leisure for the few. "In capitalist society," he wrote, "free time is created for one class by turning the entire life of the masses into working time." After exhausting labor, it is very hard for the worker to restore in his off-work time the strength and energy he has expended. Therefore free time disappears almost completely from off-work time. Capitalist production relations determine not only the amount of free time in capitalist countries but also the way the working people employ it. A survey carried out in a Brussels factory in 1955 showed that 29% of the workers read a newspaper occasionally, while 19% did not read at all; 77.7% of the working men and 85.7% of the working women in the survey never visited a library. Data accumulated by Juliet Fisher in a 1940 Washington survey showed that more than 50% of the women workers (seamstresses, textile workers and glove makers) included in the study had not been to the movies in a week and the rest no more than once; only 5% went to the theater once a week; more than 46% did no studying.

The use of free time by the working people in socialist society is of a completely different character. The advantages of socialism over capitalism appear strikingly in the fact that socialism not only ensures an uninterrupted increase in free time for all the working people but also creates the conditions necessary for its intelligent and beneficial use. According to the materials of a sample investigation of the time budgets of working people in Novosibirsk, about 21.1% of the working people's free time is spent on studying and improving their qualifications. Of the time spent on relaxation [otdykh], 21.7% is devoted to self-improvement and self-education (listening to lectures and reports, participating in amateur groups, reading literature and newspapers). About 14% of the time for relaxation was spent attending films, the theater and concerts. In the U.S.S.R. the share of time spent on taking care of personal needs, preparing food, doing housework, family games, etc., is much smaller than in capitalist countries, while the share of time spent on self-education, active relaxation, rearing children, studying, reading literature, etc. is much greater.

The structure of the working people's off-work time in our country also varies according to the separate stages of socialist construction. Unfortunately, lack of systematic data on time budgets and of a single generally accepted method for studying them makes it impossible to compare the available factual material to disclose the nature of improvements in this structure for individual years. Still, some idea of these improvements can be obtained on the basis of the following data. Whereas in Moscow in 1923 working women spent six hours and two minutes on housework on weekdays, in 1958 the figure came to three hours and 20 minutes; in Novosibirsk in 1959 it stood at four hours and three minutes and in Novokuznetsk at three hours and 43 minutes. In 1923 Moscow's women spent two hours and 54 minutes preparing food, whereas in 1959 in Novosibirsk they spent 49 minutes, in Novo-

kuznetsk (the Kuznetsk Metallurgical Combine) 58 minutes, and in Krasnoyarsk one hour and 12 minutes.

The most essential changes have taken place in the structure of free time itself. Whereas in 1924 workers in Moscow—the country's major cultural center—devoted an average of six to eight hours a month to studying, now even in cities in Siberia the figure is two to two and a half times greater; for example, among workers in Novosibirsk it is 14–18 hours, in Krasnoyarsk about 20 hours, in Novokuznetsk 24 hours and in Sverdlovsk 26 hours. Moreover, many workers who combine work with study spend more than 100 hours a month on the latter. The Kuznetsk Basin miners who are combining study with work spend three hours 11 minutes daily on study on weekdays alone; the metallurgists spend four hours and construction workers two hours 53 minutes. As for members of Communist Labor brigades, materials from time-budget studies of 30 brigades show that they spend even more time on studying than other workers and twice as much time reading literature.

The reduction in irrational expenditures of off-work time also leaves the working people more time for relaxation and leisure. The time spent on relaxation by working women in Moscow on weekdays amounted to one hour and nine minutes in 1923 and to one hour and 40 minutes in 1958; in Novosibirsk in 1959 it came to one hour and 45 minutes, in Krasnoyarsk to one hour and 55 minutes and in Sverdlovsk to two hours. Nowadays certain free-time pursuits that in 1923–1924 still accounted for a big share (religious services, games of chance, etc.) have virtually disappeared. At the same time, a large role is now played by expenditures of free time that were insignificant or totally absent in the earlier period: participation in amateur groups, people's theaters, people's volunteer detachments for preserving public order, universities of culture, etc.

The changes in the structure of the use of free time that have taken place during the years of Soviet power testify to another remarkable phenomenon— the gradual liberation of women from housework as a result of the increasing level of public service organizations, (the development of the network of children's institutions, public catering, communal service facilities, etc.), and also as a result of the rationalization and mechanization of housework within the framework of the individual family.

Typically, women's liberation from housework is also taking place as a result of redistribution of domestic duties among the members of the family, through a radical break with the old notions about the woman's role not only in society but also in the family. Thus whereas in 1923 the time spent by a working woman in housework was two to two and a half times greater than that spent by a man, in 1959 the woman's work takes only 30% to 50% longer. From another aspect, in 1923 the man had 120% more free time than

the working woman, whereas in 1959 he had only 30% to 40% more.

However, analysis of time-budget data indicates that the enormous potential for improving the structure of off-work time that has been created under socialism is not yet being put to full use, that there are still many irrational expenditures of working people's off-work time whose elimination would considerably increase the amount of free time. The basic causes of these irrational expenditures are, on the one hand, the still inadequate provision in some cities of the necessary conditions of life (housing, communal services, sanitation-medical, trade, cultural-enlightenment, transportation and other types of services, children's and preschool institutions, public catering enterprises, entertainment enterprises, etc.) and, on the other hand, shortcomings in the work of the cultural and service establishments. Geographical differences in the levels of individual types of expenditure of off-work time are quite considerable, even for data covering comparable categories of working people over comparable periods.

Boredom and Free Time

L. Zhukovitsky

...Now to the problem of free time....

First of all, it seems to me that there simply is no direct connection between

Reprinted from L. Zhukovitsky, "Boredom and Free Time," Literaturnaya gazeta (January 4, 1967). Translated in Current Digest of the Soviet Press, XIX, No. 7 (Copyright © March 8, 1967), 12–13.

the existence of free time and anti-social behavior. A man does not start a fight in the street because he happens to have a free evening. And, vice versa, even an extremely busy person can always manage to find half an hour for an act of hooliganism if he wants to. Neither a drama club nor a photography club nor even an ultramodern youth cafe with stained-glass panels on construction themes will distract our man from such action.

Incidentally, there has been wide publicity lately, fortunately without much effect, about another mighty filler of free time—the hobby. A hobby is an interest not directly related to a person's job. It doesn't matter what it is. It could be an interest in spearfishing, or it could be collecting cigarette boxes. Or thimbles. Or pink fish with transparent tails that seem to be made of nylon. Or postcards.

Advocates of the wider practice of hobbies usually cite Gorky's statement that eccentrics adorn the world. As if it were possible to mass-produce eccentrics by means of hobbies. After all, in unthinking collecting there is something of the miserliness of Plyushkin [in Gogol's "Dead Souls"], who was also an eccentric of sorts but who hardly adorned the world.

Well, fine, people can object. I am railing at hobbies. But what do I suggest instead? What else is to fill young people's free time?

Nothing. It is not necessary to fill it. It's not necessary to fight free time. It is my deep conviction that there is no problem of free time at all, but there is the problem of personality. And it is necessary to think about how to make the human personality richer, more vivid, more talented. Of course, putting the question this way also entails talking about sports and amateur activities. But how a problem is approached makes a difference, just as it makes a difference whether a samovar is lifted by the handle or the pipe. For far from every solution to the "problem of free time" fosters the sensible and harmonious development of the personality.

In recent years our young sociologists have conducted several studies to find out how young people spend their free

time. I am deliberately refraining from analyzing the results they obtained. After all, the information, for example, that on the average our contemporary young person reads five books, sees five films and attends five lectures a month does not tell us anything about his personality. He may read Chekhov, see "Wild Strawberries" and attend lectures on the latest achievements in genetics; but he can also read five detective novels and with deep personal interest attend five consecutive lectures on the evils of alcoholism.

However, this is still time that, although free, is filled with arrangements, so to speak. But what if it is not filled? If it is simply free?

At a public discussion I once heard a speech by an attractive 18-year-old girl, who said, among other things: "In our city young people have nothing to fill their free time with, so boys and girls loaf about the streets in the evenings, and everybody knows what that leads to."

Had I the power I would, despite all my hatred of bureaucracy, issue an order compelling boys and girls to walk along the street in couples at least two or three hours a week. And I'll tell you why.

The fact of the matter is that our civilized age gives people a multitude of opportunities to associate with one another without talking. Love can develop very well even if both parties maintain the silence of the graveyard.

You can get acquainted at a dance. And if you are well dressed, if you dance "modernly," three sentences of a meteorological nature will suffice for the evening. Then the young man invites the girl to go to the movies. The heroes on the screen utter lofty and mysterious words; an atmosphere of beauty and mystery envelops the girl, and the undertaking costs the young man one ruble if he gets good seats and it is not a double feature. Finally, he invites the girl to his home. Here, you would think, there is no way out, he has to talk. But, glory be to progress, we are not savages: Start the tape recorder or put a record on the record player, or turn on the radio—and keep quiet all evening long and enjoy it!

In short, today a boy and a girl can not only get acquainted but can even get married without having spoken a single significant word. And only half a year later the girl may discover that her chosen one is a dolt. . . .

Free time is useful time! It reminds the young, and not only the young, that a human personality cannot be carried around in the hand like a transistor radio, cannot be left home like a book and cannot be bought for half a ruble like a ticket to the movies.

Free time is the hallowed time of human communication. . . .

Clearly, we shall not solve the problem of personality by filling up free time to the maximum. That is, we'll solve it but the result will be sad—a mediocre, spiritually impoverished personality.

It seems to me that the evident failure of many youth cafes was no accident. A young man or girl could come to a cafe at seven o'clock and sit there until eleven, thereby obtaining some impressions in the shape of dry wine and poems recited from the stage.

But all this had a very distant relation to the development of personality. A visit to a cafe was not creative. The cafe form itself was not conducive to anything serious. At a distance of five meters from the stage the poems were drowned out by the clink of wine glasses and forks. You could talk about them only to your table partner, but you didn't even want to do that: Everybody understood that the poems were wanted here not for themselves but as a symbol of intellectual time-spending. As a result, serious, creative-minded young peo-

ple who wanted intellectual communication refused to be satisfied with conviviality. And without them the youth cafes soon atrophied as youth centers while flourishing incidentally as cafes.

Youth clubs are an entirely different matter. Especially discussion clubs, where in our troubled time young truth-seekers passionately discuss the most diverse questions, from the composition of poems to the international situation. As is known, truth is born in argument. But not only truth. Convictions and the ability to defend them are born. Respect for somebody else's opinion and, to a considerable extent, knowledge of life are born. Anyhow, if the personality is not born, at least it is shaped. Incidentally, the cafe-clubs have survived and to this day are functioning splendidly in many places.

But we have few such clubs. Moscow has a large dog club—may God prolong its days!—but there is no poetry-lovers' club (despite the enormous interest in poetry). We have excellent studios for amateur film-makers, which is all very well, but can they take the place of clubs for film-lovers? And we are in great need of a club for theater-lovers, where the most controversial productions could be discussed and where representatives of the noisy tribe of female theater admirers could admire their idols vocally and at the same time learn the elements of critical thinking.

It seems to me that if it were the aim of outing clubs to solve the problem of personality, and not of free time, they wouldn't be in such a hurry to turn outings into a competitive sport (by fitting love for local scenery into a rigid scale of norms: so many days, so many kilometers and so many nights camping out) but would give some thought to developing the creative aspect of outings.

And I think parents would be much closer to the mark if they thought not about how to fill their children's free time but about how the personality of a growing person is developed.

No, it is not necessary to occupy, to fill, free time. But it is necessary to show concern for making a person's interests broad and varied, his develop- ment harmonious and his curiosity about life inexhaustible. Then the problem of free time will disappear by itself. Or, more accurately, it will remain, but it will be quite different—there won't be enough free time. . . .

LEISURE

IN THE U.S.S.R.:

The American View

The Uses of Leisure

PAUL HOLLANDER

The emergence of leisure as an issue of public discourse, ideological concern, and sociological analysis is one of the obvious products of post-Stalin social change. While Stalin's jovial proposition in 1936 (about life having become better and gayer) somewhat overstated the case at the time of the Great Purge, from the late fifties life for the Soviet citizen did become less of a burden; consequently a quest for its available and unavailable pleasures began to gain momentum. The results, for Soviet ideologues, are yet another demonstration of the way in which "consciousness lags behind existence," or of the degree to which individual behaviour emancipates itself from the influence of institutions which were designed to guide it into

Reprinted by permission of publisher from Survey, by Paul Hollander. Copyright July, 1966.

appropriate channels. Given more (if still not enough) leisure, a great many Soviet citizens either have chosen to follow a path that shows a disturbing similarity to the ways in which citizens corrupted by capitalist societies spend their time, or they have exhibited symptoms of sincere bewilderment and paralysis of initiative. One student of such matters recently noted in *Pravda:*

If is not a secret that among some of our scientists and practical workers the conviction prevailed. . .that an increase in free time automatically leads to a rise in people's cultural and technical level and in their labor productivity. However, special research conducted by the USSR Academy of Sciences Philosophy Institute showed that it is impossible to avoid serious negative consequences when the working day is shortened without simultaneously expanding the places for cultural recreation and amusement, without improving the organization of leisure, especially for young people, and without conducting the appropriate ideological preparation.[1]

By now a veritable inventory of the undesirable responses to more leisure has been compiled by Soviet ideologues, journalists, party and komsomol officials, and social scientists. Particularly noteworthy are the time-honored reliance on alcohol, the spread of hooliganism, street-corner malingering, excessive television watching, and unseemly dances. In the following we shall deal primarily with those aspects of Soviet leisure which reflect peculiarly Soviet conditions.

How did leisure acquire such prominence in post-Stalin Russia? First of all, as Soviet spokesmen themselves point out, "non-working time" (of which leisure is a part[2]) acquires new importance in proportion to its quantitative increase. The reduction of the workday resulted in the citizens' spending less time in such well-defined settings as the place of work. The official recognition of the ideological-political significance of leisure must also be viewed in the context of diminished coercion. Since overt coercion has ceased to be the most favored way of exacting conformity, persuasion came to occupy a more prominent place in social controls. Leisure time activities provide, at least in theory, good opportunities for persuasion, yet the official intention to make it functional from the regime's point of view clashes with the popular pressures for making it private and apolitical.

The insistence that communist society is not far away also has implications for leisure (even though this insistence has become somewhat more muted since the end of the Khrushchev era). Blueprints of communism must entail, besides projections of material abundance, what people will be able and expected to do with their free time.

The current official interest in leisure is also a by-product of the concern with the younger generation. Free time plays a much greater part in the lives of the young than in those of adults, and the ways in which they spend this time have a lasting influence upon the formation of their character. Soviet spokesmen find the misuse of free time a source for the development of anti-social attitudes. "We must always remember that the morale and work of young people depend on how they spend their free time."[3] And, no doubt, how they spend their free time also depends on their morale.

Under socialism every worker can make use of his free time as he sees fit. This does not, however, mean that society takes a passive attitude toward the ways in which he utilizes his time.[4]

Two major themes permeate the official discussion of leisure. One is the interdependence of leisure and work, that is, the contribution which well-spent leisure can make to efficiency at work; the other is the relationship between leisure and the "all-round development of the personality." Thus the desired functionalization of leisure takes two forms: the morale-building, which has economic, productive relevance, and the

[1] Transl. in *Current Digest of Soviet Press* (in the following abbreviated as *CDSP*), 6 April 1966, p. 5.

[2] *'Non-working time*...that which is not directly absorbed by participation in socially productive activities....It includes routine activities of daily life and free time....Free time is the part of non-working time which includes study...voluntary public activities, leisure, hobbies, creative activities, etc....Leisure is one of the parts of free time connected with the restoration of the psychic and physical energies of man'. *Sotsiologiya v SSSR* (Moscow, 1965), vol. II, pp. 485, 495.

[3] CDSP, 8 December 1965, p. 15.

[4] G. S. Petrosian, *Vnerabochee Vremya Trudiashchikhsya v SSSR* (Moscow, 1965).

ideological, which promotes the integration of the personal and political, or the personal and collective spheres of life. The official approach is frankly utilitarian. . . .

. . . .Needless to say, the desires of the Soviet Government and the recommendations of its ideologues are far from being the sole determinants of how Soviet citizens actually spend their leisure. Among the conditions affecting leisure we find factors which are independent of the official policies or which represent the unintended consequences of them. For example, the expenditure of free time is negatively affected by poor living conditions, the scarcity of consumer goods and household labor-saving devices, the time-consuming nature of routine tasks such as shopping. The priorities of the economy are further reflected in the acknowledged inadequacy of facilities for entertainment and recreation, particularly in the rural areas, small towns, and new industrial settlements. At the same time there is a whole set of factors which exert pressure towards greater popular demand for more and better leisure. If the home, in terms of privacy, comfort, and recreational facilities leaves a great deal to be desired, public places of entertainment become all the more important and alluring.

The limited resource allocation for private telephones, cars, and household articles is also relevant here: all these services and facilities encourage private leisure. This is not to suggest that the economic factors behind these policies are not more weighty than the official fear of privacy; but when funds are available and choices have to be made, the public sector will be given primacy largely for ideological reasons. This is best shown by the contrasting development of telephones and television. The former is a largely private instrument of inconsequential and informal communications, a device for the maintenance of social life and personal relationships. Television, by contrast, is a centrally-controlled instrument of one-way communication, the contents of which are highly standardized. The figures speak for themselves: the number of telephones (this includes close to 3 million public phones and an unknown but high proportion of official ones) is 7 million, while those of TV sets is 15 million. It is unlikely that these discrepancies have much to do with the costs of installing phones vs. manufacturing TV sets and setting up TV stations.

In examining the actual expenditure of free time by Soviet citizens we can find interesting information in the newly fashionable time-budget studies designed to obtain a detailed picture of how selected groups of citizens spend their time.

A major study conducted among industrial workers of six cities, Erevan, Novokuznetsk, Kostroma, Sverdlovsk, Krasnoyarsk, Norilsk, provides many examples of the persisting deficiencies in the use of non-working time. Among them is the fact that free time constitutes only 16.8 per cent of the non-working time, while domestic work and household care consume 22.3 per cent. Activities related to work, i.e. transportation, changing from one shift to another, also account for an excessive amount of non-working time: together with domestic work and personal care, twice the amount of free time. Here lies one of the principal causes for concern and the mainspring of such studies; the large areas of inefficiency which surround the place of work and which would create problems, even if it were assumed that at the work place itself exemplary order and organization prevailed. Among the sources of the irrational use of time—which leads to its being swallowed up by domestic work and other trivia—the author mentions the underdeveloped state of "housing, communal, sanitary-medical, commercial, cultural, transport and other kinds of services...those of children's and preschool establishments, enterprises for communal feeding, places of entertainment, and so on."[5] This is seen as largely a problem of regional differences, and in particular of the surviving gap between rural and urban areas. Indeed, as all the studies show, the widest gulf in the pattern of recreation appears to be between the rural and urban population as a whole. Collective farm peasants are the single most disadvantaged group, if not in terms of absolute amount of time available for leisure, then in the accessible opportunities for its use. The most alarming expression of this lack of opportunities is the escape of the young from the villages and the resulting manpower shortage, and the reluctance of professionals and experts to accept rural assignments. However, the problem has broader implications. The current rural (and to some extent even the urban) leisure situation is the product of modernization, which has proceeded to a sufficient degree to undermine or destroy traditional forms of peasant recreation, yet not far enough to provide adequate substitutes. This has as its result a sense of cultural confusion and occasionally actual nostalgia for some of the old rural ways. Not infrequently the maintenance and enrichment of well organized non-religious, traditional holidays in the countryside is recommended.

5 Petrosian, *op. cit.*, pp. 64, 78, 127, 129. Many of his findings, and especially those connected with the inadequate availability and/or utilization of free time, were confirmed by recent articles in *Komsomolskaya Pravda* reporting the results of the newspaper's opinion poll institute. Cf. issues for 24, 25, 26 February 1966. Among the interesting findings of the latter was that, despite reduction of the workday, a high proportion of the respondents continue to work long hours at the expense of their free time.

Izvestia, in an article entitled "Holidays Need Talents," concluded that

The time has come at last to enlist our best artists...masters in all the arts, in the creation of Soviet ceremonies, holidays and celebrations...Thrilling holidays and poetic ceremonies are legitimate spiritual requirements of the people (*CDSP*, 9 February 1966, p. 32).

....Besides revealing the inequities in the distribution of free time, the sociological studies illustrate the ways in which popular preferences regarding the use of free time continue to outweigh the official ones. It is particularly interesting to compare the amount of time spent on social work (i.e., communal, public, quasi-political activities), 3–5 hours a month, with that which is spent on entertainment, namely 33.5 hours a month! A limited preference for the diversions offered by the mass media is reflected by the relatively short time devoted to radio and television—6 hours a month—against frequenting places of entertainment: 9.9 hours a month, and visiting friends and relatives: 8 hours a month. (A study conducted in Leningrad among young people similarly showed that "the majority of those polled preferred to spend their free time at home or visiting relatives.")[6] Another interesting finding of the same study was that only two hours a month were occupied by sports. In the category of self-education a significant discrepancy appeared between the reliance on reading as a means to this goal, 14 hours a month, and attendance at lectures, seminars, and study circles, totalling 2 hours. An article in *Kommunist* noted the contrast between substantial participation in civic-communal activities at the place of work and the small amount of the same at the place of residence.[7] (Such a discrepancy indicates the

6 *CDSP*, 8 December 1965, p. 14.
7 *Kommunist*, August 1965, p. 55.

superior strength of organized pressures at the place of work against the relatively unorganized character of the residential units in the framework of which people feel freer to withdraw from public-communal activities.) But the lack of adequate participation in collectivised leisure time even at the place of work is also apparent:

Particularly unsatisfactorily organized in some enterprises is mass cultural work—collective attendance at theaters, cinemas, museums, evenings of rest, touring trips, country excursions and picnics, meetings with well-known people, and so on: public organizations are little interested in the life and daily existence of the workers, and do not exert enough influence on the use of non-working time. As a rule, therefore, workers at these enterprises use their non-working and especially their free time less rationally. The raising of the general level of work of party, komsomol, and trade union organizations is an essential reserve of the further rationalization of the use of non-working time of the workers.[8]

If the use of free time by industrial workers is so different from the prescriptions, the discrepancy is bound to be more marked on collective farms. As a recent investigator reports with regret, "the kolkhozniki prefer in their free time to sit at home in their warm apartment, in a circle of friends or acquaintances over a cup of tea, or for that matter, over a glass of vodka."

...The contents of Soviet leisure are determined by the limitations on time and facilities, official policies and popular predilections. However, some of the problems associated with leisure are not peculiar to Soviet society but are also manifest, often in a more pronounced way, in other modern, secular societies. The privileged (or leisured) classes of the past always had leisure problems of their own, but these did not become major concerns for society at large,

because the number of people so afflicted was very small and they usually managed to devise elaborate, if not truly satisfactory ways to chase boredom away.

To the extent that in every modern society the young, and adolescents in particular, have more free time than the adults, it is to be expected that Soviet leisure problems are also primarily those of the young. The predominance in Soviet writings on the leisure of youth attests to this.[9]

....[A] study conducted among 1,000 secondary school students in Smolensk presents other aspects of the leisure problem, similar to the leisure problems of youth in other societies.

The teenagers' weekdays and Sundays were taken up mainly by passive activities: reading, watching television, listening to the radio, etc. Activities requiring intellectual output...were in the 10th to 20th place (*CDSP*, 25 August 1965).

Only three per cent of those polled expressed a desire to engage in public activities. The article discussing the study reached the melancholy conclusion that there is a strong relationship between free time and juvenile delinquency.

Not surprisingly, Soviet spokesmen discern a relationship between domestic leisure problems and the penetration of Western models of leisure. The trend toward the Westernization of leisure poses many dilemmas for the guardians of the ideological purity of Soviet citizens. What is the nature of the appeal of Western models of leisure? How "subversive" are they and to whom do they appeal?

As far as the Soviet public and the young in particular are concerned, inter-

[8] Petrosian, *op. cit.*, p. 180.

[9] *Cf.* F. G. Durham: *The Use of Free Time by Young People in Soviet Society*, M.I.T. Center for International Studies Monograph, Cambridge, Mass. 1966.

est in Western forms of leisure is part of the ambivalent yet voracious interest in things Western in general. Western forms and accessories of leisure are associated not only with material abundance and comforts. They are also seen by many as more exciting and "modern." Such propensities in the population are obviously unwelcome to Soviet ideologues. Borrowing from the West in the realm of leisure is undesirable because it amounts to borrowing styles of life which are tainted by apolitical and escapist values; Western leisure is fundamentally escapist, lacking in serious purpose. To be sure, escapism in the Western sense is not yet an issue. The escapist tendencies in Soviet leisure are of a more primitive kind: they originate in the desire to forget the drabness of life rather than in the anxiety generated by questions which arise *after* material and environmental harshness is conquered. The spiritual maladies—ennui, spleen, and general world weariness—which, according to Aldous Huxley, have always afflicted the leisured classes, are not yet afflicting the Soviet masses. There are, however, some indications that the Soviet social system does not confer invulnerability on them. Huxley's ironic comments on the optimists of his day who believed that "the leisured masses of the future... will do all the things which the leisured classes of the present so conspicuously fail to do," invite application to similarly unrealistic Soviet expectations.

The further Westernization of Soviet leisure is most likely, except in the improbable event of radically retrogressive political changes. It is not surprising that the more affluent and consumption-oriented societies will continue to be the models in this realm. After all, in these societies people have the most leisure and the most varied means for its use. Thus in the final analysis Soviet spokesmen are not far off the mark when they utter warnings about the "pernicious microbes" transmitted by the Western mass media, and, by implication, by many Western forms of entertainment.[10] These are the "microbes" against which the Soviet leadership wants to immunize the population. However, immunization cannot take place without exposure; "the man of the future cannot be raised in a bell-jar." Yet exposure in this context means a more permissive attitude towards the infiltration of Western ideas and models of leisure. As is often the case, Soviet ideologues face a problem analogous to the squaring of the circle.

---

[10] For example, the detective story is seen as 'a weapon that has been used long and successfully by our ideological enemies.' *CDSP* 22 July 1964, p. 16.

The Effects of Alcohol

There is very little difference between the socially problematic aspects of drunkenness in the U.S. and U.S.S.R. Drunkenness is a form of escapism carried to a state in which the individual ceases to function normally and has difficulties in performing his social and occupational roles. There are no comparative data to assess which of the two societies is more heavily burdened with the problem. If publicity is a reliable guide (which it is not necessarily), the Soviet Union has more trouble than the U.S. Recent years witnessed an enormous upsurge of public discussion of heavy drinking and the introduction of various legal and institutional measures to fight it (such as compulsory treatment, penalties, collective ostracism, etc.) Apparently heavy drinking bouts and their aftereffects undercut productivity—a matter of serious concern in the Soviet Union. While in the U.S. alcoholism and other forms of addiction are viewed increasingly as "social diseases" or psychiatric problems, in the U.S.S.R. a more punitive and puritanical official attitude prevails, and the heavy drinker is branded as "morally degraded," to be "surrounded by universal censure and contempt." This, however, is hardly the case, to the chagrin of the authorities. Unofficial public opinion treats drinking and drinkers indulgently, since drinking has been a well established, traditional form of escape and recreation. Again, it would be illuminating to know what the fluctuations in the number of alcoholics and heavy drinkers have been over the years and decades, including pre-Soviet times, but we do not have the figures.

There is a good possibility that more heavy drinking occurs in the Soviet

351

Union than in the U.S., since it is the most accessible form of escape while other kinds are less easily available than in the U.S. In America a richer variety of entertainments, a more escapist mass media, gambling, pornography, drugs, etc. compete with drinking, offering a wider variety of escapist activities than is available in Soviet society.

THE EFFECTS OF ALCOHOL
IN THE U.S.:

The American View

American Drinking Customs

ROBERT STRAUS

...A major social problem associated with alcoholic beverages today revolves around the question of drinking by young people. The press has given special prominence to this question—in part reflecting social concern, in part creating concern and misconceptions as well. There appears to be general readiness to assume that almost any untoward behavior involving young people is due to their drinking. Such assumptions are even made in the face of clear evidence to the contrary. For example, a news item about vandalism which occurred during a college outing noted in its headline and lead paragraph that

From R. Straus, "American Drinking Customs," Contemporary Social Problems, R. Merton and R. Nisbet, eds. New York: Harcourt, Brace and World, 1966, pp. 252–253, 262–263, 278–279. Reprinted by permission of the publisher.

the incident was undoubtedly the result of drinking by students, while buried in the rest of the article was a police report which exonerated the students altogether. The prevailing tendency to equate disturbed behavior in young people with drinking involves both an oversimplification of multiple factors and an exaggeration of the role of alcohol per se.

Adult attitudes toward teen-age drinking often confuse drinking with alcohol pathology, although there is no evidence to show that particular patterns of teen-age drinking are especially linked with alcoholism. Like many other social problems, the question of teen-age drinking elicits a wide variety of ineffectual social responses. Some people exaggerate the problem; others deny that it even exists. Parents tend to blame or impose responsibility upon schools or law-enforcement agencies. Equally, schools tend to blame parents or the police, while law-enforcement personnel in turn blame schools and parents, and churches frequently blame all three.

Available data on drinking by adolescents indicate that the vast majority of high-school students who drink at all do not drink very often, nor do they consume very much at a time. However, in the college age group of 18 to 21, the prevalence of drinking equals, and the quantity and frequency may exceed, that of the general population. For teen-agers, intoxication is a special problem, perhaps because they have a limited capacity for alcohol, or perhaps because their initial psychological reaction to alcohol might be hypersensitive and complicated by their lack of experience in coping with the effects of alcohol. Therefore, when adolescents do become intoxicated they are likely to get involved in other difficulties and be conspicuous. As noted earlier, some adolescents may give the illusion of intoxication when they have consumed only a single drink. Such behavior undoubtedly contributes to a stereotype of the excesses of teen-age drinking.

. . . The understanding of alcoholism has until quite recently been clouded by a persistent groping for unilateral theories of etiology. Much research and many efforts to explain alcoholism have been restricted by the blinders of single academic disciplines. Various theories have been based on a consideration of such important factors as liver metabolism, the function of the central nervous system, hormonal imbalances, vitamin and nutritional deficiencies, personality deviations, and the forces of culture and of social pathology.

There appears today sufficient evidence to suggest that alcoholism in its various forms is a manifestation of one or more of a number of underlying stress-producing conditions. The recognition or identification of primary etiological factors is complicated by the fact that the pathological use of alcohol in connection with what might be called primary forms of stress invariably results in the generation of additional stress-producing conditions which ultimately become an integral part of the overall syndrome. Harold Kalant has emphasized the problem of sorting out specific processes from the viewpoint of a biological scientist:

With the expansion of knowledge on functional interrelations, it has become clear that the metabolism of the liver affects the function of the central nervous system, that psychological and peripheral sensory stimuli acting on the central nervous system affect the release of various hormonal factors, that the resulting hormonal imbalances affect the metabolic behavior of the liver and of all other tissues, including the brain and so on and on. Because of this, it has become very difficult indeed to pick out those effects of alcohol which are primary, and those which are secondary and nonspecific consequences of the disturbance resulting from alcohol.[1]

The social scientist faces the same kind of dilemma in his effort to understand alcoholism. Most forms of alcoholism are found in association with some form or forms of social pathology. Marital discord, job instability, social alienation, economic strain, and chronic ill health can contribute to and be supported by an alcoholic drinking pattern, and each of these problems tends to interact with the others in a complex clustering of social, psychological, and biological pathology.

As yet there are no completely satisfactory theories regarding the causes of various types of pathological drinking. Although no specific physiological or

[1] Harold Kalant, "Some Recent Physiological and Biochemical Investigations on Alcohol and Alcoholism," *Quarterly Journal of Studies on Alcohol*, Vol. 23 (March, 1962), p. 53.

biochemical factors have yet been satisfactorily identified as causing alcoholism, the existence of some biological deficiencies or sensitivities as possible contributing factors cannot be ruled out.

A number of psychological traits have commonly been identified in individuals who drink excessively, and much has been written about the "alcoholic personality."[2] Alcoholics have been characterized as suffering from extreme feelings of inadequacy and chronic anxiety and as being excessively dependent on emotional support from others. Yet similar traits can be found in users of narcotics, individuals with various kinds of psychosomatic disease, persons addicted to food, as well as in many men and women who appear to function quite effectively within normal ranges of physical health and socially acceptable behavior. Knowledge about the psychological effects of alcohol in alleviating anxiety and providing a sense of well-being helps explain why alcohol is attractive to and functional for persons with deep feelings of emotional insecurity, but psychological theory cannot tell us, for example, why, of the people with a so-called alchoholic personality, only some become alcoholics, while others do not.

...It has been suggested several times in this chapter that the period since 1940 has seen a marked change in the understanding of alcohol problems and in social responses to these problems. This change has affected the attitudes and responses of the general public, of various professional groups, and of alcoholics themselves.

The stigma of alcoholism has been moderated. The alcoholic is less apt to be held morally responsible for his prob-

2 For a summary, see John D. Armstrong, "The Search for the Alcoholic Personality," *Annals of the American Academy of Political and Social Science*, Vol. 315 (January, 1958), pp. 40–47.

lem. Instead, he is depicted as the victim of a disease. He is now more likely to admit that he has a problem and to seek help.

Several different kinds of alcoholism have been identified and concepts of multiple causation have emerged, although there is as yet no generally acceptable theory of etiology. Numerous treatment resources have been developed and a variety of drugs have been found to help the alcoholic maintain sobriety, although they do not cure his alcoholism. Special clinics, special hospitals, and specially designated beds in general hospitals have become available to alcoholics in increasing numbers; even a few physicians are specializing in the treatment of alcoholism. Alcoholics Anonymous has had a significant, if unmeasurable, impact. Yet even these growing resources can serve only a small portion of the alcoholic population because they must operate within the severe limits of available knowledge. Generally, those approaches to treatment which combine medical, psychological, and social intervention have had the greatest degree of success.

A growing concept of public responsibility for the problems of alcoholism has been reflected in the increasing support provided for treatment services at the local and state levels of government and for research by the federal government. After much resistance, major employers and insurance companies are also beginning to give some attention to these problems. But, as yet, there are no sure cures and no known ways of preventing alcoholism. Nor does there appear to be any measurable reduction in the incidence or prevalence of alcoholism in the United States.

Since 1940, much progress has been made in differentiating alcoholism from some of the other problems of alcohol. Dangerously misleading educational materials used in the schools are being replaced with those designed to afford young people a basis for making intelligent decisions about drinking. The problem of drinking by young people is less often identified with the fear that they will become alcoholics. However, while most young people continue to be exposed to confusing and conflicting pressures from family, church, community, and peer groups, the use of alcohol as a way of resolving adolescent stress as well as drinking outside of the generally moderating context of the home may both be increasing.

Despite the reality of adolescent drinking, legal restrictions against drinking before the age of 21 continue and serve to enhance the symbolic status of drinking for the teen-ager. Both alcohol and the automobile have important significance in the striving for adult status, and, when combined, they comprise a potentially lethal force.

Since 1940, there is a better understanding of the impact of alcohol on driving performance. An effort is underway to redefine the public perception of this problem from that of "drunken driving" to the combination of "drinking and driving." Thus far, efforts at public education have been relatively ineffective in modifying drinking and driving behavior in this country, where the mores which uphold both the right to drink and the right to drive have prevailed against the enforcement of most laws designed to impose social control.

Conflicts between mores and laws continue to characterize many aspects of drinking behavior. The phrase "vote dry and drink wet" is an apt description, not merely of behavior associated with prohibition laws, but also of the predominant response to most other legal restrictions associated with drinking customs: the legal age laws, drinking-and-driving codes, laws regulating the hours of sale and other aspects of distribution, and laws covering manufacturing and taxation. Many people will strongly support alcohol control laws in principle but will violate them freely and, unless a violation has involved personal and direct damage to themselves, will condone their violation by others.

Experience in the United States, and elsewhere in the world, has clearly indicated that efforts to cope with problems of alcohol by legislating change will prove ineffective unless laws can be made which reflect the forces of normative behavior.

THE EFFECTS OF ALCOHOL IN THE U.S.S.R.:

The Soviet View

Harmful Indulgence

N. TROYAN

Moscow—Many alcoholics justify their unwillingness to combat their vice by claiming that it is impossible to refrain from drinking, sincerely regarding their condition as an illness. Unfortunately, this erroneous idea is shared by many nondrinkers and even by some physicians: Not being specialists in the field, they regard alcoholics as sick people and thereby involuntarily indulge them. An example of such misinformation is the letter from M. Shofman, a doctor, printed in Izvestia No. 146.[1] "We must not confuse two concepts: drunkenness and alcoholism," Comrade Shofman writes. "Alcoholism is an illness, which can in time bring on the 'D.T.s.'"

Statements of this kind are not only nonscientific, to put it mildly, but cause great harm by misleading public opinion. Nothing can "bring on" delirium tremens; it can develop in a per-

Reprinted from N. Troyan, "Harmful Indulgence," Izvestia. Translated in Current Digest of the Soviet Press, XVII, No. 34 (Copyright © September 15, 1965), 22.

[1] Current Digest of the Soviet Press, Vol. XVII, No. 27, p. 13.

son who has never used alcohol to excess. Delirium tremens, a mental disorder, may be a consequence of drunkenness, just as lung cancer may well be a consequence of smoking. But we would not call a smoker who says he cannot give up smoking ill. It is a matter of will for him to give up smoking, but when he becomes ill because he smoked, then he is indeed a patient who needs treatment. When an alcoholic wants to rid himself of his vice and exerts sufficient effort to do so, he is "cured" comparatively quickly. But what can the narcological service do when an alcoholic does not want to give up his habit? After all, the overwhelming majority of them come to the narcologist not because they want to stop drinking but in order to be registered at the clinic and to be able to tell the militia, their employers and their wives that they are "taking the cure," that they are "ill." So you have a hardened drunkard spending from 30 to 40 days in hospital—he is "taking the cure." He takes it easy, shares his "alcoholic experiences" with his ward neighbors and inquires as to how to get the antabus out of his organism as quickly as possible after leaving the hospital so he can get drunk again. Incidentally, he will be paid for sick leave, so he will have money to get drunk on. And it will start all over again.

The worst thing is that the drunkard who is registered at the clinic immediately gains a number of advantages over the "unorganized" drunks: If he doesn't report for work for a week or two, the management telephones the clinic with a request to "save the man"; if he disturbs the peace, the militia refuses to book him for the crime because "he needs medical treatment, not a trial." And if the case is nevertheless brought to court, the drunkard usually gets off all too easily. I have before me several recently issued people's court verdicts in cases of drunken hooligans, and they are all very much alike: Each describes a drunken brawl, murder threats and resistance to authorities. And the court decisions are all alike too: "Considering that Citizen X suffers from chronic alcoholism, the court finds it necessary to prescribe compulsory medical treatment at his place of residence." A completely ridiculous situation has arisen: Alcoholism and drunkenness have actually, if not officially, become an extenuating circumstance, although Art. 12 of the Russian Republic Criminal Code and the corresponding articles of the other Union republic criminal codes do not rule out liability for intoxication, while paragraph 10 of Art. 39 even makes drunkenness an aggravating circumstance.

Yet the court probably knows that general psychiatric hospitals cannot give compulsory treatment to alcoholics and drug addicts, so consequently the court's decision cannot be carried out if the penalty does not include deprivation of freedom.

Alcoholics are morally degraded people, devoid of a sense of shame. They are extremely egotistical and virtually impervious to persuasion; only the actual threat of losing their jobs or of exile will sometimes bring them to their senses. In this light, if becomes obvious how much harm is done by enterprise managements' toleration of alcoholics, by the hothouse conditions we have willy-nilly created for them. Anti-alcoholic measures will not be effective unless they are combined with compulsion.

It must be explained to the broad masses of the population that alcoholism is not a disease, that to treat the alcoholic as "an unfortunate, tormented by his serious ailment," is not only incorrect but also harmful to the alcoholic himself, since it cultivates a dependent state of mind in him. The alcoholic should be surrounded by universal censure and contempt, not by universal solicitude; he should be made to feel that society no longer wishes to see him as he is, that society wants him to reform and will compel him to do so.

Such A Law Is Needed

A. GERTSENZON

Drunkenness is an intolerable phenomenon. Scholars and writers, doctors and jurists, workers and collective farmers submit many proposals on intensifying the struggle against this social evil. However, we should examine how substantiated these proposals are and whether the measures proposed are effective enough....

It must be said that all or almost all capitalist states have laws aimed at limiting alcoholism and its further spread. But these laws have never produced the desired effect. The reason for this is the very nature of the capitalist system and its contradictions, which, in particular, create and constantly reproduce the causes spurring people to drunkenness.

The other socialist states of Europe have adopted and are enforcing special laws embracing all the norms of the struggle against alcoholism. Such are, for instance, the laws adopted in Poland (1959), in Czechoslovakia and in Hungary (1962). Typical features of these laws are, first, the priority given to purely preventive measures; second, the granting of wide powers to the public; and third, the combination of preventive and repressive measures with respect to incorrigible drunkards. It

Reprinted from A. Gertsenzon, "Such a Law Is Needed," Izvestia, (February 6, 1966). Translated in Current Digest of the Soviet Press, XVIII, No. 6 (Copyright © March 2, 1966), 29.

should be noted that in the laws of these countries the measures for fighting alcoholism have been built into a general system reflecting the incompatibility of drunkenness with socialist social relations.

Despite great transformations in all spheres of our life, parts of the population still cling to harmful survivals of the past and of ancient mores. Drunkenness in our country is to a considerable extent the result of indiscipline and of bad upbringing, customs and habits. The moral and material damage caused is obvious....

You can influence drunkards at their place of residence and at their place of work. If persuasion does not help, it is the public that must raise the question of bringing the alcoholic to disciplinary, administrative or even legal liability. In particular, it may demand that the administration of an enterprise or institution deprive the drunkard for a specified period of various benefits and bonuses, demote him and, finally, fire him. The public may even propose that such a person be exiled from the city as one who leads a parasitic existence.

The population itself must prevent the drunkards' corrupting influence on children and adolescents, assist in restricting the sale of liquor and show initiative in closing "dens of iniquity." They are able to influence in the most active manner, through the forces of the people's volunteer detachments, rowdies who disturb public order, and to hear in comrades' courts cases of unworthy actions by drunkards.

The question arises: Are the requirements of the present laws dealing with drunkards, rowdies, hooligans and home distillers being enforced precisely and steadfastly? Do all officials and trade personnel fulfill, in particular, the laws on restricting the sale of liquor? Are there enough therapeutic and labor-cure institutions? Does the public exercise its rights and broad powers in the struggle against drunkenness and drunkards in conformity with the present legislation?

The answer to all these questions is, to my great regret, negative. Although very definite tasks, forms and methods are already provided for by Soviet legislation, the struggle against alcoholism is conducted, alas, unsatisfactorily. A considerable role is probably played here by an insufficient knowledge of the laws as well as by a lack of coordination between the efforts of various agencies and those of the public.

There is no doubt that our legislation aimed at eradicating drunkenness must be further improved. I would like to express some general considerations on this score. Even a brief survey of the acts now in effect shows that their number is very great. The time has come to unite all the anti-alcoholism laws in a single unified system. All the necessary norms must be concentrated in one single law. It is advisable to renovate these norms and to supplement them with the demands of the day. In so doing, the experience of other socialist states should be considered.

While improving our anti-alcoholic code, prime attention must be paid to drawing up economic, socio-cultural and educational measures and to provide them with an appropriate material foundation. Finally, it is necessary to define precisely the rights and duties of officials and public organizations in implementing the different forms of preventing drunkenness and exerting influence on drunkards.

It would be very important to have a comprehensive discussion of the draft of such a single law in our press: in the general political, economic, medical and legal press. The struggle against alcoholism is a serious enough problem for us to spare no efforts in the study of various points of view. This will make it possible to adopt the best solutions.

Mass Culture

Strictly speaking in neither society does mass culture (i.e., the products of mass media, popular arts, and entertainment) constitute a serious social problem, with demonstrably disruptive or debilitating effects. There is merely speculation and belief that there are undesirable effects, such as spiritual impoverishment, the trivialization of interests, the distortion of conceptions of reality, the inculcation of unworthy aspirations, the undermining of character, the debilitation of taste, and the spread of conformity. Vague as they are, these accusations are widely held among many influential social critics, and even those less alarmist would not deny that at any rate the American mass media is "an enormous wasteland," which seems to offer little besides cheap excitement, sexual stimulation, and vicarious gratifications. Occasionally a causal relationship is discerned between the themes of the mass media (luxury, affluence, excitement, sex, and violence) and the development of hedonism, conspicuous consumption, short-term gratification, and even crime. More specifically it is argued that American mass media and mass culture provide unrealistic, unattainable, and worthless models of behavior and life styles which corrupt many, especially the uneducated and young.

It is in itself open to question whether or not we can apply the concept of "mass culture," as used in the West, to the Soviet Union. Mass culture, in the West, is synonymous with popular culture, one which caters to popular demands and interests. Whatever else can be said about the mass media, the arts, and mass entertainments in the U.S.S.R., they cannot be accused of being slaves to popular interests and demands. Insofar as "mass culture" in the Soviet Union represents a problem from the official point of view (i.e., from the standpoint of those who define social problems in Soviet society), it is its inadequacy in fulfilling educational and inspirational functions. Soviet controllers of the mass media would like to have the best of all possible worlds: a combination of ideological-socializing functions with lively entertainment and the provision of information. Instead Soviet mass media tends to be dull, heavy-handed, unconvincing, and hardly entertaining. These problems are enhanced by the growing demand of Soviet audiences for a new balance between entertainment and edification: with much more stress on the former. These dilemmas are reflected in the Soviet articles which follow. Today people in the Soviet Union are apparently more and more willing to voice their dissatisfaction with the entertainment the mass media provides. The demand for greater "complexity" in the mass media and artistic expression is the permissible way of conveying the desire for a less politicized and less dull mass media and art.

MASS CULTURE

IN THE U.S.:

The American View

A Dissent from the Consensual Society

ERNEST VAN DEN HAAG

The crucial issue is fully comprised in the question with which Rostovtzeff concludes his *magnum opus*: "Is it possible to extend a higher civilization to the lower classes without debasing its

Reprinted with permission from Daedalus, *Journal of the American Academy of Arts and Sciences, Boston, Massachusetts. Spring 1960.*

standard and diluting its quality to the vanishing point? Is not every civilization bound to decay as soon as it begins to penetrate the masses?"

Mr. Shils describes mass society as one in which there is "more sense of attachment to society as a whole... more sense of affinity with one's fellows." According to him, the mass stands in a closer relationship to the center; there is a "dispersion of charisma" with "greater stress on individual dignity"; "the value of sensation has come to be widely appreciated"; individuality has been "discovered and developed," as has the value of personal relationships; the masses begin to "become capable of more subtle perception and judgment" as their "moral responsiveness and sensibility are aroused."

The society which Mr. Shils describes is not the one in which I live. I am forced to conjecture that the generosity of his wishes has relaxed the customary strictness of his methods and blunted the accuracy of his perception.[1]

Progress toward the fulfillment of Mr. Shils' wishes is implied by the terms he uses. Yet there are some material doubts. Is the value of sensation more widely appreciated than it was in antiquity, the Renaissance, or even the nineteenth century? I find American society singularly anti-sensual: let me just mention the food served in restaurants, preprandial cocktails intended, often charitably, to kill sensation. The congested seating arrangements in restaurants, the way cities, suburbs, exurbs, and resorts are built do not support the hypothesis of increased value placed on privacy. Even sex is largely socialized and desensualized. Do we stand in closer relationship to the center—or are we alienated; suffering from what Wordsworth described as "perpetual emptiness, unceasing change" because in

Yeats' words, "Things fall apart; the centre cannot hold"? Has there actually been a "dispersion of charisma"?[2] Or has there been a shift from real to Hollywood queens? Does our society foster "personal relationships," "individuality," "privacy," or marketability, outer-directedness, pseudo-personalizations parasitically devouring the genuine personalities of those who assume them? Could Jesus go into the desert today to contemplate? Wouldn't he be followed by a crew of *Life* photographers, cameramen, publishers' agents, etc.? What of the gossip columns, of people's interest in other people's private lives and particularly their personal relations— don't these phenomena suggest a breakdown of reserve, vicarious living— indeed, pseudo-life and experience?

Statistical data reveal that there is now higher income, more education, and more equally distributed leisure, increased mobility, travel, and communication. Undoubtedly there is more material opportunity for more people than ever before. But if so many people are so much better off in so many respects, is culture better than ever? The lowered barriers, the greater wealth, the increased opportunities are material achievements but only cultural promises. Mr. Shils appears to have taken all the promises of the age and confused them with fulfillments. It is as though one were to take the data of the Kinsey report and conclude that since there seems to be so much intercourse, people must love each other more than ever. I have nothing against Mr. Kinsey's entomological enterprise (though it makes me feel waspish). But even though it may furnish raw data, we

---

[1] John Stuart Mill (*On Liberty*, ch. 3) concludes his discussion of the power of public opinion in egalitarian societies by pointing out that as leveling proceeds, "there ceases to be any social support for nonconformity...any substantive power in society which...is interested in taking under its protection opinions and tendencies at variance with those of the public." From de Tocqueville to David Riesman, the dangers of "cultural democracy" have been considered. I do not believe that Mr. Shils comes seriously to grips with these dangers.

[2] I am not convinced even that the greater inclusiveness of our society can quite be taken for granted. The fate of the Jews in Germany cannot be that easily dismissed. Nazism was political Kitsch as well as a rise of "brutal culture."

must distinguish it from sociological enterprise.

If people address each other on a first-name basis when they meet, do they really love and esteem each other more than people who do not use first names? Or does equal familiarity with all suggest a lack of differentiation, the very opposite of personal relations, which are based on discriminating among perceived individualities? "In America," de Tocqueville wrote, "the bond of affection is extended but it is relaxed." Mr. Shils notes the extension but not the dilution. Yet extension can only be bought at the price of lessened intensity, depth, and stability.

Of course we have more communication and mobility than ever before. But isn't it possible that less is communicated? We have all the opportunities in the world to see, hear, and read more than ever before. Is there any independent indication to show that we experience and understand more? Does not the constant slick assault on our senses and minds produce monotony and indifference and prevent experience? Does not the discontinuity of most people's lives unsettle, and sometimes undo them? We surely have more external contacts than ever before. But most people have less spontaneous and personal (internalized) relationships than they might with fewer contacts and opportunities.

We have more equality of opportunity. But the burden of relative deprivations is felt more acutely the smaller they are and the greater the opportunities.[3] People become resentful and clamor for a different kind of equality, equality at the end rather than the beginning, in short, invidious leveling. Does not the comminution of society alienate people from one another—as

the discontinuity of their existence fragments them—and replace a sense of purpose with a sense of meaninglessness? Is the increased "conviviality" Mr. Shils hails more than the wish for "togetherness" which marks the lonely crowd?

Mr. Shils contends that we have more intellectuals, consumers, and producers of "refined" culture than before. In one sense, he is quite right. But these are intellectuals by position (university teachers, authors, etc.), and having more of them tells us nothing about the number of intellectuals by ability, interest, and cultivation. Mr. Shils almost concedes as much. But he remains on the phenomenal level, and never goes to the root of the phenomenon:[4] the marginal role, the interstitial life, of intellectuals in a mass culture society. And I mean those who remain engaged in intellectual life and do not allow themselves to be reduced to the status of technicians or manufacturers of middle-brow entertainments.

Similarly, Mr. Shils mentions the possibility that intellectual and artistic creators may be seduced into more remunerative pseudo-creative activities only to dismiss it by pointing out that "the mere existence of opportunity will not seduce a man of strongly impelled creative capacities once he has found his direction." Of course, no one is impelled *only* by "creative capacities." The trouble is that the lure of mass media (and of foundation money and prestige) and the values that go with them are internalized long before the

---

[3] "The more complete this uniformity the more insupportable the sight of such a difference becomes," de Tocqueville notes.

[4] Even on that level, one might quarrel with Mr. Shils. England is not yet as much imbued with mass culture as we are. The class system and selective education have not been entirely overcome; nor have the traditions of elite culture. With only a quarter of our population—not to speak of wealth—England publishes more books every year than we do. And it has at least as many economists, philosophers, and novelists of the first rank as we do.

potential creator "has found his direction."

Mr. Shils declares that "the heart of the revolution of mass culture" is "the expanding radius of empathy and fellow feeling" which "have given to youth opportunities never available before." These opportunities, Mr. Shils concedes, are utilized mainly through "mediocre and brutal culture." But he does not point out (though noting the effect) that the appalling ignorance of educated youth is produced by reliance on the equally ignorant charisma-endowed peer group; by belief, in short, that there is little to learn from the past and its representatives. The loss of respect for learning and tradition, particularly in its less tangible aspects, is not independent of the leveling dear to Mr. Shils; it is not unrelated to the widely held view that obsolescence automatically overtakes aesthetic and moral values, as it does technological invention. It should be evident that this notion is generated by the pragmatic nature of mass culture and by the high mobility that Mr. Shils extols.[5]

To object to some of Mr. Shils' views is to agree with others. For he starts by praising and ends by deploring mass culture. This nice balance is achieved, I feel, at the expense of a coherent theory of mass culture. Let me suggest a few prolegomena to such a theory.

The most general characteristics of mass culture are deducible from premises on which there is no disagreement: they are concomitants of any industrial, mass production society. Included among these are increased income

and mobility, more equally distributed leisure, egalitarianism, wider communication and education,[6] more specialization and less scope for individuality in work. The consequences that I deduce from these premises are consistent and fit my impressions. But there is no strict empirical proof, although I do believe it may be possible to test some of these hypotheses after appropriate reformulation. Further, other hypotheses may be consistent with these premises, and the real question turns on their relative importance and their relevance. With these qualifications, I submit that this quasi-deductive method which relates the ascertainable to the less tangible is the only one that can yield a "theory" of mass culture deserving the name.

Let me outline some of the most important characteristics of mass culture.[7]

(1) There is a separation of the manufacturers of culture from the consumers, which is part of the general separation of production and consumption and of work and play. Culture becomes largely a spectator sport, and life and experience become exogenous and largely vicarious. (Nothing will dissuade me from seeing a difference between a young girl walking around with her pocket radio listening to popular songs and one who sings herself; nor am I persuaded that the tales collected by the brothers Grimm remain the same when enacted on television or synthetically reproduced by Walt Disney.)

---

[5] The phenomenon is part of mass culture everywhere, but the ignorance and rejection of the past were particularly fostered in America because of the immigrant background of many parents, the melting-pot nature of the school system, and the rapid rate of change which makes the experience of the old seem old-fashioned and diminishes their authority.

[6] Note that more has to be learned through formal instruction, partly because less culture is transmitted informally and individually. This is no advantage because our school system helps bring about the spread of a homogenized mass culture intentionally and unintentionally.

[7] For a fuller exposition of my view, see Ralph Ross and Ernest van den Haag, *The Fabric of Society* (New York: Harcourt, Brace and Company, 1957), ch. 15.

(2) Mass production aims at pleasing an average of tastes and therefore, though catering to all to some extent, it cannot satisfy any taste fully. Standardization is required and necessarily de-individualizes—as do the techniques required by mass production and marketing.

(3) Since culture, like everything else in a mass society, is mainly produced to please an average of consumer tastes, the producers become (and remain) an elite by catering to consumer tastes rather than developing or cultivating autonomous ones. Initiative and power to bestow prestige and income have shifted from the elite to the mass. The difference may be seen by comparing the development of ritual dogmatic beliefs and practices in the Protestant denominations and in the Roman Catholic church. The latter has minimized, the former maximized, dependence on consumers. In the Protestant churches, there is, therefore, no body of religious (as distinguished from moral) beliefs left, except as an intellectual curiosity.

(4) The mass of men dislikes and always has disliked learning and art. It wishes to be distracted from life rather than to have it revealed; to be comforted by traditional (possibly happy and sentimental) tropes, rather than be upset by new ones. It is true that it wishes to be thrilled, too. But irrational violence or vulgarity provides thrills, as well as release, just as sentimentality provides escape. What is new here is that, apart from the fact that irrelevant thrills and emotions are now prefabricated, the elite is no longer protected from the demands of the mass consumers.

(5) As a result of the high psychological and economic costs of individuality and privacy, gregariousness has become internalized. People fear solitude and unpopularity; popular approval becomes the only moral and aesthetic standard most people recognize. This tendency is reinforced by the shrinkage in the importance and size of primary groups, which have also become looser; by a corresponding increase in the size and importance of secondary groups and publics; and finally, by the shift of many of the functions of primary to secondary groups.

(6) The greatly increased lure of mass markets for both producers and consumers diverts potential talent from the creation of art. (Within the arts, the performing do better than the creative ones.) Here interesting empirical questions arise: to what extent is talent bent endogenously and exogenously; to what extent can it be?

(7) Excessive communication serves to isolate people from one another, from themselves, and from experience. It extends bonds by weakening them. People become indifferent and indiscriminately tolerant; their own life as well as everything else is trivialized, eclectic, and styleless.

(8) Mass media for inherent reasons must conform to prevailing average canons of taste.[8] They cannot foster art; indeed, they replace it. When they take up classics, they usually reshape them to meet expectations. But even when that is not the case, they cannot hope to individualize and refine taste, though they may occasionally supply an already formed taste for high culture. Half a loaf, in these matters, spoils the appetite, even with vitamins added, and is not better than none. The technical availability of good reproductions and the paperback editions of noncondensed books are unlikely to change this situation; they often add alien elements

[8] In Frank Stanton's words, "Any mass medium will always have to cater to the middle grounds...the most widely held, or cease to be."

which merely decorate lives styled by mass culture.[9]

(9) The total effect of mass culture is to distract people from lives which are so boring that they generate obsession with escape. Yet because mass culture creates addiction to prefabricated experience, most people are deprived of the remaining possibilities of autonomous growth and enrichment, and their lives become ever more boring and unfulfilled.

This very brief sketch of the general features of mass culture should make it clear that I do not agree with those

[9] Joseph Bram has called my attention to the several distinct phases of mass culture. It often begins with a rather moving attempt of the uneducated to become seriously educated. One sees this in countries beginning their industrial development. The adulteration of, and disrespect for, education comes with full industrialization, when the mass culture market is created and supplied with goods manufactured for it.

mass culture optimists who favor the wide presentation of "refined" culture through the mass media. I do not think this desirable or desired. Nor, for that matter, practicable. People get what they wish and I see no way of imposing on them anything else. I have to disagree with those who appear to think that the issue is to improve the culture offered the mass of men and to try to reach the masses in greater and greater numbers. My conclusion is different: high or refined culture, in my opinion, is best preserved and developed by avoiding mass media. I should go further and give up some advantages of mass production for the sake of greater individualization. This would reverse many present policies. For instance, I should favor fairly high direct taxes on most mass media, or a tax on advertising. Perhaps we might still be capable of replacing the noise that would be thus eliminated with conversation.

MASS CULTURE

IN THE U.S.S.R.:

The Soviet View

See the Chief Goal

G. MDIVANI

...Two or three years ago certain workers in the theater and the arts were

Reprinted from G. Mdivani, "See the Chief Goal," Izvestia (June 16, 1966). Translated in Current Digest of the Soviet Press, XVIII, No. 24 (Copyright © July 6, 1966), 19–20.

arguing quite seriously about a "single style of the epoch," and there were some defenders of this, so to speak, universal human phenomenon; citing the rhythm of life, cosmic speeds, the improved technology of the 1960s, the splitting of the atom and many other things, they proved that the "style of the epoch" is the same in New York as in Moscow, in Bonn as in Prague, in Rome as in Sofia.

But in the epoch of the most bitter conflicts between two worlds, only frivolous people who flirt with uncritical imitation of Western "fashions" can reason in this way. Besides, is fashion applicable in the arts and literature?

If a Moscow student or a young worker at the Red Proletarian Plant is dressed in the same way as an American youth, there is nothing unnatural about it. But when on the stage of a theater or on a movie screen there is almost no difference between the characters of a young Soviet man and a young man from Broadway, it becomes lamentable.

You experience the same sense of displeasure, and even outrage, when you look at a certain show or read a certain play and suddenly discover that you already know from somewhere this manner of writing, this manner of staging, this manner of creating characters, so unlike the characters of representative Soviet people.

Character is the internal world of a person, the essence of his world outlook, his past, present and future. Character is the fruit of the social structure. Unfortunately, even certain of our talented playwrights and directors sometimes forget this.

I am alarmed primarily by the errors of talented people who are certainly capable of creating works that glorify the life and exploits of the Soviet people. I am absolutely confident that sooner or later they will come around to this— such is the logic of our Soviet life. But our criticism must help them, not confuse them, as, unfortunately, so often happens.

For example, when the young playwright E. Radzinsky appeared with his first play, "You Are Twenty-Two, Old Men," we were delighted. True, the young author still lacked mastery, but the freshness of his thought, his ability to pick out what is basic and life-affirming in the lives of our contemporary youth, gave all grounds for supposing that Radzinsky was following a correct ideological course. But suddenly, along came Radzinsky's plays "One Hundred and Four Pages About Love" and "Shooting a Film," with an obvious orientation toward "fashion." And our critics began to lavish praise on these works without restraint, instead of telling the young playwright about the dangers lying in wait for him if he continued heeding the Philistine tastes of certain audiences.

The chief line of our art has been and still is determined not by fashion but by service to great and noble ideas.

Were Stanislavsky and Nemirovich-Danchenko, Ye. Vakhtangov and V. Meyerhold, K. Mardzhanishvili and A. Tairov the fashion in the Soviet theater? Not in the least. These outstanding masters of the stage created an original art of lofty thoughts, great generalizations and brilliant revolutionary passions. Their artistic work enriched not only our Soviet theater art but the world's progressive theater in the 20th century.

Unfortunately, a majority of the characters in today's plays are either "angry" young men or ninnies who grumble about their personal grievances. Does this kind of de-heroization really correspond to the spirit of our ideology and the truth of our life?

You will recall that in Gorky's play "The Lower Depths" even the riffraff speak like heroes, but in a number of our plays and shows, the heroes often speak in slangy gibberish. Is this not shameful?

Can one really look indifferently on the fact that revolutionary heroism has almost disappeared from our contemporary theater, for that "whispering from the stage" now so widely advertised in articles and statements by certain of our "fashionable" directors and critics kills in advance everything heroic, because the heat of great passions demands a dialogue from the stage in a loud, full voice. . . .

Works marked by apolitical tendencies, a partiality for portraying the negative phenomena in life, now frequently make their way onto the stages of our theaters and our movie screens, into our literature.

Of course, the artist cannot disregard negative phenomena. A passionate struggle against whatever hinders our forward movement is one of the chief tasks of literature, cinema and theater. But concentration of attention on the negative aspect, on only the negative phenomena of our life, inevitably leads to a distortion of reality. . . .

Of course, it is far easier to arouse an audience's pity for the luckless character, to squeeze out tears of tender emotion, to speak from the stage about quirks of fate and life, of love that flares up like a spark and then dies slowly like a tongue of flame from a tallow candle, than to talk in a grand way about the thoughts that whirled through Yury Gagarin's mind as he rushed through space, where not one person in the world had ever been before him.

In centuries to come, wondering, grateful descendants will write about Gagarin with more admiration than peo- ple now write about Copernicus or Galileo. The feat of the conquerors of space is one of the heroic subjects that our reality generously supplies to contemporary artists. A genuine talent cannot fail to be ignited by its life-giving fire.

Attempts are sometimes made to justify departures from the chief subjects of our heroic times by citing independence of artistic thinking and originality of talent.

We do indeed have more than a few talented directors who are charged with guiding the theaters of Moscow and the Union republics. Among them are Ye. Simonov, B. Ravenskikh, A. Efros, G. Lordkipanidze, Yu. Lyubimov and many others.

Talent presupposes a whole aggregate of qualities: an acute sense of truth, emotional purposefulness, a flair for imaginative thinking and much more. But the direction of the artist's talent and his ideological strength play the dominant role. Unfortunately, certain of our critics ignore this—one of the main qualities of talent—in their judgments. . . .

The heroes among whom we live, who are our contemporaries, are inexhaustible material for the artist.

To speak of our victories and our great times in a full voice means to embody in artistic images the idea of a bright future for mankind. And, after all, its embodiment is the central task of the art of socialist realism.

What the Contemporary
Hero Is Like

Y. RAIZMAN

...It is difficult to overrate the significance of the hero's image and his role in disclosing a work's ideological design. A hero must express the ideals of the age and the features most characteristic of his time.

It is therefore natural that for Soviet film makers there is no problem more important than the problem of the hero. Reality sets forth new themes and new conflicts and, of course, molds a new type of people. Our contemporaries today differ in many ways from their fathers and grandfathers. Our focal heroes in the pictures of the 1920s and 1930s were properly representatives of the popular masses, workers and peasants cast up by the wave of revolutionary enthusiasm, people for whom the class struggle had become the school of life. . . .

The power of the influence of these heroes on the audience was determined first of all by their emotional infectiousness and their revolutionary impetus.

But it would be a mistake to use the same yardstick for the heroes of the present, the 1960s, for the prototypes of today's heroes are people of another age, another outlook and another cultural make-up.

Who, then, is the hero of our time,

Reprinted from Y. Raizman, "What the Contemporary Hero Is Like," Izvestia (October 10, 1965). Current Digest of the Soviet Press, XVII, No. 41 (Copyright © November 3, 1965), 32–33.

the hero who can become the ruler of men's minds? What new traits does he possess, how must he be presented in our films?

In my view, it is most characteristic of the man of today that, no matter what he does, he cannot stand aloof from the anxieties of the modern world.

This whole world, full of crucial events and contradictory ideas, is continuously intertwined with the facts of life's daily routine and is sometimes in conflict with them. Therefore, it seems to me that contemporary heroes should be above all people who are able to think historically, people who by virtue of their qualities are capable of understanding the most complicated phenomena of the life around them, particularly the progressiveness of the processes of our social development, even when these processes are very complicated.

The film maker must accustom audiences to these people's way of thinking, to the play of their thoughts, to their disputes with opponents, sometimes with one another and often with themselves. And, of course, the struggle of views must not look like a rigged game, a kind of dialogue between two vaudevillians, one asking naive questions to give his partner the chance for witty comebacks.

In the sharp and serious duel between differing points of view, let him win whose world view is more robust and profound, who can see life's phenomena as moving progressively toward the ultimate goal.

These are precisely the tasks that the scenarist Ye. Gabrilovich and the present writer set ourselves while working on the script I am beginning to direct. We want to tell about people of today, principally the Communist Vasily Gubanov. Life raises more and more new questions for him, large and small, social and personal. He has to ponder them constantly. It could be that he by no means always solves them correctly, but what is important to us is how he thinks and what he thinks, how and with whom he argues. The assortment of questions that disturb our hero also disturbs us, the authors. The questions he seeks to answer, we too are seeking to answer.

It seems to me most essential that the dramatic action of a film be built not only on conflicts arising when the hero clashes with the outside world but also on the hero's searches and his decisions on the particular ideological and moral problems important to him.

Audiences, especially young people, expect from us a hero who thinks and reflects, not just in a simple way, but interestingly. This, it seems to me, is a sign of the times.

When one succeeds in creating an infectious image of the positive hero it is always a great triumph for art and a great joy to the artist. But this is a far from easy task, and it cannot be solved through the hopeful enumeration of the virtues a hero should possess. There really aren't too many of these virtues, nor are they very diversified: nobility, courage, honesty in labor and high morality.

But if this arithmetically composed standard is deprived of clear individuality and a lively, distinctive character, he will never interest anyone. This is a blank cartridge, which more often than not compromises the author's good intentions. True, in films, and also in literature, a whole system for "enlivening the stereotype" has been worked out. Thus, certain characteristics have come to be imparted to heroes: They are made either hot-tempered or somewhat crude. A checklist has been compiled of the stock traits that "humanize" the positive hero.

These contrived heroes wander from film to film, ready to be of service to everyone. They sneak in under the pen and force their way onto the screen. They are the first to arrive and the last to leave. The artist must make a constant, titanic effort to guard against them. Therefore, we experience a feeling of genuine joy when every now and then there flashes on the screen characters that delight us with their uniqueness and originality, such as Serpilin in the film "The Living and the Dead," Kulikov in "Nine Days of One Year" and the charming hero of the film "There Is Such a Young Man" and, unfortunately, very few others. . . .

Of course, a hero whose moral principles can become a model is the paramount task of art. However, I think we should not confine the movie's methods of influence strictly to the image of the positive hero.

In my view, his absence does not necessarily deprive a picture of active influence. A film in which the author's position is distinctly expressed, a film that administers a direct, open blow to negative phenomena—philistinism and emotional blindness, as well as moral narrow-mindedness and facts impairing people's lives—can also have tremendous educative significance.

But sometimes we have a surprisingly primitive notion of the ways and means of the influence of art. There is the notion that what is seen on the screen excites immediate and direct imitation. But this is usually the elementary copying of purely superficial observations, such as the style of a dress or the heroine's hairdo, a manner of bearing, speaking, etc. The process of a film's moral influence is considerably more complex. In carrying over what is seen in a film into his personal life experience, the viewer sometimes discovers that the thought presented in the picture aids in the ripening and formulation of certain of his own heretofore unclear thoughts. In presenting this or that ethical problem, the film urges the viewer toward its solution and makes him examine the correctness or error of his own views—in a word, it makes him reflect. It seems to me there is no more worthy goal than to teach a man to comprehend on his own the phenomena of the life around him.

New tasks, born of the artist's deeper and more intense penetration into the spiritual world of man, naturally need new artistic methods. The time has come when the scope and depth of problems confronting modern film art cannot be expressed in the film language of past decades. In their search for new modes of expression, many film makers have begun to lean toward the form of the novel—consecutive, detailed narration.

Viewers first became accustomed to the off-screen voice of the author telling what the hero was thinking and feeling. Then the so-called interior monologue appeared: We see a silent actor but hear a voice coming from off the screen, as if transmitting his thoughts. There is no doubt that these devices have enriched our palette. But their artistic potential is still purely literary. Such "commentary" is not capable of fully expressing a character's underlying psychological state and the psychological totality out of which a man's internal world and spiritual disposition are formed.

But how are these reflections and experiences to be expressed? How is this state, so familiar to everyone, to be conveyed when a man lives, as it were, in several dimensions?—first, in real, everyday life, and second, in the realm of his reflections and ideas, which, through the power of imagination, can become no less real than life itself. How many times has it happened to each of us that, while walking down a crowded street, we have stopped noticing what was going on around us and have become completely submerged in our own thoughts? They can be evoked by a book or article you have read, or perhaps something that has to be done or a conversation you are faced with. The conversation can be so real in your mind that you even hear the intonations of your partner.

But then something suggests a new thought to you and you are, as it were, in a new dimension, sinking into the realm of memories. Certain associations arise, and you are far, far away from what had just been the subject of your intense reflection. And the street continues to flow past you. You pass the blocks of houses and cross intersections, but everything around you has ceased to be reality. You move mechanically and notice nothing. At this moment your memories constitute a considerable reality.

No less interesting is the circumstance that you can never precisely determine at what moment your imagination snatched you from the real world.

Have film makers learned to convey this particular amazing feature of our psyches? Or, for that matter, the many other traits inherent in homo sapiens?

At present, interesting searches are being made for new devices to expand the language of cinematography. Now here and now there, now in one film, now in another, appear elements of an expressive new movie language. Of course, new artistic modes make the audience's perception difficult at the outset. But should we be afraid of this?

Readers were not immediately accustomed to Mayakovsky's language. Close-ups, dissolves, complicated panoramic shots and the off-screen voice did not catch on immediately.

The course of Soviet film art is marked by a constant search for new forms of expressing a new view of the world. It is our duty to continue this search.

I have touched on only certain questions that film makers are today faced with resolving. The creation of films in which general problems of the modern world are profoundly and absorbingly disclosed and the creation of films peopled with intelligent, reflective and interesting people is one of the most important tasks of cinematography.

Youth

In both American and Soviet society the gist of the "youth problem" is that young people (or many of them) behave in ways of which their elders disapprove and find puzzling, irresponsible, or unconstructive. The extent to which this is a matter of perception or of more solid reality is debatable. In any event, many adolescents in both societies tend to behave in ways which are substantially different from their parents' youthful behavior and from what the older generation finds appropriate. It is also possible, and particularly in American society, that these aspects of youthful misbehavior appear more pronounced and more deviant because of the exaggerated awareness and the distortions created by mass media. The deviant portion (a minority) creates the impression of a "youth problem."

The youth problem has many components, some of which we have considered elsewhere. Actually many more specific social problems are concentrated among the younger age groups: crime and delinquency, misuse of leisure, escapism, as well as political dissent (discussed in the section dealing with political institutions). Perhaps the basic common denominator of youth problems is what some would designate the unwillingness to grow up. This implies the rejection of routine, conformity, stable social and occupational relations, and suggests compulsive anti-authoritarianism, hedonism, short-term orientations, impulsiveness, and the like. Many believe that these not entirely novel attributes of adolescence are more widespread in contemporary American society (as in other parts of the world) than before. There is at least one theoretical proposition that lends plausibility to this belief; namely, the acceleration of social change in the modern world leading to instability, disruption, mobility, confusion, and the intensification of expectations. It is also quite possible that some aspects of youthfulness, in the U.S. at any rate, are to some degree subject to commercial manipulation. An atmosphere of faddism, short-term orientation, impatience with delayed gratification, and hedonism creates a favorable climate for consumption—for the marketing of forever newer products, styles, and fashions. Advertising copy writers are having a hard time constantly devising novel and more emphatic terms for an almost hysterical affirmation of the present, the most recent, the most up-to-date, the latest, the now-generation and all the rest. (At the same time it should also be noted that many of our problematic youth are thoroughly repelled by the consumer ethos. Nonetheless faddism is a common denominator of the mass media, advertising, the consumer ethos, *and* youthful nonconformity.)

The Soviet youth problem has some features in common with the American, but as most things in the Soviet Union, it is more controlled. There is first, a similarity in the presence of a generation conflict which is frequently denied by the authorities with the vehemence customarily reserved for the refutation of easily observable truths. The strong official reaction is related to the political-ideological implications of the issue. If the young are, for example, more apolitical than the older generation (which is a major issue), this would signify a resounding failure of the Soviet system of education, indeed the whole institutional environment. (This concern with the ideological purity and commitment of youth is instructively revealed in the article entitled "Rear Young People in the Spirit of Revolutionary Ideals.") However, if the young are not apolitical, but instead keenly aware of political matters, and idealistically bent on a return to the old revolutionary purities, they could also be a disturbing phenomenon in a basically conservative social system. There is every indication that the latter group does not represent sizeable numbers, although nonconformist tendencies without a necessarily significant political implication have increased among young people in the Soviet Union since Stalin's death. Much of the nonconformity has little to do with politics, and more with entertainment, consumption, and the desire for a more colorful, enjoyable life. Yet in the Soviet political system political apathy is almost as abhorrent as active opposition, or at least such is the impression publicly conveyed. There is every indication that the restlessness of Soviet youth has been exaggerated in part by the wishfulness of Western observers, in part by the tendency of Americans to discover the echoes or counterparts of their own social environment in other parts of the world. It might also have been exaggerated by Soviet leaders who seem to fear that the younger generation will become soft, individualistic, hedonistic, and increasingly apolitical. It is difficult to tell how genuine or justified is the publicly expressed anxiety. One would assume that Soviet political leaders know better than anyone outside the Soviet Union how little active or genuine participation the stability and maintenance of their political system requires. Perhaps their occasional anguished cries for greater political-ideological awareness and participation need not be taken too seriously.

Still the familiar spectacle of expectations rising faster than the opportunities for their gratification applies to Soviet youth more than any other group in Soviet society. As already noted, they expect a higher standard of living, more freedom of choice (not political), more contact with the world outside, better entertainment, and better jobs. Specific problems have arisen in the latter sphere. The problem is not unemployment, but a shortage of jobs which are in demand because they are considered interesting, well-paid, or otherwise desirable. Apparently job placement for the young is a creaky, bureaucratic process that creates much frustration. Supplementing the problems of job placement are problems of higher education, which is also in short supply in many parts of the country in relation to the demand. American youth also face severe employment problems, but the problem is generally limited to those with little education. The job placement of Soviet youth is complicated by the unattractiveness of the vast rural areas of the country which reduces the number of desirable positions people want to take. The overall American situation is worse than the Soviet, however, since there are millions of unemployed, many of them young. Also, there is no concentration of unemployment in the U.S.S.R. among a particular ethnic group, such as the Negroes and other ethnic minority groups in the U.S.

Finally we must briefly comment on the complex of negativistic attitudes Keniston discusses under the heading of "alienation," since they certainly represent a crucial component of "youth problems," at any rate in American society. While the types of alienation he is concerned with are not very widespread, they can easily be placed on a continuum and fitted into a broader pattern. Since Keniston did his research, the emergence and spread of the hippie sub-culture has added yet another dimension to the problem and has partially confirmed the significance of the phenomenon he was concerned with. There is an obvious kinship between the forms of alienation he considered and the retreatism of the hippies. The problem does not exist in such forms in Soviet society, which simply does not permit the development of retreatist sub-cultures and styles of life. Similar tendencies may and evidently do exist, but the institutional framework of Soviet society stifles their luxuriant growth. Alienation and retreatism cannot become a way of life without a high degree of permissiveness in the broader social environment. Certain forms of alienation require a minimal material basis, a measure of affluence, freedom to dispose of one's time, freedom of association, freedom to be idle and to reject prescribed, respectable social and occupational routines and roles. In the absence of these conditions the alienation of Soviet youth, whatever its exact nature and degree, cannot approximate that of the American. But, apart from institutional restraints, there is also reason to believe that, at least until very recently, Soviet society has not been conducive to the development of the attitudes and values which make up alienation and retreatism. However, since no one has carried out empirical research among Soviet youth comparable to Keniston's, our comments are bound to be tentative and speculative.

YOUTH
IN THE U.S.:

The American View

The Uncommitted-Alienated Youth in American Society

KENNETH KENISTON

We began from a definition of alienation as an explicit rejection of American society, and we have seen that rejection in several contexts: in agreement with statements like "the idea of adjusting to American society as now constituted fills me with horror"; in a rejection of active political and social involvements; and above all in the many statements which deny any "feeling of relationship with American society as a whole." Thus, the young men we are discussing clearly fit this initial definition of alienation by rejecting what they see as the dominant roles and institutions of their society.

But what is puzzling is that these youths share so many other outlooks apart from their rejection of their society. With almost monotonous regu-

From K. Keniston, The Uncommitted. New York: Harcourt, Brace and World, 1965, pp. 75–83. Reprinted by permission of the publishers.

larity, these young men (who rarely know one another and form part of no group which might give them a common ideology) express essentially the same views about human nature, about intimacy, about the metaphysical structure of the universe, about the nature of philosophical truth, about the relative importance of the present, about the likelihood of future felicity, and so on. Yet there is no a priori reason why the rejection of American society should entail any one set of supporting or associated beliefs. In other eras and in other societies, the concomitants of alienation have been far from invariant. Men have rejected their society for a variety of reasons: because they had some ideal future society in mind (as with youthful socialist and communist revolutionaries the world over); because they harked back to some earlier social order, often romanticized, which they sought to re-create in the present (as with reactionary revolutionaries); or at times because they held in higher regard some non-material kingdom of the spirit for which the "real world" was but an anticipation, a purgatory, or a preparation. Men and women can refuse their allegiance to a society that asks too much of them or to one that asks too little; they can revolt against an order that promises only poverty and suffering when they aspire to better things, or against one where lowly birth, color, or race denies them opportunities afforded the more fortunate. If we were to survey alienations throughout history (or even in other sectors of American society), we would not find the unanimity of concurrent belief that we have seen in these students.

Why, then do these young men agree about so many other things in addition to the worthlessness of contemporary American society? One key difference between this and other alienations stands out: most rebels and revolutionaries rebel *in the name of* some higher principle or value which they hold more dear than the existing social order. But these young men do not. Historically, most of the alienated have concurrently served some positive goal in whose name they are estranged—be it the radical reconstruction of society, the restoration of ancient verities, the salvation of the soul, national sovereignty, abundance, or opportunity. But these young men find it hard to articulate any clear programs or objectives; and when they do, their values turn out to be private, "aesthetic," and often explicitly irrelevant to the vast majority of men. With these students, then, we are dealing with what we can call *"unprogrammatic alienation,"* rebellion without a cause, dissent without a fully articulated foundation.

In contrast with rebellions with a cause, unprogrammatic alienation tends to be unselective—to take the entire culture as its target. To understand why this is, we must acknowledge that acts of rejection spring from complex personal motives, some related to the now-forgotten frustrations of childhood, some to the difficulties of current living, some more directly and consciously to the difficulties of current living, some more directly and consciously to the inequities and evils of the society that is repudiated. A rebel often supports his rejection of society by that universal human potential which has been called "characterological anger": resentment, rage, and hostility which stem from early life and which are available, in all of us, to inspire and intensify our indignations, irritations, repudiations—and at best our creativity. Like "free-floating anxiety," such diffuse resentment tends to attach itself to any and all objects at hand—sometimes regardless of whether or not they merit anger—unless it is somehow channeled to a few specific and appropriate targets.

The social critic and the revolutionary are often men who have a great storehouse of this free-floating indignation, repudiation, and anger available to motivate their rebellion, and who at the same time have learned to express their anger in attacks against some aspect or all of their surrounding society. Criticism of one's society is, of course, not the only possibility for a deeply angry man: others express their inner frustrations in ritualistic conformity and rejection of those who deviate; others torment their intimates. Nor do I mean to imply that the criticism of society is to be deplored as nothing but the displacement of childhood angers; on the contrary, the world would be a poorer and more stagnant place without men who could appropriately mobilize their own private discontents to improve their society. But when in any society a large number of men and women have a deep reservoir of potential anger because of shared frustrations in the process of growing up, or because of common frustrations in their current lives, or because of actual inequities in their social order, or (most often) because of all three—then it takes little catalyst to direct this anger against the prevailing social order and, sometimes, to channel it into the effort to reconstruct society.

Given a program—a revolutionary ideology—diffuse characterological angers can be focused negatively on specific targets (what the ideology points to as the *causes* of current frustrations) and positively on specific goals (what the ideology specifies as its *objectives*). At best, diffuse anger can be transformed first into concrete criticisms of actual evils and then into "aggressive" efforts to transform the society for the better. Indeed, it is partly the ability to capture such collective angers which enables political leaders to create revolutions, to make men risk death and hardship, take chances with the future of civilization, and (at times) transform their societies for the better. The same angers and resentment, however, inevitably remain unfocused, diffuse, and free-floating without a program or an ideology which pinpoints the problems to be attacked, enumerates the areas in which the social order is in need of change and those which are peripheral. With no criterion for selecting *the* targets, everything becomes a potential target. Without an articulate conception of what is desirable, energy which might have been channeled into construction is available only for rejection. The enemy is the entire status quo—not merely pernicious aspects of the social order which must be changed to permit improvement, but the entire social and cultural ethos. And this is precisely what unifies the ideologies of these alienated students—their rejection not only of selected visible aspects of American society, but of the basic assumptions

and values of traditional American culture as a whole.

In ordinary usage we think of "culture" as meaning primarily the standards of taste, manners, art, and, in our own day, mass media; "low standards of culture" are low standards of taste, of beauty, or art; and "cultural" are those interests traditionally cultivated primarily by women in our society having to do with reading, flower arranging, music, poetry, and so on. But anthropologists use "culture" in an extended, almost botanical sense, as the medium of values and assumptions within which an individual grows, flourishes, and dies. Standards of taste and cultivation are of course part of this surrounding environment, but more important are those usually implicit and unexamined assumptions about the nature of life, man, society, history, and the universe which are simply taken for granted by most members of a society. Thus, every viable culture has characteristic cultural configurations, guiding and unifying assumptions about itself and its members, notions of what it is to be a man or a woman, of the purposes of life, the relationship of man to himself, history, nature, and the invisible world. These assumptions are learned early in childhood as those "facts" of life without which existence would be unthinkable, as those ways of dealing with others, the impersonal environment, and oneself which are simply taken for granted.

Seen in these terms, then, what unifies the ideology of these alienated young men is their generalized refusal of American culture. As we will later see, this refusal of culture goes beyond matters of philosophy and belief, and extends deep into the personal lives of these youths. But even on the level of explicit values, virtually every alienated outlook can be seen as a rejection (often unstated) of American assumptions about

ALIENATED OUTLOOK

OPPOSITE
("American culture")

DISTRUST OF COMMITMENT:
Low view of human nature
Repudiation of intimacy
Rejection of group activities
Futility of civic and politial activities

Rejection of American culture
Vacillation, hesitation to act

COMMITMENT:
Human nature basically good
Closeness, togetherness
Teamwork, social-mindedness
Usefulness, need for civic and political
activities
Praise of democratic culture
Resoluteness, decisiveness

PESSIMISTIC EXISTENTIALISM:
Pessimism about future
Anxiety about world
Universe chaotic, unstructured, meaningless
Truth subjective and arbitrary
Meaning "created" by individual
Impossibility of "true" communication
Appearances usually misleading

Short-range personally centered values

OPTIMISTIC "IDEALISM":
Optimism about future
Confidence about world
Universe orderly, structured, purposive
Truth objective and necessary
Meaning found in universe
Possibility of mutual understanding
Appearances trustworthy, taking at "face
value"
Long-range universally grounded values

ANGER, SCORN, AND CONTEMPT:
Justification and admission of resentment;
rejection
Intolerance, scorn
Self-contempt
Egocentricity in egocentric world

FRIENDLINESS, RESPECT, AND ADMIRATION:
Disapproval and denial of resentment;
acceptance
Tolerance, respect
Self-confidence
Sociocentricitity in friendly world

AESTHETIC QUEST:
Awareness, experience, sentience, "being"
Living for today
Self-expression and creativity
Passion, emotion, feeling
Isolated individualism
Social outsider
Rejection of "success"

ACHIEVEMENT GOALS:
Activity, manipulation, "doing"
Saving for tomorrow
Instrumental work
Reason, self-control, self-discipline
Socialized individualism
Social participant
Drive to succeed

life and the universe. Where Americans have traditionally lived for the future, and still sometimes see history as progressive, the alienated value the present and see history as retrograde, moving downward or backward. Whereas the individualism of most Americans has traditionally been tempered by an acute sensitivity to public opinion, that of the alienated is opposed to social pressure and is "realistic" in its emphasis on personal needs. The point-by-point contrast of an alienated ideology to this "traditional American ethos" can be best seen by simply taking the opposite of each alienated outlook; the result is a recognizable portrait of the traditional American world view.

This contrast between alienated beliefs and their opposites makes clear the extent to which alienation constitutes a total reaction against values long associated with a characteristically American outlook. The opposites of alienated outlooks are those which students of American society have pointed to as the basic assumptions of our culture. What unifies the alienated outlook, then, is its point-by-point denial of each of these historical verities and their replacement by the opposite notions.

This is not to say that every American today holds all of the beliefs I have labeled "traditionally American"; nor is it to assume that every one of these beliefs is clearly articulated and explicit in each of its adherents. "Culture" is most often taken for granted, imbedded in the structures of thought, usage, and language, and is articulated only in times of crisis, when—as in our Declaration of Independence—a new nation seeks to define its future identity, or when—as now—an old nation faces a profound questioning of the values which have supported it for generations. Indeed, the fact that the list of non-alienated values reads more like a mild caricature than an accurate description of our current outlook points to the recent weakening of our unquestioning and implicit acceptance of this world view. Without such widespread questioning, it would be difficult for these young men to sustain an ideology that is so fundamentally opposed to that of a majority of their fellows. It is probably only to the extent that lesser alienations are "in the air," part of the cultural climate of the times, that individuals can find their way to so total a repudiation.

For if we take alienated beliefs one by one, virtually all of them find some support in some current of modern thought. I have already noted the parallel between pessimistic existentialism and alienation, a parallel made more meaningful by the fact that existentialism, too, grows out of rejection of the traditional pieties of what Kierkegaard called "Sunday Christianity" and what Nietzsche saw as the life-denying blindness of bourgeois society. One can also find substantial support for many other alienated views: many schools of psychoanalysis would support their darker assertions about human nature, the inherency of destructiveness, and the fundamental nature of self-seeking. And distrust of appearances is not only a cardinal tenet of much depth psychology (which alerts us to the unfathomed impulses beneath our civilized rationalizations), but of Marxism (which shows class interest lurking beneath most statements about society), and even of philosophical analysis (which behind traditional philosophical questions discovers "misunderstandings" about the way in which words are normally used). Even the traditional American belief in the importance and efficacy of individual political participation is fading before the complexity of the problems which face our nation. In all these areas the alienated can find support and ammunition for their rejection of the traditional American world view—if only a few would follow them so far in their total rejection of this ethos, many would support them on individual points.

This interpretation of alienation as a refusal of traditional American culture is not, however, one that most alienated youths would accept, or that, if they accepted it, they would find relevant or meaningful. For them, alienation is not part of a deliberate effort to locate and systematically oppose the basic values of our culture, but rather a set of conclusions about life that grew relatively un-self-consciously out of their own experience, that appears to be confirmed by it, that makes sense of the way they experience the world. For all of its oppositional quality, and indeed perhaps because it so embracingly and comprehensively opposes that coherent, well-organized, and self-consistent world view traditionally associated with America, alienation is itself a coherent and consistent view of the world. The alienated are in general true to the logic of their position: denying universal truth, they accept that their own assertions are subjective and arbitrary; believing in the evilness of human nature in general, they accept self-contempt along with contempt for others; convinced of the difficulties of human communication, they point to their own isolation. For them, alienation is but an expression of an experience of life, of feelings, and of fantasies, which they cannot comprehend within traditional American culture.

YOUTH

IN THE U.S.S.R.:

The Soviet View

Youth Enters Life

V. SHUBKIN

The growth of productive forces, the scientific and technological revolution and the profound changes in all areas of the life of our society have resulted in a high degree of occupational and social mobility and have placed various and rapidly changing demands on Soviet young people who are entering independent life. The problems pertaining to the young generation's start in life are highly complex and cover a wide range —labor, family, education, upbringing, preparation of cadres, production training, choice of occupation, etc.

The correct and prompt solution of these problems always has both social and economic effects. On the one hand, it diminishes the possibilities of mistakes, dissatisfaction and disappointment linked with young people's first steps in life, thereby reducing all kinds of anti-social phenomena (drunkenness, crime, immorality, etc.). On the other hand, it furthers the more rapid and effective enlistment of young men and women in the labor process, reduces labor turnover and migration, ensures a high degree of acclimatization of young people in newly developed areas of the country, and raises the quality of selection and preparation of cadres for all branches of the economy, science and culture.

The social problems of young people cannot be solved automatically. If the

Reprinted from V. Shubkin, "Youth Enters Life," Voprosy filosofii. *Translated in* Current Digest of the Soviet Press, *XVII, No. 30 (Copyright © August 18, 1965), 3–4, 7.*

entry of young men and women into independent life is to be facilitated and they are to be helped to cope promptly and successfully with the conflicts that arise, there must be systematic scientific research into the social problems of the young generation in a socialist society.

Some of these problems are being studied by the sociological group of Novosibirsk State University's Laboratory for Economic-Mathematical Research.

Our program of work covers a fairly broad range of socio-economic, sociological and social-psychology questions linked with the young generation's start in life. These include: the social prestige and attractiveness of different occupations and types of work; objective and subjective factors influencing the education, occupation inclinations, choice of occupation, job placement and paths in life of various groups of young people; social, occupational and geographical mobility in choosing an occupation; the effectiveness of the system of production training in schools; some ways for improving the planning and preparation of qualified cadres; and improving the system of vocational guidance and counseling. One of the objectives of our research was to discover how far it is possible to forecast personal plans, job placement and occupational, geographical and social shifts in connection with choice of occupation among those young people who in effect make their choice freely.* Prognoses of this kind are essential before the social planning and regulation of these processes can be carried out with any degree of accuracy. To a certain extent the broad range of our research was unavoidable, for objec-

* [bez vsyakoi reglamentatsii, literally "without any regulation." The sense is that the choice of occupation has not been entirely or largely predetermined through attendance at a trade or factory school or other factors.— Trans.]

tivity of analysis can be ensured only by considering the greatest possible number of facets of the process under study.

Novosibirsk Province was chosen as the field of investigation. The survey covered graduates of secondary and incomplete secondary schools. Of all the groups of young people starting out on their work careers, these seemed to us of special interest not only because their choice of occupation was not predetermined but also because with the development of our society the schools are becoming an increasingly important source for replenishing the economy, science, and culture with skilled cadres.

The research was carried out in three stages:

The first stage (1962), during which a trial survey of 300 secondary school graduates was conducted in order to evolve methods of evaluating questionnaires and to bring out certain interdependencies;

the second stage (1963), consisting of a large-scale survey embracing all the secondary schools and 10% of the incomplete secondary schools of the province (approximately 9,000 questionnaires in all were sent out);

the third stage (1964), consisting of a follow-up survey on the same scale and with the same subjects as the second stage, for the purpose of verifying the stability of information and studying the possibilities for the scientific forecasting of certain social processes.

With support from Party and public education bodies and the active participation of school directors and educators, the research program has now been basically completed.

The data assembled are now being processed at mechanical computer centers and the Electronic Computer Center of the U.S.S.R. Academy of Sciences' Siberian Division. Although analysis has not been fully completed, we feel it worthwhile to publish certain materials and conclusions connected mainly with the second stage of the study, dwelling in particular upon the following questions: the specific nature of job placement of young people in the near future in connection with the "demographic echo" of the war; production training; certain social questions of education; and, finally, the attractiveness of various occupations for young men and women just completing secondary school.

JOB PLACEMENT OF YOUNG PEOPLE

The young men and women we studied in 1963 represent the last generation born during the war years. We know that in all the combatant countries the war years brought a sharp decline in the birthrate, and the decline was sharper in proportion to the given country's involvement in the war. Conversely, after the war the birthrate rose sharply.

We are now observing a peculiar "demographic echo" of the war. It is expressed in an avalanche-like increase in the number of young people of 17 or 18 starting out in independent life. Thus calculations carried out by Novosibirsk State University's Electronic Computer Laboratory show that the number of 17-year-olds in Novosibirsk rose by 60% and of 18-year-olds by 70% in the period 1963–1965. There will be an even sharper rise in the size of secondary school graduating classes in the near future; the number of pupils graduating from the general education schools of Novosibirsk Province will increase several-fold in the next few years.

The socialist countries, unlike bourgeois society, have the objective conditions for solving questions linked with the job placement of young people successfully and in planned fashion. But we must not count on merely letting

matters take their course. If these questions do not receive the attention of Party, Young Communist League and economic bodies, if we do not study the economy's requirements for cadres of specialists, the structure of production and vocational training and the occupational preferences of young people, there may be negative consequences.

In our conditions, the problem of job placement has three aspects: geographical, branch (i.e., industry, construction, transport, agriculture, etc.) and vocational. With our labor resources very unevenly distributed throughout the country at present, we may rightly expect great differences in the job-placement prospects of young people in various regions. In regions that have surplus manpower—specifically Moldavia, the western part of the Ukraine, the western part of Belorussia, the Transcaucasus and the Central Asian republics—the job placement of young people has been quite a complicated task for a number of years now. However, specific problems connected with the job placement of young people may also arise in the near future in some of the eastern regions of the country in which heretofore there has usually been a manpower shortage.

Calculations for Novosibirsk Province show that even in the conditions of 1963, when there were many fewer graduates than there will be in years to come and when the percentage of young people entering higher educational institutions and technicums was substantially higher, approximately half of those completing secondary school went to work, most of them in industry. In the next few years, given the same (or approximately the same) number of admissions into higher schools and technicums, both the relative and the absolute number of young men and women who will go to work will increase sharply. Special attention must be given to the fact that the sharp rise in the number of secondary school graduates resulting from the termination of the effects of the wartime decline in the birthrate will be augmented—in fact, will be doubled—for the next few years because of the shortening of the period of secondary schooling, that is, the changeover from 11 to ten years. Clearly, job placement is becoming an important socio-economic problem in our society.

To what extent are we prepared to deal with these questions? What steps must we take to solve them with maximum effectiveness in the new five-year-plan period?

Problems linked with the job placement of young people cannot be solved in the new five-year period separately from the overall problems of the utilization of manpower.

Right now this task is complicated by the serious weakening and neglect during the years of the Stalin personality cult of the "labor services" that existed in our country. I have in mind the abolition of the People's Commissariat of Labor and relevant research institutes and journals; the curtailment or complete cessation of social research (in demography, social psychology, social statistics, public health, etc.) and of research on the scientific organization of labor and management; the lack or scarcity of information on employment and the utilization of manpower. The neglect of the "labor services" has had an extremely negative effect on the growth of labor productivity, the planning of public education, the preparation of skilled cadres and job placement, and it has often created many complications for young men and women starting out in life.

In addition, some of our economic and scientific cadres underestimate the importance of the problem of job placement. Here we still feel the effects of the peculiar "theory" of automatism or spontaneity, according to which the socialization of the means of production will in itself automatically ensure full employment for the entire population. Actually, this does not happen automatically, since public ownership of the means of production merely creates the objective preconditions, the possibilities, for solving these problems. As for automation and technological progress in general, under our conditions they, too, usually lead and should lead to curtailment of the need for manpower at a given enterprise or in a given branch of the economy. It is something else again that we can foresee such developments and that in a planned economy we can promptly redistribute and retrain cadres released as a result of technical progress, automation, changes in the structure of production, etc. This is why painstaking, day-to-day work is necessary to realize the advantages of socialist means of production, and in particular to ensure systematic full employment for the population.

A complete, comprehensive picture of the use of manpower in the country as a whole and in regional and branch cross sections is the first essential. Effective management of labor resources, we feel, requires not only a highly authoritative state agency such as a Ministry of Labor but also interdepartmental and territorial administrations and centers for planning the redistribution of manpower. In the first place, they could keep the population informed about requirements for cadres, and in the second place, they could provide essential information to economic, design and economic-planning bodies concerning the labor resources available in a given district, city, province or territory. This would reduce the losses resulting from having to search for a job in one's specialty, and problems of planning and economic development of an area could be considered with regard for available labor resources and their distribution, sex, age, occupations, skills, etc. At the same time, it seems advisable to charge these institutions with the job placement of workers released from enterprises as a result of the introduction of new technology, change in specialization, etc.

The territorial administrations, as we see it, should also make long-term calculations of requirements for cadres according to specialty. Experience shows that the province planning agencies now charged with this task are in general unable to solve it because of their small staffs. Often, so far from being able to supervise and guide this work, they are not even in a position to collect all the requests for manpower from enterprises.

Under the territorial administrations there should be a network of educational institutions where workers released from enterprises could be retrained and taught new skills. At the same time, it is very important that the territorial administrations not be subordinated to various agencies but that they embrace the entire territory, all branches of the economy and the entire population of the given region. Often, for example, the effect on agricultural labor resources of the construction of factories or industrial complexes is ignored, and agriculture suffers as a result. It must be clearly understood that unless there is an overall approach, work with labor resources will not produce the required effect.

All these considerations on the utilization of manpower should be taken into account when approving the five-year plan. Because of the special urgency of the problem of the job placement of young people in the coming five-year period, it would be advisable for the new five-year plan to have a special section on the job placement of young people. It would be a good idea to review the basic indices of the five-year plan for the U.S.S.R. as a whole and region by region from this point of view. This is particularly important with respect to the drafting of measures for the distribution of production and the utilization of capital investments.

JOB PLACEMENT AND PRODUCTION TRAINING

One of the most important means for successfully solving the problems of job placement of young people in the new five-year period is the efficient organization of production training. The system of polytechnical education, which both cultivates positive attitudes toward labor and provides vocational training in specialties required by the national economy, makes it possible to facilitate the entry of young people into work careers.

What role does production training in the schools play in present conditions?

In Novosibirsk Province, of all those who completed secondary school in 1963, only 11% worked in the specialties for which they had received vocational training in school; that is, the majority of graduates did not work in the occupations they had learned in school. This means that the state has to make further expenditures (material facilities, machines, raw materials, wages, tools, etc.) to retrain boys and girls who have just been trained in some specialty. This is not even to mention the cost in morale.

But may it not be true that the purpose of production training as it is conducted in most schools today is achieved indirectly, insofar as it inculcates love of work, provides for the labor upbringing of young people?

We know that one of the tasks of labor upbringing in the schools is to ensure a correspondence between young people's personal aspirations and the interests of society. If, for example, 90% of the graduates are needed for work in industry, construction and agriculture and 90% of the graduates do in fact intend to go to work in those branches, then there is no problem. But if only 10% intend to go to work in those branches, serious problems arise, which the recent reorganization of the schools in general and the introduction of production training in particular were expected to solve.

The mass survey conducted among Novosibirsk Province pupils just before their graduation from secondary school and after their placement in jobs reveals substantial differences between personal plans and actual job placement. For instance, 80% of the graduates intended to continue their studies. These personal plans were substantially changed by objective conditions. Not 80% but 44% of the graduates went straight from secondary school to higher studies (a very high percentage, which is explained by the small number of graduates in 1963).

As we can surmise, the highest proportion of those continuing their studies after completing secondary school is to be found among the children of the urban intelligentsia. In second place are the children of industrial and construction workers, in third and fourth places are the children of workers in the service branches and the rural intelligentsia, and in fifth and sixth places are the children of workers in transport and communications and of agricultural workers.

While we are categorically opposed to an overly broad interpretation of these selective data, we nonetheless have a basis for asserting that the paths in life of young people in various social groups at present differ substantially. Of 100 graduates from families of agricultural workers (state farm workers and collective farmers), only 10 continued their studies after completing secondary school, while 90 went to work; of 100 graduates from families of the urban intelligentsia, 82 continued their studies and only 15 went to work.

An examination of the factors influencing education gives us reason to believe that the sharp rise in the number of young people starting out in independent work during the new five-year period will give rise to a number of trends contrary to those observed when, because of the decline in the birthrate, there were fewer young people. If special measures are not taken promptly, this will mean an increase in the number of drop-outs from the secondary schools and a reduction in the proportion of pupils completing their secondary education. At the same time, it is apparent that competition for admission to higher schools and technicums will increase. The efficacy of production training, given the observance of the conditions referred to earlier, will grow.

It must be especially emphasized that the intensification of competition for admission to higher educational institutions in connection with the rise in the number of secondary school graduates may lead to a reduction in the percentage of children of workers and peasants entering the higher schools. Therefore steps should be taken in advance to counteract this trend. This is a complex problem. On the one hand, we must try to provide equal educational opportunities for all. But on the other hand, because of differences in the material circumstances of the families, in the education of the parents, in place of residence, in the distribution of the network of educational institutions, in level of instruction, etc., young people with equal abilities but with different preparation have in fact different educational opportunities.

In examining this question, we must not forget that the principal way to overcome social differences in education is to alter the objective circumstances. Attempts to create preferential conditions for admission into higher educational institutions for certain social groups regardless of level of preparation not only will not help solve the problem but will lower the general level of education, to the detriment of scientific and technical progress.

Such is the contradiction. It cannot be solved quickly, but it must be perceived and definite steps for solving it must be outlined in accordance with the level of development of productive forces. Specifically, in working out measures connected with the sharp rise in the number of 17- and 18-year-olds, it is important that the new five-year plan not permit a reduction of the opportunities for the children of workers and peasants, and especially for rural youth, to enter higher educational institutions.

Rear Young People in the Spirit of Revolutionary Ideals

M. KHALDIYEV

...Youth and its militant vanguard, the Leninist Young Communist League, boundlessly devoted to their mother the C.P.S.U., are actively struggling for the implementation of the Leninist policy of the Party. In these days millions of young men and women, enthusiastically preparing for the 23rd Party Congress, are holding a labor vigil in honor of the Congress and are displaying an example of patriotic concern for the development of production, for the successes of science and culture....

It must be stated frankly that successes in the development of the economy and culture and the victory of our great cause, of our ideals depend in

Reprinted from M. Khaldiyev, "Rear Young People in the Spirit of Revolutionary Ideals," Pravda (Nov. 28, 1965). Translated in Current Digest of the Soviet Press, XVII, No. 48 (Copyright © Dec. 22, 1965), 5–6.

substantial measure upon the correct rearing of our younger generation, on its readiness to absorb and continue the revolutionary traditions of the older generation. Society's responsibility for bringing up the rising generation is now growing immeasurably.

Yet it would be wrong not to see, behind the general traits and qualities of youth that gladden everyone, serious shortcomings in ideological upbringing work with youth as well.

In the rearing of youth the processes underway in the life of society are often disregarded, and a differentiated approach to various groups of young people is not observed. As we know, the formation of the world outlook, convictions, views and characters of today's young men and women took place in the postwar period. They have not gone through the school of life and struggle that was the lot of the representatives of the older generations, at the cost of sacrifices and deprivations on the part of those who won and consolidated the victory of the socialist revolution in our country. The young people did not see with their own eyes the great labor victory of their fathers and mothers, the first people in the world to build a socialist society; they did not see their heroic struggle in the harsh years of the Great Patriotic War.

There are also other phenomena the true meaning of which some young men and women cannot clearly grasp. We have in mind questions linked with the struggle against the consequences of the personality cult, and also against subjectivism and voluntarism in leadership.

Nor can we leave out of our reckoning the endeavors of bourgeois ideologists and their masters to disarm ideologically a certain segment of Soviet youth, to shake its faith in communist ideals and instill pessimism and apoliticism in its ranks. To these ends they resort to direct ideological diversions, adapt themselves to new conditions and make their insidious tactics increasingly refined.

The complicated and diverse phenomena in domestic and international life must be correctly understood and interpreted. But at times young people do not have the necessary preparation for this. They do not always, unfortunately, receive from their older comrades a correct explanation of questions that are not clear to them. Certain young men and women, being unable to understand independently the events that are taking place, sometimes fall under an alien influence and slide into a position of skepticism and nihilism. It must be taken into account here that ardor and emotion are attributes of youth, that youth, as Lenin stressed, is the turbulent, searching part of mankind.

Upbringing work will not be effective if we do not take into account the processes occurring in life, do not skillfully and truthfully explain to young men and women the complex questions of the revolutionary transformation of society, help them perceive the essence of events and phenomena and strengthen communist conviction in them.

The tasks of communist construction insistently demand a decisive improvement in the ideological-political rearing of young people, raising the effectiveness and efficiency of all sectors of the system of communist education. These questions have been comprehensively discussed at recent plenary sessions of the committees and meetings of the aktivs of the Moscow City and Province, Leningrad, Kemerovo, Gorky and other Party organizations.

Communist construction is taking place in conditions of acute class struggle in the international arena between the moribund system of capitalism and the constantly growing socialist system. This raises as a major task the instilling in young people of class consciousness, an ability to evaluate events from Marxist-Leninist positions, the fashioning in each young person of the features of a communist fighter, revolutionary, patriot and internationalist. . . .

The tasks of building the new society demand the rearing of a young generation in which spiritual wealth, moral purity and physical perfection are harmoniously combined. Health, creative principles, a striving toward knowledge, inquiry, discoveries, exploits in science, labor and art must be developed in young people. The entire education and upbringing of young men and women must be permeated with the confirmation of communist morality, with the spirit of conscious fulfillment of the principles of the moral code of the builder of communism.

But the rich possibilities for the class, communist rearing of the rising generation are by no means being exploited to the full. This applies to oral and printed propaganda, to literature, the theater, the cinema, radio and television.

Of especially great importance is the patriotic rearing of the young generation, the inculcation in its members of the revolutionary morality of the working class, a readiness always to uphold resolutely the proletarian revolutionary cause. Party and Young Communist League organizations, workers in literature and the arts, the press and radio are faced with a concrete task—to rear young men and women in the heroic traditions of the struggle of the working class and the collective farm peasantry, in examples of the selfless labor of the older generation in building socialism and communism, in their exploits in defense of the great gains of October.

In this regard, rich positive experience has been amassed by the Party organizations of Leningrad. Meetings of three generations have become a tradition in all boroughs of the city. They are held in Palaces of Culture, factory clubs, shops, institutes, workers' and students' dormitories. Veterans of labor and revolution pass on to their sons and daughters, like a glorious relay baton, revolutionary behests and traditions. Many plants and factories have set up rooms and museums devoted to the enterprises' history. Meetings with participants in the Great Patriotic War and with soldiers of the Soviet Army and evenings and lectures on military-patriotic themes enjoy great popularity.

The inculcation of Soviet patriotism is one of the fundamental questions of work with youth. A feeling for the motherland—a great, the loftiest of human feelings—manifests itself, takes root and grows strong under the entire tenor of our life and history, of the whole of socialist reality.

Broader use must be made of Soviet holidays and revolutionary anniversaries in the patriotic rearing of youth. The celebration this spring of the 20th anniversary of the victory over fascism showed how receptive young people are to the patriotic and heroic achievements of the Soviet people, how they love our glorious Soviet Army. Preparations for the 50th anniversary of Great October and the 100th anniversary of the birth of V. I. Lenin must become a school of the revolutionary education of the young generation, of its tempering in the glorious traditions of the Party and the people.

Taking into account the sense of romance characteristic of youth, we must encourage Y.C.L. committees to hold various demonstrations, parades, mass athletic and military-patriotic games, agitational motorcycle marathons, walking tours to battle sites of the Great Patriotic War, etc.

The rearing of youth includes also the formation of such a feature of the new man as a lofty sense of civic duty, the responsibility of the individual to society. It is completely reasonable and humane to act everywhere—in the family, school, institute, factory, collective farm, institution—in such a way that solicitude and consideration for young people are accompanied by demands upon them, exactingness and serious trust.

It is understandable that the secondary and higher educational institutions play a large role in forming in young people a communist world view. The schools lay the foundation for the world view of young men and women and mold their convictions. An important place in this belongs to such subjects as social science, history and literature.

It must be admitted that instruction in these disciplines in the schools is still insufficiently exploited for molding a scientific world view and communist conviction in pupils. Such instruction is often not linked with current events. Some instructors confine themselves to what the textbooks say, disregarding the events of the stormy current of political life and evading the acute questions that arise among young people.

The teaching of the social sciences in the higher educational institutions, which are called upon to prepare highly skilled and ideologically convinced cadres of specialists, requires all-round improvement. In a number of higher schools lectures on social science disciplines are delivered dryly and without the necessary documentation; insufficient encouragement is given to developing in students independent thinking, the creative assimilation of Marxist-Leninist theory. Concern for improving the teaching of the social sciences is an urgent task for the professors and instructors and the Party committees of the higher educational institutions. . . .

The great tasks of the ideological-political upbringing of young people require a significant improvement in the activities of Y.C.L. organizations, increased activeness and initiative in their work. And this in turn presupposes the strengthening and improvement of Party leadership. It is called upon to contribute to the development in the Y.C.L. of a creative approach to the cause, of activeness and initiative, and it must unfailingly be permeated with profound attentiveness and consideration, paternal concern and exactingness. . . .

In some places there is an incorrect understanding of labor upbringing; it is limited to the inclusion of young people in the labor process. But the labor process in itself does not provide revolutionary tempering if the ideological content of production matters is not disclosed and interpreted, if there is no concern for man's spiritual growth. Labor upbringing is not merely the instilling of work habits in young people

but also an important part of the communist rearing of youth.

The task is to enhance in every way the authority and role of the Y.C.L. organizations, to help them correctly combine participation in economic construction with the ideological-political and moral upbringing of youth. The Y.C.L. must always look upon the communist education of young people as its main task.

At the plenary sessions of a number of Party committees, Communists have mentioned with deep concern the fact that of late the number of Party members engaged in Y.C.L. work has begun to decline. We, too, believe this is wrong. In the interests of the cause it is essential that Party representation in the Y.C.L. be strengthened.

The entire system of education and upbringing in our country must serve the tasks of the ideological-political upbringing of young men and women. Such important sectors of ideological work as literature and the arts should be mentioned in particular.

The creative intelligentsia helps the Party rear the young generation as active builders of a new society. Writers, composers, artists, directors have produced many books, films and stage shows, works of music and art that are permeated with life-affirming optimism and that help mold staunch, convinced fighters for the ideals of communism. They clearly reveal the spiritual beauty of the man of labor, the great feat of the Soviet people, their unshakable faith in the triumph of the ideas of communism.

But we must not fail to see that, along with works that help our Party solve successfully the tasks of the communist education of the rising generation, there have also appeared, unfortunately, those that have no clear class position, that do not engender in the readers and viewers a feeling of selfless struggle for communist ideals. The contest of good and evil presented in them frequently loses sight of social positions and proceeds on a detached moral-psychological level. This is understandably of little help in molding a class consciousness in young people.

In recent years certain works of literature and art have portrayed individual periods in the life of the Soviet people in a one-sidedly subjectivist fashion, and at times have cast doubt upon our indisputable accomplishments. Certain authors, in treating the events of the Great Patriotic War, concentrate their attention only on the difficulties and mistakes of the initial period. With other creative workers the so-called "prison camp theme" has overshadowed everything. An artistic chronicle of the formation and development of Soviet society is an important means for educating our youth. It enables the young person to experience for himself, as it were, what happened long before he was born. It must assist in the spiritual formation of the individual, in patriotic upbringing.

V. I. Lenin said that young people need the authority and experience of the old fighters grown wise through revolutionary practice and traditions and possessing a broad political horizon. It is precisely by the example of the courage and heroism of the grandfathers, fathers and mothers in the Civil War, during the first five-year plans, in the harsh time of the Great Patriotic War and in the struggle for the building of communism that today's youth is tempered.

But recently a number of works have appeared that offer a false treatment of the reciprocal relations of the generations, the role of the older generation in the life of Soviet society.

Departure from the great civic themes and the replacement of what is heroic in our days with the narrowly personal and intimate experiences of the characters are clearly noticeable in the repertoires of certain dramatic theaters; this applies in particular to the Leninist Y.C.L. Moscow Theater.

Soviet people, particularly the youth, expect that in the theater, as in other kinds of art and literature, a worthy place will be occupied by works of heroic plan, of lofty civic resonance, that show the great achievements of the Soviet people, of the Party and the Y.C.L., and in which contemporary man emerges in all the fullness of his life-loving, strong character.

*   *   *

Youth is our future. The rearing of youth is a great task of the entire Party and the entire state. All Party, Soviet, Y.C.L. and public organizations are called upon to devote themselves to the rearing of the rising generation. We must do everything so that the young generation may grow and be tempered and may worthily continue the great revolutionary cause of the older generation.

Initiation into Life

R. NISHANOV

...Recently a mass poll was taken among the young men and women of our republic for the purpose of ascertaining the interests, tastes and views of the most varied categories of young people. It is significant that to the question: "What do you see as the meaning of your life?" 93% of those polled answered "Service to the people." We can only be gladdened by and proud of the pure thoughts and the ardent impulses of our young people. . . .

The years of youth are a time of character formation, of searches for a course in life and bold plans. These years are full of reflections, evaluations and reappraisals, doubts and the restless testing of ideals, enthusiasms and disappointments. Youth is always inquisitive, especially in our time. Characteristic of the young people of today is the striving for independent understanding of the complex phenomena of reality. This cannot be ignored, any more than we can discount the fact that the subjectivism of recent years, the self-willed treatment of Marxist-Leninist theory, and the overestimation of a number of events in our history furthered the appearance in a certain segment of young people of such phenomena as political apathy, nihilism, the rejection of authority and an egocentric attitude to-

Reprinted from R. Nishanov, "Initiation Into Life," Izvestia (Oct. 17, 1965). Translated in Current Digest of the Soviet Press, XVII, No. 42 (Copyright © Nov. 10, 1965), 33–34.

ward life. Therefore it is very important that we give timely support to everything good in young men and women, that we develop their positive qualities and give full play to their noble impulses, that we direct their curiosity and seething energy into the proper channels.

There are in the West many "poisoners of wells" who have not given up their attempts to drive a wedge between the older and younger generations of Soviet people or between the peoples of the U.S.S.R. and to slander and distort the essential points of our party's national policy. But the ideological unity between the generations in Soviet society will never be shaken by anyone. No one will ever muddy the pure spring of our fraternity, because the political basis of our society is internationalist, our economic base is internationalist and, in the broad sense, our culture is internationalist.

We say to our young people: "Preserve and strengthen the friendship of peoples as the holy of holies, cherish our socialist fraternity as the apple of your eye." Repudiating any manifestations of nationalism means serving one's people.

There is no stronger substance cementing the friendship of people of various nationalities than free labor together for the good of the homeland. There is in Uzbekistan no enterprise, collective farm, state farm or higher educational institution where representatives of many nationalities do not work or study side by side. . . .

At times one still has occasion to hear this kind of talk: Young people today, the argument goes, aren't what they were in the 1920s and 1930s. There were heroes then, and there was enthusiasm! Yes, the memory of these heroes of the first five-year plans and the glory of their feats live on in the Y.C.L. But is the present generation of builders of communism really any less heroic? Who is not aware of the enthusiasm with which our young men and women are creating the country's big chemistry today, or what trials were endured by the young builders of the Bukhara-Urals Gas Pipeline, the largest in the world, or what an utterly historic feat was accomplished by young Soviet patriots when they blazed the first trails in space!

True, we sometimes come across the kind of young people who grumble and whine about everything and go for years without finding their place in the labor system. They have changed occupations once, twice, three times, but nothing is to their liking. Sometimes older people are to blame for this. They did not inculcate respect for labor in time, they did not impress upon them that the labor of the worker or the farmer, as well as the labor of the sales clerk, the tailor and the barber, is honored and respected in our country. We create an aura of romance around certain vocations and forget the many others.

However, it goes without saying that no aura will help if a basic concern for the individual is lacking at an enterprise. Building is the vocation of the twentieth century, youngsters want to become builders, but many construction organizations have an indifferent attitude toward young people, toward their labor and daily life.

This is the kind of "concern" for young people shown by the managers of Construction Trust No. 150 in the city of Samarkand. The trust dormitory,

where 300 young builders live, is dirty, the furniture is no good at all, the laundry facilities and showers do not work and the radio loudspeaker system is in bad condition. In the Red Corner you won't find a single newspaper or magazine. The man employed here as the house adviser is not at all qualified for the job. This is how he "planned" a mass-political function in the dormitory one day: "From three to five, spin records; from eight to ten, holiday greetings; from ten to 12, spin dance music." While this house adviser, if such he can be called, was busy "spinning," the young people were killing time with cards and intoxicating beverages.

It is time to call those who work side by side with young people and guide them to more strict account. The director of the enterprise, the shop chief, the foreman and the brigade leader are all as responsible as the public organizations for the moral image of the young generation of workers and its work qualifications.

The novice needs guidance from older people, not only on the job but also beyond the factory gate. His living conditions, how he spends his free time, where he studies—all this should be of interest to the manager of the enterprise, to the Party and Y.C.L. workers.

At a number of enterprises we recently made inquiry as to how young people spend their free time. To the question: "Where do you study?," 45 out of 100 answered "Nowhere." To the question: "What literary heroes do you remember best from the books you have read during the last two months?" only 27 gave an answer. To the question: "How many times have you gone to the theater this month?" 68 people gave no response. To the question: "Do you engage in physical culture and sports?" only 37 gave an affirmative answer. To the question: "Do you engage in amateur art activity?" 87 answered in the negative.

As you see, the results of this study lead us to disquieting reflections. The free time of the majority of the young people polled is still being spent thoughtlessly and, in some cases, to the detriment of the individual and society. This does not speak well for the managers of enterprises and the public organizations. . . .

Old Age

The hardships of old age exemplify a social problem which is manifestly unrelated to any deliberate policy, or design, and which represents a classical accumulation of "unintended consequences." The problems of the old are truly peculiar to modern societies where, to begin with, the number of people who reach old age is much larger than in the past or in contemporary primitive societies. Changes in the family structure are another commonly observed source of old age problems, since the old are, to a greater or lesser extent, left outside the narrower confines of the nuclear family of parents and children. Consequently, they tend to lose both a sense of importance and familial roles as well as sources of financial support. Modern societies also weaken the status of the old by their emphasis on change and innovation. While in relatively unchanging, traditional societies the experience of the old has been a useful guide for the young and a valuable asset to transmit, in modern ones the experiences and values of one generation may become totally obsolete and irrelevant from the viewpoint of the next.

It is likely that this is another problem which is more acute in the U.S. than in the Soviet Union. Three explanations suggest themselves. One is that American family patterns are further removed from the traditional ones than the Soviet, and the coexistence of the generations in the Soviet Union is also reinforced by the housing shortage. Because of the higher proportion of Soviet working mothers, grandparents also have a greater role in child care than in the U.S. Secondly, the obsession with youth, youthfulness, and novelty is more pervasive in the U.S. and correspondingly little respect is shown for the old, who often end their life in degrading circumstances of neglect, poverty, and social isolation (see the article by Jules Henry). Thirdly, inexpensive or free medical care is still not easy to obtain in the U.S. (although recent legislation brought considerable improvements), creating additional problems for an age group most in need of it. A large proportion of old people in the U.S. also suffer from the prevalent attitude that if a person could not save enough money for his old age and must seek public assistance, then something must be wrong with him. This, of course, is a widespread attitude toward all those in need of public welfare assistance for whatever reason: poverty, ill health, old age, or illegitimate children.

As the Soviet selection indicates, old age is also becoming a problem in the Soviet Union although its symptoms and dimensions are different from those in America. In the U.S.S.R., according to the article, the "largest group of old age pensioners live with their children as one family"—an entirely different situation than the American. (Whether or not the children prefer this solution is another question.) There must be a great scarcity of institutional facilities, if in the entire Russian Republic, by far the largest of the Soviet Republics in area and population, only 150,000 old people are cared for in institutions. This, of course, need not be an undesirable state of affairs as long as living with the younger generations is a matter of choice rather than necessity. But apparently more old age homes are needed and the demand for them is growing. It is quite likely that with the improvements in the standards of living, housing, institutional child care, and higher expectations of comfort, the problem will get worse before it gets better.

OLD AGE

IN THE U.S.:

The American View

Human Obsolescence

JULES HENRY

Public institutions for sick "social security paupers"—those who have no income but their social security checks—are ruled by the social conscience; that is to say, obvious things that readily excite conventional feelings of right and wrong are taken account of within the limits of miserly budgets, but everything else is slighted. For example, an institution may have plenty of medicine and an abundance of sterile gauze, but the medicine is often administered by ignorant persons and the gauze contaminated by ill-trained aides. Bedding, even when sufficient, may be dingy grey because of penny-pinching on soap and bleach. Food may be adequate but distributed in assembly-line fashion and eaten within obligatory time limits. Every bed may have a thin blanket sufficient for the regulated temperature of the institution, but if the heating breaks down or the staff decides to open the windows when the outside temperature is freezing, the patients are unprotected. Thus, were the social conscience to inquire whether the inmates

had enough of what they need, the answer would be "yes," and the social conscience, easily lulled by appearances and small expenditures, would sleep on.

Always interested more in outward seeming than inner reality, always eager not to be stirred or get involved too much, always afraid of "pampering" its public charges and more given to the expression of drives than of values, the social conscience cannot be stirred to a concern with "psychology" unless some terrible evil, like juvenile delinquency, rages across the land. Hence, the spiritual degradation and hopelessness of its obsolete charges seem none of its affair. The social conscience is affected by things having "high visibility," like clean floors, freshly painted walls and plenty of medical supplies, rather than by those having "low visibility," like personal involvement. A nurse in a mental hospital once put it to me this way: "When you go off duty they can tell if you've got a clean dressing room, but they can't tell if you've talked to a patient." In an institution for obsolete social security paupers the supervisor can tell whether or not a patient has been bathed but not whether the aide who did it spent a little extra time bathing the patient as if he was a human being rather than something inanimate. Since too many minutes devoted to being human will make an aide late in getting her quota of patients "done," they are washed like a row of sinks, and their privacy is violated because there is no time to move screens around or to manipulate the bedclothes in a way that preserves the patient's sense of modesty.

In many primitive societies the soul is imagined to leave the body at death or just prior to it; here, on the other hand, society drives out the remnants of the soul of the institutionalized old person while it struggles to keep his body alive. Routinization, inattention, carelessness, and the deprivation of communication—the chance to talk, to respond, to read, to see pictures on the wall, to be called by one's name rather than "you" or no name at all—are ways in which millions of once useful but now obsolete human beings are detached from their selves long before they are lowered into the grave.

...Every institution establishes a "national character" of inmates and staff in accordance with the remorseless requirements of the institution and in relation to the characteristics brought to it by inmates and staff. Given the commitment of Rosemont to profit, the laughable social security checks of the inmates and the cost of food, comfort, and a high standard of living, certain consequences have to follow. In order for Mrs. Dis to be comfortable and make a good profit, according to her lights, she has no choice but to extract as much as she can from the pensions of the inmates and the salaries of her help and to limit the standard of living of both. That of the inmates is cut to a level just above starvation but below that of a good prison. In order to do this a fundamental transformation has to be brought in the mode of life and the self-conception of the inmates and in the staff's way of perceiving them. In short, Mrs. Dis makes it necessary for her institution, as personified in her staff, to conceptualize the inmates as child-animals, and to treat them accordingly. This in turn is made possible because in our culture personality exists to the extent of ability to pay, and in terms of performance of the culturally necessary tasks of production, reproduction, and consumption.

But the transformations are possible in Rosemont only because of the acquiescence of the inmates; and this is obtained not only because the inmates are old and powerless, having been abandoned by their relatives and a miserly Government, but because with one or two exceptions, they recognize that, being obsolete, they have no rights; because they understand that, having nothing, they are not going to get anything. Meanwhile their degradation is intensified by the fact that while economically poor they are intellectually poor too; for the schooling they received, and the culture in which they have lived, provide no resources for making life in a filthy hole more bearable. They can neither read nor carry on conversations of interest to one another; nor, having lost faith, do they have the culture of worship. Rather they spend their time staring into space, defending their beds against the gropings of the blind, the incontinent, and the disoriented, or watching the behavior of their blind and psychotic fellows, while they wait obsessively for the next meager meal.

Thus the "national character" of all the inmates becomes reduced to several simple components under the tyranny of the institution. These components are apathy, obsessive preoccupation with food and excreta, the adoption of the role of child-animal, and defense of the bed. To this may be added general acquiescence in everything the institution does, decline of the disgust function, and preoccupation with reminiscence.

...If one were to attempt to derive but one law from this section it would be that *culture outlasts body and mind,* for even as the body remains barely alive and the mind declines into a senile rigidity, beset by hallucinations, the cultural configuration remains as part of mind. Long after she can no longer move, the American upper-middle-class woman is concerned with appearance and status, and her capacity to hate and to hurt follow channels determined by the culture. Bedridden though she may be, listening for her heart to stop beating, she still retains the lesson she learned when she was strong: that it is easier to be hostile than compassionate. So, cooped up in narrow quarters with others, she is unable to sacrifice an illusory autonomy to the wishes of those with whom she shares her room.

Since the frames of reference of the cultural configuration are the *content* of mind—if not, indeed, mind *itself*—the extent to which these frames are retained by aged people becomes an index of the intactness of their minds. Sensitivity to space–time, to moods of weather, to the importance of appearance and status, alertness to competition and luck, and the capacity to participate in amiable misrepresentations, are all measures of the mental state of an aging person of either sex. So also are insistence on one's rights and the capacity to enmesh another person in a meaningful conversation. This involves an understanding of the cultural theories of causality and probability.

As one reads these conversations between the researchers and the patients in Tower, one is impressed with the uniqueness of our culture's orientation toward aging and death: its denial of death; its expectation that at death's

very door women will dress up; its acceptance of the fact that the aged may be bound even while all the ingenuity of science is used to keep them alive. Meanwhile the vast effort to maintain life is technical and impersonal; and at the patient's death, those who exerted the greatest efforts to keep him *alive*—the technical staff—are least moved, for his personal death is his family's affair.

One is also impressed with the gulf between the aged and the young, even when the aged are mentally alert; and this is because our culture is an avalanche of obsolescence hurling itself into the Sea of Nonexistence. And so it is with the personal community: our friends and those we love are a bit of string that falls from our hands when we die, and youth will never use it to tie up anything.

An effort to formulate a "national character" for Tower yields the following: the staff, though animated by *solicitude* and *kindliness* seems to maintain an attitude of *indulgent superiority* to the patients whom they consider *disoriented children,* in need of care, but whose confusion is to be brushed off, while their *bodily needs* are assiduously looked after. Tower is oriented toward body and not toward mind. The mind of the patients gets in the way of the real business of the institution, which is medical care, feeding, and asepsis. Anything rational that the patient wants is given him as quickly as possible in the brisk discharge of duty, and harsh words are rare. At the same time the staff seems to have *minimal understanding of the mental characteristics of an aged person.*

As for the patients, they live out their last days in long stretches of *anxiety* and *silent reminiscing,* punctuated by outbursts of *petulance* at one another, by TV viewing, and by visits from their relatives. There is no inner peace, and *social life is minimal.* Meanwhile the patients *reach out* to the researcher and would engage her endlessly in conversation if she would stay. There is a *yearn-*

ing after communion but no real ability to achieve it. In this we are all very much like them.

OLD AGE

IN THE U.S.S.R.:

The Soviet View

The Third Age of Man

G. DROZDOV

[On May 20 *Literaturnaya Rossia*, No. 21, published an article by Varvara Karbovskaya entitled "The Third Age of Man," containing excerpts from letters written by old people complaining about the difficult and sometimes humiliating conditions in which they are compelled to live. The article discussed the need for more old-age homes. The following article was written in response to the numerous letters received by *Literaturnaya Rossia* and the Russian Republic Ministry of Social Security.]...Statistics for the past 50 years show that the number of old people increases every decade. For example, according to the 1939 census 6.8% of the people in the Russian Republic were over 60, and according to the 1959

census 9.4% of the people were over 60. And what if we compiled statistics on people of retirement age throughout the country?

According to data from the Institute of Labor, by 1961 the number of men over 60 and women over 55 constituted 12.5% of the total population. A stable trend toward a continued increase in the proportion of old people in the total population has been observed. There are many reasons for this.

According to forecasts made in a report by the Housing and Urban Construction Committee of the U.N. Economic Commission for Europe, in many countries the proportion of aged people over 60 will amount to 20% of the population by 1980.

The problem of the "third age" is becoming ever more urgent throughout the world. It is of considerable importance in the Soviet Union too. The Soviet state has done a great deal for the material security of old people.

Reprinted from G. Drozdov, "The Third Age of Man," Literaturnaya Rossia *(Aug. 12, 1966). Translated in* Current Digest of the Soviet Press, *XVIII, No. 34 (Copyright © Sept. 14, 1966), 15–16.*

Never before has so much state-budget and public money been spent on this. In the Russian Republic alone more than 6,000,000 people receive old-age pensions.

Nearly a quarter of a million old people and invalids in the U.S.S.R. live in old-age homes and are fully supported by the state. The Directives of the 23rd Congress provide for a further increase in minimum old-age pensions.

However, neither pensions nor the rise in the general prosperity of the people in the country have removed the "third-age" problem from the agenda. The fact is that as the over-60 population increases, so does the number of single elderly people who require medical supervision and everyday care and services.

The war left many parents and wives without spouses. As sociological studies show, the Soviet Union has the greatest longevity difference between men and women. There are two and a half times as many women as men over 80. Consequently, many elderly women are alone, and care must be provided for them. The growth of the urban population owing to the influx of young people from the villages often divides families and increases the number of aged people who also need collective service by the state.

The article "The Third Age" and the responses to it have raised several problems. The first is the attitude toward elderly people within the family; the second is housing for single elderly people; the third is everyday and medical service for the elderly.

These old-age problems cannot all be solved by any one method, by a single approach, or by the efforts and resources of the state alone. The problem is much more complex than it appears to be at first sight.

In the first place, the largest group of old-age pensioners live with their children as one family and wish to continue to do so. Second, there is a group of single old people who find it difficult to get along without outside help in their everyday lives; although some have relatives who are obliged by law to support them, they cannot live with them for various reasons. For example, the old people may live in a village and the children in a city. Or parents and children may live in different cities. Housing conditions may be unsuitable, the mutual relations between the old and young in the family may be incorrect, etc. The reasons are many and diverse. Third, there is quite a large group of single, chronically ill old people who require constant medical attention and who are incapable of taking care of themselves.

For the old people in the first group, those who live with their families and receive pensions, a tranquil life depends on correct mutual relations within the family. However, when deciding housing questions, local Soviets should always consider that there may be elderly people in a family. Things should be arranged so that old people have their own room. Their work for the benefit of society has earned them this.

The problem is more difficult with regard to the second group, the single old people, especially those of advanced age. Many of them have good modern apartments and receive sizeable pensions. But with each passing year they find it more difficult to cook, launder, shop and clean house. Therefore, many of them apply for admission to state-supported old-age homes. Between 10,000 and 15,000 people are admitted to such homes in the Russian Republic every year. Of course, this is not enough. There are old-age homes built on the State Building Organization pattern, with rooms for one, two and three people, dining rooms, club rooms, workshops, medical rooms and an auxiliary farm. But there are not enough of these.

New old-age homes with a total capacity of 7,000 to 10,000 people are built every year, but all the same this does not fully satisfy the demand.

Altogether the Russian Republic has 815 homes for old people and invalids. In them live approximately 150,000 people who are wholly supported by the state. Many of these homes have excellent reputations. Examples are the Bersky Home in Novosibirsk Province, the homes for labor veterans in Krasnoyarsk, the Ordzhonikidze home in North Ossetian Autonomous Republic, Vidny in Moscow Province and the new homes in Mazilovo, Leningrad, Pushkino, Pavlovsk and Strelna. It should be said that the Leningrad City Soviet and the Leningrad Party agencies have done a great deal to build new homes for old people and invalids and to improve the old homes. Their example is worthy of imitation.

In the last five years the Moscow City Soviet has been paying more attention to the building of old-age homes. Fine homes have been built in Lyublino and Izmailovo, and construction has been planned for Khimki and other places. But the need for such old-age homes in Moscow remains very great.

The draft five-year plan for developing the Russian Republic's national economy provides for the expenditure of 180,000,000 rubles on construction of old-age homes with space for 72,000 people. In addition, in the Russian Republic alone the state spends more than 140,000,000 to 150,000,000 rubles annually on maintaining old-age homes. And nevertheless, the state construction plan will be unable to satisfy the demand for old-age homes during the five-year-plan period.

The trouble is that for many years, right up to 1952, no new old-age homes were built; various accommodations, turned over to social-security agencies by local Soviets, were adapted for such purposes. Many of these buildings were poorly appointed, shabby and unsuitable. Only 110 old-age homes with space for 30,000 people have been built in the last 14 years. And there are some provinces and autonomous republics where not a single old-age home has been built in the 20 years since the end of the war.

Among those are Belgorod, Bryansk, Irkutsk, Kurgan, Penza, Chita and Archangel Provinces, Stavropol Territory and the Mari and Udmurt Autonomous Republics.

Nothing can explain this situation except underestimation of this important matter and a heedless attitude toward old-age-home construction on the part of local Soviets and the social-security departments of building organizations. What is more, on pretexts of insufficient manpower for construction, priority of other projects, and the inadequacy of the building organizations, some province executive committees are reducing the allocations for old-age-home construction and are changing the dates for their completion after the State Planning Committee and the Russian Republic Council of Ministers have already approved the plans for their construction. This happened in Bryansk, Archangel and a number of other cities. And in the Kalmyk Autonomous Republic an old-age home for 100 people has been under construction for eight years.

The attitude of Soviet executive committees, planning agencies and the building organizations toward developing the network of old-age homes must be radically changed; fulfillment of the plan must be ensured.

Nor should construction be limited only to old-age homes that have been envisaged in the national-economic plan. During the years 1952 to 1955 many Union ministries took the initiative, and that initiative was approved by the

U.S.S.R. Council of Ministers. The ministries built special old-age homes for their retired employees. Such homes were built for railroad, oil, steel, and textile workers. The construction of a home for elderly actors and singers was started in Moscow this year. There has long been a home for elderly theater workers in Leningrad, built on the initiative and with the funds of the All-Russian Theater Association.

The Russian Republic Ministry of Social Security has proposed that ten Union ministries build homes for their retired employees. Only three ministries found such construction feasible—the Ministries of the Chemical Industry, the Petroleum Industry and Highway Transportation.

Could it be bad to have such homes for steelworkers, miners, schoolteachers, medical workers, journalists and writers?! But certain executives do not wish to understand this. For example, the Board of the U.S.S.R. Writers' Union has rejected our repeated appeals that the union build a home for aged writers.

In "The Third Age of Man" and the responses to it, a proposal was made to build homes and boarding houses construction of and maintenance at which is to be paid for from the savings of the pensioners themselves and by contributions from children and other relatives obliged by law to support aged relatives.

The Ministry of Social Security has examined the proposals made by *Literaturnaya Rossia,* has supported them, and has requested the Russian Republic Council of Ministers to instruct the province executive committees of Moscow, Leningrad, Rostov and other provinces to examine these proposals for the experimental construction of cooperative boarding houses. The idea is that province executive committees and city

Soviets should each build one old-age home in the course of the five-year period, and the old people living in them should be provided for by deductions from their pensions and by payments by relatives.

Construction should not be limited to isolated old-age homes. In our country a multitude of new towns spring up every year; plans are being made to build thousands of new microboroughs in the cities. Apartment houses, stores, schools, hospitals, kindergartens and Palaces of Culture are being built, but almost nowhere are old-age homes and boarding houses for unattached old people going up. In our opinion, this is not right. Homes are needed for people of the "third age," especially given the population's changed age profile.

The construction practice of our neighbors, the northern countries, and of France, Britain and others also confirms this. Finally, there is the tested and proven experience of planning the splendid new city of Volzhsk, where, unlike other new cities and microboroughs, an old-age home was built along with schools and children's medical and sports facilities.

In recent years collective farms have altogether ceased building homes for elderly collective farmers. There are only 160 such homes in the republic, accommodating a total of 2,000 people. Moreover, 90% of all these homes are in Voronezh and Belgorod Provinces, Krasnodar and Stavropol Territories and the Tatar Autonomous Republic; no such homes exist in most other provinces. And yet the need for them in the villages is no smaller but greater than in the cities.

The Russian Republic Council of Ministers has instructed the Russian Republic Ministry of Agriculture and Ministry of Finance to draft proposals on this question. It would be a good idea if the draft Collective Farm Statutes obligated collective farms to build homes for single aged collective farmers and invalids as well as provided for pensions for collective farmers.

Institutions for the chronically ill, including the aged, who require constant medical attention, treatment and care should be built entirely differently.

Before the war there were special departments in hospitals, and even earlier, under the system of public health agencies, there were special hospitals for the chronically ill. Now hospitals do not as a rule admit the chronically ill, who must be cared for by the social-security agencies. Thus, homes for chronic psychiatric patients have appeared in the system of social security agencies, and in some old-age homes nearly half the inmates are bedridden.

At the end of 1965 the Housing and Urban Construction Committee of the U.N. Economic Commission for Europe held an international conference in Belgium on housing construction for elderly people, which a delegation from the Soviet Union also attended. Several recommendations were drafted at the conference. They should be discussed by our architects, planners, builders and social security employees. . . .

Rural Areas

The principal problem of rural areas in the Soviet Union is economic and cultural backwardness. In these regions a spectacular concentration of disadvantage abounds. The standard of living is low, even in comparison to that of poorly paid urban workers and employees. Cultural-recreational facilities are inadequate, and communications, transportation, schools, the choice of occupations, and the range of consumer goods are all inferior to what is available in urban areas. The stagnation of the countryside, combined with the low productivity of agriculture, is probably the biggest social problem in the Soviet Union. The Soviet countryside bears the marks not only of the legacy of a traditional peasant society but also of decades of neglect, peasant resentment against agricultural policies, the long-standing official attitude of mistrust of the peasants, and consequent treatment of them as second-class citizens (reflected among other things in the restrictions on his freedom to leave the farm). The situation could aptly be described as a vicious circle or a self-fulfilling prophecy. Since Marx, through Lenin and Stalin, communist theoreticians and political leaders (at least in Europe) considered peasants backward, non-revolutionary, and corrupted by private property aspirations. They were treated accordingly by Stalin in particular, who institutionalized their exploitation and coercion. As a result, the countryside stagnated despite the sweeping economic and administrative restructuring represented by collectivization. The countryside has failed to produce enough food; almost half a century after the Revolution, years after Soviet space achievements, and decades after Soviet atomic bomb production, the Soviet Union has been compelled to import wheat.

The articles on the problems of Smolensk province (situated in European Russia and far from being the most backward) provide graphic, candid illustrations of these points. The major expression of rural discontent is the flight of the young to the city, which leaves behind a growing manpower shortage, an unbalanced age structure, and further impairment of agricultural production.

Another ramification of these problems is the arrival of young peasants in the overcrowded cities. One article presents a classic description of the processes of social disorganization which follow the sudden transplantation of rural people to the cities. It could almost come from the writings of early American sociologists concerned with the anonymity, the weakened kinship and community ties, and the demoralization that face the newly arrived, rootless city dweller:

> When the age structure of the population is normal, the fundamentals of ethical experience are assimilated through the lively communion of the generations. . . . The artificial partitioning off of the generations destroys this mechanism. The old folks remain in the village, while the young find themselves in the city with their views as yet unformed. They live in dormitories or rent corners in the rooms of strangers, people whom they meet quite by chance. Could this be one of the reasons for the shortcomings in the behavior of some young people?

There is a striking appeal here to traditional forms of socialization one would not expect to find, an appeal that betrays little confidence in the surrogate communities which the Party, Youth Organization, school, or place of work provide.

Apparently the stagnation of the countryside is not limited to collective farms and villages. Small towns have also been left behind in the march of modernity—unchanged unimproved, and bleak—as shown in another article. It is worth noting that two of the three articles on rural areas appeared in literary magazines (which in recent years have become the most outspokenly critical voices in Soviet society) and that they have not been written by professional sociologists.

The problems of the American countryside are different— in part because a much smaller proportion of the population lives in rural areas, and in part because the gap between town and country is much narrower than in the Soviet Union. As with most American social problems, even those associated with the rural areas have a racial-ethnic component. It is the rural Negroes, Mexican farm laborers, and migrant farm workers who live in the most abject poverty. Many rural areas, particularly in the deep South and the Appalachians, are indeed underdeveloped—if not by Soviet standards, by those of the rest of the United States. There is also massive rural unemployment, resulting from automation and the decreasing economic viability of small farms, and an attendant rural depopulation, which causes problems analogous to or possibly worse than the Soviet problems. There is an indissoluble link between rural and urban problems in the United States: city slums are fed by the surplus population of the countryside, especially Negroes. These problems are the subject of Harrington's famous exposé, excerpts of which will follow. Paradoxically, while many of the problems of the Soviet countryside are rooted in technological backwardness, many of those in the United States are linked to rapid technological development which makes a large agricultural labor force obsolete and unnecessary. That Negroes are the prime victims of this process is understandable, since they have traditionally supplied labor for unskilled, unmechanized agricultural operations.

It would be difficult to guess which society will be more successful in solving the problems of its rural areas. Possibly the Soviet Union will be more successful, since it does not have the added problem of an uprooted, underprivileged racial minority, as does the United States. However, the entrenched backwardness of the Soviet countryside and the animosity of the peasants toward the regime has proved remarkably resistant to change for half a century. Moreover, Soviet rural problems and insufficient food supplies are inextricably joined together; whereas the spectacularly high level of U.S. agricultural production is in no way undermined by the hardships of big segments of the rural population, and production continues to rise despite an ever-shrinking agricultural labor force.

RURAL AREAS
IN THE U.S.:

The American View

Pastures of Pleasure

MICHAEL HARRINGTON

There are those in the city for whom progress is upside-down, a threat rather

Reprinted by permission from Michael Harrington, The Other America. *Baltimore: Penguin Books, © Copyright 1963, 43–51, 60–62.*

than a promise. But this is even more true of the rural poor.

In the postwar period American agriculture continued to transform itself in the most basic way. As a result of mechanization, a vast exodus to the city took place. And yet, even given this agricultural revolution, this complete restructuring of farm life, the poor remained behind and, incredibly enough, by about the same proportion.

The big corporate farms gained, of course. So did the urban consumers. As a result of the technological gains, Americans spend less of their income for food—an average of 20 per cent—than any other nation in the world. And the cost of food has risen less since 1949 than almost any other item in the cost-of-living index. Clearly, agriculture is one of the major successes of the affluent society.

At the same time, perhaps the harshest and most bitter poverty in the United States is to be found in the fields.

In recent years, quite a few people have become aware of the migrant workers. They are not only the most obvious victims of this triumphant agricultural technology; their plight has been created by progress. In the new structure of farming, a great number of human beings are required for a brief period to do work that is too delicate for machines and too dirty for any but the dispossessed. So the Southern Negroes, the Texas-Mexicans, the California Anglos are packed like cattle into trucks and make their pilgrimage of misery.

The migrants are not the only victims. In a nation where Fourth of July speeches about the virtue of the "family farm" are still being made, there are nearly a million such farms that are centers of poverty and backwardness. The stationary farm workers, the factory hands of the new agricultural technology, suffer along with the small owners. And, as industry comes to the South and other rural sections of the nation, the independent proprietors of low-income farms have become the

human reservoir for low-paying industry. There is, to be sure, a well-publicized farm program in Washington. Yet here, even more than in the cities, the welfare state is for the middle class and the rich. The impoverished who dwell in the pastures of plenty have simply been left out.

These are the people who have hardly received a cent of the money spent for the subsidization of agriculture. The surplus foods are scrupulously cared for and controlled; the human beings are not. So these men and women form their culture of poverty in the midst of abundance; they often go hungry while the fields produce more than ever before in man's history.

Beauty can be a mask for ugliness. That is what happens in the Appalachians.

Driving through this area, particularly in the spring or the fall, one perceives the loveliness, the openness, the high hills, streams, and lush growth. Indeed, the people themselves are captivated by their mountain life. They cling to their patches of land and their way of living. Many of them refuse to act "reasonably"; they stay even though misery is their lot.

It is not just the physical beauty that blinds the city man to the reality of these hills. The people are mountain folk. They are of old American stock, many of them Anglo-Saxon, and old traditions still survive among them. Seeing in them a romantic image of mountain life as independent, self-reliant, and athletic, a tourist could pass through these valleys and observe only quaintness. But not quite: for suddenly the mountain vista will reveal slashed, scarred hills and dirty little towns living under the shadow of decaying mining buildings.

The irony is deep, for everything that turns the landscape into an idyl for the urban traveler conspires to hold the people down. They suffer terribly at the hands of beauty.

Though the steep slopes and the narrow valleys are a charming sight, they are also the basis of a highly unproductive agriculture. The very geography is an anachronism in a technological society. Even if the farmers had the money, machines would not make much difference. As it is, the people literally scratch their half-livings from the difficult soil.

The seasons are vivid here. The tourist perceives this in the brilliance of spring, the bracing air of fall, the lush charm of summer. The tourist will not, of course, come here in the winter. Yet the intensity of the weather also means a short growing season. The land is resistant, and even unapproachable, for great portions of the year.

But, the traveler may say, granted that there is a low level of income, isn't it still true that these folk have escaped the anxiety and the rigors of industrialism? Perhaps this myth once held a real truth. Now it is becoming more false every day. Increasingly, these are a beaten people, sunk in their poverty and deprived of hope. In this, they are like the slum dwellers of the city.

During the decade of the fifties, 1,500,000 people left the Appalachians. They were the young, the more adventurous, those who sought a new life. As a result of their exile, they made colonies of poverty in the city. One newspaper in Cincinnati talked of "our 50,000 refugees." Those who were left behind tended to be the older people, the less imaginative, the defeated. A whole area, in the words of a Maryland State study, became suffused with a "mood of apathy and despair."

This, for example, is how one reporter saw the independent yeomanry, the family farmers, and the laid-off industrial workers in the Appalachians: "Whole counties are precariously held together by a flour-and-dried-milk paste of surplus foods. The school lunch program provides many children with their only decent meals. Relief has become a way of life for a once proud and aggressively independent mountain people. The men who are no longer needed in the mines and the farmers who cannot compete with the mechanized agriculture of the Midwest have themselves become surplus commodities in the mountains."

Perhaps the most dramatic statistical statement of the plight of these men and women occurred in a study produced in Kentucky: that, as the sixties begin, 85 per cent of the youth in this area would have to leave or else accept a life of grinding poverty. And a place without the young is a place without hope, without future.

Indeed, it is difficult to find any basis for optimism in this area. And yet, the various states of the Appalachians have come up with a program to offer some basic relief for the incredible plight of these people. Still, the very candor of their analysis defeats much of their purpose. One study, for instance, estimated that the Appalachians would need slightly more than one million new jobs if the area were to begin catching up with the rest of America. As of now, the vicious circle is at work making such a development unlikely: the mountains are beautiful and quaint and economically backward; the youth are leaving; and because of this poverty, modern industry hesitates to come in and agriculture becomes even more marginal.

The roads are bad. Less than half of the population has had more than one or two years of high school. There is no human backlog of ready skills. The industrial incentive is for the low-paying, manpower-exploiting sharp operator. In the Appalachians this has meant the coming of textiles and apparels plants. (This is the classic association of low-paying industry with low-paying agriculture, to be described in greater detail later on.)

Some things could be done. The roads could be improved and brought up to the standards required by modern industry—but only with Federal grants. Education and the cultural life of the area could be improved. There could be regional planning. (Significantly, the Kennedy Task Force on depressed areas recommended only one regional planning commission specifically and by name: for the Appalachians.) The whole structure of backwardness and decay, including bad public facilities, lack of water control, and the struggle with soil erosion, could be dealt with.

But such a program would be truly massive. It would require a basic commitment from the Federal Government. As the sixties began, the nation cheered a Depressed-Areas law which provided that the bulk of the funds should be spent in the South. Yet even its proponents admitted that the money for bringing in industry was minimal, and the allocation for retraining and education almost miniscule. It seems likely that the Appalachians will continue going down, that its lovely mountains and hills will house a culture of poverty and despair, and that it will become a reservation for the old, the apathetic, and the misfits.

For the city traveler driving through the mountains, the beauty will persist. So too, probably, will the myth about the sturdy, happy, and uncomplicated mountain folk. But behind all this charm, nestled on the steep hills and in the plunging valleys, lies an incredible social ugliness.

The Appalachians are a dramatic and obvious part of a larger process. For behind the plight of these mountain folk, and of the rural poor all over America, is the working of a curious dialectic: how a technological revolution in agriculture created the conditions for the persistence of poverty.

One of the main groups in the rural culture of poverty has a peculiar characteristic: It is composed of the property-owning poor.

During the last three decades, mechanization has recreated the American countryside. According to the United States Department of Agriculture, the average investment per farm increased some six times between 1940 and 1959. The amount of working hours spent on food production has been in almost steady decline since the end of World War I (and right after World War II the average dropped by 700,000,000 man-hours a year). As a result, there has been a decline of almost 2,000,000 units in the number of farms since 1930.

At the top of agricultural society are the minority of corporation farms and big farm owners. For them, the technological revolution has meant enormous profit and fantastic feats of production. In 1954, the year of the last comprehensive farm census, some 12 per cent of the operators controlled more than 40 per cent of the land and grossed almost 60 per cent of the farm sales. These were the dramatic beneficiaries of the advance in the fields.

At the bottom of American farming, there are over a million farms. They constitute 40 per cent of all the commercial farms in the United States, yet they account for only 7 per cent of the sales. Their plight is similar to that of the slum dweller who lacks education: as the big units become more efficient and modern, as invention mounts, the poor fall further behind.

So it is that this progress resembles nothing more than a treadmill when it is viewed from the rural culture of poverty. For example, in 1954 a farmer had to double his 1944 production in order to maintain the same purchasing power. This was easy enough, or more than easy, for the huge operators with factory-like farms. It was an insuperable task for the small independent owners. Even though tens of thousands of them were driven off the land and into the cities, their proportion within agricultural society remained the same.

The centers of this property-owning poverty are in the South, the Pacific Northwest, the Rocky Mountains, and New Mexico. It is here that one finds the people so aptly described by the Department of Agriculture as "farmers dependent on their farms as the main source of income but unable to make an adequate living from farming." The houses are often dilapidated and without running water or sinks. In the case of Southern Negro farmers, the 1950 Housing Census reported that 98 per cent of their dwellings were either rundown or lacked some plumbing facilities.

It has already been noted that the proportion of these people in American agriculture shows an amazing persistence, staying at the same rate despite the most profound transformations and an exodus from the land. Their location is a similarly obstinate fact. In the mid-fifties two agricultural sociologists, Charles P. Loomis and J. Allan Beegle, made a survey of depressed farming areas. These were, they found, exactly where they had been in the thirties. The New Deal and postwar prosperity had passed over these areas without really touching them.

For years, however, the main concentration of rural poverty has been Southern. In Virginia, West Virginia, and South Carolina, for example, over half of the farm units are in the bottom-income categories of the Department of Agriculture. Kentucky, Tennessee, Alabama, Mississippi, Arkansas, and Louisiana are not far behind in agricul-

tural backwardness. Taken together, these states make up a belt of misery that runs from the Middle Atlantic coast to the South and to the West.

One statistic should illuminate this problem dramatically. These poor farm owners live in a society with an incredibly productive agricultural system. Yet, according to Government figures, in the mid-fifties some 56 per cent of low-income farm families were deficient in one or more basic nutrients in the diet. The rural poor who did not live on farming were even worse off: 70 per cent suffered from this deficiency. Thus, there is hunger in the midst of abundance.

Food, of course, is only one item in the rural culture of poverty. In a study of the southern Appalachians made at Tuskegee Institute, it was found that this area had higher rates of infant mortality than the rest of the nation, higher rates of rejection by Selective Service, fewer doctors per thousand people, and older doctors. Schooling is, in many cases, inferior to that of the urban slum.

Mississippi, as one might expect, is one of the extreme cases of property-owning impoverishment in the United States. In 1956 the state had 211,000 farms. Of these, 60 per cent were under 50 acres; 60 per cent had product sales of less than $1,200; 8 per cent used machines; and 81 per cent harvested cotton by hand picking. The resultant poverty, it must be emphasized, was not that of the migrants. Out of 628,000 persons working, and 200,000 farm workers, there were only about 2,000 migrants. The majority of these people were members of families who owned the farms; and a sizeable minority were regular hired hands.

By saying that rural poverty is most heavily concentrated in the South, one is also indicating that it has a racial aspect.

In a state like Mississippi, the Negro poor farmer is not simply impoverished; he is terrorized as well. The Southern Negroes who have been making integration news by boycotts and sit-ins are city people. Concentrated in large numbers, forming communities, they have a cohesion and social strength that is able to stand up to the forces of racism. But the rural Negro is isolated, living in a place of backwardness and ignorance. As such, he is the perfect subject for the traditional methods of terrorism.

Two means are employed in making this Southern Negro farm poverty a special horror. The Klan or the Citizens' Council can use physical violence or intimidation. The car that approaches a shack in the middle of the night is a threat. Or the racists can call in the bills at the local store, or even eliminate sharecropping units. (Hundreds of thousands of them have disappeared in the last two decades.) In Fayette County, Tennessee, both techniques have been employed. Negroes who registered to vote suddenly discovered that they could not buy supplies, get a doctor, or any other assistance from the community. Then the recalcitrant ones who still stood up for their rights were driven off the land.

The poor farmers of Fayette County demonstrated extraordinary courage and competence. They made their plight a national symbol, and built their own "Freedom Village." But for many other Negroes of the Deep South, the terror is too overwhelming. They are poor, and part of their poverty is fright and the acceptance of their own humiliation.

I remember talking to one of the Negro leaders in Mississippi. He told me of all the tricks of intimidation that I have described. When he went with some other Negroes to register, they were surrounded by state police. They had to take a lengthy examination— they were, of course, failed by the white examiners—and he said that it was difficult to remember the Mississippi Constitution while hostile and well-armed officers of the law surrounded the group.

The details of the poor farmer's situation could be multiplied almost endlessly: the Southern states where rural poverty is concentrated are statistical simplicity incarnate, the poorest, lowest, and meanest living areas of the nation by every index one can imagine. But perhaps the most dramatic and summary statement of the problem was made in a dry statistical chart published by the Department of Agriculture. The Government economists had noted that the number of low-income farm units was declining (the inevitable result of the flight from the land). Some people were seizing upon this development to argue that all was getting better in a slow, effortless, evolutionary way. In probing this theory, the Department of Agriculture worked out a measure of "relative" low income that charted the income of these farmers in relation to the gains made by the rest of the society between 1929 and 1954. Their conclusion left the complacent theory in a shambles.

In 1929 there were almost 1,700,000 low-income farms. They constituted 35.8 per cent of the total of commercial farms. During the depression their number rose as the unemployed came back to the land. In 1939 they were 39.2 per cent of all the commercial farms. During the war the figures dropped sharply. (The agricultural population gained because of the way in which price and wage stabilization worked during the war.) But in the postwar period the old pattern reasserted iself. In 1949 these low-income farms were 30.3 per cent of the total, and in 1954, 32.2 per cent. In a period of a quarter of a century, the number of low-income farms had declined to about a million. But despite this enormous change, their percentage drop was only a little better than 3 per cent. In 1929 a third of the commercial farms in America were centers of poverty; in 1954 the same relative figure still held.

However, there is still another theory which argues that the situation is not so bad as it seems. Industry, some say, is coming to these areas. All the Government figures indicate that more and more people from low-income farms are going into factory work. Consequently, the problem will be eliminated in the long run. (The penchant for looking for an easy way out when people consider the other America of poverty is ubiquitous.)

The basic assumption of this theory is true enough: part-time farming is on the increase, if only because the bottom third cannot support the people who live there. But once again the ironic dialectic that threads its way through the culture of poverty is at work. The industry that comes to these places is not concerned with moral or social uplift. It seeks out rural poverty because it provides a docile cheap labor market. There is income supplementing as a result, but what basically happens is that people who have been living in the depressed areas of agriculture now live part-time in the depressed areas of industry. They get the worst of two worlds.

A Tennessee Valley Authority study put the situation neatly: there is developing, it said, an association between low-income farming and low-income industry. Poverty, it would seem, can be quite useful it is properly manipulated and exploited.

...Thus, in the face of a massive problem involving millions of people, the political power of conservatism was able to reduce the provisions to the barest minimum. And the rural poor had no powerful spokesman of their own to plead their case. If they benefit,

it will be through no fault of the power system.

This situation is one on which the public is tremendously confused. For most middle-class Americans, aid to "farmers" is a gigantic giveaway, a technique for robbing the urban millions and giving to the countryside. Yet the poor farmers do not, for the most part, receive a cent as a result of these laws. Parity, and the other sensational provisions, are pegged to farm units with big market crops. The poor farmers are left out. (This is yet another case of "socialism for the rich and free enterprise for the poor," as described by Charles Abrams in the housing field.)

Yet the farm poor must pay a political price for this lopsided program. They are excluded from the benefits of the welfare state in the countryside, but the public does not know that. When legislation comes up, these impoverished and defenseless people must bear the onus which rightly belongs to the rich farmers alone.

So it is that those who go hungry in the pastures of plenty, those who lack education and doctors, have no one to speak for them. Their needs are enormous and continuing. As Big Agriculture continues its revolution in the fields, their plight will get worse. And those who finally flee to the cities will discover that they are almost completely unprepared for the complexity of metropolitan life. They are part of the selective service of poverty; they are sent from one culture of the poor to another.

Where, then, is hope for these people?

It is one of the terrible ironies of political life in America that there are social problems that could be dealt with, where the basic research has been done and the techniques of solution demonstrated, but where there is no political force strong enough to enforce progress. This is the case with farm poverty. It is, for example, completely obvious that these areas require comprehensive inventories, careful planning, and coordinated programs. The battle for this concept, lost in the debate over the depressed-areas law, will be one of the crucial social conflicts of the sixties.

If there is not a massive and planned program, then the conditions of misery described in this chapter will continue.

The other chief avenue of hope is the labor movement. After years of ineffective but dedicated work, a major effort is being made among the migrants of California. It is still much too early to say that the present campaign will succeed. Ultimately, migrant unionism must gain some measure of control over work in the fields, through a hiring hall, or possibly, as some unionists have proposed, through a union employment agency that could enforce decent wages and rates. The growers, however, have tremendous political power. When hearings are held, they produce works of scholarship demonstrating that a few cents more an hour would nearly bankrupt the richest agricultural system in the world. (In California a great deal of agricultural research is subsidized by, and subordinate to, the big farm owners.)

But the union's importance is not confined actually to raising the money income of those who toil in the fields.

Equally important is the fact that it will enfranchise these voiceless citizens and that it will finally produce a movement in which the rural poor speak out in their own name. This could happen in California; and there are now attempts to move into the South where the new agricultural technology, by creating factories in the fields, may well create the social conditions for union organization; it could also happen throughout the nation.

When Edward R. Murrow's "Harvest of Shame" appeared on television, there was a moment of national shock. Suddenly, millions of people became aware of what one part of the other America really looked like. Any union campaign to help the migrants can count on greater support from the middle class than any labor project one can think of. In this, there is great potential.

But as of now, all this is a matter of potential and of hope. The present reality is one of misery. The image of the old America, so dear to the rhetoricians and Fourth of July orators, was of a nation based on a sturdy and independent yeomanry. That is no longer true. The old America of the fields has been replaced by the other America. What was once the nation's pride is now the nation's shame.

RURAL AREAS
IN THE U.S.S.R.:
The Soviet View

Sociological Essay: Anxieties of Smolensk Province

G. SHINAKOVA and A. YANOV

Editors' Note.—...It is well known how sharply many areas of our country are confronted by the problem of the departure of young people from the countryside. There has been no lack of newspaper and magazine articles dealing with this theme.[1] Unfortunately, these have sometimes been of a more emotional than analytical nature. *Literaturnaya gazeta,* in cooperation with Moscow State University's Labor Resources Laboratory headed by Candidate of Technical Sciences V. S. Nemchenko, attempted a trial exploratory investigation of the migration of rural youth in Smolensk Province....

*   *   *

1.—...In a number of the central provinces the heart of the problem lies

Reprinted from G. Shinakova and A. Yanov, "Sociological Essay: Anxieties of Smolensk Province," Literaturnaya Gazeta *(July 23 and 26, 1966). Translated in* Current Digest of the Soviet Press, *XVIII, No. 33 (Copyright © Sept. 7, 1966), 9–12.*

[1] See *Current Digest of the Soviet Press,* Vol. XVIII, No. 2, pp. 10–13; Vol. XVI, No. 47, pp. 21–22.

in ensuring the normal replenishment of labor resources in the countryside. This question arises most sharply, perhaps, in Smolensk Province....

Nature in this area, as distinct from the lavish but capricious South, offers the guarantee of stable harvests—on condition that the soil is sound and that there are sufficient hands to nurture it carefully. This has been incontrovertibly borne out by the experience of the German Democratic Republic, Holland and other northern countries, which on land just like the land here have stabilized grain yields at a level of 30 centners per hectare.

Smolensk Province achieved a grain yield of 8.7 centners per hectare in 1965. This was its highest flight, its peak, for the past ten years. The average yield does not exceed six centners.

Incontestible figures also tell us that there are far fewer working hands in Smolensk Province's villages now. No one will dispute that the migration of the rural population to the city is an historically legitimate, progressive process, the natural result of the growing productivity of labor in agriculture.

But it is not natural that the rapid

migration of Smolensk Province's rural population has been proceeding at the expense of the healthiest and most vigorous age groups. When it comes to people over 50, there are considerably more of them than in 1953, for instance. The rate at which young people have been departing from the countryside may be judged by the declining number of Young Communist League members. Five years ago there were 12,771 Y.C.L. members or the state farms of the province; in 1965 there were 6,258. "If the young people continue to leave at this rate," remarked Yu. Anisimov, secretary of the province Y.C.L. committee, when the subject was broached, "we'll have no one left to work the state farms." The collective farms present a similar picture: In 1960 there were 21,043 Y.C.L. members, while five years later there were only 8,788.

On the Red Tractor Collective Farm in Kardymovo, Yartsevo District, there are only two Young Communists left. It has been impossible to set up a primary organization there, since a third Y.C.L. member has been lacking for years. In the Smolensk District village of Pomogailovo, the brigade leader S. M. Baranovsky recalled that the last wedding was celebrated five years ago and it it three years since a child was born. Already there are villages in Smolensk Province in which, as N. I. Kalmyk, First Secretary of the Smolensk Province Party Committee, put it, the voices of children are not heard for years on end. In many cases the migration of the young from the villages of Smolensk Province precludes the very possibility of the reproduction of the rural population. Hardly a fifth as many children were born in the villages in 1965 as were born 25 years before, while the natural increase in the rural population of Smolensk Province has dropped by almost sixteen-seventeenths in the past 17 years!

The shortage of working hands on farms that grow a number of labor-consuming and practically unmechanized crops leads to scandalous phenomena. The collective farmers are compelled, quite officially, to decide which crops they have grown shall be permitted to perish. How can a worker deliberately doom a harvest watered with his sweat? The province has more than 200,000 hectares of flax and potatoes and about 500,000 cows and pigs—and all of this is supported to an enormous extent by manual labor. Now let us solve a little problem of arithmetic. The province will need 50,000 equipment operators by the end of the five-year plan. At present it has a third of that number. The farm mechanization schools alone trained 15,500 equipment operators in the seven-year period, but the number of equipment operators on the farms has risen by only 4,000. How many equipment operators will have to be trained in the next five years if this proportion continues to prevail? The figure is fantastic, to put it plainly, utterly unrealistic for the province. The disruption of the process of the reproduction of labor resources, the distortion in the structure of growth of the rural population and the direct effects of the migration of young people thus pose a threat to technical progress itself these days. It is not the 50-year-olds, surely, who will get behind the wheels of the machines furnished to the province during the five-year plan. . . .

We went to Smolensk Province precisely to examine the approaches to this problem.

We began by questioning rural school children—321 pupils in the eighth, ninth, tenth and 11th grades. The schools were located in different districts; some were collective farm schools and others state farm schools. Only 5% of the pupils had not made up their minds about such a fateful question, so to speak, as where they would live after finishing school; of the rest, 72% chose the city and 23% the countryside. It was considerably more complicated than that, actually, since the city had been chosen by 65% of the eighth-grade pupils, 83% of the tenth-grade pupils and 96% of the 11th-grade pupils. As we see, with the rise in the educational level, the standing of the village, the prestige of rural life drops sharply in the eyes of the pupils. . . .

Let us briefly review the basic motives for migration. The majority of the pupils were going to leave the village to continue their studies. Of the 85 tenth-grade pupils questioned at the Kardymovo school, 83 were leaving for that reason. . . . The motive is merely the form through which various circumstances are reflected in people's minds, through which they perceive those circumstances and through which the latter shape their behavior. Therefore the conditions that make for migration do not always coincide with the motives given for it. Just remember that 35% of the eighth-grade pupils and 17% of the tenth-grade pupils we questioned had no intention of leaving for the city. Nevertheless, they would do so.

Everyone in our country, of course, has a right to education. If some little fellow in the village wants to become another Lomonosov, more power to him! But there are others who would like to become tractor drivers.

The concentration of educational institutions, including those preparing cadres for the countryside—right down to the agricultural vocational-technical schools—in the cities and the utter impossibility of acquiring a specialty in the village had been leading to the alienation of rural young people from their native soil. Such alienation, though temporary at first, in most cases becomes permanent.

The result is, in a sense, a dramatic situation. Let us assume that a boy has passed through eight grades of schooling and that he is not tempted by the laurels of an Academician but wants to stay in his native village and raise grain. However, even if he is 16, he may not, according to our labor legislation, be put behind the wheel of a tractor. To go to school he must be sent to the city, and he begins to lead a life in two places. Buying 35 kopeks' worth of pretzels on Saturday, he sets out for home; on Monday he returns on the crowded bus to his dormitory, laden with goodies from the village.

The city rises like a huge filter between the young peasant and his need for specialization, a need that is inseparable from the spirit of the 20th century and is as imperious in the countryside as in the cities. Once the offspring of the village finds himself in the city, still another important factor of migration makes itself felt—the difference between urban and rural standards, a difference stemming from the centuries-old economic and cultural backwardness of the countryside.

A differentiation should certainly be made among school children, who are not equally susceptible to the pull of migration. The 11th-grade pupils, who have been in school for more than half their lives, aspire for the further heights of education. The eighth-grade pupils, however, are more attracted by the possibility of mastering for themselves the magic of operating a mechanism. In view of this, it would evidently be expedient to review the entire structure of the preparation of cadres for agriculture. Schools should be opened on the big farms, giving those farms normal opportunities for training their own cadres, as any large industrial enterprise does. Legal status should be given to individual-brigade apprenticeship on the state farms. Possibly, too, it might be expedient to provide for exceptions in the labor legislation, permitting 16-year-olds in the proper circumstances to operate machines. If a teenager can avoid loafing and quickly learn, right then and there, a job he likes, a job through which he can help his family and farm, he will be spiritually cemented to the countryside. If migration is to be regulated, it is necessary to take advantage of the modern teenager's enormous bent for mechanisms, so that the spirit of the 20th century will work for and not against the countryside.

Second on the list of motives for migration is the fact that there are no fixed hours in the countryside, that manual labor predominates and pay is low. "I see my mother working from morning until late at night, and I am not attracted by the prospect"; "The same work pays more in the city than in the village; it's hard to live on low earnings."

Behind this motive, of course, are the actual living conditions of rural toilers in Smolensk Province. It must be remembered that in 1965 the province's collective farms had 9,000 equipment operators and about 85,000 people engaged in unskilled, unmechanized work [literally, "horse-and-hand work"]. For every equipment operator, there are about ten people engaged in general farm work. Such work means low pay; it is carried out only at certain times, but during those periods the worker is kept busy from morn till night. And no special skills are involved. Is this a job fit for a person with a secondary education?

The third motive set forth in the questionnaire was the low level of cultural and everyday services in the village. In talks with the young people, they complained about this even more often than about the other two factors. They answered differently, however, when the question was raised in practical terms. Seventy per cent of the tenth-grade pupils in the Kardymovo school, in opting for the city, cited working conditions and low pay as the motive for moving. One cannot avoid the thought that constant reiteration of this motive in the press implants it in the minds of school children, much like a cliché implanted by literature.

But to return to our teenager, whom we left oscillating between town and village like a shuttlecock. Let us assume that he has withstood the temptations of the city, has come home and taken his place behind the wheel and has finished the duties expected of a novice. During his second year, when he might really be expected to be an asset to the farm, he goes off to the army. When he has finished his military service, he will take a job on a construction site (for his trade, happily, is in demand everywhere), or will marry a city girl, or will be talked round by his comrades or "come to his senses" by himself—but he will never return to his native village, for he has been sliced cleanly away from Smolensk Province. And once the young men have gone, the young women are sure to follow; they are not inclined simply to wither away on the vine. Through the force of objective circumstances, through distortion of the sexual structure, we have simply been "driving" the girls from the countryside....

But let us see what would happen should they stay where they were "collectively," as an entire "classroom" of young people, if that classroom of young men and women were given a section of land to work and were turned into a brigade. The boys in the brigade would become tractor drivers, but the girls— what would they do? They would have to go to work in the fields, engage in those same general tasks referred to before. There would be a difference in pay and skill. Because of the shortage of hands, moreover, the farm's management would put them to work singly, wherever they might be needed—one to work with the flax, another in the potato field, a third on harvesting, etc. The brigade would surely fall apart.

This is no figment of our imagination. All this has been tried before. An entire class of 11th-grade pupils of the Syr-Lipetsk school stayed on in 1964. They had addressed an open letter to all who were finishing school and had already found emulators.

But what happened to the whole thing in a few months? The girls turned up in town after all, although "cultural and everyday conditions," as they are called, had been created for them on the farm. They had been given apartments, and sports equipment had been bought for them.

It is time we realized that we are dealing with a powerful objective process not to be stemmed with enthusiasm alone, nor by offering the proper "cultural-everyday conditions" alone. Those conditions are important, but no less so than the art of working with the young —for this truly an art, and its absence leads directly to conditions making for migration. "The young get no attention at all in the rural localities," the young people write. "Little attention is given to their guidance."

Added to these conditions, there is the exceptionally low educational level of the middle-echelon managers on the farms. Imagine an enthusiastic 18-year-old 11th-grader making a start under a brigade leader who, as the young people put it, had only an incomplete church-school education behind him, and many things will become clear. Of the 1,667 collective farm brigade leaders in Smolensk Province, 141 have had a secondary education and 628 an elementary education. The situation is hardly better on the state farms. Of 1,190 leaders of integrated brigades on these farms, 173 have had a secondary and 390 an elementary education.

Can one imagine shop chiefs such as these in industry? The number of specialists on Smolensk Province's farms has grown hardly at all for many years. As Young Communist League statistics show, there were 1,091 agricultural specialists who were Y.C.L. members in the province in 1958, as against 785 seven years later. In that period, moreover, 4,973 specialists trained by the province's agricultural technicums alone —most of them, of course, Y.C.L. members—were sent to the farms.

The young people engaged in general farm work are not the kind who finished ten years of school. There are hardly any people on the farms who have a secondary education—those go off to the cities. The general farm workers as a rule are people who for one reason or another failed to finish school and figure as "drop-outs" in the records. We looked into the educational levels of the various categories of workers at the Red Tractor Collective farm. Here is what we found. There were 22 equipment operators (all with four to seven years of schooling), 29 livestock tenders (all with four to seven years), 66 general farm workers (all with four to seven years), two brigade leaders (with four to seven years), four specialists (one with a higher education, one with a secondary education and one with four to seven years of schooling) and one chairman, who had a higher education.

It is precisely the school, as we see, that serves as the main channel of migration, precisely the school that "skims" the upper, the strongest and healthiest, section of the rural youth and pumps it into the city (though, as the extensive and fruitful work done in Kostroma Province to keep school graduates in the countryside has shown, the school can turn into almost the chief factor for the solution of the migration problem; once again, we cannot but regret that no one has generalized this experience). The young men who remain in the village drift away through the second channel of migration—service in the armed forces, from which by far the greater number of them never return to their former homes. It would be well, probably, if the young men could be given the correct orientation in the army, if they could be convinced that now, at a time when skilled hands are needed in the countryside, farm work is as honorable and necessary to the country as work on the remote construction projects.

The third channel consists of family ties in the cities. No sooner has one member of the family left the countryside and settled in town than he turns into a magnet attracting the growing members of the family one by one. Only the old folks stay behind, the parents serving as caretakers in the deserted dwellings, which the others may visit for a while, for a rest in the lap of nature. The parents also serve as suppliers of rural delicacies. On the Pravda Collective Farm, 119 peasant homes out of 164 have turned into "caretaker houses" since 1953, with an old man or an old woman in each eking out the days: 119 families have moved to town.

Needless to say, under certain conditions this channel could function in the opposite direction. This is all the more so since certain, at times interesting, experience has already been garnered in regulating migration in the villages of Smolensk Province. But about this in the second part.

2.—How and when did this habit come about—the habit of leaving for the city? Strange as it may seem, the grain grower who has worked on the land all his life is ashamed to let his children stay at home, ashamed of what people will say. Even such an objective advantage of rural life as strong public control, the force of public opinion—incomparably more real in the country-

side than in the city—has in these circumstances been operating for migration. Yet the oldtimers in the countryside clearly remember the time, 15 years ago, when village youngsters could hardly be induced to go to those same trade schools and factory apprenticeships. . . .

An analysis of statistical data shows that the first waves of migration from the collective farms broke in the years 1950–1954.

By the beginning of the 1950s the collective farms of Smolensk Province could as a rule ensure the peasant neither bread nor money. Overtaxation of the peasant household was another source of trouble. Each able-bodied member of the family, especially if single, was a source of taxes; is it surprising that his family should try to get rid of him?

By no means every household, moreover, had anything to sell in order to pay those taxes. Some families had to have help from the city, had to have someone there to send a little real money now and then. In 1950, therefore, 18 young men left a village of 15 households to go to trade school in Moscow together.

This may be the way the tradition of leaving for the city came into being. It is possible, too, that the well-known arbitrary limitations set on personal plots at the beginning of the sixties precipitated the second wave of migration that undermined the stabilization, and even a numerical growth, of rural young people that had been observed since 1955.

The picture, understandably, is quite different now. At the Pravda Collective Farm, by no means the best in the province, each toiler receives 250 rubles a year in cash, a ton of grain and as much hay as needs. Baked bread is bought at the counter. Each worker is able to sell 500 rubles' worth of suckling pigs on the market. In short, these people are well fed, though they do have to work ten to 15 hours a day in the harvesting season, and their livestock are well fed and productive too. Those who have stayed on the collective farm are satisfied with life. Had people only been able to live like that in 1950, the habit of leaving the countryside might never have been formed. But now that habit exists, and the young people are no longer interested in selling suckling pigs, or mowing hay, or receiving a ton of grain for their workdays, since they have oriented themselves to another set of values—those of the city. And their elders, owing to the moral and psychological effect of former years, encourage that orientation.

The production-training school of the Smolensk Meat-Packing Combine has been monopolized by girls from the countryside. Only five of its 100 trainees originally came from the city. Their work is hard and comparatively low-paid. In the poultry-processing shop, saturated with the odor of blood, the girls finish plucking the dead but still-quivering chickens by hand. The place is damp and untidy. We asked the girls if they were aware that—in addition to the healthy country air, the blue skies and being with their mothers—they would earn about twice as much on the dairy sections of their farms as they were earning in the city, besides not having to live in corners rented from single old ladies.

No, they hadn't been aware of this, and they didn't even argue that the working conditions of a milkmaid are hard, since they knew nothing about these conditions. Nor did they believe us when we told them that the average pay of a cattle tender in the province is 80 rubles a month, and that the milkmaids have long since become the most privileged category of rural toilers. What did this indicate? It indicated a lack of occupational orientation on the part of the young people from the countryside, something that in certain conditions could turn into a lack of social orientation. Chiefly, however, it showed that the selfsame moral and psychological effect fixed in the social consciousness of the Smolensk Province peasantry had acquired comparative independence, turning into a perfectly real force.

This is no simple force, as we see, but one conditioned by diverse and even unrelated phenomena. And no amateurish and primitive methods of combating it—methods such as a promise to build a club or to raise pay, or a refusal to issue passports—will solve anything by themselves. Life has demonstrated their futility. It would be difficult to find an instance in which a clubhouse has kept young people in the countryside.

The officials of the rural Soviet in Kardymovo assert that as far as they know, no young person had ever been kept in the countryside by the present passport system. This is borne out by the migration itself, by the figures.

From numerous confidential talks he had had with the school children, moreover, L. G. Ulenkov, director of the Kardymovo school, had become convinced that this system has had a most negative effect on the decisions made by the young. For if they were to spend so much as a year on the collective farm after finishing school, they would lose the right to free self-determination. This is what lends a rather hysterical, hasty air to their wish to be off to the city at once. As for those who finish eight years of schooling, they are in a hurry to get to the city before they reach 16 so that their passports will be issued to them there.

Then what purpose does such strictness serve? It serves only as a symbol of the administration by fiat that has been so decisively condemned by the Party....

Let us look at the farm run by Sergei Ivanovich Bizunov, for example. . . .

He has explored all the possibilities available to an individual farm for regulating migration and has concluded that this matter should be decided at least at the province level. This is no longer the arithmetic of migration but its algebra.

It is a matter of specialization on the scale of the whole province. The trend of specialization in Smolensk Province, as Bizunov sees it, should be agrarian-industrial. This would mean that the industrialization of the province that has been proceeding since 1958 would no longer be an end in itself but would be harnessed to the development of the countryside, to its industrialization. If the villages of Smolensk Province are to give their young people to the city, it is imperative that these young people in the city work for the countryside.

The city, in short, must serve the countryside effectively and efficiently. It is a poor state of affairs when the retting section of a flax mill cannot be completed for several years simply because 100,000 bricks' are lacking, when the procurement of the peat so necessary to keep the soil in good condition has not been put on a sound basis, when the production of organic fertilizers is dropping rather than rising, when there are no machines to haul those fertilizers to the places where they are needed, when the province's chief products— flax, potatoes, milk and meat—belong to all intents and purposes within the sphere of manual labor.

In Bizunov's opinion, the forces of the city should be put at the service of the land. All of the city's progressive engineering thought, all of its means of propaganda and information should work to raise the prestige of the countryside. Only on such a basis can the rural young people be brought to love the land.

When the Americans boast that it takes only 7,000,000 people to feed their country, they are concealing and actually falsifying the basic fact that another 7,000,000 are engaged in the preliminary stages of the "agricultural business" in their country as suppliers of goods and services to agriculture. Furthermore, 11,000,000 more people work in the processing, storing and marketing of farm produce. It is simply that these two stages of the "agricultural business" are sharply separated from agriculture per se there and are highly industrialized; this is what accounts for the high productivity of labor. The average number of people annually engaged in agriculture in the U.S.A. dropped by 3,000,000 between 1947 and 1960, but the army of labor engaged in the branches of industry producing the means of production for agriculture rose by 2,000,000! In our country the process has been one-sided for many years. The young people have been leaving the villages at a rapid rate, but the number of people engaged in the production of farm machinery has increased at a far slower rate.

We are concerned here not with some sort of one-time delivery of machinery, materials, specialists and engineering ideas to the villages of Smolensk Province but with a reorientation of the province's development. . . .

Nor should we forget that there is a moral side to the problem, apart from all the socio-demographic aspects. When the age structure of the population is normal, the fundamentals of ethical experience are assimilated through the lively communion of the generations. This experience is indeed distinguished from all other experience in that moral criteria cannot be assimilated by mere repetition, without the specific personal example and supervision of the older generation, without the development of the habits on which the moral heritage of the generations rests. The artificial partitioning off of the generations destroys this mechanism. The old folks remain in the village, while the young find themselves in the city with their views as yet unformed. They live in dormitories or rent corners in the rooms of strangers, people whom they have met quite by chance. Could this be one of the reasons for the known shortcomings in the behavior of some young people?

The regulation of migration from the villages of Smolensk Province should be seen to at once, without delay. And a radical approach is necessary. The benefits of economic experimentation have been splendidly illustrated by life. What we are proposing is in essence a sort of *social experiment* something like the economic experiments of recent years, an experiment incorporating a series of simultaneous and integrated measures. It goes without saying that such an experiment calls for the introduction of special conditions in the province.

One measure could be the stepped-up vertical mobility of rural young people, their bold advancement to command posts. As we have seen, the educational level of the managerial links on the province's farms is very low. The Party is bold in promoting the young.

Another measure could be the expansion of housing construction in the countryside, first of all in the zone of the most intensive migratory influences —the areas near the big cities.

These and other measures (better pay for work, the reorganization of the system of training rural cadres, the molding of the occupational and social orientation of rural youth, the integrated mechanization of animal husbandry, solution of the question of modernizing the villages, a resolute end to the so-called organizational hiring of labor, the specialization of the province, etc.) could in our view create a sharp turning point in the social consciousness of the peasantry of Smolensk Province, without which it will be difficult to so much as approach the regulation of migration. . . .

Thoughts and Concerns
of Village Youth*

A. ALEXANDROV, M. GARIN, and N. SHTANKO

From some provinces of the country the editorial mail brings letters saying that too many young people are leaving the villages and that this is having an unfavorable effect on the rate of growth of agricultural production. Smolensk Province is characteristic in this respect. In Smolensk District, for example, only one-third of this year's rural secondary school graduates are remaining on the state and collective farms. For the second year in a row four-fifths of the graduates in Pochinok District have left for the city.

What is the reason for this phenomenon? *Izvestia* correspondents decided to ask young people who have grown up in the villages and are now choosing their life paths.

A young man has emerged from his native Smolensk Province village. He carries a neat suitcase or rucksack; in his pocket is his graduation certificate. He stands at the crossroads. A rural road leads to the neighboring village, where the collective farm office is

Reprinted from A. Alexandrov, M. Garin, and N. Shtanko, "Thoughts and Concerns of Village Youth," Izvestia (Nov. 22, 1964). Translated in Current Digest of the Soviet Press, XVI, No. 47 (Copyright © Dec. 16, 1964), p. 21.

* For related articles, see "How Ya Gonna Keep 'em Down on the Farm—?" *Current Digest of the Soviet Press*, Vol. XIII, No. 2, pp. 10–13.

situated. A wider road leads to the district center, where there are an agricultural technicum and a school for equipment operators. And there is the highway, which runs to Smolensk and then to Moscow and on through the whole country, past thousands of other crossroads.

Which road will he choose? And why? Let us go up to him and ask.

CROWDED ROADS AND EMPTY ROADS

We selected Pochinok District, which is highly typical of Smolensk farming, and in this district we took five rural schools (two eight-year and three secondary): the Stodolishche, Trostyanka, Balvanichskaya, Dankov and Galeyevskaya schools. Children from 15 collective farms study in these schools; the 15 farms include 149 small settlements. We submitted to the graduating classes of these schools a questionnaire asking which road the pupil had chosen in life and why. It was decided not to ask that the replies be signed.

Before us lie 430 answers. Let us quote several of them:

"Almost everyone tries to go to the city after graduating from school. Some pull others along with them; still others, seeing that no one is left, themselves rush off to the city as fast as they can. The culture of the countryside is far below city culture. My dream is to make the village like a city in every respect, so that country dwellers will not envy city people. I want to become an agricultural economist, for it seems to me that one cannot raise the cultural level without economics. So I want to dedicate my life to work in the countryside, because no one will do for us the job of making it what we want it to be."

"I shall not remain here on the state farm because I do not want to tie my life to agriculture. In general it is uninteresting here. We do not even have a good library. And my mother advises me not to remain here. It is livelier in the city, of course. And in general one cannot compare the village to the city. I talked it over with other girls, and they too say: 'Try to get into some educational institution!'"

"If I don't get into a technicum I shall go off somewhere to a construction project in Siberia. I don't like it in the country. After all, in cultural level the village lags behind the city. There are no sports groups in the village, and I would like to engage in sports. Couldn't a trainer be sent? Of course it is interesting to spend a vacation in the village, but there is no place there to develop in rounded fashion. I would like to hear opera and attend concerts. Couldn't performers come from town more often? Many of the houses don't have electric light. And who wants to sit by a kerosene lamp? They have been promising for several years to wire our street for electricity, but they have done nothing about it."

"When I pass the exams I shall remain on the collective farm. There are few young people on our collective farm, and young workers are very badly needed. I want to become an agronomist. Agronomists are sent to us, but they don't stay; they work three years and leave. I want to bring as much benefit to our collective farm as I can. We have a great deal of land, and it is interesting to work here. How good it would be if my girl friends also remained at our collective farm! We would compete in the work and solve difficult problems together."

"I shall remain on our collective farm because it is a very weak one. I want to become an equipment operator, since equipment operators play a big part in the progress of agriculture. The future of the collective farm rests on the equipment operator's shoulders."

"After completing school I want to enter an institute. I shall try until I achieve this wish. I want to get into a pedagogical institute in order to work in a village afterward. I would want everything here to be improved, and I would like more young people to be here. The chief thing is for the public of the villages to be better served culturally. The trouble is also that after army service the boys leave the villages, and the girls remain unwillingly when only they are left. In my opinion, work in agriculture should be more mechanized. Manual labor is one of the reasons why young people leave the collective farms."

All 430 replies are just as detailed and serious as the answers above. Evidently each young person has given careful thought to deciding how to embark upon his or her independent life.

Here are the answers to the first question:

1. I shall stay here and work on the collective farm 27
2. I shall go to an agricultural school, technicum or higher educational institution 56
3. I shall go off to work elsewhere in industry or transport 31
4. I shall enter a technical higher educational institution or technicum 102

5. I shall enter a university, pedagogical or medical institute or
other educational institution . . 124
6. I shall continue my studies, but
have not yet chosen a spe-
cialty 90

Thus only 83 persons intend to dedicate themselves to agriculture. Less than
20%. Let us also count 48 graduates
who did not choose agricultural higher
education but intend to return to the
countryside as doctors, teachers or
engineers. Of the 90 who have not yet
chosen a specialty, probably some will
also remain in agriculture. But nevertheless a clear majority of them are leaving for the city.

On the Threshold of a New
Five-Year Plan—Kuzma

I. BURKOVA

Editor's Note.—This is a small town
of Russia. No Tyumen oil nor Yakut
diamonds have been discovered in its
vicinity, and its name is not to be found
among the big new projects. The Directives of the 23rd Party Congress, however, provide not only for the development of the major complexes of the
national economy, but also for the participation of small- and medium-size
towns in the general upsurge of the
country's economy.

In offering Inessa Burkova's essay on
Kozmodemyansk we appeal to readers
of *Literaturnaya Rossia* to present their
views on the problems of small towns.

*   *   *

Kozmodemyansk—"One ticket to
Kuzma, please," I said to the cashier at
the airport, and realized that I had

*Reprinted from I. Burkova, "On the
Threshold of a New Five-Year Plan—
Kuzma," Literaturnaya Rossia (May 6,
1966), Translated in Current Digest of the
Soviet Press, XVIII, No. 19 (Copyright ©
June 1, 1966), 16–17.*

abbreviated the name of the town, as
everyone does there.

Its proper name is Kozmodemyansk.
Have you ever heard of it? If not, it's
not surprising, for this is one of those
small towns that leads a quiet, secluded
existence. There are no big factories or
plants here, no huge construction projects staggering the imagination. There
is nothing at all the little town can
boast of, and nothing is ever written
about it. It lies hidden away, far from
noise and bustle and the fast pace of
life.

But don't get the idea that this is an
outlying backwoods town, for it stands
beside the great Volga, seething with
life from time immemorial.

Yet Kozmodemyansk does stand
alone and apart.

And a handsome town it is, little
Kozmodemyansk, cosily perched on
two setbacks of the high bank of the
Volga. You can see the whole town
from the river. Every alley, every house
and shrub—it's all there before you,
with nothing hidden.

It's an old town. In 17 years it will celebrate its 400th anniversary. But springtime smooths its ancient wrinkles every May. It is clad in shining white when its orchards are in blossom, it is young again then, dazzling and beautiful.

This town has many memories. How it came to be called Kozmodemyansk, for instance. This happened on Saints Cosmas' and Damian's Day, on Oct. 17, 1552, when Tsar Ivan the Terrible, sailing up the Volga with his Cheremis vassals after subduing the khanate of Kazan, camped for the night where the town now stands. The Tsar then ordered a fortress erected here to keep the conquered Cheremis in bondage. A prison rose in 1583, and the town began with that.

Kozmodemyansk also remembers how Peter I undertook to turn Russia from a backward country into an advanced one, and set out first to seize an exit to the Black Sea for this purpose. The *streltsi* [musketeers] of Kozmodemyansk joined his Sea of Azov campaign and built a belfry with their own means and own hands to commemorate the event when they returned. That belfry is still there, on the high bank of the Volga.

As for the 19th century (getting close to our times now), Kozmodemyansk remembers it very clearly. That was when industrial timber-felling began in the Gorn-Mary District. The song of the Volga boatmen was heard over the city from dawn to dusk all summer long then. The timber rafted from the Vetluga and Kerzhenets was tied into *belyani* [barge-like rafts] and floated down the Volga. To keep the work rhythm, the people never stopped singing. The town was especially lively in the summer, when the timber rafting drew so many strangers to the spot: workers, merchants and wandering players. Stalls and show-booths crowded the squares.

Some of the traces of the 19th century have survived here, and I walked about the streets wondering at the sights. This was not the mid-20th century, it seemed to me, and I was not I, but a character out of a film about the pre-revolutionary past of our province.

There were log houses all around, small and buried in the earth to their brows, or solid two-story affairs built by the merchants. Now and again I saw a brick house, too, with molded stucco in imitation of carved wood. Invariably carved, too, were the eaves and window frames of the richer houses. I had never seen so much tracery, so many carvings, anywhere. Not even in Kizhi, where examples of ancient architecture of the North have been assembled.

Then came the central square, once known as the Bazaar. Everything was sold here in the summer: edibles of many kinds, Kozmodemyansk apples, baskets and suitcases woven of heat-dried reeds, and the famous chairs and divans wrought of cherry wood, for which the Kozmodemyansk handicraftsmen won prizes at all-Russian and international exhibitions. From May to August the city never slept: It cooked vats of cabbage soup, baked cakes for the market, wove baskets, or ferried the workers across the Volga in rowboats. In autumn the square was bare again, and the town fell silent. The strangers had gone then, and with them some of the people of Kozmodemyansk. They would be gone until spring. There was seasonal work to be done. And those who stayed behind settled down to a quiet, dull existence.

Walking along, I pictured the scenes of the past and kept trying to guess in which houses our great forefathers, Radishchev, Pushkin, Hertzen, Shevchenko, Korolenko and Gorky, the pride of our people, had lived. Each had come through this town. Some had come of their own accord, others with convoys of prisoners. The road through Kuzma, along the Volga and the Yamsk Highway, had been traversed by many, both the unknown and the famous [on their way to exile].

"What a lovely house!" I stopped, surprised.

The austere gray lines of logs had been tastefully, tenderly decorated with the laciest of patterns. What clever fingers had wrought those designs for the joy of man? This was a delightful building, graceful and fairy-like. It was occupied too, for there were curtains on the windows. "Kindergarten No. 1," read the plate on the gates. "What a happy idea—to put the children in a fairy tale!" I thought.

I opened the door and heard the cheerful voices of children on all sides. There was a steep stairway leading up, and another down to the cellar. The door to the latter was open, revealing white cots and a flurry of children. I descended, and found the bedroom crowded with small folding beds. There was a huge round stove in the middle, occupying a full third of the room. Twilight, dank air, walls marred with the stains of leakage—a cellar, in short.

I went upstairs, found the manageress, and walked from room to room with her. Nina Ivanovna recounted a series of misfortunes and complaints. They were crowded, short of funds, and the place had been renovated only once in 20 years.

"Can you call this a good kindergarten?" she reiterated bitterly. "Yet this is our best, the basic establishment, the place which others visit to learn from!"

In each room the nurses were plodding to and fro, piling bedding into one corner, vigorously stacking the cots and other objects on improvised trestles in a second corner, and hauling chairs and tables from a third corner to fill the spaces made free. It was lunch time. The children, meanwhile, stood aside, huddled together, or tried to help the nurses, but got in their way.

And what wretched furniture! Club-footed tables and chairs slapped together by some amateur, anything but skillful. There were worn, ponderous washbasins and clumsy, unpainted cupboards for toys. Could any of this teach good taste?

A flaxen-haired, snub-nosed girl, so tender I could not take my eyes from her, came up to Nina Ivanovna, asking her something. How incongruous she seemed in this coarse, old, wretched setting. If only one could snatch her up, carry her to another kindergarten, and set her down on the floor with a group of children where everything was bright, spacious, graceful and modern!

I kept directly behind Nina Ivanovna, for it was painful to look the children in the eye.

Back in the street, I took a deep, sweet breath of air. Then I hurried away, but did turn to look at the house again. It wasn't beautiful anymore. This was the wrong fairy tale. Not a tale for children.

Beauty is a virtue if it is clean and serves well. But this? No! This was only the former home of the rich merchant Gubarev. The roof had rotted, and the building was heated with a wood stove. It was dark and decrepit, ready to be torn down. Or it could be touched up and preserved as an example of old architecture. In that case it would be really beautiful, just as it looked to me at first, for people would enjoy it then.

As for me, I had had my fill of exotica. It was secondary now. It might be interesting and enjoyable to come here to observe the unblemished 19th century for a day or two, but live here? What kind of a life would it be?

I walked about the town for many

days, trying to get to know it well, familiarizing myself with the local industry, with life, talking to people and asking all about the past and the present.

This was the picture:

A typical little town out of an old-time province. Privately owned houses. Each with its own garden, its own fruit trees, snugly behind its own fence.

Not a single public building had risen here in all of 48 years, except for the bath house. The legacy from the merchants served to house the children's establishments, the hospitals, the cinema and the lunchrooms. The cinema, called the Central, operated in the erstwhile grain merchant's shop. The House of Culture and the two stores beneath it occupied the former mansion of the merchant Ponomarev. The regional museum, with its rich collection of paintings, had settled in the Smolensk Cathedral, and the town library in the cellar of the fire department.

Makeshifts? But what else could one do? People wanted to read new books and see new films. And the young folk wanted their parties, even if in the former home of a merchant, where there was no cloakroom or buffet, where everything was rickety and inconvenient. They wanted to sing, dance, talk and argue about their Y.C.L. affairs, compete in a quiz like the television quiz shows, or watch an amateur theater production.

Only the school children have been lucky in Kuzma, for the merchants left them the quite adequate town school and two gymnasia—classical secondary schools. Only the youngsters who live "uptown" (in the upper section of the town) have been cheated, for they have no school up there. They have to come way "downtown" and climb the steep incline on their way back. This is far from easy sometimes in the spring and autumn, when the roads are washed

away and rivulets rush down. The water flows everywhere, and there is no dry spot on which to set foot. The town stands on clay and the water rolls irresistibly down to the Volga, flooding everything in its path; it fills the cellars where supplies are kept, pours in through the windows of the tiny sunken cottages, and prevents people from getting to the shops or to work. Traffic comes to a standstill, and everybody comes out into the streets in high fishermen's boots, armed with shovels and planks to build temporary "dams."

This is what happens in an emergency. But how do the people of Kozmodemyansk live ordinarily, from day to day? Local industry consists of a brewery, a fruit cannery, a small dairy and a brickyard. There is also a timber rafting office, though the town no longer lives off timber. Technology has by now reached a stage in which far fewer people are needed than before. About 1,000 Kozmodemyansk residents are employed by the rafting office.

That is all the industry in this town of 13,500. There are a few more establishments, such as the district services combine and a motor vehicle office. Of the town's 6,900 able-bodied persons, 5,400 are employed by various organizations and establishments.

What do the others do? In the autumn they go off to Gorky, Volgograd and Kazan for seasonal work. Until spring. They set out to look for seasonal work, as they used to in olden times, but always return to Kuzma in the spring. Back with their home gardens and fruit trees, they poke about from morning till night, each behind his own fence. When the first crops are gathered, several households band together to charter a barge. And off they go to Kazan while the market prices are still high. Then they make more trips up or down the Volga. They earn a living.

Is there anything wrong with this?

Everyone is working for a living. What if they fill the markets of the big cities with fruit and vegetables? There is no harm in this. Not for others. Nor do the old folk of Kuzma complain. This is the customary thing, the tradition.

But what about the young? Are the youths and girls really attracted by the prospect of continuing the agricultural and mercantile traditions of their fathers and grandfathers? Not at all. Lofty and enticing vistas have been opened to them by school, literature and art— sciences, different and attractive; the latest industries, gigantic and intricate; and agriculture, mechanized and up-to-date. Their home town can give them none of these, and that is why they are leaving to try their luck in other cities, attempting to enter the universities and technical colleges, or going to work in factories, while staying with distant aunts and uncles and other relatives. Those who remain in Kuzma manage to become truck drivers or mechanics at the motor vehicle base or timber rafting office. Some of the girls settle in the district villages as kindergarten nurses (the specialty they trained for at school).

Very soon, too, things, will be far worse, for an acute problem of the year will crop up in a month or two—the result of the school changeover: There will be two simultaneous graduations, the 10th grade and the 11th. Which means that 289 citizens will be entering upon adult life. Where can they be put to work? And be given jobs to their liking, the jobs they were trained for? These young people are about to begin an independent existence.

This is the most difficult aspect of the Kozmodemyansk employment problem.

That is what Kuzma is like today. Very little has changed here. Attempts were once made to uproot what is old, to change the appearance of the town and its entire way of life. But then time seemed to come to a standstill in Kuzma. The town bogged down, unable to budge.

Urban Areas

In this section we present selections which highlight the primarily physical-environmental (rather than directly social) problems that city life creates. These are problems of comfort, health, transportation, aesthetics, and access to services. Cities are criticized for overcrowding, traffic congestion, air pollution, inadequate recreational areas, and general squalor. Two societies as different as the U.S. and U.S.S.R. manage to produce very similar problems of this kind as though proving the vision of the Chicago School of urban sociology, which perceived cities as uncontrollable, monster-like entities whose growth, decline, and general development obeyed apparently mysterious laws of their own, defying human will and planning. These visions were rooted in the American experience of urbanization, which was indeed uncontrolled, haphazard, and unregulated. (It is interesting to note that this American image of the city finds its Soviet counterpart in a surprisingly similar representation of the city as a "living organism.")

In both American and Soviet society, most urban problems are closely related to the rapid and uneven growth of cities. In the U.S. conditions have been aggravated by real estate speculation and weak and fragmented municipal governments; in the Soviet Union, by insufficient resource allocation for housing and services. Soviet cities have so far been largely unaffected by the encroachments of the car, although recently they slowly began to "catch up" with American cities in this regard. Good city planning is apparently uncommon in the U.S.S.R. too, as the perceptive criticisms of the Soviet architect will show. On the other hand, Soviet public transportation is superior to the American in its coverage and possibly in other respects. Soviet cities have some other advantages over the American ones. Although drab, their physical structure is not marred by pockets of ghettos which contain disadvantaged ethnic minorities. In Soviet cities there is little residential segregation, either along racial or social class lines. (Members of the highest political elite groups are the major exception to this.) Soviet housing, with all its inadequacies, is far more uniform than American. At the same time, air and water pollution are increasing as is the despoiling of other natural resources.

The following articles show that some urban problems, social in their consequences but not necessarily in their origin, are least directly traceable to the prevailing political order, being primarily determined by technology, resources, and population pressures.

Since planning is more readily used in the Soviet Union to solve both economic and social problems, but used reluctantly and piecemeal, if at all, in the U.S., Soviet urban problems are likely to be resolved or alleviated sooner than American ones. As far as overall resources are concerned, American cities could be rescued more quickly from their present state of congestion and decay, than Soviet ones. However, the American political climate and tradition abhors the large-scale social engineering and long-range planning required for urban redevelopment. It is also likely that the summer riots in 1967 will have a lasting effect on residential segregation, reinforcing the current division of most American cities into a decaying central core and livable suburbs.

Traffic, Transportation, and Problems
of the Metropolis

SCOTT GREER

No society in history has ever controlled space as well as the American society of mid-twentieth century. Never before has the average man had, at his command, instruments which are able to turn a coast-to-coast journey into a five-hour sojourn in a jet liner, while a machine in his garage places distant cities and diverse places within easy reach. If we remember the peasant of the past, who rarely traveled as far as 50 miles from home in a lifetime, the magnitude of the contemporary accomplishment is more striking. Americans have domesticated the great barrier of space, rendered the tool of its conquest into an individual weapon, and distributed it to the populace as a rightful consumer article.

Because the United States is the extreme example of modern, mobile, urban society (in 1957 Americans

From Scott Greer, "Traffic, Transportation and Problems of the Metropolis," Contemporary Social Problems, *R. Merton and R. Nisbet, eds. New York: Harcourt, Brace and World, 1961, pp. 605–606, 608–609, 614–615, 636–639. Reprinted by permission of the publisher.*

owned 64 per cent of all motor vehicles on earth) we shall confine this discussion to our own society. As other nations approach our own intensive use of the automobile, they will face the identical problems. Large-scale society demands large-scale motion—and America is a nation in motion. In 1956 Americans traveled 628 billion miles, in 65 million vehicles, over 3,400,000 miles of public roads and streets.[1] In fact, automobile ownership and travel by Americans has been increasing much faster than the population in recent decades. Since 1920 the rate of increase for automobiles has been 10 times that for people and today there is a motor vehicle for every 3 Americans. The average American family spends one-eighth of its income for transportation, while the nation as a whole will spend a trillion dollars on transportation in the next 15 years. The entire economy is heavily dependent

[1] *Automobile Facts and Figures* (Detroit: Automobile Manufacturer's Association, 1957). For the world comparison see *Statistical Abstract of the United States,* Commerce Dept., Bureau of the Census (Washington, D. C., 1959), Sect. 34.

upon the automobile complex; our city layout and our new building assume mobility; we are committed because the very conditions of the society require such movement of people and goods to carry on the business of survival.

. . . Because the cities are particularly dependent upon the daily, reliable circulation of millions of persons in a small space, and because they experience congestion, traffic accidents, and air pollution, regularly and predictably, they are the focus for the general concern with traffic and transportation as social problems. Almost half of all American driving in 1958, 267 billion miles, took place upon a mere tenth of the road surface in the nation.[2] The most congested traffic in the nation is a direct consequence of the fact that two-thirds of us live and pass most of our days within a space which is only a little more than 1 per cent of the United States. This relatively tiny space is, however, crucial, for the United States is an urban nation. A preponderance, not only of the people, but also of the governmental and economic centers, the cultural and economic values, of the nation is concentrated in the areas of urban development.

Thus metropolitan traffic and transportation problems have become a matter of widespread concern, for they affect the everyday life of the average citizen in our urban society. The traffic jams, noise, confusion and congestion of the peak rush hour are universal occurrences in our cities. And in each city the use of the automobile has allowed the suburbs to spread farther and farther from the center of the city —with a consequent increase in the traffic from periphery to center. Furthermore, in most cities the automobile has competed so successfully with other

[2] *Automobile Facts and Figures*, p. 63.

transport media that it has greatly weakened the financial and economic position of the rapid transit and the bus line, yet the disappearance of public transportation today would leave an impossible situation, in which most of the space within the center city would have to be used for roads and parking. Public transportation, once among the most lucrative investments in the society, is today a cripple looking to the government for a subsidy in order to survive. Much of the clientele of bus and subway use it only for peak rush hour travel to work and back; many abandon it completely as their incomes go up and they move to suburban areas far from the dependable bus service of the central city.

It is against this background that the alarm of political leaders and experts in the field of transportation makes sense. The American nation is growing at a rapid rate, and most of its growth is within metropolitan areas. Estimates of 50 million new residents by 1975 may be overexuberant, but certainly the population will continue to increase rapidly in the near future. And with the population, in fact ahead of the population, the automobile and truck population will also increase. Owen predicts that 100 million vehicles will be operating on American streets and highways by 1975. Most of them will be used in urban areas for the daily journey to work which moves the suburbanites to the center of the metropolitan area and back.

The continually increasing investment in giant, divided-lane expressways is one method of preparing for this increase of traffic, but such preparation may not be adequate, for the more roads are provided, the greater the automobile ownership becomes. In fact, the Hollywood Freeway in Los Angeles carried, within one year, almost twice the number of vehicles it was expected to carry in the remote future.[3] Thus the increase in expressways does not solve the problem; at least until now it has resulted in an increase in automobile traffic. This in turn has further weakened the public transportation system; since it provides worse service, more people use the automobile. There are vicious circles within vicious circles; as we will note throughout the chapter, such patterns are not odd accidents, but are characteristic of problems in metropolitan society. They interest the social scientist because they indicate structure and interdependence. To the layman, leader, and policymaker, however, they are more likely to seem indications of doom and despair.

...Nor is the "problem" of the desirable shape of cities a simple one; it also breaks down into a multitude of problems, many of which when examined seem ambiguous or nonexistent, and others of which seem to be special pleading for special interests. The struggle to support public transportation in the metropolitan area is, in large part, an effort to retain the present division of activities between the core of the city, the industrial districts, and the outlying residential areas.[4] It is certain that the gradual decay of public transportation will result in greater automobile traffic into the central city, or less traffic of any kind, or both. This is not, on its face, evidence that a problem exists.

In short, from our temporary position of extreme skepticism, it seems that the various "problems" exist only if we assume that certain values are held by everybody, or at least by all right thinking men. This may be so, but it is a question which requires an empirical answer. One way to test the assumption is to ask: Who is concerned? For the same events are seen and evaluated very differently, from different vantage points in the social structure.

Most observers leap immediately to one conclusion—those who own business and properties in the central city are concerned with its accessibility as a marketplace. However, cheap and speedy transportation downtown is not considered such a general good by the suburban merchant. Those who have cast their economic lot in the outer areas, whether in corner groceries or giant shopping centers, have a real and personal interest in the decline of retail trade in the central city. It is money in their pockets.

As for those who would be called upon to subsidize improved mass transportation to and from the center city, most of them do not use it, and many will resent supporting a transit line in addition to their automobile. You may question their rationality in choosing the automobile over the bus or streetcar, but you must remember that the family car is evidently of great value to them. The American people spend more for automobile transportation than they do for doctors, religion, charities, telephones, radio, television, furniture, electricity, gas, books, magazines, and newspapers combined.[5]

This is the crux of the matter: the population is, by and large, choosing what it wants and getting what it chooses. To be sure it is getting many other things, which it does not want,

[3] Wilfred Owen, *The Metropolitan Transportation Problem* (Washington, D. C.: The Brookings Institution, 1958), p. 35.

[4] To be sure, it is sometimes justified as an effort to maintain adequate transportation for the "needs" of the portion of the population which cannot afford to own an automobile. However, such justification must be seen for what it is: a redistribution of income, with taxes upon the entire population paying for the movement of one part of the population.

[5] W. Owen, *Annals of the American Academy of Political and Social Science*, Vol. 320 (November, 1958), p. 4.

in the package. Still, the steady increase in automobile ownership, until 75 per cent of American families are now wheelborne, testifies to the value of the automobile. Its increasing daily use, reflected in the traffic congestion and expanding freeways of the cities, indicates that heavy driving, polluted air, accident and death, the decline of public transportation, blight of the central city, and other "problems" are not overriding arguments. They are the price we pay.

...The central city and its suburban ring are as much a unity economically and socially as was true in the days of the compact urban mass, even though the geographical division of labor and rewards within that unity is different. However, the populations moving outward from the center have not been included in the governmental boundaries of the central city; beginning in the first decade of this century, the "outside" populations have resisted annexation by the central city, and have incorporated themselves into small residential enclaves, called variously "villages," "towns," and "cities." And, despite considerable recognition that the growth of such governmentally autonomous suburbs may be related to various urban problems, the process continues.

Between 1952 and 1958 alone, 170 new municipalities came into being in metropolitan areas and 519 new special districts were created. By 1957, there were over 3,000 governments that could be said to possess more or less general municipal powers, and there was, of course, that awesome figure of 15,658 legally distinguishable local units [in metropolitan areas].[6]

Despite the fact that a majority of

[6] R. C. Wood, *Suburbia,* p. 69. There are many other studies of these phenomena; a recent work oriented toward policy problems is John C. Bollens, *The States and the Metropolitan Problem* (Chicago: Council of State Governments, 1956).

those who live in the suburban rings work in the central city, including a disproportionate number of the wealthiest and most powerful, and despite the fact that social ties of many kinds cross the boundaries from city to suburbs, the suburbs and the central city have no local government in common. Political boundaries fractionate the metropolitan complex.

This disjunction between political and social boundaries has important consequences for the polity of the metropolitan area. It means that no local governmental decision applying to all of the residents of the metropolis is possible. Yet many of the conditions which the citizens expect their government to control ("problems," that is), can be controlled only by an areawide normative order. As the Air Pollution Control Officer of Los Angeles County says, "Air pollution does not recognize political boundaries,"[7] nor do crime, epidemics, and other conditions which require governmental action. The change in the space-time ratio which has permitted a close integration of many activities within today's metropolitan areas has not been accompanied by any increased governmental integration.

Nor is there a public treasury for the metropolis as a whole. This creates continual problems of assessing the costs of public improvements, which, in terms of American political norms, are supposed to be paid by those who benefit, or at least by their neighbors and fellow citizens. For a great deal of the use value of facilities in the central city is realized by those who live in the suburbs; when the daytime population of the central city is increased by a million people, the public utilities, police force, buses and streetcars, and other services of the urban center must provide for them. Yet much of the suburban popu-

[7] S. S. Griswold, *Unburned Hydrocarbons,* p. 108.

lation which works in the city is extremely resentful of the city's efforts to tax them—through taxes on earnings and city sales taxes.

The inability to pass and enforce laws for the metropolitan area, and the inability to tax and spend for the area, mean, in brief, that there is no single polity for the metropolis. Such problems as those we have discussed earlier, the provision of a better transportation system for the area, the lessening of the strain on the transportation system through planning the locations of activities differently, cannot be carried out except through negotiation among whatever share of the 15,658 governments are located within a given region. The magnitude of this task is clear when we reflect upon the 97 municipalities in St. Louis County, ranging in size from 53,000 people to 60 people— or the 1400 governmental units in the greater New York metropolitan area.

Integration of policy is further handicapped by the differentiation of interest among the various governmentally defined subareas of the metropolis. The central city faces a problem of renovating or rebuilding much of the structure of the eotechnic city which is no longer useful for the fluid metropolis of today. Antiquated business buildings, deteriorated housing pre-dating the Civil War, and deteriorating public monuments on narrow streets which are nearly impassable by modern automobiles, all require great expenditures of public funds. At the same time the city's share of the metropolitan population is disproportionately made up of newcomers to the area who are poor and disadvantaged and require more public aid. Thus the central city has very specific and pressing interests and a need for a larger treasury.

But taxable resources steadily declined, and as residential areas deteriorated, the slums took up 20 per cent of the non-business area, siphoning off 45 per cent of total municipal expenditures but contributing only 6 per cent of the revenue. As a further complication, as the city became more and more the educational or civic center of the region, the amount of tax-exempt property increased steadily. With service demands at least as high as when most of the urban population lived within its limits, and with the tax base declining relatively or absolutely, most American cities ran out of money.[8]

For those identified with the fortunes of the central city, the pressing metropolitan problems are: what should be done and what can be done for the central city? Should the central city, housing a large and necessary portion of the unskilled and semiskilled labor force which makes the industrial complex of the metropolis possible, alone be forced to pay the deficits associated with such a population, while those who profit most from the city's work retreat to the suburbs? Similarly, should the city alone pay taxes for universities which serve the entire metropolitan region? art museums? symphonies?

Meanwhile, those who identify with the suburbs see different problems. Living in the seas of subdivision, where new public facilities must be developed from scratch, their taxes move steadily upward. The major child-producing regions of the country are in the suburban municipalities, and the bill for public schools is ordinarily two-thirds of the local tax bill. It climbs each year with each new generation of school children. Local taxes fall almost entirely upon homeowners in many suburban districts, for the commercial and industrial plants (which yield massive tax payments) are highly concentrated. The very smallness of most suburban municipalities, together with their definition by their residents as cities of homes, tend to eliminate all but the home-

---

[8] R. C. Wood, *op. cit.,* pp. 71–72.

owner as taxpayer. While a few suburbs are tax rich because of the industry located within their boundaries, most of the others consist of nothing but single-family dwelling units.[9] The suburbanite sees the problems of the central city as no more pressing than those of his suburb, and feels, at most, that payment of an earnings tax through his employer in the central city should allow him to call it even.

From these divisions of interest, com-

plex and lurid ideologies arise. The spokesman for the central city, manifesting little sympathy for the suburbs, proposes that they solve their problems by abandoning their "toy government" and acknowledging their unity with the city. The suburbanite retorts that the central city is old and decaying, taken over by Negroes, labor unions, and crooked political machines. Each side says, in effect, "Why should I pay taxes for the benefit of those others?" And, at the same time, the tax bill rises in central city and in suburb, while people in each area complain about problems common to both.

[9] This variation is illustrated in suburban St. Louis County, where the assessed valuation (that is, taxable property) *per capita* in the wealthiest school district is 18 times that in the poorest.

URBAN AREAS
IN THE U.S.S.R.:
The Soviet View

The City Awaits a Reply

B. SVETLICHNY

Immediately after the Second World War, statistics reported an exceptionally high birthrate. This raised a commotion in the camp of the bourgeois demographers.

Reprinted from B. Svetlichny, "The City Awaits a Reply," Oktyabr, No. 10. Translated in Current Digest of the Soviet Press, XVIII, No. 48 (Copyright © Dec. 21, 1966), 11–15.

The news spread throughout the world, like the worried sound of a tom-tom: "Baby boom! Baby boom! Baby boom!"

At first this was what this remarkable phenomenon was christened. The birthrate was rising everywhere, and particularly swiftly in the developing countries.

As the years passed it was no longer anxiety, but a real note of panic that resounded in the chorus of pessimistic prophets:

"Attention! Beware! Demographic explosion!"

What could have frightened the modern neo-Malthusians so?

The number of people in the world was snowballing and by the end of the century would clearly double and exceed 6,000,000,000 souls. Last year alone 65,000,000 new inhabitants appeared on the globe.

How are they to be fed? The growth in the production of foodstuffs persistently lags behind population growth.

Urban population has been increasing at a rapid rate. Whereas in 1800 the number of urban inhabitants was only 2% and cities were rare islands in a boundless sea of rural settlements, now one-third of mankind has gathered within city walls. In the past 40 years alone the proportion of city dwellers in India's population for instance, nearly doubled. In 30 years the number of city dwellers in Venezuela more than doubled. From 1940 to 1960 the cities of Latin America experienced an unprecedented invasion of hungry people seeking any kind of work. In 20 years the population of Sao Paulo in Brazil increased nearly threefold, and the population of Caracas in Venezuela nearly fivefold. Since 1800 the total number of urban inhabitants has increased 26-fold. And food must be provided for all of them because they have lost touch with the land and can produce neither grain nor meat nor vegetables. Analyzing and comparing these data, bourgeois sociologists forecast for the near future the emergence of mass unemployment and the material and cultural impoverishment of mankind, and they created "theories" justifying the predatory laws of the capitalist world.

At a recent international city-planning congress, the main speaker, D. Sekkaldi, touched on the problem of the giant cities and bitterly remarked that the city forced many limitations on man that are felt all the more painfully as people's needs keep growing. Limited space has dictated high buildings and has separated man from living nature, lack of contact with which makes normal rest, sleep and steady nerves impossible. The "rationing" of water and clean air has had a bad effect on people. They do not receive as much of either as they want. Finally, in spite of the reduced workday, the rhythm of life in the giant city is so tense that man constantly feels short of time. There is not even enough light.

There is an ominous note in these prophesies of the irremediable harm that urban civilization causes man, of the inevitable collapse of the big cities under the weight of their own defects. The mass flight, by all who have the money, to distant suburban spots is cited as evidence. The architects of the West are gripped with anxiety: The city created by man is slipping from his control.

But are the notorious defects of the modern, capitalistic giant cities really the invariable and inevitable marks of the large city as a whole? These defects arise not because a city's population has reached a certain critical size, but because the capitalist system itself is daily and hourly creating them.

The cities in our country are also growing. Since the Revolution the urban population of the U.S.S.R. has increased from 29,000,000 to 125,000,000. However, demographic "explosions" do not yet frighten our country, where industry has been developing at a tempestuous rate, where people are drawn into new enterprises in a planned manner and are given not only work, but the necessary living conditions as well.

The growth of our largest cities is another matter.

We architects, builders, and doctors find much to think and worry about as we read and ponder over and over again the decisions of the 23rd C.P.S.U. Congress.

There is a general problem that is always on the agenda both in our country and abroad: What direction should urban construction take so that the city dweller can improve and perfect his mode of life from day to day, instead of complicating his existence, spoiling his health and shortening his life expectancy? Nearly two-fifths of our city dwellers now live in cities with populations of more than 250,000. Not long ago we had only two cities with populations of more than 1,000,000—Moscow and Leningrad. Now there are seven; Kiev, Kharkov, Novosibirsk, Tashkent and Gorky have been added. If our cities continue to grow at the present rate—and this apparently will happen —the number of our giant cities will double in ten years and treble in 15. It is possible that there will be more of them here than in any other country.

Sweeping toward the million mark are Kuibyshev, Sverdlovsk, Chelyabinsk, Donetsk, Baku, Tbilisi, Dnepropetrovsk, Perm, Kazan and Minsk. There are more than 20 cities where the population exceeds half a million. And cities that are a stone's throw from half a million inhabitants are catching up with them.

The cities keep growing despite our city-planning theories, which long ago declared verbal war against giant cities, and despite the bans on building new industries in them.

What makes us say one thing and do another—against our own will and convictions? There is nothing mysterious about it. It is simply that present-day economic considerations often supersede theoretical principles. Today it is almost always cheaper to build new plants in a large city with a developed industry and adequate transportation facilities, electricity, and water than in a remote town where as yet there is nothing,

where everything has to be built almost from scratch, even though this is often anything but sound for the greater economy of tomorrow. This is why people keep streaming into the cities and why all local measures—limitations on registration, establishment of "rigid" city limits and building "barriers" of woods and parks—prove useless.

All artificial measures, including bans, will lead nowhere until the [effectiveness of the] process of city planning mounts by virtue of organic social and economic factors.

IN QUEST OF THE OPTIMUM

Of course, if it were possible to stop all growth of industrial and service cadres in the city (something which in itself can hardly fit in with life), nobody who came to the city would be able to settle in such an inhospitable place and would have to flee it in order to avoid unemployment. This would probably put an end to the penchant for the large city.

It seems to me, however, that a city, especially a big one, cannot be fenced in. For its socio-economic and cultural significance alone it belongs to the whole of society, to the entire country, and cannot and must not turn into an egoistic "thing to itself." Even if the number of inhabitants is fixed, a city will grow for many years, as if in some inner ferment. The amount of housing for those now living in it now must be constantly increased. Medical, cultural, and service institutions must be built up and enlarged. A case in point is Moscow, where construction has spread many kilometers beyond the former city limits and continues to advance further.

With the purpose of stopping the growth of big cities, the construction of satellite cities was at one time suggested and carried out. Life, however, has shown that as a rule these separate, deliberately created "branches" soon turn into new cities with their own independent destinies, while the cities which propagated them become neither smaller nor more comfortable.

...A city is like a living organism. It is born, it grows, it eats, it breathes and often even "multiplies," acquiring a family of daughter or satellite cities. However, all processes usually flow harmoniously in the living organism, which is inherently wonderfully balanced, while in the developing body of the city much remains unchanged, fossilized, as it were—the dimensions of the center, the width of the streets and the height of the buildings—and it is sometimes difficult to remove the disproportions that have been established. Nevertheless everything cannot be left as it is when a puny center can no longer serve its growing population, when its streets no longer accommodate the traffic and when factories built in the suburbs find themselves in the heart of the city. In designing new cities one must look many years into the future; and in foreseeing the future one must deliberately create some seeming disproportion in the initial period of the city's life, in the years of its childhood: Spacious squares and wide avenues must be built with "room to spare," leaving enough spaces for large buildings, and industry must be distributed with an eye to the future limits of the city's construction. At first such extraordinary generosity of scale may surprise some people, but later everyone will fully appreciate the city planners' farsightedness, since the construction of the city will prove less expensive on the whole than if it had to be rebuilt later on.

Of course not every ship is destined for the long voyage. We have quite a few towns with deliberately circumscribed destinies, and it would be unwise to dress them up in the clothes of "up-and-coming" towns. Our chief trouble, however, is that we often cannot discern the great strapping fellow that the unprepossessing adolescent promises to grow into, just as we once failed to discern the future of Magnitogorsk and Novokuznetsk, which outgrew their original dimensions dozens of times over. The general plans of Angarsk, Sumgait, Volzhsk and Togliatti were repeatedly revised, for in the process of their development they upset all the planners' calculations. It would be silly to blame the architects alone for this, of course. A considerable part of the blame belongs to our economists, who were unprepared to solve many important problems. Our ignorance of our country's potential possibilities and productive forces also played its role.

If only long-term projects for planning the chief industrial centers and inhabited points were worked out on the basis of integrated schema for the economic development of the country's main districts! The national-economic plans, however, often say one thing, while the general plans for the development of cities say something altogether different. Often cities are planned in isolation from the long-term plans for developing the entire area, i.e., they are planned unscientifically.

Isn't it time resolutely to reject this worthless practice, since it has a highly negative effect not only on the country's economy and settlement pattern, but also on the destinies of the cities and every person's living conditions?

The general plans of cities, worked out on the basis of district planning and coordinated with the national-economic plans, should henceforth become the law of Soviet city planning.

Some think that the general plans should be flexible enough to cope with any "unforeseen" [read *unplanned*] changes in the life of a city, such as suddenly locating new industrial enterprises in it. But such a universal project suitable for all life's exigencies, fixing on nothing and offering no guidance, is actually tantamount to no project at all and is therefore no good to anyone. In short, "the dog should wag its tail, instead of the tail wagging the dog."

Perhaps some of what has been said here will seem contradictory, but life itself is woven of contradictions. Ideally we strive for one thing, but life compels us to adjust to something else; no one can give a simple answer to the question of whether the small city or the giant city is good or bad, for there are positive and negative aspects in both. Only our economy's system of planning can overcome the negative features. Here the matter rests primarily with us, with the depth of our understanding of the laws of economics and the social life of society, with the strength of our conscious influence on them.

TRAFFIC IS LIFE

Perhaps the most intricate problem in city planning is transportation, plotting out a street system, which must take into account traffic, safety, and the shortest distances. But even seasoned city-planners sometimes view the merits of a given city's planning system in different lights. When discussing the reconstruction of Moscow, for instance, some architects proposed putting an end to the "medieval" radial-ring network of streets and replacing it with a system of long parallel avenues. Others overly idealized the old system of planning, alleging that it was the most progressive and socialist.

The rectangular network of streets is the most widespread in our cities but it has the disadvantage of often compelling us to cover a distance almost half again as long as the shortest distances (the two sides instead of the hypotenuse). This is also true of the radial-ring system of planning, for it too requires half again as much time, gas, conveyances and funds.

It is, of course, impossible to plan streets so as to be able to get somewhere directly, "as the crow flies," but it is perfectly feasible to improve the rectangular system with additional diagonal routes. The radial-ring system could be supplemented by arteries directly linking one district with another and bypassing the center. All this has long been known in theory. But in practice even simple ring boulevards are not being built. Moscow, for instance, has the only complete transportation ring—the Sadovoye Ring with a radius of slightly more than two kilometers. In the 19th century the Sadovoye Ring performed its role ideally, linking all the main sections of the then small city. Now the radial avenues cutting across new boroughs fan out for scores of kilometers; almost nowhere do they link up with one another.

Just try, for example, to travel the Peschanaya Street-Sokolniki-Enthusiasts' Highway-Tula Highway route. It is a vain undertaking! Impenetrable "forests" of buildings will stand in your way. To say nothing of straight arteries, it is at least time to build the ring avenues mapped out in the general plan for the capital 30 years ago. Too expensive? No more expensive than the hundreds of millions of kilometers of "extra" distances covered by motor vehicles over the years! All this is equally applicable to our other large cities. It is, of course, difficult to build in old cities a new network of streets suitable for speedy, safe traffic. But to provide for such a network when planning new cities is something else. This is when the designers hold all the trumps, so to speak. But more often than not, outdated methods are applied here too for some reason. Novosibirsk's satellite Science Town is a case in point.

The chief obstacle to speedy and

safe traffic within a city is its abundance of crossings. It is the constant stopping that costs transportation its inherent possibilities, especially now that there are more than enough motor vehicles. According to French statistics a horse and carriage (manned by an ordinary coachman) moved through the streets of Paris at a speed of nine kilometers an hour, while nowadays the average speed of motor vehicles traveling the same streets does not exceed seven kilometers an hour.

Transportation must be emancipated. It must receive full freedom of motion, for which, properly speaking, it was created. But on no account can this be at the expense of the pedestrian, the city's mainstay. After all, the city itself, with all its streets and conveyances, was, in the last analysis, created for man.

Underground crosswalks have been built intensively in our largest cities in recent years. Vehicles, especially trucks, have been the winners, of course. What about the people? I would hardly be mistaken if I said that Muscovites would be glad to return to the "good old times" when they could cross a street without descending and ascending steep underground stairways. It is a fact, after all, that in many cases pedestrian traffic has grown more inconvenient. In addition, the crosswalks are still too few, and one often must make a detour of nearly a kilometer to cross the street. But, while we regard extra mileage for motor vehicles as a great evil, even though this does not cost them much time, owing to their speed, the "extra mileage" for pedestrians is of scant interest to the traffic organizers.

Can underground crosswalks solve the problem of pedestrian traffic in general? I think not.

One often finds abroad designs for two- and three-level streets. The natural ground surface is sacrificed to transportation and turned into a dank urban cellar, as it were, while pedestrian traffic is elevated to suspended platforms. I am sure this will never do for our cities. Man must have a place on the ground, cleared and beautified as it deserves, while transportation must be moved underground—wherever the two are incompatible, of course. The construction of underground transportation tunnels should be warmly welcomed. The designs for new cities must even now provide for special open strips, subsequently to be turned into enclosed corridors for the main transportation arteries and for laying utility lines.

The situation is most complicated with respect to traffic in the city centers. This is what prompted the idea, now very popular, of prohibiting the construction, in the center, of buildings that could attract great streams of people. The solution to this problem, however, is complicated by the contradictory nature of the task itself. The center has to be cleared, but cleared of what? Not of itself? For after all, this is where social, political, cultural, business and trade life, embodied in hundreds of buildings, is concentrated. This is what makes a center a center; this is the source of its enormous city-planning, transportation, and social significance. Nevertheless, only what is indispensable should be located in the center. For instance, the persistent proposal to supplement the city's three largest department stores by putting a fourth in the center of Moscow, on Sretenka, seems rather strange.

The difficulty of solving this problem has produced yet another concept: Enclose the central district in large cities with a sort of magic transportation ring that would allow you to ride "around and near it," yet that could be entered only on foot. But severing the vitalities between the city and its center by force is like severing the carotid artery of a human being. In Vienna, for instance, a transportationless zone was planned within the "Ring," but nothing came of this, though, considering the medieval congestion there, it really should have been done. It is impossible to confine a living, developing center within a ring.

As for transit vehicles—particularly trucks—it would be best to reroute them from the center and from residential districts in general to bypass thoroughfares.

The best solution is to be found in speedways lined with greenery and flanked by residential districts, but as far from the houses as possible. Though these roads, without crossings at any level, have been much discussed, few of them have been built. Yet the future belongs to them.

...The organization of traffic in a large modern city requires painstaking research, extensive polling of the inhabitants and scientific investigation. We often act in a crudely empirical manner and attribute all our setbacks and mistakes to the notorious shortcomings of the large cities. This highly complex problem can be properly solved only on the basis of an integrated, thoroughly thought-out and interlinked system of all forms of urban transportation—from electric railways to taxis. It is not by chance that the Directives of the 23rd Party Congress on the forthcoming five-year plan provide for the further development of all types of passenger transportation, with an increase of at least 50% in the number of passengers conveyed, and the introduction of more spacious and comfortable cars.

A final word on transportation. How do we view the prospects for the automobile's further penetration into the life and daily round of our cities? At one time some of our "theoreticians" posited the absurd doctrine that the development of auto transport was unnecessary in our conditions, that all problems of urban and suburban traffic could be fully solved by public transportation; this, they said, was why we could do without not only a large number of automobiles, but also (even worse) without good roads.

True, we favor primary development of public transportation as the most capacious and economical means of travel in a large or even medium-sized city. It is indispensable for providing city dwellers with transportation to their jobs and back. Nor can there be any doubt that it will keep this role in the future. However, for all its merits, public transportation can replace neither the taxi nor the automobile of personal use, just as the electric railway cannot replace the bicycle, nor the bicycle the electric railway. These are essentially different things, especially if we remember that our transportation needs do not always coincide with the major routes.

The number of automobiles will grow and is in fact growing now. It is an inflexible command of life, of material and cultural progress, of economics and our growing needs.

Freedom of movement is the most precious achievement of culture. And it is not surprising that we have included the automobile in the arsenal of the communist mode of life, so to speak, just like air travel, radio, the cinema and television.

We have equal need of both public transportation and personal means of conveyance. The Directives of the 23rd C.P.S.U. Congress on the new five-year plan provide that the production of automobiles will increase almost 300%. And this process will certainly continue to develop.

This being so, urban thoroughfares, squares and parking areas should be designed and built to use all the advantages of our planned socialist system, taking into account the further development of automobile transportation: The streets must gradually be widened, and old districts must be reconstructed in a planned manner.

We do not yet know just what the transportation of the near future will look like. But the requirements can be defined in advance: speed, safety, absence of fumes, quiet and comfort. The designers' tirelessly probing creative thinking should aim at these qualities in the automobile, the friend and helpmate of man.

But the essence of the task is by no means to deliver man from moving about on his own feet wherever possible. It is, after all, technically feasible to create the kind of supertransportation that would enable a man to be whirled, without so much as putting on his hat, straight from the door of his apartment through underground tunnels and elevators to work and to emerge in front of his office door. I think this would be the beginning of man's degradation. Probably even a century from now, people will prefer to spend the 15 "saved" minutes on a walk through the frosty streets, at least as far as the subway station.

This is why I think pedestrian movement will not decrease but on the contrary increase as transportation develops and the workday is reduced. And the faster transportation moves, the more time there will be for walking.

Who exists for whom?

When a huge city is filled and surrounded with scores of mighty enterprises spewing forth hundreds of millions of cubic meters of gases like volcanoes day and night and hurling enough ashes and dust on people's heads to fill scores of giant dump trucks, when trainloads of gasoline are consumed in the streets and ultraviolet rays no longer penetrate the polluted air, it is no longer a place for man to live normally.

In many large capitalist cities the pollution of the atmosphere has become a truly national misfortune often culminating in real catastrophes. Londoners still remember how enormous smoke and gas wastes mixed with dense fog killed 4,000 people in December, 1952. Similar smog claimed 4,000 more lives four years later. The health of the population in our cities is protected by a whole system of laws, sanitary norms and rules. In recent years coal has been replaced by harmless gas at many enterprises and in the boiler rooms of apartment houses. Gas filtering installations are being put into operation.

But these are only half-measures and cannot be depended upon to clear the air of our cities completely. Meanwhile every year the problem of clean air becomes more acute. Our industry is developing intensively: there are chemical, oil-refining, metallurgical, cement, and pulp-and-paper enterprises. They give people many useful products, but nonetheless they are polluting air, water and land.

The residential sections of many cities are subject to the effects of industrial wastes. The concentrations of carbon monoxide, sulphur dioxide, fluoride compounds, chlorine, nitric oxide and other harmful gases often considerably exceed the permissible limits. The people in such districts cannot open their windows or relax in a square somewhere, for everything around them is covered with soot. It is hardly necessary to say how badly this affects the health of the public, particularly the children.

Here are some characteristic facts.

After the war the former Ministry of Metallurgy decided to build an agglomeration plant in Novokuznetsk, a city already crowded with huge plants, including a giant metallurgical plant. It was a heavy blow for the city. Novokuznetsk had been left with a single air vent in its ring of factory smoke, and now this too would be shut with the construction of the new factory. Despite all the city's protests, the ministry insisted on having its way. The factory was built and later was even expanded.

Several years later the same story was repeated in deciding whether to build a second (!) metallurgical plant, the West Siberian Metallurgical Combine, in the same city. This time the problem arose of where to erect a new residential district. It turned out there was no room for it. But the plant was built nonetheless, the first blast furnace is already smoking, and the town is laid out between the two combines. There was "no time" to look for a new site for the plant.

One cause of our cities' deterioration is the pursuit of false economy in the early stages of construction. It is far easier and cheaper, of course, to throw together a factory settlement beneath the chimneys of an enterprise than to find a suitable site for a future city and build it soundly, taking into account its long-term prospects. Nor does it take much wisdom to see that it is much cheaper to build a plant without filter installations than with them. But why doesn't somebody seriously reflect on what such "economy" leads to?

The city of Gubakha, for instance, for many years was built up right next to industrial enterprises, but the enterprises had no filter installations. Everything was done "temporarily," as an "exception to the rule." But the time came when it was impossible to live in the city, and the residential sections of Gubakha had to be moved to another site. The cost of that operation came to 200,000,000 (!) old rubles.

If we continue to pursue so-called economy and be short-sighted in our city planning, we shall certainly have to move to other sites entire districts of some industrial cities. Just think what that will cost!

The most important point is that the state does not demand such "economy" from anybody. On the contrary, estimates for the construction of plants always provide funds for filter installations; according to the existing rules, it is impermissible to commission enterprises without them.

Industrial wastes do not pollute just the air. Newspapers and magazines have been sounding the alarm increasingly often.

An extraordinary event took place in Sverdlovsk on the eve of 1965: The Iset River caught fire. Who had set the river on fire? Many of the city's enterprises had been dumping their sewage, filled with fats and oil by-products, into the Iset. The concentration of combustible materials in the river grew so dense that a burning cigarette butt thrown into the water was enough to ignite it. Once a transparent stream abounding in fish, the Iset lies dead for hundreds of kilometers below Sverdlovsk, turning into a collector of sewage.

Many a river in the Urals has suffered the same fate. The Aiva River, which flows into the Salva River, passes near Krasnouralsk. But don't try to drop a fishing line in it, and don't take it into your head to go swimming there, for what flows between its blackened banks is not water but a solution of acid. The Krasnouralsk copper-smelting combine dumps its waste into the Aiva without purification. Enormous forest and haymowing areas in the river's floodlands were laid waste.

In January, 1965, the foreman of a diving station near Dzerzhinsk on the Oka River descended beneath the ice and gasped with surprise: The entire bottom of the river was covered with dead fish. The Chernorechensk Chemical Plant had dumped waste into the Oka several times that winter; this had killed everything alive in the water. Participants in a special investigation committee of community activists, specialists and journalists have written about this.

Many inhabited points along the banks of the Belaya and Kama Rivers must obtain their water from remote sources, since it is impossible to use the water from these rivers. Even such large rivers as the Volga, Ob, Yenisei, Ural and Northern Dvina are highly polluted over considerable stretches. Needless to say, the waters of hundreds of smaller rivers can be used neither for drinking nor for bathing.

"The people of some riverside villages would give a lot to have their homes as far as possible from such a river as the Uvod," V. P. Prokhorov, from the town of Shui, remarked in Pravda. "Once one of the loveliest rivers in Ivanovo Province, it now carries its stench three or four kilometers below the city of Kokhma."

According to press reports, the filtering of sewage in a number of soda factories in the Ukraine and at the Rubezhansk Chemical Combine is thoroughly unsatisfactory. At the Syzran oil refinery, for instance, an industrial installation was commissioned that is polluting the Volga. A paper mill without any purifying installations was put into operation at the Solikamsk pulp-and-paper combine. Where there are purifying installations, moreover, they often either do not work at all or function almost ineffectively.

What is really the trouble and who is to blame: the city in itself, or we, its bungling creators? The culprits are evidently as numerous as the causes of the absence of production culture and our lack of discipline.

Population Movements
and Imbalances

The population problems of the two countries have three shared features: too many people in some areas, too few in others and too much movement from one place to another. The undesirable consequences of all this are obvious: some areas become overcrowded in relation to their resources, employment opportunities, and available services, while others remain unexploited, fail to develop, or become depressed for lack of manpower; high rates of movement from one area to another in turn tend to disrupt both economic activities and social cohesion. Furthermore, population movements are usually selective and result in an uneven, unbalanced age or sex structure with concentrations of old and infirm in some areas and younger and more able groups in other ones. In all these respects the U.S. and the U.S.S.R. have much in common partly because of the size of both countries and the unequal opportunities found in their different regions. Probably the Soviet Union is in a worse position, since it has proportionately larger areas which are unappealing for reasons of climate, resources, and lack of urban development. The problem has become particularly acute in recent years since many of the restrictions on domestic travel and change of employment which, under Stalin, curbed spontaneous population movements have been removed. Moreover, under Stalin there was considerable organized, coerced or semi-coerced population movement in the form of deportations, political exiles, and resettlement of certain minority groups and unreliables, many of them filling the so-called corrective labor camps. While these measures were motivated primarily, though not exclusively, by political rather than economic

448

considerations, they enabled the leadership to be in firm control of population movements—apparently no longer the case, as our Soviet selections indicate. Sometimes the control measures themselves backfire as did the regulations limiting residence rights in Moscow, resulting in a redoubled and sometimes irrational determination of old residents to cling to the city for fear of forfeiting their rights to live there in case of leaving. Even when officially encouraged population movements occur (under pressure or stimulated by the incentive of higher wages) to areas like Siberia, the newly settled tend not to stay. Professional and highly qualified people in particular dread rural assignments or those in remote regions of the non-European Soviet Union. Sometimes "shock projects" attract the young, in part because of the credit they receive upon return (e.g., better chances to get into universities), in part because of the ideological glamour of such assignments. On the whole, however, revolutionary romanticism has ceased to be an important factor in volunteering to distant, underdeveloped parts of the country.

In the U.S., population movements are totally uncontrolled and often also quite irrational from the point of view of the overall economic efficiency of the system. People flock to California because of its climate, leaving other areas denuded of manpower; physicians congregate in big cities while entire towns and huge parts of states have hardly a doctor left; marginal farmers escape into cities to exchange rural under-employment for urban unemployment, etc. The common denominator of American and Soviet population movements is a sometimes unrealistic pursuit of better living conditions. In the U.S. there is also a connection between geographical and social mobility: a rise in social status often entails taking a new job at a new location, rather than moving up within the hierarchy of the same firm or place of employment. In both societies geographical mobility is quite wasteful of resources and time. In both, such mobility gives rise to a host of social problems since it weakens established informal social controls. It also disrupts continuity in the educational experience of the young and prevents or weakens the development of sustaining community ties and social relationships, reduces motivation to participate in local and public affairs, and in general contributes to the proverbial triplets of modern life: anomie, alienation, and anonymity. Presumably these population movements also reflect the heightened expectations, the restlessness, and the decreasing sense of attachment of modern man to any particular social setting or physical environment.

POPULATION

IN THE U.S.:

The American View

Selected Population Problems
in the U.S.

LEO F. SCHNORE

Most attention today is properly focused on the problems of world population, for the magnitude of the problem is immense. We live in one world, and the birthrates in India and China must be of interest to us. It is a matter of importance that we be aware of the demographic situation around the world. But we must also be aware of population problems facing the United States.

At first glance, the United States has no severe "population problems." We are the wealthiest nation in the world. We occupy a wide continent, rich in natural resources. Far from having a food problem, we are faced with an embarrassment of riches—agricultural surpluses that cost millions of dollars to store. This is not to say that some of our citizens do not go to bed hungry; recent discussions have made clear that in the midst of our affluence there are "pockets of poverty" that will be diffi-

Reprinted by permission from Leo F. Schnore, "Population Problems in Perspective," Social Problems, H. Becker, ed., New York: John Wiley & Sons, © Copyright 1966, pp. 629–633.

cult and costly to eliminate. But most of us are not aware of pressing population problems, and for good reason: compared to the problems of, say, our Latin American neighbors, our problems seem insignificant. The Latin American countries make up the most rapidly growing region in the world, many of them growing at 3 per cent annually, while our rate of growth is less than the annual world average of 2 per cent.

These rates may seem low. We must remember, however, that population grows by multiplication and can compound rapidly. This compounding can be shown by considering the number of years required for a population to double its numbers at given rates of increase.

The United States now has about 200 million people, which is an enormous increase over the last two generations. (Our population was only a little over 76 million in 1900.) Despite this tremendous increase, our population density is only about 50 persons per square mile. This is a moderate "man-land" ratio compared to that of most major nations. (India has about 300

Annual Average Percentage Increase
1
2
3
4
5

Number of Years Required to Double Population
69.3
34.7
23.1
17.3
13.9

people per square mile, China about 150 per square mile, and Japan well over 600 per square mile.) We seem to be in no immediate danger of "standing room only." In fact, nearly half our counties *lost* population between 1950 and 1960 (the dates of our two most recent censuses). There is, too, an increasing unevenness of population distribution in the United States. Some regions and states are losing population while others are growing rapidly. To take the outstanding example, California gained over five million people between 1950 and 1960, an increase that more than exceeds the current total population of Wisconsin. These figures testify to the dynamism characteristic of the American population.

The physical mobility of the population is such that one out of every five of our citizens changes his place of residence every year. One result of this high rate of internal migration is that we have become an increasingly urban nation. Until the census of 1920, just after World War I, the United States continued to register rural majorities; such has been the force of urbanization, however, that by 1960 over 70 per cent

of our people were urbanites. One out of every four Americans now lives in our twelve largest metropolitan areas.

The point of these statistics is that some of the most significant changes in population are changes in population *composition* and *distribution*. The very fact of change brings problems. Every change in population distribution, for example, means that new facilities have to be provided in the areas that are growing, and that existing facilities in areas of out-migration are likely to be underused. This holds for housing, schools, roads, and all other things that people need and use.

What are some pressing problems? Consider urbanization. The rural-to-urban population shift is far from complete. Many areas, especially in the South, still contain surplus numbers of farmers engaged in subsistence production. Most of their meager output does not find its way into commercial market channels so they are not contributing to the food surplus that gives much trouble. What they have to export is themselves. We may reasonably assume that this "marginal" farm population will ultimately be drawn into other sectors of the economy. Trends in recent years indicate that the elimination of this relatively unproductive group is well underway. Nevertheless, a key policy problem persists beneath the surface, a problem that is not ordinarily taken up in the continuing political debates over parity, price supports, and the proper disposition of farm surplus. The hidden issue has to do with the role the government should play in aiding the adjustment of displaced farmers, many of whom become rural-to-urban migrants. The available evidence indicates that under laissez-faire conditions the farm-reared migrant typically enters the urban labor force at or near the bottom of the occupational scale, taking the jobs requiring the least training and receiving the smallest rewards.[1]

The problem faced by the migrant is worse, of course, if he is not white. One of the most striking population statistics concerning the United States is that in 1910 over 70 percent of all Negro Americans were rural dwellers. Most of them lived in the South; but in 1960 over 70 percent of Negro Americans were urbanites, increasingly concentrated in Northern cities. Almost 30 percent of the nonwhites in this country now live in the twelve largest metropolitan areas —New York, Los Angeles, Chicago, Philadelphia, Detroit, San Francisco, Boston, Pittsburgh, St. Louis, Washington, Cleveland, and Baltimore. It is not just the handful of large cities that is undergoing this specific change in population composition. Outside of the South, nine out of ten metropolitan areas experienced gains in the proportion of nonwhites between 1950 and 1960.[2] Thus our great cities are generally faced with the problem of absorbing massive numbers of people who are often—through no fault of their own— totally unprepared for life in the metropolis. They have neither the training nor skills to allow them to be readily assimilated into the social and economic life of the great city.

Urbanization, the continuing concentration of our population, has been going on for a long time, though the pace has quickened in recent decades. In one sense, the increased tempo of urbanization has simply meant that old solutions have had to be applied more quickly. Other population changes, however, have not had this character. This is

[1] See Ronald Freedman and Deborah Freedman, "Farm-Reared Elements in the Nonfarm Population," *Rural Sociology,* 21 (March 1956), pp. 50–61.

[2] See Leo F. Schnore and Harry Sharp, "Racial Changes in Metropolitan Areas, 1950–1960," *Social Forces,* 41 (March 1963), pp. 247–253.

especially true of changes in the age composition of our population over the past 30 years. We have had our attention repeatedly called to the so-called "baby boom" that followed the low fertility years of the Depression in the 1930s and World War II. From a compositional standpoint, the result is a series of indentations and bulges in the "population pyramid," the graphic device that demographers use to portray the age-sex structure of the population.

Stated simply, we are confronted with the problem of age groups of radically different size, passing through various age-graded institutions and services. In the 1950s, as a result of the limited number of births in the Depression and war years, small numbers of people were going into high schools and colleges of this country, and subsequently into the labor market. Over the past several years primary and secondary schools have been feeling the impact of the tremendous revival of the birthrate. Today these large numbers are beginning to reach our colleges, and shortly thereafter they will burst on our labor and housing markets and enter the "marriage market." At that time the small number of Depression cohorts (people born in a given year) will be having children, and in such reduced numbers as to lower the birthrate and the absolute number of births to a certain extent. This is, in fact, already happening; the American birthrate has been falling since 1957.

Only a few years will pass, however, before we will witness the reassertion of higher birthrates when the postwar cohorts themselves marry and have children. The overall prospect, then, is for a more or less rhythmic series of "delayed reactions" to the fluctuations in fertility that marked the period between the early 1930s and the late 1950s. The influences on the housing market, educational facilities, and industries oriented to the needs of infants and children are obvious. To the extent that population size determines levels of output in an economy closely geared to the mass market, we may thus anticipate a long-term alternating sequence of expansion and "stagnation" in at least some industries.[3]

The amplitude of these fluctuations is probably narrow enough to permit adjustment on the part of the American economy as a whole. The real problems appear when we consider the *localized* manifestations of these trends, especially

when we give simultaneous attention to both population distribution *and* composition. Any resident of a mushrooming suburb will testify to the high costs of providing school facilities for a rapidly expanding child population. One disturbing possibility not considered by many local authorities is that an equally sudden shrinkage in the demand for educational services may eventually follow the completion of suburban families. Newer suburbs with heavy concentrations in a narrow parental age range are especially vulnerable. In short, some of our most pressing population problems will stem from peculiarities in age composition, peculiarities now "built into" our population structure.

[3] For a very lucid account of this matter, see Norman B. Ryder, "Variability and Convergence in the American Population," *Phi Delta Kappan,* 41 (June 1960), pp. 379–383.

POPULATION

IN THE U.S.S.R.:

The Soviet View

Population Movements, the Economy, and Science

V. PEREVEDENTSEV

Reprinted from V. Perevedentsev, "Population Movements, the Economy, and Science," Literaturnaya gazeta *(March 10, 1966). Translated in* Current Digest of the Soviet Press, *XVIII, No. 11 (Copyright © April 6, 1966), 10–11.*

WHERE IT IS CROWDED AND WHERE IT IS DESERTED

Statistics show that most of the adult inhabitants of our country have changed

their place of residence at least once in their life.

In no other country of the world do population shifts have such scope and importance. In 1926, for instance, only one inhabitant out of six was a city dweller. Today more than half of the Soviet people live in cities. Vast urban conglomerations have formed in the central part of the country, in the Urals and in the Donets and Kuznetsk Basins. The populations of many remote provinces (Murmansk, Kamchatka and others) have increased tens of times. All this is the result of migration, which is inseparably linked with major economic processes. It is clear to everyone that without population shifts it would have been impossible to carry out the industrialization of the country and much else besides.

However, I did not undertake to write this article in order to eulogize migration. Our successes in this respect are incontrovertible. Still, as a specialist I am well aware of the shortcomings in this great phenomenon.

I am deeply convinced that the rationalization of migrational processes will be of great help to the growth of our national economy.

Rather than trying to cover too much ground, I shall speak of migration only as it concerns the distribution of the population. On the solution of this problem depend in large measure the effective use of the country's labor resources and the productivity of social labor.

The economic reform set forth in the decisions of the September, 1965, plenary session of the Central Committee will lead to more prudent use of labor. The steady progress of the national economy also requires a constant redistribution of manpower. Then, too, the demographic situation has changed sharply in recent years: The many young people born after the war are now reaching working age.

The draft Directives of the 23rd Party Congress say: "*To ensure the rational use of labor resources* in all areas of the country and the enlistment in production or study of young people and adolescents who have graduated from general education schools; to make better year-round use of rural manpower."

This is a task of great importance, and its solution will not be easy. Moreover, there is no effective system of regulating migrations in the country.

The chief shortcoming in the distribution of population, from the economic standpoint, is its unevenness, the disparity between available labor resources and the need for them in *each given* place.

This disparity is most evident in agriculture. For instance, in 1959 the collective farms of the Georgian Republic had twice the labor resources they needed, while such major agricultural areas as Kazakhstan and Western Siberia had only about two-thirds of the required manpower.

The surplus of labor resources in the agricultural areas of the Ukraine, Belorussia, Moldavia, the Northern Caucasus, Transcaucasia and other regions, which numbers millions of people, is one of the chief reasons for the low labor productivity of agriculture. At the same time, a shortage of people in other rural areas is holding back the growth of agricultural production.

Our cities also vary greatly in their supply of labor resources.

The manpower shortage has substantially retarded the economic development of such promising economic regions as Siberia and Kazakhstan. Yet surplus labor resources in a number of provinces in the western part of the country necessitate increased capital investments in the economy that run contrary to considerations of prudence.

At the beginning of the seven-year period a plan was compiled for the interregional redistribution of the population. Among other things, it was intended to substantially augment Siberia's population and to draw off surplus labor resources from the Northern Caucasus.

What actually happened?

Calculations we made on the basis of

data from the Central Statistical Administration show that in the five years 1959–1963, the number of people who left Siberia exceeded the number who arrived there by 250,000, while 500,000 more people arrived in the Northern Caucasus than left. And this despite the fact that hundreds of thousands of people came to Siberia from various places, including the Northern Caucasus.

In the same period the rural population dropped (in other words, the number of people leaving the countryside exceeded the natural population growth) in a number of areas that were already experiencing a manpower shortage. And conversely, where there was already a surplus of labor resources, the population sharply increased.

What are the reasons for this state of affairs?

Population movement is a phenomenon that follows its own logic and has its own causes. Chief among these is the desire of those moving to better their living conditions. Naturally, a person will move only to a place where he can find means of livelihood. Therefore the need for additional manpower is an essential condition for the flow of population to one or another area of the country. Let me stipulate that it is only the chief cause—many other complex, interlinked factors are involved. For example, we must by no means ignore the great importance of moral factors in, say, the migration of young people to new, undeveloped areas. But the point is that these factors play a smaller role in a decision to stay in a new place than they do in a decision to go to Siberia or Kazakhstan.

The efflux of people from Siberia results from the fact that conditions there are inferior to conditions in the areas to which the population moves (the Ukraine, Moldavia, the Northern Caucasus, the Baltic republics, etc.).

Places where there is a shortage of manpower should offer better living conditions than places where there is a surplus. The person who moves should find himself better off, not worse, in the new place than in the old one. Consequently the planning agencies must work purposefully to establish the proper correlations of living conditions in various places in order to regulate population shifts according to the needs of the national economy.

ODDITIES OF THE POPULATION SHIFT

Is such work being done? How do these correlations take shape? Strange as it may seem for a planned economy, no one has any precise idea of the correlation of the conditions and, more narrowly, the living standards of the populations of different areas. Some planning indices are drawn up only for entire Union republics. In the most recent scientific literature we read that "among the planning indices drawn up for economic regions, those for real income, public consumption funds and real payments for labor are completely nonexistent"—that is, the chief indices of the standard of living, as well as many other important indices.

In addition, the various departments of the State Planning Committees work without sufficient contact with one another. One department, for example, plans investments in housing construction while another department is responsible for planning the construction base. As a result, it sometimes happens that money allocated for housing construction cannot be used—there are no materials or facilities for building the housing.

Precisely because of such shortcomings in the work of the planning agencies, the abnormal correlations that have formed often take a long time to correct. Let me give an example. Back at the beginning of 1960, the Institute of the Economics and Organization of Industrial Production of the U.S.S.R. Academy of Sciences' Siberian Division submitted to the Russian Republic State Planning Committee the results of an analysis of the migration of the population of Siberia, accompanied by a description of the reasons why people were leaving for the western areas plus a suggested system of measures for preventing the continued efflux from Siberia. No one disputed the institute's conclusions. But nothing was done. Moreover, in the three succeeding years Siberia fell even further behind other parts of the country in housing conditions for the population.

That is one side of the matter. But there is another side. Besides moves by individuals, there are also organized population shifts. Resettlement agencies, agencies of vocational-technical education, ministries and departments, public organizations and certain enterprises are concerned with this. It would seem that here, at least, population shifts should occur when necessary and to and from the necessary places. But closer examination reveals that these organizations act independently, and often in diametrically opposite directions.

For instance, the resettlement agencies each year send many thousands of families from the western parts of the country to the collective and state farms of Siberia, while the agencies of vocational-technical education do their best to attract young people from those same collective and state farms to their industrial, transportation and other schools. The resettlement agencies and public organizations of the western regions send large numbers of workers to construction projects in Siberia, while the officials of many construction projects and enterprises in manpower-rich areas invite workers from Siberia under the transfer system (i.e., paying their moving expenses, etc.).

Finally, the lack of a clearcut migration policy leads to the most bizarre incidents. A few years ago I saw the following picture at one of the largest plants in Krasnoyarsk: One inspector in the personnel department was registering the release of young people being sent to work in agriculture in response to public appeals; at the very next table another inspector was signing up for work young people from villages in the very areas where the released workers were being sent. In essence, the new arrivals were taking the places of those who were being sent to the countryside.

The unfavorable migratory tendencies and inadequate knowledge of the laws governing migration have led to attempts to regulate population movements administratively, by limiting the number of newcomers to places where an influx of people is undesirable. Applied first to Moscow, such measures spread to many large cities. It can already be said that, most disconcertingly, they have not brought the anticipated results. The consequences have been unexpected. As it happens, they have been felt most appreciably in Moscow. On the one hand, it has been necessary, because of the capital's manpower shortage, to adopt special decisions on bringing in workers of certain categories (construction workers, for example). On the other hand, many tens of thousands of skilled specialists for whose knowledge and experience Moscow has no use (agronomists, zoo-technicians, veterinarians, reclamation experts, lumberman, etc.) but who are needed elsewhere do not leave Moscow because this would mean they could not return. For the same reason elderly people will no longer leave Moscow, although its conditions are by no means ideal for them. Evidently it is necessary to evaluate on their merits the results that have been obtained, so that we may arrive at a more flexible migration policy.

"DEEP DRILLING" IS NEEDED

Finally, there is the matter of research. At first glance everything would seem to be fine in this respect.

Indeed, in the past five years far more literature on contemporary migration has been published than appeared in the preceding 30 years. Many scientific meetings have been held, and their discussions of problems of migration appears thorough. The study of migration has been taken up in many places.

But let us look a little more closely. We will see that in general those engaged in this work are lone-wolf enthusiasts, most of whom are burdened with another job; that in recent years there has been no scientific advance (this, by the way, was correctly noted by the writer A. Smirnov-Cherkezov in his article "The Extremes of the Far North," published in *Literaturnaya gazeta* on Dec. 28, 1965); that scientific workers embarking on the study of migration are forced to go over from the very beginning the ground covered by their predecessors, since the methods of studying the migration of the population have never been published (even though they were worked out long ago); and that some research divisions that should concern themselves with migration (for example, the former Department of Labor Resources of the Labor Research Institute) have been sidetracked.

I am deeply convinced that all this is the result of an underestimation of the national-economic and social impor-

tance of migrations and of the complexity of their study.

Scientific research in one respect resembles geological drilling—the deeper the drill goes, the harder the drilling becomes. Often the first 1,000 meters are easier to get through than the next 100. And in the study of migrations it is precisely "deep drilling" that is needed.

I shall name only one problem that needs solution. At present migration is studied for the most part qualitatively. Instances of migration are described. The factors of population shifts are established, described and classified. The direction in which each one acts is known. The relative importance of the major ones is also known. Some consequences of migration are described. But after all, if migration is to be guided successfully, it is necessary to know the measure of influence of each of the major factors. This can be established only by the industrious teamwork of demographers and mathematicians, making extensive use of our statistical methods.

One recalls the 1920s. Shortly after the Revolution a special State Colonization Institute was set up in the country, and to judge from materials published in the press it did a great deal of work in the study of migrations and the conditions of settlement of the North, Siberia and other areas.

In recent years the scientific community has more than once proposed that all work on the migration of the population be headed and coordinated by a single center.

In conclusion I will mention the most important point. In order to create the optimum conditions in migratory processes, it is first of all necessary to work out a scientifically based complex of economic and organizational measures and to establish a single system of agencies for calculating, distributing, releasing and redistributing labor resources. These proposals are not new. It is obvious that their implementation will require some effort. However, there cannot be the slightest doubt that these measures will pay for themselves quickly and many times over in economic results.

Concerning Demographic Ignorance
and the Problem
of the Birth Rate*

V. PEREVEDENTSEV

Novosibirsk—I won't say that an economist should be a demographer and a demographer need be an economist. I shall merely try to demonstrate that an economist should be *knowledgeable in demography* and a demographer should be *knowledgeable in economics*. This means that an economist should be able to foresee, at least in general outline, the demographic consequences of economic decisions and measures, while a demographer should foresee the economic consequences of demographic processes. It is particularly important for economists to take a demographically knowledgeable approach to problems of the distribution of productive forces, the utilization of manpower, and the distribution of consumption funds.

I shall begin with a widely known

Reprinted from V. Perevedentsev; "Concerning Demographic Ignorance and the Problem of the Birth Rate," Literaturnaya gazeta (Aug. 13, 1966). Translated in Current Digest of the Soviet Press, XVIII, No. 32 (Copyright © August 31, 1966), p. 8.

* Published by way of discussion.

example. An abnormal ratio of women to men is characteristic of the majority of the country's textile centers. In 1959 there were 136 females between the ages of 20 and 24 per 100 males in this age bracket in the cities and towns of Ivanovo Province. (The ratio for the country as a whole is 102:100.) The disproportion has many negative social consequences in marriage and family relationships, child upbringing, etc. In 1959 there were only 444 married women per 1,000 females above the age of 16 in the cities and towns of Ivanovo Province, whereas in nearby Tula Province the figure for married women was 548, and in distant Magadan Province as high as 774. Only in the popular song does it sound touching to hear the line: "Most of the women textile workers are single." The women textile workers themselves are not a bit enchanted by it.

How did this demographic problem arise?

It is customary nowadays to speak of the textile industry as a "women's" industry. Yet it became so not very long ago. The Ivanovo-Voznesensk textile workers who established and defended Soviet rule under the leadership of M. V. Frunze were *men,* not women. Then why does one need a searchlight in daytime to find a male textile worker nowadays? Because in the thirties the textile industry was placed in such wage conditions (second category!) that even today men do not want to work in it. And even now pay is comparatively low in the textile industry. As we see, the demographic problem owes its appearance entirely to economics.

Of course, socialist society is capable of solving this problem. Both by suitable adjustment of wages and by building male-employing enterprises in the textile towns. That the problem has not yet been solved is due, I believe, to an underestimation of the demographic and social aspects of the distribution of labor power, to inability to consider these aspects and to relate them to the purely economic aspects.

Now let us try to look a little farther and deeper, tracing the consequences of the abnormal sex-age structure of the population of the textile towns.

Visit the textile mills in Central Asia and see who is working there. In 1964 *half* of all the employees of the huge textile mill in Dushanbe had come from the central and Volga regions. Why do women residents of Ivanovo, Kalinin, Kamyshin and many other cities head for Central Asia? Personnel department officials and the newcomers to Central Asian cities themselves are of the same opinion: the difficulty of establishing a family and the impossibility for many of them of finding husbands in the textile towns of Russia. These "subjective" answers are thoroughly confirmed by an analysis of the migration statistics. Several times as many persons per thousand inhabitants leave Ivanovo Province as leave Tula Province. And, per thou-

sand, the number coming from Ivanovo Province who remain in Central Asian cities is several times as large as the number from Tula Province who remain there.

The mill executives naturally have a stake in the influx of skilled workers. Why bother to train workers from among the unskilled local rural youth, when already trained workers come themselves? But, with the high natural increase in the rural population of Central Asia, surplus manpower is increasing in many districts there. See what a long chain of demographic, economic and ethnographic consequences go back to an economic factor—the relatively low pay in the textile industry.

Try to draw sharp lines between the economic, demographic and ethnographic problems, divide them among the respective narrow specialists, and you may be sure that the real relationships that exist among these life problems will not be uncovered, that there will not be a rounded understanding of the life processes, that no way will be found for purposeful regulation of the various processes. Specialists of different fields must understand one another, must be able to share scientific problems, must be able to apply the conclusions of related sciences.

I am convinced that many economically undesirable demographic phenomena are due in the final count to the utter demographic ignorance of economists and planners. Here is another illustration. Siberia is marked by a very high mobility (migration) of its population. Each year two or three times as many residents leave its cities (per 100 population) as leave cities in the western parts of our country. This mobility is particularly high in the new cities that are springing up. Some construction projects have turned into "revolving doors." There are many reasons for this, one of the chief reasons being that the demography of these towns has been completely ignored. Most of those who come to the new construction projects are between 18 and 30 years old. There are many marriages and many children are born. In the new cities of Siberia the proportion of children in the population is usually two or three times as high as in the old cities of the western regions. Yet the norms for the number of accommodations in children's institutions are the same for all cities. Thus, the planned norms already doom the residents of the new towns to difficulties arising from the impossibility of placing children in nurseries and kindergartens. The situation is aggravated by the fact that there are very, very few grandmothers and grandfathers, those natural "nursemaids," in the new cities. They cannot be asked to come because of the difficult housing conditions. The young mothers quit their jobs and the family income drops. Often the young mother and father prefer to move to where their relatives live. Thus does the Olympian neglect of elementary demographic problems take economic revenge. Labor turnover is the plague of many of the new construction projects. . . .

Religion:

Decline and Survival

When discussing religion as a social problem in the U.S. and the Soviet Union, we are actually talking about two different issues. In the U.S. what is seen as problematic is the decline of religion, or its failure to achieve a new role under the new social conditions of mid-twentieth century America. Thus religion remains to be viewed as a useful institution and religious beliefs praiseworthy. The Soviet treatment of religion is quite the opposite. It is regarded as a social problem insofar as it survives; it is actually designated as one of the harmful vestiges of the past, along with crime, drunkenness, acquisitiveness, sloth, hedonism, individualism, and many others. The Soviet condemnation of religion has deep philosophical-ideological roots, going back to Marx at least. In all the modifications and reinterpretations of Marxism— by Lenin, Stalin, Khrushchev and other minor Soviet philosopher-kings— there has never been any attempt to alter the original "opiate theory" of religion. Indeed the position taken on religion remains probably among the most stable parts of Marxism-Leninism and its periodically reformulated versions. The anti-religious attitude is based on these premises: religion is unscientific; it arises out of ignorance, oppression and the incomprehension of the physical and social world; it is also a tool of the exploiting classes deliberately used to mislead, placate, or divert the masses and prevent them from taking action against the injustices of their society. In short religion is regarded as antithetical to social progress, justice, rationality, and mastery over the natural and social environment. Occasionally more concrete charges have also been made against specific churches, denominations or religious functionaries, claiming that they deliberately engage in political activities, in or outside the U.S.S.R., intended to undermine the Soviet system. In the light of these propositions it is hardly surprising that religion is viewed as an undesirable phenomenon, the extinction of which is to be accelerated. This position is fully reflected in the Soviet selections included.

In addition to the reasons enumerated, Soviet hostility toward religion can also be appreciated on certain sociological and social-psychological grounds. Religious beliefs represent ideological competition; they may also imply a degree of indifference toward the social-political environment predisposing to apathy and withdrawal from participation in the numerous tasks the Soviet regime has set out to accomplish. Religious moral injunctions often clash specifically with the practices of the regime. Religion, at least in theory, can be conducive to the development of an inward-looking, reflective mentality alien to the attributes of the type of citizen, the New Soviet Man, the regime has tried to create. In short the regime makes claims on the totality of psychic energies and emotional commitments of the citizen.

Curiously enough, although the U.S. is also essentially a highly secular society (perhaps even more so than the Soviet Union), religion is not regarded as threatening or in conflict with the operational values, pursuits, and activities which are predominant. This is in part a consequence of the peculiarities of American religious institutions and practices, and of their flexibility which allows them to depart from the more traditional, otherworldly orientation. This at times makes it difficult to distinguish the religious from the non-religious, social or charitable institutions. Belief in God in American society is still an ultimate value for most people, firmly entrenched in the framework of the somewhat mythical dominant values or mainstream of American thought. The overwhelming majority of Americans, also according to the testimony of public opinion polls, claim to believe in God and engage in some kind of religious participation with some regularity—whatever the meaning attached to it. Moreover, in the U.S. the conflict between religion and science has been solved for most people by compartmentalization or by the simple denial of the conflict. Religion has two major roots in American life. One is its unquestioning acceptance as something vaguely good and valuable which does not make any serious claims on one's life; the other is the complex of social, symbolic and communal functions it has assumed. Belonging to a church is on the same plane as belonging to a club, chapter, or organization of an explicitly secular character. American churches are in fact preoccupied with a variety of activities only remotely relevant to traditional religious concerns. What then is socially problematic about religion in the U.S.? The problem is seen not in the decline of formal religious participation, the number of people belonging to churches, the money spent on church construction and the like. In terms of such indices religion is thriving in American society. The decline is detected in the areas of genuine belief and commitment, in the ever-shrinking extent to which religious values inform the life of Americans or answer, or help raise questions, about meaning and fulfillment in life; or in the gap between professed belief and behavior, not a new problem in itself. Also as the American authors quoted below put it: (the church)..."is not seeking to make explicit how men ought to behave, to what ends and for what reasons." In other words organized religion in the U.S. might be called a consumer religion: it does not make demands on the faithful; it does not set standards; it is permissive and merely wants to "sell" itself in areas and by methods which will provoke the least resistance.

As these remarks suggest, religion as a social problem has very different implications in the two societies. In the U.S.S.R. the major issue is to make the official system of values the only functioning alternative, or to fill the value-gap created both by the institutionalized official attacks and by the unintended erosion of faith in modern urban, industrial society. It is the lesser problem to "decontaminate" those still clinging to religion or to keep small scale religious revival, such as accomplished by the Baptists, within bounds. In the U.S. the institutional framework and tradition in themselves are not under attack. The problem lies in filling the old structures with new meaning and relevance, or simply in finding a place for traditional religious values in a thoroughly secular modern society.

RELIGION

IN THE U.S.:

The American View

Religion and Society
in Tension

CHARLES GLOCK and RODNEY STARK

...The basic normative structure of American society derives in large mea-

From C. Glock and R. Stark, Religion and Society in Tension. *Chicago: Rand Mc-Nally, 1965, pp. 182–184.*

sure from the high value placed on democracy as a basis for political and social organization. At the present time, this commitment to democracy rests primarily on secular beliefs and values. It is nevertheless fair to say that the respect for human individuality which underlies democratic conviction is rooted in and has been informed by the Judeo-Christian heritage as it has been interpreted in the light of history.

This capacity of religion to inform the secular normative structure seems to be largely a thing of the past. In a complex society, and particularly in a democratic one, contributions to the normative structure come from many sources—the body politic, the economic order, the mass media, labor unions, and private citizens, as well as the church. These sources at once inform the norms and values for our society and are informed by them. The process is a dialectical one but it is not necessarily a matter of even exchange. Any particular institution may at times be influenced by the surrounding value structure considerably more than it is able to exercise influence over it.

Organized religion in the United States, we would assert, is currently much more on the receiving than on the contributing side of the value process. This is not because of lack of opportunity to make explicit what secular values should be, to elaborate on the implications of religious faith, or to question the existing normative structure. The avenues open to the church for making a contribution are many—sermons, church periodicals and educational materials, official pronouncements, church programs, discussion groups. The available audience is large: the majority of the population is regularly exposed to the church's influence through Sunday worship as well as in other ways. Yet, the evidence indicates that the church is not availing itself of its manifold opportunities. It is not, in fact, seeking to make explicit how men ought to behave, to what ends, and for what reasons.

This is not to say that norms and values are ignored in what the church seeks to communicate. On the contrary, they are the major themes of much that it talked and written about. But the level of abstraction at which the topic is pursued has the consequence of leaving to other sources the final say in determining everyday norms and values. The church's emphasis is overwhelmingly on man's relationship to God. The implications of the faith for man's relation to man are left largely to the individual to work out for himself, with God's help but without the help of the churches. Man is exhorted to be a steward of God; to exercise choice and initiative in his use of leisure time in keeping with the new life in Christ; to manage economic wealth in terms of Christian responsibility and leadership; to accept the political responsibilities of Christian citizenship on the basis of his citizenship in the Kingdom of God.

However well grounded these injunctions may be theologically, and whatever symbolic or psychological functions they may serve in the lives of individuals, the result from the standpoint of influencing concrete behavior is very little. How the majority of Americans behave, and what they value, is not informed by religious faith but by the norms and values of the larger society of which he is a part. Confronted on the one hand by the abstract prescriptions of religion and on the other by the concrete norms and values made explicit by law, by the context in which they labor, and by secular groups, men are almost inexorably led to follow the latter—partly because these sanctioning systems are more salient, but also because the nature of a religiously inspired choice is not clear.

There are good and perhaps sufficient reasons, aside from theological ones, to account for the church's failure to contribute significantly to informing present-day values. The implications of the faith are simply not clear enough to be expounded authoritatively and unequivocally. Also relevant, most noticeably on the contemporary scene, is the high value which the church appears to place on harmony and the avoidance of conflict. Wherever choice is between maintaining harmony and taking a stand on an issue which would produce conflict, the church most often chooses harmony. This is seen in the way that local congregations are governed as well as in situations where the church has an opportunity to inform the general community, for example, in the recent events in Little Rock, Arkansas. What is being here spoken of is perhaps no more than another facet of the frequently commented upon "dilemma of the churches." Were the church to insist upon strict obedience to a set of norms, values, and beliefs, it would probably lose whatever power it now exercises in the larger society.

Because of this dilemma, it is unlikely that the church could succeed in generating a general commitment to its standards even were it to make explicit the behavioral and attitudinal implications of the faith. Insofar as it has made its position explicit on given issues, its constituency has not widely adopted its values, at least not in situations where there are conflicting secular norms. Witness, for example, the relative failure of the churches to foster racially integrated congregations though this is an

issue on which most major denominations have spoken out in unequivocal terms.

That the church is being informed by, more than it is informing, the values of the larger society is an indicator that our society no longer appeals to religious suprasocial authority and its sanctioning system to validate its norms. It is also a sign that organized religion is committed, implicitly at least, to maintaining the society as it is rather than to fostering its regeneration along lines formulated by the church. In this latter sense, religion is indeed making a contribution to social integration though perhaps on terms which compromise its distinctly religious character.

It is not being suggested that the contemporary church cannot inform the lives of individuals and exercise an influence on society through them. Nor can it be said that, within particular minority religious movements, suprasocial authority may not still have precedence over other forms of authority. Looking at American society as a whole, however, organized religion at present is neither a prominent witness to its own value system nor a major focal point around which ultimate commitments to norms, values, and beliefs are formed.

RELIGION

IN THE U.S.S.R.:

The Soviet View

On Measures for Intensifying
the Atheistic Indoctrination
of the Population

The Ideological Commission of the C.P.S.U. Central Committee has worked out "Measures for Intensifying the Atheistic Indoctrination of the Population." The C.P.S.U. Central Committee, having approved these measures, has instructed the Central Committees of the Communist Parties of the Union republics and the territory and province Party committees, taking local conditions into account, to work out and implement concrete steps aimed at a radical improvement in atheistic work.

The measures for intensifying the atheistic indoctrination of the population may be summarized as follows.

THE SCIENTIFIC ELABORATION OF THE PROBLEMS OF ATHEISM AND THE TRAINING OF ANTI-RELIGIOUS SPECIALISTS

It has been decided to set up an Institute of Scientific Atheism in the

Reprinted from the Ideological Commission of the CPSU Central Committee, Partiinaya zhizn (Jan. 1964). Translated in Current Digest of the Soviet Press, XVI, No. 9 (Copyright © March 25, 1964), 3–4.

C.P.S.U. Central Committee's Academy of Social Sciences. The institute is charged with guiding and coordinating all scientific work in the sphere of atheism carried on by the institutes of the U.S.S.R. Academy of Sciences, higher educational institutions, and institutions of the U.S.S.R. Ministry of Culture; the preparation of highly skilled cadres; the organization of the integrated elaboration of pressing problems of scientific atheism; and the holding of all-Union scientific conferences and creative seminars. The Learned Council of the Institute of Scientific Atheism is to be composed of representatives of the C.P.S.U. Central Committee's Ideological Department and of central scientific and ideological institutions, and also of public organizations.

The presidium of the U.S.S.R. Academy of Sciences and the collegium of the U.S.S.R. Ministry of Higher and Specialized Secondary Education will examine the question of the active participation of institutes of the Academy and departments of higher educational institutions in the scientific elaboration of the problems of atheism, as well as in atheistic propaganda.

The Institute of Scientific Atheism is organizing the semiannual publication of the collection "Problems of Scientific Atheism," based on the collection "Problems of the History of Religion and Atheism," published by the U.S.S.R. Academy of Sciences' History Institute, and the annual publications of the Leningrad Museum of the History of Religion and Atheism. During the current year the Institute of Scientific Atheism and the All-Union Knowledge Society will conduct scientific-methodological conferences of specialists and propagandists of atheism on questions of the criticism of various trends in contemporary religion.

Beginning with the 1964–1965 academic year, the U.S.S.R. Ministry of Higher and Specialized Secondary Education will introduce the specialty of scientfic atheism for some of the students in the university faculties of history and philosophy and in the history-philology faculties of higher pedagogical schools (in full-time, evening and correspondence divisions). It is planned to set up scientific atheism departments at a number of universities and pedagogical institutes, as well as atheism sections in the institutes for improving professional skills at Moscow and Kiev Universities.

The C.P.S.U. Central Committee's ideological departments for Russian Federation industry and Russian Federation agriculture and the Central Committees of the Union-republic Communist Parties are organizing permanent courses for propagandists of atheism (lecturers, leaders of theoretical seminars, consultants and others).

THE ATHEISTIC TRAINING OF CADRES

Beginning with the 1964–1965 academic year, a required course (with examinations) in the principles of scientific atheism will be introduced in the univer-

sities and higher medical, agricultural and pedagogical schools, and an elective course will be offered at other institutions of higher education. The principles of scientific atheism will also be taught in medical, pedagogical and cultural-enlightenment academies. Programs and textbooks for the course are being prepared that take into account the different forms of instruction. Study plans and programs envisage a required course of seminar studies, the preparation of course work, and credit for practical atheistic work. The atheistic orientation of courses in the natural sciences and the humanities will be intensified.

With the new academic year, the course "Principles of Scientific Atheism" will be introduced in the correspondence Higher Party School of the C.P.S.U. Central Committee, in the four-year higher party schools, in the Central Young Communist League School, and also in Soviet-Party schools. The study program in philosophy at two-year Party schools will include an increased number of hours in the study of scientific atheism.

Party and Y.C.L. committees are instructed to make active use of the political-enlighenment system for the atheistic training of cadres. For this purpose it has been decided to set up in all areas—especially in regions where there is a relatively high incidence of religious belief among the population—seminars, schools and circles for the study of atheism, combining the instruction of students with atheistic work. In conformity with contemporary requirements, programs on atheism will be improved and appropriate materials on atheism for the political-enlightenment network will be prepared for publication by the beginning of the 1964–1965 academic year.

It is recommended that seminars on questions of atheistic indoctrination be put into effect for Party, Soviet, Y.C.L.

and trade union workers and activists, teachers, physicians, Young Pioneer group leaders and workers in children's preschool institutions, instructors in vocational and technical academies and schools, cultural-enlightenment workers, journalists, administrative workers, chairmen and members of women's councils, apartment house committees and pensioners' councils.

THE UTILIZATION IN ATHEISTIC
INDOCTRINATION OF ALL MEANS
OF IDEOLOGICAL INFLUENCE

The All-Union Knowledge Society, together with the Y.C.L. Central Committee, the All-Union Central Council of Trade Unions and the U.S.S.R. Ministry of Culture, will hold a conference on questions of improving the organization and content of scientific-atheism propaganda lectures.

Party committees are instructed to examine the question of the more active enlistment in atheistic lecture propaganda of scientists, instructors, teachers, physicians, writers, journalists and students at higher educational institutions in the humanities, agriculture and medicine. The people's universities will be utilized actively for atheistic indoctrination.

The U.S.S.R. Council of Ministers' State Committee for Cinematography envisages the release each year of feature films, popular science films, newsreel-documentaries and animated cartoons on atheistic themes. It is planned to introduce the practice of showing atheistic films, including feature films, on television and at free film showings in cultural-enlightenment institutions and schools, and also to increase the number of prints of atheistic films and to duplicate them on narrow film.

The collegiums of the U.S.S.R. Ministry of Culture and the U.S.S.R. Council of Ministers' State Committee for Cinematography and the secretariats of the boards of the artistic unions will discuss at a joint meeting the question of enhancing the role of literature and art in atheistic indoctrination. The holding of competitions (with incentive prizes) for the best artistic works on atheistic themes (in the fields of literature, drama, films and painting) is envisaged. The question of improving the atheistic repertoire for amateur performing groups will be examined.

Measures are planned for stepping up the publication of atheistic literature, broadening its subject matter, utilizing varied genres and raising its ideological-political and publicistic level. The U.S.S.R. Council of Ministers' State Committee for the Press has been charged with compiling an overall long-range plan for the publication of atheistic literature, envisaging expanded printings of editions in the national languages and of editions for children and adolescents; the publication of mass "Atheist's Library" editions and of popular series (philosophical and other) designed for believers; the reprinting of the best works of classical atheistic literature; and the translation into the national languages of the U.S.S.R. of the best books published in Russian and other tongues.

In the interests of the qualitative improvement of atheistic literature and the elimination of duplication in its publication, it has been decided to set up an Editorial Advisory Council under the U.S.S.R. Council of Ministers' State Committee for the Press, and to set up scientific-atheistic editorial boards within the framework of the existing staff of large republic and interprovince publishing houses.

With the object of intensifying the publication of atheistic materials, it is planned to introduce appropriate sections in the periodicals *Agitator, Politicheskoye samoobrazovaniye, Voprosy filosofii, Voprosy istorii, Nauka i zhizn [Science and Life], Znaniye—sila [Knowledge Is Strength], Priroda [Nature], Zdorovye [Health], Rabotnitsa [The Woman Worker], Krestyanka [The Peasant Woman],* and *Smena,* and also in the analogous republic magazines. In the interests of strengthening the presentation of atheistic. themes by newspapers, magazines and publishing houses and on radio and television, it is recommended that the U.S.S.R. Council of Ministers' State Committees for the Press and for Radio and Television and the Union of Soviet Journalists, and their organs in the republics and provinces, conduct regular creative seminars for journalists specializing in questions of atheistic indoctrination, work out in practice methodological recommendations on these questions, strive for greater attention on the part of the press to the unmasking of religious ideology and the generalization of practical work in atheistic indoctrination, and draw specialists more actively into the work of the press.

The All-Union Radio and Central Television, and also republic and province radio and television studios, are called upon to broadcast regular atheistic programs on radio and television for various categories of listeners and viewers (especially lecture cycles and public-events series, round-table discussions and question-and-answer sessions), to enlist the best propagandists of atheism and scientists in this work, and to produce television films on atheistic themes.

It is recommended that the All-Union Central Council of Trade Unions, the U.S.S.R. Ministry of Culture and the Knowledge Society strengthen the material and technical base for lecture and cultural-enlightenment atheistic work,

enliven the atheistic activity of museums, especially historical and regional-lore museums, planetariums, traveling exhibits and mobile clubs [*avtokluby*], increase the production of slide-projector films, etc.

It is planned to heighten the role of medical workers in atheistic indoctrination, to set up permanent courses on atheism for medical workers at medical institutes, and also to organize atheistic work in Houses of Health Education, hospitals, maternity homes and women's and children's consultation clinics.

In order to introduce nonreligious holidays and rituals more actively in the everyday life of Soviet people, a conference of Party, Soviet, Y.C.L. and trade union workers, ethnographers, propagandists and registry-office workers will be held on this question; local Soviets will provide for the construction of Palaces of Happiness in plans for urban and settlement construction and for the active utilization of Houses of Culture for these purposes and will establish ceremonial forms (taking specific local features into account) for official participation in the registration of births and marriages, the issuing of passports, and other important events in the lives of Soviet people.

Seminar-conferences will be held for the purpose of generalizing experience and working out recommendations for work with believers. Party committees and local Party organizations, together with trade union and Y.C.L. committees, are instructed to investigate the state of religious belief in every center of population and every collective. Taking the findings into account, people of authority and possessing a knowledge of life will be assigned to work with believers (at either their place of work or their residence) and to organize atheistic instruction for them. The staff of propagandists and discussion leaders on atheistic themes will be strengthened, and atheist groups will be assigned to organize individual work with believers in each community. Believers will be drawn into general-education circles and schools.

THE ATHEISTIC UPBRINGING OF CHILDREN AND ADOLESCENTS

The anti-religious trend in school programs, especially in the social sciences, is gaining strength. Methodological textbooks for anti-religious education in schools will be issued to teachers. The widespread utilization in the atheistic indoctrination of school children of various forms of extracurricular and afterschool work (young atheists' clubs and corners, lectures, discussions, evening meetings, excursions, cultural trips to the movies and the theater, etc.) is directed.

It is recommended that the Union-republic Ministries of Education, together with Y.C.L. committees and the Academy of Pedagogical Sciences, hold local, province and republic seminar-conferences of teachers, Young Pioneer group leaders, and workers in preschool institutions on questions of atheistic work with children and adolescents, and also with parents. Permanent courses on atheism for workers in the categories listed above are being set up at pedagogical institutes. People's universities of pedagogy and schools for mothers will be actively utilized for the atheistic instruction of parents.

CONTROL OVER THE OBSERVANCE OF SOVIET LEGISLATION ON CULTS

In order to put a stop to illegal activities on the part of clergymen, groups of believers and individual believers, control is being strengthened over the protection of children and adolescents from the influence of churchgoers and from parental coercion of children to perform religious rites.

Measures are planned to enhance familiarity with the legislation on cults. The magazines *Sovety deputatov trudyashchikhsya, Sotsialisticheskaya zakonnost* [*Socialist Legality*] and *Sovetskoye gosudarstvo i pravo* have been instructed systematically to elucidate questions of the legislation on cults and its application in practice.

The work of the committees for control over the observance of legislation on cults under the district and city Soviet executive committees is being stepped up.

THE ORGANIZATION OF ATHEISTIC WORK

Local Party organizations are obliged to select Communists who will be responsible for the organization of atheistic work and who will unite around themselves groups of public-spirited people engaged in the propaganda and organization of atheistic work at enterprises and construction projects, on collective and state farms, in institutions, schools, Young Pioneer organizations, etc., and to strengthen control over the fulfillment by Communists of the Statutes' requirements for participation in the struggle against religious survivals.

It is recognized as desirable that large Party organizations, district committees, Party committees of production administrations, and city, province and territory committees have under their ideological commissions councils (or sections) on atheistic work that would consolidate and direct the work along these lines of Party, trade union and Y.C.L. organizations and committees, the Knowledge Society, cultural-enlightenment institutions and schools. Certain workers in the ideological departments of the Party committees should specialize in questions of atheism, especially in those territories, provinces, cities and districts where the incidence of religious belief among the population is relatively high.

Public volunteer atheistic councils (commissions, editorial groups) will be set up in central ideological institutions and in publishing houses and the editorial offices of newspapers and magazines.

Atheistic Indoctrination is the Concern of the Entire Party

I. BRAZHNIK

The Party Program has set the task of forming a scientific world view in all members of Soviet society, of fully emancipating their consciousness from survivals of the past, including religious prejudices. This is a prerequisite for the building of communism. . . .

As was noted at the June plenary session of the C.P.S.U. Central Committee, the imperialist bourgeoisie in its struggle against us is now placing its hopes chiefly in ideological subversion. It is counting on religion to further the penetration of bourgeois ideology into our midst. . . .

In recent times, the scientific and ideological-political level of atheistic work has risen significantly; it is becoming more and more diverse in form. Many people have broken with religion and become atheists, hundreds and thousands of religious communities have disintegrated. But many of our people are

Reprinted from I. Brazhnik, Partiinaya zhizn (December 1963). Translated in Current Digest of the Soviet Press, XVI, No. 9 (Copyright © March 25, 1964), p. 5.

still held captive by religious ideology. In this connection, the decisions of the June (1963) plenary session of the C.P.S.U. Central Committee pointed out anew the necessity of furthering by all possible means the intensification of work on forming a scientific world view and on the atheistic indoctrination of working people.

Questions of atheistic indoctrination were thoroughly discussed at an expanded session of the Ideological Commission under the C.P.S.U. Central Committee that was held at the end of November. Participating in it were Party workers, scientists, propagandists of atheism, and workers in higher and secondary schools, cultural-enlightenment and other ideological institutions. A report by Comrade L. F. Ilyichev, Secretary of the C.P.S.U. Central Committee, on "The Formation of a Scientific World View and Questions of Atheistic Indoctrination" was heard and discussed at the session. Comrade Ilyichev and those who spoke at the session emphasized that atheistic indoctrination is an important task of the entire Party. Party committees and local Party organizations have been called upon to employ all forms and means of ideological work for its solution. . . .

If the struggle against religion is to be waged successfully, it is necessary to have a clear view of the extent and character of the religious beliefs of the population in every specific area of the country, every community, collective, house and apartment, to know each believer, his views and attitudes and the reasons for his beliefs. Furthermore, it is important to arm our cadres (by teaching the principles of atheism in higher educational institutions and technicums, through the political-enlightenment network and schools for agitators, etc.) with the ability to expose contemporary religion, to work concretely and effectively with believers, encompassing all strata and groups of the population.

It must be acknowledged that until recent times some Party workers and propagandists were poorly acquainted with contemporary religion, since they did not understand its essence, the nature of its adaptation to new conditions, and the trends of its development. In the recent past, deviations from Lenin's decree on the position of religion and the church in our country were tolerated. Conniving in favor of clergymen took place, illegal privileges and indulgences; this gave them the opportunity to step up their activities, to violate grossly the legislation on cults, to nurture idlers playing the role of church activists and choristers. In Tadzhikistan and other Central Asian republics, the illegal activity of mullah-charlatans who shamelessly fleece trusting believers is tolerated to this day; one can encounter mosques masquerading as tearooms.

The inability to do battle against religion is manifested on the one hand by a complacent attitude toward it and on the other by the impatient desire of some zealous administrators to "be done

with" religion as quickly as possible, to be rid of the believers. . . .

It is hard to say which of these extremes is worse. One thing is certain: Both of them are inadmissible. But they also are indicative of something else. Not everyone sees that no alterations of church policies in specific conditions, no trimming of religious ideas, has ever changed or can change their antiscientific character, which is alien to communism. The letter of church sermons and even canons can and does change, but their spirit, basic content and objective meaning remain in opposition to a scientific world view, and religion as a whole is a component part of the hostile bourgeois ideology. First of all, the failure to understand this explains the fact that the unmasking of contemporary religious ideology has not yet become the basic content of scientific-atheist propaganda. Some workers, lacking the ability to expose it under present-day conditions, strike in the main only at the victims of religious ideology, while religious ideas themselves often remain intact.

Truly militant atheism presupposes irreconcilability toward religious ideology and a considerate attitude toward its victims, the believers. It is very important that everyone who wants to organize atheistic work correctly understand this side of atheism, know how religious survivals are concretely manifested in the consciousness and psychology of various groups of believers, and know the reasons for their religious feelings.

It is no secret that Party workers can be found among us who have an excessively general, somehow abstract notion of a believer. Such workers often fail to see even that religious people are by no means all alike. Zealous disseminators of religious ideology, wild fanatics who use the people's religious feelings for their own selfish purposes, often covering up their malicious anti-Soviet views by outward religiosity, are one thing. Ordinary believers, stupefied by religion, are quite another.

The C.P.S.U. Central Committee pointed out the necessity of distinguishing between the former and the latter last year in its resolutions on the guidance of ideological work by the Kuibyshev and Minsk Province Party Committees. The former should and must be brought into the open with the support of the power of Soviet law, exposing their ideological core to the eyes of atheists and believers alike. We have a different approach, a different method for the latter—the method of persuasion, a comradely, friendly approach. It should not be forgotten that such believers, together with atheists, are building communism. Many of them, sincere in their delusion, attempt to reconcile the irreconcilable—scientific truths and religious dogmas, the moral code of the builder of communism and religious precepts. A split consciousness, in which our socialist ideology occupies an ever larger place, is characteristic of the contemporary believer.

A necessary condition for work with believers is differentiation, taking into account the degree, the nature of, and the reasons for people's religious feelings. In each specific case, as V. L. Lenin pointed out, it is important to determine why people went astray, how they became lost.

VI

APPRAISALS
OF SOCIOLOGY

The following readings reflect the professional self-awareness of American and Soviet sociologists and the criticisms they make of each other's work and orientation. As has often been the case with the American side of our equation, it is more difficult to generalize about American sociology than about Soviet. It is not too difficult however to summarize the American views of Soviet sociology, partly because rather limited attention, critical or otherwise, has been devoted to the subject. By contrast, Soviet sociologists are dedicated to a massive critical analysis, or rather an "unmasking," of American sociological activities. This is not purely a matter of scholarly interest but also a programmatic task, a part of the ideological struggle which, however, benefits not only those determined to expose the wily maneuvers of American sociologists but also the curious Soviet sociologist who wants to become acquainted with the work of his American colleagues. Second-hand information is often better than no information.

There is an element of symmetry in the vision American and Soviet sociologists have of each other, although it does not necessarily reflect the realities of the two disciplines. Nor should we assume, if both sides accuse each other of the same failings, that they are in fact evenly distributed. To begin with, neither group believes that the other is free to pursue sociological research unhindered by ideological restraints or outside political-economic interference. Soviet sociologists see the Americans as lackeys of capital (or the Ruling Circles, the Power Elite, Neo-Imperialism, etc.); while in less colorful language many Americans tend to believe that Soviet sociologists are essentially servants of the State or the Party—primarily ideological functionaries in a respectable professional disguise. At the same time, American sociologists are willing to give more credit to Soviet sociology than vice versa; their criticisms are sorrowful rather than angry and they often try to ignore what is unappealing to American sensibilities by accentuating the substantive, less ideological aspects of the discipline. Even the highly critical discussions of Soviet sociology embody some attempt to strike a balance between denigration and praise. Perhaps this is merely a matter of professional conventions which require a modicum of objectivity or balanced judgment or the capacity to see more than one side.

Soviet sociologists tend to attribute more deliberate malice to their American counterparts than vice versa. Even when Americans comment on the absence of intellectual freedom in Soviet sociology or the presence of ideological cant, or on the lack of institutional-professional autonomy of Soviet sociology, their manner is regretful and they tend to voice the belief that these circumstances do not reflect on the integrity or intellect of their Soviet colleagues but on the limitations of their political environment. Such attitudes might be dismissed as hypocritical by the Soviet spokesmen but this would be a mistake. Most American sociologists concerned with or aware of Soviet sociology are hopeful well-wishers and not acrimonious critics. They prefer an optimistic projection of their hopes about the further liberalization of Soviet society and its reflection in a richer sociology, to a bitter, pessimistic appraisal. When Soviet sociologists consider American sociology, however, their basic posture is one of suspicion, hostility, and a readiness to seize on falsehoods and distortions. These two attitudes are rooted in the two generally different perspectives each side has of the other: Americans want and tend to believe that Soviet society is moving in a desirable direction—toward more freedom, more affluence, more modernity. (Of course, the American and Soviet conceptions of social progress or freedom are not identical.) A corresponding optimism is conspicuously absent from the Soviet perspectives of the future development of American society. They see the latter as riddled with crises and contradictions, and heading toward even more severe crises, indeed, toward disaster and collapse. The Soviet view is that things are getting worse, not better, in the United States, and that this situation should exist, according to the laws of historical development. It is logical that a doomed society could hardly sustain a flourishing, fruitful social science. If there is a crisis in American society at large, there must also be one in American sociology, and Soviet observers are not slow to provide an inventory of its signs and symptoms.

In criticizing American sociology, Soviet writers list its theoretical and practical fragmentation, its lack of a truly scientific theory (such as Marxism-Leninism), its "crude empiricism," its refusal to investigate serious problems, its apology of the status quo, its subservience to the ruling classes, its assistance in maintaining the capitalist system and in ideological disarming of the masses, its overly psychological, biological, quantitative, or abstract orientation (as the case may be), and its underplaying of the conflicts in American society. The list could be extended.

American criticisms of Soviet sociology are perhaps fewer in number but no less severe, even if presented in more moderate language and interspersed with some positive observations. American sociologists do make allowances for the youthfulness of Soviet sociology, which is seen as a mitigating its real shortcomings. In particular they criticize two failings: one is the structured, systematic neglect of important areas of inquiry, and the other is the refusal to draw a clear dividing line between fact and value, wish and reality, ideological proposition and empirical finding. (With some effort the two can be disentangled, more easily in some cases than in others, depending on the subject of the inquiry.) These difficulties are seen as the result of the commitment to vindicate, or at least to avoid reaching, conclusions which conflict with the propositions of Marxism-Leninism. Less serious, because they are more easily corrected, are the methodological weaknesses still reflected by the products of Soviet sociology. It is widely recognized that this shortcoming is directly related to the novelty of the discipline and can be remedied with little trouble; not so the other flaws, which cannot without changes in the entire intellectual-ideological climate—indeed, the entire social order.

We must also note that American sociologists, no matter how critical of Soviet sociology, are likely to accept without question all its findings which have negative implications for the Soviet social-political system. This is a propensity they share with their Soviet colleagues, who, in the spirit of "even American sociologists are compelled to admit..." draw more frequently and systematically on the works of Americans to supply ammunition for their criticism of American society and sociology.

What of the professional self-conceptions current among the two groups of sociologists? How do they see the accomplishments and weaknesses, the present and the future of sociology in their own society? We included two American writings which establish, so to speak, the perimeters of the outlooks current among American sociologists, ranging from bitter indictment and criticism, represented by Barrington Moore, to an optimistic and confident appraisal voiced by Shils.

Barrington Moore regards much of American sociology as an exercise in futility. He is primarily critical of its refusal to engage in significant issues and of its flight from reality, into either abstract theorizing or trivial research. He deplores its ahistorical orientation and its preoccupation with methodology. He foresees retrogression rather than progress.

Shils, on the contrary, feels that the discipline has made much progress in the U.S. He is primarily concerned with outlining the major stages in its development and the principal controversies surrounding it and in its establishment at the universities. He does not think that American sociology failed in its role as a provider of social criticism. His far more optimistic evaluation of the discipline is not unrelated to a more positive conception of American society than that entertained by Moore.

Aside from these two views, we might note that American sociology is, by and large, past the stage of the self-conscious examination of failures and accomplishments. Whatever they may be, they tend to be more readily accepted and the sharp disputes about the proper concerns, methods, directions, and ethical contents of sociology are fewer. American sociology is established, i.e., no longer overly anxious about its intellectual identity.

This is not true in Soviet sociological circles. In this respect, if no other, there are similarities between early American and present-day Soviet sociology. The position of Marxism-Leninism in Soviet society complicates the issue for our Soviet colleagues, since Marxism, besides being the foundation of the official value system and the major pillar of legitimation of Soviet society, is considered *a science of society, the* science of society. Thus, defining the exact nature of the relationship between Marxism and sociology is a delicate task, still not fully resolved. This also accounts for the affinity between Soviet philosophy and sociology and the fact that most Soviet sociologists are by training philosophers and economists or, to a lesser extent, journalists. There are also institutional identity problems in the Soviet Union. Sociology departments do not yet exist, although there are growing demands for establishing the academic-institutional autonomy of the discipline. At the same time there is little official or popular hostility toward sociology; in fact, it has become very fashionable in the last few years and is surrounded by hopeful curiosity and expectations which are exceeding its professional and financial resources. Many untrained amateur sociologists are active, and dilettantish investigations are being conducted by party or youth organization officials or journalists. While the underlying essential superiority of Soviet over Western or bourgeois sociology is never in doubt (at least as far as can be judged from what is printed), there is awareness of the weaknesses and growing pains of the discipline, particularly its lack of methodological sophistication. Soviet sociologists are also aware that their discipline could not exist without the changes in the political climate during the last decade, allowing a more open-minded, empirical, and at least partially objective approach to social reality. The emergence of Soviet sociology is also explained in terms of a response to the growing complexity of Soviet society and its social, economic, administrative, and other requirements.

We might offer a few summary conclusions as to the principal differences between American and Soviet sociology. Sociology in the U.S. is a far more developed and differentiated discipline, in which divergent orientations and schools coexist (though some are more popular or prestigious than others), in part because it is a more mature and more secure field of inquiry. Though the type of investigations and the problems studied are unequally distributed, no aspects of social life completely escape sociological scrutiny.

Much of American sociology is actual or implied social criticism. Sociology is fully autonomous, firmly entrenched in the universities, well endowed with research funds, and not lacking professional manpower. In society at large it is regarded with a mixture of scepticism, curiosity, and incomprehension, but it no longer attracts violent criticism. Soviet sociology is much more homogeneous in its theoretical orientation, more applied in its long-range goals, and more limited in its scope, partly for ideological-political reasons and partly for lack of manpower and research facilities. It focuses on industrial sociology, juvenile delinquency, family instability, leisure and time-budget studies, and problems of rural underdevelopment. Perhaps because of its relative novelty, it is characterized by more excitement and a sense of discovery than American sociology. The methodological differences between the two disciplines are the least significant. The association of the Soviet sociologist with officialdom is a burden which American sociologists do not have to face when collecting data.

ON AMERICAN
SOCIOLOGY:

The American View

The Calling of Sociology

EDWARD SHILS

...In its largely inchoate state, sociology in the 1920's scarcely engaged the public mind. *Middletown* was, perhaps, the first work of academic sociology that aroused and partially satisfied the need for self-understanding. It left no lasting

Reprinted with permission of The Macmillan Company from Theories of Society *by T. Parsons, E. Shils, K. Naegele, and J. Pitts, eds.* © *The Free Press of Glencoe, Inc., a Division of The Macmillan Company, 1961. Pp. 1407–1409, 1421–1424.*

impact other than the awareness that such efforts were possible and would be welcomed. *Recent Social Trends* and *The American Dilemma,* in the 1930's refreshed the memory of *Middletown* and prepared the way for a more general reception of sociology.

Except, however, for the occasional trajectory of an isolated report across the field of public attention, sociology lived mainly within the walls of the university, emerging only for material and then returning to digest and assimilate the facts of the outer world into an academic discipline. In the United States, it led a quiet, crudely respectable life, largely confined to the universities, where it was popular among students and disesteemed among the practitioners of the other academic disciplines. In Britain, it hardly found academic tolerance until the end of the Second World War, and its infiltration into the larger public occurred much later. In Germany, too, in the universities, sociology—after the First World War and until the beginning of the Nazi regime, when it went into exile—led a fruitlessly solitary, usually neglected, sometimes dimly stormy career. The seed of German sociology ripened only when it was transplanted to America. The seed of sociological theory could not grow without being fertilized by empirical research and by the diversification of its objects; the German universities offered little opportunity or motive for this kind of research. In France, its establishment was still scant and scattered; but, in so far as it existed at all, it was in universities.

So, for many years, sociology lived its life, despised and scarcely tolerated by publicists, amateurs and professors of philosophy, economists, and students of literature. Even when it obtained academic establishment, its lot was not a happy one. Its intellectual right to existence was often denied, even when it was allowed academic survival. Many were the debates in Germany about the possible existence of sociology—debates which often ended in negative conclusion. Sociologists themselves felt the pressure of this contempt and expended much energy in attempting to justify their existence—not by works, but by the demonstration that they had a proper place in the hierarchy of the sciences, that they were practitioners of a branch of learning that had an important subject matter and a logically defensible claim to respect. They spent much time in the assertion of methodological principles that received neither reinforcement nor guidance from a matrix of experience.[1]

Even in pragmatic America, the country of legendary theorylessness, sociology could not resist the feeling of obligation to prove itself by the argument that the fully assembled family of the sciences necessarily required the existence of sociology. No one was convinced by these arguments—the sociologists no more than the professors of other subjects with a longer history and more glorious achievements, in the strength of which their own mediocre efforts could seek protection. By an obdurate tenacity, sociologists finally found their vocation in research. In Britain and then in the United States, utilitarian and humanitarian concerns with the poor opened the way to empirical sociological inquiries. The roaring flood of immigrants to the large cities of the United States disturbed a Victorian calm. Humanitarian social workers were alarmed by squalor and delinquency, and sociologists came to share this alarm, which they tempered with curiosity and the pleasure of concrete discovery. At the end of the second decade of the twentieth century, the crisis in the relations between Negroes and whites—which had been uncovered and aggravated by the northward urban movement—gave sociologists a further extension of their domain. It also gave them a parochial self-confidence, which

[1] It was at this stage of sociological development that Henri Poincaré said that sociology was a science that produced a new methodology every year but never produced any results. Because there was so little substance, theory remained empty and directionless. Because there were no results, the methodological self-justifications of sociology remained empty and, quite naturally, possessed no persuasive powers.

muted their larger intellectual uncertainties. Within the universities of America—nothing much was happening in Europe—a sympathetic skepticism replaced disparagement among the neighboring disciplines: the conventional humanistic departments took abborrent note of the sociological goings-on, and the real sciences showed a patient condescension.

In the 1930's, American sociology underwent a marked expansion at its peripheries. Its population grew, and so did its output. It was helped by the Great Depression, by the influx of German and Austrian refugees, and by the coming of intellectual age of the first generation of offspring of the Eastern European immigrants of thirty years before. Research became more sophisticated through the development of a new statistical discipline, and through the improvement in interviewing techniques under the influence of psychoanalysis and the public opinion polling industry. Substance became a little more sophisticated under the impact of psychoanalysis, Marxism, and a greater knowledge of Emile Durkheim's and Max Weber's writings. These owed much to the influence of the Central European refugees and to indigenous developments in American intellectual life.

The Second World War gave sociologists the evidence they desired for their usefulness. Their employment, in many military and civilian roles, as sociologists, conferred on them the conviction of full-fledged intellectual citizenship that they had hitherto lacked. To this growth of a sense of belonging to the central circle of the intellectual cosmos, there corresponded a growing belief, among public and civic officials, publicists, and the educated public at large, that sociology had something to contribute to the national life.

Sociology has moved forward in the academic hierarchy. Its spokesmen are often among the leading lights of their universities. The other disciplines have become deferential or have at least suspended their derogation and replaced it by attentive distrust, furtive curiosity, or sheer resignation. Political science is eager to learn from sociology. Anthropology, solid in its knowledge of facts and linked with the real sciences through physical anthropology, is ready to assimilate a little of it. Even the proud economists are willing to concede its right of existence and to allow that it might have something to say. A few American sociologists are known and respected throughout the academic world. A few sociologists have become public figures in America, prophets on the same order as famous scientists and publicists; their fame has spread to England, Germany, and Italy—and even France, intellectually self-satisfied but discontented, has heard of them.

The improvised sociology of the war years, increased attention to American intellectual affairs after the war, and—probably most important—the change in fundamental sensibility opened the way for the admission of sociology into the theater of public intellectual life.

...The criticism of sociology from the outside has dwindled very markedly. There is still criticism, usually neither friendly nor understanding. It is not what it once was—neither in volume, in acerbity of tone, nor in the objects criticized. Thirty years ago, sociology was belittled for not being scientific. It was scorned because it could not make its case for a place in some problematical classification of the sciences. It was accused of gathering "mere" facts without regard to their meaning. It was charged with only rediscovering what every intelligent man already knew—and doing so only with great effort and high cost. It was derided for its preoccupation with the trivial. It was ridiculed for its propensity to cumbersome terminology of sometimes obscure and sometimes too obvious reference. It was abhorrent to humanists, who were apprehensive that its "scientific" procedures would destroy what is essential in the human being, would falsify his nature and degrade him. Sociology was accused of abolishing individuality, of degrading man by an inhumane determinism. It was charged that it aspired to the erection of a Machiavellian regime of scientists. The poverty of its historical knowledge and imagination was underscored; its excessive and unthinking readiness to obliterate the uniqueness of historical events by cramping them in general categories was often bemoaned.

Somehow, for no good reason—since what was valid in the criticisms still retains some validity—these accusations have evaporated. It is not that sociologists confronted these criticisms and refuted them by reasoned argument, or that the actual development of sociology rendered them completely nonsensical. They simply faded away. The critics and those who accepted their criticisms ordinarily were not very knowledgeable about sociology or perceptive of its deficiencies; the silence of their heirs is no more reasonable than the volubility of the preceding generation of critics. Sociology, by the magnitude of its exertions and the grand scale of its establishment, by some of its achievements, and especially by the groping discovery of its true vocation, has simply succeeded in imposing itself on its critics. Only a few echoes of the older arguments still resounded after the Second World War, and they were faint.

A rear-guard action expresses apprehension about the literary inelegance of sociology and its imperialistic relationship with the treasuries of foundations and governments. Sociologists are now accused—and often rightly so—of not presenting their thought in readily intelligible and grammatically correct language. But their intellectual right to do what they are doing, and the interest and value of their results, go on the whole, unchallenged. Only among the dwindling old guard does it still encounter the otherwise long-expired complaints that sociology has not properly defined its subject matter and its boundaries vis-à-vis other academic disciplines, that it is not really a science after all, that it is too concerned with the contemporary, or that it is one of the madnesses in which rich, enthusiastic, and juvenile America might well indulge itself, but which sober countries would do well to eschew.

Most of these external complaints belong to the past. They did not help sociology to outgrow its faults when the faults were more obvious and the criticisms more harsh and numerous. The criticism sociology receives from outside the circle of its practitioners is still, because of the limitations imposed by ignorance and ill-will, bound to be of limited helpfulness in the movement toward improvement. Improvements are necessary in every aspect of sociology, and not just because it is a science and, as such, committed to the postulate of progress. Its improvement, however, will have to be generated from the inside of the sociological enterprise, because only long exposure to and permeation by the sociological outlook can provide the preconditions for its deepening, differentiation, and extension, for the transformation it requires.

...Sociology is not a normative science according to the sensible but simplistic view that distinguishes between "norm" and "fact." It has, however, the greatest ethical—and therewith political—implications, by virtue of its construction of the elements of human action. Man's existence as a moral and rational being is a fact of a different order from his existence as a biological entity. Our perception of these properties in him is possible only through organs involving our own moral and rational powers. These qualities that we perceive in man call to the like qualities in ourselves and demand the recognition of an affinity that has ethical and political implications. Sociology also possesses ethical and political dispositions, by virtue of its ancestral traditions.

It is the fruition of some of the tradtions of sociological theory, in their confluence with the growing humanity of this still so distressing age, that leads toward the attenuation of the alienation that has long been characteristic of sociology.

The traditions from which the theory of action springs are not all equally oriented toward the more consensual position of contemporary theory. The powerful impulsion given by Hobbes and the utilitarianism that came from it contained an alienative tendency, which the moderate political views of its nineteenth-century proponents did not eradicate. Nor did Durkheim fully overcome such elements in his inheritance from St. Simon and Comte. For many years, sociology was viewed by its adherents as something outside the existing social order and as necessarily at odds with it. Sociology conceived of itself as a necessarily dissensual factor in society; its observations emphasized the dissensual processes, toward which it took a tone of severe disapproval.

It is still a proud boast of some sociologists that sociology is an "oppositional" science. Some of those who take pride in the oppositional character of sociology are former or quasi-Marxists —who, without giving their allegiance to Marxism, wish nonetheless to retain its original disposition.

It is, however, not only the Marxian influence in sociological analysis that has sustained this alienated standpoint.

It came into sociology much earlier than the first contacts of sociology with Marxism. Marxism and late nineteenth-century German sociology both drank from the wells of inspiration provided by German Romanticism and by the radical Hegelian version of alienation. Rationalism and scientism, from Bacon to Descartes, although not producing a substantive influence on sociology, helped to create the still prevailing culture of sociology.

The original association of sociological research with poverty and the miseries of the poor left a precipitate that has lasted long after these subjects have ceased to preoccupy sociologists. After first focusing attention on the miserable, the homeless, the parentless, the insulted, and the injured, sociologists later generalized this particular condition into one which was put forward as representative of all of modern society. While the subject matter of sociology was extended and even shifted from the poor into the other sections of society, and to problems other than the description of poverty and its attendant troubles, the original conception remained more or less intact. The great efflorescence of empirical inquiry took place in America in the 1930's, during the Great Depression and at the time of the awakening interest, among American sociologists, in Marxism, psychoanalysis, and German sociology. Very few of the investigators of that period underwent all these influences simultaneously, and not many bore them directly; but they permeated the intellectual atmosphere and could not be avoided. They increased the sophistication of American social sicence; but they also raised to a more abstract level the orientation that had, at least in urban sociological studies, already been very much alive, albeit in a more callow form. The great efflorescence of empirical inquiry in the second half of the

1930's—in industrial sociology, in the study of race relations, in the interest in mass communications, and in the introduction of psychoanalytic conceptions—differentiated but did not otherwise change the basic attitude toward contemporary society.

The movement toward theory that accompanied this lively activity in empirical research had no difficulty in giving a more elaborate expression to this "oppositional" science. The theory that came forth has been largely constituted by "middle principles." It has not aspired to reach the level of abstraction and scope of the sociological theory of action, and for this reason the fundamental divergences of the two orientations in sociology have not come to a full confrontation.

The numerous investigations into industrial sociology, mass communications, criminality and delinquency, educational institutions, elites, urban communities, adolescents, and the aged are conducted in a radically iconoclastic mood. This iconoclasm is not merely the realistic dissipation of erroneous views; it is almost always directed against authority. There is often an overtone to the effect that those in authority have acted wrongly, out of incompetence, blindness, or disregard for the common good. This is frequently not a result of a personal attitude; it is a product of the setting of the problem and of the establishment of a certain set of subject matters as the appropriate ones for investigation. The power of the tradition in which sociologists work dominates their own not especially strong or clearly defined moral and intellectual impulsions.

The result is an outlook that radically distrusts the inherited order of society. It is an outlook that has much to recommend it on the moral side and many intellectual achievements to its credit. It is nonetheless defective intellectually, and it will not sustain juxtaposition with experience or systematic theoretical reflection. Society is not just a "congeries of atomized individuals"; nor has bourgeois society "reduced the family relation to a mere money relation." Contemporary society does not consist of anonymous faces in the crowd; political life is not just a scene in which self-interested pressure groups determine every policy. Yet these are notions that many sociologists have believed until quite recently and many still believe. To the extent to which they have given up believing in them, they have done so out of submission to the pressure of a wider experience and of the theory of action, which has undermined the extremer utilitarian and romantic assumptions of this alienated sociology. Much of the resistance against the theory of action comes from this obstinately alienated sociology, which contends that the theory of action purports to see consensus where there is only a concert of interests or an equilibrium of coercive powers. The sociological theory of action is, moreover, charged with an unjustifiable attachment to the status quo, and with a conservatism that denies the reality of revolutionary social change because it is ethically and politically unsympathetic with such change.

The criticism, from the standpoint of the theory of action, of the alienated outlook of much of the sociological work of recent years does not rest on political grounds. The primary reason for criticizing the oppositional conception and outlook is that they provide a distorted picture of contemporary society and of society in general. They greatly overestimate the extent to which the Hobbesian state of nature prevails in society; they overestimate correspondingly the role of deception, manipulation, and coercion, and the degree of deliberate concerting of action by the elites against the rest of society. It is not that these observations are entirely without foundation; but they do not merit the preponderance that "oppositional science" accords to them.

There is another reason for rejecting this standpoint. Insofar as it is not entirely contemplative, it is manipulative because it does not accept the possibility of a consensual modification of conduct through self-control. It is not necessarily committed to a manipulative attitude by its analytical schema. That is too seldom sufficiently well worked out to impel commitment, and often its inclinations are in the direction of the theory of action. The manipulative orientation is a product of a political and ethical attitude that has little to do with the fundamental sociological orientation.

The argument for the alienated standpoint, aside from the allegation of the correctness of the results it produces, is twofold. First, it is alleged that it is the most fruitful point of departure for understanding a society; and second, it is alleged that the main and inescapable function of sociology is to be the critic of its society. The first argument need not detain us here. The second is more germane to our consideration of the calling of sociology. One may grant its correctness and yet deny that the critical attitude necessarily entails the kind of criticism that has implicitly and explicitly been associated with this standpoint in sociology during the past century.

If the theory of action is capable of integration with certain ethical standpoints and not with others, then it stands to reason that it also affords a range of alternative points of view from which to criticize the performance of any particular society. If the sociological theory of action is an act of self-interpretation, it also carries with it the possibility of self-criticism, individual and collective. In neither case does it provide either the sole foundation of criticism or a single determinate standpoint. It simply leaves open the possibility. Indeed, if by "criticism" is meant rational criticism, which is intended to be effective through appeal to the cognitive and ratiocinative powers of those to whom it is addressed, it might be said that only a theory having much in common with the theory of action is in a position to criticize. Otherwise, criticism must take the form of manipulation, subversion, etc.

...Sociology, both in its theory and in concrete analyses, possesses, in contrast with Marxism, a critical potentiality all the greater for the flexibility which its implicitness confers on it. It appeals more to the mind of the contemporary intellectual by the freedom of experience it permits; it allows a man to make his own personal contact with reality, to test it by his own experience, and to criticize it in a way that does more justice, as he sees it, to that experience. This is especially true of concrete sociological research on particular topics.

Can the same be said for sociological theory? Would a theory that is not just a theory of *contemporary Western* society be equally attractive for those who wish to make contact with their society and to criticize it realistically? Sociological theory as it stands today is, to too large an extent, an abstraction of concepts formed in the historical context of the second half of the European nineteenth century, and extended by the assimilation—in part—of the experience of the United States in the twentieth century. As such, it has the possibility, often realized, of illuminating major trends of contemporary and recent society. It is a sort of shorthand description of the chief features of "modern society," with occasional extensions to non-Western and nonmodern societies. It is the aim of general theory to become genuinely universal and transhistorical, and there is nothing in principle that would obstruct the attainment of this aim. If sociological theory attains a generality of scope and a differentiation that render it equally applicable to all societies of the past and present, will it still retain the potentiality of criticism and self-location that makes it so attractive today?

With respect to the former, it might well be that the more genuinely *general* and abstract the propositions of sociology become, the less they will contain of a genuinely critical response to any contemporary situation. Criticism that is not just a grim hopelessness about the condition of man is always particular and concrete. It is directed against particular persons, particular classes of persons, and particular institutions; it is about things that exist *at present* and that have a prospect of being made *not to exist in the future.* The terms for referring specifically to such conditions are rather concrete— in any case, more concrete than the abstract language that a well-founded sociology of universal scope would be likely to employ. The key words that are crucial in a critique of society have not only a relatively particular reference; they also have a tone that they share with current opinion and that they lose when they are replaced by terms of greater generality, of greater historical and territorial inclusiveness.

These observations refer only to a general theory of sociological analysis. They do not apply to a theory of "middle principles." The latter kind of theory will undoubtedly still exist even under conditions of a higher theoretical achievement. There is no necessary incompatibility between these two kinds of theory, which will, in any case, as they already do in their present very imperfect forms, overlap and intertwine with each other.

The "theories of the middle range" will be the vehicles of the critical outlook that is essential to sociology. In its function as a critique of any contemporary society, Marxism will be replaced by middle principles and not by a general sociological theory. As the theories of "the middle range" become more general and abstract, the critical element will become more attenuated and more generalized. An element of ethical or moral orientation will always remain, by virtue of the fundamental categories of intellectual orientation that are integral to sociology; but it will be in the same relationship to the concrete critical disposition as serious publicistic analysis bears to moral and political philosophy.

What, then, of the value of sociology as self-interpretation, as "self-location," which is so closely related to the critical function of sociological theory? A similar process will be at work. Sociological theory, as it becomes more abstract and general, will be more significant as the location of man in general. Its value in the location of particular and more concrete, historically singular variants of the human possibility will diminish as it turns its attention toward the determinants of human possibilities on a more universal scale. It will then provide the instrument of self-location of the sort that "philosophical anthropology" presents, and more differentiatedly and less nebulously than that considerable intellectual achievement at present permits.

Strategy
in Social Science

BARRINGTON B. MOORE, JR.

Let us now examine the ideal social science sets up for itself. What do its leading practitioners think it ought to be? What are the characteristics of the intellectual structure they are trying to create? Here again I shall speak mainly of sociology with an occasional glance at other social sciences.

As physical science moved away from the mechanical determinism of the nineteenth century, social science tended to abandon the corresponding grand syntheses of historical determinism to the point where the latter are now generally in very bad repute. In their place there has grown up a body of deductive theory, widely referred to as structural-functionalism. The key idea in this body of theory, the reader may recall, is the view that for every society there exists a certain limited number of necessary activities or "functions," such as obtaining food, training the next generation, etc., and an equally limited number of "structures," or ways in which society can be organized to perform these functions. Essentially, struc-

tural-functional theory searches for the basic elements of human society, abstracted from time and place, together with rules for combining these elements. It gives the impression of looking for something in human society to correspond to the periodic table of elements in chemistry.[1]

The ultimate objective in this line of thinking is the establishment of abstract quasi-mathematical formulae about human society from which it should be possible to derive the particulars of human behavior in any specified situation. Or to put the point in another fashion, the proponents of this view hope to subsume more and more individual facts that now appear as isolated observations about soicety in a single logically coherent structure. This viewpoint corresponds very closely with the natural science ideal of being able to reduce all phenomena to a series of related propositions.[2] The fundamental statements in this structure are expected to be universal propositions of scientific law. Let us see to what extent social science has succeeded in this goal of imitating natural science.

Reprinted by permission of the publishers from Barrington Moore, Political Power and Social Theory, *Cambridge, Mass.: Harvard University Press, Copyright, 1958, by the President and Fellows of Harvard College, pp. 125–140.*

[1] Talcott Parsons', *The Social System* (Glencoe, 1951), is the leading statement of this point of view, though the above characterization is, of course, my own.

[2] "A process is any way or mode in which a given state of a system or of a part of a system changes into another state. If its study is an object of science any process is assumed to be subject to laws, which will be stated in terms of determinate interrelations of interdependence between the values of the relevant variables." Talcott Parsons, *The Social System,* p. 201.

Natural scientists seek in the main two kinds of universal propositions. One takes the form of a static correlation, asserting that when A occurs B also occurs, as when we say that water freezes at 32 degrees Fahrenheit. Ordinarily natural scientists try to go beyond a mere static correlation to explain why the relationship holds. The other kind of proposition takes the form of a mathematical function,* asserting that X varies as Y does, as in the relation between pressure and volume in a gas. Again some kind of an explanation is given. While scientific explanations are tied together as firmly as possible, ultimately they take the form of descriptive propositions.

When we compare this model with the actual performance of social science, the contrast is striking. As even those most enthusiastically committed to the model will admit in candid moments,[3] social science, after some two hundred years, has not yet discovered any universal propositions comparable in scope or intellectual significance to those in the natural sciences. The situation does vary, of course, from one discipline to another. Sociology, as one of my colleagues is fond of remarking, constitutes from this standpoint the science with the hollow frontier, since it lacks any core of established theory, or any framework of general propositions strong enough to convince a substantial part of the profession.[4] Psychology is perhaps somewhat better off. Pavlov and those who have followed in his footsteps have established through laboratory methods a fairly large body of propositions. However, their significance in explaining more than a tiny segment of human behavior remains very doubtful. Though the explanatory power of Freudian theory is much greater—perhaps even too great—its scientific status is less secure. Classical economics managed to erect at one time a comprehensive and elegant theory to organize its subject matter in a scientific manner. Somehow the facts have changed since the formulation of the theory. It may be significant that one of the leading figures in the tradition of classical economics, Professor Frank H. Knight, is also one of the most sharp-tongued opponents of a literal-minded transfer of natural science methods into the study of human affairs.[5] Whatever the variety among the different disciplines, it is safe to assert that the generalizations of social science nowhere approach the range and cogency of those in physics or chemistry.

The fact that we do not yet have any laws in social science comparable to those in the natural sciences does not by itself prove that such laws will never be discovered. Nevertheless it justifies raising once more the question whether social science is on the right track in making the search for such laws its chief *raison d'être*. The differences between natural science and social science may concern more than the relative crudity of social science. The logical structure of the kinds of knowledge we

---

* It should perhaps be pointed out that the mathematical concept of function is not identical with the sociological one.

[3] In conversation with the writer more than ten years ago, Professor George Lundberg, the leading advocate of a strict natural science model for sociology, confessed that he was at a loss for a good example of a scientific generalization and was unhappy that the only one he could point to was a rather limited one about migration. See his *Can Science Save Us?* (New York, 1947), p. 41. His remark, as far as I can recollect, was one of the earliest impressions leading me to doubt that the search for scientific laws should constitute the primary task of sociology.

[4] Compare George C. Homans, *The Human Group* (New York, 1950), chap. 1.

[5] See for example his "The Limitations of Scientific Method in Economics," in *The Ethics of Competition and Other Essays* (London, 1935), pp. 105–147.

seek in social science may not be identical with that in the advanced natural sciences. It may be profitable to consider this possibility through examining the relationship between abstraction and additions to knowledge.

Natural science and social science both make use of abstraction from the raw data of experience in order to frame concepts and theories. Nevertheless the procedures of abstraction vary from one field of knowledge to another in accord with the nature of the materials studied and the purpose of the inquiry. In many fields, perhaps all of them, there is a certain tension between the desire to do justice to all the facts and the need to frame a logically coherent and esthetically satisfying theory. There is in other words a tension, perhaps an irreducible one, between particulars and universals.

Abstraction is not an end in itself. Indeed the end or purpose for which the scientist makes abstractions and seeks propositions lies, to some extent, outside the realm of empirical science. Even strict positivists now recognize this point. Philipp Frank has recently asserted that the validation of scientific theories "cannot be separated neatly from the values which the scientist accepts."[6] Therefore any system of abstraction that omits facts which the investigator wants to understand is automatically inadequate. There are then strong grounds for suspecting that we have so few universal propositions in the social sciences because such propositions frequently do not give us the kind of knowledge we really seek.

In human affairs the mere fact of uniformity or regularity, expressible in the form of a scientific law, may often be quite trivial. To know that Americans drive on the right hand side of the street is to know something that permits predictions about American behavior and meets all the formal requirements of a generalizing science. Such knowledge does not, however, meet the criterion of significance. The same comment applies to many generalizations that social scientists seek with a technical apparatus and logical rigor that contrasts ludicrously with the results. Here is a recent example. From a study of "Male Sex Aggression on a University Campus" we learn that:

Of the 291 responding girls 55.7 per cent reported themselves offended at least once during the academic year at some level of erotic intimacy. The experiences of being offended were not altogether associated with trivial situations as shown by the fact that 20.9 per cent were offended by forceful attempts at intercourse and 6.2 per cent by "aggressively forcely attempts at sex intercourse in the course of which menacing threats or coercive infliction of physical pain were employed." ...A 3×3 table yielding a Chi square significant at the .05 level suggests that episodes of lesser offensiveness are concentrated in the fall and more offensive episodes in the spring.[7]

The professional journals are full of similar articles where careful methodology is used on trivial problems. Unfortunately most of them are not as amusing as this one. If the demonstration of uniformities like these were all that social science had to offer, it would constitute no more than an enormous diversion from more important problems.

Uniformities in social behavior become significant for us only when they concern important problems, such as freedom and compulsion. What is im-

---

[6] See the introduction by Philipp Frank, editor, in *The Validation of Scientific Theories* (Boston, 1957), p. viii.

[7] C. Kirkpatrick and E. Kanin, "Male Sex Aggression on a University Campus," *American Sociological Review*, Vol. XXII, No. 1 (February 1957), 53.

portant is not a matter of subjective whim, but is the consequence of a specific historical situation. The important regularities in human behavior, as well as some of the trivial ones, are found within the context of historical change. For example, one can observe recurring patterns in the behavior of a slaveholder and still other patterns in those of a feudal lord. There may even be some common features in all the major historical forms of domination. To find them would be a worthwhile task, and in an earlier essay I have suggested possible common features in the "natural history" of systems of domination. But we certainly cannot stop there, even if we arrive at such a point. Accurate knowledge requires that we understand each social type, slaveholder, feudal lord, capitalist entrepreneur, and socialist bureaucrat, within its proper historical context, that is, in relation to previous forms and possible subsequent ones.

Above all we must not make the mistake of thinking that some universal necessity inheres in social relationships that are limited to a particular historical epoch, such as capitalism or, for that matter, socialism. To abstract from all historical situations in the hope of discovering some pan-human or universal kind of social necessity does not seem to me a very promising procedure. Can we really make any worthwhile generalizations that apply equally well to the Stone Age and to twentieth-century America?[8] Perhaps one cannot answer this question with a flat negative in advance, though I remain most skeptical. One certainly has the right to object vehemently to any science that eliminates from its vision all change

that has taken place between the Stone Age and the twentieth century merely for the sake of formulating universal propositions like those in the natural sciences.

Let us look more closely at some of the procedures modern social science theorists use when they try to arrive at universal propositions. As noted earlier, these scholars often tend to abstract from the reality of historical trends in order to concentrate on resemblances and differences in the hope of formulating scientific laws. For them, history, if it is used at all, becomes merely a storehouse of samples. Using historical data, one can supposedly discover the social correlates of democracy, tyranny, class struggle or class peace,[9] and the like. The existing body of theory should, from this standpoint, indicate the likelihood or unlikelihood of finding a particular combination of traits. Historical and social facts are then drawn upon as if they were colored balls from an urn, and the results subjected to tests for statistical significance in order to disprove the hypothesis or derive additional support for it.

The trouble with this procedure is that it starts with the assumption that the facts of history are separate and discrete units. This assumption is basic to statistical analysis. "The fundamental notion in statistical theory," says an advanced theoretical text, "is that of the group or *aggregate,* a concept for which statisticians use a special word—population. This term will be generally employed to denote any *collection of objects* under consideration, whether animate or inanimate. The notion com-

---

[8] Here the Oedipus complex comes to mind, but there are grave doubts as to its universality. See B. Malinowski, *The Sexual Life of Savages* (New York, 1929).

[9] Rather than cite other writers, I will point to one of my own works that displays all the faults criticized here. See my article, "A Comparative Analysis of the Class Struggle," *American Sociological Review,* Vol. 10, No. 1 (February 1945), 31–37.

mon to all these things is that of aggregation."[10] The modern social scientist searches for invariant laws that govern the relationship among these atomized observations reflected in statistics. Such laws are implicitly or explicitly thought to apply to masses of single facts of equal importance, which are expected to display at least the statistical regularity that molecules do in a gas under specified conditions.

It is in this conception, I think, that the modern social scientist goes astray. Though I too would reject any thorough historical determinism, I do not believe that the significant facts of history are mere mechanical aggregates. Instead, they are connected with one another over time.

The point may be clearer if we refer to a concrete problem. Franz Neumann has pointed out how dictatorship has at certain times in history served to prepare the ground for democracy by breaking the resistance of privileged social classes.[11] This is a crucial point that helps us to understand dictatorship, class struggles, and democracy in a context of continuing historical growth. Now, such a point would necessarily be hidden from an investigator who proceeded by some widely used procedures in deductive social science. Dictatorship and democracy would be separated into air-tight compartments with carefully worked out definitions of each. Then other facts would be sorted into neat piles labeled "dictatorship" and "democracy." The whole process by which one social structure passes into the other would become invisible. Such a procedure might, to be sure, uncover some

important and unsuspected connections. One cannot reject it as totally useless. But the most significant problem would remain hidden.

I doubt very much that the logic of sampling is at all appropriate to historical problems of the type just mentioned, where the investigator is studying the change from one type of social structure to another. In sampling techniques, as shown by the familiar image of drawing balls from an urn, the researcher examines the numerical distribution of traits in the sample to make inferences about the universe from which they are drawn. His main problem is whether or not the same is representative of the whole. The historian too looks at some of the facts in order to make inferences about the rest of the facts. He also, in other words, has to make a connection between the parts and the whole. But the historian's connection has a different form. The notion that he works with frequently is that of stages of historical development. Now any given stage of historical development is to some extent the product of a preceding stage and the source of subsequent stages. Even the most anti-determinist historian uses such a notion. This kind of connection is missing, as I see it, in the logic of sampling. In an atomized universe the numerical character of the sample does not "cause" the universe to have a corresponding numerical character, nor does it by itself affect the character of subsequent samples drawn from the same universe.

From a strictly logical standpoint one could avoid the preceding difficulties by including the concept of time as a specific variable, and working with some form of mathematical function. Historical writings often do have the logical form of a mathematical function, as when they assert that political changes have accompanied economic

10 M. G. Kendall, *The Advanced Theory of Statistics* (5th ed., Hafner; New York, 1952), I, 1. [Emphases added.]

11 Franz Neumann, *The Democratic and the Authoritarian State* (Glencoe, 1957), chap. ix.

advance or economic decline. Perhaps even some of the Hegelian insights into revolutionary upheavals as the final result of slow cumulative structural change can be expressed in the form of discontinuous functions. Mathematics does not limit itself to the study of quantity, and cannot be excluded from any field of knowledge merely because the latter seeks knowledge that goes beyond quantitative relationships.[12]

Whether one can leap from such observations to the claim that mathematics can weave a web around *any* body of facts is a question I am not competent to answer. This claim does seem to imply potential omniscience in the manner of a Laplace, and therefore strict determinism, a position from which natural science has been retreating rather rapidly for some years. This question does not seem to be a very fruitful one to ask just now. We can easily afford to wait until a mathematical genius encompasses all history with his mathematical net, and decide then if it improves our understanding. In the meantime there is work to be done.

The real question then concerns the gains and losses involved in mathematical abstraction. Here again we cannot give a firm answer because we cannot know what discoveries in mathematics may come along that might some day constitute a powerful analytical tool. But we do know in a general way that we do not want our gains in logical rigor and ease of manipulation to be at the expense of too much historical content.

Nor can mathematical sophistication do much to help us out where our data

12 On this ground I disagree with the Hegelian strictures against mathematics presented in Herbert Marcuse, *Reason and Revolution* (London, 1941), p. 144.

are inadequate for other reasons. There is no use drawing intriguing curves and computing intricate functions on the basis of badly collected statistics. Such devices merely conceal the real problem. Good judgment on all these questions requires training on problems that lie outside mathematics as such. We can use the mathematical notion of function, but it will not do everything for us. Current overuse and misuse of statistics and abstract mathematical models in social science stem in my opinion partly from the failure to present fledgling students with other adequate criteria for distinguishing important truth from accurate triviality. For this reason it is not a problem that can be solved merely through the improvement of mathematical techniques.

Certain virtues in the mathematical way of thinking deserve explicit recognition here. The use of mathematics compels the investigator to state his propositions in an unambiguous manner that automatically permits a tight chain of deductions leading to a firm result. If the original premises are corrcet, and the chain of deductions made without error, the truth of the conclusion is guaranteed. The difficulty, on the other hand, is that at present the act of putting statements about society in the form of mathematical premises requires such simplification that the essential elements in the facts are likely to be lost or seriously distorted. The lack of ambiguity in the original propositions may therefore be spurious. The trouble here may lie as much in mathematics as in social science proper. So far, at any rate, the results have not been striking. As one of the most enthusiastic advocates of mathematical methods in the social sciences has observed recently, "Even the most ardent optimist would not claim that mathematics has yet led to important discoveries in the behavioral sciences."[13]

The decline of the historical perspective and the rise of a formalist deductive tradition in search of laws has been accompanied by an increasing static bias in much contemporary social science. For this there are several reasons. The search for categories that apply without reference to time or place easily introduces a static bias unless we are extremely careful to notice the historical limits of our generalizations. The very notion of a scientific law implies a relationship that holds whenever and wherever it occurs. Naturally if one could really demonstrate that any given law really held for human affairs, it would be nonsense to assert that formulating such a law and writing it down introduced a static bias into thinking about society. What often happens, however, is something else. The investigator discovers, or thinks he has discovered, a relationship that actually holds for a limited period of history, and extends it unjustifiably into the future. Most scholars are too cautious to make flat statements like this in print, and a clear example from recent writings does not come to mind readily. The bias is in the air more than in print. Not long ago social scientists used to say to one another in informal conversations that Soviet experience "proved" the need for inequalities of income, prestige, and authority in any form of industrial society.[14] Actually Soviet experience merely tends to demonstrate the necessity for such inequalities at a particular

stage of industrial and technological growth. The Stalinist era also shows that totalitarian methods are effective for catching up rapidly with advanced industrial countries. Future technological progress, such as more advanced automation, may make possible very gross changes in the structure of authority, prestige, and inequality. If we looked at this problem with nothing but dubious laws in our heads about the "functional imperatives of industrial society," we could easily go astray. Though the notion of functional imperative has its uses and can lead to valuable insights, we must be careful to realize its limitations.

Closely related to the preceding difficulties are those derived from the importation of equilibrium theory into social science, which may also produce a static bias. In equilibrium theory the key assumption is that any social system tends toward a state of rest in which the conflicts and strains among its component parts are reduced to a minimum. Most people are aware that in real life this movement toward a state of rest may not actually take place. Some try to get around the difficulty by asserting that the equilibrium assumption is not one about empirical facts, but a purely theoretical assumption that serves to order the factual material into a consistent whole.[15] No one would object if this were the case, but it is difficult to see how the equilibrium viewpoint can account for certain fairly well established facts. For example, in the judgment of some historians, the attempts made by later Roman emperors to strengthen the empire contributed to the growth of feudalism, or, in other words, to the

[13] Paul F. Lazarsfeld in his "Introduction" to *Mathematical Thinking in the Social Sciences* (Glencoe, 1954), p. 3.

[14] My own writings came close to taking this position. See *Soviet Politics: The Dilemma of Power* (Harvard University Press, 1950).

[15] Compare Talcott Parsons, *The Social System*, p. 481.

replacement of one social system by a quite different one. In technical language, meeting the "functional imperatives" of the system had destroyed one social system and led to its replacement by another. Again, in modern times the New Deal may be plausibly regarded as an attempt to shore up American capitalism. But the effort to do this led in turn to marked modifications of American society. Perhaps structural-functional theory could somehow account for these changes by saying that these efforts to restore equilibrium led to unanticipated and dysfunctional consequences. We may leave aside the question of what gain to real knowledge such statements bring. To my mind they amount to throwing the equilibrium assumption overboard by saying the tendencies toward equilibrium are unexpectedly producing change.

The Hegelian dialectic with its conception of developing contradictions that lead to intermittent abrupt changes provides, one may argue, a better heuristic guide to the explanation of many important processes of historical growth. In any case it would appear that the decision whether equilibrium theory applies or not is basically an empirical one, to be decided after careful study of the facts.

We come then to the conclusion that a static bias and a tendency toward triviality pervades much contemporary social science quite largely, though not entirely, because of the model that it sets for itself in copying the successful procedures of the natural sciences. Other social factors play a part in this. They may even be the more important ones, though I have purposely left them aside to concentrate on the smaller problem of the way in which social science may limit itself through its own ideals. In closing this part of the discussion it may be worthwhile to men-

tion briefly some of the social factors which favor the present direction of social science.

One factor may be that the United States, where the kind of social science just discussed flourishes best of all, is at the present juncture a prosperous country at a high point in its power. American society has some of the qualities of an *ancien régime,* though it is worthwhile remembering that the Soviet Union has a good many of these too. The critical spirit may not flourish just now because our social and economic problems are mild relative to those of other times and other places. Furthermore, the historical point of view is likely to remind us of the transitory nature of social institutions, generally an uncomfortable thought in an *ancien régime.*

At a more detailed level of analysis, one may note that many modern social science research projects are very expensive affairs. They require the collaboration of a large number of persons with a variety of skills and training. Often their cost exceeds several hundred thousand dollars. It may be unfair to remark that the results are not always in proportion to the costs. But it is true that the present situation in social science is the exact reverse of what prevailed during the great theoretical discoveries in physics in the nineteenth and early twentieth centuries. Revolutionary advances were made with limited funds and, by modern standards, crude laboratory equipment. Today, in social science at any rate, the effect of large grants is to give to those in control of the allocation of research funds a highly strategic position for determining which problems will be investigated and which ones will not. It is also true, of course, that older systems of economic support for intellectuals, such as patronage and direct dependence on the market, exercised some influence over the ideas developed by professional intellectuals. The varying impact of all these factors is certainly not understood in any detail. But it is clear that in older times patronage and the market did not succeed in shutting off thought critical of the existing social order. Under the present situation the need to be a cooperative member of a research team may do more to stultify original and critical thinking than direct economic pressure. At the same time it is difficult to conceive of the foundation director who will readily allocate several hundred thousand dollars for a research project that is likely to come up with conclusions that reflect very seriously on important interest groups in the United States. The result is that creative thinking has to take place, if it can take place at all, mostly in the interstices between Big Theory and Big Research.

ON AMERICAN SOCIOLOGY:

The Soviet View

Learned Henchmen of Capital

S. EPSTEIN

Books on sociology are not gathering dust in the shops. It is already impossible to find the recently published collections "Marxist and Bourgeois Sociology Today" (based on materials from the Fifth World Congress of Sociologists) and "Contemporary Philosophy and Sociology in the Countries of Western Europe and America." The two-volume "Sociology in the U.S.S.R.," published as late as 1965 and containing research by Soviet sociologists, has

Reprinted from S. Epstein, Novy mir, *No. 6. Translated in* Current Digest of the Soviet Press, *XVII, No. 30 (Copyright © August 25, 1965), 11–12.*

sold out just as fast. Andreyeva's book "Contemporary Bourgeois Empirical Sociology" was also snatched up.

The appearance within a brief period of a number of large works on sociology and this demand for them are in themselves symptomatic. In fact, until just recently sociology, the Cinderella of our social sciences, was kept in the background. Even the very word "sociology" was in effect banned. Social research, like the study of facts in general, was neglected. Many sociological terms and concepts elaborated in the classical writings of Marxism were banished from science.

In recent years the situation has changed and greatest attention has been focused on sociology. But G. Osipov, the author of the book under review,[1] does not overestimate our successes in this field. Only the first steps have been taken here. Not all of the consequences of the personality cult have as yet been fully overcome in this field, G. Osipov writes.

The renewed interest in sociology is connected with enhancing the role of science and scientific analysis in the conduct of public life and overcoming elements of subjectivism and arbitrariness. The nature of the science is also changing; it is beginning to conform more and more to the Leninist requirement: "A little more knowledge of facts, a little less logomachy pretending to be communist points of principle."

G. Osipov set himself a difficult task —to present in systematic form all the trends of contemporary bourgeois sociology. He criticizes its basic conceptions, shows the substantial changes in this science in the period of the general crisis of capitalism, reveals its class nature and epistemological roots as well as its place in the present-day ideological struggle, and shows what philosophical conceptions underlie various sociological theories.

Individual sections of the book are devoted to the treatment by bourgeois sociology of such problems as the social consequences of automation, the use of atomic energy, and urbanization.

In the U.S.A., in the words of the American sociologist R. Merton, there are 5,000 sociologists and each has "his own sociology." There is no single bourgeois sociology. At times schools are distinguished only by nuances. In addition, sociology breaks down into a

[1] G. V. Osipov, "Contemporary Bourgeois Sociology (A Critical Essay)." Science Publishing House, Moscow, 1964. 416 pp.

mass of specialized, petty "sociologies" —"the sociology of the city," "the sociology of the country," "the sociology of the family," "the sociology of crime," "the sociology of alcoholism," "the sociology of small groups," "the sociology of the elite," "industrial sociology," etc. There is even a "sociology of advertising" and a "sociology of prostitution."

What is most characteristic of bourgeois sociology as a whole, disregarding differences between individual sociologists?

First of all, its custodial function: This is how it's always been, this is how it always will be! "The majority of sociologists occupying leading positions in contemporary sociology," writes the English sociologist L. Cozier, "are far from regarding themselves as a body of reformers.*** They concentrate their attention on problems of adjustment rather than conflict, on social statics rather than dynamics. Of key importance to them is the maintenance of existing structures and the ways and means of doing this." They justify the status quo referring sometimes to the laws of biology, sometimes to the nature of man and sometimes directly to divine decree. Every violation of "stability" or "equilibrium" is social "disorganization." "As soon as they" (sociologists—S. E.) "stop performing this task," writes G. Osipov, "they are deprived of all their privileges and benefits—chairs, high salaries, means for carrying out empirical research, etc. —and are declared 'Reds' or 'undercover Communists.' "

Today's sociologists, as a rule, are distinguished from their predecessors by pessimism. It is now difficult to prove that capitalism is the best of systems. Bourgeois science cannot fail to reflect the fact that capitalism has entered a period of decline. Human society, states G. Moreno, is in a stage of dangerous illness. "Doesn't the entire universe," he writes, "begin to resemble more and more an enormous insane asylum, with God as the head physician?" "Society of fear," "schizoid culture"—these terms have become current in sociology.

A sick society must be treated. Moreno proposes a magic means against the fatal ailment—"social psychology." The neo-Malthusians call for birth control, the technocrats for handing power over to the engineers, the school of "human relations" for arranging cooperation between workers and administrators. Others recommend the regulation of economic life. As a rule these recipes are intended merely to remove the negative consequences of capitalism while preserving inviolate the social structure that gives rise to them.

Bourgeois sociology is, naturally, against struggle and does not acknowledge its inevitability. Revolution is regarded as an anomaly, a "pathological" phenomenon brought about by a great number of accidental causes. Equally abnormal are conflicts between workers and enterprises. Their causes, the sociologists teach, lie not in economics but in defects of the human psyche, just as it is not imperialism but the "aggressive nature" of man that gives rise to war. Leaving aside the problem of classes, the sociologists concentrate their attention on small social groups (particularly groups of workers in enterprises), trying to determine their behavior and subject it to their control.

Apart from a small group of sociologists who constitute the brain trust of the monopolies and seek out "great ideas" for the justification of capitalism, the great majority of sociologists have taken refuge in "microsociology," in petty practical details. "Despite the fact that wars and exploitation, poverty and injustice, and lack of confidence poison the life of people and society or threaten their very existence, many sociologists treat problems so remote from these catastrophic phenomena that they appear irresponsibly petty," stated the prominent American sociologist R. Merton.

G. Osipov dwells in detail on the characteristic feature of bourgeois sociologists—their neglect of the popular masses. They depict the people as a senseless crowd moved by blind instincts. They exalt an "elite" of select personalities, "chief conductors." They have even fabricated an "iron law of oligarchy." According to a statement by the American sociologist E. Lederer, the leader is endowed with "charisma," that is, prophetic powers, and is the spokesman of the will of God. Some bourgeois scholars attempt to demonstrate that there is a special genius peculiar to heroes and prophets. American sociology has created a cult of "powerful personalities" of business. Subjective idealism, voluntarism, empiricism have always been peculiar to bourgeois thought.

The author does not confine himself to an analysis of bourgeois theories; he cites factual material, figures in particular, against them. In doing so, he draws his figures chiefly from the works of bourgeois scholars themselves, who at times are driven by the very logic of research to correct conclusions. Lenin, warning against a nihilistic attitude to bourgeois science, instructed Marxists "to learn how to sever their" (bourgeois professors.—S.E.) "reactionary tendency, to learn how to pursue their own line and to fight against the entire line of the forces and classes hostile to us." Lenin himself often gave us examples of such a dialectical approach to bourgeois science (take even his attitude toward the Taylor system, in which

Lenin saw both a reactionary and a progressive side). There is something to be learned from Western sociology in the field of techniques and methods of research, the selection and processing of information.

A struggle is being waged in bourgeois sociology between reactionary and progressive forces. Certain sociologists take a critical approach to capitalism. Suffice it to mention W. Mills or M. Harrington, author of the book "The Other America," which has been published in Russian in the U.S.S.R. A different approach is necessary to the various sociological schools, as G. Osipov rightly points out.

Whoever reads the book, and many will read it—scientific workers, students, workers on the ideological front —will get a picture of Western sociology and find many interesting thoughts.

Unfortunately, the book is unevenly written and is not easy to read. To some degree this derives from the author's intent. He has tackled a very broad theme, and this has resulted in a certain schematism. The book often suggests a summary through which hundreds of names flash. The most prominent sociologists (Durkheim, Weber, Comte) get only a few short pages, sometimes even less. In a mere three pages (169–171) he cites 17 definitions of culture given by bourgeois sociologists and just as many refutations. We are told, for instance, that the "functionalist" school, one of those influential in contemporary American sociology, "works out means and methods of preserving and maintaining the existing system of oppression and exploitation" (p. 154). But our legitimate curiosity as to how it does this remains unsatisfied.

Nor is the reader told what useful things may be learned, at least in the field of specific research, from our

adversaries. But perhaps applied sociology exceeds the bounds of this work and requires special investigation.

We also read in the book: "Sumner attempted*** Small attempted*** Cooley attempted***" Or: they "developed" Spenser. Inasmuch as the word is in quotation marks, the reader is at a loss to know whether they did or did not develop. On page 332 it is said that induction predominates in American sociology, but on page 333 we read that the empiricist sociologists deny the importance of induction. On page 334 it is explained that they "exaggerate the importance of analysis and induction and ignore the role of synthesis and deduction."

The shortcomings of G. Osipov's work are, alas, peculiar not only to it and are typical not only of sociology. Of course, a scientific work is not belles lettres, and the book under discussion is not even intended as a popular scientific book. But is dryness, the difficult form of interpretation through which the reader must force his way to reach the content, an indispensable companion of erudition? Shouldn't even a scientific book carry the reader with it? Should the reader "entering into science" abandon hope beforehand of any emotion and prepare himself to surmount the language and similar barriers by the sweat of his brow?

M. Baskin, who contributed an introduction, recalls that rarely in a scientific treatise can one find so much "heart," so many burning and passionate words against the representatives of backward views, as in Marx's *Kapital*. And what about all the works of Lenin? What is involved is not merely the reader's convenience but also the effectiveness of the scientific work.

The stylistic errors of the book are all the more annoying in that the author has permitted them in a big and useful work. He relies on the research of many Marxists sociologists, both Soviet and foreign. His book is an important step in the development of a reviving science.

Certain Characteristics and Features
of Bourgeois Sociology
in the Twentieth Century

G. OSIPOV

THE ORIGINS OF MODERN BOURGEOIS SOCIOLOGY

Modern bourgeois sociology is not merely a set of theoretical constructs whose function is to provide a "scientific" validation of the right of present-day capitalism to exist. It is a distinctive weapon of state monopolist organization, one of the means for the ideological disorientation of the masses and for the modification of their consciousness in a direction advantageous to the ruling class.

Bourgeois sociological research has been prepared to perform this function by a rather lengthy evolution, in the course of which the incompatibility of its fundamental concepts with scientific materialist principles of analysis of social life has become more and more obvious. Four major stages may be traced in this evolution.

The first stage, resulting from the socio-political changes occurring in a number of the countries of Western Europe during the first half of the 19th

Reprinted by permission of International Arts and Sciences Press, Copyright 1962, from Soviet Sociology, *No. 8, (Winter 1962) 48–56.*

century, coincided with the publication of the six volumes of Auguste Comte's *The Course of Positive Philosophy* (1830–1842), in which he set forth the basic principles of a "positive" science of society, which he termed sociology. The positivism of Comte's sociological views was based on his faith in the stability of the capitalist society that had come to take the place of feudalism, and also in the rapidly advancing progress of science. The social and political changes that had occurred were regarded by Comte as an obvious witness to the arrival of the epoch of "social order" and "social progress."

Research into the foundations of "social order" and "progress," according to Comte, should become the major objective of sociology, which he declared to be one of the exact social sciences. Reflecting the social processes of the first half of the 19th century, the sociology of Comte was, as it were, a distinctive reaction to the profound and insoluble crisis of bourgeois political economy due, on the one hand, to the decay of the school of David Ricardo in England and, on the other, to the ever more evident limitations of Utopian socialism. Comte built his sociological concepts without considering the economic factors in society. From that time on the separation of social from economic processes was in general transformed into one of the guiding principles of bourgeois sociology.

Comte's sociological system did not stand the test of time. The relative stability and seemingly progressive nature of bourgeois society were disturbed by periodic socio-economic earthquakes, accompanied by economic chaos, mass demonstrations of the working people, etc. Efforts to find a foundation for social order and progress within the bourgeois system itself proved vain. One school of sociologists (M. Kovalevskii, C. Ellwood, etc.) published sharp criticisms of Comte, proposing to replace the concepts of "order" and "progress" by the more neutral concepts of "organization" and "evolution," which corresponded to the political and economic status of capitalist society. Another segment directed its attention to non-social and technological factors which, they claimed, sufficed to explain social life in its entirety.

Thus did bourgeois sociology begin the transition to the new stage in its development.

The second stage is characterized by the appearance of a number of trends in sociology: the biological with its numerous branches (Herbert Spencer and others), the mechanistic (G. Kern and others), the technocratic (Thorstein Veblen and others), and many others. The appearance of these trends was associated with a loss of faith in the stability of capitalist relationships and an attempt to find criteria for the improvement of social organization outside the life of society itself, which is increasingly subjected to spontaneous change, anarchy and disharmony. A significant role in this process was played by the rapid development of the natural and technical sciences and, in particular, by the vast influence of the evolutionary teachings of Darwin. The founders of the new sociological teachings regarded social phenomena in the light of the laws of the organic and inorganic worlds. Thus Herbert Spencer drew an analogy between biological and social organisms. His follower, Paul von Lilienfeld, identified biological with social organisms; Thorstein Veblen declared the social mechanism to be "measurable" and believed that "energy" bonds could be used to measure it, etc. The appearance of all these trends testified to a tendency toward reductionism, an effort to impose the logic of the natural and technical sciences upon the phenomena of social life and to introduce into that life, on the basis of cognition, ties between the social and non-social phenomena of "progress" and "order."

Gradually these trends, too, lost their significance. The ever-deepening contradictions of bourgeois society also exercised a decisive influence upon the nature of development of science and technology. Evolutionary development in these fields was replaced by irregular progress, reinforced by the general disorganization of the capitalist system. In the investigations of bourgeois sociologists social phenomena as such began to emerge into the foreground.

The third stage owed its origin to the changes in economics, politics and ideology, characteristic of modern capitalism. The earlier forms of private property were replaced by the property of monopolies, which are corporate bodies. An endless number of mass organizations appeared. The further division of labor resulted in the appearance of various specialized groups. The individual as such lost, to a considerable degree, his former significance and was transformed into a representative of some particular social group, class, party, organization or whatever. The ever more complex interweaving and conflict of interests of various social groups made it possible to pass over to consideration of social progress as an interaction among groups, free of the influence of natural and other "external factors." This turning point in the development of bourgeois sociology was the work of the Austrian, Ludwig Gumplowicz, and the American, Lester Ward. The first held that only "purely" social phenomena (the social group), presented *sui generis,* could be the subject matter of sociology. The second attempted to explain the motivation of group behavior by the operation of so-called "psychic forces." A peculiar process began whereby bourgeois sociology was "liberated" from orientation toward non-social factors.

The conversion of sociology into a science of "social groups" and "group processes" was a distinctive type of reflection of the rising contradictions of modern capitalism. The course of development of bourgeois society as a whole, spontaneous and not subject to social control, is combined with rational organization and relatively successful functioning of certain of its components (individual industrial enterprises, corporations, associations, and so forth). Shying away from analysis of the nature of modern capitalist society as a whole, bourgeois sociologists proceed to investigate its component parts. By a study of the rational organization of the latter, they strive to subordinate the fundamentally uncontrollable evolution of capitalism to conscious social control.

The refusal to investigate the development of society as a whole and the transformation of the "social group" into the major subject matter of sociological investigation constituted, at the same time, the beginning of the transition from theoretical to empirical sociology. The German philosopher and sociologist Wilhelm Dilthey offered a theoretical justification for the inevitability of this transition. He sharply denied the pretensions of Comte and Spenser to an interpretation of social processes in their entirety. His point of view was empirical. Identifying the previous sociology with pseudoscientific alchemy and recognizing the "social group" as the subject of sociology, Dilthey asserted that the social group could be understood only with the aid of a number of specialized social theories. Dilthey's views had a major influence upon the later development of sociology. Thereafter one saw the beginning of abandonment of investigation of fundamental social problems and a transition to the elaboration of a number of specialized sociological theories embracing various aspects of the most diverse social groups. This new trend was typified by bourgeois sociologists such as W. G. Sumner, A. Small, G. Tarde, E. Durkheim, F. Giddings, F. Tonnies, G. Simmle, Max Weber, G. Cooley, K. Mannheim, E. Ross, W. Thomas, R. Park, C. Ellwood, and others. Their doctrines formed what amounted to a theoretical foundation on which empirical sociology was erected during the three following decades.

The transition to empiricism and the appearance of a number of specialized sociological theories signified an abandonment of analysis of the social organism as a whole as it combines the most various social processes. As a result, a break-up of sociology into a number of special disciplines was observed. A theoretical validation of this process was provided somewhat later by the French sociologist Emile Durkheim.

The fourth stage in the development of modern bourgeois sociology embraces primarily the past three decades. This is the period of break-up of the colonial system of imperialism, the weakening of its position in economic competition with socialism, and the acute exacerbation of all its internal socio-economic contradictions. Under these conditions bourgeois sociology has been converted into a practical means of shaping human thought in the direction necessary to the ruling classes. The change in the role of sociology in bourgeois society was combined, in the words of bourgeois sociologists themselves, with the development of a consistent system of empirical sociology and its reduction to psychological terms.

The center of attention for bourgeois sociologists became the problem of human behavior in social groups and the factors governing this behavior. They sought explanations for group behavior, joint acts by human beings and the like, in the operation of psychic factors. However the "psychic forces" of Ward, which bear solely on the motivation of personal behavior, could not serve as the basis for a theory of group behavior. The combination of psychological factors determining the acts and behavior of a social group is fundamentally a new thing when compared to the combination of psychological factors determining the behavior of the individual. In a group the individual loses, to a considerable degree, the characteristics distinguishing him alone, and his behavior comes to be determined fundamentally by the combination of psychological factors characteristic of this group as a whole. In order to determine the factors influencing group behavior, it was necessary to find the connecting link between psychology and sociology. This link was social psychology, which arose as an independent discipline as a consequence of sociological investigations in the sphere of group behavior.

According to bourgeois sociologists, the subject matter of social psychology consists of what are termed behavior-patterns, customs and their development, which are examined in isolation from the economic system of the given society.

With the appearance of social psychology and its merger with sociology for all practical purposes, the term "the social group" comes to be employed only "to create a complete picture of the interaction of all factors acting on the psycho-social level, as with the term 'organism' which is employed to establish a general picture of all factors operating on the biological level" (J. Moreno, *Sociometry*, Russ. ed., Moscow, 1958, p. 177).

Subsequently the doctrine of social groups was influenced by Gestalt psychology, as a consequence of which the social group came to be regarded as an isolated psychological phenomenon, and by the ecological teachings of Ernst Haeckel which provided the impetus for the founding of what was called "social ecology." It holds that the origin and development of the social group as a distinct socio-psychological phenomenon is due to geographic, industrial and other factors.

Thus, whereas in the 19th century the individual personality held the center of the attention of bourgeois sociologists, in the 20th century the social group, as a distinct socio-psychological complex, came to be the main factor considered. The individual is considered only as a part of this group.

PSYCHOLOGIZATION OF CONTEMPORARY BOURGEOIS SOCIOLOGY

The behavior of social groups in approximately equivalent geographic and other circumstances often shows distinct differences. Solution of the question of the causes of this phenome-

non became possible for bourgeois sociologists with the appearance of social
anthropology as an independent science.
Its separation from physical anthropology was determined to a considerable degree by research in the field of
"tribal psychology" done by American
social psychologists, particularly Ruth
Benedict. In the course of her study of
the psychology of two Indian tribes and
of the factors determining differences in
human psychology and causing it to
change, she came to the conclusion that
all these factors may be received to culture differences, and these differences in
her opinion are determined by various
relationships among geographical, biological, technological and other factors.

Thereafter the concept of culture and
cultural ranges became the basic concept of sociology. "The nature of
human society and the direction that
may be taken by the life of society may
be understood," says the American sociologist Charles Ellwood, basing himself
on the conclusions of the social anthropologists, "only if we have understood
the distinctive factor separating the
human group from the animal world.
This distinctive factor is culture. Only
human groups are possessed of culture
in the form in which we know it. In
the broad sense of the term, a culture
consists of 'behavior-patterns,' socially
acquired and socially transmitted
through the mediation of symbols and
their corresponding meanings" (C. A.
Ellwood, "Social Evolution and Cultural Evolution," *J. Appl. Sociol.*, XI,
p. 303).

According to bourgeois sociologists,
"behavior-patterns" are based on a system of values elaborated in the course
of mental development and accepted by
the given social group. There is a great
variety of opinions with respect to the
concept of the essence and nature of
social values. The definition of values
most generally accepted (although

with various qualifications) by bourgeois sociologists is that offered by the
American sociologist Henry Pratt Fair-
child in his *Dictionary of Sociology.* "A
value," he writes, "is an article of
faith. Its existence may be discovered in
the process of social or psychological
research, but neither its real significance
nor its truth are demonstrable. At the
same time, they (values—G.O.) are
only the motives of all rational conscious behavior" (*Dictionary of Sociology,* N.Y., 1944, pp. 331–332). By
the reduction of social values to psychological terms and their consideration
as a particular system of "behavior-
patterns" accepted in the given society,
the bourgeois sociologists attempt to
present that which is dominant (but
special) as the universal; in other
words, they proclaim the class interests
of the capitalists to be the interests of
society as a whole. As a consequence of
this approach, they treat the social conflicts of capitalism not as clashes among
"behavior-patterns" characteristic of
different classes and social groups, but
as conflicts between a given system of
"behavior-patterns" and the individual.

But this poses a problem. How is one
to explain the deviations in individual
behavior from established "behavior-
patterns" that underlie changes in
"social values"—i.e., the problem of
"culture versus the individual"? The
process of individual behavior is regarded by bourgeois sociologists as a
process of adaptation of the individual
to the value system established in the
given social group. "Usually," writes
the American investigator Nikolai Timascheff, "sociologists emphasize the
form of reciprocal interaction between
the individual and his culture (as they
do between him and his society). The
individual personality takes shape
under the influence of the culture characteristic of the society to which he
belongs. Its formation occurs through

channels of socialization, of which the family is the most important. But socialization is never complete. Moreover, the majority of cultures, if not all, leave the individual a given degree of freedom and initiative. It is in terms of the latter that an individual performs acts that result in a change in culture" (N. Timascheff, *Sociological Theory*, New York, 1955, p. 100).

The motivation of a given behavior (adaptation) by an individual is explained by bourgeois sociologists to a considerable degree by return to the "psychological forces" of Ward and their biological foundation. In the words of Engels, "The awakening consciousness of the fact that the existing social scheme of things is irrational and unjust, that 'the rational has become the irrational, that a blessing has become torment,' is only a symptom of the fact that changes have taken place imperceptibly in the modes of production and forms of exchange, to which the social system, rooted in the old economic conditions, no longer applies" (*Anti-Dühring*, Russ. ed., 1953, p. 251). Being incapable of understanding this, bourgeois sociologists attempt to base their search for motives of change in the individual behavior of man, on certain of the concepts of Freudianism and the latest data in physiology, neurophysiology and psychology.

Thus, contrasting the individual and the "social structure," the American sociologist Talcott Parsons takes as his point of departure the Freudian dichotomy between the ego, driven by instincts, and the superego, constituting a system of "strategic social roles." "From the viewpoint of the sociologist," writes Parsons, "the most important problem in the relationship between psychoanalysis and the social structure is the possibility of employing these categories (the ego and superego—G.O.) to explain the social structure and its

changes as such. This is a field in which it is particularly dangerous to approach the explanation too directly, inasmuch as the structure of the personality and the social structure do not correspond" (T. Parsons, *Essays in Sociological Theory*, 1954, p. 336).

Regarding the lack of correspondence between the personality and the "social structure" as the basis of all social changes, Parsons sees the cause for these changes in the fact that the individual cannot find an appropriate sexual outlet for the discharge of his psychological energy and is compelled to sublimate and transfer this energy to something else that will provide it with appropriate satisfaction. Therefore the human psyche turns to social, economic and cultural activity.

This explanation of the motivation of "individual adaptation" leading to social changes is by no means the only one of its type. Some bourgeois sociologists supplement it with references to motivation induced by disturbance, guilt feelings, a desire to experiment, curiosity, subconscious defense against imagined and real dangers, and the like. In his book *The Psychology of Communication* the American social psychologist S. Schachter, considering the motivation of the human desire to communication, states that man hopes, through communication, "to unburden his soul," and so forth. But all bourgeois sociologists have in common a recognition of the subconscious and of various instincts as the motive forces of individual behavior, resulting in deviation from the accepted value system, and then in social changes interpreted in accordance with the Freudian idea of "sublimation."

The meaning of this large-scale resort to psychoanalysis is manifested in the efforts of a number of bourgeois sociologists to interpret the impelling motives of individuals inclined toward revolution as being allegedly in the sphere of the "psychologically abnormal." The neo-Freudian "theories" to the effect that a man who actively opposes the existing social structure of society is primarily a "personally maladjusted" individual suffering from personality disorder is adopted with increasing frequency.

The behavior of social groups is given a rational explanation by bourgeois sociologists only as long as it remains static. Changes in them are ascribed to irrational motives. Most recently, in conjunction with rising interest in the physiology of higher nervous activity, in particular the teachings of Pavlov, an attempt has been made to explain the behavior of the individual leading to social changes, in terms of physiological conditioning of mental processes. The bourgeois sociologists assert that the latest achievements of neurophysiology, such as the discovery of new hormones, make it possible to control certain psychological acts of the personality. However, they leave completely out of consideration the decisive, social conditioning of the human psyche.

In analyzing the social group and holding the individual personality to be a socio-psychological unit in it, bourgeois sociologists inevitably return to the individual, explaining the "kinetics" of the group by the acts of the individual and ascribing those of the individual to unconscious psychological processes. The process of psychologization of contemporary bourgeois sociology reaches its logical end by referring its problems back to subconscious strivings of the individual personality which are not subject to further sociological analysis.

The psychologization of sociology has resulted in conversion of all the bourgeois schools of sociology which have hitherto been regarded as mutually "hostile," into "absolutely compatible and absolutely convergent" trends.

The interaction of the individual with the factors surrounding him is analyzed as a social act occurring "in a situation that exists independent of the wishes and goals of the given individual. But action within the limits of this situation takes place with the employment of possibilities which are subordinate to the control of the individual and are based on knowledge of a system of goals and desires" (ibid.).

This "situation," which different bourgeois sociologists interpret differently, constitutes what they term a "social situation." An act, understood as a process of interaction between the individual and the "situation" and leading, under given conditions, to social changes, takes the form of a system: "the acting individual—the social situation" (T. Parsons, The Social System, 1954, p. 4).

The chief fault in the theories of bourgeois sociologists lies in the fact that, having identified the concept of "social situation" with that of the "socio-psychological," they attempt to analyze "purely ideal" phenomena apart from their relationship to and conditioning by material factors. Making a fetish of the socio-psychological, they completely ignore the fact that any social phenomenon (social situation), which is in the final analysis conditioned by an economic factor, is, in Engels' expression, nothing but the result of the collision of a multiplicity of individual wills, "and each of these wills becomes what it is again thanks to a great number of circumstances of life. Thus, we have an infinite number of mutually intersecting forces, an infinite group of parallelograms of forces, and one common result emerges from this intersection. . . ." (K. Marx and F. Engels, Selected Works [Izbrannye proizvedeniia], Vol. II, pp. 468–469).

Individual social phenomena cannot be understood if they are torn out of their interrelationship and examined in isolation from the major laws of the development of society, for they constitute special manifestations of those laws.

STRUCTURE AND THEORY OF EMPIRICAL SOCIOLOGY

Sociology consists of a number of special theories revealing various aspects of a single whole, constituting the subject area of the given field of scholarship. It was Emile Durkheim who laid the foundation for the dissection of sociology into a number of independent fields. In the past decade this process has been significantly reinforced. In the United States alone there are more than 100 different sociologies (industrial sociology, agricultural sociology, urban sociology, the sociology of religion, of the family, of crime, of alcoholism, of politics, and so forth). Each of these sociologies studies particular social groups. In the study of these groups various common empirical theories are employed. They constitute sets of extremely abstract empirical concepts. Essentially these theories are a conglomeration of distinctive social ideals expressing the class consciousness of the bourgeoisie and its dreams of social unity and solidarity. In the opinion of bourgeois sociologists, attainment of these ideals is possible by empirical investigation of the given social situation and appropriate social control.

In their analysis of social life they reason as follows: Social integration, leading to social solidarity both within the given social group and of society as a whole, is a good. The socialization of the individual, leading to conformity of the interests of the individual with those of society, is also a good, and so on. These processes are capable of being understood and explained rationally. Those social phenomena, i.e., "social disintegration" or "social disorganization," which cannot be rationally understood and explained by bourgeois sociologists, are proclaimed to be anomalous deviations from the rational norm, due to psychological disturbance in the given individual. In bourgeois sociology, study of all these deviations constitutes the subject area of what is termed "social pathology." Adherents of that school regard operation of the general laws leading to disorganization of the entire social system of capitalism as random pathological deviations (the theory of social deviations) from standard, rational norms, in the behavior of individual personalities. Thus, all that corresponds to the social interests of the bourgeoisie is rational, and what does not correspond to them is irrational. Investing the social objectives of the bourgeoisie with the form of sociological theories, the bourgeois sociologists are simultaneously attempting, with the aid of empirical investigations, to develop a system of means for influencing the social behavior of a given group, and thereby of establishing constant "social control" over this behavior for the purposes of preserving and strengthening bourgeois social organization.

These social goals of the modern bourgeoisie have been reduced by bourgeois sociologists to a consistent and extremely abstract system incorporated in the general structure of empirical sociology, which includes three major fields: a) investigation of the social process; b) study of the structure and functions of social groups; and c) research into the interrelation between the individual, the social group and social processes.

In the eyes of empirical sociology, the social process is the process whereby conflicts arise and are resolved between social interaction, which is constantly changing in nature, and the relatively stable structure of social relationships. Ignoring the materially-conditioned nature of social interaction, regarding it merely as psychological, and assigning to this psychological phenomenon the role of the motive force of the development of human history, bourgeois sociologists substitute psychological contradictions characterizing the contradictions not of classes but of the separate individuals comprising a given social group for the material contradictions of capitalist society.

Basing themselves on this interpretation of social process and social contradictions, bourgeois sociologists develop various methods and means allegedly making possible prompt discovery of change in the nature of social interaction and adaptation of the structure of social changes to it. In this regard, many bourgeois sociologists base themselves, in the first place, upon the sociometric method of Moreno, the essence of which resolves to a procedure for "discovering" changes in the structure of social interaction and to adaptation of social relationships to this structure (by shifting individuals from place to place). Secondly, they rest upon the theory of "Verstehen" of Max Weber, according to which the observers themselves, as they accustom themselves to a given situation and, if possible, completely identify themselves with the real participants in this situation, reproduce in thought the social interactions of interest to them and thereby "penetrate" into their essence. Thirdly, they base themselves upon the theory of strategic games, which makes it possible to determine the nature of contradictions and to find the most rational means of resolving those that have become conflicts. Fourth and last, they base themselves upon the method of statistical correlation between the totality of the acts of a given individual and actions that follow.

The lack of a scientific methodological approach to analysis of social reality has the consequence that all the methods listed above can, at best, make possible merely a temporary solution of some particular contradiction without at all touching upon the universal social contradictions that are constantly giving rise to an endless multiplicity of the most various special and partial contradictions.

The problem of the interrelationship between the individual and the social group, between personal and social ideals, is the subject area of what is called "socialization" theory. Bourgeois sociologists divide all social groups into two major types: "primary groups," or communities, and "secondary groups," or societies. Groups of the first type are based upon the sense of personal contact, blood relationships, etc. (for example, the family), while groups of the second type are based upon specialized functions (for example, political, legal and other social institutions). Each of these is characterized by a solidarity specific to it, which gives rise to the social unity or disunity of these groups. Thus, according to Durkheim, groups of the first type achieve unity due to their homogeneity; groups of the second, due to specialization of functions, etc.

The American sociologist Charles Cooley attempted to offer an explanation for the interdependence of these two types of groups, explaining it by specialization of social functions. Thus, a group of the first type predetermines the process by which an individual acquires the major values, ideals and points of view underlying social solidarity. A group of the second type determines the influences or pressures upon the individual, effected by means of communications, public opinion, social institutions and so forth.

Abstracting the social group from all social relationships prevailing in bourgeois society and regarding it as a closed social phenomenon, bourgeois sociologists analyze its activity in the categories of function and structure. They define the activity of a social group as a striving to attain particular goals; this is what constitutes the function of the group. The form of organization of this activity constitutes the structure of the group. Analysis of the structure-function relationship is proclaimed by bourgeois sociologists to be fundamental in the investigation of the given social group. The cause-effect relationship is replaced by the structure-function relationship.

Empirical studies in this field are based upon what are called theories of social order, social disorganization, social deviations, social planning, etc. The basic content of all these theories resolves itself to determination of the factors giving rise to social changes, and to an attempt to establish, on the basis of a rational cognition of these factors, the appropriate social control over social changes so as to eliminate the disorganization of social life and establish social order, i.e., what the bourgeoisie has dreamt of ever since it won political ascendancy.

With the conversion to empiricism there came a transition in the social function of bourgeois sociology. The place of the earlier sociology, confining itself to a general theoretical interpretation of social processes, was taken by an applied sociology, offering an operative system of theories and means whose function it was to direct the consciousness of man along the channel needed by the bourgeoisie. Empirical sociology may be compared, within certain limits, to applied eugenics. Eugenics offers a means for what is called the

physical renewal and strengthening of the human race. Empirical sociology proposes a number of methods and means for the subordination of the human consciousness and for shaping it in the direction needed by the bourgeoisie.

Many industrial enterprises in the U.S.A., West Germany and other capitalist countries have established a ramified system of sociological and psychological laboratories with a very specific practical objective—the development of methods and means of systematically influencing human consciousness. It is not for nothing that enormous sums are contributed by the Rockefellers, Morgans and others for purposes of empirical studies, as is admitted by the bourgeois sociologists themselves.

TOOLS OF SOCIAL RESEARCH AND DEGREE OF GENERALIZATION OF RESULTS

Basing themselves upon the general empirical theories set forth above, bourgeois sociologists connect researches into the greatest variety of social groups. In so doing they make use of a variety of tools of social investigation, which there is no need for us to pause to analyze. It need only be observed that among these most various methods (tools) of empirical investigation there are those that may, after critical reinterpretation, be used for specific sociological researches based on Marxist-Leninist theory. Specifically, note must be taken of the possibility of critical investigation of the rules of observation and interview developed by various bourgeois sociologists: the method of the participant observer; mass surveys; various social scales; the use of mathematical methods in analysis of certain special social phenomena; various forms of social model-making in choosing the subject of investigation (stratificational, probabilistic, multi-stage, multiphasic); mathematical methods of determining the degree of error in various types of social sampling, etc.

Definitely of interest is the use of mathematical methods to determine whether the number of persons to be surveyed is sufficient (representative) to yield objective answers, characteristic of the given social group, to the questions posed. In conducting mass surveys of particular population groups, bourgeois sociologists have arrived at the conclusion that errors occurring in mass interviews by the sampling method are more or less standard. They depend upon the size of the sample and the diversity of the material, but make it possible to employ a mathematical formula to determine the standard error.

Mathematical methods make it possible to determine the number of persons who have to be questioned for the purposes of a survey to determine the public opinion prevailing in a given social group. However, this opinion cannot always correctly reflect the given social reality and is frequently distorted. Techniques developed by the sociology of knowledge are widely employed to determine the degree of falsity of individual or social (group) consciousness.

All these tools of social investigation may, upon critical reexamination, be of truly scientific value only if their use rests upon a scientific methodology. To conduct specific sociological researches means a study, with the aid of Marxist-Leninist methodology and the special methods (techniques) of sociological analysis, documents and records, regional and factory statistics, systematically to observe social phenomena, to conduct interviews with workers, peasants and the intelligentsia, for the purpose of a deep cognition of life and a scholarly generalization of the data collected and systematized.

Here we find one of the fundamental distinctions between Marxist sociology (the theory of historical materialism) and bourgeois empirical sociology. Marxist sociology, being the universal theoretical science of society, regards specific sociological investigations as a means of resolving most important general problems of theory as they face society. However bourgeois sociology pursues the objective of "curing" particular "ills" of capitalist society, while completely ignoring the general social processes of which these ills are particular manifestations.

Bourgeois sociologists hold that the process of deriving general conclusions from sociological research may be carried out on four levels.

The first level is that of deriving primary empirical conclusions pertaining to a particular social phenomenon. The second level is that of obtaining more general results: empirical generalizations.

The generalizations of empirical sociology are confined to these two levels. Bourgeois sociologists reject any other conclusions, claiming that they are allegedly not subject to verification. They say that social thought has not yet "matured" to the point of further generalization and that inadequate empirical material has been gathered for that purpose. Before sociology can rise to the level of drawing general sociological conclusions it must, according to Merton, elevate itself to a third level.

The third level, in his opinion, is the elaboration of theories of "the middle range." This process must include: a) carrying out broad-gauge empirical researches in various fields of social life; b) systematization and comparison of the scientific results of these investigations and elaboration, on the basis thereof, of specific sociological theories for various areas of social life; and c) carrying out broad-gauge sociological investigations on the basis of these theories. Merton, for example, regards conclusions with respect to the shaping of behavior stereotypes of various classes to be a prerequisite for the development of a specific theory of this nature and of a "middle range" theory.

The fourth level is reduction of the "middle range" theory to a unified sociological theory. Efforts to create such a theory are, it happens, currently underway. Such efforts are being made by at least three schools of sociology— microsociology, the sociology of natural science, and analytical sociology.

The microsociological school seeks to extend the theory of small groups to the social process as a whole. Its founder, J. Moreno, who regards the basic conflict of modern society as that between the "official" and "concealed" structures, due to the presence of "attractions" and "repulsions" within the latter, proposes that a so-called "microsociological revolution" be carried out: that the entire population of the globe be resettled on the principle of mutual "attractions" and "repulsions."

The sociology of natural science, a school headed by the American sociologist George Lundberg, applies the laws of natural science to social processes as a whole. Such an approach inevitably leads to reductionism.

The analytical school, represented by Parsons and his followers, seeks to create a unified social picture of the world through the device of various connecting links. This school advances an extremely abstract and scholastic theory constituting a set of various speculative constructions.

It is significant that all these schools rest, to a substantial degree, upon various psychological trends: microsociology upon Gestalt psychology, the

natural science school upon behaviorism, and the analytical school upon Freud and neo-Freudianism.

*   *   *

The limitations upon, and then abandonment of, theoretical thinking in sociological investigations and the reduction of the results of these researches to narrow empirical conclusions and generalizations—this is the historically inevitable cul-de-sac entered by bourgeois sociology in the middle of the 20th century.

Its spokesmen carry out numerous empirical studies at the greatest variety of industrial enterprises, in offices and the like, and on the basis of generalization of the results of these investigations they strive to develop a system of "definite conditions," the creation of which would enable them to control and plan the social behavior of a given social group at any given moment in a given enterprise, a particular office, etc. Sometimes they are successful in doing so. But the rational organization and conscious control of the given specific social phenomenon inevitably come into conflict with the true nature of the development of capitalist society as a whole. As a consequence, the "ideal order" and "ideal unity" of social groups, previously deemed stable, are destroyed, the antagonistic contradictions of capitalism become more profound, and the revolutionary movement of the masses grows irrepressibly.

Cognition of the major laws of development of the existing society is possible only on the basis of broad theoretical generalizations.

But to take that road means to abandon the "positivist" attitude toward capitalist reality and to recognize the historical need for its "negation." Such an approach is unacceptable to bourgeois sociology in the light of the social role it is called upon to play in capitalist society. Empiricism is a specific expression of the class essence and historically limited nature of bourgeois sociology.

Specific sociological researches acquire force and a vast theoretical and practical value only when they are based on a scientific dialectical-materialist sociological theory.

Under the conditions of socialism, specific sociological study of the quality and direction of change in social life corresponds to the needs of a planned economy and permits, as Lenin long since observed, "the planning of social changes" and thereby rational control over the progress of society.

ON SOVIET

SOCIOLOGY:

The Soviet View

Historical Materialism—
Marxist Sociology[1]

F. KONSTANTINOV and V. KELLE

The construction of socialism and communism confronts the social sciences with tasks of an unprecedented scale. This is, above all, because the communist social formation arises and develops on the basis of conscious appli-

Reprinted from F. Konstantinov and V. Kelle, "Historical Materialism—Marxist Sociology," Kommunist (January 1965). Translated in Current Digest of the Soviet Press, XVII, No. 8 (Copyright © March 17, 1965), 3–8.

[1] The questions of historical materialism raised in Comrades F. Konstantinov's and V. Kelle's article are attracting the attention of the scientific community. The discussion of pressing problems of historical materialism will promote the development of Marxist-Leninist theory.

cation of the laws of social development. The building of communism is a process of the creative activity of millions of people; it rests upon the thoroughgoing application of science. Only scientific thinking can determine the direction of society's development and set forth the concrete tasks of the masses' activity in accordance with the objective laws and requirements of social progress. The social sciences, says the Program of the C.P.S.U., represent the scientific foundation for the guidance of society's development.

But only social science that stands firmly on positions of historical materialism and is closely linked with the practice of communist construction, only social science that thoroughly studies and generalizes everything new and progressive arising in life, is capable of performing its extremely important creative social function. Therefore the C.P.S.U. not only relies on Marxist-Leninist science in its work, it provides an example of a creative attitude toward science, enriching it with new theses and conclusions which accord with the conditions of the era.

The development of scientific knowledge about society, as well as about nature, is connected with numerous complex processes of differentiation and integration of sciences, their interpenetration and the establishment of new mutual links among them. With the development of concrete sociological researches, questions arose about the place that Marxist sociology should hold in the system of knowledge about society, what the relation of concrete sociological researches is to historical materialism and scientific communism, whether social and sociological research can be equated, and so on. In the course of discussion of these problems, a more general issue was raised in the literature —the problem of the subject and tasks of Marxist sociology.

Since the problems raised are of fundamental importance for Marxist sociology, we should like to turn anew to consideration of them, using the materials of past discussions and the experience accumulated in concrete sociological studies.

THE PLACE OF MARXIST SOCIOLOGY IN THE SYSTEM OF KNOWLEDGE ABOUT SOCIETY

The social sciences can be divided into at least three main groups. World history, with its subdivisions—the histories of individual countries and peoples— constitutes one group. History studies the past of peoples in all its actual diversity. Hence it turns not only to laws, to the general and the necessary in history, but also to the particular and the accidental.

Individual social sciences, the subject of which is specific forms and aspects of social relations (economics, government, law, art, language, etc.), with their special laws, constitute another group of the social sciences. Political economy studies the development of people's economic relations; it explains the laws governing the production and distribution of material benefits in society at different stages of its development. Linguistics studies the laws of development of language as a social phenomenon. Jurisprudence concerns legal relations, and so on.

But at each stage of historical development society represents a whole, a specific social organization with its particular relations and laws. The study of society as a historically developing whole, the study of the laws of the succession of socio-economic formations, the investigation of the internal relationship of various aspects and phenomena of social life—these constitute the subject of sociology, the third essential sphere of social science.

Various philosophical-historical conceptions used to fill this sphere of social knowledge in the past. But the philosophy of history, developing on the basis of historical idealism, could not provide a scientific understanding of the interrelationship of social phenomena and the essence of the historical process.

The rise of historical materialism was a very great achievement of philosophy, a revolution in social science. Marx and Engels, who disclosed the dependence of social ideas upon the conditions of social existence, who singled out from the totality of social relations the material production relations as basic and determinant, and who linked the latter with the development of productive forces, showed that social development represents a process governed by laws and independent of the arbitrary will of individuals, of historical personages. In rejecting the abstract, metaphysical reasoning of bourgeois sociologists about society in general—reasonmg that employed fixed, non-historical laws— K. Marx, according to V. I. Lenin, "was the first to place sociology on a scientific foundation, establishing the concept of socio-economic formations as a totality of given production relations, establishing the fact that the development of these formations is a natural-historical process" (*Works,* Vol. I, pp. 124–125).

V. I. Lenin regarded historical materialism as a part of Marxist philosophy and at the same time as a social science —sociology. Lenin did not see any contradiction in the fact that historical materialism combined the qualities of a philosophical and a social science.

Other points of view, however, appeared in Marxist literature, particularly in recent years, on the question of the relationship of historical materialism to philosophy and sociology. Some assume historical materialism to be a sociological discipline and claim that it should therefore not be regarded as part of Marxist philosophy. Others, on the contrary, on the grounds that historical materialism is part of the philosophy of Marxism, refuse to consider it a sociological science and at best assign it the place of a general-theoretical and "methodological" basis for sociology. They pose the question of the need to create a new sociology, or even several sociologies, alongside historical materialism and distinct from it or resting upon it. Still others take the path of compromise, claiming that the philosophical and sociological aspects should

be distinguished within historical materialism itself.

Historical materialism is the philosophical science of society, since it provides a scientific resolution of the fundamental gnoseological problem in application to society. Without a materialist resolution of the question of the correlation of social existence and social consciousness it was impossible to establish a scientific theory of historical development. People—beings endowed with consciousness and will—make history, and for a scientific understanding of social life and its development one must first of all explain the consciousness and will of people from their material existence, one must discover the objective laws of the historical process. It was as a *philosophical* science of society that historical materialism was first able to resolve fundamental *sociological* problems and thereby to make its appearance as scientific sociology.

But consistent application of materialism and the dialectic to history is impossible by mechanical application of general philosophical categories to society. Only after determining the specific features of social existence and the special nature of the dialectic of the historical process, only after disclosing the social essence of man—that is, only by operating as a *sociological* science— was historical materialism able to provide a solution of the *philosophical* problems of social development. Therefore it is not subjective wishes but the very object of research which determines that scientific sociology cannot but be at the same time a philosophical science.

The application of materialism and the dialectic to cognition of social life provided the possibility of discovering the secret of the historical process, the secret of the processes and antagonisms of the capitalist social formation, to understand social development as a complex, many-faceted and contradictory process, and to disclose its more general laws.

The laws studied by Marxist sociology are general in two respects.

First, they operate throughout all history or several formations. This includes the laws constituting the subject and content of historical materialism: the law of the determinant role of the mode of production in the development of society, the law of the correspondence between production relations and productive forces, the law of the determinant role of social existence in relation to social consciousness, of the base in relation to the superstructure, the laws of class struggle, and so on.

Secondly, they [the general laws studied by Marxist sociology] apply not to one or another individual sphere of life but *to society, to the social formation as a whole; they constitute laws of interaction, of internal ties among various aspects of social life.* The general laws mentioned above are at the same time laws of the interaction of various aspects of social life— existence and consciousness, economics and politics, the productive forces and production relations, and so on. The forms in which the general laws manifest themselves and operate in different specific conditions are not identical. It is the task of Marxist sociological research to study specific forms of the general laws' manifestation and the mechanism of their operation.

Ordinarily, the laws constituting the subject of historical materialism include only laws operating throughout many formations of the whole of history. It seems to us that, in addition, there are *sociological* laws of specific formations. These laws determine the forms of interaction of various aspects of social life specific to each given society. For example, the development of the communist formation, in distinction to that of capitalism, is connected with the processes of bringing mental and manual labor closer together, of eradicating class distinctions. Here the tendency to turn labor into a prime human need develops. Specific laws determining these processes and tendencies also constitute a subject of sociological analysis.

It is not enough to learn a law in its general form, it is necessary also to trace the nature of its action and manifestation in specific processes. Here sociology encounters the diversity of relations that are characterized by the categories of cause and effect, possibility and actuality, necessity and accident, and so on. People's actions, which carry out social laws, are causally determined. But the causal conditioning of human actions cannot be viewed as simple dependence upon the environment, that is, cannot be treated in the spirit of mechanical Laplacian determinism. Therefore it would be wrong to regard the process of the realization of social laws as unavoidable operation of the laws. The conditions existing in a given society and a given country hold various possibilities of development, and which of them will be realized depends on the correlation of forces, on the actions of people, on the class struggle and on the struggle of a people to resolve pressing historical problems.

The downfall of capitalism as a social system and its replacement by socialism throughout the world is inevitable. But how, when, how fast it is happening or will happen in each capitalist country is determined by many factors: historical, political, ideological; by the specific balance of forces in the international arena and in the given country at the given moment, including the character and farsightedness of the public figures heading the working class. Therefore, in studying the operation of a law, it is necessary to disclose the existing possibilities and strive for the realization of those that most closely suit the requirements of steady development of society, the interests of the masses, of the revolutionary classes around which peoples unite.

The view that all problems of the theory of scientific communism belong to the sphere of Marxist sociology has become current of late. Of course, the component parts of Marxism are organically related to one another, and this connection is expressed in the works of the founders of Marxism-Leninism. V. I. Lenin described Marx's "Das Kapital" as not only an economic but also a philosophical (including sociological) work. When a representative of scientific communism analyzes the process of the revolutionary transformation of capitalist society into socialist society and the process of the construction of the new (communist) formation, and in doing so relies on the method of historical materialism, he unquestionably cannot and should not avoid sociological conclusions and generalizations. In this sense scientific communism, especially in our era, when it has ceased to be only a theory and is embodied in an actual society, likewise contains a sociological side. But it would nevertheless be wrong to see scientific communism as a sociological theory, since it includes above all a large range of its own socio-political problems. Among these are the theory of socialist revolution and the dictatorship of the proletariat (and now also the doctrine of socialist statehood), the doctrine of the Marxist-Leninist party, of the strategy and tactics of the proletariat's class struggle, the doctrine of the proletariat's allies in the struggle for socialism, in the national-liberation movement, and so on.

The content of the theoretical problems of scientific communism as an international doctrine of the world proletariat is determined for various national detachments of the working class also by whether the detachment is operating in a capitalist or a socialist country.

In our times the theory of scientific communism is called upon to take up questions of the international workers' and communist movement, the mutual relations of parties and the countries of the socialist camp, the struggle for peace, and problems of the national-liberation movement. In the conditions of the U.S.S.R. the subject of scientific communism includes the policy of the C.P.S.U., directed at a carrying out the program of communist construction; study of the leading role of the Party and of the socialist state; and analysis of concrete socio-political problems of the transition from socialism to communism.

Thus there is a deep organic connection, as well as a certain distinction, between Marxist sociology and the theory of scientific communism. While bearing in mind the internal differentiation among scientific disciplines and the consequent unavoidable specialization of scientists (economists, philosophers, law scholars, etc.), we must always direct no less attention to the synthesis of Marxist sciences and remember that the economist, the sociologist and the specialist on the theory of scientific communism are all representatives of a single Marxist-Leninist theory; that impassable boundaries cannot be set up in science, any more than in nature. It is always important to keep in mind that the component parts of Marxism are not separated from one another by a Chinese wall. Marxism is a single, unified doctrine. The separation of individual sciences from one another impoverishes science and retards the process of cognition.

SOCIAL AND SOCIOLOGICAL RESEARCHES

The founders of Marxism-Leninism, in describing historical materialism, always stressed its *methodological* significance. The soul of Marxism is method. Marxism-Leninism never turns theory into a hard-and-fast schema into which reality is twisted and which is used as "a lever for erecting constructs in the manner of Hegelianism" (F. Engels). Marxism as a whole—and historical materialism in particular—is a living, creative method of cognition, of investigation of constantly developing and changing reality. By virtue of this it is at the same time also a guide to revolutionary activity in the practice of socialist and communist construction. Marxism-Leninism is incompatible with stifling dogmatism, which distorts the living spirit of Marxism—its revolutionary method, the dialectic—and does not see what is new that is being born, and which applies conclusions and theses appropriate in some circumstances to other, changed circumstances, where they are false and untrue.

All the social sciences rely on the method of historical materialism in their researches and apply it in accordance with the particular features of their respective subjects. On the other hand, historical materialism, Marxist sociology, by its very nature as a science of general theory, must always rely in its generalizations and conclusions upon the discoveries of particular sciences, on broad social researches and on well-organized statistics. But, in addition, the method of historical materialism has been and is employed for the analysis of actuality in those spheres that constitute the subject proper of Marxist sociology. Historical materialism as a method would turn into some-

thing dead if it were not used for studying what is new that is born, arises and develops in the sphere of social relations, in the material and spiritual life of society. Scientific research in the sphere of sociology includes generalization of the experience of the creative activity of the masses, study of the mechanism of operation of social laws in concrete processes, and generalization of the information obtained. This presupposes study of the social relations that take shape in concrete social groups, communities and collectives, the interrelationships of objective (external) conditions and the consciousness of people, the role of ideas, of consciousness and of material interests in the conditions of the construction of socialism and communism. We employ the term "concrete sociological research" to define this direction of scientific research work.

Sociological research in our country cannot follow the path of imitation of bourgeois and, in particular, American empirical sociology. Marxist sociology is fundamentally hostile to all kinds of bourgeois sociology. In the U.S.A. bourgeois sociologists have splintered into a host of different "sociologies," depending on the subject of research: labor, the family, law, medicine, art, crime, alcoholism, prostitution, sports, the city, the countryside, religion, etc.

The dozens of such sociologies view various aspects and phenomena of the country's public life out of the context of the whole, because bourgeois sociologists do not have a single, harmonious scientific sociological theory. They accumulate heaps of diversified material, sometimes valuable and interesting but at times unnecessary and worthless. The chief thing, however, is that this material does not serve as a basis for penetrating the social essence of the studied phenomena and processes, since bourgeois sociology is not interested in this and does not possess the scientific theory and scientific method for generalizing the assembled material.

Despite this, bourgeois sociologists in effect substitute sociology for other social sciences that study contemporary social life. This expanded interpretation of sociology contradicts a scientific understanding of it, which requires that account be taken of the distinction among social sciences according to the special features of the object studied and the subject of the given science.

For us, concrete sociological research is a form of development of the single Marxist sociological science.

The striving of some Marxists to set up a new sociology, distinct from historical materialism, comes not only from a failure to understand the essence of historical materialism and from a kind of imitation of bourgeois, particularly American, sociology. It is also a reaction against a purely dogmatic, doctrinaire interpretation of historical materialism as some kind of sum or system, a collection of truths and theses established once and for all—an interpretation that arises when one forgets that historical materialism is first of all and chiefly a living method of studying social life.

A creative attitude toward historical materialism, as also toward sociological theory and method, requires, first, the elimination of the existing separation between historical materialism and the individual social sciences; second, the conducting of specific sociological researches in the sphere that constitutes the proper subject of sociology; third, participation in broad, complex researches involving the cooperation of sociologists, economists, historians, law specialists, ethnographers, art specialists and representatives of other social sciences.

It is the custom among some scientists and practical workers to describe any studies of phenomena relating to people's everyday life—economic, legal, historical, even technico-economic phenomena—as concrete sociological researches. Some consider, for example, that problems of the organization of bus service, improving the work of retail shops, devising measures for reducing fatigue at work, etc., belong to the sociologist's tasks. All these questions are important, of course. But such attempts to expand inordinately the interpretation of sociology and of concrete sociological research signify dissolving sociology entirely and in actuality lead to liquidation of Marxist sociology as a science.

A distinction should be drawn between Marxist social researches and sociological studies. Social research is a wider concept. Concrete sociological research is a specific form of social researches. The latter are conducted in political economy and specific economic disciplines, jurisprudence, ethnography, pedagogy and other social sciences that directly study social reality. Concrete sociological research cannot substitute for or replace social researches. Each specialized scientist knows best his own subject of research. Sociologists should rely on these special researches and draw sociological conclusions and generalizations in studying individual aspects of social life. If the subject of Marxist sociology is society, the socio-economic formation as a total social organism, the laws of its development and functioning, its motive forces, then it follows that concrete sociological researches should cover study of the action of these laws and motive forces in the given country, in the given segment of time. And in so doing the discovery of new forms of relations of phenomena and of laws hitherto unknown, as well as of the mechanism and conditions of operation of previously known laws, is important.

The systematic pursuit of social, including concrete sociological, researches is an old tradition of Marxist-Leninist social science.

Take F. Engels' early work "The Condition of the Working Class in England [in 1844]." What a vast array of factual data it is based on! For a year and a half Engels studied the life of workers in a number of British industrial centers, including Manchester, before starting to write this work. As we know, "Das Kapital," the chief work of all of K. Marx's life, generalized a "Mont Blanc of facts" and relied on the most diverse economic and sociological researches.

In "The Development of Capitalism in Russia," in works on the agrarian question and in many other books, V. I. Lenin summed up a colossal amount of factual information about the economic, political and other aspects of the life of Russia, about the countryside, industrial and agricultural production, and social relations in the country in the reform period.

V. I. Lenin's famous article "A Great Beginning" can serve as one of the fine examples of a broad Marxist sociological approach to the phenomena of contemporary times. The experience of the first communist *subbotniki* [volunteer work for the state in free time], which the Communists of the Moscow-Kazan Railroad initiated, served as the point of departure for sociological generalizations of the widest scope—about the communist forms of labor that were coming into being, about the new discipline, about socialist competition, etc. A Marxist sociologist must learn this ability to perceive in the mass of phenomena those that are particularly valuable for the development of the communist way of life.

One could cite a host of other examples showing that the classical writers of Marxism always relied on social and sociological investigations, on the data of statistics and practical experience, on study of the creativity of the masses. Only thanks to such social researches could Marxism-Leninism develop, be enriched with new data and conclusions, and win victories over bourgeois science. The development of social sciences is impossible without social research, just as historical materialism without concrete sociological research faces a danger of turning into a system of frozen, unchanging concepts and categories, divorced from reality.

The scientific traditions of Marxism were distorted or cast into oblivion in the period of the Stalin cult. Concrete sociological research on socialist society was often replaced with a presentation of general theoretical schemata, divorced from real life; instead of analysis of living and typical facts taken in their interrelationships, a haphazard and one-sided selection of "examples" and illustrations of various schemata was often resorted to, which gave rise to dogmatism and pedantry and deprived science of its nutrient medium, its tie with life, with the facts, and consequently of a creative, effective foundation.

The Marxist-Leninist traditions began to be restored in the sphere of social researches after the 20th Party Congress, but this process has nevertheless proceeded more slowly than the practice of communist construction required and requires. The development of research was retarded to some extent by underestimation of its importance in resolving practical problems of the building of communism, by manifestations of voluntarism and administrative methods in the management of the economy.

Social research, including concrete sociological research, has not yet become a mandatory component part of the scientific guidance of social development in our country. This gap must be closed, for without such research the rise of communist relations and the shaping of the new man and of communist consciousness cannot be concretely guided. We also require good statistics, in establishing which the sociologists as well as the economists should take part—statistics that have been checked and are public. Without these statistics social sciences, including Marxist sociology, cannot exist, live and develop. The program of collecting statistical data should depend not only on the Statistical Administration but also on the economic institutes, the Philosophy Institute and other scientific institutions on which our statistical agencies should firmly rely.

CONCERNING THE SUBJECT OF CONCRETE SOCIOLOGICAL RESEARCH

Under socialism the *possibilities* and the necessity of cognition of social processes increase immeasurably. But the *utilization* of the new possibilities for science is not achieved automatically. The active creative work of scientists and a demand for scientific data on the part of society are required for the development of science.

The more widely communist construction develops in our country, the more society needs a sociological science that would constantly keep within its field of vision the dynamics of development, the process of perfecting social relations; that would generalize factual data and on this basis would work out as initial methodological principles an approach to reality itself, as well as specific recommendations stemming from the results of study of social processes.

A widely developed and constantly operating system of concrete social and sociological research, organically linked with the program of communist con-

struction, is a historical necessity in socialist society.

The basic direction of sociological research in our conditions is study of the working masses in the construction of communism. Living and creative communism is the cause of the masses themselves, the result of the creativity of millions. This creativity functions under the leadership of the Communist Party, which relies on a scientific theory. The Marxist-Leninist theory, reflecting the laws of social development, makes it possible to use these laws in practice, to foresee the basic directions of historical development, to determine the ways and means of building communism. But in practice this construction is always a many-faceted and contradictory process that should be under the Party's constant observation so that one may know precisely where and when there appear various difficulties and new contradictions, whether distortions and weak links are arising, and where, on the other hand, progressive "growth points" arise. Science has the duty of showing the causes of these phenomena, studying the favorable and negative factors, and helping to disclose the realization in the activity of the masses of those mighty creative potentialities that are contained within the socialist system.

In Marxism, concrete-sociological research is connected with posing and solving big social problems. Among these, first of all, are changes in the social structure of society in the process of the transition to communism. The Soviet Union has reached a level of development at which the creation of a classless, socially homogeneous society has become a practical task of the people. This is a majestic and at the same time complicated task, which cannot be accomplished offhand. Its accomplishment presupposes the final elimination of all survivals of social inequality, that is, overcoming the existing distinctions between city and countryside, eliminating differences between mental and manual labor, eradicating all class differences.

The questions of how this task is concretely solved, what the real dynamic of the social structure of society is, what difficulties and contraditions we are still encountering and shall yet encounter—these are of tremendous theoretical and practical interest. In studying them we must bear in mind that the distinctions between the workers, the collective farm peasantry and the intelligentsia are eliminated through the development and strengthening of the comradely cooperation of all strata of Soviet society. The study of the numerous forms of this cooperation, forms that are constantly growing in the course of building communism, is an important sociological problem.

When analyzing the interrelationship of the large social groups of Soviet society—the working class, the collective farm peasantry, the intelligentsia—one must not forget that these groups themselves are not homogeneous. In guiding the process of bringing persons of mental and manual labor closer together and eliminating social distinctions, one should take strict account not only of the concrete conditions of material life and activity and the level of education and culture of the basic social groups as a whole but also the distinctions within them.

When, for instance, there is posed the general task of raising the cultural-technical level of manual workers to the level of engineers and technicians, it is accomplished in different ways for different groups of workers and collective farmers (and some office workers). Therefore it is necessary to study sociologically not only the interclass relations but also the relations within the working class, the collective farm peasantry, and the intelligentsia.

The solidarity of various national and occupational detachments of the working class plays a tremendous role in the revolutionary struggle. Without this spirit of proletarian solidarity, the working class could not have defeated the bourgeoisie, maintained and strengthened its rule and led the non-proletarian masses of the working people.

Under socialism the solidarity of the working people is expressed also in the fraternal mutual aid of the socialist countries; in the city's help to the countryside and the help of the working class to the peasantry; in the cooperation of workers of manual and mental labor, and in the mutual relations of various collectives of working people within them. To develop the sense of comradely solidarity among the working people of our country as a component element of socialist consciousness means to heighten the responsibility of each individual for the common cause, to influence the development of socialist and communist social relations. Solidarity in our conditions is a natural and logical expression of socialist production relations, and it should be regarded as an important sociological category.

Thus the study of the dynamics of the social structure of socialist society presupposes study of the situation not only of individual classes and their interrelations as entities, but also study of the various groups within classes.

One of the chief subjects of sociological research is the forms of political organization of socialist society, their improvement and development, the process of evolution of socialist statehood into communist public self-government. These problems are studied by a whole complex of political and legal sciences. The sociological aspect here consists in studying the interaction of the political system with all other aspects of public life—as an element of the communist formation, as the organizing of the socio-political life of the masses and their enlistment in active building of communist relations in accordance with objective laws. This includes working out, on the basis of concrete research, the methodological problems of the science of administration, of conscious utilization of objective laws in the process of administration, study of questions of the thorough and comprehensive development of socialist democracy, of the elimination of survivals of bureaucracy, of the formation of elements of self-government.

Concrete-sociological research should find very great application in studying problems of labor, particularly the process for formation of communist labor as a prime vital need, as well as study of questions connected with the relationship of man and technology, the role of science in production, and the social consequences of the scientific-technical revolution.

Many sciences—technical, economic, psychological and others—study production, labor, and man at work. Here sociology has its own range of problems: the interrelationship of labor and other aspects of public life, the dynamic of the interrelations of material and spiritual labor, and particularly the process of molding man, the individual of communist society.

A whole series of sociologists' collectives of Moscow, Leningrad, Sverdlovsk and other cities of the Soviet Union is engaged in studying problems of labor. Interesting data have been collected, but the published materials show that the sociologists are not always capable of distinguishing their own aspect of research, and often set out to substitute for economists and psychologists; sometimes, instead of deep and creative theoretical research, they engage in superficial observation. Of course, as already noted, one cannot draw an absolute line of demarcation between the social dis-

ciplines, but nevertheless, for example, devising recommendations for eliminating elements of monotony in work or for assigning workers their places at the bench is not the task of sociologists. But problems of the role of labor in the formation of personality; of a rise in the cultural-technical level of the working people as a necessary element in overcoming the distinctions between persons of mental and manual labor; of working out the communist attitude toward labor and communist work relations—these are the direct job of sociologists, and here they can bring genuine benefit.

Family and everyday living relations constitute a quite important and special object of sociological research. Changing everyday life over to a communist basis is a complicated process. Everyday life, of course, depends on production, but at the same time the planning of the changes in everyday life, organizing people's everyday living, is a sphere of personal life in which man is not tied by production discipline and presents definite difficulties. In addition, we cannot say that the question of what communist everyday living will be like is already entirely clear. To this day the most contradictory views are expressed. Sociological research in the sphere of everyday living is still in embryo.

Everyday living cannot be studied without research on the family, the essential cell of society, reflecting within itself the totality of the relations existing in society. It is hardest of all to eliminate the survivals of harmful ways and hoary traditions in the sphere of family and everyday life. But it is very important for society that this sphere develop in step with the general progress: After all, it is in the family that the new generation of the country's citizens begins its life path, and the development of the individual, and consequently his success in labor, depends on the organization of everyday life. The family and everyday living are, along with work, the major sphere of people's lives, and study of them by the methods of Marxist sociology is one of the elements necessary to socialist society's self-understanding—an element of prime importance for communist construction.

We should like to draw attention also to the following important spheres of sociological research, closely linked with the above—research on the spiritual life of socialist society, on the role of science in the modern world, on the reasons for the existence of religion and the conditions for its withering away, the change from socialist consciousness to communist consciousness, the formation of communist culture, and comprehensive development of the individual personality.

The study of society's spiritual life has two interlinked aspects. One is the analysis of the progress of science and of the trends of its development, the dialectic of interaction of the forms of social consciousness, morality and law, science and philosophy, the process of ideological development. The second is the analysis of the process of formation of the communist consciousness of the masses, their introduction to the discoveries of science and culture and their participation in the development of culture, elimination of survivals of the past in the mind. Here Marxist sociology is in arrears to society.

Scientific sociological analysis of spiritual life is possible, of course, only insofar as people's consciousness is taken in organic connection with life, practice and material conditions, not in isolation from them. Therefore, in concrete research on spiritual life, sociology turns to the study of the life of collectives, of man at work, in everyday life and in real life. It is this approach that makes it possible to free oneself of abstract talk about survivals, to seek real ways and means of raising the communist consciousness of the masses, the true reasons for anti-social acts and ways of eliminating them.

The study of all these questions is of great practical significance. Quite naturally, the researcher should give an objective picture of reality, should disclose what is new, advanced and progressive, as well as what is negative, obsolete and distorting of the nature of socialism. A subject of sociological research is the nonantagonistic contradictions in the development of socialist society, which are connected with the inner dialectic of socialism's evolution into communism as well as with the difficulties of growth and the operation of the subjective factor. The Marxist sociologist, in disclosing and analyzing these contradictions, has the task of seeking ways of solving them in the process of the further development of socialist society.

Thus the sociologist studies a variety of social relations in society. When studying social relations, we are at the same time studying man, the human personality. *The focus of attention of Marxist sociology is man in his relationship to surrounding reality, in all the diversity of his real ties and relations.* "***The Marxist sociologist," wrote V. I. Lenin, "in making definite social relations of people the subject of his study, is thereby ipso facto studying actual *personalities,* of whose actions these relations are composed" ("Works," Vol. I, p. 395).

While noting the specific nature of sociological research, the sociological aspect of the approach to labor, to the social structure of society, to the public consciousness, etc., we must bear in mind that Marxist sociology in its conclusions rests on a wider range of data of various social sciences and, consequently, on a broad range of economic, ethnographic, pedagogical, psychological and other social researches. What is more, the requirements of practice and theory often require *integrated* Marxist social research, combining the efforts of specialists of various fields of social knowledge for the comprehensive study of various phenomena or processes of social life. The cooperation of scientists and of practical workers is necessary and useful in carrying out social researches. Unfortunately, such integrated researches as yet constitute a quite rare phenomenon.

Concrete sociological and social investigations can be conducted both on the scale of the whole society or within the framework of republics, territories and provinces, or even within the narrower and more local framework of enterprises, collective farms, factories, offices and institutions. In the first case research can yield data for comprehensive theoretical generalizations, in the second it can provide the basis for less sweeping generalizations. Only the accumulation of this material makes it possible to turn from partial to more comprehensive sociological generalizations.

Concrete sociological researches cannot be divorced from Marxist sociological theory, before which life sets big tasks. Sociology should enlarge the range of its problems. For example, sociologists have as yet given insufficient study to the problem of material self-interest, the dialectic of incentives and needs, specific features of the interaction of the subjective and the objective factors under socialism, the relationship of the individual and society, etc. Efforts expended on carrying out concrete sociological researches will not be wasted if they really serve the development and concretization of sociological theory, the accomplishment of the practical tasks of communist construction.

THE METHODOLOGY OF CONCRETE SOCIOLOGICAL RESEARCH

As we know, science distinguishes between methodology and research methods. This distinction exists in the social sciences, including sociology. The general laws and principles of dialectical and historical materialism constitute the methodology of concrete sociological and social research. The methods bear a more limited and essentially applied character, since they concern specific devices, ways and means of obtaining and dealing with factual data. Methodology and method are closely related to one another. The general methodological principles of Marxist philosophy manifest themselves in the specific methods of research. The methods—and this is their purpose—should, so to speak, technically ensure application of the methodology in concrete research and in generalizing the information. It is scientific methodology and correct method that make it possible, first, to assemble non-haphazard details and the totality of facts—since it is only in this form that the facts are "not only 'stub-born' but unquestionable proof" (V. I. Lenin, "Works," Vol. XXIII, p. 266) and furnish the basis for objective conclusions; and, second, to draw true conclusions from these facts.

Without going into narrowly professional details of these problems—the place for such details is on the pages of specialized journals—we wish to point out several questions that are of general interest.

One of the shortcomings of some of the sociological research previously conducted in our country was that new theoretical conclusions, even limited ones, were not drawn from them. These "investigations" merely supported theses that were already known and had long been stated in Marxism; at best, these researches could serve as specific illustrations of them, which has quite, quite limited value for science.

The emergence of research beyond the bounds of mere illustration is connected primarily with the advancing of scientific hypotheses. F. Engels termed the hypothesis "a form of development of natural science insofar as it [natural science] cogitates" (K. Marx and F. Engels, "Works" [Russian ed.], Vol. XX, p. 555). This applies in no smaller measure to the social sciences, including sociology. Yet among us were persons who in effect denied the right of specialists in the social sciences to advance hypotheses. It was held that economists, sociologists, *et al.*, should mouth only ready-made truths. But a new truth, after all, is the product of research and not its prerequisite. To deny the right of the specialist in the social sciences to advance scientific hypotheses is to doom these sciences to stagnate and vegetate. "If we wanted to wait until the maerial is ready *in pure form* for a law, this would mean stopping [all] thinking research until such time, and ipso facto never getting the law" (*ibid.*).

In this connection let us recall V. I. Lenin's statement that the materialist interpretation of history was itself a hypothesis until K. Marx showed in "Das Kapital" what brilliant results it yielded in the study of the capitalist formation. Only after the appearance of "Das Kapital," said Lenin, did the materialist interpretation of history become a synonym for social science, since its truth had been scientifically demonstrated.

A hypothesis means a scientifically grounded presumption which requires appropriate testing in experience and becomes the basis for observation and experiment. Even if the hypothesis is not confirmed, by that very fact it helps to define a truer direction for research. The hypothesis in science is closely connected with experimentation. But until recently sociology hardly used this method. Experimentation in the sphere of social investigations differs substantially, of course, from natural-science experimentation, since it concerns people and social relations.

It is not by chance that the question of the very possibility of conducting experiments of a limited, local nature has been raised more and more insistently in sociological and economic literature. The social experiment makes it possible to check in practice this or that hypothesis or innovation and can serve as a source of factual data. It makes it possible to move from hypothesis to theory and from theory to practice, to drafting scientifically well-grounded recommendations for regulating various processes of social life and the guidance of them.

Social experimentation is particularly important in the conditions of the building of communism, for we are pursuing untrod paths and do not have historical models to follow. Our society is seeking wiser and more effective forms of organization and administration, the best means of construction, more effective methods of upbringing. And here social experimentation, affording a practical test on a local scale for new ideas and methods, can render an incalculable service.

Unfortunately, we have had the sad experience of hastily adopting and immediately introducing on a nationwide scale thoughtless and untested ideas and proposals. Such "experiments" are expensive; they lead to waste of efforts and means. Thus it was with the economically groundless reduction of the collective farmers' individual plots, the division of local Party bodies into industrial and agricultural, and the introduction of 11-year schooling. The

Party revoked these "innovations," but it has not renounced further improvement of the forms of organization and administration. However, in order that the improvements be wise and the decision be adopted only after comprehensive analysis and practical testing of proposals, experimentation is needed.

The organization of social experimentation and working out methods for it are one of the responsible tasks of sociological science.

Both in devising the methods of concrete sociological research and in applying them, sociology encounters specific difficulties and problems. The natural scientist uses devices to "hear" what nature "tells." But consciousness, subjective opinions and interests do not exist in nature outside of man. And the sociologist, whatever he may be investigating, is dealing first of all with man.

Sociology has at its disposal various means of social research. One group of means is used to study the "inner world" of people, their thinking. This group includes questionnaires, interviews, personal documents, observation. These methods, however, must be skillfully employed if the data gathered through them are to provide a real and comprehensive reflection of actuality and not a distortion of it. In other words, questionnaires must be carefully drafted, control questions must be used and interviews and observations conducted. One must know the means of classification and treatment of facts; scientific methods exist for this. Finally, study of the "subjective data" must be combined with analysis of the objective conditions. Sociology's arsenal of means of research includes modeling, statistics and other mathematical methods. The problem of the representativeness of research has great importance in sociology. The sociologist must be able to reckon the minimal size of the object of research (group of persons, number of enterprises, their composition and diversity) required in order to draw general conclusions from the data obtained from this object of study. Here, of course, the utilization of mathematical calculations is necessary.

The importance of quantitative methods in sociology is great, and will unquestionably increase. These methods meet the requirements of objectivity and limit the possibility of mistakes and arbitrariness. One can express important aspects of social phenomena with the help of mathematics. For example, in the formula of the norm of surplus value K. Marx mathematically expressed the relation of capitalist exploitation and the magnitude of this relation. There are tremendous possibilities for the use of mathematical methods in sociology, and here we should not invent any a priori limitations. At the same time, one must bear in mind that sociology cannot be reduced to mathematics, to quantitative calculations, that mathematics is only one of the methods used in sociology. The subject of sociology is such that here the quality, the type, the nature of social relations has prime and definitive importance.

Constant and widely developed sociological research suits the interests of communist construction. But it is important that this research be systematic, not haphazard, that it stem from the real needs of practice and science and not from the caprices and subjective wishes of various persons, that it disclose the objective picture of reality and not serve as "confirmation" of preconceived schemata. All this demands of the sociologists the highest sense of responsibility, scientific honesty and principle, impartiality and objectivity, a Communist Party attitude, firmness and the ability not to stop halfway in one's conclusions.

We must realize quite clearly that

the interests of communist construction require not the prettifying or blackening of our reality, but exact cognition of it: After all, we are building our own future, and science can help the Party and the people only by providing an objective picture of this reality, disclosing the objective truth. Historical truth, objective truth, the interests of the peoples and the interests of communism coincide.

*   *   *

The analysis of the questions reviewed here shows that the requirements of development of Marxist sociology, that is, historical materialism, demand wide application of concrete sociological research. Of great importance to the success and effectiveness of this research are the development and utilization of data of the sociology-related disciplines—social psychology, statistics, anthropology and demography.

The development of Marxist sociology presumes also the further development and enrichment of its categories and improvement of methods and the techniques of sociological research.

Obviously, solution of all these problems is impossible without the training of qualified specialists. Yet the training of cadres in our country is being conducted on an insufficiently high level. Most of those graduated from the philosophy departments do not have the skills for employing the methods and techniques of sociological research or applying formal-logical and mathematical methods to generalization of the data of social research.

It is difficult to overestimate the practical state significance of sociological research. Socialist society has opened up the possibility of conducting sociological research on a wide scale. It will be successful and objective and bear results only if it is conducted on a strictly scientific basis. Therefore, evidently, the U.S.S.R. Academy of Sciences should not only stimulate more actively the conducting of such research but should also be an organizing center for it and provide the necessary scientific level in such researches.

Sociology:
Discoveries and Possibilities

A. ZDRAVOMYSLOV

Leningrad—Sociological research: It is being written about more and more frequently in the newspapers and magazines. True, the subjects of this research

Reprinted from A. Zdravomyslov, "Sociology: Discoveries and Possibilities," Sovetskaya Rossia *(May 21, 1964). Translated in* Current Digest of the Soviet Press, *XVI, No. 22 (Copyright © June 24, 1964), p. 12.*

and the benefits it can bring to society are still not clear to everyone. But the fact remains: Laboratories for sociological research have been established in Moscow, Leningrad, Sverdlovsk, Novosibirsk and Kiev. They have been operating at the universities for several years now.

Interest in this area of knowledge is

constantly growing. We at Leningrad University's laboratory for sociological research alone were visited during March and April by more than 100 persons, representatives of higher educational institutions and Party organizations from various regions of the country. And as a rule everyone wanted to learn about the problems of research, its methods and techniques, and about the practical results achieved.

What is the explanation for the recent heightening of interest in sociology?

Before answering this question, it would be proper to ask: Do we know the man of today? Are we able quickly, and at the same time scientifically, to provide answers to whole series of problems arising in the course of the formation of new social relations? I have in mind questions relating to the psychology of labor, to the attitudes of members of one trade toward those of another, etc.

Resolutions of congresses and the Party Program disclose the laws and paths of communist construction. But it must not be forgotten that the process of the transition to communism is so many-sided, complex and unexplored that each day of our swift-moving life poses ever new problems, on whose solution depends the success of the general cause.

For example, let us take such a problem as labor turnover. From the standpoint of an enterprise director, this is unquestionably an undesirable phenomenon. Judge for yourselves: A trained worker leaves the plant. In order to place a person in the vacancy created, it is first necessary to train him. Finally, a worker frequently changes his specialty when transferring to another place; he also requires retraining. In the final analysis, all this amounts to a loss to society in time and in rubles.

But there is also another side to this problem. Imagine for a moment that all production collectives were absolutely stable. And then a new enterprise is placed in operation and must be staffed with cadres. But from where can we draw resources of trained manpower?

Can it be that the turnover of cadres is not only an evil but a kind of means of technological progress as well?

At present, probably no one can fix the optimum, most acceptable range of labor turnover. But this natural phenomenon can be used for the good of society, if it is regulated scientifically and not by guesswork, and it must be so used. Given a questionnaire survey of a large group of workers' objective observations, and conclusions that can be drawn after the answers have been processed by electronic computer, sociologists will be able to offer scientific recommendations on the problems of the natural turnover of cadres. Incidentally, our Leningrad laboratory for sociological research already has experience in such work.

Or another problem: the choice of an occupation. The schools are turning out millions of young citizens annually. Some of them enroll in educational institutions, others enter plants, factories and construction work. How well prepared are we for this? Do we know which occupations are popular with the graduates and which are not? And does the gravitation toward one occupation or another always correspond with the requirements of the national economy?

For the time being, such questions also cannot be answered precisely or altogether scientifically. But this problem will cease being a problem if sociologists come to our aid. By analyzing the results of surveys, they can provide planning agencies with invaluable information. Materials provided by sociologists will help in determining the scale of the training of cadres in various specialties and in regulating the measure of manpower requirements in each occupational group. Finally, data provided by sociologists will indicate the direction in which indoctrinational work with graduates should be intensified, instilling in them a liking for one or another specialty that is for some reason unpopular, although it may be extremely vital.

In other words, we will receive answers to an entire complex of questions and problems and, relying on a scientific analysis of the social attitudes being formed, will be able more flexibly and precisely to assist society in managing the national economy.

But this is still not all. So far, the question has been only one of research that facilitates the development of the country's economy, yielding a direct profit. But sociological research will also help in solving a number of problems of another nature, linked with the long-range prospects for the upbringing of the new man, the bearer of communist morality.

For example, how do working people use their free time? It is no secret that they as yet are not all able to organize their time but squander it aimlessly, thereby robbing both themselves and society. But in which part of the population and for what reason is this especially prevalent, and what is the effect here of the specific peculiarities of one or another category of working people? For answers to these questions as well, sociological research is indispensable.

In short, the problems of sociological research are not merely dreamed up in the silence of offices and libraries. They are dictated by life. In precisely this lies the interest in sociological research.

One may ask: If the work of sociologists offers, or at any rate can offer, tangible practical results (and there need be no doubt of this), then where is the trouble, what is hindering its development?

The trouble is that the success and practical significance of this research are in many ways dependent on its organization. There is now no small amount of amateurish work being done in sociology, and there is a tendency toward empiricism and illustrative methods. Scientific search is in many cases supplanted by a selection of examples from already known theses. In this way the meaning of the research becomes absurd and pointless. Furthermore, the sociological laboratories do not coordinate their plans but work independently.

A problem has arisen that enthusiastic sociologists do not have it in their power to solve alone. I have in mind the setting up of a center that would direct and coordinate all work in this field. Perhaps such a center should be created in the form of a Central Institute for Social Research.

Of course, this would require large expenditures. And the question of whether the game is worth the candle is a completely natural one. It should be emphasized here first of all that as sociological research develops, it can be conducted more and more on a self-supporting basis.

Of course, besides studying problems on a scale applicable to the entire country, sociological research of an applied, local nature must also be carried out. On the basis of contracts with economic councils or plants, sociological laboratories would be able to solve many questions in the life of an industrial enterprise, assisting in the improvement of the organization of labor and in raising its productivity.

The development of such a practice would undoubtedly facilitate, in the first place, more flexible management of enterprises, and secondly, the strengthening of the material base of the sociological laboratories.

On a Scientific Basis:
Apply Social Research
to Party Work

E. LISAVTSEV, V. MASLIN, and N. OVCHINNIKOV

The vast scale of the economic and social transformations being carried out in our country and the complexity of the tasks of the building of communism are making increasingly high demands on the work of Party organizations.

One way to raise the level of Party leadership is to introduce scientific social research in the daily practical activity of Party organizations and Party bodies. This research is necessary not only for theoretical generalization: Without it, skilled, scientifically grounded leadership is impossible in any area of economic or cultural construction or in the upbringing of the masses.

Social research is used in the practical activities of Party organs in various ways. In some cases, Party committees rely on already available data of concrete analyses obtained by research institutes, higher schools and other institutions. Thus a study of the question of unutilized reserves of manpower in Siberia embraced a total of some 44,000 families in the city of Novosibirsk and Novosibirsk Province. The research

Reprinted from E. Lisavtsev, V. Maslin, and N. Ovchinnikov, "On a Scientific Basis: Apply Social Research to Party Work," Pravda (May 11, 1965). Translated in Current Digest of the Soviet Press, XVII, No. 19 (Copyright © June 2, 1965), 11–12.

was conducted over a period of six years. Attentive study of it guarantees against one-sidedness and haphazard conclusions.

Research on general and specific problems is frequently organized and conducted by the Party committees themselves, with the cooperation of a broad aktiv and of scientific institutions. Some studies are organized with long-range ends in view, and have not only practical but also theoretical significance. Party committees in Lithuania, for example, have analyzed the effectiveness of ideological work. This has made it possible not only to expose shortcomings but also to outline ways for improving matters.

A great deal of the research is of an applied nature. The Karelia Province Party Committee conducted a research project in connection with the preparation and discussion of the question of how the Party organization of the Leather Materials Industry Construction Trust (a Young Communist League shock construction project) was inculcating in the builders pride in their work and respect for their jobs. In the process of the study, questions of the correct organization of work and the rational use of working time were placed at the center of attention: Production training was organized at the construction project, pay rates for the workers were reset and 12 economically accountable (*khozraschetnykh*) brigades were formed. In addition, the Party and Y.C.L. organizations intensified educational work.

A number of Party committees are also undertaking research on a larger scale, with the broad cooperation of scientific forces and the application of modern means of scientific analysis. Social research centers uniting teachers, scientific personnel and workers of Party and public organizations are being set up on volunteer principles. In close connection with Party committees, they conduct day-to-day research activity on important problems.

For example, a social research laboratory was set up in Orel with the help of the pedagogical institute's philosophy department. Together with Party organs, it undertook a study of the important problem of ways for increasing the effectiveness of ideological work in the villages.

The methods of research employed were extremely varied: questionnaires, interviews, analysis of statistical data and the documents of local agencies, the collection of the reminiscences of old residents, observations made in the fields, at collective farm meetings and at political talks.

The research yielded a great deal of material, which has made it possible to draw a number of interesting conclusions and generalizations. Thus the pattern of the formation of public opinion in the villages and the shortcomings in such work on the part of rural Party, public and state organizations were disclosed.

Obviously, the nature and content of the research carried out with the participation of Party organizations should be determined first of all by the tasks that confronted the Communists of the enterprise, collective farm or district. There is no need for the Party committee to undertake research that can be carried out without its participation and that has particularly urgent significance. Why, for example, should a city Party committee occupy itself with studying the student's time budget when the personnel of a higher educational institution can themselves look into it? The effectiveness of, say, one or another form of Party propaganda is another matter—such a question cannot but concern the Party committee.

The materials of serious scientific analysis are a great help to the Party worker. They introduce a fresh current in his activity and compel him to ponder the style and methods of Party leadership. Therefore the conducting of social research must, of course, be approached not like some fashionable fad but as an important cause that helps one to work more purposefully, with perspective, to look ahead and to build leadership on a scientific basis.

However, research is not an end in itself. Scientific analysis in Party work precedes the measures adopted for improving the leadership of political and economic life. It permits the fuller use of the opportunities for improving the guidance of social phenomena and processes and the more skillful conduct of the organization and education of the masses.

It goes without saying that the practical orientation of concrete social research in Party work has nothing in common with creeping empiricism, with the blind worship of facts. The task consists in the ability to extract from the facts meaning and a program for action, and not to be satisfied with what happens to lie on the surface. "We Marxists," wrote V. I. Lenin, "must strive with all our strength for scientific study of the facts that underlie our policy" ("Works" [in Russian], Vol. XXV, p. 254). Such a scientific approach is ensured first of all by the correct choice of forms and methods of conducting research.

In a number of organizations the questionnaire method of studying processes and of learning the moods of the people and the motives for their behavior has become widespread. Party organs resort to it in checkups of various sorts. Questionnaire inquiry is an important and responsible stage in research work. It is most expedient to use this method when the state of affairs cannot be studied by the usual methods. But why, for example, resort to the questionnaire method when a collective of only 50 to 100 people is involved? Here face-to-face talks with people are much more effective. Yet in some places the questionnaire method is looked on as the only one, and such well-known and well-tested methods as analysis of documents, statistical data and letters from the working people are forgotten. Another thing must also be remembered: The questionnaire can be useful only if it is carefully drawn up.

There are quite a few cases where far-fetched research is carried out for the sake of form; it turns into a kind of game, and polls with random questions are conducted. Such research is a waste of forces and time and yields nothing practical. There are instances when the data obtained are used ineptly, in a one-sided way, and as a result disorient the Party worker rather than help him.

Correctly conducted research, and the objective information obtained as a result, makes it possible to expose in time and nip in the bud undesirable processes (the embellishment of matters, hoodwinking) and is a good means for studying advanced experience and the initiative of the masses. Truthful information is a kind of mirror of life. At the same time, one must not forget that statistics, for all their value, can never replace living contact with people, heart-to-heart talk. A well-thought-out discussion with individual comrades, as well as with an entire collective, yields much interesting material both for theoretical reflections and for the verification of conclusions.

It is appropriate here to remember Lenin's approach to discussion. N. P. Gorbunov in his memoirs describes V. I. Lenin's astonishing capacity for drawing the necessary facts and information from a thousand sources and for extracting something valuable from every encounter. In discussions with workers and peasants he caught the pulse of life, perceived even imperceptible changes in the correlation of class forces and was able on the basis of the facts reported to him to find the correct line. By posing simple questions, Vladimir Ilyich was able to verify the seriousness of the informtaion of the person with whom he was talking, to analyze it critically, to grasp the essence of the matter quickly and to single out the necessary facts, which seemed at first glance to be insignificant, of little importance.

To revive Lenin's approach to scientific research and to methods of concrete social analysis under the new conditions is an urgent task of the day.

Party cadres are called upon not only to master the methods of concrete social analysis but also to arm Y.C.L., trade union, and other public and state organizations with them. The Party Program emphasizes the importance of the study and theoretical generalization of the practice of communist construction. One means of fulfilling this task is the broad use of social research.

Sociology and Sociologists

G. GRUSHIN

It can no longer be denied that concrete sociological research has become a reality in our country. A large number of books, pamphlets, articles and compilations is evidence of this.

Yet the arguments over sociology—concerning, among other things, its significance and even sociological research's right to existence—do not subside. They go on in university auditoriums, in scholarly journals and—particularly—in endless oral debate.

It goes without saying that debate is necessary in science. However, debate can be useful only if conducted on the level of science's real needs, that is, if it deals with the real problems that face science at any given moment. Yet it seems to us that the arguments over sociology are becoming more and more obsolete. In many respects they ignore the fact that in recent years sociology in the U.S.S.R. has taken a number of theoretical and—more important—practical forward steps and that its advances have altered the plane of the problems discussed.

That philosophers[1] have turned to concrete sociological research and that

Reprinted from G. Grushin, "Sociology and Sociologists," Literaturnaya gazeta (September 25, 1965). Translated in Current Digest of the Soviet Press, XVII, No. 40 (Copyright © October 27, 1965), 15–16.

[1] Sociology has been placed under the aegis of the philosophy department of the Soviet educational and research establishment.—Trans.

such research has spread through the country with comparative speed cannot be regarded as something that concerns science alone. This has come about primarily because Soviet society's entry into a new period of development has sharply increased the need for pursuing a scientifically grounded policy, for scientific analysis and programming of the social process. The development of society has confronted us with a host of new questions concerning the economy, the social structure, the state, law, the family and upbringing. Whereas these questions used to be raised only in very general terms, now we are concerned with their practical—that is, their supremely concrete—content; the daily activity of the masses in various spheres of public life raises scores of concrete "hows" and "whys" and demands concrete, scientific answers to these questions.

It is important to note that the concrete scientific analysis of social phenomena has become possible not only because of the increased practical need for it but also because since the 20th Party Congress the Party has established social conditions in our country that are conducive to satisfying this need.

After all, there was also a very great practical need for social theory in our country before—a quarter of a century ago, for example. But at that time many philosophers were not inclined to give concrete answers to the questions raised by society's development. Far be it from us to belittle the achievements of Soviet philosophy in the prewar and postwar years, yet the fact remains that in that period thick walls were erected between theory and practice in the field of historical materialism.

It would clearly be naive to see the root of the evils of this period in the subjective qualities of the philosophers themselves. The chief difficulty lay elsewhere: The vitality of philosophy, as of all the social sciences at the time, was affected by the atmosphere of the personality cult. In conditions when only one person was recognized as having the right to scientific creativity in this field, all that remained to the others was to comment, popularize and—admire. The work of most philosopher-scholars took the form of the armchair development of theory on the basis of analysis of general philosophical categories or of the classical writers of Marxism, while the chief method of structuring science was that of formal logic, with its rules of deduction and the noncontradiction of judgments. The concrete study of reality might in a sense have been risky, as there was the danger of arriving at conclusions that differed from those proclaimed by the unquestionable authority.

How sternly this impotence of theory was subsequently criticized is well known. In the past ten years there has probably not been a single Party document having to do with the social sciences that has not mentioned the need for philosophers to undertake immediately the investigation of urgent questions of social construction, to invade life more boldly, to study seriously all aspects of the process of social development. It was then, sometime in the mid-1950s, that the word "sociology" turned up in literature and discussions.

This term was not a new one in Marxist philosophy. It was new neither in the sense of a general theory of social structure and social development nor in the sense of concrete research into social phenomena. As for the former, Marxism itself was just such a theory, and was the first to raise it to the status of a science—it is known that "sociology" is precisely the term Lenin applied to Marx's historical materialism. As for concrete sociological research, it was conducted most extensively and in diverse forms by the classical writers of Marxism-Leninism—it was on the foundation of precisely such studies that they erected the tremendous edifices of "Capital," "The Condition of the Working Class in England," "The Economic Content of Populism" and "The Development of Capitalism in Russia."

For all that, many greeted with mistrust, and even hostiltity, the term "sociology" as applied to Soviet Marxist philosophy. A question that had been clear to Marx and to Lenin became controversial: A discussion began among Soviet philosophers, the crux of which was the relationship between sociology and historical materialism.

The reason for this paradox was clear enough. First of all, in the circumstances described above the word "sociology" had to a great extent lost its practical significance. The term had been surrendered to bourgeois philosophy, which, incidentally, had a long and strong tradition in the field. The vast scope of the sociological research begun in the 1920s and 1930s in the West, particularly the United States, fostered such identification of sociology in general with bourgeois sociological research.

However, the discussion was not an argument about words alone; in fact, that was the least of it. Questions of terminology unquestionably play an important role in science, but had this been the only aspect of this particular argument, it would surely have been comparatively easy to agree on whether historical materialism was to be called Marxist sociology or not.

The primary issue was the tasks, field and very validity of concrete sociological research. And in this sense it was an issue of the struggle between the new and the old in philosophy. The main question behind the discussion was clear: Would philosophy remain an "armchair" science, or would it fully restore to its rights the creative principle lying at its basis?

Meanwhile, as the theoretical arguments thundered, life moved on; practice called for the solution of a multitude of important questions having to do with labor, mass communications, the family, urban development, culture, human relationships, etc., and the demand, as always, determined the supply. Even before any decision was reached on the cardinal questions "on the subject matter of sociology," "on the relationship between sociology and historical materialism," on the validity of concrete sociological research, etc., some people got down to actual research.

This concrete sociological research cleared up a great deal in the abstract arguments. The first concrete sociological research to be carried out after so long an interval immediately produced significant results. Of course, it cannot be denied that there were shortcomings and errors (some of them quite serious) in specific projects by specific researchers. But the main thing is that their experience disclosed the unquestionable need for and importance of such research.

Today it is no longer possible to imagine the normal existence of a social science that does not base itself on concrete study of its field, on the analysis of empirical data. Concrete sociological research is a necessary component of and foundation for the theoretical structure of any social science—political economy, history, law, ethnography,

esthetics or ethics. And also of historical materialism. This last science, which studies the most general laws of society's development, arose, developed and is developing on the basis of the theoretical generalization of the data of all the concrete social sciences, from anthropology to political economy. But at the same time its appearance and development are unthinkable without concrete research within its own field— the relationship of social existence (in its various forms) to social consciousness (in its various forms).

The first experience also confirmed the validity of raising the question of the existence of a number of independent sociological subjects with their own specific fields—for example, the sociology of the family, the sociology of sex, the sociology of religion, social psychology and others. In any case, it would seem undeniable that there are many phenomena in social life—in social relations—that urgently require the most thorough, profound and close analysis. Whether this analysis is conducted within the framework of the existing sciences (historical materialism, ethics, demography, etc.) or whether it develops into an independent science will be determined by practice. From the practical standpoint this is secondary; the main thing is that as of today no science is studying these phenomena with the necessary depth, although the interests of social development acutely require that they be so studied.

The experience of the development of sociology has placed a number of new problems on the agenda, problems to which we feel sociologists and public opinion should give close attention.

The first is overcoming the danger of empiricism. It is common knowledge that this is the greatest failing of contemporary bourgeois sociology, in the first place American: Since Western sociologists do not have a general scientific theory of social structure and social development, they are literally drowning in a sea of "umbrellalike" studies concerned with the tiniest, very often completely unexpected, problems. If we leave aside here the prevailing trend in all bourgeois social sciences to justify the existing system, then very few bourgeois sociologists engaged in concrete research can explain what they hope to achieve by their research.

In this respect Soviet philosophers are in a fundamentally different position. However, a knowledge of theory is clearly not in itself sufficient protection against empiricism in concrete research.

The overcoming of empiricism is all the more important because the recently intensified arguments concerning the "need" or lack of it for sociology have concentrated on this point. Those opponents of sociology who accepted it somewhat earlier than the "critics from the threshold" but considerably later than the people who began to carry out concrete research have now come forward with new counterarguments: We were "for" sociology, they say, but it has not justified our expectations: Where are the researches that have advanced the social sciences, provided new theoretical formulas, helped solve fundamental practical questions, etc.?

Obviously, such an attitude really testifies to a lack of understanding of the essential nature of the scientific process: It ignores the circumstance that new theoretical formulae arise very infrequently and are inevitably the result of generalization of an enormous quantity of processed factual data, which, given the distribution of labor that characterizes the sciences, makes the existence of "empirical" researchers, on the one hand, and theoretical researchers, on the other, possible and even necessary.

At the same time, this irrational—as I would call it—form of objection does conceal a real problem: Empirical research should be conducted in conformity with the demands of theory and with a view to the theoretical or practical solution of definite questions. Yet we have by no means always achieved this.

The point to be made is that the two aspects of social science must be organically linked. Furthermore, it is clear to everyone that the concrete study of social reality, which always proves to be new social reality, perforce must enrich general theory, just as it is clear that existing theory must guide concrete research, determine its structure, methodology, etc. The task is to carry over this clarity into actual work; only then will we eliminate "blind" research projects that, however many facts and figures they turn up, are incapable of enriching theory or practice.

The next problem is the problem of the methodology and methods of social research. The crux of the matter is that the comparatively extensive scope of concrete sociological research in our country exists side by side with a very poorly developed methodological and methods base. Researchers often have a superficial attitude to this aspect of the work, and the consequence is a large number of errors, including gross ones, which not only cancel out the significance of the research but also undermine the reputation of concrete sociology as a whole.

C. Bushnell, describing the state of American sociology in 1919, wrote that the working equipment of sociology in those days resembled a museum of ancient relics more than a well-stocked workshop. Applying this apt metaphor, one might say that as late as two or three years ago our sociology resembled a modern workshop with too few tools. At that time sociologists had been given premises that only needed to be equipped with up-to-date tools—partly from abroad but principally, of course, of local manufacture. The equipping of the sociological workshop has not yet been completed, and this remains a pressing problem of Soviet sociological science.

Finally, there is one more question of extreme urgency today, one that in a sense has top priority (inasmuch as the answer to the problems mentioned above depends largely on its solution). We are referring to the problem of the organization of sociological science in our country. The substance of it is that the further development of our sociology requires the establishment of serious scientific centers. Its activities cannot be limited to a few university laboratories and a division of the Philosophy Institute of the U.S.S.R. Academy of Sciences working under a circumscribed program and lacking the necessary means (manpower and material), and even less to the amateur groups that have sprung up spontaneously at many enterprises and also in Party, Soviet and Young Communist League groups and that operate without the appropriate (often without even elementary) scientific guidance. Sociology will not begin to produce tangible benefits for the theory and practice of social construction until it receives the "lawful" organizational and material expression that every "normal" science must have.

The minimum should be the establishment of a Sociology Institute and at least one sociological journal, which could head up the scientific research conducted at all levels, provide skilled guidance, coordinate work, etc. And it is necessary to start training specialized sociological cadres on an extensive scale. It would seem perfectly obvious that no science can exist without its scientists, yet in the entire country there is no one (!) sociologist who received special training in sociology under a full program at the present-day scientific level.

Only by solving all these problems can we eliminate the "question of sociology" now under discussion. And, what is most important, only by solving these problems can we create the conditions for the functioning and development of a science that is called upon to play so important a part in the scientific guidance of social processes.

ON SOVIET SOCIOLOGY:

The American View

Current Soviet Work in Sociology:
A Note in the
Sociology of Knowledge

GEORGE FISCHER

...In rough outline, the early history of the post-Stalin "new sociology" is well known by now.[1] While it hardly existed under Stalin, academic research on social problems became the object of official concern at the turn of the 1960's. Groups of Soviet scholars began

From George Fischer, American Sociologist, May, 1966, pp. 127–132. Reprinted by permission of the American Sociological Association. Copyright 1966 from AS by Fischer.

[1] René Ahlberg, Die Entwicklung der empirischen Sozialforschung in der Sowjetunion (The Development of Empirical Research in the Soviet Union), Report No. 60 of the Osteuropa Institute (Free University of Berlin), Wiesbaden: Harrossowitz, 1964; Robert V. Allen, "Recent Soviet Literature in Sociology and Cultural Anthropology," Quarterly Journal of the Library of Congress, Vol. 22, No. 3 (July 1965); Leopold Labedz, "The Soviet Attitude to Sociology," in Walter Z. Laqueur and George Lichtheim, editors, The Soviet Cultural Scene, New York: Praeger, 1958; Leopold Labedz (or unsigned), articles in Survey since the mid-1950's; Elizabeth Ann Weinberg, "Soviet Sociology, 1960–1963," Cambridge: Massachusetts Institute of Technology. Center for International Studies, October 1, 1964, multilithed; as well as my Science and Politics.

to take part in international congresses of sociology. In the field of Marxist social philosophy, a few young scholars made plans to add "concrete" research to the deductive Soviet forms of social analysis. And scholars as well as officials argued with each other about the proper role of the "new sociology" within Marxism-Leninism.

My present note does not deal with the early sixties, when Soviet sociology was embryonic. Instead, the focus here is on the years since then. We now have on hand the actual "first steps" of the new sociology. Along with a large amount of lesser writing, the first steps consist of a dozen or so books put out by Soviet sociologists in the mid-1960's. I shall use these books here to specify the type of knowledge found in current Soviet work.

THE STATE OF THE PROFESSION

For the new Soviet type of sociology, its "first steps" meant no full separation from the parent field of philosophy. On the contrary, most sociologists still teach and do research within philosophy faculties and institutes. Yet they now ask for

537

organizational distinctness and expansion. One statement is not atypical:

Sociology will not begin to produce tangible benefits for the theory and practice of social construction until it receives the 'lawful' organizational and material expression that every 'normal' science must have.
The minimum should be the establishment of a Sociology Institute and at least one sociological journal, which could head up the scientific research conducted at all levels, provide skilled guidance, coordinate work, etc. And it is necessary to start training specialized sociological cadres on an extensive basis. It would seem perfectly obvious that no science can exist without its scientists, yet in the entire country there is not one sociologist (!) who received special training in sociology under a full program at the present-day scientific level.[2]

In some other ways, the state of the profession has changed a good deal in just the past few years. The number of people and academic institutions doing social research has risen greatly. So has the number of books and journal articles on sociology. Late in 1965, a volume came out that was billed in advance as the first issue of a sociological annual. Its name is Social Research (*Sotsialnye issledovaniia*). The first national meeting of Soviet sociologists took place in Leningrad last February. About 600 people took part. The same month, the leadership of the Soviet Sociological Association passed from the veteran philosophers and ideologists who set it up in the mid-1950's to the younger

sociologists most active in the profession. The new president is Professor Gennadi V. Osipov of Moscow. He heads the social research division of the top-level Philosophy Institute of the U.S.S.R. Academy of Sciences, and writes widely.

Most important, perhaps, is that the big debate on the scope of sociology seems to be settled, at least for the moment. That can be seen from a 1964 speech by the Communist Party's then top ideology official, Leonid F. Ilichev. He put forth an open-ended formula that a number of Soviet sociologists have quoted:

At present there exist among both Soviet and foreign Marxist scholars varying views on [the subject matter of] Marxist sociology. Some hold that Marxism as a whole makes up our sociology. Others link Marxist sociology with the theory of scientific [building of] communism. Still others believe that between historical materialism and Marxist sociology there exists roughly the same contrast as between theoretical and applied areas of the same branch of human knowledge. One can find other shadings in outlook as well. In a word, as yet we have no common point of view.

So what about it? Should we forbid the representatives of this or that point of view the right to defend their opinion? Hardly.

...we must give up intolerant attitudes toward the opinions of each other, all the more since each of the points of view mentioned has in it a rational core which cannot be simply brushed aside.[3]

[2] The statement, made by Boris A. Grushin, came out on the front page of *Literaturnaya gazeta*. A translation of it can be found in *Current Digest of the Soviet Press* (issued at Columbia University once a week and cited hereafter as CDSP), Vol. XVII, No. 40 (November 27, 1965). *Izvestiia* published a long interview with Gennadi V. Osipov. The English text appears in CDSP, Vol. XVII, No. 51 (January 12, 1966). On March 13, 1966, *Pravda* carried a piece by Vladimir N. Shubkin.

[3] *Metodologicheskie problemy nauki* (The Methodological Problems of Science), Moscow: "Nauka," 1964, p. 134. The best Soviet summary of the debate appears in Chapter 6 of A. Verbin and A. Furman, *Mesto istoricheskogo materializma v sisteme nauk* (The Place of Historical Materialism in the System of Sciences), Moscow University Press, 1965; for some source references, see also pp. 3–4. In passing, a *Pravda* resume of readers' letters on a related matter brought out one effect of the debate: "Everyone knows of the rather melan-

In all of the current Soviet work, a few main elements stand out:

1. Quantitative research is emphasized but limited in method and content.
2. Criticisms of Western sociology get much attention.
3. Doctrines about the future are treated as the main guide to analyzing the present.
4. Soviet sociologists face the common problem of critical analysis.

In the rest of this note, I will outline each of the elements.

QUANTITATIVE RESEARCH

A strong Soviet emphasis on quantitative social research does not call for as much change in outlook as may be thought. At all times, as Dahrendorf has noted, "the party organization and its varied affiliations serve as a gigantic institute of opinion research..."[4] In this context, the post-Stalin state favors both mass opinion polling[5] and scholarly

survey research as added channels of information and communication. Many scholars, too, welcome "concrete sociological research...." Selected social problems remain the focus. The scope is widening from attitudes to work to include occupational choice as well as the uses of leisure. The major Soviet output of "concrete" research consists of three big studies. All of them are related to work. The only one on which no book has yet appeared is the Gorky study. Carried out under Osipov, it has to do with the tasks and daily lives of factory workers, and how technology changes them. Two other studies were done in Leningrad and Novosibirsk.[6]

---

choly experience connected with the development of concrete sociological research. This question was raised as far back as the middle 1950s. But at that time there were people who focused their attention on discussion of the legitimacy or illegitimacy of the term ["sociology"], and as a result the organization of concrete sociological research was delayed for a long time" (CDSP, Vol. XVII, No. 23 [June 31, 1965]), p. 15.

[4] Ralf Dahrendorf, *Class and Class Conflict in Industrial Society,* Stanford University Press, 1959, p. 313.

[5] The Public Opinion Institute of the main daily for youth, *Komsomolskaia Pravda,* still holds a leading place in nonacademic polling. Thus recently a big *Komsomolskaia Pravda* poll "replicated" a Gallup poll on how youth views life (*Soviet Life,* English-language monthly, November 1965). But by now many other polls appear as well. In late 1964, for instance, the central press told of at least three polls: attitudes to village life, to army life, and to theater-going. The accounts are translated in CDSP, Vol. XVI, Nos. 46, 47, and 48 (all December 1964). Allen Kassof commented on the early *Komsomolskaia Pravda* polls in

"Moscow Discovers Public Opinion Polls," *Problems of Communism,* May–June 1961. The methods used in these polls are sketched (by Boris A. Grushin) in G. K. Ashin *et al,* editors, *Voprosy organizatsii i metodiki konkretno-sotsiologicheskikh issledovanii* (Questions of the Organization and Methods of Concrete Sociological Research), Moscow, "Rosvuzizdat," 1963. This spring, a number of speeches at the 23rd Party Congress cited an official interest in quantitative social research. The interest, especially on the part of youth officials, is summed up in an article, "The Student and the Social Sciences," in *Komsomolskaia Pravda,* April 20, 1966.

[6] *Leningrad Study:* I. Andrei G. Zdravomyslov and Vladimir A. Yadov, editors and senior authors, *Trud i razvitie lichnosti* (Work and Development of the Personality), Leningrad: "Lenizdat," 1965; II. article by Zdravomyslov and Yadov in *Voprosy filosofii,* Vol. 18, No. 4 (April 1964)—translated in CDSP, Vol. XVI, No. 24 (July 8, 1964); III. article by Zdravomyslov and Yadov in Gennadi V. Osipov, editor, *Sotsiologiia v SSSR* (Sociology in the USSR), Vol. 2, Moscow: "Nauka," 1965; IV. due to appear in 1966 is an overall report on the study, with methodological and statistical appendixes: *Chelovek i ego rabota, Konkretno-sotsiologicheskoe issledovanie* (Man and his Work, A Concrete Sociological Study), Moscow, "Mysl."

Novosibirsk Study: I. Vladimir N. Shubkin *et al.,* Part II (pp. 152–267) of Shubkin, editor, *Kolichestvennye metody v sotsiologicheskikh issledovaniiakh* (Quantitative Methods in Sociological Research), Novosibirsk

TABLE 1. THE INTERACTION OF VALUE ORIENTATIONS AMONG SOVIET YOUNG WORKERS*
(Percent of Secondary Orientations for each Primary Orientation)

Primary Orientation	Number	Secondary Orientations				
		Family	Education	Civic Work	Job	Pay
Family	1,100	..	15%	14%	10%	10%
Education	627	23%	..	20%	15%	5%
Civic Work	329	42%	42%	..	21%	7%
Job	207	55%	48%	37%	..	12%
Pay	161	66%	21%	15%	16%	..
No Orientation	970	..	..	..	..	..
Distribution in Whole Sample	2,667	38%	23%	12%	10%	6%

* Source: Leningrad Study—adapted from table in Andrei G. Zdravomyslov and Vladimir A. Yadov, "Attitudes to Work and Personal Value Orientations" (in Russian), in Gennadi V. Osipov, editor, *Sotsiologiia v SSSR* (Sociology in the USSR), Vol. 2, Moscow: "Nauka," 1965, p. 205.

The Leningrad study was led by the co-directors of the Social Research Laboratory of Leningrad University, Vladimir A. Yadov and Andrei G. Zdravomyslov. Much of the study draws on a sizeable questionnaire, filled out by a stratified random sample of 2,665 workers under the age of 30. Findings cover such topics as their technical creativity

University Press, 1964; II. article by Shubkin in *Voprosy filosofii*, Vol. 18, No. 8 (September 1964); III. artcile by Shubkin in *Voprosy filosofii*, Vol. 19, No. 5 (May 1965)—translated in CDSP, Vol. XVII, No. 30 (August 18, 1965); IV. article by Shubkin in Nikolai V. Novikov *et al.*, editors, *Sotsialnye issledovaniia* (Social Research), Moscow: "Nauka," 1965; *Gorky Study:* the title announced for a forthcoming book on it is *Tekhnicheskii progress i rabochii klass, Konkretnoe sotsialnoe issledovanie na materialakh Gorkovskoi oblasti* (Technical Progress and the Working Class, Concrete Social Research with Data from Gorky Province), Moscow, "Nauka." Three research reports on the Gorky study appear in Osipov, editor, *Sotsiologiia v SSSR, op. cit.*, Vol. 2. These reports take up technical creativity (B. I. Yeremeev), the relation of psychological traits to the nature of work (N. G. Valentinova), and how time is used outside of working hours (Osipov and S. F. Frolov).

(the "rationalization" proposals made to raise output), attitudes to manual occupations, how levels of skill and education affect attitudes to work, and reasons for changing jobs. A separate essay goes into value orientations toward work and leisure. Table 1 shows the links it reports between various value orientations.

The Novosibirsk study pioneers in Soviet social analysis of occupational choice. The study is headed by Vladimir N. Shubkin, chief of the social research section of a Laboratory of Mathematical Economics at Novosibirsk University. Like the one in Leningrad, the Novosibirsk study relies in large measure on individual questionnaires. They were completed by a simple random sample of 2940 high school seniors throughout Novosibirsk province. A follow-up survey asked for information from school principals, on initial career steps of the respondents. One finding of the study revolves around the ratings assigned to seventy typical occupations. Some of the ranking appears in Table 2.

The Novosibirsk study relied on open-ended questions; the Leningrad one on

TABLE 2. OCCUPATIONAL PREFER-
ENCE* OF SOVIET HIGH SCHOOL
GRADUATES**

	*Professional Work in Science****	
	Rank	Points
Physics	1	7.69
Mathematics	2	7.50
Medical Research	3	7.32
Chemistry	4	7.23
Geology	5	6.84
Economic-Mathematical Research	6	6.33
History	7	6.17
Philosophy	8	6.05
Philology	9	5.75
Economics	10	5.52
Biology	11	4.66

	Sub-Professional and Manual Work	
Transport and Communications****	1	5.28
Education, Culture and Public Health	2	4.82
Industry	3	4.26
Construction	4	4.07
Agriculture	5	3.75
Services (e.g., Sales and Clerical)	6	2.63

* Evaluation on point scale from 1 to 10: (N = 280).

** Source: Novosibirsk Study—adapted from tables in Vladimir N. Shubkin, "...Problems of Job Placement and Occupational Choice" (in Russian), *Voprosy filosofii*, Vol. 19, No. 5 (May 1965), translated in CDSP, Vol. XVII, No. 30 (August 18, 1965), p. 7.

*** Outside science, three occupations fall between rank 3 and 4: doctors, writers, and artists. The mean rating of fourteen engineering occupations puts engineers, as a group, between rank 6 and 7.

**** The occupations of pilot and radio mechanic got the second highest rating in the whole survey, just below physics.

a more complex set of pretested multiple-choice questions. The same contrast appears in the analysis of data. The measure of association between variables used in the Novosibirsk study was a simple correlation. In the Leningrad work, the chi-square significance test was used to measure relationships. Within the Leningrad study itself, some of the research reports stand out technically over the others (notably a longer report on why workers change jobs).

As against its lower technical level, the Novosibirsk study covers a cross section of urban and rural strata. Thus it goes beyond the usual scope of workers and perhaps professionals and subprofessionals in industry.[7] It also has as one of its major indicators the occupations of the parents. In Soviet terms, these are innovations. They lead to some real differentiations, as can be seen in Table 3.

For drawing comparisons between modern societies, the new Soviet research is rich with at least preliminary data. I cannot begin to do justice to it here. Let me cite just one example of such data. It comes from a research report of the Leningrad study. According to the report, one positive correlation was found consistently. Men in occupations calling for higher skills wanted their work to be interesting. Those in lower-skill jobs tended to put much more stress on pay. In his essay on "Industrial Man," Inkeles held that in all modern societies a relation seems to exist between the nature of an occupation and what part of it led to the

[7] In 1962, at the world congress of sociology, Andreeva gave a list of studies she and other Soviet sociologists were doing on intellectuals, professionals, and leadership groups in Soviet society. See Galina M. Andreeva, "The Formation of New Representatives of the Intelligentsia and Leaders in the Course of the Building of Socialism," *Transactions of the Fifth World Congress of Sociology*, Vol. III, Louvain: International Sociological Association, 1964, pp. 233–234n. None of the research has come out in book form.

TABLE 3. THE SOCIAL ORIGIN AND EARLY CAREER OF SOVIET HIGH SCHOOL GRADUATES*

	Proportion of Graduates Wishing to:			Proportion of Graduates Who Did:		
		Combine Work with			Combine Work with	
Group to Which Parents Belong	Work	Study	Study	Work	Study	Study
Urban Professionals	2%	5%	93%	15%	3%	82%
Rural Professionals	11%	13%	76%	42%	..	58%
Sub-Professionals and Workers in Industry and Construction	11%	6%	83%	36%	3%	61%
Sub-Professionals and Workers in Transport and Communications	..	18%	82%	55%	..	45%
Sub-Professionals and Workers in Agriculture	10%	14%	76%	90%	..	10%
Sub-Professionals and Workers in Service Work	9%	15%	76%	38%	3%	59%
Other	12%	38%	50%	63%	12%	25%
Percentage of the Whole Sample	7%	10%	83%	37%	2%	61%

* Source: Novosibirsk Study—same source as Table 2, adapted from table on p. 6.

most satisfaction. As far as young Soviet workers go, the Leningrad study bears out the surmise that Inkeles had made.[8]

What, then, are the Soviet ways of doing "concrete" research? As of now, the answer can be brief. Soviet sociologists pay much more heed to the gathering and measuring of quantitative data than to its later analysis and interpretation. Nearly all of the current research belongs to the descriptive type of survey and not the explanatory, "causal" type. As yet no one has tried anything like the structural, "relational" analysis. . . .

The data revolve around attitudes and a few objective individual traits. This is why, as Parsons concluded after a visit, "a considerable part of the group's empirical research would be classified by American sociologists as social psychology."[9] Finally, on the selected social problems that Soviet sociologists study, their policy recommendations neither say nor imply that all is well at present. Yet these recommendations turn out to be quite unsystematic and lacking in novelty.

The technical contrast between the two big surveys, and within the Leningrad study as well, suggests that specialists are quite open to new research methods. If that is so, however, why is current quantitative research limited in a variety of ways? To begin with, Soviet scholars have had little time to try out new techniques. As important is the effect of divergent types of knowledge. What we may call the concrete orientation in Soviet sociology does not see firsthand experience as the main test of reality. That test lies in ideological knowledge. Quantitative social re-

[8] V. V. Vodzinskaia, "The Attitude of the Young Worker to his Occupation" (in Russian), in *Trud i razvitie lichnosti, op. cit.,* and Alex Inkeles, "Industrial Man," *American Journal of Sociology,* Vol. LXVI, No. 1 (July 1960), p. 12.

[9] Parsons, "An American Impression of Sociology in the Soviet Union," *American Sociological Review* (Feb. 1965), p. 124.

search is but a better way to collect data.

CRITICISMS OF WESTERN SOCIOLOGY

On no other subject have so many leading Soviet scholars in the field written books as on sociology in the West. The more solid of these books contain documentation, and show some real knowledge. Most of them treat specific questions.

As far back as 1959, the main Soviet writer on stratification—Vadim S. Semenov, of the Philosophy Institute—published a volume on "problems of classes and class struggles in contemporary bourgeois sociology." In 1962 came out the only book on management by a Soviet sociologist (Dzherman M. Gvishiani): *The Sociology of [American] Business*. Two years later, a couple of sociologists at Leningrad University put out specialized studies on Western social theory. Igor S. Kon wrote on positivism and neo-positivism, and Andrei G. Zdravomyslov on the concept of interests. In the one recent Soviet book on the sociology of religion (1965), Yuri A. Levada deals almost wholly with Western theory and research. About to be published are books by two Moscow sociologists: N. V. Novikov (Philosophy Institute) on Parsons and the general theory of action, and Yuri A. Zamoshkin (Academy of Social Sciences of the CPSU Central Committee) on personality and "the crisis of [bourgeois] individualism."

Two major works, however, treat the subject of Western sociology as a whole. One is by Osipov, the other by Galina M. Andreeva of Moscow University.[10]

Osipov's book, which came out in 1964, deals with the main concepts of Western sociology. His book takes up three sets of concepts: society, social classes and groups, social change and social progress. Andreeva, on the other hand, centers on the methods of empirical research. Her book, published in 1965, has chapters on the main fields of empirical research, on the procedure and techniques of research, and on the main themes of empirical methodology. A concluding chapter contains a critique of Merton's case for theories of the middle range, and the Parsons theory of action.

Perhaps because the subject is a bit more limited, Andreeva's book seems more systematic. It gives the reader more relevant facts, has fewer bibliographical errors, and does not go back to quotes from Marx and Lenin as often or as extensively as does the book by Osipov.

Beyond these contrasts, though, the two books have much in common with each other and with other Soviet works on Western sociology. Most revealing here is the overall mode of writing about the ways and means of sociology. A Manichean dichotomy overshadows all else. One side embodies darkness and failure. The other is all light and success. True, from time to time a line is drawn between more enlightened scholars in the West and those beyond redemption. Passing note is made of technical advances which Marxist sociologists can and should use, if they do so with care. A few of the Soviet works, too, deviate from the usual mode. By and large, however, the tone continues to be one of fierce and total combat, of

10 Gennadi V. Osipov, *Sovremennaia burzhauznaia sotsiologiia* (Contemporary Bourgeois Sociology), Moscow: "Nauka," 1964; Galina M. Andreeva, *Sovremennaia burzhauznaia empiricheskaia sotsiologiia* (Contempo-

rary Bourgeois Empirical Sociology), Moscow: "Mysl," 1965. A revised edition of Osipov's book is to appear in 1966. As a new step, a Soviet translation just came out of *Sociology Today,* the 1959 collection sponsored by the American Sociological Association.

true believers set to battle infidels to the bitter end.[11]

In Mannheim's terms, this mode of writing reflects both a "total" and a "special" conception of ideology. In the case of any opponent, not just some ideas must perforce be "ideological," in the negative sense of false consciousness, but all of them. And not every group, but only an opponent, is bound to ideas that mirror his group's place in society.[12] In her book, Andreeva shows how Soviet sociologists put these "total" and "special" conceptions of ideology today:

The values recognized in a society are, of course, always values of definite social forces. Bourgeois sociology does not see a possible objective criterion for weighing the values themselves. But that is just the problem. Such a criterion does exist. It reveals itself in social science if it bases itself on certain philosophical principles— on the principles of that world view which is the world view of the leading progressive force of history in the contemporary era, the working class.

Any other philosophy cannot, indeed, offer objective criteria of values. The approach to values which marks, for instance, the philosophy of neo-Kantianism gave nothing except a new variant of subjectivism. In rejecting the "speculations" of philosophy, empirical sociology rejects along with them the value approach. It is right in that part

where it admits the fruitlessness of the approach of idealistic philosophy. It is not right when it does not see the possibility of a fundamentally different approach to values within philosophy itself. But on this question [empirical sociology] cannot be right, for its class and theoretical position rules out such a possibility (Andreeva, pp. 186 and 187).

What accounts for the strong emphasis on criticizing Western sociology—and the mode of doing it? One likely reason is the strain of swift acculturation and legitimation of a science. The strain must be great.

As salient is an outlook which Soviet sociologists find all too rare in the West. As far as their writings show, all members of the profession share a strong, unambivalent rationalism. Theirs remains a highly optimistic and activist rationalism. It is collectivist and statist as well. To some degree, the lack of any such outlook among most Western sociologists make them seem alien and their work dubious.

In the Soviet Union, lastly, sociologists share with officials an ideological view of how societies should be either organized or analyzed. On matters of doctrine, moreover, Soviet ways of thinking and arguing have changed much less than they have on many other things. The Soviet sociologist of today believes deeply in Mannheim's "total" and "special" conceptions of ideology.

DOCTRINES ABOUT THE FUTURE AND ANALYSES OF THE PRESENT

The future-oriented element in Soviet ideology has long been familiar. Within sociology, several books now offer examples of the same future orientation. For them, overall analysis of society has as its frame of reference not the present but the future. The books differ a great deal from the "concrete" studies cited.

---

[11] Soviet views on Western sociology are discussed by Lewis S. Feuer, "Meeting the [Soviet] Philosophers," *Survey,* No. 51 (April 1964); Allen Kassof, "American Sociology Through Soviet Eyes," *American Sociological Review,* Vol. 30, No. 1 (February 1965); and Paul Hollander, "The Dilemmas of Soviet Sociology," *Problems of Communism,* November–December 1965. Within the sociology of knowledge, a comparative way of looking at such national patterns is suggested by Merton, "Social Conflict over Styles of Sociological Work," *Transactions of the Fourth World Congress of Sociology,* Vol. III, Louvain: International Sociological Association, 1961.

[12] Karl Mannheim, *Ideology and Utopia,* New York: Harcourt, Brace, 1946, pp. 68–69n.

TABLE 4. COLLECTIVE FARMERS WHO TAKE PART IN LOCAL ADMINISTRATION*

Name of Collective Farm**	Mechanics	Animal Husbandry	Construction and Maintenance	Farm Field Work
"XXI Congress of CPSU"	23%	12%	8%	5%
(N: 1359)	(177)	(210)	(60)	(912)
"Lenin"	14%	9%	9%	4%
(N: 1564)	(257)	(167)	(32)	(1108)
"Young Communist"	29%	10%	9%	4%
(N: 273)	(31)	(72)	(11)	(159)

* The percentages in the table are based on totals which appear below them. Source: adapted from table in Vladimir I. Razin, editor, *Stanovlenie kommunisticheskogo samoupravleniia* (The Development of Communist Self-Government), Moscow University Press, 1965, p. 174.

** Located in Tomsk Province, in Siberia. "N" refers to the number of members in each collective farm.

And, as of now, they are quite a bit more typical of the field.

Aside from the future orientation, three things set these standard works apart from the surveys. They draw their data from a melange of casually cited sources. These range from census and output data to anecdotes from the mass media. As the main evidence, quotes from official documents and doctrinal classics stand out. From time to time, small pieces of survey research are now added. One study, for instance, gave such data to support the view that skilled workers take part in local administration more than do others. Table 4 shows all of this evidence.

Secondly, the topics of these studies come much closer to the central institutions of the society than do topics of the "concrete" research. This is true of all four studies I shall mention. Thus Anatoli A. Zvorykin, a member of the Philosophy Institute and a veteran student of science and technology, takes up the nature and social effects of technology. One of the books contains an attempt to study an entire community, a Moldavian (ex-Rumanian) village named Kopanka. Although this study includes only the least analytical type of quantitative research, two survey specialists—Osipov and Shubkin—were among its project directors. A group of sociologists under Vladimir I. Razin, of Moscow University, wrote a book on the trends toward a popular share in government. Still another book with a future orientation was put out under the auspices of the party's own Academy of Social Sciences. The topic of the book reaches the very heart of classic Marxian sociology, the make-up and relations of classes.[13]

Studies like these have one more feature in common. All of them talk of the society of today as no more than a

[13] Anatoli A. Zvorykin, *Nauka, proizvodstvo, trud* (Science, Production, Work), Moscow: "Nauka," 1965; V. N. Yermuratski *et al.*, editors, *Kopanka 25 let spustia* (Kopanka After 25 Years), Moscow: "Nauka," 1965; Vladimir I. Razin, editor, *Stanovlenie kommunisticheskogo samoupravleniia* (The Development of Communist Self-Government), Moscow University Press, 1965; and E. N. Chesnokov *et al.*, editors, *Puti preodoleniia sushchestvennykh razlichii mezhdu umstvennym i fizicheskim trudom* (The Patterns of Overcoming Essential Differences Between Mental and Physical Labor), Moscow: "Mysl," 1965.

passing way station en route to an ideal future. What makes progress certain are above all else the bounties of science and technology. That remains a major theme in post-Stalin doctrines about the future. Especially the sociologists with a future orientation echo this theme time and again. Any futuristic elements in the here and now are not only singled out but portrayed with euphoria. Despite their broad topics, therefore, these books say little about the whole of any present-day structure.

THE PROBLEM OF CRITICAL ANALYSIS

My brief overview of current Soviet work in sociology brings out two orientations, the future and the concrete. When we consider the type of knowledge these orientations embody, the conclusion seems clear. Both orientations belong wholly to the ideological type of knowledge. This is equally true whether Soviet sociologists do quantitative research on selected social problems or whether they put forth random evidence that life today is moving toward a future ideal. Throughout, the social theory is ideological. So is the methodology.

No sharp line can be drawn between the scholars that follow one orientation or the other.[14] Nonetheless, some contrast does appear. In form, at least, work in the future orientation shows a good deal less change from earlier Soviet analyses of society. And if we look at

Soviet sociologists who are now most active professionally, they tend to be closer to the concrete orientation (as well as to documented criticism of Western sociology).

This raises a set of questions about the concrete orientation. At present, it seeks rigorous quantitative methods of studying reality. Yet can Soviet sociologists move from limited descriptive surveys to some that aim at causal analysis? Can they move from studying individual responses to the environment to a structural analysis of the environment itself? And if they eventually do both, which is quite likely in the years ahead, can Soviet scholars ever do so as far as any central part of the society goes?

Some of the answer is political. In Eastern Europe, several communist states give sociologists more leeway.[15] Of late, the Soviet state itself has gone far in "secularizing" the field of economics. Soviet economists can now be wholly empirical about a range of quite basic questions as they could not just a few years ago. While sociology differs greatly in its history and functions, such a shift cannot be ruled out altogether.[16]

Yet politics is no more than part of the story. The rest of it can probably be found within sociology. In this field, what kind of empirical research can Soviet sociologists do without giving up an ideological outlook? As yet, no school of sociology has combined an empirical concern with human behavior and the

---

[14] One work especially cannot be assigned to either orientation. It fits somewhere in between. I have in mind a book by a leading Soviet specialist on the family, a member of the Leningrad Branch of the USSR Academy of Sciences: Anatoli G. Kharchev, *Brak i semia v SSSR* (Marriage and Family in the USSR), Moscow: "Mysl," 1964. Up to half of this book, I might add, deals with family life not in the Soviet Union but in the West.

[15] Jerzy J. Wiatr, *Political Sociology in Eastern Europe, A Trend Report and Bibliography* (*Current Sociology*, Vol. XIII, No. 2), Oxford: Blackwell, 1964; Gabor Kiss, "Soziologie in Osteuropa" (Sociology in Eastern Europe), *Osteuropa*, Vol. 15, No. 11–12 (November–December 1965).

[16] I touch on this question in *Slavic Review*, Vol. XXIV, No. 3 (September 1965), pp. 581–582.

much broader philosophical and ideological concern with existential or ideal forms of social organization. Wolff has pointed up this deep gulf between "American" and "European" sociology, between individual-psychological realism (and social-historical nominalism) on the one hand, and the very opposite metaphysical tendencies on the other.[17]

In the recent quantitative research by Soviet sociologists, we see a lot of the "American" individual realism and social nominalism to which Wolff refers.

[17] Kurt H. Wolff, "The Sociology of Knowledge and Sociological Theory," in Llewellyn Gross, editor, *Symposium on Sociological Theory,* New York: Harper and Row, 1959, especially pp. 580–582.

That does not mean at all that some Soviet sociologists are giving up the ideological type of knowledge for the empirical one. Rather, in our time the two types of knowledge themselves may have developed a basic epistemological likeness.

As long as any type of knowledge involves no methodically critical view of reality, sociologists using it are apt to treat the existing institutions and values as a given. Hence they look not at society as a whole but at lesser units within it, or at individual attitudes and adjustments to it. Today this pattern applies to the Soviet kind of sociology, and to the main American kind.

American Sociology
Through Soviet Eyes

ALLEN KASSOF

Sociology has been one of the incidental beneficiaries of the halting political thaw in the Soviet Union since Stalin's death. Banned as a discipline until less than a decade ago, it now is accorded tentative and limited official tolerance. An increasing number of academicians identify themselves as sociologists; philosophy journals carry articles on sociological themes; a few empirical studies and public opinion

Reprinted from A. Kassof, American Sociological Review, *February, 1965, pp. 114–112. Reprinted by permission of the American Sociological Association. Copyright 1965 from* ASR *by Kassof.*

polls have been published.[1] Release from Stalinist restrictions has also given Soviet sociologists their first opportunity to read and write about foreign sociology and to participate in international conferences.

These developments have raised the hope that exchanges in the dispassionate language of the social sciences might help bridge the bitter ideological gap

[1] These developments are reviewed by George Fischer in *Science and Politics: The New Sociology in the Soviet Union,* Ithaca: Cornell Research Papers in International Studies, I, 1964, and by Leopold Labedz in "Sociology as a Vocation," *Survey,* July, 1963, pp. 57–65.

between East and West. But Soviet sociological writing has not been very encouraging. Soviet sociologists have declared an ideological war against what they call bourgeois sociology, and the result is a badly distorted, but fascinating, version of what sociology is like in the "capitalist camp."

The main attack centers on the United States, not only because the Soviets consider it preeminent in "bourgeois" sociological teaching and research but because the crisis of sociology in the "most advanced" capitalist nation is sharply exposed to the trained eye of the Marxist critic. The basis of their attack is that American (Western) sociology, because it refuses to recognize the universal validity of Marxism-Leninism, is politically reactionary and scientifically sterile. Bourgeois sociology is said to be incapable of formulating general theory, hopelessly mired in insignificant and non-cumulative empirical studies, worthless as a tool of social analysis or as a basis for intelligent social action. At the same time, "monopoly capitalism" and "imperalist ruling circles" use sociology as an ideological weapon to hide from the masses the evils of an exploitative system and to divert their attention from the tasks of the proletarian revolution.

The comments of sociologist G. M. Andreeva, of Moscow University, are typical:

The critique of contemporary empirical [bourgeois] sociology is an important part of the struggle of sociologist-Marxists against bourgeois ideology in the current stage....

Empirical sociology has had a widespread propagation in the capitalist countries. It is a very subtle weapon in the arsenal of bourgeois means of apology for contemporary capitalism. Hiding behind the "scientific" nature of its methods, choosing some very narrow objects of research, it easily creates the appearance of full objec-

tivity, non-partyness [that is, representing the interest of no social class], full "freedom from ideological influences."

...in certain narrow realms of research empirical sociology sometimes achieves useful results. Bourgeois sociologists use this as a demonstration of its "productiveness," its "link with practice," and they try to sow harmful illusions concerning the possibilities of empirical sociology in the reform of contemporary capitalism.

...now that concrete sociological research in our country is being organized on a broad front, it is very important to clearly illuminate and to determine the principal differences between these researches and the researches of bourgeois empirical sociology, to contrast the methodological richness of the Marxist science of society with the theoretical impotence of bourgeois empirical sociological thought.

...finally, bourgeois empirical sociology is now undergoing a period of deep crisis ...and our criticism should take account of these changes.[2]

SOCIOLOGY AND CAPITALISM

The scientific vacuity of bourgeois sociology and the crisis that it allegedly faces are closely related, say the Soviet critics, to the historical development of the capitalist order that it serves. G. B. Osipov, of the Institute of Philosophy, writes:

It is a special tool of the state-monopolist organization, one of the means of the ideological disorientation of the masses, of a transformation of the latter's consciousness into attitudes useful to the ruling class.[3]

[2] G. M. Andreeva, "Burzhuaznaia empiricheskaia sotsiologiia v poiskakh vykhoda iz krizisa" ("Bourgeois Empirical Sociology in Search of a Way out of Crisis"), *Filosofskie nauki*, 1962, No. 5, pp. 32–41.

[3] G. B. Osipov, "Nekotorye cherty i osobennosti burzhuaznoi sotsiology XX veka" ("Some Features and Peculiarities of Bourgeois Sociology of the 20th Century"), *Voprosy filosofii*, August, 1962, pp. 120–131.

...While rejecting bourgeois sociology as scientifically void, Soviet writers have not hesitated to cite the descriptive works of American sociologists as evidence of the insoluble problems generated by capitalism. Iuryi Zamoshkin, a member of the Moscow University faculty and an editor of *Voprosy filosofii* (*Problems of Philosophy*) who has travelled in the United States, specializes in writing critical commentaries on American life.

In one article, Zamoshkin concludes that the "objective contradictions" of capitalism lead "inevitably" to anomie, crime, and delinquency.[4] Merton, Parsons, Cohen, Cloward, and Ohlin, he writes, have demonstrated that the inconsistency between the individualistic doctrine of success and the severely limited opportunities available to Americans today are the basis of social problems. But, he argues, their bourgeois outlook blinds American sociologists to the obvious fact that capitalist production relations are at fault and that the only solution lies in the revolutionary overthrow of capitalism in America. Meanwhile, the development of "modern state-monopoly capitalism" continues to produce amorality and delinquency, for the "demagogic slogan" of equality for all only creates intolerable frustrations among the masses of "helpless servants" of the capitalist class.

On a related theme, Zamoshkin extracts from the social commentaries of Max Lerner, C. Wright Mills, Eric Fromm, Karl Mannheim, David Riesman, and others, to show how the "ruling circles" of contemporary capitalism attempt to enslave the individual by promoting bourgeois forms of group

activity and how the encroachments of monopolistic bureaucracy have dehumanized American society and threaten to destroy personality.[5]

The personality of the simple American —that is the realm where there is now developing a serious class struggle, a struggle between bourgeois consciousness, bourgeois psychology, and the new, revolutionary consciousness and psychology directed against imperialism and its vices. From this also stems the attention on the part of the "collectivist" groups and organizations created by state-monopoly capitalism of the USA.

This drive for pseudo-collectivism, writes Zamoshkin, is closely linked to the "fascist tendencies characteristic of an imperialistic bourgeoisie, with the policy of militarization of the economy and all of social life."

The ideology of "groupism" attempts to subordinate the American workers to various types of military, political, and church and other organizations created in abundance by contemporary capitalism in the USA.

In another essay,[6] Zamoshkin seeks to demonstrate that monopoly capitalism with its increasingly fierce exploitation of the working class has destroyed social respect for labor. Reliance on the raw stimulus of self-interest and on the profit motive is becoming less and less effective, because the real income of workers steadily decreases as the fruits of their labors are siphoned off by capitalists. To support his contentions, he offers quotations from the writings of Mills, Merton and Nisbet, Riesman,

---

4 IU. A. Zamoshkin, "Problema amoralizma i prestupnosti v sovremennoi amerikanskoi sotsiologii" ("The Problem of Amoralism and Crime in Contemporary American Sociology"), *ibid.*, April, 1961, pp. 25–26.

5 IU. A. Zamoshkin, "Biurokratizatsiia burzhuaznogo obshchestva i sud'by lichnosti" ("The Bureaucratization of Bourgeois Society and the Destiny of the Personality"), *ibid.*, April, 1961, pp. 71–85.

6 IU. A. Zamoshkin, "Krizis 'amerikanskoi delovitosti'" ("The Crisis of the 'American Business-Like Character'"), *ibid.*, November, 1962, pp. 52–55.

Vidich and Bensman, Daniel Bell, Paul Goodman, Ely Chinoy, and others.

FUNCTIONALISM IN THE SERVICE OF POLITICAL REACTION

Among the chief ideological offenders in contemporary bourgeois sociology, according to the Soviet critics, are the functionalists. Marion Levy, for example, is taken to task for favoring "multifactor causality" as superior to Marxist economic determinism, and charged with oversimplifying and "flagrantly misconstruing" the Marxist understanding of causality.[7] Robert Merton's "theories of the middle range" are dismissed as unscientific, while Ely Chinoy's *Sociological Perspectives* is described as a blatant piece of functionalist propaganda.[8]

The main target is Talcott Parsons, whose theory of social action is said openly to serve capitalist class interests. The official summary of N. V. Noviskov's "Contemporary American Capitalism and 'The Theory of Social Action,'" succinctly states the Soviet argument:

...the theoretical constructions of the "theory of social action"...represent an attempt to translate into scientific idiom the intuition of an enterpriser, who is affected by the changes entailed in state-monopoly capitalism....

The model of the "social system" in the theory of action is based upon a fetishization of the elements of personal relations contained within social relations, on an interpretation of all kinds of emotional relations as the essence of social relations. This model is an imprint of the illusions cherished by agents of the present-day

bureaucratized business, who believe that the network of personal contacts determines the world of business...

...T. Parsons regards the subjection of individuals to a code of personal relationships that has spontaneously emerged, as a prerequisite for multiform human activity ...the "theory of social action" attempts to throw the veil of "naturality" over the transformation of American society into a bureaucratic machine.[9]

"The theory of social action," Novikov writes in a different essay, "is linked by thousands of threads to an openly pro-capitalist, propagandistic literature which, in its attempts to hide, to paint over the obvious defects of capitalism, often goes to open absurdities and falsehoods."[10] Far from constituting a genuine innovation in social analysis, action theory is merely a restatement of commonplace, banal psychologism and philosophical idealism (as opposed, that is, to philosophical materialism). In particular, the teachings of action theory are used to convince the masses that their unfortunate condition results, not from the objective facts of economics (which can be altered by revolutionary action), but from the subjective (and not susceptible to revolution) evaluations of others in the society. These efforts to deny the division of capitalist society into mutually hostile classes reveal the essentially reactionary nature of bourgeois sociology; they are the basis for the "openly pro-capitalist doctrine of human relations," which supposedly demonstrates new, humanitarian

[7] M. Sh. Bakhitov, "Problema prichinosti v sotsiologii i kritika funktsionalizma" ("The Problem of Causality in Sociology and the Critique of Functionalism"), *ibid.*, September, 1963, pp. 78–88.

[8] *Ibid.*

[9] N. V. Novikov, "Sovremennyi amerikanskii kapitalizm i 'teoriia sotsial'nogo deistviia' T. Parsonsa" ("Contemporary American Capitalism and the Theory of Social Action' of T. Parsons"), *ibid.*, March, 1963, pp. 118–129; the official summary is on p. 185.

[10] N. V. Novikov, 'Ideologicheskii smysl 'teorii sotsial'nogo deistviia'" ("The Ideological Meaning of the 'Theory of Social Action'"), *Filosofskie nauki*, 1961, No. 4, pp. 54–61.

conditions under contemporary capitalism and which proclaims "a spiritual unity between workers and entrepreneurs."

In the same vein, action theorists are charged with belittling the importance of economic factors in social life in order to foster the myth that members of contemporary bourgeois society are "collectivists" motivated by far more admirable goals—self-respect, prestige, the good opinion of others—than a crude hungering after money. Parsons and Smelser, for example,

hide the fact that in the United States these things are obtained only with money, that the drive for prestige is the drive for wealth. . . . With the help of "non-economic factors in economic behavior" the partisans of "human relations" try to prove that in the last decades the main thing for the worker in the capitalist enterprise is allegedly not economic interest but love of work, striving for moral recognition from peers and management, and so forth. From another side, management and entrepreneurs are depicted as altruists, for whom, allegedly, profit in general has ceased to play the role of stimulant in economic activity.[11]

Although action theory is partially effective as an instrument of propaganda, it is powerless in fact to solve social problems under capitalism, for its stress on socialization leads bourgeois students of social disorganization to the false conclusion that social problems arise from inadequate personality training—rather than from the rotten fabric of capitalist life.

INDUSTRIAL SOCIOLOGY AS A TOOL OF MONOPOLY CAPITALISM

The reactionary political orientation of bourgeois sociology, according to the Soviet critics, is reflected especially in

industrial sociology, or "managerism," which constitutes an effort to still the burgeoning class conflict, to patch the growing rift between capital and labor. Because bourgeois sociology is incapable of grasping the true nature of contemporary society, however, industrial sociology is confined to minor empirical research concerning the internal administration of enterprises. D. M. Grishiani, in an essay on American industrial sociology, writes:

The meliorist and pseudo-optimistic conceptions existing in managerism, its firm link with concreté problems of the administration of business, have led to its rapid and widespread propagation among business people in America. Today it is possible to call it a kind of "pocket sociology" of the American businessman.[12]

But in the long run the discoveries of industrial sociology will not save capitalism.

Monopoly capitalism, incapable of escaping the inevitable ruin of the capitalist system as a whole and not being in a position to create an entire scientific system of outlooks on social life, tries to substitute the "science of organization and administration" of production as a basis for the viability of capitalism, turning it into a party theory and giving it one of the foremost places in the arsenal of sociological means for the defense of capitalism.

Useless as science, impotent to stem the rising revolutionary consciousness of the working masses, bourgeois industrial sociology, Grishiani points out, nevertheless provides the Marxist observer with further evidence of the crisis of capitalism. The rapid development of industrial sociology in America testifies to the inherent contradictions and strains that the sociologists have been

11 *Ibid.*

12 D. M. Grishiani, " 'Menedzherizm'—amerikanskaia sotsiologiia biznesa" (" 'Managerism'—the American Sociology of Business"), *Voprosy filosofii,* May, 1961, pp. 80–92.

commissioned to paper over: the anarchy of a capitalist economy has led to a futile quest for secrets of rational organization and administration. No solution will ever be found under capitalism, but meanwhile the practical advice of industrial sociologists helps entrepreneurs to increase profit margins through better techniques for exploiting employees. The urgency of these efforts, Grishiani concedes, has produced certain minor applied successes which Marxist sociologists should study closely for their own purposes, even while rejecting their bourgeois basis.

C. WRIGHT MILLS: TRAGIC HERO

Only one prominent American sociologist, the late C. Wright Mills, escapes the charge of being an out-and-out reactionary propagandist. E. D. Modrzhinskaia wrote in a commemorative article on the anniversary of his death:

> In the twilight of the capitalist structure and the strengthening of political reaction in the USA, he found in himself the courage to come out against the American "ruling elite," against militarism and the arms race, in defense of revolutionary Cuba, and also to pronounce sharply critical judgments on the limitedness of contemporary bourgeois sociological theory.[13]

Yet Mills is a tragic figure: his insights concerning the evils of capitalist society failed to yield sound, Marxist conclusions, and he remained a victim of bourgeois ideology.

Not only in his critique of American society, says Modrzhinskaia, but in his understanding of international affairs as well, Mills fell short of realizing his full potential because he "did not free him-

[13] E. D. Modrzhinskaia, "Progressivnye iavlenie v sovremennoi amerikanskoi sotsiologii" ("Progressive Phenomena in Contemporary American Sociology"), *ibid.*, November, 1962, pp. 3–18.

self from fruitless, scholastic, and antihistorical bourgeois sociology," and made the fatal error of equating the USA and the USSR alike as "two powerful national centers," failing to distinguish between the reactionary nature of one, and the progressive, humanitarian strivings of the other. He "could not recognize the general nature of imperialism," and this "prevented him from understanding that imperialism is the sole source of the war danger."

Like many of his bourgeois colleagues, Mills wrongly looked for signs of a convergence between capitalism and socialism; he erred in regarding Marx as only another Victorian social theorist and Marxism as outdated and utopian; he was negatively influenced by Max Weber's spirit of "pessimism" regarding the bureaucratization of modern society. Nevertheless, he "approaches an understanding of contradictions as the moving force of social development," and his critique of the "groundlessness, abstractness, and apologetic nature of contemporary bourgeois sociology," especially his disapproval of Parsonian theory and Lazarsfeld's empiricism, meet with an enthusiastic Soviet response. Concluding on an optimistic note, Modrzhinskaia offers the opinion that the crisis of bourgeois sociology may yet produce more such progressive figures.

SOCIOLOGY, POLITICS, AND IMPERIALISM

The bitterness of the Soviet attack on American sociology is partly explained by the Marxist conviction that ideas have immediate consequences in social affairs. Not only do Soviet sociologists regard non-Marxist sociologists as wrong in some abstract sense, but they fear that bourgeois ideas will have politically harmful effects.

F. V. Konstantinov, head of the Soviet delegation to the Fifth World

Congress of Sociology in Washington, D.C., held in September, 1962, reported afterward to readers of *Voprosy filosofii* that the main theme of the Congress was precisely this struggle of ideas between Marxist and bourgeois sociology. And he hints that ideological errors of the kind committed by bourgeois sociologists may even lead to nuclear warfare.

Mistaken sociological theories in our time can have especially harmful consequences for policies, for nations, for the cause of peace and progress. Among the theories must be named, first of all, subjective theories that deny the presence of objective laws of the development of society; they are characterized by voluntarism, arbitrariness, and adventurism in politics which, in an epoch of nuclear weapons, can lead to unfortunate, tragic results.[14]

There is only one truth, writes Konstantinov, the Marxist truth:

At the Congress, bourgeois sociologists spoke of Protestant, Catholic, and similar sociologies.... The truth about one and the same phenomenon, event, process, can only be one—not three. In this sense, scientific sociology, which gives the objective truth, is only one. It carries the name of Marx, is called Marxist sociology (historical materialism) because Marx discovered the laws and the moving forces of societal development.

In a more detailed report on Congress proceedings, V. S. Semenov reviews the lines of the "battle."[15] The keynote at the Congress, he writes, was sounded in Konstantinov's presentation on behalf of the Soviet delegation. Commenting on the complaints of American and other Western sociologists that their voices are too little heard by policy makers,

Konstantinov contrasted their unhappy position with the advantages enjoyed by sociologists in the Soviet Union and

pointed out the enormous role of Marxist sociology in the societal development of the socialist countries. When the speaker told what enormous successes the Soviet nation has attained over the years of socialist construction thanks to the fact that our nation was guided by Marxist sociology, friendly applause was heard in the hall.

Efforts to overcome the positive impression left by Konstantinov were useless, and only confirmed the weakness of the bourgeois position.

It is characteristic that the argument of P. Hauser that sociology should stand at a distance from politics, be independent of it, was supported by S. Eisenstadt (Israel) and other bourgeois orators. This speaks of how, in capitalist conditions, when the link between science and politics is not effected, many bourgeois sociologists try to preserve their independence [so as] not to be absorbed by the capitalist government....

The speech of E. Hughes clearly showed that in the USA and other capitalist countries not only are the ties of sociologists to society weak, but that there are no ties among sociologists themselves. One of the main reasons for this is that bourgeois sociologists are not united by general problems, to the extent that even large and general problems are absent from bourgeois sociology.

The weakness and disunity of bourgeois sociology, however, did not prevent its partisans from trying, at the Congress, to prove to representatives of the uncommitted and underdeveloped lands the superiority of capitalist economic and social patterns. Konstantinov noted in his own report that

The imperialist countries, with the USA at the head, attempt by any means to direct the development of the underdeveloped countries according to the capitalist path welcome and advantageous to themselves. And the bourgeois ideologists of the USA, including [W.W.] Rostow and others,

14 F. V. Konstantinov, "Sotsiologiia i politika" ("Sociology and Politics"), *ibid.,* November, 1962, pp. 3–18.

15 V. S. Semenov, "Na V vsemirnom sotsiologicheskom kongresse" ("At the Fifth World Congress of Sociology"), *ibid.,* November, 1962, pp. 19–35.

attempt to give a "sociological" foundation to that path.[16]

Semenov, in his article,[17] points to Arnold Feldman and Wilbert Moore as typical of bourgeois scholars who try to obscure the differences between capitalism and communism in order to discredit the superiority of the Soviet pattern.

The secret of the propaganda of the theory of "industrial society" is altogether simple. From a social point of view, capitalism long ago has outlived itself; the countries of the West for an entire epoch have fallen behind the USSR and the countries of socialism in social development. The sole trump card remaining to the capitalist world are a few technological achievements. Capitalist countries can still compete with the USSR in technical-economic indicators, and the USA is even ahead. This is why bourgeois sociologists suddenly have forgotten completely the social differences between socialism and capitalism and combine in "industrial society" the development of all countries by technological indicators.

In this way, the theory of "industrial society" for the time being "works" for bourgeois ideology and with the aid of bourgeois scholars tries to propagandize the empty "superiority" of the capitalist path of development. The paper of Feldman and Moore served basically this purpose....

It is altogether symptomatic that the "calculations" of Feldman and Moore received neither sympathy nor support in the auditorium.

Summarizing the activities of bourgeois sociologists at the Congress, Semenov identifies S. M. Lipset as the worst offender against Marxist science: "...known for his openly pro-capitalist position," Lipset described the United States as the original new nation and tried to whitewash the well-known posi-

tion of the United States as the leading imperialist power, asserting that "the USA is not the oppressor of colonies, not an imperialist government, but the leader of all new states." This "substantially false speech," asserts Semenov, "was greeted accordingly by the audience."

DISCUSSION

Space does not permit a more detailed exposition of the Soviet view of American sociology, nor a complete listing of individual sociologists who have come under attack in Soviet publications. By and large, however, the line of criticism reported here is characteristic of Soviet commentary.

Some of the criticisms are familiar enough; many have been voiced by American sociologists themselves and are very much part of the self-critical professional atmosphere necessary to the growth of the discipline. Unresolved questions concerning the relations between theory and research, problems in the formulation of theory, debate about the proper place of sociology on the contemporary scene and, of course, about the condition of American society itself, are staples in the sociological literature. That these issues are so eagerly seized upon and enlarged as signs of weakness and sterility reveals less about the state of "Western" sociology than it does about the tendentiousness of its Soviet critics.

Other elements of the attack—the portrayal of American sociologists as lackeys of imperialism and capitalism, and the decay of American society—are now being applied to American sociology for the first time, but the insistence that social science cannot be politically neutral, that social scientists necessarily represent a "ruling class," that Marxism is the only true science, that contem-

---

[16] Konstantinov, "Sotsiologiia i politika," op. cit.

[17] Semenov, 'Na V vsemirnom..., op. cit.

porary capitalism is undergoing its final death struggle, that imperialism is the guiding motive of American politics, all go back at least to Lenin, if not to Marx. The present position of Soviet sociologists on non-Marxist sociology could have been predicted in detail simply by reading Soviet philosophers—from whose ranks sociologists largely were drawn when the subject was destigmatized after Stalin's death.

Still, the attack on American sociology as such is new. In part it may represent the efforts of communist ideologists to neutralize the potentially corrupting effects of cultural and scientific contacts with the outside world. Although the present regime has granted greater access to a growing number of topics, including Western sociological literature, it has not surrendered the principle or the practice of Party control over dissemination and interpretation. Formerly forbidden sociological writings from America and elsewhere, then, have been made available to specialists, but simultaneously a campaign has been launched to discredit the sources.

The vigorous attack on American sociology may also represent the efforts of Soviet sociologists to avoid the charges of ideological deviationism they risk in their acknowledged borrowing from "bourgeois" social science research methods. Despite Soviet claims concerning the vast superiority of Marxist sociology, the actual record of empirical—or "concrete"—research is so far quite limited. Very serious efforts are being made to overcome the handicaps resulting from the long-standing ban on empirical research, but they involve a rather embarrassing dependence on Western technique. Hence, "bourgeois" sociology is carefully disavowed even while Soviet sociologists adopt many of its research methods.

One is tempted to respond to the Soviet charges in kind, to make the obvious point that the critics' view of the propagandistic functions of American sociology and the ideological servitude of American sociologists is a remarkably faithful projection of their own situation in the Soviet Union. Factual misrepresentations of course must be brought to light, but engaging in an ideological dog fight is not likely to be scientifically productive. Serious discussion about substantive matters is something else again, and here the Soviet criticisms—never mind their motivations—raise some potentially worthwhile questions about the practice of sociology in the West. However preposterous some of the charges are, a certain amount of intellectual discipline, at least, is required to formulate reasoned and responsible replies.

If the extreme and doctrinaire viewpoint of the Soviet sociologists is not always constructive, its lively disputatiousness is better than the total silence and isolation that prevailed only a few years ago. It is encouraging, too, that among Soviet sociologists themselves, many have revealed in private conversation a willingness to take a more sober look at the activities of their overseas colleagues. Face-to-face exchanges between Soviet and American sociologists can be carried out in an atmosphere of personal cordiality, despite seemingly insuperable intellectual differences; certainly this has been the case in my own contacts with Russian colleagues at home and in the USSR, and in Talcott Parsons' experience, reported elsewhere in this issue, as a guest of several Soviet institutions. More important, Soviet academies and universities have lately displayed an admirable propensity to listen, and a small but growing number of foreign sociologists (including some identified as ideological archenemies) are being invited to deliver lectures and seminars. Scholars from the West who take visits from foreign colleagues for granted may regard this still limited program as small consolation, but those who recall the conditions under Stalin will surely appreciate its great importance.

Less welcome are signs that Soviet representatives to international sociological organizations are prepared to apply their own traditions of domestic censorship in suppressing ideas that they find unflattering or disagreeable. F. V. Konstantinov, at the January 1963 meeting of the International Sociological Association's Executive Committee, demanded that British sociologist Leopold Labedz' paper on the Soviet intelligentsia be banned from the Association's publications on grounds that it was "unscientific and slanderous."[18] (The Committee rejected the demand but the Soviets won the privilege of appending a rebuttal.) This double standard—that their criticisms of other societies are legitimate while observations that do not coincide with their own image of the Soviet Union are slanderous—shows that Soviet social scientists are not yet emancipated sufficiently to appreciate genuinely free discussion and exchange.

Meanwhile, it would be an error to accept the current Soviet position as the final word on Marxist sociology as practiced in the communist lands, or as it may one day be in the USSR. In Poland and Yugoslavia, where sociologists clearly are no less Marxist, they go about their scientific tasks with less heat and more light. In this connection, a 1960 Soviet attack on Yugoslav sociology is highly revealing. The Yugoslavs were accused of "revisionism" and of kowtowing to capitalist imperialism because they questioned whether the theoretical propositions of Marx, Engels, and Lenin adequately substitute for "concrete-inductive" research, and whether historical materialism entirely preempts the subject matter of sociology.[19] This contrast between the Soviet and Yugoslav positions suggests that the contention is less between Marxists and non-Marxists than between open- and closed-mindedness, between the willingness to suspend judgment in searching for the truth and the dogmatic insistence that truth is the exclusive possession of a political party.

We would be wise, then, to approach future contracts with the knowledge that the differences between the Soviets and ourselves are very severe, yet with the conviction that the scientific and humane rewards of achieving mutual understanding are well worth the effort. Sociologists on both sides stand only to benefit from a continuing exchange.

18 V. S. Semenov, "Mirnoe sosushchestvovanie—osnovnaia tema predstoiaschego foruma sotsiologov" ("Peaceful Coexistence is the Basic Theme of the Forthcoming Forum of Sociologists"), *ibid.,* May, 1963, pp. 163–164.

19 E. G. Kuziukova and V. I. Ugriumov, "V plenu empiricheskoi burzhuaznoi sotsiologii (ob odnom soveshchanii iugoslavskikh sotsiologov)" ("In the Captivity of Bourgeois Sociology [Concerning a Conference of Yugoslav Sociologists]"), *Filosofskie nauki,* 1960, No. 4, pp. 32–34.

VII

ARE THE
TWO SOCIETIES
BECOMING ALIKE?

Seeking an answer to this question, we confront the resolute and resonant "no" of Soviet sociologists and a chorus of tentative disagreement among the Americans.

The Soviet position is simple and can be easily predicted. The two societies are not becoming alike because one is just, progressive, and ascendant (we may try to guess which), while the other is corrupt, reactionary and historically doomed. Seen in this light, there is little to support the convergence hypothesis. Beyond the simple denial of such a possibility, Soviet sociologists (as well as other social scientists, propagandists, and ideologues) have made it their task to wage war on the notion that there are growing similarities between the two societies, a proposition contained in the convergence hypothesis: what the Soviet commentators call "single industrial society theory." Since this theory bears the marks of economic determinism, the furious Soviet denials and refutations may be surprising at first. Certainly it is overly optimistic to believe that the two competing and opposing societies are in the process of gradually borrowing from one another their best features or to perceive of the Soviet Union's becoming like the United States minus its major socio-economic problems. Such is one hopeful version of convergence. A more realistic, though still questionable, variety of it maintains that modernization (i.e., industrialization, specialization, functional differentiation, or simply economic development) alters the socio-political structure of every society in basically similar ways. Since only a very limited number of socio-political institutional arrangements are

557

compatible with modernization the existing ones must converge as comparable levels of modernity are attained. This, of course, is not unlike the old Marxist notion of structure and superstructure, the economic basis of society shaping the rest of the social institutions. In the U.S. four types of social scientists favor the notion of convergence (whether they use the term or not). The first is the economists (not all, of course) for obvious reasons. One of the originators of the theory, W. W. Rostow, is an economist. In the second group are social scientists in search of a general theory of social development which would apply to every society. To the third type belong the deviant (or orthodox) Marxists and some American businessmen who believe that growing productivity resulting in an abundance of goods and services will transform the Soviet Union into a relaxed, rich, and truly democratic society of "fat communists" who will be very unlike the mean and aggressive "lean" ones. Finally, a fourth type sees convergence as a process by which the U.S. and U.S.S.R. attain similarity in adopting each other's worst features. For example, the Soviet Union might acquire popular culture, obsession with cars, perhaps even advertising and pornography, while the U.S. might borrow more efficient methods of suppressing freedoms of thought, expression, and political organization. Obviously, these are mere sketches of the types and implications of the convergence theory and the motives behind it.

In the Soviet eyes the convergence theory is not only wrong, but also a new, cunningly dangerous *weapon* in the ideological struggle and subversion, which the U.S. conducts against the Soviet Union. It was designed to confuse and disarm the masses in both the Western and socialist countries and even the Third World. What indeed could be more subversive ideologically than confusing the U.S. and the U.S.S.R.? At the same time the convergence theory could also be seen as a reflection of the desire for better relations between the U.S. and the Soviet Union. Most adherents believe that if the two societies become more similar they will also become friendlier toward each other (which is an optimistic American non sequitur). However, the official Soviet value and belief system is firmly anchored in the Marxist propositions of historical development. As modified to suit the Soviet case, Marxism supports the claim of historical superiority and advantage over all other societies extant. Convergence would deprive Soviet society of this claim, detract from its distinctiveness, and nullify much of the ideological, indoctrinational effort expended to boost the morale of the Soviet people. The historical vanguard conception of the Soviet social order is a firmly established myth, a major pillar of legitimacy, and a justification of the sacrifices made to create Soviet society. Moreover if the convergence theory is correct, the U.S. could hardly be a social system inferior to the Soviet—or not for long. That of course would be a totally unacceptable position from the Soviet point of view.

The convergence theory is open to serious questions, but not necessarily along the Soviet lines. Both Wilbert Moore and Alex Inkeles make a good case for rejecting it. Sorokin, on the other hand goes further in affirming it than most. His long-standing interest, indeed involvement, in the matter might explain this. The first time he expressed belief in the growing similarities of the two societies was in 1944 in the book discussed by Inkeles. His recent version of convergence is also highly and improbably optimistic. The new type of society to emerge from the amalgamation of the American and Soviet "is going to incorporate most of the positive values and to be free from the serious defects of each type."

Parsons' belief in convergence is in many ways similar to Sorokin's although more qualified and based, to a greater extent, on an historical argument. As Sorokin, he stresses the desirable, positive goals shared by the two systems and treats their ideological differences as being relatively ephemeral, as concealing the underlying similarities which the protagonists have overlooked in the heat of the argument, so to speak. His discussion specifically differs from Sorokin's in that the latter addresses himself explicitly to Soviet-American relations, whereas Parsons talks about the "West," which includes of course the U. S. It is unlikely, however, that substituting the United States for the "Western system" would significantly alter his analysis. Parsons appears convinced that since the two systems share "the same basic cultural roots" the conflict between them cannot be truly serious and enduring. In particular he argues that both are oriented toward progress, modernization, science, and the welfare of the masses and that neither questions "the basic desirability of industrialization." It is doubtful that similar ultimate ends promote harmony between political systems and still more doubtful that "the primary issues" between the two systems are "the benefits of the process [of industrialization] on the one hand and the mechanisms by which it is to be controlled on the other." He likes to think of the two systems in kinship terms: the Western is sketched as a more sedate, secure, permissive, and patient parental figure, while the impetuous offspring (the Soviet) is brash, brusque, and intolerant, not unlike some American teenagers in relation to their middle-class parents. At another point he refers to the socialists (and the leaders and founders of Soviet society) as " 'young men in hurry' who have professed not to believe that their slower elders really 'meant it,' that the general patterns of industrialization—with respect not only to the total productivity but to distribution and other aspects of the process—would be implemented."

This benevolent view of the relationship between the two systems is predicated on an evolutionary vision, which sees political democracy as an almost inevitable final outcome and which considers coercion a relatively short-lived aberration. This approach is also closely related to the author's commitment to a general theory of social order: Just as he is inclined to regard societies as well integrated, so he anticipates "an eventual integration in a wider system which includes both" (Western and Soviet, that is).

It all adds up to a generous, optimistic, and somewhat unrealistic picture of Western (especially American) and Soviet relations, which underestimates the magnitude and consequences of the differences between Western and Soviet institutions and values. In this perspective the cold war is reduced (with some qualifications) to some "very hard things...said on both sides," but the basic message is that these amount to barks rather than bites. The discussion unfolding is more a hopeful and reassuring look into the distant future (the long run) than an assessment of the past, present, or near future.

Are the two societies becoming alike? The answer would be inconclusive even if we could have presented a far larger sampling of opinion and evidence. Had we done that, the consensus might have been that they are becoming similar in some ways, but not in others. Even if the structural-institutional similarities rise well beyond their present level, there still remains the accumulation of diverse antecedent historical circumstances and experiences. This accumulation might be compared to the effect of hereditary endowments on individuals. It is equally difficult to pinpoint and ascertain the influence of historical and of genetic heredity. Unmistakably, if elusively, present, the effects of "historical heredity" complicate the task of the sociologist looking for the forces shaping social institutions in the observable social environment.

If the Soviet position on the similarities and differences strikes the reader as unconvincing and the American seems too inconclusive, perhaps this volume as a whole will provide him with some basis for reaching his own conclusions.

ARE THE TWO SOCIETIES BECOMING ALIKE?

The American View

Mutual Convergence of the U.S. and the U.S.S.R. to the Mixed Sociocultural Type

PITIRIM A. SOROKIN

1. *Three Prognoses.* Leaders of the West assure us that the future belongs to the capitalist ("free enterprise") type of society and culture. In contrast, leaders of the Communist nations confidently expect a Communist victory in the coming decades. Differing from both of these predictions I am inclined to think that if mankind avoids new world wars and can overcome today's grave emergencies, the dominant type of the emerging society and culture is likely to be neither capitalistic nor communistic, but a type *sui generis* which we can designate as an *integral type*. This type will be intermediary between the capitalist and Communist orders and ways of life. It is going to incorporate most of the positive values and to be free from the serious defects of each type. Moreover, the emerging integral

Reprinted by permission from Pitirim Sorokin, Basic Trends of our Times. *New Haven: College and University Press, 1964, pp. 78–79, 86–89, 129–130.*

order in its full development is not likely to be a mere eclectic mixture of the features of both types but a unified system of integral cultural values, social institutions, and of the integral type of personality essentially different from those of the capitalist and the Communist patterns. If mankind does not avoid new world wars and cannot mitigate today's grave emergencies, then its future becomes problematic and dark. Such in brief is my prognosis about the alternative future of mankind.

My main reasons for this prognosis are three: First, in their pure or extreme form, both the capitalist and the Communist orders are very defective and cannot meet the needs of a good, creative life for future mankind. Second, both orders are serviceable only under specific conditions for specific periods. In different conditions and periods both become disserviceable and therefore unneeded. Third, progressively both orders in the Western and the Soviet blocs of

561

nations[1] for the last three decades have been increasingly losing their specific features and "borrowing" and incorporating in themselves each other's characteristics. In this sense, both types have been withering more and more and are becoming more and more similar to each other in their cultures, social institutions, systems of value, and ways of life. This means that both types, exemplified by the United States and Soviet Russia, have been increasingly converging to the intermediary type, different from communism and capitalism. This intermediary type, for the time being, represents an eclectic mixture of the characteristics of both orders.

. . . Nobody can predict with certainty which of these alternatives will take place in the future. If mankind can avoid the catastrophe of a world war, then other emergencies can be mitigated

[1] In this article I limit my analysis to the Euro-American continent concentrating on the changes for the last forty years in the United States and Soviet Russia. In regard to China, where the Communist system is still largely in its first, coercive phase, I simply can state that, if the Chinese Communist order is given the peaceful conditions for its free development, in due time it also will experience a transformation essentially similar to that of Soviet Russia. The first phase of any violent revolution, and especially of the Communist revolution, is always predominantly destructive, coercive, and inhumanly cruel. Eventually, if the revolution is not suppressed, it passes from this destructive into an increasingly constructive phase. The predominantly destructive phase of the Russian Revolution is already over and it has now entered into its constructive phase (unfortunately interrupted by World War II and greatly hindered in its progress by the subsequent cold and hot wars), while the Chinese revolution is still at the end of its destructive phase and is just entering its constructive stage of development. See on these phases in the development of practically all great revolutions P. Sorokin, *Sociology of Revolution* (Philadelphia, 1924) and in P. Sorokin, *Society, Culture and Personality* (New York, 1962), Ch. 31. A Spanish edition of this work is entitled *Sociedad, Cultura y Personalidad* (Madrid, 1960).

or eliminated to a great extent. In these conditions the eventual decline of all forms of totalitarianism appears to be probable. If the emergency of such a war cannot be abolished, then there is no chance to eliminate other emergencies. In these conditions the temporary triumph of various forms of totalitarianism is to be expected. So far the international policies of the governments of both blocs of nations have been unsuccessful in abolishing the threat of a new world war and in establishing lasting peace. And there is no guarantee these policies can abolish this emergency in the future. If our hopes in this matter were dependent entirely upon the policies of the existing governments, then the future of mankind would be dark and uncertain.

Fortunately for all of us, the course of human history is only partially dependent upon the policies of governments. In a much greater degree it is determined by the collective, anonymous forces of humanity—by the totality of actions and reactions of every human being, every human group, and, ultimately, of the whole of mankind. If the policies of governments contradict the course of history which these collective, anonymous forces consciously and unconsciously, in planned and unplanned, and in organized and unorganized forms endeavor to realize, then in due time such governmental policies are "cancelled" and replaced by the policies promoted by these collective forces. Under these conditions, often the governments themselves are "dismissed" and replaced—in an orderly or violent way—by governments that are willing and capable of realizing the demands of the collective forces of humanity or, if you prefer, of the forces of historical destiny or of guiding Providence.

The discordancy between the course of history required by the interests of mankind and the course of the governmental policies of the United States and Soviet Russia for the last forty years, and especially since the Armistice, gives a good example of this sort of historical situation. While the politicians of both countries have been feverishly carrying on the policies of mutual vituperation, enmity, cold and hot war; while they have been madly engaged in the armament race and in preparation for a suicidal world war; while both governments have been trying to discredit, to hurt and destroy each other by all means available; while for this purpose in their propaganda they have been extolling their own virtues and magnifying the vices of the other government and fantastically exaggerating the irreconcilability of the values and of the biological, social, and cultural differences between the two governments and the two nations; while the governments have been promoting this policy of war, the collective forces of both nations, of mankind, and of history have been engaged in a different kind of work and have been performing a task opposed to the policies of both governments, of their politicians, and of their "power-elites."

Instead of a magnification of the allegedly irreconcilable differences in the system of values, in social institutions, in culture and in the ways of life of both countries, these forces have been mitigating and decreasing these differences and making both countries more similar to each other in all these fields. Often silently but relentlessly, these collective forces have been progressively eliminating the irreconcilability of the values and the real interests of both nations and have been building a bridge for their peaceful coexistence and co-operation. Instead of separating both countries from each other, these forces have been converging them toward the intermediary type different from the pure capitalistic as well as from the

extreme communistic type. Both countries have been increasingly borrowing and adopting the values, institutions, and cultural features of each other. This convergence has already progressed so far that at the present time both nations are much more similar to each other—socially, culturally, and in practical ways of life—than they were at the beginning of the Russian Revolution.[2]

The net result of this convergence is a progressive mitigation and elimination of practically all the justifiable reasons for continuing cold or hot wars, the mad armament race, and the policies of armed conflict. The convergence has already progressed so far that at the present time there is no justifiable reason for these policies and relationships between the two nations. If the belligerent policies continue and if they eventually result in a new world war, the only reasons for this sort of catastrophe will be the inexcusable stupidity, greediness, power-lust and poorly understood tribal interests of the governments, power-elites, and of "the brainwashed" masses of both countries. There is no certainty that these blind and irrational forces will not temporarily prevail in the future, but if such a catastrophe occurs, its reasons or motives cannot be

---

[2] One of the gross blunders committed daily by the belligerent politicians is their assumption that neither the USSR nor the U.S. has changed for the period of forty-six years since the beginning of the Russian Revolution in 1917. American politicians still talk about Russia in terms of the Russian Revolution of 1917–20 and Russian politicians talk about the United States as it was some forty or fifty years ago. If these politicians had studied the enormous changes which the United States or France or England had forty-six years after the beginning of the American, great French and Cromwellian revolutions, the politicians would have understood the big error they commit daily in their silly utterances. Their criticisms applicable to either of the two countries forty-six years ago is quite inapplicable to each of the nations, as it is today.

qualified as justifiable, rational, and excusable.

...The preceding brief analysis of the changes and tendencies in the main segments of culture, social institutions, systems of values, and the sociocultural life of both nations demonstrates indeed that in all these basic fields both have been becoming increasingly similar to each other and converging mutually toward a mixed type, neither communistic nor capitalistic, neither totalitarian nor democratic, neither materialistic nor idealistic, neither totally religious nor atheistic-agnostic, neither purely individualistic nor collectivistic, neither too criminal nor too saintly. At the present time this mixed type represents an eclectic mixture of the characteristics of both countries devoid of the unity of the new integral cultural, social, and personal system.

If a peaceful and unimpeded government of today's mixed type is given a real chance, there is hardly any doubt that eventually it will grow into a unified type of a magnificent integral order in both coutnries as well as in the whole universe. Each country will build this new order in its own variation and each variation is likely to be nobler, more creative, and better than most of the previous sociocultural orders in human history. Viewed in this light, this convergence is a hopeful symptom and a healthy process. As such it can be heartily welcomed by all who really care about man, culture, and all the immortal values created by man on this planet.

The survey also shows that at the present time, among all the different values of the two nations, there is not a single value which justifies the continuation of the present belligerent policies, and absolutely no value which in the smallest degree can redeem the great crime of starting a new world war. This does not mean that such a war cannot be started: Despite his great progress, man still remains, to a considerable extent, an irrational, passionate, destructive, cruel, and greedy creature; and human wickedness still remains rampant in human beings and especially in the ruling groups. If the present destructive struggle between the two countries and the two blocs of nations is continued, and if, especially, a new world war is started, the real reasons for these catastrophes are to be found not in the high-sounding great values invoked by the culprits of the world conflagration, but in our own stupidity, irrationality, greed, irresponsibility, and plain human wickedness.

Russia and the U.S.A.:
A Problem in Comparative Sociology

ALEX INKELES

No doubt there are important, often striking, similarities in Soviet and American social structure, and in some respect they may have followed parallel paths in the course of their development. In addition to those developed by Professor Sorokin, I have pointed to several others in the comparison of the two systems in the preceding section. Both nations are large-scale societies, composed of populations of diverse ethnic origins, sharing a diffuse secular culture. The United States and the Soviet Union are outstanding in their devotion to the maximization of industrial production through large-scale organization, the exploitation of science, and reliance on widespread popular education. In both countries physical and social mobility is taken for granted in an open class system which stresses equality, challenges tradition, and encourages individual and collective progress.

This list of similarities could be expanded to great length. The same is unfortunately true of the list of differences. Dictatorship, or at least one-party oligarchy, as against a multi-party democratic political system; state control and planning as opposed to corporate management and the dominance of the market; controlled communication and governmental dictation in art as against free expression and private pursuit of the arts. Here again the list could be expanded to greater length.

We are therefore faced with the same difficulty which sooner or later confronts all efforts at the systematic comparative analysis of social structure, namely that of combining or weighting similarities and differences to yield one composite judgment. Unfortunately, sociology does not provide any equivalent for such measures as gross national product, per capita income, or rate of growth of industrial output, which permit us to combine diverse economic factors into one common and standard measure. There is no unified scale to the metric with which we can reduce the similarities and differences in social structure, leaving us with a single score for the comparison of the Soviet Union and the United States.

Professor Sorokin stresses the fact of change. However wide apart their starting points, he says, the two systems are "now little more than the ghosts of their former selves."[1] Indeed, he argues that "economically and politically the two nations have been steadily converging toward a similar type of social organization and economy."[2] There are many

[1] Pitirim A. Sorokin, *Russia and the United States* (New York: E. P. Dutton and Company, 1944), p. 179.
[2] *Ibid.*, p. 208.

who would challenge this assertion, especially as regards the political structure and the economic organization of the two countries. Yet, even if the two nations were moving closer together, the fact of convergence could be much less important than the nature of the differences which persisted. How can we then assess the relative significance of one or another similarity or difference between two social systems? Although he does not explicitly state them to be such, Professor Sorokin's study suggests implicitly two relevant tests or standards of judgment. One is a test in action, the other a judgment based on values.

The test in action is provided by the pattern of relations between the United States and the Soviet Union after World War II. In the first edition, published in 1944, Professor Sorokin at a number of points asserted quite vigorously a prediction about Soviet-American relations in the postwar period. Since the two nations were not separated by deep-seated value conflicts and were socioculturally "congenial," this was "bound to perpetuate [the] noble record of peace between the two nations, regardless of the personal whims of their rulers." Professor Sorokin went even further, to declare: "If and when these rulers become unwise and begin to commit one blunder after another, there may conceivably be some temporary differences and quarrels between the countries. But even these conflicts are bound to be minor and can hardly lead to an armed conflict."[3] At a later point he commented that the same forces making for similarity and congeniality of the two systems "presage still closer cooperation in the future—a welcome destiny, beneficial to both peoples and to the rest of mankind."[4]

We need not labor the point that the

development of "cold war" relations after World War II, an unceasing arms race with indescribable powers of mass destruction, and actual armed conflict in Korea, all lead to the conclusion that Professor Sorokin's prediction of cordial relations was hardly borne out by subsequent events. In the second edition of *Russia and the United States*,[5] which appeared in 1950, Professor Sorokin acknowledges these facts, and seeks to explain why, when "there was every apparent reason for the postwar continuation of American-Russian friendly relationships, and no apparent reason at all for the 'cold war,' " the latter nevertheless suddenly replaced the previous cooperation of the two countries.[6]

In considering this change, Professor Sorokin argues that the popular explanation in terms of ideological, social, and economic differences is not adequate, because there are so many historic examples of cordial relations and alliances between the United States and other countries which were even more profoundly different from it than is the Soviet Union. It is not appropriate to enter here into a discussion of the alternative explanation Professor Sorokin does offer. We should note, however, that he has here shifted the basis of his argument. In the first edition he did not restrict himself to saying that differences did not preclude understanding. Rather, he mainly emphasized the similarities, and asserted that the two nations were "steadily converging toward a similar type of social organization and economy."[7] Furthermore, he argued that it was above all these "similarities" and the "congeniality" of the two sociocultural systems which made for such good prospects for cordial relations. We

---

[3] *Ibid.*, p. 162.
[4] *Ibid.*, p. 209.

[5] London, Stevens and Sons, Ltd., 1950. Page citations for the second edition refer to this source.
[6] Sorokin, *op. cit.*, p. 165.
[7] Sorokin, *op. cit.*, first edition, p. 208.

must conclude, therefore, either that the theory is inadequate and that similarity in social structure does not make for a greater probability of cordial relations, or that Professor Sorokin was incorrect in his assessment of the degree of congeniality between Soviet and American social structure. It is, of course, possible that he was incorrect on both counts.

The test of values provides quite a different basis for dealing with the fact that social science provides no single standard scale on which any two nations may be placed, but rather always confronts us with a list of discrete similarities and differences. Clearly, the mere number of similarities and differences, however important, is unlikely to be decisive. The critical question will be the weight each of us assigns to one or another factor according to his own scheme of values. On this score Professor Sorokin makes his position quite explicit in the second edition. While acknowledging some important differences between the United States and the Soviet Union, he judged them to be unimportant relative to certain other overriding common values such as survival. In the face of this common interest he ruled that all other "seemingly conflicting values...are so insignificant that their 'incompatibility' amounts to no more than the 'incompatibility' of the advertisements for this or that brand of cigarettes, each claiming superiority over all others."[8]

We do not deny Professor Sorokin the right to his perspective, but we need not automatically accept it for ourselves. Professor Sorokin chooses to judge the Soviet Union and the United States from a great distance, an Olympian height. Yet, if we get sufficiently distant from the immediate and concrete, any two contemporary large-scale systems will seem basically alike, just as any two men, no matter how different in character and action, are alike as "men." No doubt there are similarities in the two societies as great industrial nations. Without question we can in each and for both point to flaws, defects, failures, denials of liberty, denigration of values, and the like. When we have completed such a tabulation, however, there remain stubborn facts with which we must reckon. Probably the most important are the differences in the freedom of political activity, the share people have in deciding their future, the opportunities for free expression of the spirit in art and religion, which in the United States are at a level comparing favorably with most periods in history, but which in the Soviet Union remain at a point very near the bottom in the experience of Western European society.

It is very difficult to believe that in the judgment of history the differences in the political structure of the Soviet Union and the United States, and in their role in the period following World War II, will be seen as inconsequential. It may be true, as Professor Sorokin asserts, that in both societies "germs" of the "disease" represented by the disintegration of the sensate Western culture are equally abundant and active. Although the germ may be the same, and the illness equally advanced, this hardly makes the organism infected the same. Many features of the Soviet system violate the most profound principles of the liberal political tradition painstakingly built up in European culture over several hundred years. With regard to these differences we cannot agree with Professor Sorokin that "any sane person pays no attention to such incompatibilities."[9]

---

[8] Sorokin, *op. cit.*, second edition, p. 176.   [9] *Ibid.*

The Impact of Industry

WILBERT E. MOORE

...The conflicting ideologies of development fostered by major political blocs in the modern world do not exhaust the relevant differences of opinion. Scholars, too, espouse divergent views, though on presumably different grounds. Whereas the ideological differences are normative —that is, how change ought to be—the scholarly differences are factual—that is, how change has been or will be. It is always most dramatic to represent divergent views as diametrically opposed. Usually, however, there are intermediate positions, and at times even the notion of a scale oversimplifies the disagreement.

One position emphasizes the similarity of industrial societies, and asserts or implies that newly developing areas will move toward a common social model as they industrialize. The supporting arguments are both empirical and theoretical. Inkeles and Bauer,[1] for example, summarize a variety of ways in which the Soviet Union resembles the "capitalist" industrial countries, despite differences in political systems. From their own and related studies they note similarities in access to education and the use of education as an occupational sorting mechanism; the relative evaluation

Reprinted from Wilbert E. Moore, The Impact of Industry, © 1965. Reprinted by permission of Prentice-Hall, Inc., Englewood Cliffs, New Jersey, pp. 10–11, 14–19.

of occupational categories; and intergenerational mobility rates. Where they can construct temporal trends, it appears that convergence is increasing, that is, that the Soviet Union has been "developing toward" a kind of standard model of advanced societies. Rose[2] adds some other common features, over a fairly wide range of economic advancement, and particularly highlights the uniform appearance of the small-family system as economies become industrialized. With respect to developing areas, Moore stated his position, since modified, as the "creation of a common culture."[3] Kerr, similarly, has argued for the predictability of the future of industrializing countries on the basis of the common characteristics of advanced countries:

This particular history gets written mainly from the future into the present— what is currently happening comes from what is to be. The future is the cause and the present is the effect.[4]

[1] Alex Inkeles and Raymond A. Bauer, The Soviet Citizen (Cambridge: Harvard University Press, 1959).

[2] Arnold Rose, ed., The Institutions of Advanced Societies (Minneapolis: University of Minnesota Press, 1958).

[3] Wilbert E. Moore, "Creation of a Common Culture," Confluence, 4 (July 1955), 229–38.

[4] Clark Kerr, "Changing Social Structures," in Wilbert E. Moore and Arnold S. Feldman, eds., Labor Commitment and Social Change in Developing Areas (New York: Social Science Research Council, 1960), Chap. 19; passage quoted from p. 358. See also Clark Kerr et al., Industrialism and Industrial Man (Cambridge: Harvard University Press, 1960), esp. Part III, "The Road Ahead."

Feldman and Moore used the typological characteristics of industrial societies as constituting the organizational and normative requirements for "commitment": performance of appropriate actions and the acceptance of the appropriate rules of conduct.[5] They too have since questioned the rigidity or invariability of the model they then employed;[6] they were criticized at the time by Singer,[7] who argued for the diversity of social evolution, and by Herskovits,[8] who argued that the hope for generalization across patently diverse cultures in transition was to be found in processes of change rather than in precise forms of social organization.

The underlying theory that leads to the expectation of growing similarity of industrial societies and of newly developing areas as they join the club might be phrased as "the theory of structural constraints." The essential idea is that a commercial-industrial system imposes certain organizational and institutional requirements not only on the economy but also on many other aspects of society.

. . . The search for uniformities in the impact of industry, though legitimate and even laudable, cannot be totally successful in view of the crude and stubborn facts of variability. It will be useful to recapitulate the prime sources of variation, and the implications of that

variation for the theoretical conception of social systems.[9]

By far the most common sociological approach to the transformation of underdeveloped areas of the world has rested upon a kind of model of change that was rarely made explicit. By exclusive attention to societies "in transition" students of economic development implied a preceding, traditional stage and a succeeding, industrial or advanced stage. The premodern stage was taken to be essentially static, the social structure persisting through a balance of interdependent forces and actions. Even more unrealistically, the fully modernized society was also taken to be static, though this assumption had to remain implicit because of its patent falsity.

Now what is initially interesting and instructive about this approach is not its crudity but its utility. By concentrating on the manifold sources of contemporary evidence, by formalizing the kinds of structural changes to be expected from changes in so essential a societal feature as its system of production, scholars have compiled an impressive list of predictive principles, along with a partial accounting for variations.

The virtues and failures of each part of this conceptual model merit scrutiny. The conception of societies prior to modernization has not been so naive as to assume that they were or are alike. Sociologists have been in sufficiently close touch with anthropologists, if not with historians, to be aware of cultural diversity. Indeed, general textbooks commonly emphasize the range of social patterns and leave to the chapter headings the inferential fact that these are

---

[5] Arnold S. Feldman and Wilbert E. Moore, "Spheres of Commitment," and "Postscript," in Moore and Feldman, eds., *Labor Commitment. . . ,* Parts I and V.

[6] Feldman and Moore, "Industrialization and Industrialism. . . ," *op. cit.* See also Arnold S. Feldman, "The Nature of Industrial Societies," *World Politics,* 12 (July 1960), 614–20.

[7] Milton Singer, "Changing Craft Traditions in India," in Moore and Feldman, eds., *Labor Commitment. . . ,* Chap. 14.

[8] Melville J. Herskovits, "The Organization of Work," in Moore and Feldman, eds., *Labor Commitment. . . ,* Chap. 8, especially pp. 123–25.

[9] Much of this section has been adapted from Wilbert E. Moore, "Social Aspects of Economic Development," in Robert E. L. Faris, ed., *Handbook of Modern Sociology* (Chicago: Rand McNally & Co., 1964), Chap. 23.

variations on themes rather than a random assembly of odd social practices. No, the mischief has arisen not primarily from the assumption of uniformity among traditional societies, but from the static connotations of the very term *traditional*. Traditional they may be in the sense of commonly justifying present practices in terms of precedent, and even in the extended sense that change in the past has not been rapid, continuous, and pervasive. Yet change is an intrinsic characteristic of all societies,[10] and the historic paths to the present inevitably and significantly affect the continuing paths to the future.

The lack of historical perspective has proved embarrassing. At the extreme this conceptual model has led to the *sociologistic error,* the assumption that history began yesterday, if not early this morning. This kind of temporal myopia has neglected not only the intrinsic sources and courses of change in all societies but also the important circumstance that most of the world has been under some form and degree of "Western" influence for periods of years and in some instances (such as, say, Latin America) for over four centuries. The results of this prolonged contact have been a great intermixture of cultural forms and social organizations. This intermixture of civilizations in turn has built new barriers to modernization or raised old ones while obviously starting the slow process of modernizations in some other sectors of social life. The imposition of a radical racial or ethnic distinction between managers and the managed, for example, has in many places added an irrational barrier to labor mobility on top of the real impediment of simple lack of trained skills. On the other hand, the commercialization

of subsistence economies has clearly started them "on the way" to full participation in modern forms of production and distribution.

The identification of consequences and of impossible inconsistencies in the social order environing a modernized economy has been greatly aided, again paradoxically, by the unrealistic assumption that industrial societies are both static and homogeneous among themselves. This assumption has had sufficient proximity to fact in certain major respects to permit the use of the generalized features of industrial societies as a predictive destination for those now in the process of modernization.

Yet the future is still being created and at an accelerating pace of change in industrial societies. As they change, their resemblance to each other increases in some respects and scarcely at all in others. To match the unrealistic timelessness of the sociologistic error there is a kind of determinism of social structures that may be called the *functional equilibrium error*. The useful and indeed essential conception of social action as taking place in interdependent systems can be carried to the improper extreme of assuming not only that nothing changes from intrinsic sources, but also that any feature of the system is a key to all others. Societies are far looser aggregates than any biological organism, and at least the more complex animal species permit considerable ranges of structural variation and of individual differences. What the future imposes on the present for the developing areas is a resemblance but not a replication.

The assumption of uniformity among premodern societies must overlook manifold differences or treat them as essentially inconsequential. It must also incur the dangers of the sociologistic error by neglecting all sorts of cross-currents in the history of colonial and other socie-

10 See Wilbert E. Moore, *Social Change* (Englewood Cliffs, N. J.: Prentice-Hall, Inc., 1963).

ties that have experienced various external influences for various periods of time. The argument tends to go, however, that these variations, even if otherwise significant, wash out under the homogenizing influence of a compact and uniform set of requirements imposed by economic modernization. Feldman and Moore[11] argued against this view, maintaining that the way barriers to modernization are overcome not only affects the course of social change for a transitional period but also leaves a lasting residue in the social structure as a consequence of the measures taken for dealing with the problem. If, for example, underutilized land in large estates such as the Latin American *haciendas* gives rise to political discontent as well as low levels of agricultural production, the development measures will sooner or later include a land reform, and the kind of land reform will have enduring consequences for income distribution, capital formation, and labor recruitment.[12] Though such examples might be regarded as a tedious attention to detail, their significance is somewhat deeper, for they bear on a major theoretical (and practical) question in the contemporary world: namely, the degree to which "advanced" societies are becoming alike. The legacy of history is one major reason for introducing a cautionary note in the recitals of the manifold ways in which industrialized societies resemble one another.

Variable conditions such as the size of countries, their natural resources, and their political and economic relations with other societies will affect not only the ease and speed with which they may be able to modernize, but also the type and scale of the industrial development that may take place.

Perhaps the major variable affecting the route or trajectory of change is the era or stage at which a political unit enters on a course of rapid economic change. Latecomers have available several models of historical transformation and of forms of political regime. They are bound neither by the rate nor by the sequence established by their predecessors in adding products and processes, forms of social organization, strategies of communication, or scientific knowledge. The new (or newly modernizing) nation might be compared with the shopper in an extensive and well-stocked supermarket. The shopper can select products from the shelves with virtually no regard to the date or order at which the goods entered the market's inventory.

The metaphor is exaggerated, of course, because a random or whimsical selection of the components available will violate all sorts of principles of interdependence and the functional relation of elements in social systems. Nevertheless, atomic power may be introduced before coal, radios before telephones, antibiotics before aspirin, and airfields before highways. And the supermarket analogy can be translated into somewhat more austere and significant terms. For some purposes it is useful to regard the entire world as a single social system, marked by extensive internal disharmonies but marked also by extensive transit of ideologies, knowledge, and products across conventional political boundaries.

A society persists not only through orderly continuity of established patterns but also through tension-management and change. This conception of society has certain advantages in terms of the "fit" of the model to observed characteristics, even those of a persistent

[11] Feldman and Moore, "Industrialization and Industrialism...," *op. cit.*

[12] See Wilbert E. Moore, *Industrialization and Labor* (Ithaca, N. Y.: Cornell University Press, 1951), Chap. 9.

or recurrent quality, such as social deviation. It has overwhelming advantages
in dealing with the phenomena of leads
and lags in situations of rapid transformation. An outstanding way in which
both industrializing and industrial societies differ in social structure is in the
allocation of power and the political
structure of the state. If societies differ
in their characteristic tensions, because
of varying historic legacies and the ways
these intersect with current problems of
achieving social goals, then it is readily
understandable that the principal
agency functionally responsible for tension-management for the system as a
whole, the state, will differ in its structure and forms of action.

The tension-management model also
permits explicit recognition of one
grossly evident fact difficult to reconcile
with a kind of self-balancing mechanical
system. That fact is the widespread use
of deliberate change both in the
attempted solution of identified problems and in the attempted achievement
of goals associated with, say, economic
development. A principal kind of tension, in other words, is the failure to
achieve social ideals, whether those
ideals be simply those of reliable conformity with norms or the approxima-
tion to new standards and aspirations.

If societies, whether industrializing
or industrialized, differ one from the
other in their characteristic tensions, it
is not surprising that one outstanding
structural correlate of those differences
is to be found in the *political* structure
of the state. Though the formal administrative structure of one ministry may
look much like another, the kinds of
controls imposed by the state and the
ways the state maintains its own authority do differ substantially. This is true
even among the "stable democracies,"
and the differences are greater as one
encounters socialist and communist
regimes.

Nor can these differences, at least, be
derogated by reference to "mere
details," or "lower levels of generalization." The problem of order is universal and thus highly general, and the
variability in its partial solutions must
be taken seriously as impairing the
notion of social convergence through
industrialization.

The world may be viewed as a single
system for some purposes, particularly
in view of the common pool of knowledge, ideas, and techniques. But that
system retains strong elements of persistent pluralism. As developing areas
accommodate their diverse cultures and
histories, importing and inventing novel
techniques and patterns in somewhat
novel combinations, the disappearance
of their archaic customs will not imply
a total homogeneity of social life everywhere. Some of the new customs may be
as exotic as the old despite their novelty.

In brief summary of the reasons for
expecting some persistent divergence
among industrial and industrializing
societies:

Preindustrial structural and cultural
differences may persist because the
economic system is not wholly determinate of other components of social
systems, or they may leave residues
because of the way they have been
"eliminated."

The route or trajectory of change will
differ according to historical period,
alternative models and their eclectic
combination, conditions such as size and
natural resources, and relations with
other societies.

These sources of variation argue for
differences in the "weight" of various
components of social systems, both
temporally and as between countries,
and in the role of the polity in tension-
management (or in falling under revolutionary pressures).

Novelty, including accident as well
as deliberately created change, may still

occur; whether it will be then widely imitated cannot be fully predicted.

DOUBTS AND UNCERTAINTIES[13]

Weaving a path through the controversial conclusions concerning the homogeneity of industrial societies would have been easier for sociologists if our basic knowledge of conditions and processes had been more complete. As we sought predictive answers to the multitude of questions posed by rapid social transformation in "underdeveloped areas," or were asked to provide answers for the use of agencies concerned with advisory policies, we naturally turned first to the kinds of intellectual equipment commonly used in our other studies. This equipment proved to be unsatisfactory in several respects, though often serving to develop and to order principles and generalizations that were both sound and, occasionally, useful. In particular, we found that "stable integration" models of society, interrupted only in a transitional stage, overstated both the similarity and the stability of all societies everywhere.

The manner in which history prevents its own replication creates difficulties in generalizations that will unite historical and contemporary experience and deal with the diversity that optional paths of change introduce. The situation is by no means desperate, as subsequent discussion of highly general patterns will demonstrate. It is, however, sufficiently serious not to be brushed aside lightly.

In addition to minimum, required sequences and results, what is needed, and is mostly not at hand, is the construction of limited-alternative or typological sequences where total generalization is improper. The first part of the desiderata can be partially fulfilled by the distinction between social preconditions of economic modernization and the concomitants and consequences of modernization. A summary of the reliable propositions relating to these components of social organization and its changes comprises the following chapters of this book. Even here the state of knowledge is far from satisfactory, for it provides little information on processes and rates of change and virtually nothing on the interplay among variables as they change. The "before-and-after" comparison is no mean achievement but it does not provide a clear map or timetable for the journey from one to the other.

[13] Several paragraphs of this section have been adapted from Moore, "Social Aspects of Economic Development," *op. cit.*

Communism and the West:
The Sociology of the Conflict

TALCOTT PARSONS

Without underestimating the seriousness of the elements of conflict between the two systems of social organization which seem to dominate the contemporary scene, I should like to use this opportunity to suggest a few respects in which the dichotomy is more relative than it tends to be painted in the ideological interchanges from both sides and to present reasons why there may be a better prospect of an eventual resolution than appears on the surface.

In spite of the very hard things which have been said on both sides which seem to imply absolute irreconcilability; both are outcomes of the same basic cultural roots; both are involved in promoting the social changes which have come to be called "modernization"; and, I venture to say, both in the last analysis are concerned with promotion of a general pattern of "human freedom and welfare" which transcends their differences. It will sometime become clear that on both sides there is more concern with the substance of this welfare than with whether it has been arrived at by our path or by theirs. Clearly this implies that the two paths in fact converge more than is generally realized.

Let us attempt to formulate what

Reprinted from Talcott Parsons, "Communism and the West: The Sociology of the Conflict," Chapter 42 in Social Change, Amitai Etzioni and Eva Etzioni, eds. New York: Basic Books, Inc. Publishers, © 1964, pp. 390–399.

seem to be the principal issues between the systems, issues which are only imperfectly expressed in their respective ideological pronouncements. Then let us try to explore a little bit the paths by which the main forces of social change are making for convergence which, under favorable conditions (which are possible but by no means necessary), may lead to an eventual integration in a wider system which includes both.

It is an essential premise of this analysis that movements and conflicts of this magnitude are involved with the great developmental trends and stages of social change. There would be little doubt that in this case it is in the broadest sense the industrial revolution and its consequences which are the focus of the problem. The process has of course been going on for some two centuries, and even now is far from complete, even in the most advanced countries of its development. However complex the variegated threads which run through the history of industrialization, there seem to be some main trends. The focal one is perhaps the increase of productivity through the division of labor and technological advancement, including of course effective organization of the factors of production. This promises an altogether new level of facilities available in society for *whatever* purposes may be valued. These purposes, however, may on a general level be classified as economic "welfare," whatever the reference to group or subgroup, and political—in an analytical sense broader than governmental—power. In the former context, a major reference is to the egalitarian spread of welfare to the masses of a population—the "end of the line" in this sense being consumption standards.

Beyond this, of course, the facilities available for a variety of functions other than individual consumption become increasingly important in any society which is strongly impressed by developmental possibilities. The continuing furtherance of economic productivity itself must figure prominently in this picture. Then comes the concern for the foundations of power, both at the level of collective units within a given politically organized system, pre-eminently the territorial "state," and the political power of such units *vis-à-vis* each other. Of course the symbol and a pre-eminently central intrinsic fact is the impact of this general increase in economic effectiveness on the technology of war and hence the absolute imperativeness of commanding an industrial economy for any territorial unit which claims to "count" in the higher power struggle of the international world.

The basic desirability of industrialization can hardly be said to be in question; it seems to be assumed as one of the central givens of the modern world—somewhat surprisingly, in view of the recent vogue of the doctrine of an indefinite relativity of values. Thus, from the communist point of view, the essential immorality of capitalism does not consist in its having abandoned the virtues of preindustrial economic systems; nor, from the other side is it the "crime" of Soviet Russia to have promoted industrialization. Quite the contrary on both sides, as is evidenced by the continuing stress in Soviet pronouncements on their imminent "catch-

ing up" with the United States and a less obvious, sometimes indeed grudging, Western admiration for Soviet achievements.

The primary issues, then, are two, which are related to each other in a complex way. These are the distribution of the benefits of the process on the one hand, the mechanisms by which it is to be controlled on the other. Each of these issues needs, however, to be carefully interpreted and interrelated. The basic reference point is the "politically organized society," *i.e.*, the territorial unit which has been more-or-less of a "national state." The original socialist definition was internal to this unit and hence spoke of the "working class" as the claimant to an enhanced share of distributive benefits. In fact, however, the most important tendency of the socialist movement has not been directed to raising the relative standards of living of the working classes within predominantly socialist countries, but rather to bringing new and previously underdeveloped countries under the socialist movement and accelerating their economic development. This naturally has been accompanied by a strongly antagonistic attitude toward the traditional elites of these countries. Hence, they could be said to be working class societies in one sense, namely that the new dominant groups—party people, managerial groups, and "intellectuals"—were predominantly recruited from the old lower or middle classes. On the other hand, the tendency has not been to any very pronounced internal egalitarianism—rather, to a subordination of consumption interests generally to those of rapid industrialization and political power position.

This problem presents the first major case of complication of the pattern of conflict. This results from the fact that, in the societies where the industrialization process had taken hold previous to and independent of the socialist movement, there has been a process of diffusion of the benefits to the population as a whole, including the working classes, and hence not only a generalized rise in living standards, but a substantial diminution in the inequalities of the preindustrial persists. There seem to have been three main aspects of this "equalization," which is a phase of a more general process of upgrading of standards. The one which has been most discussed is, of course, that of "consumption," with no further questions asked. The second is "welfare," in the sense of direct action, either by the state or by lower-class organized groups, such as trade unions, to alleviate their difficulties. The third, which is most likely to be overlooked in these discussions, is the increasing participation of lower groups in the general growth, not only through opportunities for upward mobility, but through the generalization of levels of education and access to cultural goods of various sorts.

Very generally, the trend in the "capitalistic" societies—i.e., those which have combined industrialization (thus Spain is dubiously capitalistic in this sense) with continuity of control and status on the part of non-"working-class" elements—has been, contrary to the Marxian predictions, clearly one of both absolute and relative upgrading of the lower elements; lower first by the standard of living and relative political power, but beyond that of levels of education, cultural interest, and the like.

This, of course, poses a critical problem for the action-collectivity which starts with espousal of a cause. If the problem is simply how to alleviate the condition of the "toiling masses," it may be that they do better within the normal framework of a so-called "capitalistic" system than they have so far and presumably ever would under

regimes which are ostensibly dedicated to the interests of the "working classes."

From the "capitalistic" point of view, it is hence not unreasonable to suggest that there is a conspicuous tendency of Communist regimes to shift away from the attempt to gain control by revolutionary overturn of the political machinery of the pioneering industrial societies, notably Britain, Germany, and the U.S., and instead to become the international role model for the process of *new* industrialization. This can then be interpreted as a "confession" that the original position was an untenable one, that there is indeed no inherent tendency to "exploitation" in the capitalistic system, but that what the Communists say they want would emerge anyway and "why all the fuss?" Indeed, the case can be pressed one stage further by pointing out that there is also a strong tendency to extension of the "metropolitan" pattern of benefits to the internal lower elements, to that of upgrading of the external dependencies under metropolitan control.

It will probably never be possible to decide the question of whether the desired developments would or would not have occurred "anyway," or under what circumstances and on what time schedule. However that may be, the accumulating sense of urgency of such a goal as not only industrialization, but its spread with maximal distributive emphasis, has in fact led to a polarization, on the one hand and more weakly *within* political societies, on the other hand and more drastically *between* them. The internal "class struggle" was for a time a major factor in Western continental Europe, less intense in Great Britain, and least in the United States, where social conflicts are well known but have never been clearly polarized about industrial production in the strict Marxian sense.

Externally, however, the polarization

has become much more marked as between so-called "imperialist" and "colonial" countries, and surely this rather than the internal one is the polarity which dominates the current scene, with of course the expected "feedback" of a counterimperialism, namely that of the control of "satellites" by the previously anti-imperialist powers.

The process I have emphasized, of gradual extension of the benefits of industrialization to the previously disadvantaged classes and nations, has on the whole occurred by relatively undramatic processes, so that it could appear to be a matter of gradual erosion of the earlier positions. On the other side, there has been the sense of immediate urgency on which I have remarked and a certain pre-eminent position in the range of ideological justification. Broadly, the socialists have, with respect to the industrial complex, been the "young men in a hurry," who have professed not to believe that their slower elders really "meant it" that the general pattern of industrialization—with respect not only to total productivity, but to distribution and the other aspects of the process—would be implemented.

The combination of being in a hurry and of basic distrust of the older "parental" auspices of the process provides the setting for what we have called the problems of political control. Being in a hurry places the immediate goals of industrialization and its concomitants in the paramount position, and distrusting the parental auspices has been interpreted to mean that the movement for implementing these goals in a hurry must be declared to be absolutely independent of any connection with the older system.

The communist system is not, however, basically divergent from the more general normative pattern of Western civilization; indeed, vis-à-vis the world outside the latter, it functions as one primary symbol and agency of Westernization. In relation to its parent system, however, it comes into an acute conflict at one major point, namely that of the system of political control over both the process of economic development itself and the allocation of claims to the utilization of the products of the developmental process. The older "capitalistic" system is permissive and pluralistic in these respects, whereas the insurgent "socialistic" system is not only suspicious of all competing claims, but tends to repress them entirely in the interest of a monolithic centralized control—claiming that all limitations on this are, if internally oriented, "exploitation" of the working class by "monopoly" interests, if external, "imperialistic" exploitation of the weak and underdeveloped. What are some of the structural antecedents of this conflict?

The key fact is of course that the initial processes of what we are calling industrialization occurred under the auspices of "private enterprise," i.e., not of political authority which could be presumed to represent the "public interest." From the point of view of the institutional matrix within which it developed, this could readily be interpreted as usurping the prerogatives of the public interest in favor of private "self"-interest. It was an innovative process of fateful scope and importance which took place within a range of public permissiveness, rather than directly in the name of a public interest.

The key concept here came to be that of *property*. It has been common to think of this as in some sense a simple "economic" category. But the main problem at issue is precisely what is meant by economic? In terms of institutional development, I think the best characterization of property is as that aspect of *political* authority—or power—which has not been kept in or absorbed in, as the case may be, the authority of government. It is the private sphere of power, which in turn serves to *control* what in a more specifically analytical sense should be called the economic aspect of societal function. To this extent Marxian theory is right; capitalism is essentially a "political" phenomenon, in that it is founded on authority to control the process of production, and this control in turn operates through the institution of property. The basic capitalist–socialist difference is, seen in these terms, a political difference, as between a diffused and a centralized distribution of power. The common presumption of course is the desirability of industrial level economic development, and a "just" distribution of benefits and opportunities.

Capitalist production was first defined as political by Marx when it became clear, in the nineteenth cntury, that the typical unit of production was no longer either the individual or his immediate household—as in peasant agriculture—but included an employed class. This feature has of course not only remained, but been vastly increased and ramified, with the development of large-scale organization of what Max Weber called the "bureaucratic" aspect of modern capitalism. What has become attenuated is not the employment of labor by organizations, but the monolithic unity of the employed class as "workers" and the character of the managerial control over them. Here "property" in the older simple sense has ceased to be the primary focus of control; and whereas, in the case of private enterprise, property has continued to play its part, it is no longer the simple private aspect of political power that it once was.

The basic issue now is no longer as such the prerogatives of "ownership" but the modes and degrees of autonomy which are to be exercised by the management and fiduciary controls of organizations, centering in the sphere of economic production to be sure, but ramifying into the fields of education, research, welfare functions, and various others what in the Western world we call the "private, nonprofit sector." Socialism therefore presents an issue of "political liberty," in the sense of the relation of functionally important operating units of the social system to the central decision-making authority. For understandable historic reasons, there is in the West a deep-seated moral valuation of rights of autonomy in these spheres, though perhaps it is correct to say also a certain pragmatism in attitudes toward the proper line of division between governmental and private agency in promoting legitimate functions. It is by no means a matter of whether it must be one or the other. A good example would be the sharing of responsibility for higher education in the United States between public, state, and privately endowed universities.

The problem, being political, is not however confined to the relations of operative units, notably of economic production, to central authority. It also concerns the political machinery of control over governmental authority as such, namely the question of "dictatorship" *versus* "democracy" in the Western sense. Property, in the sense in which it came to be the focal "enemy" of socialism, was a basis of *diffuse superiority* within the society, which may be compared to that of the religious orders within the Catholic church, or to hereditary aristocracy in postmedieval Europe. Socialism is aimed basically at abolishing the two-class system which is involved in the concept of a duality between the propertied (the "proprietors") and the propertyless worker. We have suggested that the internal process of the free enterprise system itself has, in the industrially advanced countries, been eliminating or at the least very greatly attenuating this duality.

The socialist path has, however, been to deprive private property of its power of control altogether by transferring it to government. The effect of course is not to abolish power, but to fuse the two main sectors of the power-system, the public and the private, into one. Socialist ideology has tended to claim that they always were essentially one, in that under "capitalism," government can have no genuine independence but is only in Marx's famous phrase, the "executive committee of the bourgeoisie" —a claim which is surely at best an oversimplification. This fusion, however, necessarily means a great increase in the power of government and hence again raises the question of "who is to control the controllers"?

All three of the great "reform" movements of postmedieval Western history, starting with the "Reformation" itself, have produced radical groups who have undertaken to impose their interpretation of the correct position on others, by gaining control of major political units and drastically reorganizing them. In the case of the Reformation it was the Calvinist branch which in this sense was the most radical; in the era of the democratic Revolutions it was the Jacobins, and in the socialist period it is of course the Communists.

In all three of these cases a drastically difficult position was assumed, in that in effect a *self*-appointed elite has claimed the right to control the system as a whole, whether it be in the name of a "Divine mandate" through predestinarian election, in the name of Rousseau's "general will" of the people, or in the name of the "historic mission" of the proletariat. In this process, of course, not only are the prerogatives of private property carried away but, with them, for the time being, legally protected civil liberties against both government and political democracy.

In the same sense in which strict Calvinism and Jacobinism were short-lived, it seems as certain as such things can be that Communism also will prove to be short-lived. The basis of this judgment is the hypothesis, first of all, that iron dictatorship of a self-appointed elite cannot be legitimized in the long run. Even more than other comparable movements the Communist is bound to be deeply undermined by its own success; its drastic controls can in the nature of the case apply only to the transition to the desired state, not to the state itself, as is quite explicit in the ideology. On the other hand, the orthodox Communist view of the outcome, the "withering away" not only of the state, but even more important, presumably also of the party, simply cannot happen. This is the strictly utopian element in the movement (which has never been better analyzed than by Ernst Troeltsch in the discussion of Marx in his *Historimus*). So long as there is human society there will always be government, with coercive powers and law which imposes *binding* obligations. The question is not the existence of these institutions, but their character and the modes in which they are controlled.

Just as Calvinism in time gave way to a more "liberal" Protestantism which acknowledged that all men of faith could have access to Divine Grace and Jacobinism gave way (considerably more quickly) to the conception of political democracy which has given real power to an electorate based on universal adult suffrage, so it seems a safe prediction that Communism will, from its own internal dynamics, evolve in the direction of the restoration—or where it has not yet existed, the institution—of political democracy. The basic dilemma of the Communists is that it is not possible in the long run either to legitimize dictatorship of the Party or to abolish all governmental and legal controls of behavior, as the "withering-away" doctrine would have it. Political democracy is the *only* possible outcome —except for general destruction or breakdown.

In the light of these considerations, one of the most conspicuous features of the Communist story becomes particularly significant, namely that it has not gained ascendancy in a *single* political society where the process of industrialization has become advanced under "capitalist" auspices. Indeed, as Seymour Martin Lipset in particular has made clear,[1] there is a close relation between such advancement and the decline of political radicalism of the left, a situation which of course stands in direct contradiction to the Marxian predictions. It is of course our view that this can only very partially be explained by the strengthening of vested interests opposed to change, usually referred to as "monopoly capitalism"; the most important explanation is that through industrial development under democratic auspices, the most important legitimately-to-be-expected aspirations of the "working class" have in fact been realized.

Besides the centrally important matter of political democracy, there is reason to believe that in other respects the trend of change in communist societies is likely to be in a direction which converges with that of the Western world. Two of these trends may be mentioned. One is the pressure for increasing autonomy of the proponents of elements of culture other than political ideology itself, notably in science and the arts, but also including traditional religion, which, though pushed into a very subordinate place, is by no means dead—for example, in the Soviet Union. The most immediately powerful

of these is science, because of its strategic importance to the industrialization process itself and to military technology. There seems to be inherent in the professions of science and the fields of its application, a tendency to become autonomous relative to *any* centralized system of control. In the decisively important sphere of technical competence, no one can compete with the scientist except his own peers in the field. Basically, a major component of responsibility for science and its uses must focus in the scientists themselves and cannot be carried out by persons lacking in this competence. Since, however, a modern society develops not one but many sciences and since totalitarian political control is necessarily centralized, the increasing importance of science cannot but have a centrifugal effect on the social system, the development of centers of power independent of the central authority. Not least important here is extension of scientific patterns into the sphere of social phenomena themselves where science comes into direct competition with ideology.

Similar considerations apply more generally to the effects of the increasing division of labor, which operate in the direction of pluralism. We already hear of problems of complicated balances of power among groups in Soviet society, *e.g.,* the Party, the "bureaucrats" of the central government, the industrial managers, the military establishment, the intellectuals, scientists, artists, and the like. It can, I think, be definitely said that the further this differentiation of the social structure proceeds, the more difficult it becomes to press it into the mold of a rigid line of authority from the top down.

There is one further aspect of the Communist movement, which in a broad way is shared with socialism generally, which deserves comment. This is the fact that, though by no means alone,

[1] *See* Seymour M. Lipset, *Political Man* (New York: Doubleday, 1959).

it has been one of the main forces working for the transcending of the older conceptions of nationalism. It is with justice referred to as the *international* Communist movement, which from the point of view of the antagonists makes it all the more formidable, but seen in a broader perspective may well be a major agency in the integration of society on wider bases. It is not unimportant that the two principal antagonists of the present world conflict are something more than nation-states in the nineteenth-century European sense, both are more-or-less "continental" polities, and both, in different ways, have worked out modes of assimilation of ethnically and otherwise diverse elements, the US through the absorbtion of mass immigration of very diverse origins, the USSR through assimilating the populations of many different federated republics. It is not surprising that our own time has seen another major attempt at international "community" in the British Commonwealth and just now is seeing the emergence of the European Common Market, with its tendencies toward political as well as economic integration. Without these lower level integrations beyond the earlier national level, it is doubtful that even the relative and qualified success of the United Nations to date could have been possible.

The basic conclusion seems to me clear, simple, and of the utmost importance. It is simply that the present major polarization of the world is not the collision between two deeply alien cultural and societal trends, but a conflict between two very closely related ones. They have diverged relatively recently—after all, Karl Marx was a German Jew who spent most of his mature life in England and whose ideas were built on the pre-eminently British classical economics and the German philosophical idealism of Hegel. Similarly, there is already clearly discernible a major process of convergence by which on the one hand the "social gains" of the Western democracies have already gone far to bring the older working class fully into the general social community, and, on the other hand the Communist world, notably in Soviet Russia, has already begun to move away from the rigid patterns which were the source of the most serious conflict of institutional structure with the Western world.

This is not to underestimate the seriousness of the difficulties and dangers of our world. Conflicts of interest, of nations, and of supranational groups of course remain. But the most dangerous feature of the developing Cold War situation has not been this, but the tendency to polarization which may be interpreted to be leading toward a head-on collision between two "moral crusades," each party feeling that absolute right was on its side and absolute evil on that of its opponents. The convergent trend of the development of social structures and their attendant cultures makes the further deepening of *this* order of antagonism unlikely, though the dangers involved in retreating from positions already taken—on both sides—should not be underestimated.

ARE THE TWO SOCIETIES BECOMING ALIKE?

The Soviet View

Against Imperialist Ideology

A. BOGOMOLOV

Imperialist reaction now ascribes particular importance to the struggle on the ideological front, along with its military and political plans. Bourgeois philosophers and sociologists, economists and jurists, historians and representatives of "political science" are more and more turning into preachers of the current ideological systems intended both for "internal consumption" and "for export." The substance of imperialist ideology remains the same—to defend capitalist society. But the growth of the general crisis of the imperialist system is driving the system's ideologists to search feverishly for newer and newer means of defending it.

In recently years Soviet scholars have done much work in exposing and criticizing the various ideological constructions of the defenders of modern capitalism. The typical stereotypes of anticommunist propaganda have been critically analyzed, monographs and articles have been published, scientific conferences have been held on various problems of the ideological struggle. Now the time has come for profound generali-

Reprinted from A. Bogomolov, "Against Imperialist Ideology," Pravda *(July 1, 1965). Translated in* Current Digest of the Soviet Press, *XVII, No. 26 (Copyright © July 21, 1965), 7–8.*

zation of this work, for developing a comprehensive *theoretical* analysis not merely of the individual forms of bourgeois trends of thought in the sphere of ideology but also of the deepest foundations of imperialism's ideology, the inner laws, the "logic," of its development, its basis doctrines. Decisive successes in the ideological struggle can be achieved only on the basis of criticism of the initial, determinant theories, rather than the individual forms in which the ideology hostile to us manifests itself—its *principles,* rather than individual arguments.

In this connection the attention of readers cannot fail to be drawn to interesting materials published in recent issues of the magazine of Soviet philosophers. The article by Academician M. B. Mitin and V. S. Semyonov, "Mankind's Movement Toward Communism, and the Bourgeois Conception of 'the Single Industrial Society'" (Voprosy filosofii, No. 5, 1965), and "The Individual and the Crisis of Bourgeois Ideology," by Yu. A. Zamoshkin, and "Socialist Ideology and the Historical Experience of Peoples," by T. I. Oizerman (Voprosy filosofii, No. 4, 1965), pose several central questions concerning the depth processes going on in modern bourgeois ideology. The article by M. B. Mitin and V. S. Semyonov shows that, whereas in the fifties the doctrine of "people's capitalism" was the foundation of bourgeois ideology, in the sixties the "theory of the single industrial society" has been added to it.

What is their essence? Underlying the doctrine of "people's capitalism" is the thesis that the capitalism of the 20th century is not the same as the capitalism of the previous century. The authors of this doctrine thus have tried to utilize the fact that certain changes have indeed taken place in capitalist society. Marx, as is known, foretold these changes; they were considered in V. I. Lenin's work "Imperialism, the Highest Stage of Capitalism," and later also in numerous works by economists, historians and Marxist philosophers. These changes come down to the fact that capitalism has entered a new stage of its development—the stage of monopoly capitalism, imperialism. But the bourgeois ideologists deliberately falsify the appraisal of these changes. Above all, they have advanced the claim that the "new" capitalism has for its purpose "ensuring the general prosperity of all members of society."

Objective research shows that the so-called "democratization" of capital, achieved by "dispersing" ownership, by distributing stock among the working people and by transferring the direction of the enterprises to the hands of "managers" ("the managerial revolution") has proved a means of further concentrating capital and ownership in the hands of the largest monopolists. After all, small stockholders not only cannot exert any substantial influence on the management of a monopolistic organization, they even make it easier for the monopolist to retain control over the enterprises: He does not have a rival within the framework of the monopoly who could challenge him for leadership. The monopolist, though holding only 10% to 20% of the stock, can play a decisive role in the circumstances of "dispersed" ownership, can determine the appointment of the directing organs of the monopoly, whereas formerly he had to hold a much larger "controlling block" of stock.

Thus in actuality "people's" capitalism remains that same monopoly capitalism. "The reality of the U.S.A. and other capitalist countries has shown with complete clarity that there is nothing 'people's' in the bourgeois system, that this is an exploiting system," conclude the writers of the article.

Although the theory of "people's capitalism" has suffered failure, it has not entirely disappeared into the past. Contemporary reformists in particular cling to it, seeing in it a "development" of the worn-out petty idea of the "evolution" of capitalism into socialism. It is also used to advertise modern capitalism in the developing countries. Nevertheless, the ideologists of imperialism have been obliged to change the record. Their new weapon is the theory of "the single industrial society," supplemented by the "stages-of-growth" doctrine as a general sociological groundwork. The author of the latter, the American economist and U.S. State Department adviser W. Rostow, has tried to replace the Marxist doctrine of the historical succession of socio-economic formations with the concept that society, upon attaining a certain level of development, reaches a "period of maturity" when "industrial society" arises, the structure and laws of which allegedly do not depend on the character of the social relations and form of ownership. This double-ended theory performs a whole series of ideological functions.

In the first place, in contradistinction to the Marxist doctrine of the antithesis between the two world systems, capitalism and socialism, it tries to assert a "unity" of human society as a whole. In the second place, despite the obvious, it insists on a unity among capitalist countries, and in the third place, it makes pretensions to furnishing "grounds" for the idea of an inner unity of capitalist society, for the liquidation of class contradictions in this society. The theory of the "single industrial society," supplemented by the theory of "stages of economic growth," is based on the complete ignoring of production relations and forms of ownership in analyzing social processes. Therefore it can be said that its theoretical source is the absolutization of similarities in the development of productive forces— such as the accelerated development of heavy industry, the growth of the industrial working class, the rise in the role of centralization of the economy, the increase in the role of science, etc.—in economically developed countries. But their fundamental differences caused by differences in production relations— such as the dominance and constant enrichment of the monopolists, the oppressed position of the proletariat and working people in the capitalist countries, the absence, under socialism, of the unemployment that inevitably accompanies the industrial development of the capitalist countries, and so on—are disregarded.

Whereas the theoreticians of "people's capitalism" claimed that some aspects of capitalism had undergone *change,* the conceptions of the "single industrial society" pursue a more "radical" idea: Capitalist society has, if you please, *disappeared,* it has been replaced by "industrial society."

This theory has become the leading doctrine of bourgeois ideology at the present stage because it has been able to combine the approach to contemporary problems with a "realistic" *technico-economic* approach, impressing not only the scholar but also the broad public; it attracts the latter by the fact that it presents growth of production of consumer goods as the criterion of the progress of society generally. At the same time, by "removing" the problem of production relations and form of ownership, this "theory" fully manifests its anti-Marxist line as an apologia for capitalism.

The writers of the article, who give a comprehensive critical analysis of the theory of the "single industrial society," draw the convincing conclusion that this doctrine too is already suffering a crisis and is doomed, like its predecessors, to fail.

They also point out correctly the contradiction in capitalist countries between the objective need for a general social program that would answer the problems confronting the man of modern capitalist society and the inability of capitalism's ideologists to offer such a program.

It is for this reason that we find a dual ideological policy of imperialism today. On the one hand, ever new *general social* concepts are being intensively worked out to replace the bourgeois-democratic ideals that have departed into the past. The aim of the concepts is to meet the "ideological challenge" of socialism, and their essence is frantic anti-communism. On the other hand, it is claimed that modern man's lack of "ideological doctrines" is the best possible condition one could wish.

The latter doctrine, which has received the name of "de-ideologization," has reflected the imperialist bourgeoisie's actual lack of ideas and ideals that might attract the masses. But at the same time "de-ideologization" is an attempt to implant an idea-less and apolitical state of mind, thus influencing both the public opinion of the countries of socialism and those strata of the population of capitalist countries that are drawn to democratic and socialist ideals.

The widespread (particularly in the

U.S.A.) doctrine of de-ideologization was recently presented to the Soviet reader by the magazine *Amerika*. The American historian and publicist A. Schlesinger, a former special assistant to the U.S. President, presented the propaganda of this doctrine in the magazine. Prof. T. I. Oizerman, in the article published in *Voprosy filosofii*, convincingly showed that Schlesinger was trying "to find ideological application for the very moods of skepticism and distrust generated by the crisis of values of ideals prevailing in the U.S.A."

From the failure of contemporary bourgeois ideology this theory draws the conclusion that scientific ideology is impossible in general. The slogan "No ideology" expresses an ideology hostile to the forces of progress. The "optimism of desperation" that impelled Schlesinger & Co. to depict the spiritual crisis and breakdown of bourgeois ideology as an "ideal condition" signifies above all the denial of progressive, socialist ideals.

Yu. A. Zamoshkin's article disclosed the contradictions of contemporary bourgeois thinking that have arisen from the clash between the objective tendency to give meaning to contemporary reality and the tendency to "de-ideologization" that has been engendered by the general crisis of capitalism. This clash, the writer justly points out, "is experienced by the individual as a tragedy, it gives rise to deeply morbid phenomena in the social psychology."

The magazine of Soviet philosophers may perhaps gladden the reader less often than one would wish with deep studies of timely problems of the contemporary ideological struggle; it may devote more attention to special philosophical themes. But the articles we have mentioned will undoubtedly yield great benefit. We think these efforts will be continued and that there will soon appear new works devoted to the analysis of major aspects of contemporary bourgeois ideology.

The thought suggests itself that there is a need for deep theoretical study not only of the direct apologia for capitalism so characteristic of the concepts of "people's capitalism" or "the single industrial society" but also of its indirect defense. Some defenders of capitalism try to pass off the contradictions of modern capitalist society as "eternal," "inevitable" contradictions of human existence in general. Realizing full well that modern man is a wise bird not easily caught with the decoy of "universal prosperity," many (particularly West European) ideologists emphasize the crisis situation of modern man and present the thought of the absurdity, chaotic nature and contradictoriness of the world of man's existence. A great deal is written about this "philosophy of desperation and fear," the essential nucleus of which is the doctrine of existentialism ("philosophy of existence"). The time has now come to disclose fully the social role of these concepts, which combine a sharp and sometimes even hypertrophied criticism of the actual contradictions of capitalist society with a justification of them.

This is only one of the aspects of the further development of the criticism of the bourgeois ideology of our times; this aspect is important also because existentialist positions, irrationalism, exert considerable influence not only on social doctrines but also on modern Western art. The criticism of these concepts should open up a perspective of further study of the social psychology of modern capitalist society, its inner contradictions, as well as the contradictions of the petty-bourgeois criticism of imperialism.

Admissions and Distortions

V. CHEPRAKOV

Editors' Note.—"A most important event"—this is what London radio has dubbed the six lectures on "the new industrial state" given by the well-known American economist Galbraith. The editors have asked Doctor of Economics V. A. Cheprakov to share with our readers his opinions of the new conception set forth in these lectures.

*   *   *

A certain division of labor exists in the camp of the ideological opponents of socialism. Some people—the out-and-out reactionaries—cast aside all restraint and howl in a crude, primitive fashion that capitalism "is something to be proud of," while socialism is allegedly "inefficient." Others—smooth-talking liberals—behave in a more refined manner.

The author of these lectures, Galbraith—an American scholar and influential public figure—is one of the liberals. He is a fervent devotee of the capitalist system, but his apologetics is distinguished by a certain subtlety. He is certainly an opponent of Marxism, but he does not permit himself to sink to zoological anti-communism. . . .

Galbraith evidently had set himself a twofold task: to present capitalism in a favorable light and to weaken the

Reprinted from V. Cheprakov, "Admissions and Distortions," Izvestia (April 4, 1967). Translated in Current Digest of the Soviet Press, XIX, No. 14 (Copyright ©️ April 26, 1967), 17–18.

attractiveness of socialism. To this end, he tried to put some life into the faded theory of "hybridization," according to which "capitalism is assuming certain features of socialism," while "socialism is moving toward capitalism." Recently this false theory, which was designed to undermine the ideas of socialism, has been provided with a new name, "convergence," meaning an interpenetration, a drawing together at a certain point. In trying to make the theory of the "convergence" of capitalism and socialism more convincing, Galbraith runs the risk of setting his own house on fire: He criticizes capitalism and, in talking about socialism, rejects the assertion that socialism is slipping toward capitalism, an idea widely current in bourgeois writings.

THERE'S NO GETTING AWAY FROM THE TRUTH

The initial point in Galbraith's conception, which is that the economic theory of the free market based on the law of supply and demand has already lost its significance, undermines the official bourgeois theory of free enterprise. The author is forced to admit that "the last 70 years, especially the postwar period, has been a time of far-reaching changes in the very foundations of the economy" and that "industrial firms and associations have attained very large proportions.". . .

Thus, Galbraith recognizes the fact of the concentration and centralization of capital. By the way, this is a forced admission, and a very belated one at that. After all, Marxists a long time ago established the fact that the development of the capitalism of free competition into monopoly capitalism began as far back as the turn of the century. But Galbraith goes on to make a further admission: "In the world of the monopolies" (the author does not use "oligopoly," a term of bourgeois political economy meaning rule by the many, but the Marxist term "monopoly," a very symptomatic point) "prices are fixed by those who sell." He emphasizes that one can speak of a market economy only when the initiative is with the consumer. . . .

"Who holds economic power?" the author asks. But in giving his answer he sins against the truth. From the fact that the large enterprises are managed not by the owners of capital themselves but by technical personnel, he draws the incorrect conclusion that supposedly "power passes into the hands of the managerial elite, and this power is effectively divorced from and protected against outside and conflicting influences on the part of the state as well as that of the owners and creditors themselves." "The enterprise," he goes on to write, "is now becoming a kind of self-governing independent power in the hands of its engineering and administrative staff."

True, there is something of value in these statements, although this too is a belated admission: An admission that capitalists are not necessary for modern industrial production. Marxists have been affirming this for a long time. . . .

There is yet another admission: "The harmless stockholder," the author writes, "has always been kept away from participation in any effective power in big corporations," and "the election ritual in a big modern company is a most painstakingly elaborated illusion." Thus, Galbraith has buried bourgeois propaganda's pet ideas of diffusion—the "dispersion of ownership"—and "people's capitalism."

As for the statement about the supplanting of the power of the capitalists by the power of the "technical organization" and the advent of an age of "capitalism without capitalists," this is the same decrepit theory of the "managerial revolution." The author's only innovation is that he substitutes the words "technical organization" for "managers."

The author has obviously not cleared his earthshaking conclusion of "capitalism without capitalists" with the Rockefellers, Du Ponts and other bigwigs of finance. The latter do not at all believe that they have moved into a different world and do not even seem to have noticed that they have lost the power and the opportunity to make decisions about their capital and to receive excessive monopoly profits. The fact that the small stockholder is "harmless" is beyond question. But it is equally certain that the owner of the controlling shares is in command of the corporation. Needless to say, the relationship between the millionaires and the managers is a complex one, but both the former and the latter are part of the ruling state-monopoly oligarchy.

For decades bourgeois scholars have busied themselves with refuting Lenin's views on "the unification of the gigantic force of capitalism and the gigantic force of the state into a single organization of state-monopoly capitalism." Now one of the leading ideologists of capitalist America admits that "even in the U.S.A., where free enterprise is a kind of symbol of faith, the state is playing an ever larger role in the economy," "it assumes the main risk involved in expenses on the introduction of new technology, has the necessary technological experience to offer, and firms seek its assistance and protection." Many other things should be added to this list, especially the fact that the state grants large credits and subsidies to private firms, concludes armaments contracts with these firms that are advantageous to them and has set up a number of tax advantages to them in the interests of big capital. The main thing about which Galbraith is silent is the fact that all this is conducive to increasing the profits of the big monopolies and to strengthening the positions of the financial groups.

IN CONTRADICTION TO THE FACTS

The whole lecture series is permeated by a defense of the interests of American corporations and of big business. "There are no conflicts whatsoever between our basic national goals and the goals of the leaders of today's firms," the author asserts. . . . As for the following facts—that the monopolies are pursuing their own selfish ends to the detriment of society as a whole, that they are intensifying the exploitation of the workers, that prices are rising steadily (in 1966 alone prices rose by 4% in the U.S.A.), that, with the help of the state, capital is being siphoned out of nonmonopoly enterprises into the strongboxes of the big monopolies, that the big monopolies are closely linked with the production of arms—the author is silent about all this too.

Galbraith, as we have already said, is a liberal. But he shows himself in a far from liberal spirit when he talks about the trade unions. The trade unions, don't you see, in defending the interests of the workers are guilty of bringing about a danger of uncontrolled price increases. This is because, according to Galbraith, that, when a labor dispute involving strong trade unions comes up, the firms allegedly "are obliged" to raise prices. . . .

A DEFICIENT LOGIC

. . . Galbraith speaks out forthrightly against socialism. But his arguments are quite original. "Where capitalism can no longer provide the proper control, socialism can no longer offer a real alternative. The same factors, such as complex technology, planning and its attendant deadlines and the scope of production operations, factors that have deprived the individual private entrepreneur of power and have shifted this power into the hands of the firm as an organization, these selfsame factors have placed this power outside the limits of public control." There is no doubt about one thing: The capitalist monopolies do not want control by society, they do not want state-democratic control. But this is no argument against socialism—on the contrary, it is an argument in favor of the necessity of depriving the monopolies of power while transferring the monopolies' ownership of the means of production, which now bears a public character, to society.

In passing, Galbraith also "deals with" so-called "democratic socialism," i.e., the positions of the Social Democrats and the Laborites. "When democratic socialism attains maturity, it becomes, like capitalism, a natural victim of modern technology and the planning that goes with it." Galbraith notes with satisfaction that many Social Democrats have discontinued the struggle for nationalization or pay only lip service to it.

Like all bourgeois economists, Galbraith goes to great lengths to distort the meaning of the economic reforms now being implemented in the Soviet Union and other European socialist countries. To make his case seem more convincing, he dissociates himself from the excessively crude methods of those